D1452712

Normandy to Victory

American Warriors

Throughout the nation's history, numerous men and women of all ranks and branches of the United States military have served their country with honor and distinction. During times of war and peace, there are individuals whose exemplary achievements embody the highest standards of the U.S. armed forces. The aim of the American Warriors series is to examine the unique historical contributions of these individuals, whose legacies serve as enduring examples for soldiers and citizens alike. The series will promote a deeper and more comprehensive understanding of the U.S. armed forces.

Series editor: Roger Cirillo

An AUSA Book

NORMANDY
TO
VICTORY

*The War Diary of
General Courtney H. Hodges
and the First U.S. Army*

Major William C. Sylvan
and
Captain Francis G. Smith Jr.

EDITED BY JOHN T. GREENWOOD

THE UNIVERSITY PRESS OF KENTUCKY

Copyright © 2008 by The Association of the United States Army

The University Press of Kentucky

Scholarly publisher for the Commonwealth,
serving Bellarmine University, Berea College, Centre College of Kentucky, Eastern
Kentucky University, The Filson Historical Society, Georgetown College, Kentucky
Historical Society, Kentucky State University, Morehead State University, Murray
State University, Northern Kentucky University, Transylvania University, University
of Kentucky, University of Louisville, and Western Kentucky University.
All rights reserved.

Editorial and Sales Offices: The University Press of Kentucky
663 South Limestone Street, Lexington, Kentucky 40508-4008
www.kentuckypress.com

12 11 10 09 08   5 4 3 2 1

Maps courtesy U.S. Army Center of Military History

Library of Congress Cataloging-in-Publication Data

Sylvan, William C.
    Normandy to victory : the war diary of General Courtney H. Hodges and the
    First U.S. Army / William C. Sylvan and Francis G. Smith, Jr. ; edited by John T.
    Greenwood.
        p. cm. — (American warriors)
    Reproduces in edited form the First Army's daily war diary, maintained for
    Hodges by his aides.
    Includes bibliographical references and index.
    ISBN 978-0-8131-2525-1 (hbk. : alk. paper)
    1. United States. Army. Army, 1st. 2. World War, 1939–1945—Regimental
histories—United States. 3. World War, 1939–1945—Campaigns—France—
Normandy. 4. World War, 1939–1945—Campaigns—Western Front. 5. Hodges,
Courtney H., 1887–1966. I. Smith, Francis G., Jr. II. Hodges, Courtney H.,
1887–1966. III. Greenwood, John T. IV. Title.
    D769.261st .S95 2008
    940.54'1273092—dc22
    [B]   2008028010

This book is printed on acid-free recycled paper meeting the requirements of the
American National Standard for Permanence in Paper for Printed Library Materials.
∞ ❋

Manufactured in the United States of America.

Contents

Preface

Normandy to Victory is a unique contribution to the existing primary literature on the command and conduct of American military operations in Europe during World War II. This book reproduces in edited form for the first time the daily war diary maintained for Gen. Courtney Hicks Hodges, commanding general, First United States Army, by his aides, Maj. William C. Sylvan and Capt. (later Maj.) Francis G. Smith Jr. Hodges's third aide during the war, Capt. William E. Smith, also assisted at times. Unfortunately, little is known about any of these three men and their lives following World War II.

Often referred to as the "Sylvan diary" after its principal author, Maj. William Sylvan, the First U.S. Army war diary has been cited frequently in many official and unofficial histories of the war in Western Europe. Until now, however, the diary has been available only to researchers able to use the original copy in the Gen. Courtney Hicks Hodges Papers at the Dwight D. Eisenhower Library at Abilene, Kansas, or photocopies at the U.S. Army Military History Institute at Carlisle Barracks, Pennsylvania, and the U.S. Army Center of Military History at Fort McNair in Washington, D.C.

The diary covers the entire period of First Army's active operations on the European continent. It begins on 2 June 1944, when Hodges, then deputy commanding general, First Army, under Gen. Omar N. Bradley, and members of the staff departed for Plymouth, England, their assigned port of embarkation for Operation Overlord. The diary then proceeds through the invasion, fighting in Normandy, Hodges's assumption of command on 1 August 1944, and on to the end of First Army's combat activities on 7 May 1945. According to Maj. Gen. William A. Carter, who was Hodges's chief engineer during this entire time, either Sylvan or Smith prepared the daily entries each evening and Hodges then personally reviewed and approved them. They were then entered into the continuing diary by clerk-typists. Thus, although Hodges did not personally write the diary, he controlled its contents so that it does reflect his viewpoints and concerns.

The diary's daily entries normally contain two types of information: an account of General Hodges, normally referred to as "the General," and his activities, and then an operational recapitulation that covers the operations of First Army as well as those of the other American and Allied armies. The Hodges entries provide some of the most interesting and informative material and perspectives. They are also the best available account of the day-to-day activities of an American army commander and his headquarters throughout the campaign in Western Europe. The commander's incessant travels among his subordinate units; the strategic, operational, and tactical problems of the corps and divisions; frontline actions; the innumerable conferences and meetings; operational concepts; living conditions; and misconceptions of both German and Allied operations are described in the diary, which relates important and little-known aspects of a field army at war.

Although the reader is frequently left wishing for more details and fuller explanations, it must be remembered that the diarists were not privy to all of the high-level discussions being conducted among Hodges, Dwight Eisenhower, Omar Bradley, George Patton, William Simpson, Bernard Law Montgomery, and others. Moreover, the diarists knew nothing of the supersecret Ultra intelligence that flowed to Hodges and only a very few of his senior officers. The snippets of information, along with conversations and comments overheard and then recorded, provide an intriguing glimpse into the personalities, activities, and ideas of the American and Allied military leaders.

The operational entries are based heavily on the daily situation reports (sitreps) that the First Army's G-3 Section (Operations) prepared every evening to report the army's activities to Twelfth Army Group and Supreme Headquarters, Allied Expeditionary Force (SHAEF). While rather routine, they also provide a continuing account of the progress of the war in Western Europe and the First Army's role in it.

In editing the Sylvan diary for publication, I have strictly limited any editorial comments to factual information on people, equipment, code names, and so on. From the beginning, I decided that the document must remain essentially unchanged and uncluttered, as its value lies in its basic contents, not in detailed endnotes added more than five decades after the events described. Hence, the endnotes are simply to provide the reader with the factual details necessary to understand the "whos" and "whats" of the story as noted by the diarists. Except in rare instances where fuller information would aid the reader's understanding, no attempt has been made to correct or explain the events narrated in this diary. All of my editorial annotations in the main text are in brackets.

As for the "whos" in the diary, I have made a reasonable effort to identify all the key personnel mentioned. In some cases, especially for lower-ranking American officers who were not graduates of the U.S. Military Academy, any significant information was difficult if not impossible to obtain. For the West Pointers, the Association of Graduates, U.S. Military Academy, publishes a regular *Register of Graduates,* which provided sufficient information on their careers for brief biographical sketches of those who did not reach the rank of general officer. On the American general officers and senior civilian leaders of the War Department, sufficient information existed in official army and War Department biographies to draw accurate biographical sketches. Again, no attempt was made to draw subjective evaluations of the individual's personality or competence unless that aspect specifically affected the actions described in the diary. Unless otherwise noted, the biographical sketches of U.S. Army and Army Air Forces general officers, civilian leaders, and consultants in the War Department and U.S. Navy admirals are based on official releases of biographical information now contained in the individual's biographical file at the Historical Support Branch, U.S. Army Center of Military History, at Fort McNair, Washington, D.C.

While the integrity of the content of the original text as it appeared in the typewritten ribbon copy of the diary that is in the Courtney Hicks Hodges Papers in the Dwight D. Eisenhower Library has been preserved, certain changes have been made to produce a readable text free of too-numerous bracketed corrections. Obvious typographical and spelling errors have been silently corrected (for example, "shightseeing" appears simply as "sight-seeing"). When the diarist occasionally used the wrong word ("penetration" rather than "permission," for example), the original word appears in the text followed by the intended word in brackets. The names of people and geographical places were frequently misspelled, as the diarists often tried to spell names phonetically. These errors remain in the text, and the correct spelling is provided in brackets once in each chapter, rather than repeatedly interrupting the text to repeat the same correction. Where place names have changed, insofar as possible the current name is given in brackets so that readers can find the locations mentioned in the diary. The punctuation and grammar remain as they were in the original. The style used for the day and date of the daily entries varied slightly throughout the original diary, and has been regularized to a standard format.

As originally recorded, the diary was a running collection of daily entries with no organization other than by day of entry. To organize the material and provide a contextual reference for the reader, I have arranged the diary into nine chapters with subchapters that closely follow the operational framework established by First U.S. Army for its combat operations from the invasion of France through the end of the war. This structure is laid out completely in the operational volumes of the three sets of the First U.S. Army's *Report of Operations.*

For the reader who wishes to learn more about the organization and activities of the First U.S. Army during the campaign in Europe, there are some particularly important publications that must be consulted. Dr. David W. Hogan Jr., U.S. Army Center of Military History, has published the best existing coverage of the First Army's headquarters, operations, and personalities in his *A Command Post at War: First Army Headquarters in Europe, 1943–1945* (U.S. Army Center of Military History, 2000), which is available from the Superintendent of Documents. To obtain the full operational and organizational story of the First Army and its headquarters during the campaign in Europe, the reader must consult the massive but difficult to find *Report of Operations* published in 1945–1946 in three separate series: (1) 20 October 1943–1 August 1944 (6 volumes); (2) 1 August 1944–22 February 1945 (4 volumes); and (3) 23 February–8 May 1945 (3 volumes). Much of the nitty-gritty of the First Army's wartime organization and operations is also contained in *Combat Operations Data, First Army, Europe, 1944–1945,* which the First Army published in mimeograph format at Governor's Island in 1946. Another useful overview of First Army was written by Col. Elbridge Colby, himself a veteran of First Army headquarters, and published as a U.S. Senate Document (No. 91–25) in 1969 as *The First Army in Europe, 1943–1945,* at the request of Sen. Strom Thurmond of South Carolina, also a combat veteran of First Army.

There are many whom I wish to thank for making the publication of this book possible. At the Association of the United States Army (AUSA), Gen. Gordon R. Sullivan, U.S. Army (retired), president, and Lt. Gen. Theodore G. Stroup Jr., U.S. Army (retired), vice president, education, have consistently supported Dr. Roger Cirillo, director of the AUSA's Book Program, in his efforts to make important works such as *Normandy to Victory* available to a wide reading audience. Steve Wrinn and

Anne Dean Watkins at the University Press of Kentucky have offered encouragement and support, and David Cobb oversaw the transformation of the manuscript into a book. The copyeditor, Cheryl Hoffman of Hoffman-Paulson Associates, made an enormous contribution to the effort. Above all, I wish to thank my wife, Mary Ann, for assisting me throughout the editing process and for diligently reviewing and reading every page to catch my errors; to our son, James, for assisting in reviewing and selecting illustrations at the National Archives and Records Administration; and to our daughter, Anne, a budding historian in her own right, for tolerating her parents' preoccupation with this manuscript.

John T. Greenwood

A Biographical Sketch

Courtney Hicks Hodges

Courtney Hicks Hodges was born in Perry, Georgia, on 5 January 1887. He entered the United States Military Academy at West Point, New York, with the incoming class of 1908 in June 1904, a member of the same class as George S. Patton Jr. He was "found deficient" in mathematics, as was Patton, and left West Point following his plebe year of 1904–1905. Unlike Patton, who reentered and graduated with the class of 1909, Hodges enlisted in the army as a private in Company L, Seventeenth Infantry, on 5 November 1906 and was commissioned a second lieutenant of infantry on 13 November 1909. He served in the Philippines and the Mexican Punitive Expedition; in France during World War I he was as a battalion commander in the Sixth Infantry Regiment, Fifth Division, in the St. Mihiel and Meuse-Argonne campaigns of 1918. He received a Distinguished Service Cross for valor during the Meuse-Argonne operation.

After occupation duty in Germany, Hodges spent the years 1920 to 1924 on the staff at West Point before attending the Command and General Staff School at Fort Leavenworth, Kansas, from August 1924 to June 1925. He then served as an instructor at the Infantry School, Fort Benning, Georgia, until 1926 and in a similar capacity at the Air Corps Tactical School at Maxwell Field, Alabama, until 1929. For the next four years he was assigned as a member of the Infantry Board at Fort Benning, where he was closely associated with Col. George C. Marshall, assistant commandant of the Infantry School from 1927 to 1933. Hodges then completed the Army War College in 1934–1935. After tours at Vancouver Barracks, Washington, and in the Philippines with the Philippine Division and Department, he was named the assistant commandant, the Infantry School, in 1938. With his former mentor, George C. Marshall, now the War Department chief of staff, Hodges became commandant of the Infantry School at Fort Benning in October

1

1940, six months after being promoted to brigadier general. In this position, he oversaw the massive expansion of the school and the addition of important new training programs and missions during the prewar mobilization period that began in 1939–1940. Omar N. Bradley became commandant in March 1941, succeeding Hodges, who was promoted to major general and appointed as the chief of infantry in May 1941. He held that post until it was abolished in the March 1942 reorganization of the War Department.

After commanding the Replacement and Training School Command (March–May 1942), Hodges commanded the X Corps at Fort Sam Houston, Texas. In February 1943, Hodges was promoted to lieutenant general and commanded the Southern Defense Command and the Third U.S. Army, then in preparation for its deployment to England, until December 1943. In January 1944 he moved to the European theater of operations ahead of Third Army's movement. There he soon became deputy commanding general to Lt. Gen. Omar N. Bradley, commander of the First U.S. Army and also of the fictional First U.S. Army Group (FUSAG), which was a key part of the Allies' deception operations. First U.S. Army was the major American ground component of Operation Overlord, the forthcoming invasion of France. As soon as the amphibious assault (Operation Neptune) was successful and a lodgment in Normandy was consolidated and sufficient American forces were ashore, Bradley would move up to command the Twelfth U.S. Army Group, which initially would consist of First Army, under Hodges, and Third Army, under Lt. Gen. George S. Patton Jr. On 1 August 1944, this realignment took place, and Hodges took over the First Army. He commanded the First Army throughout the rest of the war in Europe, through the months of hard fighting following the breakthrough at St. Lô and the exhilarating drive past Paris into Belgium and Germany, the costly and difficult fight along the Siegfried Line along the German border, the dangerous days of the German Ardennes counteroffensive and the Battle of the Bulge, across the Roer and Rhine rivers, and on to meet the Russians at the Elbe River in April 1945.

Although he possessed a fine military reputation as a firm and skilled commander, Hodges was quiet and little known to his troops despite significant efforts to enhance his image and popularity. Promoted to full general in April 1945, he moved with his staff to the Pacific and was preparing for the invasion of Japan when the war against Imperial Japan ended. He remained in command of the First Army at Governor's Island, New York, from its return to the United States in late

1945 until his retirement on 31 January 1949. Following his retirement, he served as military adviser to Sir Owen Dixon, the United Nations mediator in Kashmir. During his retirement, he unfortunately never wrote of his wartime experiences. He died at Brooke Army Hospital, Fort Sam Houston, on 16 January 1966.

In his postwar memoirs, *A Soldier's Story,* Omar Bradley, who knew Hodges as well as anyone, provided this sober assessment of Courtney Hicks Hodges as a soldier and commander:

> A spare, soft-voiced Georgian without temper, drama, or visible emotion, Hodges was left behind in the European headline sweepstakes. He was essentially a military technician whose faultless techniques and tactical knowledge made him one of the most skilled craftsmen of my entire command. He probably knew as much about infantry and training as any man in the army. But because he was unostentatious and retiring, Hodges occupied an almost anonymous role in the war. Yet as a general's general his stature among our U.S. commanders was rivaled only by that of [William H.] Simpson. For Hodges successfully blended dexterity and common sense in such equal portions as to produce a magnificently balanced command. I had implicit faith in this judgment, in his skill and restraint. Of all my Army commanders he required the least supervision.
>
> Hodges' claims to greatness as a commander will endure in the achievements of his First Army. Without the flair of Patton's Third Army and the breeziness of Simpson's Ninth, First Army trudged across Europe with a serious and grim intensity. Yet it was the first Army to cross the German border, the first to cross the Rhine, the first to close to the Elbe and join hands with the Russians. En route it ticketed more prisoners than any other American Army. It also buried more American dead in the wake of its long advance.[1]

Chapter 1

The Invasion of France and the Lodgment in Normandy, 2 June–24 July 1944

Mounting the Invasion and Establishing the Beachhead, 2–10 June 1944

Friday, 2 June 1944: The General [Lt. Gen. Courtney Hicks Hodges], Bill [Capt. William E. Smith, aide), and I [Maj. William C. Sylvan, senior aide][1] left Bristol at 9 o'clock in the morning on exercise "Brass Hat"[2] (see next page for inclosure). Passing thru Bridgewater and Exeter, we stopped briefly at noon for some sandwiches at the side of the road and then drove on to Plymouth, arriving at 1330. In a few minutes, an LCVP [Landing Craft, Vehicle and Personnel] took us to the Headquarters Ship—the USS Achenar [*Achernar*],[3] 13,000 tons of the A53 class, commissioned in February, 1944 and considered by officers and men alike as a "lucky" ship. No member of her crew had been hurt, she had met with no incident on her trip across and down from Gourock, Scotland, her engines had always kept whirring. Perhaps most remarkable of all, at least to the officers, was the fact that 85% of her crew had never been to sea before, and yet after three months were discharging their duties with considerable skill. The commander was R. F. [Cdr. H. R.] Stevens, Naval Academy, Class of 1922; the Executive [Officer] [Lt. Cdr. M. Berner] a jolly (but sometimes wrathful) W. C. Fields character who had been 22 years in the Merchant Marine and before assigned to the Achenar had had charge of a division of mine-sweepers under Admiral Ingraham [Ingram][4] in the South Atlantic.

The Operations Room, two decks below the hatch, was a small white-walled room most of which was reserved for the Air Corps, its

31 May 1944.

SUBJECT : Movement of Phase II, Command Echelon, Headquarters and
Headquarters Company, First United States Army (Group A-1)

TO : Chiefs of all General and Special Staff Sections.

1. The personnel of Phase II, Group A-1, Command Echelon of
Headquarters and Headquarters Company will depart from this Headquarters
for Exercise "Brass Hat" at 0600 hours, 2 June 1944.

2. Officers in this movement will eat at "B" Mess between 0430
and 0530 hours. Commanding Officers of troops will designate mess hours
for enlisted men. "D" and "S" components of ration K will be issued at
breakfast to all individuals for consumption enroute.

3. Officers and enlisted men will be at place of departure prepared
to leave at least 15 minutes prior to the time scheduled for the departure
of the convoy.

4. Officers hand luggage will be placed in the last 2½ ton truck
in the convoy.

5. Uniform : Full Field.

6. Convoy will be formed on Guthrie Road facing College Road at
0530 hours.

1. 1/4 ton a. Convoy Commander : Col. R. F. Akers Jr.
b. TQM : Lt. Thompson.

2. Sedan Lt. Gen. Hodges, Maj. Sylvan, Capt. F. G. Smith
3. Comdt.Sedan Col. Carter, Col. Hart, Lt. Col. Roberson
4. Ord. Sedan Col. Johnson, Col. Patterson, Lt. Col. Huntsberry
5. A-A Sedan Maj. Locke, Maj. Bristol, Mr. Wertenbaker (WC)
6. C & R Maj. Rozamus, ███████
7. C & R Lt. Magilow, Lt. Pritchard, Lt. Dolloff.
8. Truck # 1 :

M/Sgt. Bennett	T/Sgt. Watson	S/Sgt. Wilson
M/Sgt. Kerrigan	S/Sgt. Beshore	T/3 Smith, A. B.
T/Sgt. Chamberlain	S/Sgt. Spratt	Sgt. Komnotz

9. Truck # 2 :

	T/4 Fronzo	Cpl. Lindsey
Sgt. Orcutt	T/4 McIntyre	T/5 Loving
Sgt. Vorgason	T/4 Yarbrough	T/5 Morrison
T/4 Bahl		T/5 Thomas

(2)

10. Truck # 3 :
Officers Baggage : M/Sgt. Kunkel, Sgt. Weidman

11. C & R : Maj. January, Maj. Dwyer.

7. a. Route : As directed by convoy commander.

b. Speed : 20 MPH

c. Interval : 60 yds.

d. Halts : 10 minutes every even hour plus 30 minutes at 1230 hours.
No halts in built-up areas.

Harry F. Goslee

HARRY F. GOSLEE
Lt. Col., F. A.
Hq. Commandant.

May 31, 1944. The movement order from Headquarters, First
U.S. Army, for Exercise Brass Hat.

plotting board and communications system on either side were two smaller rooms, likewise reserved for the Air Corps. The Navy personnel representing Rear Admiral [Alan G.] Kirk[5] (headed by Captain E. A. Mitchell; Lt Commander Roger Putnam,[6] ex-mayor of Springfield, Mass.; and Lt. Commander Oren Root, Jr.,[7] the young New York lawyer who started the Willkie-for-President clubs throughout the country in 1940) were seated against one wall; the other wall went for an operations map, the third for various Army personnel; the table in the middle for the General, G-2 and G-3.[8] The one newspaperman on board was Charles Wertenbaker,[9] representing Time & Life.

In the evening the weather did not look promising. Ugly clouds were overhead, and there was a swift little chop to the waves, though we were anchored far inside the inner harbour, along with countless LCTs [Landing Craft, Tank] and mine-sweepers, all flying the American flag.

Saturday, 3 June 1944: The General conferred in the Ops Room with the staff headed by Colonel Ed. Johnson[10] AGF [Army Ground Forces],[11] TD [temporary duty] with First Army, and Colonel [Russell F.] Akers,[12] G-3. At 1430 General Bradley,[13] General [William B.] Kean,[14] the four G's, and Chief of Staff [15] to Admiral Kirk [Rear Adm. Arthur D. Struble] were piped aboard for a brief visit. At 1640 the Mayfield [U.S.S. *Bayfield*],[16] flagship for the VII Corps, passed us, followed by a steady stream of LCIs [Landing Craft, Infantry] and LSTs [Landing Ship, Tank], and by 12 mine-sweepers. The weather seemed promising for The Day. The General spent the evening in the war room. Just before retiring for bed, Colonel [W. C.] Roberson,[17] G-2, brought the message that the ships radio monitor had picked up, from the OWI [Office of War Information] station WRUX in New York, the report that the Associated Press had announced, in word from General [Dwight D.] Eisenhower's[18] headquarters,[19] the beginning of the invasion. This was followed by an urgent "Kill Story, Kill." We discussed briefly who could be responsible for such a dangerous, irresponsible blunder.

Sunday, 4 June 1944: Tomorrow is the day, and the harbour is deserted. It is a chilly day, with grey clouds passing low but with little real wind. But at breakfast we learn the bad news; at 5 AM the General had been awakened with notice of postponement because of unfavorable weather. General Kean, Colonel [Truman C.] Thorsen [Thorson],[20] and Colonel [Benjamin A.] Dickson[21] arrive for a conference in the morning, and at 1135 General [Omar N.] Bradley and General [Ralph] Royce,[22] also with General Kean and Colonel Thorsen. At 1500 the General goes ashore to Admiral [Don P.] Moon's[23] headquarters for another conference with American and British leaders. At 1715 that evening the harbour is filling up again with boats turned back from their mission. The General returns with the news that, given good weather, the invasion could take place any day between now and Friday, 9 June, but that if postponed beyond that, another two weeks would have to pass before the tides would be favorable.

Late that evening we learn that the meteorologists now say everything will be all right, so the show is on again. In the west, at 2300, the sky is still cold and clear.

Monday, 5 June 1944: General Kean and Colonel Thorson came aboard at 0930 for a last-minute settlement of plans with the General. A little later the *Augusta,* famous cruiser which is Admiral Kirk's flagship and on which General Bradley, General Kean and the four G's are travelling lifts anchor, and at 12 two tugs push and guide us down to the entrance of the harbour, where we drop again. At 1550 the *Augusta* slides through the narrow breakwater passage, followed by two British cruisers and dozens of LSIs [Landing Ship, Infantry], all tossing little sausage balloons in the air. To our left a coastal battery fires on a towed target—this seems a strange time for British coastal batteries to be practicing, and to our right giant Sunderlands [Sunderland] flying boats[24] start on their routine anti-sub patrols. At 1800 the General says that the weather report is the best thus far received; to be honest, it looks none too good. There are angry clouds in the sky and the sea is commencing to boil.

At 2100 we listen to the BBC announce the fall of Rome [4 June 1944] and the wild scenes of celebration with which the Allied armies were greeted. We celebrate by putting our operations map up in the War Room. Everything is ready to go. The Achenar starts on her adventure on the dot of midnight, escorted by two American destroyers. In the words of Commander Bermer [Berner] (see incl. #2), "The rest depends on us and the will of God."

Tuesday, 6 June 1944: At 0800 there are still no reports. There is blue in the sky above and the sun is out but there is a strong breeze blowing, and our procession of LCIs, marching in two columns behind us, dip and toss in the whitecaps. Also in the procession is a lumbering LSD, Landing Ship Dock, which can accommodate a half dozen smaller craft in its innards and repair them. Ahead of us our two destroyers proceed carefully through the mine-swept designated channels past flagged buoys; overhead are Thunderbolts [P-47s][25] and a mission of 36 B-26s,[26] returning from a job done in France.

At 0930, exactly as promised, we hear the first communique over the radio, very vague, as was to be expected, stating only that landings are being made on the north coast of France. At 0945 General Eisenhower broadcasts his message; telling the people of France to act only if they have received definite orders to act, and assuring the peoples of other occupied countries that their day will come. He was followed by King Haakon of Norway and other United Nations leaders. At 1030 we slow down to six knots as we approach a huge convoy ahead. "Now is sub time, if ever," says the Chief Engineer [Col. William A. Carter Jr.].[27] It is a beautiful warm day, but getting rougher every minute.

```
                    U.S.S. ACHERNAR(AKA53)
                     c/o Fleet Post Office
                       New York, New York


                                      Tuesday, June 6 1944.


     0415 - Call Police Petty Officers
     0425 - Call all hands and all officers.
     0445 - General Quarters
     0602 - Secure from General Quarters.
     0615 to 0715 Breakfast period.



          THE REST OF THIS DAY DEPENDS ON THE WILL
          OF GOD AND US.

               GOOD LUCK!!

                                   M. BERNER,
                                   Lieut.Cdr., USNR.,
                                   Executive Officer.

     Copy to:  All officers,
               offices, OOD,
               CPO Qtrs, BB's.
```

June 6, 1944. Lt. Cdr. Berner's order of the day.

By 1215 we have two convoys on our left—convoys which stretch as far as the eye can reach, every ship flying his barrage balloon, the sole means of determining how large the convoy actually is, for with the glasses, the balloons can be counted. There are 100 in one convoy.

By 1300 we can sight land—a thin purple haze some twenty or twenty five miles away. At 1400 we pass the *Augusta,* and an hour later reach the transport area, some 12 miles off shore. At 2000 we take

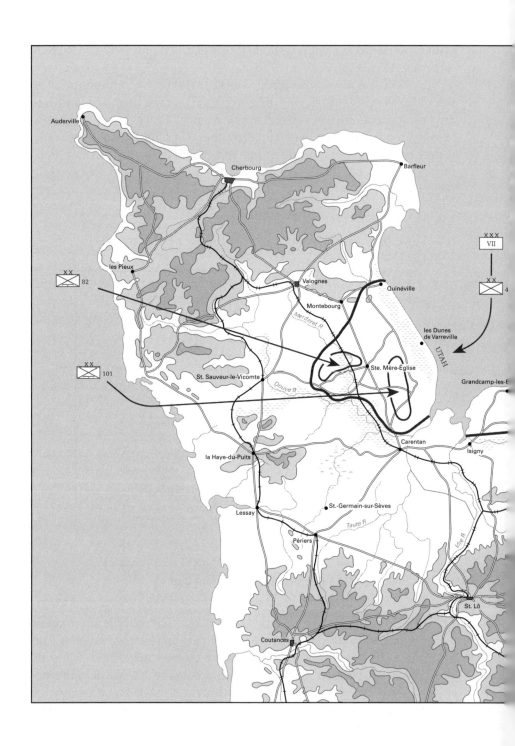

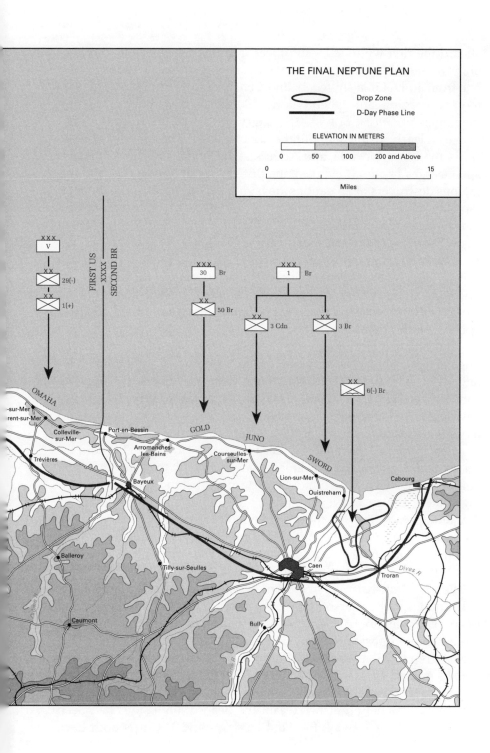

THE FINAL NEPTUNE PLAN

Drop Zone
D-Day Phase Line

ELEVATION IN METERS

0   50   100   200 and Above

0   15

Miles

XXX
V

FIRST US
SECOND BR

XX
29(-)

XX
1(+)

XXX
30 Br

XX
50 Br

XXX
1 Br

XX
3 Cdn

XX
3 Br

XX
6(-) Br

OMAHA

-sur-Mer
rent-sur-Mer

Colleville-
sur-Mer

Port-en-Bessin

GOLD

JUNO

Courseulles-
sur-Mer

SWORD

Lion-sur-Mer

Cabourg

Trévières

Arromanches-
les-Bains

Ouistreham

Bayeux

Dives R.

Balleroy

Tilly-sur-Seulles

Caen

Troran

Caumont

Bully

aboard the first wounded—an officer from the 1st Division, and later on, several enlisted men. The waves are so high it took an hour to land one from an LCI in a stretchers buoy. Early reports from land are none too encouraging, and when before 2100 the *Achenar* moves to within four miles of *Omaha Beach*.[28] The angry flashes of fire from the cliffs above is clearly visible without the use of glasses. The American battleships, the Texas, Nevada, and Arkansas; the French cruisers Montcalm and Georges Legues [Leygues]; the British cruiser, Enterprise, and numerous destroyers of all nations are laying in a murderous fire, both on top of the cliffs and in the enemy's rear, and the town of Port en-Bessin, which marks the boundary between the First Army and Second British Army, is ablaze in several spots.

One of the first reports of V Corps ends: "God bless the American Navy." Our crew has been on General Quarters most of the day, and are called out again at 2200. We have our first air-raid; every ship is having a trial with its guns, and the story is that we have accounted for three Boche.[29] Nothing drops close.

The situation at midnight was as follows: *Omaha Beach*, from which original reports had been very pessimistic, is improving, with the 16th Infantry [1st Infantry Division] reported at Colleville-Sur-Mere [Colleville-sur-Mer]; the 116th [29th Infantry Division, then attached to the 1st Infantry Division] at St. Laurent [St. Laurent-sur-Mer]. The 1st Division had set up its CP [Command Post], and at 2030, V Corps had gone ashore.

Utah Beach,[30] 12th Infantry at Les Forges. 4th [Infantry Division] CP set up. Still no positive contact made, however, with the 82nd and 101st Airborne Divisions, which had been dropped behind the beach, starting at 0001, D Day. However, gliders are coming in, against no visible AA [antiaircraft] fire, and the situation looks promising.

Wednesday, 7 June 1944: It is murky and cloudy, a 2,000-ft ceiling which as the morning progresses, opens up. The sea is still choppy, and very little seems to be getting into the beach. Major Dwyer and Colonel [Walter A.] Huntsberry [G-4 Section][31] go into Omaha Beach, and Colonel [Charles. G.] Patterson [chief, Antiaircraft Artillery Section][32] and Major [D. L.] Bristol [Artillery Section] to Utah to see if they can obtain more definite information; communications are slow and erratic. The report from Omaha was that a German division, had moved into the Omaha area on an exercise the night before the invasion, and that consequently the First Division had found itself up against four German regiments. Colonel Huntsberry said the dead of both sides had been pretty well cleared away; the First Division and V Corps both have their CPs set up, close together, and only a mile off the beach, on the side of the road off Easy-Red,[33] up which whatever traffic that is unloaded seems to be moving. There is some shelling of the beach going on; General [William M.] Hoge[34] has been slightly wounded; the Rangers are having a very tough time around Pointe de Hoe [Pointe du Hoc] and Grandcamp [Grandcamp-les-Bains], with casualties high and ammunition running low. Snipers and machine guns are still placing fire on the beaches, and sporadic artillery fire is also landing.

Much artillery has been lost in landing, and the beach is so crowded with wrecked or disabled craft that unloading is a terrific problem. Junction has been made between the 101st Division and the 4th, but the situation of the 82nd is still obscure. Contact has been made between the Rangers and the 29th Division at St. Pierre-de-Mond [St. Pierre-du-Mont]; and the 2nd Division was beginning, late in the afternoon, to unload. By 2400, the schedule of unloading was exactly one tide behind.

The report from Utah appears very satisfactory. Opposition to the landing was light, the 4th has pushed well inland, and the Corps CP is set up. This news was quite surprising to some, as it had been generally estimated that Omaha was the easier of the two beaches to conquer.

At 2030 General Hodges, accompanied by Colonel Akers [G-3 Section] and Lt Colonel Huntsberry visit V Corps Headquarters, returning at 2400. The situation seems slightly improved.

We have another sharp air-raid after 1330, and intermittent attacks throughout the night. A far greater show of strength from the German Air Force had been expected; these raids appear to be made by groups of two or three aircraft.

Thursday, 8 June 1944: Two of the wounded brought into our sick bay yesterday died during the night. One, an ensign, had been twelve hours on the beach without treatment; shock and the loss of blood were too great for his body to endure. Plasma brought the rest around to a condition described by the doctor as "satisfactory."

General Hodges goes ashore in a PT [patrol torpedo] boat at 0845, with Colonels Carter and Akers to Utah beach, to see General Collins[35] and review the progress made.

The boat gets fouled up with some mine sweeper on return and is slowed down; the General does not return until 1800. He reports the situation there splendid, with one Glider [Infantry] Regiment alone taking 1,200 prisoners.

During the day the Americans and British joined with patrols at Port en-Bessin. The 90th Division was continuing its unloading on

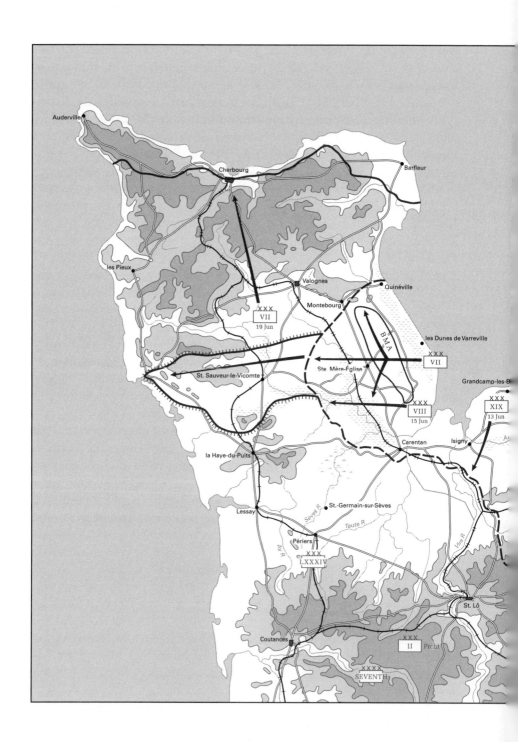

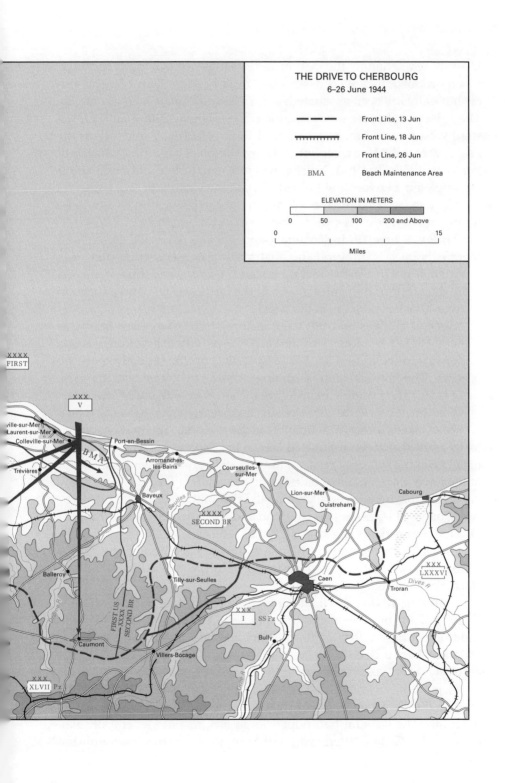

THE DRIVE TO CHERBOURG
6–26 June 1944

- - - Front Line, 13 Jun

Front Line, 18 Jun

Front Line, 26 Jun

BMA   Beach Maintenance Area

ELEVATION IN METERS

0   50   100   200 and Above

0   15

Miles

XXXX
FIRST

XXX
V

ville-sur-Mer
Laurent-sur-Mer
Colleville-sur-Mer

Port-en-Bessin

BMA

Arromanches-
les-Bains

Courseulles-
sur-Mer

Trévières

Lion-sur-Mer

Cabourg

Bayeux

Seulles R.

Ouistreham

SECOND BR

Balleroy

Tilly-sur-Seulles

Caen

Troran

Dives R.

XXX
LXXXVI

Drôme R.

FIRST US
SECOND BR

XXXX

Caumont

Villers-Bocage

XXX
I   SS Pz

Bully

Orne R.

XXX
XLVII Pz

Utah Beach. Though the Airborne divisions were widely scattered when dropped, they were assembling rapidly. More than 1,500 prisoners have already been evacuated, and 1,000 additional are in our hands. The 101st was driving southeast, the 175th Infantry [29th Infantry Division] west to try to make junction of the two corps, V and VII, at the bridge across the Vire river left of Isigny, the job of capturing which will fall to the 175th. The 2nd Division will move in the line, once unloading is completed, between the 1st and 29th, in the vicinity of Trevieres.

Customary raids during the night, but the Boche don't seem to be hitting much. They have yet to appear in any strength.

Friday, 9 June 1944: Reconnaissance for the Army CP began, and there is hope of getting off the boat tomorrow. General Bradley, it is reported, is not in a rush to set up on land: V Corps has still not pushed more than four or five miles inland at the farthest point, and a German counter-attack is perhaps in the wind.

General Hodges and Bill went ashore at 1500, stopping briefly at General Hoge's headquarters, and at V Corps, where a conference was underway to try to find means of speeding up the unloading on the beaches. The 2nd Division is coming ashore but without its vehicles; there is still great trouble in bringing the ships in with even flow.

They then went to the 29th Division headquarters, and to Isigny, which had been taken by the 175th Infantry in the morning. The town had been badly mauled, and the antiquated French fire department was still trying, mainly without success, to put out the fires still burning. A few miles south of the town, they ran into a battalion under artillery fire and spent a few uncomfortable minutes in ditches by the side of the road. They met General [Charles H.] Gerhardt[36] on the road and after attending a conference of division commanders at V Corps CP, they returned at 2230.

"They" were over again this morning and close enough to crack a couple of outer plates on our destroyer escort, some 300 yards off our stern. Four injured.

Saturday, 10 June 1944: The unloading went faster, today and Mulberry[37] is being built up in good time to permit unloading, whatever the condition of the sea. At first it was planned that we should go ashore at 1300, but there is delay with the vehicles, and the Rhino ferries[38] do not get away until 1900. We are scheduled to leave tomorrow at 0800.

General [Charles H.] Corlett[39] and General [Leland S.] Hobbs[40] arrived in the afternoon, and were taken ashore to V Corps Headquarters by Smith. The General had hoped to go ashore, but General Bradley is over with General [Bernard Law] Montgomery[41] and later with the

101st, and apparently does not want to risk having General Hodges ashore at the same time.

Situation: The 4th Division kept on its attack northward, with the 8th and 12th Infantry on Montebourg; the 82nd driving west. The condition on the beaches continued to improve slowly. Two battalions of the 9th Infantry [2nd Infantry Division] entered the Forest Cerisy [Forêt de Cerisy] (where powerful concentrations of German arms were foreseen) without any opposition. The 9th Division began unloading on Utah.

Another raid. This is getting to be routine now.

The Campaign to Capture Cherbourg, 11–25 June 1944

Sunday, 11 June 1944: We went ashore on an LCVP at 0900, the General's two vehicles having preceded us the night before. Despite a message sent to Army CP requesting that we be picked up at General Hoge's headquarters, there was no one to meet us; Bill finally borrowed a jeep from the Engineers, and the General, Captain Mitchell and Colonel Akers went on ahead.

The CP is located three kilometres east of Grandcamp-les-Bains, about a mile in from the coast, in an apple orchard which had been badly torn up by heavy naval gun fire. This is in the area bitterly fought over by the Rangers; thirty-two bodies were removed by the Advance party before the CP was set up. In the lane which borders the CP on the left are four German 155s, and great piles of ammunition of light and heavy calibre.

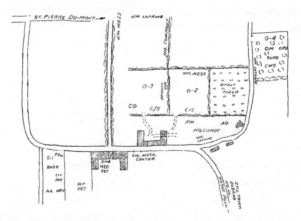

The initial First U.S. Army command post in France was located in an apple orchard and fields near Grandcamp-les-Bains from June 9 to July 2, 1944.

The General and Bill leave in the afternoon to make a tour of the front. Two companies of the 2nd Armored Division, attached to the 29th Division, holding a bridge outside Isigny, were first on their itinerary, followed by a visit to the CP of the 327th Glider [Infantry] Regiment [101st Airborne Division]. They then went forward in the direction of Carentan, which was the objective at that time of the 101st Division. On this road two miles outside the city the General and Bill had a tight squeeze. They heard a sudden yell of "Stop, there's a sniper in that house there." They braked and backed the jeep up behind the protection of a wall; the house in question was only some 10 yards ahead. The next car to follow was occupied by a parachutist Major (he had fought his way back to his lines with 28 men, after having been dropped a little off course); the sniper let loose at him and missed. The Major swung his tommy gun[42] around and sprayed the windows of the house, and then tossed a few hand grenades in for good measure. But no body was found; the sniper apparently had taken to his heels through a rear door.

The General returned to the CP where he met General [Anthony C.] McAuliffe[43] and went over the plans with him for the attack on Carentan planned for the next morning, and returned after 2000 to the CP. The customary planes overhead, and furious fire from AA—we have a gun battery to our right, and an AW [automatic weapons] battery to our left.[44] It is quite impossible to sleep through the night without awakening, but no bombs have been dropped in this vicinity.

As of 2400, the situation was as follows: No great change. The 101st has Carentan encircled, but not as yet captured the town proper.

Monday, 12 June 1944: No trip today for the General, as there are some "guests" coming—supposedly a secret, but everyone on the beach knows about it.

At 1200 General [George C.] Marshall,[45] General [Henry H.] Arnold,[46] Admiral [Ernest J.] King,[47] Admiral Kirk, and General Eisenhower drive into the CP, followed by two cars of newspaper correspondents and photographers. After a conference in the war room, they eat at the General's mess, and leave shortly afterward for Isigny, General Hodges riding with General Marshall and General Eisenhower. They were apparently very pleased with the way operations were proceeding and asked many questions on the capture of Isigny and Carentan, taken at 8 o'clock today, with which General Hodges was extremely familiar. He left them there, and returned to the CP.

The trailer arrived this afternoon; and after the camouflage net is placed, and the electricity set into motion; it is ready for occupancy. The General moved in.

Progress has been marked on all fronts, and though G-2 continues to report the arrival of new enemy units, the enemy has nowhere been able to launch a counter-attack in greater than battalion or, at the most, two battalion strength. The 1st Division made the greatest progress, capturing Caumont (26th Inf) late in the evening and are now dangerously ahead of the British who, after a remarkable swift advance in the first four days of the invasion, have since been stopped dead by heavy concentrations of German armor. The 39th Infantry [9th Infantry Division], attached to the 4th Division, took Brisbecq [Crisbecq], and Montebourg, where the Boche have been putting up a good scrap, fell to the 8th Inf [4th Infantry Division]. Contact between the V and VII Corps was being maintained by elements of the 29th and 101st Divisions in the vicinity of Lenauderie.

Tuesday, 13 June 1944: No trip today. The General spends it in almost continual conference with General Bradley, General Corlett, General Kean and other members of the staff. Chief point of discussion was where to place the XIX Corps and what its particular mission [will be]. The decision finally agreed upon was to place it between the V and VII Corps, with the 29th and 30th Divisions as its troops, with the mission of deepening our hold along the Vire River, and the Douve Canal [River], our lines here being nowhere farther inland than three miles.

Reports as of midnight indicate Montebourg held but not completely mopped up. The 101st supported by CCA of the 2nd Armored,[48] attacked southwest of Carentan but met heavy resistance and made only slight progress. The 90th Division continued its attack to the west with but small gains, in the vicinity of Pont L'Abbe. The V Corps front is relatively static.

Colonel [Samuel L.] Myers,[49] DC/S [Deputy Chief of Staff], announced this morning that the Army Commander wished no officers or men to cover up the designation of rank indicated on their helmet or sleeve. It should be noted, however, that front-line divisions, which have to deal with whatever number of snipers are around (and their number may be exaggerated), have taken this safety precaution.

Wednesday, 14 June 1944: The General and Bill started off a tour of the complete front this morning with a trip to the 1st Div CP (Brig Gen [Willard G.] Wyman,[50] and later on, General [Clarence R.] Huebner[51] and General [Leonard T.] Gerow[52]). From there he went to Caumont, to visit the OP [Observation Post] of the 2nd Bn [battalion], 26th Inf. A nervous

MP [military policeman], who had cause for his nervousness, tried his best to hurry the General through the square; a few seconds later, the reason became evident—a Boche shell landed nearby and tore a piece off a building. The 1st is square in possession of the town, but from the OP, it is plain that the Germans have the high ground south and are using it to advantage. The 1st will not move on until the British advance on the left—the 1st has now pushed far ahead, and there are obvious risks.

The General then took in the CP of the 2nd Armored Div, where he conferred with Colonel [Charles D.] Palmer,[53] the Chief of Staff, and down the road a few yards, met General [Edward H.] Brooks,[54] CG [Commanding General]. At the forward CP, he met General [Walter M.] Robertson,[55] of the 2nd Division who reported that they had had quite a bit of trouble with Frenchmen, who were continually cutting the signal communications. He said that he had issued a blanket order for his division to kill, on the spot, all Frenchmen caught sniping; and his Signal Officer had warned the French that evacuation of the population would inevitably follow any further cutting of the lines. Since the warning, there had been none.

At the V Corps Hq, the General talked with General Gerow (the latter said that V Corps had reached all its objectives, and the General smilingly reminded him that the objective was Berlin); at the 29th CP, he chatted with General Gerhardt, and later saw General Corlett, General [Leroy H.] Watson[56] (3rd Armored Div), Brig Gen [Norman D.] Cota,[57] and Brig Gen D. O. [Doyle O.] Hickey,[58] CCA of the 3rd Armored.

The Germans dropped a bomb a few feet from the enlisted mens' mess tonight; it splintered the tent but luckily injured no one. The plane escaped safely through a terrific barrage.

The town of Montebourg was recaptured by the Germans in the morning, but by evening it was again in our hands. The 22nd and 39th Inf took Quineville at 6 o'clock tonight.

The 90th and 9th Infantry divisions and 82nd A/B [Airborne] Div launched a coordinated attack at 1000—the general plan of which is to cut the [Cotentin] peninsula, and then, this done, drive on to Cherbourg.

Some elements of the VIII Corps Headquarters, being brought in ahead of schedule, and the 79th Div arrived over Utah Beach. The 83rd has been phased up to an approximate date of 23 June; the beach on which it will land will not be selected until the last minute—the decision resting on the success of the drive toward Cherbourg.

Thursday, 15 June 1944: The General spent the day witnessing the debut of the 30th Division.

Its assignment was to drive down the right bank of the River Taute (below Isigny), seize Montmartin-en-Graignes and take the high ground overlooking the [Vire-Taute] canal. In the attack were the 120th Inf, supported by four battalions of FA [Field Artillery], a Battalion of tanks (2nd Armd Div) and with the 119th [Infantry Regiment] in reserve. Naval gunfire opened the assault at 0800.

When the General arrived at the 30th Div CP at 0930 (just below Isigny), not much progress had been made. He conferred there with General Corlett, General Hobbes [Hobbs], and General McLean [Raymond S. McLain] (Div Artillery Commander)[59] and then went out with General Corlett to view the action from an OP the other side of the river overlooking the town under attack. The town was under our artillery fire at the time, and the crack of machine-gun and small arms fire was sharp and near. Six or seven Boches crossed a field more than once which led up from the river to a copse of trees near the church, and the General was about to direct fire on them when there was a whine from the clump of woods some 400 yards down the road leading to St. Lo, and then another, another, another. When the whine and bright flashes went on again, the location of some boche "Screaming Minnies" (Nebelgranat)[60] was set, and the previous target was cancelled in favor of these. After several rounds of smoke, and one or two for effect, the fire order was given, and the spot was covered, drenched with shell and fire. There was no further response from the Minnies.

At 1330 the General left to visit the CP of the 120th, where he met and talked to Col Hammonds [Hammond D.] Birks,[61] CO, and Lt Col Peter Wood, Executive. The town had not yet been taken, and there were conflicting reports as to the strength and nature of the opposition. After lunch there, and another chat with General Hobbes, the General returned to the OP, which had been occupied by two companies of the 117th Inf. The Boche was still using the open field below the church with apparent impunity, and it did not appear progress had been made. However, at 1640, the small arms fire did seem to be moving south of the town, and our artillery was now laying its fire several miles further down the road. The General paid a final visit to the 30th Div CP. By nightfall the town was ours—our casualties light. The Boche was over weakly during the night, but no bombs were dropped.

Good progress was made in the drive across the peninsula, by both the 9th and the 82nd.

The VIII Corps became operative at noon. At the present time they have the 101st Div with CCA of the 2nd Armd Div attached; their Headquarters are at Blosville, above Carentan, at the main road leading to Valognes. V Corps section quiet except for battalion counter-attacks on 1st and 2nd Div lines, both of which were repulsed.

Friday, 16 June 1944: The General and Bill spent a crowded day at the VII Corps front. The VIII Corps and General Troy Middleton[62] were first visited, and up the road, past St Mere d'Eglise [Ste.-Mère-Église], the VII Corps where, in the absence of General Collins, the General talked with Col [Richard G.] McKee.[63] Lunch, with salad and hot biscuits among other delicacies, put the Army mess to shame. There the General also saw General [Ira T.] Wyche,[64] CO, 79th Division.

After a short stop at the 9th Division CP (Col [Jesse L.] Gibney, C/S)[65] and 90th Div CP (General Landrum,[66] who succeeded Gen McKelvie [Jay W. MacKelvie][67] on Thursday as the CG, was absent but General Collins was present), the General went on to the forward CP of the 82nd Division which was viciously attacking west, trying to cut the peninsula. The route brought him through the tiny town of Pont L'Abbe, what was left of it, a powdery mass of masonry and rubble, nothing standing. Bombs and artillery had made, of the village, a mess unparalleled since the beginning of invasion. The CP was at St. Sauvuer Le Vicomte [St-Sauveur-le-Vicomte] where the General talked to General Ridgeway [Ridgway][68] and General [James M.] Gavin.[69] The 82nd has apparently found that the boche have slit the throats of several of their boys, and are asking for no quarter and giving none. All along the roads in this area were smashed gliders, some stripped of their clothing, others completely burned out, hung and draped against trees and hedges. How the men came out alive to fight as they have fought is something of a miracle.

The line, except in this vicinity, remains substantially unchanged. The 4th is holding; so are the 1st, 2nd, 29th and 30th. Air opposition is feeble, the Boche artillery extremely weak, and the G-2 reports that among troops in that sector there is an approaching demoralization, because of lack of ammunition and supply. The Germans, however, opened up with "Crossbow"[70]—the operation employing pilotless rocket bombs. One report has it that these bombs have traveled as far as North Ireland; first report casualties in the London area are 100 killed, and several hundred injured.

Saturday, 17 June 1944: A quiet day finishing out the tour of the VII Corps sector. The General first visited VIII Corps where, in the absence of General Middleton, he talked with Col [Walter C.] Stanton,[71] DC/S;

then to the 90th Division for a long chat with General Landrum; and then to the 4th Division for a talk with General [Raymond O.] Barton,[72] General Wyche (79th), and a brief howdy-do with Teddy Roosevelt.[73] Lunch was had, at three o'clock, beside four stout boche block-houses at Azeville, some three miles from the beach, which the 4th Div had taken. They were well-camouflaged, but the General pointed out, badly placed—all four in 100 yards' straight line. A group of enlisted men had apparently found the Boches' wine cellar in one of them; they brought out a full case, together with assorted bottles of vermouth and brandy.

The day finished with a long conference with General Middleton at VIII Corps Hq (The VIII now has control of the 101st alone). The latter reported that the Boche has been shelling the Isigny-Carentan bridge fairly steadily since 0300 that morning, but there was no artillery fire when we passed, shortly after 1700.

It appears that Army will maintain its present CP indefinitely.

The front line in VII Corps tonight runs north from Quineville-Montebourg-Le Han [le Ham]-bend in the Souve [Douve] River. The 9th Div cut the neck of the peninsula at 2330 when the 1st Bn, 47th Inf, gained a position just north of the town of St. Lo D'Ourville, and two Bns of the 60th Inf [9th Infantry Division] near St. Pierre d'Artheglise. Although troops are not actually at the waters' edge, the peninsula is cut by fire, we holding the commanding terrain. G-2 gives indication that some but not many Boche have been able to escape to the south. Other sectors: No change.

Sunday, 18 June 1944: The General and Bill spent the day at the XIX Corps Sector, starting at the CP with lunch with General Corlett and staff—a lunch featured by steak and french fried potatoes. After lunch, the General went on to the 29th Division, which has suffered heavy casualties (in comparison with other divisions) and had a talk with General Gerhardt. A conference at the 30th Div CP, where the General had his picture taken congratulating Colonel Hammond Birks on the capture of Montmartin-en-Graignes (see June 15), finished off the day.

All fronts quiet but VII Corps, where final plans were being made for a coordinated attack on Cherbourg, using the 4th, 79th and 9th Divisions.

The 60th Inf meanwhile occupied Barneville-sur-Mere [Barneville-sur-Mer], on the west coast of the peninsula, and the 357th RCT [Regimental Combat Team] [90th Infantry Division][74] relieved the 47th RCT [9th Division] along the line Portball [Portbail] to Newville en-Baumont

[Neuville-en-Beaumont] to hold that line against all attacks from the south.

The attack—"Blitz"—that Monty [General Montgomery] has been long planning on the British front has again been postponed—this time to June 20th.

Monday, 19 June 1944: A cold, heavy rain did not prevent the General from his scheduled visit to the 1st and 2nd Divisions. He started with talk, at V Corps Headquarters, with Colonel [Henry J.] Matchett,[75] C/S, and Colonel [Karl E.] Henion,[76] DC/S, Planning; and also with Colonel Hurley Fuller,[77] who had just been relieved of command of the 23rd Inf [2nd Division] and was pleading for another regimental assignment. A delicious lunch was served up.

At the 2nd Div CP, where General Gerow and General Robertson were found hunched over a map, operations were not progressing according to hopes. The day's plans called for seizure of Hill 192 from the Boche, but the 3rd battalion of the 23rd was finding the Boche well entrenched (according to General Robertson) and despite the fact that the Div had 60 guns available (with all the ammunition needed) the nature of the terrain was such as to deny good observation. (Later, privately, the General expressed the opinion that if they had gone about the attack correctly, and had not tried so many intricate flanking maneuvers, they would have reached their objective). When departure was made from the CP—situated in a grove formed by two rows of double-planted beeches more than 100 feet high—the Bn had reached only the first phase line. (CP just one mile from Cerisy-la-Foret).

The General then visited General Huebner at the CP of the 1st Div, occupying the ground surrounding one of the many estates of the Marquis de Balleroy (it was rumored that he had lost possession of this particular estate in a card game some years before), unoccupied when the Americans arrived. The 1st was still holding, pending catch-up of the British on their left flank, though aggressive patrols were being sent out all the time (General Huebner said he'd be "damned" if he'd have any no man's land in front of his division). After an hour and one half chat in General Huebner's work trailer, the General returned to Army CP, arriving at 1730.

The VII Corps attacked at 0500 this morning, and except in the 4th Div sector, encountered little opposition on the western side, rapid advances were made—the 9th passing thru Bricquebec, reaching St Christophe du Foe [St Christophe du Foc] and firing on the fortress of Cherbourg itself with 4.5 [inch] guns. The 79th Div, with the 4th, flanked whatever was left of the city of Valognes. The 4th reached La Maison Range, Les Fosses and Logis de-Savigny. Large fires in Cherbourg are evidence that the enemy is going about systematic destruction.

Effective at 1800, the 90th and 82nd Divisions were detached from VII Corps and attached to VIII Corps.

Tuesday, 20 June 1944: The General and Bill made a routine trip to VII and VIII Corps Headquarters in the afternoon. General Collins told the story of one evacuation hospital which put twenty German Prisoners of War to work one evening, only to find to their astonishment, twenty-five working in the wards the next morning. No one knew exactly where they came from, but the conclusions seemed obvious.

Operations are proceeding satisfactorily in the drive toward Cherbourg, though continued high winds hamper the unloading of supplies, and especially ammunition, which still remains a semi-critical item. All quiet on other fronts, active patrolling only.

At day's end, the 4th, approaching Cherbourg from the east and southeast, were seven miles away, the 79th, 3½ miles south. Valognes was passed through by the 8th Inf before noon; not a shot was fired. The 9th encountered stiffened resistance and prepared defensive position southeast of Flottemanville-Hague.

The 90th Div regrouped near Reigneville in preparation for an attack to secure the line Lessay Le Coutrie. The 82nd secured a deep bridgehead over the Souve [Douve] River south of Pont L'Abbe.

Wednesday, 21 June 1944: The General and Bill again visit the VII Corps area, the Divisions in which are still making good progress toward the port. There is every indication that they have retired to their fixed defenses and will put up a stiff fight there.

On the way, they passed through the towns of Montebourg and Valognes—wrecks of towns now, with huge masses of rubble blocking the streets, the main street of the latter pitted with gigantic bomb craters. The damage done is such that repair work is out of the question; the towns must be rebuilt in entirety. A search was made for the CP of the 4th Div, but the MPs in Valognes were ignorant of any location, many roads leading out of the town were blocked, and after an hour's search, the General called off the hunt. A stop at the CP of the 79th Div was made and on return, at VII Corps, which was then in the process of moving forward its CP.

In the evening Lt General [Carl A.] Spaatz[78] and Mr. [Robert A.] Lovett,[79] Ass't Secretary of War for Air, were in conference with General

Bradley and General Hodges in the former's trailer, making final plans for air operations against Cherbourg

Thursday, 22 June 1944: The General this morning presented Distinguished Service Crosses to twenty officers and men of the 2nd and 5th Ranger Battalions at a ceremony at Colombiere [Colombières], headquarters of the 2nd Battalion which turned out in mass formation for the awards.

After the "blanket" General Order of First Army was read announcing the awards, the General pinned the Cross on the shirt of each soldier, shook his hand and congratulated him. Among those decorated were Lt Col J. E. Rudder,[80] commanding the 2nd Bn, and Lt Col Max Schneider,[81] commanding the 5th.

In a brief address, the General told the men that these awards were the first that had been processed through, that General Bradley wanted him to tell them that there would be other awards shortly for similar deeds of gallantry in action. He said he liked to think of these awards as representing the will of the American people who, through their Congress, had created these awards; and that, in their presentation, the people back home were thanking them for a job well done in defense of their country. At the close of his talk, he saluted those decorated, and drew aside Lt Cols Rudder and Schneider for a brief chat.

The next stop was made at the CP of the 29th Div, just in time to hear the report of four patrol leaders who had gone out at midnight with their men and returned at 0330 with information of value.

Three were lieutenants (two of whom had only joined the Division as replacements the Saturday before); the fourth was a Sergeant. All of them had met with some reaction from the enemy—flares, rifle fire, in some cases machine pistol and machine gun fire. One of the 1st Lts said his patrol had knocked out a German machine gun position twice and had accounted for at least seven dead (at the loss of one man). But as he had not brought in any evidence of same—in the form of German soldiers' book[82] or similar proof—it was possible that the patrol may have been less successful than thought.

However, General Gerhardt was pleased with the performance and pinned Bronze Stars on all four men, saying that the medal was "not much" but that it should mean a great deal to them as proof they had done a dangerous job to the very best of their experience and ability. General Hodges shook hands with the men, who were as proud as punch, and looked it.

The General next went to the CP of the 115th Regiment (commanded since last Saturday by Col Goodwin [Godwin] Ordway,[83] replacing Col [Eugene N.] Slappey[84]) to see his nephew, 2nd Lt. Sam N. Hodges, Jr. who had just been assigned, as a replacement, to command a heavy weapons platoon. The General chatted with him for twenty minutes, learned that the casualties among officers of the Division ran everywhere high, and after a few minutes talk with Col Ordway, went on.

A twenty-minute stop was made at the CP of the 30th Div where, in the absence of General Hobbes, Lt Col Hassenfelt [Harold E. Hassenfeldt], G-3, brought the General up to date on the situation. Return to Army CP was made over the marsh and inundated area across from La Cambe.

All during the day missions of medium bombers had been droning overhead, on their way to batter Cherbourg. That evening, at 1930, a B-24,[85] sputtering into flames directly over the CP, went into a scream power-dive and crashed about two miles south of the CP, sending up a thick spiral of black smoke.

AA only expended about twenty shells last evening, and no one complained of lack of sleep.

Situation: Cherbourg took an 80-minute shellacking from light and medium bombers today, and by dark the 79th and 9th Divisions had gained approximately 1800 yards in their respective sectors. The going is slow and tough. The 24th Rcn Sqdn [Reconnaissance Squadron] completed patrol of the northeast horn of the peninsula and reported no German troops in the area.

The scheduled attack by the VIII Corps has been postponed pending seizure of Cherbourg.

All quiet on other fronts.

Friday, 23 June 1944: At the War Room conference this morning, General Von Schliefen's [Generalleutnant Karl-Wilhelm von Schlieben][86] order to the Fortress Cherbourg troops was made known to those present. In it, the General said that all officers and non-commissioned officers were to shoot, on the spot, all those who left their presently occupied posts. He also laid down certain regulations concerning the use of ammunition—not to fire, for instances, unless a concentration of so and so many Americans were spotted—indicating a shortage, of which there has been much evidence before.

Shortly after the conference, the first line of a steady stream of C-47s[87] droned overhead. Five hundred are due to arrive today, and every day until further notice, bringing ammunition. Though the beach unloading was better yesterday—the week-long high winds having subsided—there is still not much leeway. Supply on hand this morning was 2.8 units of fire.[88]

The General drove this morning to the CP of VII Corps, located in a Chateau one mile west of Valognes. On the way, a mile beyond Carentan he met General [Maxwell D.] Taylor[89] of the 101st who, with Colonel [Howard R.] Johnson,[90] was just completing his "Historical Research" on the scraps his division had had. Fire from the USS Quincy had helped these men, dropped into marshland between the road and the sea. He said there were only 1300 men in his division now counted missing, and that a few were wanderers returned every day.

When he arrived at Corps Hq, "Monty," in blue beret and light blue sweater, was conferring with General Collins. When Monty left the General went upstairs to talk with him and Colonel McKee.

The 79th had just pushed beyond one of the objectives they asked to be bombed. General Collins said, and they did not know yet whether the Air Corps had properly followed the smoke (which the 79th had heavily shot out in front of its lines) or had followed the original plans. The 4th, General Collins said, were receiving some fire from their rear, from troops collected around the airfield 5 miles east of Cherbourg, and he favored General Hodges suggestion of having the Rangers used to clean up that horn of the peninsula and protect the rear. Five ships, of undetermined size and purpose, had just been sighted steaming west toward the harbor; our Long Toms[91] were laying it on, and the Air Corps had been advised. It was now a question of whether to use the Navy off-shore as aid or not. General Collins favored their concentrating on four forts, which were shown on all aerial mosaic of the region as well as on a general map of the defenses, captured by the 4th Div the day before. The discussion went on when General Bradley arrived at noon. (General Collins was anxious to use his Corps in the drive after seizure of Cherbourg; General Bradley reminded him that "Troy [Middleton] likes to fight too." General Bradley also had some definite words to say about Divisions and Commanders who appeared to be fighting the war for newspaper headlines alone. This competition for publicity, he told General Collins, will have to cease).

The General was also informed that Colonel [Charles Bowler] King,[92] Corps G-2, was missing and presumed to be a prisoner. The evening before, acting on a tip that there were Boche surrendering along the coast below Barneville, he went down there with a small group. When they reassembled, Colonel King was missing, and a subsequent search by the Provost-Marshal and Colonel King's brother, ended in the wounding of the Provost Marshal, and the shell-shock of the brother. The area in which Colonel King met with accident was well within VIII Corps boundary, outside VII Corps jurisdiction.

Following lunch, the General finally found—through no help of the MPs (who knew nothing) the CP of the 4th Div, stuck off on a dusty side road six miles north of Valognes. He talked over the situation with Colonel [James S.] Rodwell,[93] C/S, and then with General Barton and Teddy Roosevelt, who had just returned from the 22nd Inf. They, like General Collins and Colonel McKee, had been strafed by their own planes the day before, but they regarded the incident as "inevitable" with the bomb line so close to troops. Both of them requested General to ask General Bradley to have issued some statement to the effect that the 1st, 4th and elements of the 29th had assaulted the beaches at the same time. They said the Division had been furious that publicity had been given the 1st Div as the first to land.

We arrived back at 1800. The only other news of the day is that the 83rd and 3rd Armored Divisions have come ashore and are assembling north of the Isigny-Colombière area.

Saturday, 24 June 1944: The General and Bill spent the day in the XIX Corps sector—talking with General Hobbes and General [William K.] Harrison,[94] and staying at the Div CP for lunch.

After lunch, the Generals drove to the 120th Inf CP and then to an OP which overlooked the now fairly static sector. Upon return to the regimental CP, General Hobbes presented the Silver Star to a Captain, and Bronze stars to four enlisted men.

The General then paid his first call on the 3rd Armored Division now half ashore, the CP of which is at Les Oubeaux, two miles south-west of that of the 30th Div. In the absence of General Watson, Colonel [John A.] Smith,[95] C/S, talked with the General.

During the course of the day in which General Eisenhower paid a brief visit to General Bradley and the newly-arrived 83rd Div, a general advance against the Cherbourg defenses was made by all divisions, aided materially by close air support missions, and the outskirts of the city are, tonight, from 1200 metres away (79th Div) to 3500 metres (4th Div). Twenty three hundred prisoners were taken during the day. The VIII Corps continued active patrolling, and picked up a few isolated groups west of St Sauveur Le Vicomte trying to infiltrate south. No change on other fronts.

An indicator to the fierceness of the first few days' fighting and also, perhaps, to the respective skills of the divisions is furnished by the casualty figures for the period covering up to 22 June. They are, in numerical order, as follows:

Unit	Killed	Wounded	Missing	Captured	Total
82nd A/B	475	1587	2577	14	4653
29th Div	751	2599	524	155	4029
4th Div	524	2717	505	7	3753
101st A/B	447	1773	1360	0	3580
90th Div	434	2455	36	82	3007
2nd Div	309	2270	320	24	2923
1st Div	224	1829	303	0	2356
9th Div	151	966	77	0	1194
79th Div	84	345	87	0	516
30th Div	59	301	37	0	397

The grand total, including tank battalions and their spare parts units, is:

Killed	3640
Wounded	18023
Missing	6401
Captured	292
Total	28346

The estimated strength of the Army was put at 250,000; the wounded evacuated to the United Kingdom at 16,808. Prisoners totaled 11,141.

Sunday, 25 June 1944: The General made an early start this morning, leaving with his guest, Major General F. W. [Francis B.] Wilby,[96] Superintendent of the US Military Academy, at 7:30 to visit the 1st and 2nd Divisions, with which the latter had served during the First World War.

First stop was the CP of the 1st, the engineer regiment of which General Wilby had formerly commanded [formerly the First Engineer Regiment and now the First Engineer Combat Battalion]. During General Huebner's absence at Mass, General Hodges and General Wilby visited the G-3 Room which, during the interval between our last visit, had moved underground. There had been shelling of the CP two nights before—one killed and four injured—and now, over our heads, instead of canvas, were two thicknesses of heavy pine log, atop of which were sandbags and dirt. The British on the left had that morning launched an attack, and indications at 0845 were that they had reached their first phase line.

General Huebner said, with a twinkle and with his mouth curling into a smile, that he had "no idea" of whom his Division was up against, because his men refused to take prisoners—"could have taken four yesterday easily, but preferred to kill them." He said relations between his Division and the British were excellent; that he had discovered one, and possibly two German batteries yesterday, and had laid it on them heavily, with good results.

A visit to General Robertson followed. The 2nd, as the 1st, was beginning to feel a healthy respect for the Boche artillery, and engineers were scooping out great shovels of dirt to move the CP underground. General Robertson reviewed his Division's battles, and said that Hill 192, which they had held with one company overnight but had been forced to abandon because of lack of reserve, was still the main problem. He said he had been conducting two experiments (1) TOT—Time on Target, in which the guns are so phased that shells from all cascade into the target at the same time, thus preventing the enemy from taking cover or digging in and (2) communications between a tank and infantry by means of a telephone coming out of the rear of the tank. In this way, the platoon leader, protected by the armor ahead, could direct the tank which, buttoned up, was proceeding in the dark.

A stop was made at V Corps, but General Gerow was out, and after a brief chat with Colonel Matchett, General Wilby was driven to Mars Headquarters[97] for embarkation on a PT boat back to England.

After lunching at the CP, the General returned to V Corps for a long conference with General Gerow, and then a visit to the 83rd Div CP at Bricqueville (as usual, badly marked). There he met and talked with General [Robert C.] Macon,[98] Brig Gen [Claude B.] Ferenbaugh,[99] Col Krathoff [Samuel L. Krauthoff],[100] C/S; and Col [John C.] Whitcomb,[101] an "extra" regimental commander. During the afternoon some novel detours through the back country roads of France were made, but fortunately ended up in the general intended destination.

During the day, the assault on Cherbourg continued unabated. Reports of patrols entering the city, and then withdrawing were reported—these patrols stating that a great deal of resistance was not encountered. Street fighting in the outskirts of the entire city was going on constantly. The 9th Div delivered an ultimatum to the Boche at 1630 by officer courier, but no reply had been received at midnight. Other fronts: No change.

A 25-mile wind was predicted for today by the "weather experts" and many smaller craft had taken refuge in the nearest harbor, but the day was hot, the sky clear, and there was no suggestion of breeze, even less wind.

Expanding the Lodgment, 26 June–24 July 1944

Monday, 26 June 1944: The General spent the morning in conference with General Bradley, General Kean, and Colonel Thorsen, planning the course [of] action to be taken, and the movement of divisions to be made, following the fall of Cherbourg. General Macon of the 83rd Div arrived at Headquarters and his division started to move at 2230 into the line, to replace the 101st around the Carentan area.

Last night and today there continued to sound the thunder of artillery from the XIX Corps sector. In the afternoon the General visited their CP for a chat with Gen Corlett. The Boche may be building up strength in this area, but the XIX Corps will be ready.

In the evening it was expected that the CP would have as its guests General von Schlieben, commander of Fortress Cherbourg (who issued the "fight or be shot" order) and Admiral [Walther] Hennecke,[102] captured during the afternoon. General Bradley said that he had no desire to see them—if they had surrendered a few days before he might have been interested in their comments, he said—and Col Dickson, G-2, finally decided that security-wise, it would not be a good idea to bring [them] into the CP. They were consequently stopped at Isigny and interviewed there. Both were found extremely uncommunicative.

At the end of the day all organized resistance had ceased in Cherbourg, except in the arsenal. The Fort de Roule [Fort du Roule], just to the right of the Valognes-Cherbourg highway, on the outskirts of the city, fell after a tough fight in which elements of the 79th Div overran the top floor and then blasted their way from floor to floor, finally captured 180 men at the bottom. The 79th Div is being relieved at noon tomorrow by the 4th, while the 9th will turn west to mop up Cap de Hague [Cap de la Hague]. Approximately 8000 prisoners have been taken during the past 24 hours; 15,000 during the past four days, it is estimated. First estimates as to the condition of the port ranges from fair to very good. On other fronts: No change.

Tuesday, 27 June 1944: The General spent a half-hour with General Middleton (VIII Corps) discussing the coming offensive, his Corps moving south along the west coastline of the peninsula, VII Corps moving down into the area directly west of Carentan, and moving, after start of the VIII Corps drive, upon issuance of orders from General Bradley. General Ridgway and General [Hobart R.] Gay,[103] DC/S of Third Army, were at the CP at the time but did not take part in the discussion.

Then on to VII Corps, (passing many prisoners in trucks, on their way to the PW cage,) where General Collins was told details of the coming drive. He requested the Corps rear area be enlarged north of Carentan to give his artillery and other supporting troops necessary movement space and sufficient roadways.

Word had just come through, at our arrival, that the Arsenal and its troops had surrendered and before we left, the German general in Command [Generalmajor Robert Sattler, deputy fortress commander], with a Lt Col and his orderly, arrived at the Chateau, to be liberally photographed, and then offered the facilities of Gen Collins' quarters.

General Collins said that Von Schlieben, a gigantic six-foot, four-inch-tall Prussian, had been most uncommunicative, preferring not to answer the one question General Collins was most interested in: why had the Germans not defended the high ground around Cherbourg (a good outer ring) instead of retreating to the inner ring of forts to make their stand. He said that von Schlieben had surrendered in a tunnel along with 800 other troops but that the Boche had declined to command the other still resisting groups to do likewise.

General Collins said he expected some tough opposition in the western horn of the peninsula; that the 9th had encountered more artillery fire from forts there than during the entire campaign; that the air corps, after some argument, had finally agreed to go after some of these batteries; and that he hoped he could call the business ended in two or three days, but was not certain. He was going to Cherbourg at 4 o'clock where, in the Place de la Republique, he and the Mayor were going to trade appropriate words in celebration of French-American friendship.

The General decided that, under the circumstances, it would perhaps be better not to go to Cherbourg, so he returned to Army CP, arriving at 1500.

During the day the 9th Div moved up to take on the enemy resisting in the Cap de Hague area—estimated at 3,000, remnants of the 709th and 243rd Divisions. In the NE sector, stiff resistance at Maupertus airport was overcome; other troops in the area have agreed to surrender, some 10 officers and 400 men. The garrison of Fort de L'Ile Pelee likewise is also to surrender.

The 79th Div was relieved by the 4th and will move south to Fierville (0996*) [map coordinate]. The 83rd opened its CP at the location at Carentan formerly occupied by the 101st A/B which moved to 180944 [map coordinate].

The British VIII and XXX Corps continued slow advance against tenacious opposition. A bridgehead on the Odon River at 930630 was established, and the town of Juvigny occupied by the 146th Brigade [southwest of Caen].

Wednesday, 28 June 1944: The General spent the morning completing, with General Bradley, the plans for the coming push.

The General and Bill inspected Cherbourg this afternoon, after a brief stop at VII Corps headquarters on the way.

They found it a city in which war had certainly passed through, scarred and hit, but not to the extent that Montebourg and Valognes had been punished. They passed the Hotel Atlantique, Headquarters of the 12th Inf, and along the waterfront; the harbor seemed moderately normal in appearance, and one ship was in. Roads leading in and out of the city were jammed, many a truck sardined with prisoners. On the way home, boche artillery shelling the Carentan bridge forced a detour across the Doube [Douve] bridge.

During the day, there were no startling developments on any front. The mopping [up] of the Cap de Hague area continues; VIII Corps moved its CP westward near St Sauveur Le Vicomte; the British are advancing at snail's pace and finding the going exceedingly hard.

Thursday, 29 June 1944: The General witnessed another division's introduction to fire—that of CCA of the 3rd Armored Division which, under command of XIX Corps, attacked in the zone of the 29th Div to reduce the Villiers Fossard salient.

CCA was divided into three task forces[104]—X, Y and Z—and was supported by 10 Bns of artillery, its own, that of the 29th, and that of Corps. When the General arrived at the 29th CP (after a brief stop at Corps Hq), where Gen Corlett was awaiting "first returns," the news was that the attack was progressing slowly, despite a terrific pasting given the boche by five squadrons of aircraft starting at 0825. The nature of the opposition seemed to be in small arms fire principally, though later in the day ten different German batteries were spotted. Gen Watson, Gen Hickey, and Gen Cota were all at the front but did not seem to be able to push the advance forward with the hoped-for speed.

It was a noisy day—Gen Corlett admitted that "perhaps" they had exceeded their ammunition allowance—and conversation was, at times, postponed until the batteries behind us, and to right and left, had ceased firing. Early in the morning small arms fire had penetrated the CP, one spent bullet hitting in front of the War Room tent, another slicing a hole through the Chaplain's quarters, at which point, Gen Gerhardt remarked, he probably knelt to pray. The Boche, denied good observation and with no aircraft in the sky, was firing many high bursts in the 175th area, a mile or two to our right flank, but left the CP area strictly alone.

The General had lunch at the CP and returned to the War Tent, hoping the afternoon would bring decisive results. Gen Watson kept telephoning back that the objective would be reached but though Force X on the left was going ahead, Y was making little advance. Observers said only one tank had been disabled, and casualties were at 1500 light. Col [Edward H.] McDaniel,[105] C/S, who returned at 1500, said that the terrain—the usual story of "too many hedges"—and not the enemy were the real deterrent to quick success. When the General left at 1730, not too pleased with the advance (which, considering the power of the attacking force, was small indeed) the situation was still fairly obscure, but it was definite that the objective on the right, at any rate, had not been reached.

The first real batch of mail arrived tonight—after nine days of "no mail today."

Progress by the 9th Div was satisfactory in the Cap de la Hague area. The three forts on the outer breakwater to Cherbourg surrendered. On the British front heavy fighting continued; no advance was made, but the bridgehead south of River Odon was widened by the 43rd Div.

Friday, 30 June 1944: The General spent the morning in conference with Gen. Bradley, Gen Gerow and Gen Brooks and did not leave the CP until 1630, when a visit was made to Pointe de Hoe, a half-mile directly north of us.

The Pointe was a scene of complete destruction—huge bomb craters, shell holes, masses of concrete from broken forts tipped crazily on side, the ground littered with small cartridge belts, hastily discarded clothing, boche administrative papers, flares, grenades. Only a few green spots had been left untouched by the bombardments, and all the forts had received one or more hits. On the cliff, some 100 feet high and almost perpendicular, still hung one of the ladders the attacking Rangers had used. The General remarked that the boche must have suspected an attack on this position (so perfect a view it commanded over the Omaha and Utah beaches) for there were everywhere signs that he [was] still digging in, reinforcing his position, and close to the cliff itself was a machine-gun position, a hole covered with wooden logs, obviously not completed. On a path 150 yards behind the main forts were a helmet liner and helmet of a soldier of the 2nd Bn, a bullet hole directly in front which had spread the steel wide on emerging in back. There was still present the sweet, cloying smell of the dead.

During the day, the 9th Div continued advance up the Cap de la Hague peninsula, enemy resistance collapsing after capture in the late afternoon of the strong point of Greville. About 2400 prisoners were taken, and resistance was ended with the surrender of Lt Col Kiel [Oberstleutnant Günther Keil], commanding troops, at 0230 (1 July).

The 4th Div moved south and closed at Gouresville [Gourbesville] (2896) at 2300. The area about Cherbourg is being policed by the 101 A/B; the city itself by the 99th Bn.[106] CCA of the 3rd Armd Div continued its attack in the Villiers-Fossard salient and reached its objective—520668–530662–550658. The 115th Inf relieved them at night. On other fronts: no change. On the British front, elements of six panzer divisions have now been identified on the VIII and XXX Corps fronts. To 28 June, an estimated 100 British tanks have been lost as against 95 boche casualties. Casualties in man-power are just over 20,000; 5,700 prisoners have been taken.

Saturday, 1 July 1944: The General and Bill left in the afternoon to tour the peninsula sector, stopping first at the new CP of the VIII Corps, some four miles north of St Saveur Le Vicomte, for a conference with General Middleton, Col [Cyrus H.] Searcy[107] and Col [Andrew R.] Reeves.[108] Then they went on to the 90th Div, which is located in a fine old Chateau just south of the causeway leading across the marshes from Pont L'Abbe. Gen Landrum was out, so a conference was held with the C/S and Col Hurley Fuller, who has just been appointed DC/S. On the way home, the General stopped briefly in at the new CP of the VII Corps which, running true to form, is handsomely established on an estate just south of the crossroads above Blosville. VII Corps has captured a German frigidaire[109] and now have ice, among other "luxuries." There was no action of importance along any front, as all divisions are bent on moving up troops and supplies for the offensive starting Monday morning. The bad weather continues without letup.

Sunday, 2 July 1944: Headquarters moved its CP this morning, starting at 0600, and closing and opening at 1600. It is located, as before, in several apple orchards, and on both sides of the Isigny-Bricqueville road at a place (several houses) called Le Haut Chemin. The Germans had formerly occupied the field housing the Generals conveniently leaving a six-foot-deep fox-hole, in front of which the General's trailer is parked. The new location is comfortable, but noisy—Artillery from XIX Corps and anti-aircraft being active throughout the night.

In the afternoon, despite heavy rain, the General and Bill paid a short visit to the CP of the 3rd Armd Div where they met Gen Eisenhower and Gen Bradley. The former arrived last night for a visit of two or three days. This evening Gen Corlett and Gen Gerow were among those invited for dinner and after-dinner conference.

On the fronts: The 8th Div is arriving off UTAH beach and will go into assembly position W of Montebourg, to be attached to the VIII Corps. The 9th Div completed its concentration after mopping up the Cap de la Hague peninsula and moved north of Les Pieux. The 2nd Armd Div completed relief of the British 7th Armd Div at 0300, placing the 41st Armd Inf in defensive position in the area recently taken over from the Second British Army on the left of our sector. CCA, 3rd Armd Div (Army Reserve) moved under cover of darkness tonight to the area in the V Corps Sector vacated by the 2nd Armd Div. The Second British Army continued to consolidate their previously-won bridgehead over the ODON River.

Monday, 3 July 1944: The VIII Corps opened its offensive at 0530 this morning, and at 0930, the General started his rounds to see what success it was having. It was still raining, and for the first time we traveled with the top of the jeep up.

The General spent only a few minutes at the VIII Corps with Gen Middleton. As we left, Gen Eisenhower drove up with Gen Bradley, and a few minutes later the Boche, whether with malice aforethought or not is not known, dropped some 20 shells beyond the CP—deflection good, but range happily inaccurate.

We next visited the CP of the 79th Div, stuck off in the hills on a dirt road (off the main road to Portball) and, according to the General, very badly placed and set-up. Dispersion, he pointed out, was such that if any shelling was done, casualties would be infinitely greater than warranted. Gen Wyche was out, so the General talked with Gen [Frank U.] Greer,[110] Asst Div Comdr. The 79th was making very slow progress, though the prisoners taken (some 60 at noon) attested to the accuracy of our artillery fire. Everyone regretted, naturally, the forced cancellation of air bombardment.

After a stop off the roadway for K-rations[111] and coffee, we drove next to the CP of the 82nd Div where the Gen had a brief chat with [Lt] Col [Robert H.] Wienecke,[112] acting C/S (he had met him previously in

Africa) and then picking up Lt Col [Frederick M.] Shellhammer, G-1, as guide, drove on to the forward CP, located in a farmhouse a mile down the main road leading to Periers. The General there had a long chat with Gen Ridgway. Despite the fact they are operating at only 50 percent of strength, and have been in action, almost without letup, for a month, the Div was making good progress, the 505th and 508th [Parachute Infantry Regiments] going steadily forward, the 325th Glider Inf [Regiment] moving somewhat slower.

At our next stop, the Chateau CP of the 90th, we likewise found the CG to be ahead in a forward echelon so again picking the G-1 as guide (Lt Col [Frank G.] Adams) we drove down dirt roads to a farmhouse near Hotteville. There, deep in the Opns Room (an old wine cellar with ceiling four feet thick) the General discussed the situation with Gen Landrum. Gen Landrum said that Bn commanders were still not calling for artillery support as they should, and that infantry-tank coordination left much to be desired (the tank bn supporting them was having its baptism of fire) One of the American tanks had been captured by the Germans intact and was now being used against us, along with two of their own. (The American Tank apparently stalled in a hedgerow, and the Germans took it over). The 90th was encountering some mines and booby traps—six dead as of 1600. Artillery was putting on a great show of noise, and the Germans were counter-battering to the extent that some mud thrown up by a nearby shell splattered the courtyard in front of the CP. At 1630 we drove back to Army.

At the end of the day, the situation was as follows: the 79th, on the right, advanced their forward elements about 3,500 yards; the 82nd, in the center, about 4,000, reaching their initial objective, Hill 131 in the middle of the afternoon and extending their front to the La Haye du Puits–St Saveur Le Vicomte road; the 90th, on the left, about 3,000 yards, entering St Jores but being driven out by a counter-attack later in the day. On other fronts: there was no change.

Tuesday, 4 July 1944: The General and Bill this morning first visited the CP of the 83rd Div which was having its baptism of fire, and in the absence of Gen Macon, talked with Col Krauthoff, C/S. They then went on to VII Corps for a conference with Gen Collins and Col McKee. At noon they stepped outside to hear the Noon Salute—every gun in the Army firing one round in honor of the day.

The next stop was made at the forward CP of the 90th Div for a talk with Gen Landrum; then back to the CP of the 83rd and the CP of the 329th Inf where, in addition to Gen Macon and Gen Ferenbaugh, they again saw Gen Collins and Col McKee. There was an extended conference here, then on to Army.

The situation during the day was as follows: the 79th after only small advances the opening day did far better, advancing approximately 4,500 metres and being driven back only 1,000 by a tank-spearheaded counterattack by the Germans during the afternoon. In the left of the division good progress was made by the 314th to positions 1000 metres north and northwest of La Haye du Puits. The 82nd A/B occupied all their objectives and withstood a counter-attack on Hill 95. The 90th Div on the left made only slight progress and by midnight had reached the main road running from La Haye du Puits in the right sector and the north bank of the stream running NW from La Butte [La Hutte] in the left sector. The 8th Div reported 85% unloaded in its assembly area between Montebourg and Valognes.

The premiere of the 82rd [83rd] Div was disappointing. Advance of 1,200 metres was made, but casualties were high, particularly among officers, and only a few prisoners were taken. [At] 1900 the 330 and 331 Inf made a coordinated attack to seize Coulot but were driven back to their previous positions after a slight advance.

Wednesday, 5 July 1944: The General made his opening stop today at the VII Corps, where Gen Collins was in the process of trying to find out, without success, exactly what front lines the 83rd Div occupied. There were conflicting reports coming in every minute, and the General was exasperated (to put it mildly).

The 4th Div was at the time in the process of changing its CP from Gourbesville to the sector occupied by the 90th Div, but the General decided to take a chance on meeting Gen Barton at the old CP. We went through Gourbesville and were directed by the MPs to a road running left. After covering six or seven miles, with Fran [Capt. Francis Smith, one of Hodge's aides] hopelessly lost and with the General despairing of finding the location, Gen Barton drove by and in ten minutes we had reached their CP, located overlooking the marshy area at coordinate 319893. Teddy Roosevelt came in shortly after the General's arrival with a report from the situation at the bridge at Baupte, which the boche were trying to hit. As the General remarked later, the entire Div gave the impression of being all the way "in" this war and, so far as conditions allowed, enjoying it—full of vigor, enthusiasm, will to win.

After a 30-minute conference with Gen Barton in the latter's trailer, the General paid a call on the 83rd CP, which had moved, since his previous visit, from the canal at Carentan to a farmhouse on a dirt road

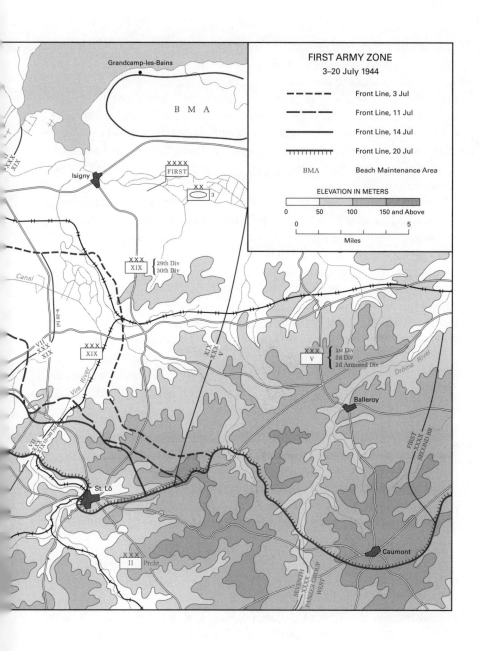

FIRST ARMY ZONE
3–20 July 1944

Front Line, 3 Jul

Front Line, 11 Jul

Front Line, 14 Jul

Front Line, 20 Jul

BMA   Beach Maintenance Area

ELEVATION IN METERS

0   50   100   150 and Above

0   5
Miles

Grandcamp-les-Bains

B M A

Isigny

FIRST

3

Canal

XXX
XIX   29th Div
       30th Div

VII
XXX
XIX

XXX
XIX

XXX
V

XXX
V   1st Div
       2d Div
       2d Armored Div

Vire River

Drôme River

Balleroy

FIRST
SECOND BR

VII

St. Lô

XXX
II   Prcht

SEVENTH
PANZER GROUP
WEST

Caumont

approximately three miles southwest of the city. As all Div CPs, it was badly marked; no MP was by the cut-off to direct traffic, and once the turn-off was made, the dirt road was entirely without marking of any nature. The CP was only a mile or so from the then front lines, but soldiers were walking around unconcernedly without helmets or side-arms; the General wondered whether nonchalance or stupidity was the primary cause of such behaviour. The situation at the Div did not look very promising, but the General patted Gen Macon on the back and told him to go to it.

The day—no surprise to us now—was cloudy with intermittent rains. We have quite given up hope of ever seeing the sun for more than a few minutes at a time—so fickle has been the weather, so quick the change from cloudless sky to hard, driving rain.

However, the air did have a chance to put down some of its weight today, and progress generally was not unsatisfactory. By dark the 79th Div front was such as to have encircled, from the north and west, La Haye du Puits. The 83rd Div captured the town of Culot [Coulot] and repulsed a counter-attack. There was no startling news from the British sector.

Thursday, 6 July 1944: Today, fortunately, was bright and hot, be-cause, for reasons as yet not known or at least unexplained, the Gener-als' CP shifted one field to the west, into a small area nearer the road, completely without cover and concealment facilities. Extra camouflage nets were hastily requisitioned, and by 1600, the trailers were reparked, practically bumper to bumper, next to a hedgerow, back end facing out into the field.

At the request of Gen Bradley, the General spent the afternoon visit-ing the wounded at two hospitals and one clearing station.[113] Col [John A.] Rogers,[114] the Army Surgeon, and Major Gen [Albert W.] Kenner,[115] Chief Surgeon SHAEF, accompanied him.

The first stop was made at the 83rd Div CP, and then on to the 34th Evacuation Hospital, which was operating in the field for the first time. All personnel were extremely busy, handling casualties from both the 83rd and 90th Divs. A stop was then made at the Clearing Station of the 83rd and then at the 128th Evacuation Hospital, a veteran unit which had been in the original North African invasion and had been in action ever since.

At all three establishments, the majority of the wounds seemed to be those of arm and leg (small-arms and machine-gun fire) though there were also those whose bodies had been badly smashed up by heavier enemy stuff. The morale of the soldiers with whom the General chatted appeared, in most cases, to be high; there were a few who complained of being hedged in by their own artillery fire. The General and Bill both watched briefly at the operating tables; the doctors as usual were without rest, doing their great job on a 24-hour schedule.

General [George S.] Patton[116] and Gen [Hugh J.] Gaffey[117] arrived in the middle of the afternoon (D plus 30, as scheduled) and the former was the General's guest for drinks in the trailer tonight. They intend to set up their headquarters in the vicinity of St Saveur Le Vicomte.

There were no startling developments during the day. Progress along the VII and VIII Corps sectors is very slow. Artillery and mortar fire of the enemy appears accurate and heavier than before.

Friday, 7 July 1944: A terrific artillery barrage, that of guns supporting the attack of the 30th Div this morning, woke everyone up at 0400. It continued for a full hour—the 8 inch guns situated only two miles to the south of the CP furnishing most of the noise.

At 1000 the General decided to see how the show was going—the purpose of which was to establish a bridgehead across the Vire River at Aire [Airel] (505745) and exploit to the west and south in that sector. The first stop was made at the new CP of the 30th, just north of Lison, in a field and well dug-in. Gen Hobbes was away, but Gen Harrison gave the General what the latter described as a "pep talk"; everything was "going very well," "opposition was slight," casualties, as of 1000, were only 44.

The General decided to see for himself, for with Lt Col [Stewart L.] Hall, G-2, as guide, we drove to the west two miles to an OP overlooking the river and [Vire et Taute] canal. Artillery fire was hitting to our left, but it was not close. However, Lt Col Hall lead us a fast & circuitous chase through heavy ferns and barbed wire 200 yards or so until we finally reached the dugout—covered with planks and sandbags. (The General later remarked that Col Hall was an officer who believed there were two kinds of officers only, "the quick and the dead," and he believed in remaining the first).

Two hundred yards below was the railroad, and 100 yards farther on the personnel of a chemical mortar company which had supported the attack. They were strolling about, apparently unconcerned, though Col Hall admitted that one of their ammunition dumps had gone up earlier in the day. Our artillery was screaming overhead, some of it hitting the higher hills about two miles away, other shells sending up bright red flashes to our left. Part of the attacking force had pocketed an enemy force in a clump of houses to our right center, but the main force of four companies which had crossed the canal was moving ahead. The boche was sending some shells back in return, and we could hear their "screaming Meemies" and the crackle of small-arms fire, but in general opposition did not appear to be particularly rugged. Two tanks, clearly visible, did not move one tread during the entire hour and one-half that we were there.

We next visited the CP of the 120th Inf which was due to jump off from their area at Montmartin-en-Graignes at 1345 and move south. We drove, following Col Hammond Birks, Regimental CO, to an OP, heavily dug in, which overlooked the road leading up from the canal into St Jean de Daye, the objective. At first, so heavy was the barrage, we could see nothing through the smoke; there was only the fog and smoke caused by the crashing shells. One company, we learned as reports came in, had crossed but had fairly heavy casualties through enemy artillery; Col Birks ordered the following company to pass on through, giving the first time to reorganize for attack. The enemy was laying in some of their own in front of our OP and were putting down heavy mortar fire on the canal which the Engrs [Engineers] had the mission to bridge as soon as possible. When we left, at 1545, the attack had progressed some 800 metres up the road leading to St Jean—slow but moving anyhow and not stalled, as it appeared from first reports.

During the day, no material gains were made on the VIII Corps front. The 79th advanced and was then thrown back; the 90th consolidated previously-won positions in the Foret de Mont Castre (high ground). During the night, the 8th Inf Div was moved into assembly area N of La Haye du Puits. In the VII Corps sector, the attack launched by the 4th Div failed to gain foothold on the high ground NW of Sainteny [and] the 83rd made slow progress on the front SE of Sainteny.

The attack on the XIX Corps front, which we had witnessed, was more successful, the 30th Div pushing past St Jean du Paye [St-Jean-de-Daye], 500 yards west and south. CCB of the 3rd Armd Div is moving forward to pass through the 30th and resume the attack south; CCA will follow CCB. On the 29th Div and V Corps fronts, no change.

Saturday, 8 July 1944: The General and Bill spent an hour this morning with Gen Collins. The two discussed the possible advantages to be gained by the transfer of the 9th Div (now at Les Pieux) to ground south-east of Carentan, to be under VII Corps. Coincident with this, the XIX Corps would cede part of its right flank to VII. Gen Collins said he believed this plan to be sound in every way and said he was going to see General Bradley for approval. Later in the day General Bradley put his whole-hearted OK to the plan, saying it was a brilliant tactical move.

Not stopping for lunch, the Gen went on to the 90th Div for a long chat with Gen Landrum, and then to the CP of the 359th [357th] Inf (Col [George B.] Barth,[118] CO). Arriving back home, he and Gen Kean enjoyed a hot shower. (Maj-Gen [Harold P.] Bull,[119] G-3, SHAEF, arrived back an hour later from a sight-seeing tour of the front, escorted by Fran [Smith].)

La Haye du Puits was captured during the day by the 1st Bn, 314th Inf which continued to mop [up] until dark. The 8th Div passed the town on both sides and had made some slight progress to the south by nightfall. The 90th Div made no gains of mention.

The VII Corps resumed the attack with the 4th on the right, the 83rd on the left; at the day's end elements of both were only a few hundred yards north and east of Sainteny. The 9th Div moved the 39th and 47th Inf near Montmartin-en-Graignes in preparation to take over the sector created by the readjustment of the XIX-VII Corps sector boundaries (see diary for Friday, 7 July, and above).

The XIX Corps continued to exploit the bridgehead established over the Vire River and good progress was made by the 120th, 117th and 119th Inf assisted by both combat commands of the 3rd Armd Div. By dark a line had been established from a point 450765 on the Canal southeast to 492722 and then east to the Vire River.

The British launched an assault against Caen, preceded by bombardment of 600 heavy and medium aircraft, and after heavy fighting had forced their way to the high ground overlooking the eastern outskirts of the city. Elements of the XXX Corps crossed the Hottot-Caumont highway in the vicinity of Des Landes—in considerable strength.

Sunday, 9 July 1944: Another nasty day, and the General postponed his departure until 1400, when he drove up to VIII Corps. Gen Middleton was at the 8th Div, so after a brief chat with Col Searcy, he decided to follow Gen Middleton there.

The route followed was that suggested by Corps—a roundabout dirt road to Carmesnil, St Sauveur de Pierre-Pont [St-Sauveur-de-Pierrepont], La Fotterie [La Poterie]. As we approached the front lines (as indicated by the map) the General stopped a dozen soldiers. They appeared poorly instructed; not one knew the location of the CP, and there was no road markers out. Not until we were within 50 yards of it, and saw a Brig Gen's car, were we sure we were on the right track. The General found Gen Middleton gone, but had a brief chat with Gen

[William C.] McMahon[120] and learned that the 8th had made no known progress. After a shifting of guides (one of whom wished to take us back by a road even more circuitous than the one we had taken) a Lt Col was found who had traveled back to St Sauveur by the short route, and we followed him out to the main highway.

During the day, the advances made were as follows: VIII Corps, none; VII Corps, the capture of Sainteny, and advance along the Carentan-Periers road to the crossroads 338778 by the 22nd Inf.; XIX Corps, advance, despite a stiff armor counter-attack, to a line running roughly from La Meauffe to Le Desert [Le Dézert]; V Corps, none.

The 35th Div completed its concentration in the area between the Vire River and St Claire sur L'Elle [St-Clair-sur-l'Elle].

On the British front, the northern part of Caen fell to I Corps. A large pocket of enemy holding out several miles north of the city has been trapped, and it is only a matter of time before they surrender or are decimated.

Monday, 10 July 1944: The General and Bill did not leave the CP until 1430 and made their first stop at the CP of the 9th Div where they talked to Gen [Donald A.] Stroh,[121] Gen [Reese M.] Howell,[122] Gen Collins (likewise visiting) and a general officer from the 5th Div. They then drove on to St Jean de Daye where they met Gen [Manton S.] Eddy.[123] The latter was in very good form, optimistic over the way the fighting was going and confident that the enemy would not hold up very long. The General remarked to Bill later that the attitude and military bearing of the 9th was a pleasure to see; that it was one division which had remembered all it had been taught, and that discipline and self-confidence were the natural result.

They then paid a visit to the 4th Div for a chat with Gen Barton and Gen Roosevelt. The former had had a very narrow escape from death that day when an artillery shell had landed only 25 yards away; shrapnel would probably have reached him had it not been for an apple tree luckily standing in the way. The CP of the Division was located near a crossroads on which the enemy had been "working" from time to time; their artillery had also been plumping close to the CP of the 22nd, and Gen Barton advised the General against visiting it. The General didn't want to give in to this request, but finally decided that discretion was perhaps the better course to follow.

Gen Barton took the General to see some positions, 600 yards south of the CP, which had been abandoned by the defending paratroopers a few days ago. The boche had left in a hurry—machine pistols, pouches of ammunition, clothing, and rifles were strewn for yards. The positions themselves were minor masterpieces, dug in under the hedgerows, and vulnerable only, perhaps, to direct hit from very heavy stuff. They had been "flanked" out of these positions; frontal assault would have been unnecessarily costly.

The day's military news:

VIII Corps: The 8th Div captured Mobecq; the 90th Div made slight gains to the southern edge of Foret de Mont Castre. There was decreasing resistance all along the front.

VII Corps: The 83rd Div made slight advances only, the 330th Inf meeting 7 enemy tanks (believed Mark VIs[124] dug in) which TD [tank destroyer] fire failed to neutralize. The 4th Div cracked the enemy positions southwest of Sainteny and took La Mangerie [La Maugerie] and La Roserie. The Germans appeared, at one point, with a white flag and officer, but after firing stopped and we went forward to find out the situation, it turned out to be a typical German trick—they were only fooling, to provide their troops an opportunity to withdraw unmolested. The 9th Div also went ahead, against heavy mortar and machine-gun fire.

XIX Corps: The 30th Div, supported by CCB, 3rd Armd Div, advanced to within 400 yards of Le Desert and on the left took Pont Hebert and advanced to within 200 yards of the crossing over the Vire.

Tuesday, 11 July 1944: The General visited Gen Corlett, who has been in bed for the past few days with a kidney infection and then went on to V Corps for a long talk with Gen Gerow.

The 2nd Div was again after Hill 192, this time in strength, and at the time of our arrival (noon) were making slow, steady progress. The hill had been so pounded by artillery that aerial photographs showed it as a moth-eaten white blanket, but there was still "plenty of hill" left. An aerial mission had strayed off course, and four bombs had dropped among our own troops, but luckily had slightly injured only one man. Gen Gerow was confident that the Hill would be in American hands before the day was over, but if not, he would give orders to dig in and recommence the attack tomorrow.

After lunch, the General drove to the 2nd Div CP, to find Gen Robertson up forward. After a brief "lookover" of the situation with Col [John H.] Stokes[125] and Gen Hayes [George P. Hays],[126] he motored to the 1st Div CP. Gen Huebner was forward decorating members of the 16th Inf and after finding out that all was quiet—"nothing new"—the General drove back to the CP.

We learned tonight that Gen Nelson Walker,[127] assistant Div Comdr of the 8th, had been killed during the afternoon of our visit to the 8th. Machine-gun [fire] had hit him, and he had died from loss of blood before medical aid could assist him.

The day's military news:

VIII Corps: Both the 79th and 8th Divisions advanced from 1,000 to 1,500 yards, with the 313th Inf capturing the town of Angoville [Andoville] sur Ay. The 90th Div continued to mop up pockets in the Foret de Mont Castre and by nightfall were 200 yards south of the woods. The 82nd A/B was assembled in an area north of La Poterie awaiting orders to return to the UK.

VII Corps: The 4th and 83rd continued the attack, advancing during the day approximately a mile. The 9th Div, on the other hand, encountered stiff tank opposition and though artillery and bombing helped disperse them, they made slow advance. Elements of CCA, 3rd Armd Div, were attached to each RCT to strengthen the anti-tank defense, and by day's end, Corps claimed the destruction of 24 MK IV[128] or MK V[129] tanks as follows: 9th Div—11; 4th Div—7; and 83rd Div—6.

V Corps: The 2nd Div, coordinating with the 29th Div on its right, made an attack [to] seize Hill 192 and the Bayeux–St Lo road in the western part of Corps sector. By 1600 the Hill was taken, and the advance continued across the road as far east as La Cix Rouge [La Croix Rouge].

For the first time in ten days, no rain fell. General Bradley went "way out on the limb" and predicted that the day after tomorrow would see good weather, steady good weather.

Wednesday, 12 July 1944: All Corps commanders came to the CP this morning for a two-hour conference with General Bradley and General Hodges. It was not until after 1400, therefore, that the General made good his intention to see "Buck" [Charles T.][130] Lanham, one of his oldest friends in the Chief of Infantry's office, and now commanding the 22nd Inf [4th Infantry Division]. Gen Barton, Gen Collins and Gen Roosevelt joined him at the CP, and there followed another two-hour session. He arrived back at the Army CP after 1800.

The day's fighting produced the following results:

VIII Corps: 79th Div, no change; 8th Div, an advance of some 2,000 yards against light resistance, taking in Vesly and Les Vallee; 90th Div, an advance of 2,500 yards, reaching just north of Pierrepont, and taking St. Germain and Gorges.

VII Corps: 4th Inf Div met stiff opposition and there was no substantial change; the 83rd advanced slowly, but an enemy strong point at Chau de Bois Grinot [Grimot] was taken, and the 330th Inf advanced to the water's edge at Le Port; 9th Div, the 39th Inf occupied Le Desert, the 60th Inf penetrated the Bois du Hommet and crossed the Gournay–Le Remmet d'Arthenay [le Hommet-d'Arthenay] road at 4173.

XIX Corps: The 30th Div's 117th Inf advanced to a point 600 yards SW of Vents [Hauts-Vents]; the 1st and 2nd Bns, 119th Inf, 300 yards south of the Pont Hebert–Vents [Hauts-Vents] road. 35th Div: 320th Inf moved forward to about 800 yards NE of Le Mesnil–Rouxelin but otherwise no changes made. The 29th Div advanced the 116th Inf about 2,000 yards along the St. Lo–Berigny road to the vicinity of La Roulage [La Boulaye]; the 115th Inf to Belle Fontaine and La Luzerne.

V Corps: Only limited objectives on this front. The 38th Inf took possession of the St. Lo–Berigny road at La Calvaire [Le Calvaire]; the 2nd Bn, 23rd Inf, crossed the road at Berigny.

G-2's report states that elements of 2 SS Das Reich,[131] which had been used to plug the lines along the VIII Corps front, were no longer in evidence, though Pz Lehr [Panzer Lehr][132] threw some tanks in east of Bois du Hommet. Stubborn delaying action, with all advantage being taken of the protective hedgerows, is still the order of the day.

Total enemy dead buried to date: 5,423; total prisoners taken, 47,822.

Thursday, 13 July 1944: The sad news this morning is that "Teddy" Roosevelt died last night from heart attack—a few hours after the General and Bill had chatted with him. He had not been feeling very fit during the first two days of the week (though he refused to heed doctor's orders and stay in bed) but yesterday, he reported to everybody that he was "fine." His death not only robbed American soldiers of a great friend, whom they would follow anywhere without question, but the American Army of a Div Commander. Had he lived, he would have had his own command.

A Silver Star was presented to Brigadier [H. N.] Foster[133] of the Canadian Army this morning and with that, and continuous conferences with General Bradley and other Corps and Div Commanders, including Gen Collins, the General did not leave the CP until 1500.

With the road from Carentan to La Haye du Puits now open and moderately safe from enemy artillery fire, we arrived at the CP of the 90th Div in 45 minutes. There the General went over the current situation with Gen Landrum and had a five-minute chat of confidential nature with him. We then went on to the CP of the 8th, just right of the main road, only a quarter-mile from the center of La Haye. There the General had another confidential talk with Gen Stroh, who assumed command only a day ago (Five general officers have now been relieved: Maj Gen McMahon, Brig Generals McKelvie [MacKelvie], [Henry A.] Barber,[134] [Thomas L.] Martin,[135] [John J.] Bohn[136]—in addition to countless regimental commanders.)

La Haye du Puits we found crippled and battered but, like an old man with one arm and one leg, still able to get about—not so ghostly and deserted as Montebourg and Valognes. We went two miles north to the new CP of the VIII Div [Corps], a few hundred yards off the main road in several quiet meadows. The General closeted himself in General Middleton's trailer for a half-hour. We arrived back at Army at 1930.

VIII Corps: In the 79th Div sector, the 314th advanced 1,000 yards; in the center and on the right, no appreciable changes were made. 8th Div: the 13th passed through the 28th Inf and went 700 yards south of Vesly. 90th: late in the afternoon the 90th resumed the offensive and had to its credit fair gains on the right, taking St Germain and Roquefort.

VII Corps: 4th Div: no advance, as the attack was met immediately by counter-attack. 83rd Div: captured the town of Auxais. 9th Div: the 60th made good progress, taking Les Champs des Losque [Les Champs-de-Losques].

XIX Corps: The 35th and 29th met heavy resistance and gains were slight. The 30th Div sustained a strong counter-attack at 0745 but had the situation under control at 0900.

V Corps: The 5th Div is continuing its movement into the Corps area to relieve the 1st Div.

G-2, in its weekly summary, points out that break-throughs were blocked by the piecemeal commitment of mobile reserves, and at the close of the week, more particularly by sporadic counter-attacks supported by armor. "While his troops are exhausted and his local reserves gone," the report continues, "the enemy's tenacity remains." Morale is believed to be stiffening as a result of German boasts of the destruction caused by V-1,[137] but lack of artillery support and the absence of the Luftwaffe must have diminished the confidence of the man on the front-line. At VIII Corps today, one of the prisoners taken was a clerk from a Corps finance office who had been given one week's basic training and propelled to the front. Such is the shortage of man-power, all along the front.

Friday, 14 July 1944: The General witnessed this morning, with General Bradley and Col [John B.] Medaris,[138] Army Ordnance Officer, an experiment which may revolutionize the use of tanks in this *bocage* country and which will, if successful, greatly speed up our advance.

The experiment was conducted by the Tank Co. of the 102nd Cav [Cavalry Reconnaissance Squadron]. Two officers and two enlisted men, wracking their brains for an answer to the question—"how can tanks break through hedgerows without getting stuck or exposing their bellies?"—finally hit upon tetrahydra. They picked this material upon the beach and hastily welded it to the tank. The results this morning were beautiful to watch. The tanks went ploughing through the hedgerows as though they were pasteboard, throwing the bushes and brush into the air. The tetrahydra and its huge iron teeth not only cut through the growth as though slicing bread, but they help keep the tank low, nose down. Every effort is now being made to equip all tanks with this latest "secret weapon," and special welding crews are being flown from the UK to speed up the job. It is certain that the inventors will be decorated for their ingenuity and resourcefulness.[139]

Experiments were also conducted with an automatic carbine, but the consensus was that it will not replace the present carbine, semi-automatic. During the shooting, a white-faced and nervous Lt Col plucked at General Hodges' sleeve to tell him that over the next hill was his hospital, containing only neuro-psychiatric cases. At the sound of the first shot, the patients had jumped out of bed and taken to their heels, and the doctors were tackling them and bringing them down as best they could. Would it be possible, he asked, for the firing to cease? His request was granted at once, and the harried Lt Col rushed back up the hill.

In the afternoon, the General paid a visit to his nephew, Lt Sam Hodges, 115th Inf., after a brief stop at the 29th Div CP. Sam had just been given command of a "commando" unit of 23 men (chosen because there were not enough volunteers to go around) which he is training to specialize in day and night patrolling. Sam told the General of some of his present troubles: the Division was so full of replacements that it took time to get them started. The incoming officers were full of fight and vigor, but the new men were a bit more cautious, and took prodding and pushing before they advanced. However, the General stopped to talk briefly with a young lad who was unconcernedly washing his face, using his helmet as washstand. "How long have you been here, soldier?" "Three days, suh." "Seen any action yet?" "Yes, suh, already got a few of them to my credit." The boy might have been talking of shelling peas, or doing KP [kitchen police]; it was all, for him, part of a day's soldiering and nothing to get excited about.

That evening the General attended the funeral services held for Teddy Roosevelt at the American cemetery just outside St. Mere Eglise—the cemetery which the French have taken upon themselves to care for, to groom, and to cover with flowers.

First in the cortege was Captain Quentin Roosevelt, Teddy's only son (with the 1st Division), followed by Lt Marcus Stevenson, his aide, and then his driver and orderly. Behind them were the colors, the two buglers, the two chaplains, and the half-track carrying the body. The pall bearers were General Hodges, General Bradley, General Patton, General Barton, General Huebner and General [Harold W.] Blakeley.[140] The honor guard brought up the line.

Prayers were read by Col Schroeder [Col Peter C. Schroder], Army Chaplain, and the 4th Div Chaplain, and taps were sounded, by one bugler standing near the grave, by the second, his distant echo, standing a few hundred yards away. The three traditional volleys, and the ceremony was over.

There were tens of enlisted men present—men from the 4th and 1st Divisions, nameless, but alike in their admiration for the man with whom they had served.

Situation:

VIII Corps: All three divisions attacked at 1000, and progress was good. The 79th advanced some 3,000 yards and by dark the area west of the north-south Lessay highway and north of the Ay River had been cleared. The 8th Div made some 4000 yards, the 13th Inf on the right occupying Pissot, and the 121st moving 700 yards south of St Patrice de Claids. The 90th advanced 4,000 to 5,000 yards to the north bank of the Seves river from a point 700 yards to the west of the town of Seves [St. Germain-sur-Seves] to Brehou.

VII Corps: There was only minor activity, with limited attacks. The 4th and 83rd had planned to attack, but postponement of air bombardment also cancelled their plans. The 9th Div, however, went forward—the 47th advancing 1,500 yards along the Corps left boundary.

XIX Corps: No change of importance.

V Corps: Relief of the 1st Div by the 5th Div was completed at 1500 hours. Most of the interchange of units was accomplished during the early morning hours, in darkness.

Saturday, 15 July 1944: The General spent the morning in various conferences with General Bradley and other officers and did not leave the CP until 1300.

We made our first stop at the CP of the 35th Division (off the main road right from Moon sur Elle) where he chatted with Lt Col [Maddrey A.] Solomon [Chief of Staff].[141] The latter admitted that progress was slow but assured the General they were "in there, doing their very best." The General said he was sure of that.

Then on past Ariel [Airel], across the Vire, to the CP of the 30th Div., which the General described as a "boar's nest." It was just off the road, mixed in with a tank park, and exceedingly crowded. Here he had a long chat with General Hobbes, before proceeding to St Jean de Daye and then to Gouberie, for a visit with General [James E.] Wharton[142] and later, with General Eddy. He had also planned to visit the 3rd Armored Div, but since its CCA was in the process of moving, the General decided to postpone his call until the following day.

Tonight, at midnight, the boundary between the XIX and VII Corps changed to the Vire River, former boundary between the 30th and 35th Divisions. At the same time the boundary between the VII and VIII Corps changed to La Taute River, former boundary between the 83rd and 9th Divisions.

Along the fronts:

VIII Corps: Consolidation of positions, patrolling. No attacks.

VII Corps: The 60th Inf advanced 1,000 yards astride the Carentan–Marigny road; the 47th reached a point 1,800 yards south of Le Hommet d'Arthenay. The 330th Inf (83rd Div) operating in the 9th Div sector advanced about 1,400 yards SW along the Le Desert–Le Mesnil [Le Mesnil–Vigot] road. Progress by the 4th Div ranged from 400 to 1,200 yards—resistance was fairly stiff throughout.

XIX Corps: The three-divisions attack met with tough resistance. The 30th Div advanced 1,000 yards south to La Foutelaie. The 35th advanced sufficiently, taking Emile [Emelie] and Les Ifs, to be within 1,500 yards of the northern outskirts of St Lo. The 29th went along the northern side of the Berigny–St Lo road to a point 200 yards beyond La Boulage [La Boulaye]. V Corps: no change.

Sunday, 16 July 1944: The General and Bill this afternoon visited the 2nd Armored Division—and, though not in their plans, the Forest of Cerisy. When they reached Cerisy La Foret, an MP told them that the customary road cutting through the forest was temporarily blocked off, but that they should go ahead, take their first right (where there would be an MP directing) and join in that way. There was no MP guide at the turn-off, and they went ahead, taking what they presumed to be the right road. The presumption was wrong, however, and Bill frankly admitted that, before long, they were lost. But they finally reached Balleroy and after some more difficulty, the Division, where the General conferred with Gen Brooks. To cap the climax, an MP Division guide escorted them out to the main road and then went right for some distance, instead of taking them to the left, back to Balleroy. Bill said it was rather of an embarrassing day.

Along the fronts:

VIII Corps: Principal activity was the relief of the 12th Inf (4th Div) by elements of the 329th Inf (83rd Div). Active patrolling along the line.

VII Corps: The 330th Inf (83rd Div), attached to the 9th Div, launched an attack and against heavy resistance had advanced, by nightfall, to Remilly sur Luzon and had a bridgehead across the river. With the 9th, the 60th Inf advanced 1000 yards, the 47th and 39th only 300. The 30th Div, destroying 11 tanks (3-artillery; 8-bazooka[143]) went 1,000 yards on to take Mesnil-Durand. CCA, 3rd Armored Div, moved to an area just north of Le Desert; CCB just south of Rauline.

XIX Corps: Reorganization and consolidation of positions.

V Corps: No change.

British front: The 2nd Army continued the attack to the south and south-east. General advances of 1,500 yards were made, and nine small villages taken.

Monday, 17 July 1944: General Bradley went to Cherbourg this morning to meet Mr. [Henry L.] Stimson,[144] arriving for a day's visit to the front, but the General decided he would check up on plans for tomorrow's big attack, and see the Secretary upon his return to the CP.

First stop, in the afternoon, was therefore made at XIX Corps, where he conferred with Gen Corlett, Col [Hamilton E.] Maguire,[145] and Col West.[146] Gen Corlett has almost completely recovered from his recent illness and looks fairly well.

Second stop was made at the 3rd Armd Div (CP a mile east of St Jean-de-Daye) in time to hear the "briefing" by General Watson for the "big attack." In his talk, the General said that this was to be a tank show, conducted at tank speed, and that failure of the Div to reach the objectives demanded by the Army would seriously jeopardize the entire plan, and thus let escape the estimated two divisions which would be bottled up should the plan go according to schedule.

He said that, yes, certainly, tanks would be lost, but that we had overwhelming strength, and that the attack must be pushed, that where opposition was met, the tanks should go around the foe, and that thirty percent of the tanks would be equipped with the tetrahydra ["Rhinos"].

In his talk with Gen Watson, General Hodges emphasized that tanks could and must bust through the hedgerows, that the hedgerows were becoming a greater psychological hazard than was merited by their defensive worth, that he had seen tanks in action against obstacles far tougher and knew what they could do. It was dangerous business, of course; you couldn't fight a war without it, but he had full confidence in the tanks to bust on through.

Final stop of the day was made at the new CP of VII Corps, established in quiet, comfortable buildings at Goucherie [La Goucherie], a tiny villages two miles northwest of St Jean de Daye. General Hodges went over the plans in detail with Gen Collins. The attack will not take place tomorrow, as originally scheduled, but certainly before the end of the week. Ammunition supply again appears to be a troublesome factor.

Upon arrival home, General Hodges went to the War Tent to talk with Mr. Stimson, who left shortly after seven o'clock to return to the UK. He had spent most of the day inspecting the beaches, and visiting hospitals.

The military situation:

VIII Corps: The 83rd Div advanced the 1st Bn, 331st Inf across the La Taute river to secure the point at La Varde. Otherwise, no change. The 4th Armd Div completed the relief of the 4th Inf Div at 2300, but the disposition of units has not been reported as yet.

VII Corps: The 60th Inf advanced to its objectives, 200 yards N of the Periers–St Lo road. The 330th Inf went 1,100 yards west from Remelly-sur-Lozon. The 30th Div advanced some 1,500 yards to its objective, with two Bns of the 120th Inf astride the Pont Hebert–St Giles [St. Gilles] road.

XIX Corps: The 1st Bn , 137th Inf, reached a point 700 yards SW of the Pont Hebert–St Lo highway. On the left, Les Ifs and Emilie were abandoned in the morning because of heavy mortar and artillery fire but were recaptured later in the day. The 29th advanced the 1st Bn, 116th Inf to Ste Croix de St Lo—on the outskirts of the city itself. The city will perhaps be entered tomorrow.

V Corps: The 2nd Armd Div was relieved by the British 8th Armd Bde [Brigade], and is assembling west of Tournieres in [the]vicinity of their new CP, coordinates 609751.

Tuesday, 18 July 1944: The General and Bill put in a busy day. With General Kean, they first visited XIX Corps where, in the absence of General Corlett, they talked with Colonel Maguire, C/S. They then went on to

2nd Division where they had a talk with General Robertson, Col [James] Van Fleet,[147] and General [Stafford L.] Irwin,[148] CG of the 5th Div.

After lunch back at Army CP, the General set out again—this time with Gen [William H.] Simpson,[149] CG Ninth Army, who had arrived in the morning with his G-2, G-3, and G-4 for [an] "estimate of the situation." The first stop was made at the 30th Div, which Gen Simpson had commanded, before he took over XIII Corps, for a talk with Gen Hobbes. The final stop was made at VII Corps for a visit with Gen Collins.

After supper, the same group went a few yards down the road from the CP to inspect a German Panther tank, which had been captured virtually intact. Its main differences from an American medium tank were: greater thickness in armor plate, and a greater muzzle velocity in the gun, the barrel of which is several feet longer than ours. However, the motor was, in all ways, inferior to that in our tank.

The day's military news was substantially as follows:

VIII Corps: The only activity was in the 83rd Div sector where two companies of the 1st Bn, 331 Inf, were forced to fall back from La Verde across the Taute river, because of heavy, concentrated fire.

VII Corps: The 9th Div attacked with the 39th and 47th Inf to reduce the salient in the center of the division sector. By dark the 1st Bn, 39th, had pushed through to position abreast of the 60th Inf north of the St Lo–Periers road, and the 2nd and 3rd Bns, 39th, and the 47th Inf had the remaining pocket of resistance surrounded on three sides.

XIX Corps: The city of St Lo was captured by 1900 by the 29th Div. The 115th had reached the northeastern outskirts by 1200 and finding the city lightly held, had pushed on to the center. The 35th kept up its pressure from the north, taking Rampan and reaching the northern edge of the city. Positions will be consolidated tomorrow.

V Corps: No change.

2nd British Army: More than 3,000 aircraft blasted a gap 7,000 yards wide southeast of Caen through which a strong armored and infantry force poured. By noon armored elements of the 8th Corps had broken through approximately eight miles to the south, taking Hubert-Folie, La Hogue and Frenouville. The Canadians—II Corps—took Mondeville. On the right of the Army sector, the 49th and 50th Divs made good progress in the area west of Hottot [Hottot-les-Bagues] and to the south of Juvigny [Juvigny-sur-Seulles]. Fierce fighting is going on everywhere.

Wednesday, 19 July 1944: General Hodges spent the morning in conference with General Bradley, Gen Collins, Gen Middleton, and Gen Gerow, as last-minute preparations for COBRA[150] were discussed and plans made. In the early afternoon Al[151] flew General Bradley to the UK for a conference with Marshall [Air Chief Marshal Trafford] Leigh-Mallory[152] on preliminary air bombardment.

The General left the CP at 1500, for a first stop at XIX Corps. Their new location was just north of St Marguerite sur Elle [Ste-Marguerite-d'Elle] and, not unexpectedly, the General and Fran had difficulty in finding their way through the maze of tents and paths (unmarked) to the General's trailer.

On the way, a marauding boche plane (against which AA fire was thick but seemingly inaccurate) had caused all vehicles along the main road to scatter madly into the bushes bordering the highway; our jeep rode down in solitary and comfortable splendor, though if the 50-cal. bullet which fire-cracked some fifty yards ahead of us had landed in the back seat, it might have been a bit warm for both of us. Col West said that the plane was smoking when it passed over XIX Corps, and we learned later that it fell only two miles east of Army CP. The pilot parachuted safely to earth; in ten minutes there was not enough left of the plane (because of souvenir-hunters) to put in a 1/4 ton [truck].

After a long chat with Gen Corlett (who still has what the General refers to as "that hospital look"), we went on to the 9th Div, where the Gen chatted first with Col [Noah M.] Brinson,[153] and later with Gen Wharton and Gen Eddy, who, as usual, had been forward at his regimental CPs. We learned that boche aircraft had been more active than usual over this front, too—they had brought down one air OP (came up under his belly and fired a burst, killing the observer and four M-109s[154] came up under the low cloud to strafe a road, apparently without doing damage. Gen Eddy asked General Hodges to bring up with General Bradley the orders the former had received (via Corps) not to let any boche north of the St. Lo–Periers road. He said that the boche were apparently dug in deeply five hundred yards or so south of the road, and that it would expend his strength, before COBRA struck, to keep the boche to the south of the highway, without gaining any material benefit by so doing. General Hodges said he would discuss it with General Bradley tonight. Gen Eddy remarked how pleased he had been to find all officers and men of the 39th (relieved) shaven and well-dressed that morning, and the General later remarked that it was characteristic of the division—they knew military discipline and politeness, and what they were about, and the proof of the pudding was in their superb fighting quality, which had been proven so many times.

We returned to the CP shortly after 1800. After supper General

Bradley returned from the UK and immediately left for CP to see Gen Collins. General Hodges had a long talk with Gen Simpson. Shortly after eleven o'clock, several boche planes swooped over, and every AA gun within miles opened up, making a noisy and spectacular display. The boche, if [the] day's show is indicative, have apparently decided to bring up a bit of their aerial reserve and make it pay.

The fighting fronts:

VIII Corps: The little town of La Varde is still proving a tough nut to crack. The 3rd Bn, 331st Inf , took it against light opposition in the morning but for the second time, were forced to cede it back to the enemy before nightfall.

VII Corps: The 9th Div remained fairly quiet with a limited advance by the 3rd Bn, 39th Inf. The 30th Div launched a limited attack along the west side of the Vire to clean out the enemy salient, and reached its objective. The 4th Div was attached to VII Corps at 2300; the 22nd RCT to the 2nd Armd Div; and the 18th Inf, 1st Div, moved to the vicinity of 430760.

XIX Corps: The 35th Div mopped up the area North of the Vire between St Lo and Rampan and placed an outpost line across the northern bank. The 29th Div is in the process of being relieved by elements of the 35th. St Lo has been mopped up, apparently without great difficulty.

V Corps: No change.

2nd British Army: The 49th and 50th Div went forward some 1,500 yards, reaching southwest several hundred yards of Landelle. The town of Noyers is still strongly held by the enemy. The 2nd Canadian Corps made good advances—bridging the Orne [River] in three places between Caen and Fauburg de Vancelles [Faubourg de Vancelles]. The VIII Corps reorganized after the armored attack on the 16th but did not make appreciable gains. Resistance was strong, and the enemy had an effective anti-tank screen.

Four air OPs were lost during the day (along the American front) to enemy action and our own antiaircraft fire.

Thursday, 20 July 1944: Today was a day of final preparation for Cobra. Generals [Lewis H.] Brereton[155] and Spaatz arrived early in the morning to confer with General Bradley and Gen Hodges. In the middle of the afternoon General Eisenhower arrived by plane, and a brief ceremony was held at Army CP, in which General Bradley received an Oak Leaf Cluster to his DSM [Distinguished Service Medal], General Gerow the same, and General Collins his second Oak Leaf Cluster. General Eisenhower returned to the UK before dinner time.

After supper the General and Bill motored to the 30th Div CP to pick out an OP for the "air show" which, early in the morning, would be the first fang of COBRA to strike at the enemy. Everyone there was a little low in spirits—an enemy shell has just landed, a few minutes before, at the very entrance to the CP, killing three persons. General Hobbes agreed to have an officer there to take Fran to the OP early in the morning, in advance of General Hodges and his party, consisting of General Brereton and General Simpson. But shortly after 2300, definite word came through from General [Elwood R.] Quesada[156] that bad weather was in store for tomorrow, and the attack was postponed.

The day's military developments:

VIII Corps: The 4th Armored Div repulsed an attack, estimated at strength of two companies, at 2100, and again shortly after midnight. Activity elsewhere along the front was confined to patrolling.

VII Corps: The 9th and 30th Divisions continued to press the enemy but made little headway because of heavy mortar and artillery fire.

XIX Corps: The 29th Div has been relieved by elements of the 35th Div and moved, as Corps reserve, into the vicinity of St Clair sur L'Elle. No change in the front lines.

V Corps: Corps changed its CP to two miles SW of Balleroy (6667).

British Front: The 2nd Canadian Corps continued the attack in the area SW of Caen, took St Andre sur Orne, Bras and Hubert Folie. SE of Caen, all tank brigades have been withdrawn from combat for refitting. East of Caen, the I Corps is still fighting hard for possession of Troan [Troarn].

Friday, 21 July 1944: The weather people were correct—we awoke this morning to a "cats and dogs" downpour which continued, with slight abatement, until late in the afternoon. The General said he had no plans other than "try to keep dry."

It did clear perceptibly before supper-time, and there were hopes that COBRA might go on Saturday morning. However, word was received about 2200 that weather had forced another postponement.

At 0100 there were a series of shots—three minutes or so—wild shouts of "Gas," "Gas" and the alarm was sounded in the CP. Some fumbled wildly in their duffle bags, others covered their heads with blankets, still others put on their masks only to find they had not dewaterproofed them. General Bradley said he poked his head out of the trailer, asked the sentry if there had been any planes overhead and receiving a negative answer, went back to sleep. General Hodges halfdressed to see what the excitement was about, and then went back to bed, just as the all-clear sounded. However, this was not to be the end. Ten minutes later the shots and shouts started over again; again an all-clear. After the third "false alarm," a sound truck patrolled up and down the road, a quiet voice repeating: "Attention all troops, Attention all troops. There has been no gas. There has been no gas. Do not give the alarm unless you personally smell or see gas." This proved effective medicine, for there was no further alert.

The post-mortem on the alert brought several facts or rumors to light. Apparently a shell had exploded behind, the VII Corps lines during the day, exploding some dynamite, which in turn gave off its customary non-dangerous but headache-causing gas. Drivers returning from Isigny in the afternoon reported that civilians were walking around with handkerchiefs fastened to their noses. As the day wore on, rumors became bigger rumors, and by nightfall apparently everyone was "gas-conscious." It took a group of negroes in Trevieres, so runs the most reliable story this morning, to fire a few shots in celebration of "armistice" (the biggest whopper of them all) to start the cry all the way down the line, up the peninsula, and into the sheltered quarters of AD SEC [Advanced Section, Communications Zone].[157]

The day's military fronts:

VIII Corps: Active patrolling and small counter-attacks by the enemy. Nothing major to report.

VII Corps: At 2200, the 39th Inf received a strong counter-attack near the St Lo–Periers road. Tanks were employed by the enemy. The attack was repulsed, however, and enemy movement along the road was considerably lessened by strong concentrations of our artillery. Boche aviation was active along the 9th and 30th Div sectors and some flares and bombs were dropped. The enemy undoubtedly smells something coming. The 4th Div closed in assembly areas in the rear of the 9th, and the 1st Div closed in assembly area west of St Jean de Daye.

XIX Corps: Nothing startling to report.

V Corps: Heavy counter-battery fire by the enemy; active patrolling by us.

British: Continued to consolidate positions and regroup forces.

Saturday, 22 July 1944: The weather is still not fit for bombing, and COBRA is consequently again postponed.

The General and Bill leave in mid-morning, however, for a lengthy tour of the front, starting with General Middleton at the VIII Corps. The attack against Seves [probably St.-Germain-sur-Sèves] had him rather disappointed in the 90th Division; he said that had he his old

45th, there would be no question of taking the town after crossing the river. He also told the story of a German private, just captured, with whom he had talked. The private—whom General Middleton suggested as a likely member of any G-3 staff—said that the only obvious thing for our troops to do was to attack exactly as was planned. In a few brief sentences, the boche private outlined the plan of COBRA, obviously without knowledge that "his plan" had been worked on for many days previous.

After lunch at the CP, the General went on to the 90th Division (where another change in Commanding General is rumored about to take place), VII Corps, and the 9th Division. Commanders, it appears, are growing a bit impatient for COBRA to strike.

With everybody in place, waiting for the word to go, action along the front was necessarily limited. Two battalions of the 90th did cross the Seves river before dusk, encountering stiff fire from the houses in Seves, St Germain sur-Seves and Remburge, all of which appear to be fortified positions. The V Corps CP was shelled by artillery at 2000, but little damage was done, and only six men slightly wounded. The British front was likewise dormant, though a limited attack against Maltot, against light resistance, ended in success.

Sunday, 23 July 1944: The weather still says "no," though the sky did clear up during the day, auguring well for tomorrow. The General spent the morning in various conferences with General Bradley, Gen Kean, and others.

At 1500 he took General Simpson to the XIX Corps where a long conference with Gen Corlett was held in the latter's trailer. We arrived back in the CP shortly after 1700, and a little while later General [Lesley J.] McNair,[158] who has left AGF [Army Ground Forces] and will shortly assume an "important assignment," presumably in this theatre, arrived to spend a few nights at the CP.

During the day, the 15th Scottish Division moved into the area occupied by the 5th (Which had relieved the 1st at Balleroy and Caumont), and a new boundary between the First Army and the Second British Army became effective. The line approximates the line between the 2nd and 15th Scottish.

The attack on Seves faltered under a stiff counterattack from the boche, and the 358th Inf was forced to withdraw their five companies north of the Seves River. Casualties including battle fatigue are estimated to be about 400; our wounded were evacuated under a flag of truce, and with the assistance of the Germans. Aside from extensive regrouping, and the going into operation of the I Canadian Corps, things were generally quiet along the British sector.

Tonight General Hodges told us to be ready to leave in the morning, that the "show" was on, with H-Hour scheduled for noon. He would have as his guests General Henry[159] and General Salinas, chief of the Mexican Air Force.

Boche reconnaissance planes were active over the Army and CP area tonight, both early and late, but AA fire kept them moving along, and no known bombs were dropped.

Monday, 24 July 1944: The General's party left the CP at 1050 this morning—the General leading with General Simpson in his jeep, followed by Gen Royce, Gen Henry, and Gen Salinas. Just before we reached the OP—a house right by the road leading south-west from Pont Hebert [Pont-Hébert] (coordinate 458695) General Brereton, Gen Ridgway and his aide (who had been "dragged" into the party unwittingly and wore pinks[160] and had no helmets) joined us. In a few minutes we had been joined by a half-dozen war correspondents, including Harold Denny[161] and Hanson Baldwin[162] of the New York Times.

Shortly before noon, the first "foursomes"[163] of P-47 dive bombers appeared and after cruising around a bit at 1500-foot altitude to get their bearings, dove sharply into the valley before us, and there came in their wake the thud-thud-thud of their bombs. There was a rush of black smoke into the air from a spot down the road, perhaps a half-mile distant, and we learned in a few minutes that one of our ammunition trucks had been hit. Shortly after twelve another group, obviously far off course, peeled downward and let their eggs fly at a spot some 500 yards northeast of where we were. The General said he saw actually only one of their bombs released, and at the present time, there is no proof that more than one dropped, but no doubt whatsoever as to the fact that they were far off course.

One of the Air Corps colonels hastened off in his jeep to find out how this had happened, and what the damage was. But for the next half-hour or so, though we kept our eyes more firmly peeled on the sky, the Air Corps appeared to be putting their 100-pounders where they were intended to go. The party pulled out K-rations, and with our two burners operating in what was once the kitchen of the house, everybody soon had hot coffee.

Then came the heavies—some 200 of them. We could see their rocket markers flare off, designating time to drop, and then a few seconds later their clusters of bombs. We were watching unconcernedly when we heard a shrieking whistle, and knew that some were coming our way. There was a wild scramble for cover, but few reached farther than the rear of the house before the bombs hit, crunch, wham, thud, some 500 or 600 yards southwest of us. General Brereton came up with a pair of dust-covered trousers; Bill slit his finger on a piece of glass; everyone was laughing, but it was not quite so huge a joke as the laughs intended—just nervous release. For we learned that the death toll from this mis-aimed cluster was 17; the wounded, at nightfall's count, more than 80. The great majority of the casualties had been in the 120th Infantry, which was down the road not more than one-half mile, and to the right of the road.[164]

General Brereton noted the time the bombs had fallen—1250 ("Make a note of that, Colonel, we'll check that bunch") and then left. The rest of the air [Air] Corps personnel followed, and then General Simpson and his party, which were due back in Bristol. Members of the 120th Inf were trudging up the road, saying that the attack had been called off shortly before noon. It was the first word we had had of that.

At 1340 the General left for the 30th Division, where he had a chat with Gen Hobbes, who was naturally both hurt and indignant at the Air Corps show, which he termed a "fiasco." Everything had been pulled back, according to order, he said, and there was nothing to do but wait for additional instructions. The Air Corps had come north-south, not east-west, along the St Lo–Periers road, as planned; they apparently had either not seen nor needed [heeded] the various panels and smoke markers set out for their aim. Leaving Gen Hobbes, we went on to the VII Corps, where we learned that the attack from the air had been called off shortly before noon by Marshal Leigh-Mallory (then in France) and that the ground attack had subsequently been called off by General Bradley, then at VII Corps. We then set out for the Army CP. The General spent the evening discussing the new plan for the morrow with General Bradley and other air corps commanders.

Chapter 2

Operation Cobra and the Breakthrough at St. Lô, 25–31 July 1944

Tuesday, 25 July 1944: The General and Fran reached the OP—the same house at Vents—at 0927, and did not have long to wait for the opening air blow. Promptly at 0936 the first of nine groups of four P-47s each approached the target from over St Lo and then whipped down through a clear sky to plaster the road and the ground just south of it. We counted nine groups in all, the last finishing its pounding at 0958.

Not a moment too soon. The sky was filled with the weary, ear-filling drone of B-24s, and we looked through the torn corner of the house to the north. As far as the eye could reach they came—flying in twelves.[1] A mile past us, AA fire came up to meet them, bad black spots marking their silvery white. One ship faltered, tried to regain its group, and then slowly floated down to the right; out of it blossomed three parachutes. A second one was hit more squarely—possibly in its bomb bay—for in several seconds it was one ball of red fire which fell straight down through the blue sky, and this time there were no parachutes to give hope for those inside.

The last notation I made in the count I was keeping for the General of those overhead was at 1010, when another large group of heavies went overhead. The next group, three or four minutes later, was the first to strike where unwanted. The warning was the same—the eerie whistle—but it was more urgent than the previous day's, and we seemed to have more time to run. Most of the party reached the sunken road behind the house, or the ditch behind the road, when the bombs hit and tore the earth to shreds. Again, we found out later, they had smacked down the north-south road, and again to the right, and again

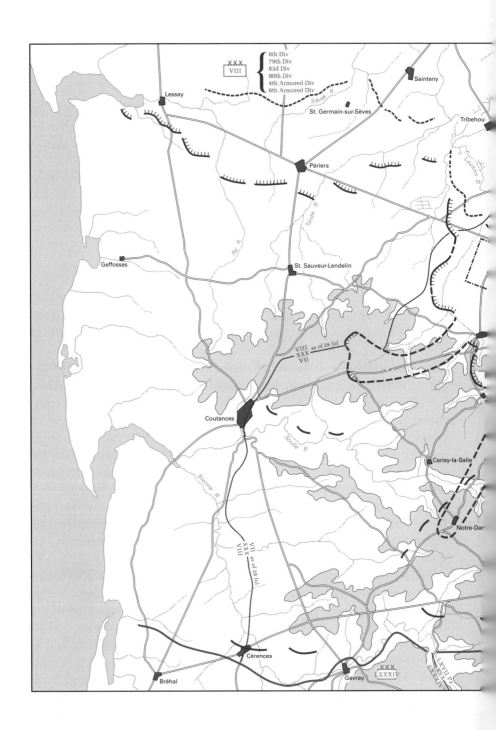

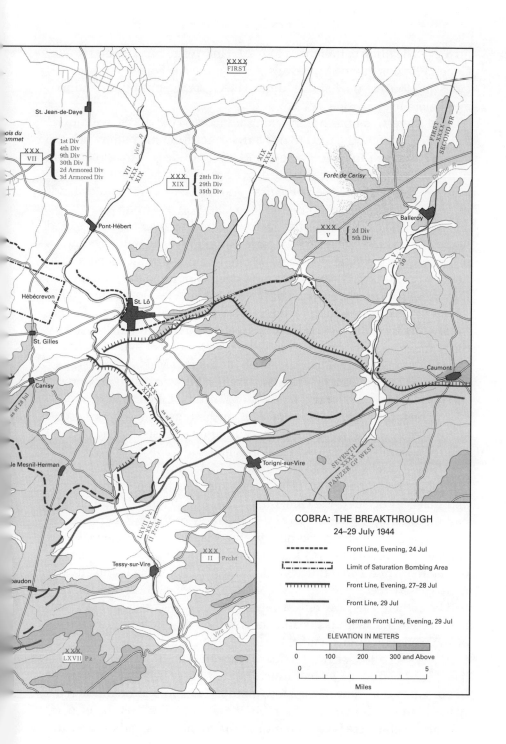

St. Jean-de-Daye

ois du
ommet

XXX
VII

1st Div
4th Div
9th Div
30th Div
2d Armored Div
3d Armored Div

Vire R.

VII
XXX
XIX

XXX
XIX

28th Div
29th Div
35th Div

XXXX
FIRST

XIX
XXX
V

Forêt de Cerisy

Orne R.

FIRST
XXXX
SECOND BR

Balleroy

XXX
V

2d Div
5th Div

XX
V
30

Pont-Hébert

Hébécrevon

St. Lô

St. Gilles

Caumont

Canisy

as of 28 Jul

as of 28 Jul

V
XXX
XIX

Je Mesnil-Herman

Torigni-sur-Vire

SEVENTH
XXXX
PANZER GP WEST

LXVII Pz
XXXX
II Prcht

XXX
II Prcht

Tessy-sur-Vire

oaudon

XXX
LXVII Pz

COBRA: THE BREAKTHROUGH
24–29 July 1944

- - - - - - - - - Front Line, Evening, 24 Jul

·—·—·—·—· Limit of Saturation Bombing Area

⊥⊥⊥⊥⊥⊥⊥ Front Line, Evening, 27–28 Jul

—————— Front Line, 29 Jul

—————— German Front Line, Evening, 29 Jul

ELEVATION IN METERS

0   100   200   300 and Above

0   5

Miles

on the two leading battalions of the 120th Inf. We got up. General Royce, General Bevins [James M. Bevans],[2] A-1 of the Air Forces,[3] and several aides and lookers-on, left in a hurry. The General, Spratt [unidentified] and I were the only ones left.

But there was no sense in taking unnecessary chances; we moved to the fields across the road to our left, farther from the path which the bombers seemed to be following, and closer to deeper fox-holes. One of the last groups, hitting at 1046, drove Spratt and me to our fox-holes, but they were not so close as the first, and the General remained standing. They did, however, hit on the road below, in our troops.

As the last of the Forts[4] disappeared, wheeling over to the west and homeward bound, we returned to the house to see the fighter-bombers bring in their incendiary bombs. Again, it seemed to the General that they were smacking the road, but not deep enough to the rear, though they were covering the length of the road in fine fashion. Some 100 P-47s and P-38s[5] dove and released; by 1130 the air show appeared over.

By this time the General had a greater worry than that caused by the bombers. As we went back into the house, Colonel Jones and Major Narramore, pilot and aide respectively to General McNair, came rather breathlessly up to General Hodges. "We're a bit worried about General McNair," were Narramore's first words. Then he told his story.

Against their advice, General McNair had insisted, for the second successive day, in staying on the very front lines. Yesterday he had not heard the bombs falling, and Col Jones had had to push him out of the car. They thought they had persuaded him to stay farther back today, but some person had said: "The troops sure like to see you up front," and that had decided the General's mind, and again this morning he had motored up to within several hedgerows of the enemy positions. When the first cluster of bombs hit, the Major said that General McNair, to the very best of his knowledge, was occupying a fox-hole just off the road, and some thirty yards from him. After the bombs had finally ceased their work, the Major hurried over. Where the fox-hole had been there was now only a gaping crater. A rescue detail was commandeered, and with picks and shovels they dug deeply, but no trace of the General could they find. After a vain search through the area, they had come to General Hodges. We waited until the air show was over—12:25—and (a cluster of medium bombs at 1210 had brought us to our knees uncertain) then a few minutes later we motored down the road about three-quarters of a mile. It was still "hot," as the General said; the boche were laying on mortar fire to the crossroads a few hundred yards to the south, and the chatter-chatter of his Schmeisser pistol[6] was clear and sharp. With one Lt-General possibly killed, there seemed no sense in risking the life of a second, and reluctantly the General decided to return to the 30th Division CP, to return a little later when the boche pockets were overrun and done for.

General Hobbes was naturally terribly upset by the air show—mad that it had happened a second time so unsuccessfully, saddened by the loss of his own troops. "We're good soldiers, Courtney, I know," he said, "but there's absolutely no excuse, no excuse at all. I wish I could show some of those boys, decorated with everything a man can be decorated with, some of our clearing stations." The Air Corps, he reminded, had been instructed not to drop unless they could see the all-important highway. It was undoubtedly obscured by smoke caused by previous bombings, but they had dropped anyhow. He said that last night, after visiting the regiments and giving them a fight talk, he thought their morale was high as could reasonably be expected; now they were shaken, justifiably so, and took to their holes when aircraft appeared, and Colonel Birks had been up at the very front, shooting a bazooka himself, in order to push the troops on. While we were there, Col Birks called and gave the latest information. Going was very slow, he said; the boche had tanks dug in, hull down, and were shooting perhaps more artillery than they had ever previously used along any American sector, and regularly laying it down along the north-south road. Gen Hobbes told him to stay in his CP, and not to get too close to the front—he couldn't spare him.

Bill arrived in the jeep, on the General's orders, and he and Colonel Jones went on to Amey [Amigny], to search through the Division Clearing Station, and then the two Evacuation hospitals. The General, Major Narramore and I went back, past the OP, and down the road. We parked the jeep next to the area occupied by the 92nd Chemical Bn (B company of which had lost 14 men to the bombing and several missing) and went forward, then branching off to the right to the 120th CP, which was strongly dug in on a reverse slope. Col Birks had lost one of his best officers in a nearby dugout, which had collapsed because of near-hit; the field itself was a mass of bomb pockets, and the wonder was that not more had been killed. General Harrison himself said that one had struck thirty feet to his right, and another a few yards to his left; he had been sitting on a pile of dirt and had received not a scratch.

A war correspondent from the Chicago *Tribune* told me that a rumor was flying around that a general had been killed up the road, but I said I had heard nothing of it. Col Birks got a guide, Captain Anthony, to lead us forward. When we had gone forward two hundred yards, Colonel [Thomas A.] Roberts,[7] 2nd Armored Division, came forward, introduced himself, and asked if we were looking for, or had heard of, the body of a "Ground Forces" General.

He led us a few yards up the road, twenty yards short of the crossroads at coordinate 446670, and there on the side of the road itself, indisputably tossed there by the explosion of the bomb, was the body of General McNair, recognizable by the shoulder patch and general's stars.[8] There was nothing to do but to order an ambulance; fifteen minutes later a jeep ambulance arrived, and we followed the body back to the 105th Medical Bn clearing station at Pont Hebert. There General Hodges put in a call to General Kean and advised him of the tragic story. We arrived back at the CP at 1830.

This day, a day to remember for more than one reason, did not bring the break-through for which all had hoped. In the VIII Corps sector, the 330th Inf, supporting the 9th Inf Div on its left, reached the St Lo–Periers road at 2200, against moderate resistance. The general line–La Butte (380665)–La Chapelle [La Chapelle-en-Juger] (408639)–Hebecrevon (442645) was reached by VII Corps, the 9th Div going the farthest, a little more than two miles. There was no question but that the postponement of the attack from Monday to Tuesday, plus two successive days of bombing of our troops, took the ginger out of several of the front-line elements, and as was to have been expected, all surprise element from the attack itself.

Wednesday, 26 July 1944: Today the General escorted a Russian military mission, consisting of Major Generals Vasiliev and Skliarov, Rear Admiral Kharlamov, and Colonel Gorbatov on a tour of the American front.

The Admiral, naval attache in London for the past three years, road [rode] with General Hodges at the head of the procession. The others, together with Brigadier Firebrace and Col Tamplin of the British War Office (interpreters) followed.

At each of the stops—V Corps and 2nd Division (then attacking) in the morning, and VII Corps, 30th Div and 2nd Armd Div in the afternoon—the visiting group was given a complete survey of the front-line situation, and were given frank answers to frank questions. (There were no restrictions placed on what they could see, other than the fact that they were to be shown no Russian PWs. At V Corps, General Gerow said they had captured a few Russians, but luckily the remark was not expanded upon, and perhaps not understood). The Russians appeared particularly interested in our artillery (they are admittedly masters of its use) and asked several questions about casualties and prisoners of war, without in any way making them pointed. At 1730 they had arrived back at Army CP and thanked General Hodges for his kindness. If they saw or learned nothing else, they certainly knew, at day's end, about Normandy dust. At noontime, when they borrowed the General's whiskbroom, their uniforms were covered; at nightfall, their caps and their faces, and ours as well.

In the evening, the General attended funeral services for General McNair, who was buried in the 29th Division Cemetery at La Cambe. The ceremony was given no publicity whatsoever. Present, in addition to General Hodges, were General Bradley, General Patton, General Royce, General Quesada, General McNair's two aides, and a color guard and guard of honor.

Two post-mortems to the last two days' action: Casualties from Tuesday's misdirected bombing were close to 600 persons, almost 100 of whom were killed and more than 90 percent of which came from the 30th Division;[9] (2) Col [Harry A.] "Paddy" Flint,[10] one of the best-known and beloved regimental commanders, died yesterday as the result of wounds. A shell fragment hit him in the head on Monday, and a brain operation failed to save his life. General Hodges said Col Flint was so sure that "his turn was coming" that he had written home, telling friends that he did not expect to survive the war. He was replaced by his executive officer, Lt Col John [Van H.] Bond.[11]

The day's military news was much more encouraging:

VIII Corps: Attack was made by all four divisions—8th, 83rd, 79th, and 90th. The first succeeded in securing the high ground 1000 yards south of La Banserie, and Joliment. The 79th crossed the river south of Pissot and extended the right flank of the bridgehead. The 90th finally made a bridgehead across the Seves, and advanced to Longuet against very stiff opposition. In the 359th Inf area, four tanks were destroyed—three by our bazookas, one by artillery. The 83rd made no gains.

VII Corps: The 1st Div with CCB, 3rd Armored, attacked along the main Marigny-Tribehour [Tribehou] road and advanced rapidly, clearing Marigny of all opposition by 2300, and the armor advancing 1,000 yards south of the town. The 9th Div, on the right, met heavy resistance and progress was slow. The 4th Div went on rapidly, and by nightfall the 8th Inf occupied high ground near La Couviniere [La Conviniere]. The 2nd Armored, with CCA attacking, entered St Gilles at 1530 and by dark had gone 2,000 yards south of Canisy. The 30th Div attacked with the 117th and 119th Inf; the former reaching the rail road line southeast of St Gilles, the latter advancing along the main highway from Hebecrevon to St Lo and reaching the river west of St Lo.

V Corps: The 2nd Div, with 2nd Inf, 5th Div, advanced to Rouxeville-Caumont highway from CR 618607 to the Vesbire River. Resistance was light on the left flank, heavy on the right.

Thursday, 27 July 1944: With the news from the front everywhere encouraging (despite bad weather, which cancelled mainly scheduled air missions), the General left after the news conference this morning for the VII Corps, to urge General Collins to throw everything in and keep pushing, for the boche was apparently on the run. While he was there, orders were issued by General Collins for the 3rd Armored to keep smashing southward to the Bois de Soulles, and once that spot was taken, to keep on going.

After learning that the attack was continuing to go well, the General left for VIII Corps. Just before entering the CP, he stopped the jeep for a chat with General Wyche, who said that extensive mine fields were slowing up his Division. The General learned from General Middleton that there was a slow but definite withdrawal along his front; one prisoner taken that morning reported that they had orders to retreat six kilometres a night until they reached the main body. The hope is, of course, not only to pocket them but the main body further south as well. The General left the CP at 1513 and arrived back at Army after an hour and twenty-five minute drive.

Tonight, to our surprise, the radio announced the death of General McNair, due to "enemy fire" in Normandy. Everyone had rather thought that the news would not be released for several weeks or perhaps months, because of the importance of his mission on the continent, and the change in plans necessitated by his sudden death.

The day's good news:

VIII Corps: The 314 and 315 Inf (79th Div) crossed the Ay River on the extreme left of the division sector. The 315th entered Lessay with one Bn at 2200.

The 8th Div advanced about 3 miles to the La Feuillie–Periers road.

Periers was taken by the 359th Inf against minor resistance, and advance made 3000 yards south of the city.

The 83rd Div (331st Inf) has two Bns in the vicinity of La Varde; other front line elements are just north of La Taute River.

Tomorrow the 4th and 6th Armored Divisions will enter the push south.

VII Corps: The 9th Div, protecting the right flank of the Corps met very tough resistance and went only some 1000 yards to the west and southwest.

The 1st Div, with CCB of 3rd Armored, ended up 2½ miles east of Coutances.

The 2nd Armored advanced rapidly to the south with three columns—left within 2000 yards of Tessy sur Vire, center at La Denisiere, right fighting in Notre Dame de Cenily [Notre-Dame-de-Cenilly].

The 30th Div also shot ahead—the 2nd Bn, 120th Inf at St Romphaire, the 1st Bn reported on the Canisy–Torigny sur Vire [Torigni-sur-Vire] road about 1,400 yards west of the river.

In the XIX Corps sector, the 134th Inf (35th Div) advanced to St Thomas de St Lo, and the north slope of Hill 101. For V Corps, the 2nd moved slowly ahead, making gains of between 1,000 and 1,200 yards.

Enemy bombers were out tonight in far greater than usual strength. The 30th Div CP and front lines of the 9th Div were hit. Over Army CP several were active, but did not drop bombs in the immediate vicinity. It was a bright moonlit night, and the bombers came in at 2,000 feet—out of 40MM range, effective range, and too low for gun batteries. The AAA [antiaircraft artillery] officer, Col Patterson, admitted it was a bad night's shooting. There were no claims of planes destroyed, though twenty were "damaged."

Friday, 28 July 1944: The General concentrated his attention today on V Corps and XIX Corps, stopping first at XIX Corps to talk with Colonel Maguire, lunching with Colonel Matchett at V Corps, and returning to XIX Corps in the afternoon for a two-hour conference with General Corlett. The subject of the conferences was not made known.

During the evening, from six different prisoners, one of whom said he had been present during the incident, testimony was received that Field Marshal [Erwin] Rommel[12] is either seriously injured or dead. The prisoners say that he was bombed by one of our planes at Lisieux about two weeks ago. G-2 rates the information as probably correct.

The drive south, the break-through, continued to prosper during the day. The main points:

CCB, 4th Armored Div, captured Coutances during the day and continued south on the Coutances-Brehal road. The 6th Armored followed behind on the Lessay-Periers road. The 90th Div made contact with the 1st Div driving to the west at Cambernon (2860) at noon.

The VII Corps continued to exploit the break-through and mop up pockets of enemy resistance by-passed in the swift advance. The 4th Div moved to Notre Dam (3750) [Notre-Dame-de-Cenilly]; the 2nd Armd Div, CCB, advanced slowly, against moderate enemy resistance, to St Denis La Gast [St. Denis-le-Gast].

The 30th Div continued to advance south along the west bank of the Vire to secure the Corps left flank. The 29th Div was going back in the line, assembling at Le Mesnil Herman, and the 28th Div was alerted and ready to move down into the line near the 29th.

Saturday, 29 July 1944: The General returned to V Corps this morning to tell General Gerow to drive ahead. Corps' primary mission, he told General Gerow, was still to protect the flank, but there was absolutely no reason why he could [not] perform that job and at the same time drive southward. "Even take Vire?" asked General Gerow. "If you take Vire," General Hodges answered, laughing, "you'll get nothing but three cheers.["]

So a bet was made. If the 2nd and 5th Division reached two spots of high ground, considerably ahead of the front lines, they'd win bottle of brandy apiece from General Hodges. If they reached Tessy sur Vire, they'd win another.

The General then went on to XIX Corps to find from Col Maguire, to his dismay, that both the 28th and 29th Divisions had made their move by motor and not by foot. He also learned the sad news that Lt Col Tom Crystal,[13] G-2, was missing in action. He and Major Weymouth had been reconnoitering south of Le Mesnil Herman when they were jumped by a group of German tanks. Major Weymouth escaped, but no word had been received, at 3 today, about Crystal's fate. The General was pessimistic, saying that from such news, a happy ending is seldom possible.

On the road to St Lo, on our way to the CP of the 29th Division, we found all the evidence the General needed to sustain his long-held and frequently-asserted conviction that motor movement, for short distances, is ridiculous. The road to St Lo was one steady stream of vehicles, closely packed, moving (when at all) at snail's pace. We finally passed through the city—of which there was barely anything left but piles [of] rubble—and crossed the bridge across the Vire on the road leading to le Mesnil Herman.

Just the other side of the bridge, we met General Brown[14] and General Hodges stopped to inquire further into the motor movement, learning that the march by foot would not have been in excess of 18 miles.

We continued along the road to the right (in the direction of Canisy), and at the crossroads, a half-mile from Canisy, stopped to look into a possible CP. It was an old, gigantic chateau, set in the midst of deep pine woods, and offered everything: cover and concealment, accessibility, office space, all the room needed. After inspecting it, we turned left, on to the 29th CP, but ran into Col [Grant A.] Williams,[15] Signal Officer, and stopped to take a look at the site, 600 yards from ours, chosen by Col Myers—a series of the customary fields, and two farmhouses.

When we reached St Samson de Bon Fosse [St Samson-de-Bonfosse], we inquired as to the CP of the 29th, but no MP was sure, and since there were rumors that it had been run out of the location originally picked, the General decided not to take unnecessary risks. So, instead, we turned left and after a three-mile drive, reached the farmhouse CP of the 30th Division, just established. General Hobbes said that his 119th had just been bombed again by our own planes, but not as badly as before, preliminary reports showing four killed, ten injured. He was generally satisfied with the situation.

We returned to Army via the Canisy–St Gilles–Pont Hebert road— over its hastily-filled bomb craters and past the wrecked German tanks and half-tracks. This road, apparently, had taken as great a beating from Tuesday's attack from the air as did the St Lo–Perier road running across it.

Our Army continues to move ahead. The 6th Armored Div, held up temporarily at the Sienne River, finally crossed and took up positions on high ground 500 yards south. The 4th Armored advanced to La Jourdannierre and Cambernon. The 79th assembled in the vicinity of St Malo de la Londe [St-Malo-de-la-Lande]. The 8th, 90th, and 83rd continued to regroup.

CCA, 3rd Armored; advanced to Nicorps, Hyenville and St Denis Le Vetu; CCB completed its mission and assembled near Belval. CCB, 2nd Armored moved to Blanchard, another column to Cambry, a third toward St Martin de Cenilly. The 4th Div moved its 8th Inf from Notre Dame de Cenilly along the main roads to assist in preventing any enemy breakthrough from the trap. The 26th Inf was attached to the 4th; the remainder of the 1st continued to mop up. The highlight of the day occur[r]ed when a considerable force of enemy tanks, vehicles, and guns was bottled up on the Roncey–St Denis Le Vetu by-highways by elements of the 2nd and 3rd Armored Div, and was pounded to bits by armor, artillery, and aircraft. Early reports from VII Corps showed 64 tanks, 204 vehicles, and 11 artillery pieces destroyed, an almost equal number damaged.

Heavy fighting took place in the area north and west of Tilley-sur-Vire [Tessy-sur-Vire], where an estimated three battalions of enemy are dug in. The 30th, the 116th of the 29th [Division], and one Bn of tanks are being employed against them. The remainder of CCA, 2nd Armored is on the high ground northeast of Percy. The 29th (115th INF) occupied the town of Percy, and the 175th was along the main East-West highway from Villebaudon to Beaucoudray. The 28th Div closed in an area northeast of Canisy.

In the V Corps sector, the enemy started withdrawing, and advances of 5,000 to 6,000 yards were made along the entire front.

Sunday, 30 July 1944: With the day of assumption of command now not far off, the General spent another busy day discussing tactics and strategy with his generals.

He first visited V Corps to keep General Gerow advised of Army plans, and to urge him to keep moving south as fast as he could. With General Gerow he next paid a call to the CP of the 35th Division, a mile southeast of St Lo, where he talked to both General Boddy [Paul W. Baade][16] and General [Edmund B.] Sebree.[17] He ended up the day with a long conference with General Corlett at XIX Corps.

There was some lack of agreement here as to the best policy to be pursued. There was no question that the 30th Division, and to a lesser extent, the 29th were taking rough treatment from the 2nd Panzer, which was fighting determinedly. General Corlett's solution was to flank them, securing high ground further south, which fact, he said, would make their present position untenable. He admitted the move was a gamble, but he thought it was a good one. General Hodges, who has felt since the beginning that too many of these battalions and regiments of ours have tried to flank and skirt and never meet the enemy straight on, was opposed to the maneuver outlined, believing it safer, sounder, and in the end, quicker, to keep smashing ahead, without any tricky, uncertain business of possibly exposing yourself to being cut off. He did not specifically order General Corlett to change his plans, but made it clear that he thought there was much against it as presented.

The big news of the day was that CCB, 4th Armored Div, entered Avranches at 2200 and secured two bridges over the La See river. Several hundred prisoners were taken during the advance. CCA, 6th Armored Div, advanced within 5000 yards of Granville and also had elements reported at Malecorne. The 79th and 8th Division were following both tonight.

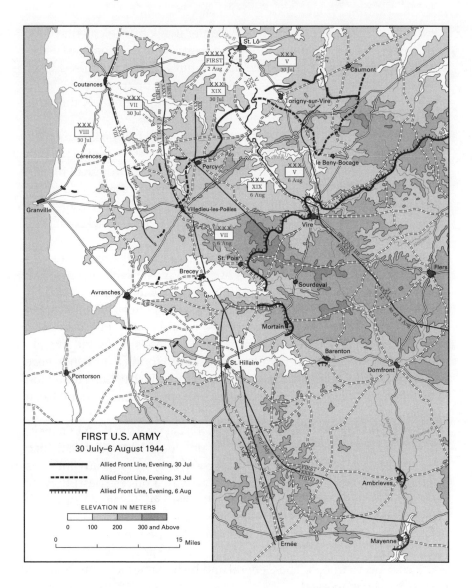

FIRST U.S. ARMY
30 July–6 August 1944

———— Allied Front Line, Evening, 30 Jul

- - - - - Allied Front Line, Evening, 31 Jul

┴┴┴┴┴┴ Allied Front Line, Evening, 6 Aug

ELEVATION IN METERS

0   100   200   300 and Above

0   15 Miles

On the VII Corps front, CCB, 3rd Armored Div, advanced to within 4,000 yards of Villedieu les Poeles. CCA reached Gavray but was held up there while the bridge was being repaired. The road between Roncey and St Denis Le Gas [St. Denis-le-Gast] was reported as impassible due to the damaged and destroyed enemy tanks and vehicles. The 4th Div continued to advance and were on a line running generally west from Percy.

The XIX Corps received a major counterattack from elements of the 2nd Panzer and 116th Panzer along the Tessy–Ville Boudon [Tessy-sur-Vire–Villebaudon] road. It started at 1300 but had been repulsed three hours later. There was, however, no gain chalked up for the day.

V Corps put the 5th Div 1000 yards ahead; approximately the same advance was made by the 2nd Div.

The British VIII Corps launched a heavy attack at 0655, preceded by aerial support of some 1400 aircraft, south of Caumont. The 15th Scottish Division made good progress and advanced through St Martin de Besaces [St. Martin-des-Basaces]. The 11th Armored was held up by mines and dug-in tanks in the area north of La Lande sur Drome. The 43rd advanced to Cahagnes. The 50th Div, 30th Corps, attacked at 0600 and took St Germain d'Ectot.

Last night, for the first time since we arrived in France, there was no AA fire. Night fighter patrol was overhead most of the evening, and theirs was the responsibility of fending off enemy aircraft.

Monday, 31 July 1944: The General left with Fran at 1030 to inspect the Chateau CP and was not enheartened to find that an Engineer combat command was still living in one wing, the place strewn with wreckage and dirt, and several details supposedly working on it not very busily or usefully engaged. He left some definite instructions for action to be taken, which he later passed on, in greater detail, to General Kean by telephone.

After lunch on the Chateau grounds, the General visited XIX Corps, where there seems to be some loosening up along the front. The British were reported in Beny-Bocage, when we arrived, and this advance has doubtless persuaded the Germans to give way a bit less [lest] they be caught between the XIX Corps and the British VIII. General Corlett reported that they had had a noisy night previous, that a dump had been fired, and some guns destroyed, and said he hoped the ban on AA fire would be lifted tonight. Even if they didn't bring any down, their firing was a comfort to troops. The General and he had another conference as to tactics to be employed.

We drove then to St Gilles and across to Marigny and just north of the town, only to find that the VII Corps had, unbeknownst to Fran, just changed, or were in the process of changing it. The General was able to get late information of the situation but wishing to talk to General Collins, he decided to push on to the new one, twelve miles south at St Martin de Cenilly. Though the roads were jammed and the MPs not very much on the job, we found the farmhouse without trouble. Unfortunately General Collins had just left in order to visit the 1st Division, three miles down the road, so after a chat with Col McKEE, the General turned back for Master.[18] The road trip was quick, though we had to wait a few minutes in St Lo to permit Army's Bomb Disposal Squad to set off an unexploded 500-pounder which showered bricks and stones for yards but did not bring down any of the tottering walls of what is left of the city.

The General was busy with General Bradley until late in the evening, making final plans for the separation into Armies and Army Group, and the zone that would belong to General Hodges' forces.

An interrogation of Captain Hardegen, aide to General Beyerlein [Bayerlein],[19] commanding Panzer Lehr, brought forth some very interesting facts. Hardegen, captured yesterday, is full of hatred against the SS,[20] which is favored at every turn over the regular Army. He says a similar hatred exists among high-ranking officers of the Wehrmacht, those who are not party newcomers. He foresees further struggle as futile, only an effort by Hitler to save his skin a few more weeks, and outright murder of German[y]. He thinks the British infantry far superior to ours; on the reverse, he praises our artillery and armor as far better than theirs, and goes out of his way to pay tribute to the effectiveness of our harassing fire, especially that at night.

Some 10,000 prisoners have been taken during the drive, and today it continued without visible abatement—on all fronts.

CCB, 6th Armored, followed by 314th Inf, advanced along the coast through Granville to a mile north of Avranches. The 4th Armored continued to exploit south of Avranches, and elements were reported to have seized bridges at Ducey, and at 365110.

The 1st Division, with CCA, 3rd Armored, crossed the Sienne at Gavray and advanced in three columns rapidly to 405305 (26th Inf), 375315 (18th) and 375260 (16th). Their division CP was bombed during the night with 25 casualties, including the wounding of Capt WALT Hillenmeyer, aide to Gen Huebner. The 4th reached 1,500 yards north of Villier-Les-Poeles [Villedieu-les-Poêles]. The 2nd Armored, less CCA, was assembling at 3951 preparing to move, upon call, to the XIX Corps.

Resistance in the XIX Corps sector continued to be rugged; the boche here shows no signs of demoralization, The 30th Div made only 300 yards, and the 29th, attacking east along the Villebaudon–Tessy road with 175th Inf and elements of the 2nd Armd Div were able to make only 800.

V Corps had things a bit easier, the 2nd and 5th Divisions making more than two miles, the 35th Div a mile. The Second British Army continued its drive but met determined enemy resistance and consequently had to be content with a stalemate.

Chapter 3

Exploitation of the St. Lô Breakthrough, 1 August–12 September 1944

The Drive South, 1–12 August 1944

Tuesday, 1 August 1944: Today, at 1025, General Hodges signed four secret copies of General Orders No 4, First United States Army, and thereby assumed command. Three of the orders went to the Corps Commanders serving under him; the fourth to the AG [Adjutant General] safe. Until SHAEF releases news of the existence of two Armies in operation under command of 12th Army Group, there will be no general publicity given to General Hodges' assumption of command.

General Bradley, and his two aides left, with bag and baggage (and the trailer) shortly after 0900, and from then on, until late in the evening, the General was in the War Room tent, either with General Kean or Colonel Thorsen [Thorson], or visiting Generals. At 1115 General Collins flew in from VII Corps, and shortly afterward General Corlett drove up from XIX Corps. General Bradley, jokingly remarking that maybe he should have left his napkin ring here, also arrived for lunch and conference.

The Third Army went operational at 12 noon, at the same time that General Hodges, officially, took command. It consists of the VIII Corps, XV and XX, though only the first-named is operational at the present time. General Hodges' Army consists of the V, VII, and XIX Corps; the 1st, 2nd, 28th, 29th, 30th, 4th, 9th; and the 2nd and 3rd Armored Divisions. Also included are the 5th and 35th Divisions, but these will revert to Third Army so soon as the tactical situation permits.

During the day the 1st Div continued to advance to the south against light resistance. The 4th Div line now runs generally along the Villedieu les Poeles–Percy highway. The XIX Corps took Tessy sur Vire with the 120th Inf and elements of CAA [CCA], 2nd Armored Div. V Corps like-wise continued its advance in the west part of the Corps sector.

Wednesday, 2 August 1944: The CP of the Army was moved this morning to the chateau of the Count of Marigny, one-quarter mile east of the small town of Canisy.

The General's van and area were placed directly south of the lake, some fifty yards from the chateau; the C/S a few yards away. G-2 and G-3 for the first time have large, comfortable, workable offices, on the second and first floors respectively of the south wing of the chateau. (The lake was noted for its fine supply of striped bass, but it was unfor-tunately bombed two nights before our arrival, and Utilities spent the best part of yesterday in a canoe, sweeping out the dead fish).

The General did not come directly to the CP but instead went out with Bill to V Corps for a conference with General Gerow, returning to the old CP (where the War Tent was kept intact) for study and confer-ence. He arrived in the new CP at 1500, and started an immediate con-ference with General Kean and Col Thorsen which was to last almost, without interruption, until midnight. The General was not pleased with the location of Air Corps trucks, which are parked in a row next to the chateau wall and obviously a dead-give-away for any boche observa-tion, but otherwise, the CP appears to be satisfactory.

There has been a change in First Army-Second British Army fronts, and the boundary now gives back to us the job of taking Vire, which originally fell to the British. First Army's general directive, as set out by Twelfth Army Group, is to swing south and southeast, with Domfront as the objective. Third Army's job is to take the Brittany peninsula, in the shortest possible time and with the minimum employment of man-power.

The day's news continued good. In the VII Corps sector, the 9th Div advanced up to three miles against light resistance and reached a line a few hundred yards northwest of the Villedieu-les-Poeles–Villiers Bocage [Villers-Bocage] road. The 1st Div shot ahead from five to six miles, and their front line, in general, is along the Avranches–Mortain road. The 4th Div likewise had light resistance from isolated pockets only and were about a mile north of Pois.

In the XIX Corps, the 29th Div made good gains but were tempo-rarily stopped in the afternoon by very heavy mortar and artillery fire. CCB, 2nd Armd Div, advanced to 448385 in a late-afternoon attack but was stopped by dug-in tanks and artillery. The 28th Div made very little advance. The front line is generally along the Villedieu-les-Poeles–Villers Bocage road from Marqueray to 5042 and then north to a point some 2,000 yards SW of Tessy sur Vire.

In V Corps, advances across the Soulevre [Souleuvre] river were made, although the 35th had trouble. The 2nd Div lost contact with the enemy early in the day and Corps cavalry was sent in to regain contact[1]—which was done, some 3,000 yards south of the river.

General Patton's troops continue to move south, and although communications are bad and very uncertain, elements of the 6th Armored were reported near Dinan and Meillac. CCB of the 4th was in the vicinity of Rennes, and it was also reported that Tremblay had been occupied.

In the British VIII Corps sector, the 11th Armd Div advanced south from Beny Bocage to points 690340 and 715340. Rcn [reconnaissance] elements placed road blocks on roads running north and east out of Vire. On the left the Guards Armored Div encountered stiffer resistance, being held up in the vicinity of Montchamp.

Thursday, 3 August 1944: After the morning conference in the war tent, the General pinned the Distinguished Service Medal on the blouse of General Kean. The latter was awarded this honor for his untiring efforts in the planning of First Army's invasion of the continent.

Later in the morning General Bradley and General "Bedell" Smith[2] arrived for a conference. The latter left before lunch to catch a plane back to London; General Bradley stayed for lunch but left immediately afterward. At 1530 the General and Bill paid a quick trip to VII Corps for a conference with General Collins.

In the VII Corps front the 1st Div continued its lightning advance. It occupied Mortain and later sent on patrols as far as Barenton without encountering enemy resistance. The 4th Div advanced to the outskirts of St Pois. The 9th advanced rapidly during the morning but met stiffer opposition in the afternoon. However, by dark, they were on the general line La Fosse–La Bigotiere, an advance of 6,000 yards for the day.

XIX Corps: The 28th and 29th Divisions made 7,000 yards up to the St Sever Calvados–Landelles et Coupigny road. Elements of CCB, 2nd Armored, were in St Sever Calvados itself and Sept Freres.

In V Corps, resistance was moderate to heavy. The 35th Div made Beaumesnit [Beaumesnil], the 2nd Div only 2,000 yards .

The Third Army continued its swift sweep through Brittany. Mauron, Broons, Bain de Bretagne and Derval fell during the day. The 83rd Div closed on Pontorson.

In the Second British Army front, the 11th Armd Div advanced to the Vire-Vassy road with elements as far south as 7080. The Guards Armd Div went 1,000 yards south of Estry. On the XXX Corps sector, the 7th Armd Div seized Hill 138 west of Aunay-sur-Odon. The 43rd Div occupied Bois-de-Buron. The British are meeting tough resistance all along their various fronts.

Friday, 4 August 1944: The General left shortly after 11 this morning with Fran to visit Tac Hq [Tactical Headquarters] of the Second British Army. Arriving at noon, he found General [Miles Christopher] Dempsey[3] to be out visiting one of the Corps, but the latter arrived shortly afterward. Tac Hq, consisting of a few staff operations officers and ADCs [aides-de-camp], acts as a forward CP to Main Hq, at Creuilly [Creully].

We left Cormolain shortly after 1430, and for the rest of the day, and until 1030 tonight the General was busy on the telephone with General Corlett, whose XIX Corps is making but very scant progress, if any, in its push toward Vire; and General Collins, whose plan to push across almost due east to Gathemo (5624), intruding a bit on the XIX Corps boundary, the General heartily approved of. There is apparently some boche strength coming west, and the General, in the absence of XIX Corps advance, wishes to stop them as short as possible.

The news from the fronts: The 1st Div consolidated its positions around Mortain, meanwhile conducting active patrolling in the direction of Mayenne and Domfront. The 4th Div met stubborn resistance around St Pois and failed to gain the town. The 9th Div continued the advance during the morning against no resistance, but later ran into scattered pockets of resistance in the Foret de St Sever and many minefields. Penetration of a mile into the forest was made before dark.

The 28th and 29th Divisions met heavy resistance late during the day. The 115th Inf was 500 yards south of Mensil Clincamps [Mesnil-Clinchamps], the 116th at the northern edge of La Tiercerie, CCA 2nd Armd Div 2,000 yards north of Vire. The 28th Inf and CCB, 2nd Armd Div, secured St Sever Calvados and were 1,000 yards south and 2,000 yards west of the town.

V Corps took the remainder of the high ground overlooking their boundary—the 35th reaching their objectives early in the day, the 2nd Div meeting with more trouble.

Third Army continued its march. CCA, 4th Armd Div, is 12 miles south of Rennes; CCB is in Derval. Task Force A—the 330th RCT and

2nd and 5th Cav launched an attack on St Malo. Order of Battle of the Third Army at present is:

VIII Corps: 4th and 6th Armd, 8th and 83rd Inf Divisions.

XV Corps : 5th Armd, 79 and 90th Inf Divisions.

XX Corps : 2nd French Armd Div (of which big things are expected) and 5th Inf Div.

On the British XII Corps front, the 53rd and 59th Divisions began an advance along the entire front, and leading elements of both have occupied Villiers Bocage, Epiny sur Odon [Epinay-sur-Odon], Villedon [Villodon], [Ste] Honorine du Fay, Maizet, and Amaye sur Orne, Esquey [Esquay-Notre-Dame] and Evrecy. The enemy offered little resistance and appeared to be staging a definite withdrawal.

Saturday, 5 August 1944: The General spent another day in the CP, almost exclusively in the war tent, directing the battle and getting the news. The CP is now so far behind the front lines that today he sent Colonel Myers in the direction of St Pois to see if we could not set the forward CP in that vicinity. Because of the swiftness with which the battle is at present moving, it is the General's intention to set up a small, forward CP with key personnel from G-2, G-3, Arty, Engr, and Signal and, in the event that the breakthrough definitely becomes a pursuit, follow right along with it.

This evening he had his three Corps commanders in for their first dinner with him, and a conference in the war tent followed. As the outcome of this conference, the General ordered the 30th Div, which has been resting for the past three days, to entruck southward at once, relieving the 1st Div at Mortain, thus enabling the latter to push southward to Mayenne, and perhaps later Domfront. This now puts five divisions under VII Corps; V Corps has only the 2nd left, the 35th having reverted to Third Army.

The day's news continued good, although the pace of advance, with all divisions tired and with resistance stiffening, was slower. The 4th Div bypassed St Pois, encircled it, and then took it. In the 9th Div, the 60th Inf advanced through the Foret St Sever until it reached Champ du Boult, a strongpoint. The 47th Inf encountered mines but few enemy and went 2,000 yards NE of St Pois.

The XIX Corps found the area around Vire tough going. CCA, 2nd Armd, and elements of the 29th were 1000 yards west and northwest of the city but suitable locations for stream crossing were heavily mined and covered by fire. On the right, the 28th Div went on 4,000 yards to the vicinity of Camp du Boult [Champ-du-Boult]. In the center of the

Corps sector, the 112th and 115th Inf advanced 3,500 yards to the town of St Manvieu Bocage.

The Third Army continued its headlong dash westward. The 6th Armd were within 15 miles of Brest; the 5th Armd were moving south toward Fougeres. The 4th Armd and attached units were generally along a line running SW from Rennes thru Redon to the Villain [Vilaine] river. The 79th is moving on Laval; the 83rd is being held up in its attack on St Malo. The 90th Div, crossing our Army boundary, is in Mayenne, but will be relieved by the 1st Div.

The only news from the British sector is that General Dempsey called this night, late, to inquire for permission to move an Armored Brigade through our lines, far south, and then to attack across Conde sur Noireau. The General is not enthusiastic over the scheme.

Twelfth Army Group Letter Instructions No. 3, which were discussed by General Bradley, General Hodges, and General Patton this morning and over the luncheon table, still call for First Army to swing Vire to Domfront to Ambrieres [Ambrières-les-Vallées]. Third Army, upon completion of the capture of the Brittany Peninsula, will swing on below us with the Loire as southern boundary.

Sunday, 6 August 1944: General Louis Craig,[4] former commander of the 97th Div under General Hodges, and now CG of the XXII Corps [XXIII Corps], visited the General this morning and stayed for lunch. He is over here to stay, he reported, but is traveling without any member of his Corps staff.

The General was not too well satisfied today with the progress in general. The 1st Division reached Mayenne as scheduled, but the 30th Div did not close until six or seven hours after the planned time, and the General has taken steps to clear up the traffic snarls which so frequently have made motor movement not only slower than foot marching but potentially more dangerous. Vire is surrounded on all sides, but the east, and all roads leading into it are under our control and fire, but still the city is not ours. The XIX Corps is not moving as fast as it had been hoped.

Still the day's progress, as recorded in the War Room, where the General was closeted most of the day, was not unimpressive. The 1st Div, in addition to having Mayenne (16th Inf) had also Ambrieres-la-Grande [Ambrières-les-Vallées]; and Task Force X of the 3rd Armd Div and some elements of the 1st were into Domfront and Lassay [Lassay-les-Châteaux]. They withdrew without encountering resistance.

The 4th Div reverted to Corps reserve. The 9th Div, meeting very strong resistance, advanced only 1100 to 1500 yards. The 30th, closing in Mortain, received a localized counterattack from enemy infantry during the night and early hours of the morning (7th) but repulsed it without difficulty.

Late reports, coming through at midnight, indicated that 2 Bns of the 116th Inf were finally in Vire, with the attack around the city continuing to mop up during the night. The 2nd Armd was held up south of St Pois by enemy counterattack coming from the southeast between the 39th Inf and the 30th Div.

The Third Army is having a far easier time. Vannes has been taken; Task Force A is on the outskirts of St Malo. Elements now extend across the peninsula from Vannes to the north coast, and elements of the 6th Armored are in Couron [Gourin] and Hulegoat [Huelgoat].

On the British front, the VIII Corps continued the attack. The 15th Div occupied Estry, 7437. A strong counterattack in vic [vicinity] Burcy 6934 was being repulsed. The outskirts of Pont Pinchon [Mont Pinçon] were reached by the 43rd Div.

Monday, 7 August 1944: The General left the CP briefly today for conferences at the XIX and VII Corps, but spent most of the time—and until 0130 in the morning—in the war tent.

The boche is attacking—with the acknowledged purpose (Hq did not leave the captured order to tell them) of cutting across from Mortain to Avranches, thus separating the First and Third Army. For this purpose he had assembled four armored Divisions—the Second [SS], the Second Panzer, the 116th, and what was left of Panzer Lehr, badly mauled in our original break-through. The counterattack was made east and south of Mortain, and later a column of armor was discovered to have penetrated to the vicinity of Le Mesnil Tove. During the day—one of the best, weather-wise, we have yet had—the air went after the enemy armor with a vengeance, claiming by nightfall a total of 109 tanks destroyed. The General is not too worried over the situation, though there is admittedly the strongest kind of pressure. The 35th and 80th Divisions are being moved to back up the line, in the event the enemy succeeds in cracking the line to any great extent. Mortain definitely belongs to the enemy, and the 2 Bn, 120th Inf, occupying high ground east of the town, is temporarily, at least, cut off.

General Bradley came for lunch, but in the absence of General Hodges, did not stay at the CP long.

Tuesday, 8 August 1944: The new advance CP was set up this morning (25 officers and 200 enlisted men) at Sept Freres, two and one-half miles north of St Sever Calvados, occupying two apple orchards and two wheat fields. Good camouflage is offered; the only drawback, and that to be anticipated since we are only some six or seven miles from the front lines, is that we are surrounded by artillery—a battery of 8 inchers a kilometer behind us—a battalion of Long Toms below the town to the south, and various other batteries, too far away for identification except by the crack of their guns. Two members of the Cavalry squadron were injured by mines this morning; a booby trap was removed from a gate leading to G-3's corner; and all day long the engineers have been busy finding and exploding Teller-mines and Schuh-mines.[5]

The General spent a good part of the day at XIX Corps and VII Corps, too busy to pay much attention to XIX Corps' visiting celebrity, the motion picture actor Edward G. Robinson. The situation appears a bit better tonight, and roughly as follows:

The 9th Div less 38th Inf repulsed several small local enemy counter-attacks in the Mesnil Tove and Charence le Roussel [Chérencé-le-Roussel] areas and made no gains during the day. The 4th Div with 8th Inf and attached 39th Inf maintained lines south of the 9th Div against strong enemy pressure. The 30th Div with attached 12th Inf was heavily engaged throughout the day. The 2nd Bn, 120th, is still cut off. The 35th Div advanced against very light resistance to the east but the 1st and 2nd Bns of the 134th were held up at 580060 by a strong enemy attack from the north. The 1st continued to consolidate positions and conduct active patrolling to secure crossings on the Mayenne river. The CCB, 2nd Armd Div, which is making an end sweep in a northeasterly direction (coming from the southwest) continued to advance in two columns on Ger (7040) against increasing resistance.

In the XIX Corps sector, the 109th Inf regrouped about 1,000 yards NW of Gathemo after having [been] forced out by the enemy. The boche, holding here with the 84th, is apparently determined to keep intact his line in the north, in order to give full play to his main effort toward the west, which, despite the pounding from the air and artillery, he does not appear yet to have abandoned. The 112th, however, on the left flank, advanced a little more [than] a mile to Les Nudieres, and leading elements of the 29th Div the same distance to St Germain-de-Tallevende.

Third Army: All radio reports to the contrary, Brest is still very much in enemy hands, while reports that the garrison at Lorient wished to surrender also appear premature, 4th Armd Div still being held up two miles north of the city.

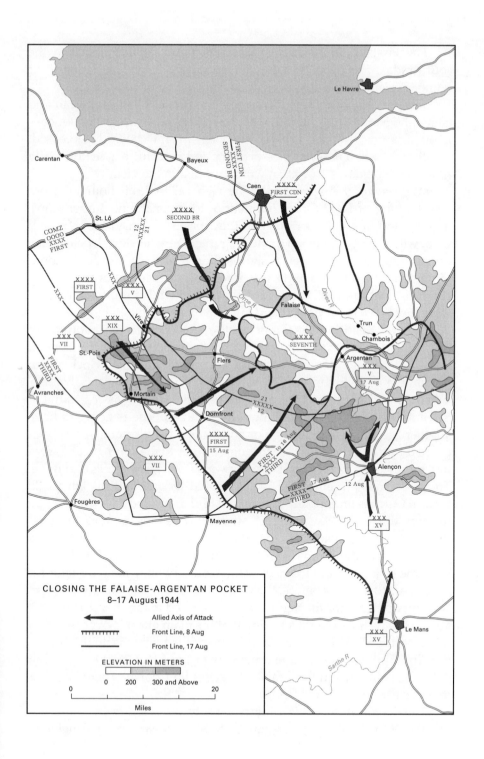

Carentan

Bayeux

FIRST CDN
XXXXX
SECOND BR

Caen

XXXX
FIRST CDN

St. Lô

COMZ
OOOO
XXXX
FIRST

12
XXXXX
21

XXXX
SECOND BR

XXXX
FIRST

XXX
V

Orne R

Falaise

Dives R

Trun

Vire

XXX
XIX

XXX
VII

FIRST
XXXX
THIRD

St.-Pois

Flers

XXXX
SEVENTH

Chambois

Argentan

XXX
V
17 Aug

Avranches

Mortain

Domfront

21
XXXXX
12

XXX
VII

XXXX
FIRST
15 Aug

FIRST to 16 Aug
XXXX
THIRD

FIRST
XXXX
THIRD

17 Aug

Alençon

12 Aug

Fougères

Mayenne

XXX
XV

Le Havre

Le Mans

XXX
XV

Sarthe R

CLOSING THE FALAISE-ARGENTAN POCKET
8–17 August 1944

Allied Axis of Attack

Front Line, 8 Aug

Front Line, 17 Aug

ELEVATION IN METERS

0   200   300 and Above

0   20

Miles

The First Canadian Army launched a coordinated attack to the south today, preceded by the now customary heavy preliminary air bombardment. Initial advances up to four to five miles were made.

Tonight at midnight, in a conversation between General Kean and General Leven Allen,[6] the 35th was attached to us until further notice—in other words, until all threat of the boche push westward has ceased.

Tonight was a noisy night—artillery and air being active until early morning. No bombs, however, were dropped in the vicinity.

Wednesday, 9 August 1944: The General took an hour off from his planning of Field Order Number 5, to cover the next operations, to greet and talk with Secretary of the Treasury [Henry] Morgenthau[7] who, with a party of eleven (including the man who signs Uncle Sam's dollar bills) came down on a sight-seeing tour from Group. Without too much difficulty, the party was safely engineered out of the way by eleven o'clock, and Bill escorted them to the 28th Division, where they were met by General Corlett and later taken to Corps.

General Kean left for Group in the afternoon to get approval of General Hodges' next field order, with its new boundaries; the General rested briefly and then stayed in the war room until six o'clock, when he made a brief flying visit to VII Corps via the St Sever Calvados–Villedieu-les-Poeles road, heretofore not very safe for passing traffic.

It still is not certain, tonight, whether the boche is going to have another "go" at a breakthrough or not. Stopped at Mortain, he has been pushed into an effort to strike through farther to the south, near Barenton, but the 35th Div, though moving very slowly, is balking him there. The audacious sweep of the 2nd Armored Div around his left flank, toward Ger, has undoubtedly surprised him. But some have argued that for him, this is a "now or never" attempt. If he fails to break through, there is a strong possibility that the Third, still making its great end sweep past Le Mans and toward Alencon, may yet succeed in drawing tight the string around his neck. This would be inevitable disaster for his forces. Tonight, as before, the General issued orders for all troops to "button up tight" for the night, and be prepared for anything, though it appears to be the General's feeling that his main effort is over, and that it has been decisively broken or at least stopped, there is no doubt.

An impudent Nazi plane cruised over the CP at 2130 tonight, but AAA [antiaircraft artillery] failed to bring him down. There was less artillery fire.

The details of the day's military activity are as follows:

The 30th Div continued to attack to St Barthelmy [St.-Barthélemy] and Mortain but were unable to advance. Second Bn, 120th Inf, is still out of contact with its other units. The 2nd Armd met heavy resistance on the road to Ger but advanced a mile. The 9th Div made no advance. The 4th Div, less the 12th Inf, remained in Corps reserve.

In the XIX Corps sector, the 29th Div attacked and made good progress—advancing some 4,000 yards (the 115th Inf) to 640268, against heavy fire. The 28th attacked to Gathemo but made very little headway.

The 2nd Div finished mopping up in Vire and moved its 9th Inf out to relieve the 116th.

In the Third Army sector, elements of the 83rd had under control all but one strong-point of St Malo. The 4th Armd Div is holding positions of Lorient; the 6th Armd Div is three miles north of Brest. The 79th Div took Le Mans, assisted by the 5th Armd Div attacking from the southeast The 90th Div moved in, mopped up, and occupied the town, and the 80th Div moved to this vicinity. The 2nd French Armd Div is enroute to this area. The 5th Armd Div, not stopping, continued to eat up the miles toward Angers.

Thursday, 10 August 1944: The General spent the morning at VII Corps, came back here for lunch , and then motored out again to the XIX and V Corps for closed-door conferences with the Corps commanders.

The boche seems to be giving way slightly, though G-2 and G-3 do not agree as to what the next steps to follow are—whether a re-groupment is in order, or whether, as G-3 believes, the enemy is making ready for a dash out of the ever-tightening noose.

The 2nd Div took Mainsoncelles Le Jourdan [Maisoncelles-la-Jourdan] and went 1,000 yards south of the town before halting on Corps order.

The XIX Corps continued the attack with the 28th and 29th Div and a special task force from CCA, 2nd Armd. The 29th did not advance perceptibly, but the 109th Inf, with the task force as its spearhead, recaptured the town of Gathemo and went 500 yards south. The special task force advanced slowly along the Gathemo–Tinchebray highway.

The 2nd Bn, 120th Inf, still held out, refusing two German demands to surrender. They were resupplied by air, and tanks of the 3rd Armd Div—five of them—broke through to them. The 35th advanced against stiff resistance, the 1st Bn, 320th, reaching the road junction south of Mortain. The 1st Div continued defensive positions guarding the crossings over the Mayenne river between that city and Ambrieres le Grand.

The Third Army sector is substantially unchanged from yesterday, except that the 2nd French Armd and the 5th Armd Div attacked to the north and east of Le Mans.

Tonight, the situation is generally satisfactory to the General.

Friday, 11 August 1944: General Bradley arrived shortly before 11 o'clock, bringing with him General [John L.] DeWitt,[8] who has just arrived to take over the post, as yet unannounced, which was to have been held by General McNair. General Corlett also arrived at about the same time, and after a long conference in the War Tent, everybody adjourned to a late lunch. One of the decisions made was to relieve General Lloyd Brown of the 28th with Brig Gen Wharton, Asst Div Comdr of the 9th Div. The other was that General Bradley wishes the 35th Div to be released as soon as possible from VII Corps, in order to take over another mission with the Third Army.

The signs today are that the enemy is trying to get out, though the resistance against leading elements has not everywhere slackened. The 30th Div still came up against tough sledding around Mortain and could not relieve the 2nd Bn, 120th. The 134 and 137 Inf reached and occupied objectives along the Mortain–Barenton road. CCA, 2nd Armd Div, made no advance against Ger. CCB, 3rd Armd, attached to the 30th, maintained road blocks along the Gathemo-Tinchebray road.

The 28th Div and 29th Division made a mile advance during the day—here resistance is not quite so tough as before. There was no change in the V Corps sector.

Saturday, 12 August 1944: General Brown and General Wharton visited the CP this morning for conferences with the General. In the afternoon General Bradley likewise returned for [a] conference with the General.

This evening the General made his first appearance before the press—some 40 correspondents, including three or four Britishers. The plan [press conference] explained First Army's plan, VII Corps to be the hammer-head of the attack with the 1st Div swinging up from the South, the 30th advancing across the Corps sector due east—the 90 degree change in Army's direction. All this was given "off the record."

The session was then open to questions—and thick and fast they came. The correspondents wanted to know when we would be in Paris, whether the German Army would be destroyed, whether the Seventh German Army was purposely committing "suicide," what Third Army was up to, what kind of fighter was the German, were we behind or ahead of schedule, did our maneuver follow the original plan—in fact, everything but what our next morning breakfast meal would be. It was the old newspaper game of trying to entice the interviewee into broad, sweeping generalization, to get the General so far out on a limb that he would either fall off, or climb down in a hurry. The General, well aware of the tactics opposed to him, refused to be trapped, answered frankly all questions which concerned his Army front but refused to let himself be drawn into the wide strategical picture, on which correspondents always seek the "answers." The session ended about 9, an hour after its start, with the General well in control of the situation, and the correspondents satisfied.

During the day—as the General pointed out to correspondents—IX Tac [IX Tactical Air Command, Ninth Air Force][9] spotted vehicles fleeing out of the sector, on roads from Flers eastward, and General Quesada reported fairly satisfactory "hunting," though the heat haze was not perfect for such activities. It is now almost without dispute that he is getting out of the noose as fast as his gasoline and feet will carry him.

During the press conference, sad news came through from XIX Corps that General Wharton had died, only three hours after inspecting the front lines of the 28th Div, the command of which he had just taken over. A sniper had fired only one bullet, but that had hit him in the chest, and he died shortly after reaching the clearing station. General Hodges immediately called Gen Bradley to suggest the name of Gen Hasbrouk [Robert W. Hasbrouck][10] to succeed, but the choice finally fell on Brig Gen "Dutch" Cota, much-decorated Asst Div Comdr of the 29th Div. General [George A.] Davis[11] will become assistant Div Comdr under him, General Buchanan[12] leaving.

At midnight the day's advances, though not great, were praiseworthy. The 2nd Div made gains up to three miles; the 29th Div, switched over to V Corps, also went two miles—both divisions meeting considerable fire resistance.

The 28th Div, in the XIX Corps sector, reported putting patrols of the 110th Inf into Soudeval [Sourdeval]. CCA, 2nd Armd Div, was progressing to the same town, but meeting tough resistance from mortars and bazookas.

The 2nd Bn, 120th, was relieved this morning by two battalions of the 35th Div, and Mortain and land two to three miles east of the city is again in our hands.

Brest, Lorient, still are putting up a fight against Third Army's VIII Corps. Alencon, in the XV Corps sector, is being by-passed. Reconnaissance elements are reported to have pushed as far forward as Chartres, then withdrawing.

The British are making some gains, none of them sizeable or of break-through proportions, generally along their entire front. The 4th Armd Div, Canadian, reached a point north of Falaise at 083455.

The Falaise–Argentan Gap, 13–18 August 1944

Sunday, 13 August 1944: The General left the CP only once today— to attend the funeral of General Wharton in Armor's cemetery at Le Neubourg north of Morigny. It was a rather unpleasant ceremony, for the smell of the dead was deep-lying, and corpses were piled in long rows, awaiting burial by the blacks. While there, the General had a brief conference with General Corlett.

The remainder of the day the General spent in the War Tent, watching the 1st Div speed up from the south, making gains which, by day's end, were as much as 20 miles. At 10, General Collins called asking for more "territory to take." The Div was, in some places, on the very boundary itself, and General Collins felt sure he could take Falaise and Argentan, close the gap, and "do the job" before the British even started to move. General Hodges immediately called General Bradley, to ask officially for a change in boundaries, but the sad news came back that First Army was to go no farther than at first designated, except that a small salient around Ranes would become ours.

The good news was not confined to the VII Corps sector. The 38th Inf, in V Corps sector, advanced to the Tinchebray–Gathemo road; the 29th Div were a mile south and southeast of St Martin de Chaulieu.

In the XIX Corps: the 109th and 110th Inf went three miles up to the Ger–Mortain highway. CCA, 2nd Armd Div, got to within a mile of Ger. CCB, 2nd Armd Div, attacked toward Domfront, with one column on the Barenton road, the other on the Passais road. The northern column by nightfall were within two miles of Domfront; the southern column within three. The 30th Div was attached to XIX Corps at 0900 today, and spent the day reorganizing in the vicinity of Mortain.

VII Corps: The 35th Div, which finally accomplished its mission under steady pushing from Gen Collins, reverted to Third Army this morning. The 1st Div, as noted above, "dusted the road with their shoes." Elements of the 18th Inf were north of La Chapelle Moche [La Chapelle-d'Andaine], while the 26th occupied Couterne. The 3rd Armd Div, composed of three task forces, likewise rolled merrily on. Task Force X advanced through Carrouges, made contact with the 2nd French Armd on their right, and then went on to Ranes—against light resistance. Task Force Y advanced to Ligmeres la Doucelle; Task Force Z took Javron [Javron-les-Chapelles].

The General had, to be on the safe side, told correspondents the night before that he expected the "hammerhead" to reach their objectives within 72 hours. He is obviously pleased tonight to find that almost all the primary objectives have been taken within 18 hours.

News from other fronts: CCA, 4th Armd Div, entered Nantes against no opposition but found all harbor facilities destroyed, and the piers heavily mined. Brest and Lorient are still German. The 5th Armd Div occupied Sees, Argentan, and Le Pin au Haras; the 90th was reported in the vicinity of Alencon; and the 79th near Le Mele sur Sarthe.

Monday, 14 August 1944: The CP was moved this morning—after General Gerow and General Corlett had arrived at 10 for an "open-air" conference with the General—to a dusty, straw-ridden field (which the General referred to, upon first sight, as a "hog wallow," one kilometre north of the switch-off on the Le Tilleul [Le Teilleul]–Barenton road. He immediately decided that the CP should move again, and General Kean went out to inspect a spot previously looked at as a possibility for Command Echelon.

Army CP was in startling contrast to that of the VII Corps, south of Gorron, which the General visited with Bill between 11 and 4—by a lake, cool and refreshing, offering decent cover and concealment. At VII Corps, the General found the news entirely satisfactory in every way. TFX [Task Force X], 3rd Armd, is meeting heavy fighting at Ranes, which was not contrary to expectations, but the other three forces (it split from three into four) had less trouble. The 9th took St Patrice-du-Desert and Houve-du-Bois [Joue-du-Bois]. The 26th Inf occupied La Ferte-Mace, and made advances one mile north and northeast.

The Third US Army likewise continued its sweep. The 2nd French and 5th Armd Div occupied Argentan–Bourg St Leonard area. The 7th Armd and 5th Inf advanced on Dreux. The 4th Armd, freed from its Brittany peninsula fights, and the 35th, freed from our sector, advanced east with Orleans and Chartres as their objectives. The area between Falaise and Argentan was reported to be completely covered by artillery fire from the 1st Canadian Army, some 2½ miles north of Falaise, and elements of the Third Army.

Tuesday, 15 August 1944: While the CP was being moved again— this time to broad, beautiful meadows a few hundred yards off the main highway leading from Le Tilleul (Lettuce) to Domfront—the General and Bill drove to XIX and V Corps for long conferences with their respective commanders for coming operations. Both XIX and V Corps are on their objectives, or a few hundred yards from them, and there soon must be a move, and another job to do. While out, the General met and talked briefly to Mr. Bryant [William Wright Bryan],[13] correspondent for the Atlanta Journal and broadcaster for NBC [National Broadcasting Company], who, as correspondent for a Georgia paper, was particularly interested in getting information. There have been many requests, already, for official interviews with the General, but thus far he has been too busy to grant them. "Winning the war's the thing right now," he keeps saying.

The day's military news:

V Corps: Tinchebray was captured by the 2nd Div against light resistance. This completes Corps' mission.

XIX Corps: The 28th Div reached the boundary; the 30th still has a few hundred yards more to go. The 2nd Armd Div is undergoing much-needed maintenance.

VII Corps: The 1st Div made good progress, capturing the entire Foret d'Andaine; the 1st Bn, 26th Inf, went 1,500 yards north of La Ferte Mace. The 9th Inf likewise advanced, part of the 60th Inf taking Joue-du-Bois. The 3rd Armd Div had the biggest scrap northeast and northwest of Ranes, with the town not definitely ours as yet.

Farther to the east, the Third Army continues to plunge its armored columns ahead. The 79th and 5th Armd were starting on Dreux; the 5th Inf Div and 7th Armd Div were attacking Chartres.

The British are slowly coming south to Falaise, but there are stronger indications, now than before, that the Boche have successfully extricated, and are extricating, far more of their force than was thought possible. Stiff fighting, as indicated above, has been going on at the northern and southern parts of the bottleneck, and the gap is still open, even if closing rapidly.

Wednesday, 16 August 1944: The General spent an exceptionally busy day—which started at 0800 and did not finish until 0230 the next morning.

He first went to XIX Corps for a conference with General Corlett. Returning here for a snack at lunch, he left immediately afterward for the CP of the 4th Division, where, with General Collins, present, he pinned the Distinguished Service Medal on the shirt of General Barton. At the same time he awarded DSC [Distinguished Service Cross] to three Battalion Commanders, and Silver and Bronze Stars to a host of other deserving soldiers, officers and enlisted men.

From there he drove with General Collins to the CP of the 1st Div, beautifully situated in the resort town of Bagnoles sur l'Orne, one of France's most famed "watering places." There the Distinguished Service Medal was presented to General Huebner for his part in the planning and execution of the landing on Omaha.

From there he drove on to Ranes, which was still burning, the roads leading in and out of which were still lined with burnt-out and destroyed tanks and vehicles, some of which were ours. General [Maurice] Rose,[14] who succeeded General Watson as CG, 3rd Armd, was likewise seen, and a conference with him held. After dinner at Jayhawk[15] CP, the General arrived back at Master Tac to commence "another day's work."

During his absence, General Kean had received word, from crosschannel, that a radio intercept had been picked up, indicating that the boche would attack strongly in armor tomorrow morning from the roads leading southeast and northeast from Ecouche. VII Corps was immediately alerted, and preparations made to move the 4th Div up closer as reserve in the event the attack should materialize.

General Bradley likewise came during the afternoon for a long conference with Gen Kean and Col Thorsen, the upshot of the matter being that V Corps will immediately take over the sector to the right of the VII, with the 2nd French Armd, the 90th and the 80th Divisions as its components. At 9 o'clock, General Gerow was ordered to Master with his planning staff; and at 1030 a night's work began. The tent was a beehive of activity—new maps to paste together, roads to select, administrative details to write, troops to start marching. By 2 o'clock, details were pretty well in order and led by Lt Col [R. M.] Low, Asst G-2, who had just returned from the Third Army sector, the party of seven jeeps started out for Alencon, to set up a new CP and get into operation at once.

From the fronts, the following was news:

V Corps: no change.

XIX Corps: Patrols contacted British armored forces, moving from the north, all along their entire front. The area is clear of boche.

VII Corps: The VII Corps, with its new objectives of Briouze and Putanges (beyond which it will not go) in mind, continued to push on ahead. The 1st Div reached La Paniliere, Les Roussiers, and Le Mesnil de Briouze [Le Ménil-de-Briouze]. The 9th Div—which refuses to be stopped anywhere, at any time—advanced along the Ferte Mace–Fromental [Fromentel] highway to Hill 270. CCA, 3rd Armored, occupied Fromental.

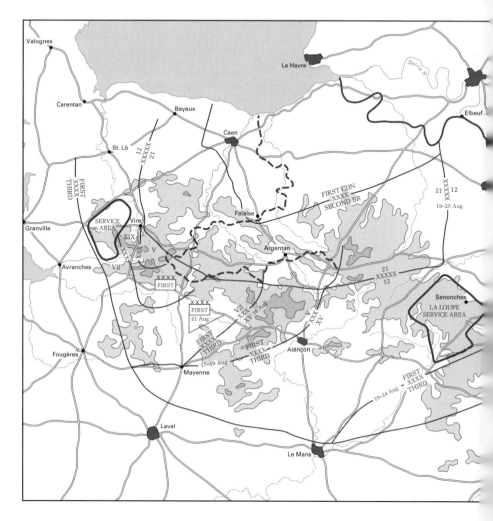

The work having been done by us, the British had no trouble, advancing from the north, in occupying Conde sur Noireau and Flers. Falaise has been encircled on three sides by the Canadians, and the Polish Armd continued to widen its bridgehead over the Dives river at Jort.

The Third Army continued to advance east of Chartres several miles; Orleans fell. On the Brittany peninsula, only Brest and Lorient still hold out. Resistance at St Malo is now negligible.

Thursday, 17 August 1944: Today was another busy day of conferences. General Corlett arrived during the morning for a preliminary orientation on the use of his Corps (now swollen by the 2nd and the

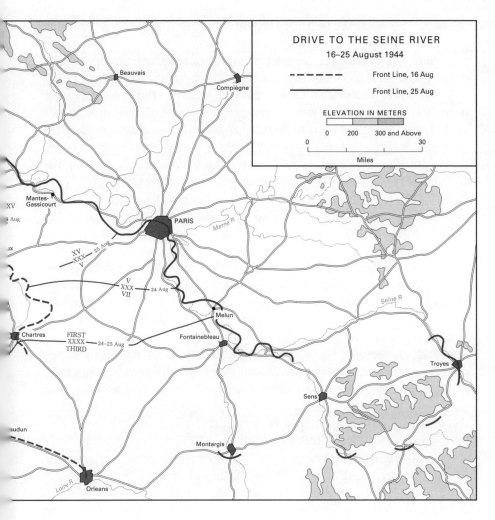

29th), and was followed by General Louis Craig, who called to pay his respects.

After a quick lunch, the General left for 12th Army Group for a long conference with General Bradley and General Patton, to decide the "sphere of influences" and "zones of action" for the next few weeks. The General apparently got what he wanted, for both he and Col Akers, who accompanied him, were pleased with the results. The preliminary indications are that the Army will swing east until just before it reaches Dreux, when it will hook off to the left, toward Mantes-Gassincourt [Mantes-Gassicourt], on the Seine. Among those with whom the General talked at Group was General Ridgway, giving rise to speculation that the fighting days of the 82nd Airborne are not over yet.

There was nothing to report yesterday from V Corps, preparing to rejoin the fight above Alencon, and XIX Corps, which had to rest quietly and watch the British take over the ground without a shot being fired. The VII Corps' activities were not in any way diminished, however. The 3rd Armd Div was heavily engaged throughout the day by all types of fire, particularly heavy in the vicinity of Fromentel. CCB, however, advanced to the east in two columns against decreasing resistance—TFK [Task Force K] reaching Mesnil Jean [Ménil-Jean], TFH [Task Force H] moving to the western outskirts of Ecouche. The expected German counter-attack did not materialize around Ecouche; instead there was, in the late afternoon, a great throng of German vehicles trying to flee northeast from it and from Argentan, and the Air Forces under General Quesada had what he commonly refers to as "good hunting." Both the 1st and 9th Divisions met slight opposition only in their march to their objectives: for the 1st, contact with the British at 9311 (11th Armd Brigade); for the 9th, the Briouze-Fromental road.

From the British, the news was that Falaise was definitely occupied by the First Canadian Army, and that the Polish Armd Div made rapid advances to the east and southeast, taking Trun, Mezidon, and Montreuil la Combe [Montreuil-la-Cambe], closing the gap to a bare three miles. Contact is established with VII Corps along the entire line up to the few remaining miles of "gap."

The Third Army continues to "fan" in every direction. Patrols of cavalry have reached Versailles. Orleans and Blois are definitely in their hands. The 35th Div is assembling at Chateaudun.

Tonight—during the course of a 12 o'clock conference in the War Tent—the 2nd Armd Div was alerted for immediate movement to the east, the assembly area being Tourouvre. No rest for the weary these days—for the boche is wearier and still disorganizedly on the run.

The bag of prisoners taken by the Americans from 11 to midnight last night has now reached 5,000. It is believed that the total, including those taken by the British, the Canadians, and the Poles will fall far below the optimistic figures of 50,000–100,000 which some people and radio commentators openly boasted of.

Friday, 18 August 1944: The General stayed in the War Tent all during the morning, ironing out a few difficulties with the British, who are set on using the Brouze [Briouze]–Putagnes [Putanges]–Argentan road, despite the fact that our troops are fighting in this area. Arrangements are finally amicably settled to let the British through, after contact is made and after sufficient time is given our men to withdraw properly.

In the afternoon the General flew to both VII Corps and V Corps Headquarters—at the former, to discuss the future employment of the Corps, at the latter, to get the most current information on operations. On returning to VII Corps, the General motored over to the 9th Division (Bill had been summoned down by air) to award the Distinguished Service Cross to General Eddy for his gallantry in the action before the port of Cherbourg. It was a fine ceremony—replete with band and flags, and a fitting close to General Eddy's career with the 9th. Tomorrow he leaves to take command of the XII Corps, under Third Army, and General Louis Craig, formerly under General Hodges' command, takes over the 9th Div, at least on temporary assignment.

The entire evening was spent in the war tent with discussion of the First Army–Third Army boundary and the use of certain east-west roads, now in Third Army area, which we must employ to send the 4th Cavalry Group on a screening mission to La Loupe. Third Army, apparently, did not look upon our entrance with favor, but a telephone call to Group (it took General Kean two hours to make it, and another half hour to make himself understood—such are communications) settled the dispute in our favor. An overlay was made at 4 a.m. of the boundaries which General Hodges proposes and the zone of action in which he wishes to see the XIX Corps, its mission around Sourdeval and Mortain finished and won, employed. Since prior approval was given to most of it, the 3rd Armored Division and 30th Div are starting their long move tonight—some 120 miles—one of the biggest and most complicated troop movements yet made by the Army.

The day's military news was not startling. The 2nd Div, now under Third Army control, started its move to Brest. The 3rd Armd Div continued to mop up a few remaining pockets around Putagnes [Putanges]. V Corps' Second French Armored remained in the Ecouche-Argentan-Le Bourg St Leonard area, having orders not to push further. The 80th and 90th Divisions pushed north against moderate to strong resistance, crossing the Argentan–Exmes road; the 359th drove on toward Chambois, to meet the Poles, reportedly near there, and thus close the "now famed gap."

The Drive to the Seine River, 19–26 August 1944

Saturday, 19 August 1944: The General flew up to with Captain Campbell this morning to make rendez-vous with General Bradley in the air in the vicinity of Vire. Both were early for their appointment with General Montgomery, and so they cruised about, following each other through the blue, until it was time to land.

The conference with General Montgomery was successful in every way. General Hodges' map, with plan, was approved without change. First Army, with its XIX Corps, is to strike north, by-passing Dreux, to Conches, Evreux, and then on further north to Elbeuf and Le Neubourg. General Corlett and his entire staff were here for luncheon, and the ensuing conferences, and left from here directly to the east and their new, as yet unselected, CP. The attack is to capture Elbeuf and prevent escape of the enemy across the Seine. VII Corps' mission will be to protect [the] left flank of the Army along the boundary extending from Sees exclusive to Verneuil [Verneuil-sur-Avre] exclusive with the 9th Inf Division and the 4th Cav Group.

The gap is now quite definitely closed, and the British are advancing at what is, for them, considerable speed toward the east. Prisoners are beginning to flow in—V Corps accounted for 5,000 today, and believe the bag will steadily mount. There are still many divergent guesses as to what the total will be; it seems generally conceded that the boche got away with what armor he had left, but nonetheless we should be able to cop from 25,000 prisoners upward.

Sunday, 20 August 1944: General [Jacques Philippe] LeClerc,[16] commanding the 2nd French Armored Division, arrived at 1030 this morning by air, though he had previously arranged to arrive at one o'clock for lunch only. His arguments, which he presented incessantly, were to the effect that, roads and traffic and our plans notwithstanding, his division should run for Paris at once. He said he needed no maintenance, no more equipment, and that he was up to strength—and then, a few minutes later, admitted that he needed all three. The General was not impressed with him or his arguments, and let him understand that he was to stay put until he gave orders otherwise.

This extended stay of the Frenchman took the General away from his primary interest and concern—the attack of the XIX Corps which jumped off at 8 o'clock this morning. Unfortunately, there was no news; communications were bad, impossible, and the General at once ordered fuller use of the liaison officers, to move to and fro from XIX Corps in continuous shifts until news was received.

Before midnight, some word, scanty though it was, came in. The 2nd Armored reached Verneuil, where the advance was held up. The 30th Div by-passed Nonancourt, on the east and west, and crossed three battalions across the Avre River, with one as far north as Droisy. The 28th Div, the last of the three divisions to make the great move eastward, closed near Duchenes.

V Corps reached all objectives given it—the 80th Div occupied Argentan, and the 90th Div continued to mop up its area around Chambois. The enemy staged small counter-attacks to try to break from the pocket, but the force was insufficient to be successful, and a large number of prisoners and enemy equipment was captured. Prize catch for the day's bag was Lt General [Otto] Elfeldt,[17] commanding the Eighty-Fourth Corps, and his staff, who are due to come to our CP for questioning. The British are taking over the area west of the end of the pocket at their customary rate of speed.

Monday, 21 August 1944: The captured German Corps commander and his staff arrived at five o'clock this morning and were given some refuge from a downpour of rain in the General's map trailer, not otherwise employed. The MP reported that they at once started to rifle the desks for papers, but the drawers were empty.

They were not liberal with their information. They admitted our artillery was better than the Russians', they didn't know where the Luftwaffe was, and in general, there was about them little of the austere haughtiness with which the German officer caste is usually associated. Colonel Dickson took one of the group (consisting of one colonel, a Lt Col, and a Major in addition to the General) to the General's mess for breakfast; colonels coming to breakfast refused to sit down until he had left. Luckily, he was shepherded out of the way before the General arrived.

General Bradley arrived at 1030, and remained in conference in the War Tent with General Hodges and General Kean until noon, when K-rations and hot coffee were served. Much of the time was spent in discussion of the Top Secret Overlay from higher headquarters, dealing with proposed operations east of the Seine, and with the passage of the British Second Army or sections of it through the XIX Corps sector, when General Corlett's mission was completed. In the rearrangement and regrouping of forces after the Seine is crossed in several places, it is probable that General Hodges will get the XV Corps, and very possibly the XX Corps also, at least for a short time.

After lunch, the CP was moved to the beautiful, two-century old Chateau de Chantepie, home of Baron and Baroness Charles de Lauriston. The chateau, which is just a mile west of the little town of Couterne, was occupied for the past year by the Germans and used most recently as a hospital, much to the displeasure of the Baron, who served during the First World War as a liaison officer with the Americans and, with his wife, speaks English with ease. The chateau itself has more than thirty bedrooms, six of which (the most luxuriant, done in brilliant red brocade, and with all walls lined with 18th century French art) were offered to the General, but he declined. The War Room is what formerly was the ballroom—hung with tall, eight-foot pictures of two old-school French women. Staying at the Chateau with the Baron and Baroness is Mr. Sosthenes Behn,[18] president of International Telephone and Telegraph, who is acting as civilian adviser to General [William S.] Rumbough,[19] Signal Officer of SHAEF [only U.S. Army, European Theater of Operations, and not SHAEF], and who will, upon our entry into Paris, enter the city and supervise the employment of his factories there for Allied use. Mr. Behn was a colonel in the last war, also assigned to First Army, and he at once wished to report to General Hodges to "receive his orders."

General Collins arrived before dinner but did not stay long, leaving after a brief discussion of when the 9th, 1st, and 3rd Armored Divisions could be moved.

Three thousand more prisoners have fallen to V Corps' troops, and the 80th Division, its job now done, had been relieved by 50th Br Div and is assembling south of Argentan. The 90th will probably move back out tomorrow.

The 30th Div, in the XIX Corps fight, advanced its leading elements to the outskirts of St Andre de l'Eure, while the 28th Division moved up to take Verneuil which the 2nd Armd, in its drive northward, bypassed.

Tuesday, 22 August 1944: General Gerow arrived early this morning to give General Hodges an up-to-the-minute picture of his front and to discuss with the General the call from the Roberts Committee[20] to come back to the United States to give testimony.

Shortly before noon, with very little advance warning, General [Brehon B.] Somervell[21] and Under-Secretary of War Robert Patterson[22] arrived, and the General gave them a full picture of Army front and activities. At 12:45, as pre-arranged, General Dempsey of the Second British Army and Brigadier Stone, Engineer of the Army, arrived and lunch was served at 1:30. When the first two guests left, on a flying visit to the 1st Division, still quartered at Bagnoles sur l'Orne (only eight miles away) General Hodges sat down for a full discussion with General Dempsey of the passing of the British XXX Corps through our territory, once General Corlett had completed his mission.

He had no sooner left—there being complete agreement on the proposal and preliminary details as to the actual working arrangements—when General Bradley arrived by cub plane,[23] unannounced. The news he had was momentous and demanded instantaneous action. Paris, since Sunday noon, he said, had been under control of the French Forces of the Interior[24] which, after seizing the principal buildings of the city, had made a temporary armistice with the Germans, which was to expire Wednesday noon. General Bradley said that higher headquarters had decided that Paris could be avoided no longer, that entry of our forces was necessary in order to prevent possible heavy bloodshed among the civilian population, and he inquired what General Hodges could dispatch at once. General Hodges said that General Gerow was ready (it was better and fairer, too, that he be put in charge of the provisional corps, since General Collins had had the honor of seizing Cherbourg) and that the 2nd French Armored and 4th Division were the best-fitted to make the move (General Hodges had decided, a week back, that when the time came to enter Paris, the French division would be among the troops included). General Bradley said that destruction of the city, by shelling or bombing, was definitely to be avoided, that if fighting grew in intensity, the Provisional Corps should draw back and hold. A frantic telephone call was put in to V Corps, and then to Group, to which General Gerow had flown in search of General Bradley. Luckily, he was still there, and he at once returned to our Headquarters, making the trip in less than a half-hour. Jeep by jeep, the Corps staff assembled in the war room, and there was repeated the scene of just a week before—the hasty assembling of maps, the hurried writing of movement orders, the determination of routes of march and march tables, the pull back of VII Corps units, the careful instructions to the French, who have a casual manner of doing almost exactly what they please, regardless of orders. Col Low was again picked out to lead the party in, and at two o'clock in the morning, the jeeps moved off—Paris bound.

The news from the XIX Corps continues to be good—the General talked tonight for the first time in two days with General Corlett. Verneuil [Verneuil–Pont-Écrepin] is occupied, and the 30th Div is continuing to move north, at rapid pace, against very light resistance.

Wednesday, 23 August 1944: Mr. Behn got his orders this morning—to report to V Corps Headquarters—and the General had a goodbye chat with the Baron and Baroness and thanked them for their kindness in giving us the use of their estate. At ten o'clock he took off [from] the landing strip with [Capt] Campbell (it was a bad morning for flying—slippery and wet—and the sergeant who took off after the General drove his ship into the hedgerow, seriously injuring himself and scratching his passenger) for XIX Corps. Bill followed with the jeep.

XIX Corps headquarters is an old chateau, which the Germans had used not only as a headquarters but also as an ammunition dump—piled high, throughout the grounds, were stocks of every calibre. General Hodges had a long talk with General Corlett and then drove back to the new CP—a pleasant chateau in the town of Maillebois, north of La Loupe, eighty-two miles distant from the one at Couterne. As before, the War Room, the General's office, and his mess, are located inside the building—in the midst of brocaded chairs, chaise-lounges, pictures, and the customary bric-a-brac of all nations with which travelers like to litter their homes.

In the evening, Brigadier Pineman [H. E. Pyman][25] of the XXX Corps came to make arrangements of the pass-through of the Corps—an operation which, he said at first, would take nine days, using daylight only. His general wished to run eight hour[s] solid the first day (which he hoped would be the 25th), but the General said four hours, off two, on four would have to be the schedule for the first day, followed on the successive days by a two-on-two off block system. The General likewise suggested that the British employ two roads, instead of one, and the Britisher admitted this was a good idea. He at first wanted to move "tactically," and then wanted to know if he could be assured that it was a "peace-time" move—i.e., assurance that we had cleaned out everything. The General assured him that our troops did not leave behind live Germans. Future details of the move will be settled tomorrow, when representatives of the XV Corps, which passed to General Hodges' control at six in the morning, are able to get here, along with representatives of the XIX Corps and British XXX Corps.

There is no word tonight from XV Corps, but the news from XIX is still bright. Le Neubourg has been taken, and Elbeuf at least partially in control of Combat Command A of the 2nd Armored Division. There has been some German armor present near the Seine, and the General instructed General Corlett tonight to "button up tight," but the situation appears completely under control. With General [George D.] Shea

[Commanding General, XIX Corps Artillery][26] loosening up his guns on the Boche retreating west in the direction of Conches and Elbeuf (at the General's orders), everything appears the way the General likes to see it.

We hope to have some news tomorrow from V Corps. General Gerow came in briefly tonight to tell of his troubles with the 2nd French Armored Division whose drivers stopped in town, been drunk, and held up traffic all along the roads. His CP is at Rambouillet and he hopes, from there, to be able to push them into Paris.

General Collins also stopped in briefly before dinner to discuss the movement to the area near Melun of his Corps, which the General has ordered.

Thursday, 24 August 1944: The news this morning is that leading columns of the French Armored are only ten to fifteen miles south and southeast [southwest] of Paris. Perhaps today the city will be occupied. The only other military news of interest this morning is that the German Air Force appeared in some strength strafing and bombing the north part of the XIX Corps sector.

XV Corps passed to General Hodges' control at six o'clock this morning and representatives from there, XIX Corps, and British XXX Corps arrived here this morning to complete plans of movement and regrouping. Two east-west roads have been given to the British and tomorrow morning at eight o'clock they will start to roll through XIX Corps area. Again at two o'clock they will have a four hour passage, and from the 26th on every two hours, a two hour block, until their movement is completed. At four o'clock General Dempsey and General Corlett arrived and in the presence of General Bradley, who had arrived shortly before, another area centering around Le Neubourg was selected for the XII Corps [British]. They also will start movement into this area early tomorrow morning. The 5th Armored Division is moving out at once from the area it has occupied along the Seine from Vernon almost up to Leuviers [Louviers] and this assembly area is reserved for XXX Corps.

General Bradley had many interesting things to announce: 1–General Eisenhower will assume command on September 1st. 2–First Army's mission, as it is contemplated now, will be to advance from Mantes [Mantes-la-Ville] to Beauvais to Albert to Antwerp. The British will be responsible for the area from there to the channel and sea. 3–Definite boundaries are not yet settled but will probably be given us tomorrow. 4–It is contemplated that First Army will be composed in this drive of nine divisions: 1, 4, 9, 2, 8, 30, 79, 2nd, 3rd, and 5th Armored, and that in addition we will get one or two of the divisions which are not [now] completing the mopping up of the Brittany peninsula. 5–General Bradley gave orders for General Hodges to move the 4th Division which was to cross the Seine and flank Paris from the south, to proceed instead directly north into the city without delay. He also said that the restrictions which he had placed on fighting inside the city would definitely not apply to the suburbs or outskirts and that General Hodges' forces could employ whatever artillery or other weapons were needed to force entry into Paris proper. He approved most definitely of the steps which General Hodges had taken in the movement of British troops through the XIX Corps area and of the success of the drive which XIX Corps had made.

There has been exceedingly bad weather all day thus preventing our air from further blocking the German retreat but the XIX Corps reported tonight that never before had they killed so many Germans and that in the vicinity of Elbeuf it was necessary to use bulldozers to clear them off the road. General Shea is again opening up with his heavy guns which can reach up the Seine, the mouth of which is only 25 miles from Elbeuf itself.

Friday, 25 August 1944: The information this morning is that the French Armored Division entered the City at seven o'clock. The situation there seems to be under control.

General Hodges flew to Eagle[27] this morning at eleven for conference at their new CP near Chartres with General Bradley and General Patton. He returned at two with our new boundaries which are substantially the same as those announced yesterday. We are to strike northeast with the British taking care of the Crossbow sites and we are to have temporarily XV Corps troops but not the Corps itself. This is now [not] the most direct road to Germany and not a route which General Hodges wished to take, but at the time at least apparently there was nothing else politically to do.

General Corlett and General Dempsey arrived again at four o'clock for the second successive day for a continued conference on the movements of the British XXX and XII Corps and our XIX Corps. Further information coming in this afternoon confirms that Paris is definitely occupied and within the city itself there is no German resistance to speak of although the war between French political parties, collaborationists and anti-collaborationists goes on. General [Charles G.] Helmick's[28] Aide was killed early today in just such a shooting affair.

Saturday, 26 August 1944: General Collins flew in at nine o'clock this morning to give General Hodges the current picture of VII Corps activities. The 3rd Armored Division he said is now crossing the [Seine] river at Melun and the 1st and 9th Divisions will cross just west of the river today. He said that the bridge situation was critical, that the Third Army had constructed their bridging badly and that he thought at least two more bridgeheads were necessary to properly move Corps and other troops across. He said that yesterday there had been extremely little fire from the Boche in that sector.

Just after the General left for XV Corps by Cub plane General Gerow arrived at the headquarters. "Who in the devil is the boss in Paris?" he asked, "The Frenchmen are shooting at each other, each party is at each other's throat, is Koenig[29] the boss, is De Gaulle[30] the boss, or am I the senior commander of troops in charge, I must know, I have no instructions on this score." "You are in charge" said General Kean. "All right" said General Gerow, "whatever you say. There will be repercussions, mind you, you will have plenty of kicks and kicks from important people but I have a military job to do, I don't give a damn about these politicians and to carry out my job I've got to know one way or the other." General Kean assured him that he was, in the absence of any other instructions, in command of the City.

The pilot, despite preliminary reconnaissance, did not seem to be able to find XV Corps landing strip and had to land on a field to inquire directions of a Frenchman before the flight was resumed to destination. He returned here at 2:30. After a long conference with General [Wade] Haislip,[31] the General left promptly again at 3:30 for a third day's successive conference with General Dempsey. He returned with a bottle of whiskey but minus one pistol and apparently with satisfactory arrangements concluded.

During his absence General DeGaulle who has been in Paris since seven o'clock last night ordered a grand parade of the 2nd French Armored Division. General Gerow informed General Hodges in a telegram received here at 2:30 that he had told General LeClerc to disregard completely these orders and proceed as previously instructed to clean up the city. Before General Gerow's telegram arrived a telegram arrived at this headquarters from Colonel Henion saying that he was doing his best "to prevent parade of 2nd French Armored Division."

During the morning Colonel Dickson had as our "guest" the former military commander of Paris[32] and a few of his staff. The military commandant insisted that only our arrival saved Paris from going up in smoke asserting that the internecine war between the French surpassed all his expectations. He added emphatically to Colonel Dickson that he was damn glad to get rid of the job of policing both Paris and the Frenchmen, both of which he apparently detests. He said that neither mines nor booby traps of any nature have been placed in the city and his attitude as brought out later by Colonel Dickson seemed to be that he realized quite a while ago that the job of trying to defend the city was hopeless and that he had taken no great steps to try to do so.

After dinner the General pinned stars on the now Brigadier Generals [Charles] Edward Hart[33] and "Tubby" Thorson. In way of celebration and to pay their respects to the owners of the chateau, the General and his party paid a brief visit to a library of Monsieur and Madame Charles Armand De Ville. Dr. De Ville is, or rather was, the vice-president of the American hospital in Neuilly a suburb of Paris. After sipping a glass of champagne [the] General returned to the war room to hear the report of Colonel Dickson and to chat further with General Quesada who had just returned from Paris, there picking up a Dutchman and an Australian flyer, both of whom had spent practically the last three years, as escaped prisoners of war, in keeping out of the hands of the Germans.

The Battle of Northern France, 27 August–3 September 1944

Sunday, 27 August 1944: The General flew this morning with Captain Campbell to the new VII Corps CP located just four or five miles west of the Seinne [Seine] at Melun. There he learned that the 3rd Armored Division had pushed rapidly, against little resistance, passed the advanced line set by General Collins for this day, the 27th, and that both the 1st and 9th Divisions had crossed the river completely. He had hoped to go to the XV Corps but, not having time, returned directly to the new Army CP near Auffargis some ten miles east of Ramboulliet [Rambouillet]. This new CP tops all we have previously had in comfort, luxury, and tradition. The chateau is only a few yards away from the Abbey of Vaux-de-Cernay, an abbey built by monks eleven centuries ago and belonging to the Ministry of Beaux-Arts. The chateau was, up until a year ago, the property of Baron Henri de Rothschild and was sold by him or by his estate (since no one knows for certain whether he is now dead or alive) to Monsieur Amiot[34] builder, before the war, of some of France's most highly touted but in action most worthless bombers. Monsieur Amiot lives here but being in Paris for the day was not present to greet the General. However, he had turned over to the Army all but his own suite—which accounts for some 200 rooms in all. The General was offered one of the prize rooms but at this writing he has not yet decided whether he will move out of the trailer. G-3 and other sections, however, intend to employ the bedrooms to the fullest.

Colonel Matchett, Chief of Staff, V Corps, flew in from Paris at five this afternoon to discuss important matters behind closed doors with General Hodges and General Kean. Early reports as received this evening of the attack by XIX Corps show that success had been made in getting out of the "loop" of the Seinne [Seine]. It is too early to see whether there will be much opposition or not. Further reports from VII Corps indicate that 3rd Armored is already beyond Meaux and that with luck the 1st Division may be only a few miles tomorrow from Soisson [Soissons].

General Dempsey flew in this afternoon for coffee and K ration biscuits and for a final agreement on the clearing of XIX Corps troops down through the sector now occupied by the British. Since XIX Corps has already cleared its divisions, it has left only an Ordnance Battalion and a few service troops to pass through British lines, and it is expected that this movement will be completed before mid-morning tomorrow.

Monday, 28 August 1944: Today was rather an "unhappy" day for the General. Communications with our Corps were non-existent throughout the better part of the day and the 5th Armored Division which said was ready to move then insisted it was not.

The General left about ten o'clock to visit General Haislip whose Corps is having a fairly tough scrap east of Mantes-Gassicourt. They have pushed out a few kilometers however, widened the bridgehead, and the drive is generally going satisfactorily. The General flew back here at 11:45 to greet General Bradley and General DeWitt. General Bradley brought with him plans for the parade in Paris tomorrow afternoon in which will be represented the 28th Division, AA, TD [tank destroyers], and perhaps a battalion of light tanks. The 28th will move on directly through the city to begin operations under V Corps in their drive northeast. General Bradley and General Hodges also discussed the problem of supply at length, which has for the last two weeks been critical with no relief in sight. The gasoline line to Chartres is coming along rapidly but General Bradley stated that there had been considerable difficulty in obtaining the necessary French labor to repair a railroad line direct to Paris—first in priority. His instructions to General Hodges were to keep going just as far as he could. He could rest as-

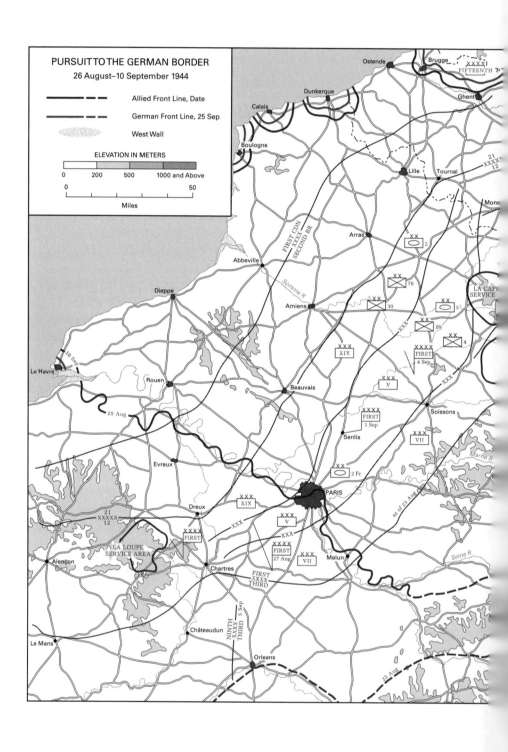

PURSUIT TO THE GERMAN BORDER
26 August–10 September 1944

Allied Front Line, Date

German Front Line, 25 Sep

West Wall

ELEVATION IN METERS

| 0 | 200 | 500 | 1000 and Above |

0   50

Miles

Ostende

Brugge

XXXXX
FIFTEENTH

Dunkerque

Ghent

Calais

Boulogne

Lille

Tournai

21
XXXXX
12

Mons

Arras

XX
2

Abbeville

Somme R.

XX
79

Dieppe

Amiens

XX
30

XX
5

LA CAP
SERVICE

XX
28

XX
4

XXX
XIX

XXXX
FIRST
4 Sep

Rouen

Beauvais

XXX
V

Soissons

25 Aug

XXXX
FIRST
1 Sep

Senlis

XXX
VII

Evreux

XX
2 Fr

Marne R.

Dreux

XXX
XIX

PARIS

as of 25 Aug

21
XXXXX
12

XXX
V

XXX

Seine R.

LA LOUPE
SERVICE AREA

XXXX
FIRST

XXX

Alençon

Chartres

XXXX
FIRST
27 Aug

XXX
VII

Melun

FIRST
XXXX
THIRD

Châteaudun

Le Mans

NINTH
XXXX
THIRD 5 Sep

Orleans

25 Aug

FIRST CDN
XXXX
SECOND BR

Le Havre

10 Sep

sured that Group appreciated the difficulties and were doing everything in their power to alleviate them.

Shortly after five o'clock General Gerow flew in from Paris to receive final instructions on the parade and on his Corps drive.

VII Corps on the right is travelling at whirlwind speed. They took Chateau-Thierry and late this evening reported also that they captured Soissons. The 1st and 9th Divisions are following rapidly behind against little or no opposition. After dinner General [Lunsford E.] Oliver[35] from the 5th Armored Division reported to the General of his difficulties in regrouping.

Tuesday, 29 August 1944: The General left the CP shortly after twelve o'clock to attend the triumphant parade up the Champs D'Elysees [Champs-Élysées] of the 28th Division, three Field Artillery Battalions, a TD Battalion, and of the troops. General Bradley and General De Gaulle, General Koenig and General Le Clerc were among those who stood on the reviewing stand at the Place de la Concord [Concorde] and after the parade the party drove up the great avenue itself stopping at the Arc de Triumphe [Triomphe] to permit General Bradley to lay a wreath on the tomb of the unknown soldier. General De Gaulle left the reviewing stand before the parade was over—a departure which, although General Bradley had no objections to it, nonetheless impressed most present as an impolite gesture, and one more incident to the now accepted opinion that De Gaulle is indeed a very temperamental person to handle. General Hodges was very much impressed with the appearance of the 28th Division which marched smartly and the Parisians lining the streets showed their enthusiasm by wildly shouting and cheering. The General returned here about five o'clock.

General Collins appeared to be a little worried tonight because V Corps on his left flank had made little progress but the General assured him that they would break under way tomorrow. VII Corps itself has pushed on beyond Soissons and its infantry units already occupy Chateau-Thierry and Soissons. XIX Corps is gradually pushing out of the once narrow bridgehead across the Seine at Mantes [Mantes-la-Ville], XV Corps having been withdrawn at twelve o'clock noon today to reassemble and then return to Third Army. The weather was bad again today thus restricting the air activity.

Wednesday, 30 August 1944: The General flew this morning to XIX Corps to discuss the situation with General Corlett. He found that the 2nd Armored Division, was at its old tactics again and the news by nightfall should be very good indeed. He wished to fly to VII Corps this afternoon but General Quesada advised against the trip because of bad weather.

General DeWitt and his two aides arrived for lunch and will stay as the General's guests overnight.

VII Corps keeps on rolling, having taken Laon with advance reconnaissance elements being considerably beyond the town already. Although it requires 103,000 gallons of gasoline to keep the Corps in motion, General Hodges promised to do his best to furnish same and instructions given General Collins tonight were to keep on moving as far as Sedan, holding the bridges there defensively until V and XIX Corps should make more progress. So great apparently is confusion among the Germans that they have very little idea exactly where the Americans are. Into Laon this afternoon pulled three troop trains packed with Boche. Those that were not killed were captured. Precisely the same thing happened at Soissons where Germans retreating by train from the Rouen–northern France area puffed into the station and were promptly dealt with.

Both V and XIX Corps today made considerable progress. The 5th Armored Division passed through the 28th and 2nd French Armored Divisions and was pushing out rapidly toward Senlis and Compeigne [Compiègne]. The 28th was making good progress on the left flank and the 4th on the right. Opposition was limited to small delaying detachments and the general consensus is that the Boche neither can nor intend to try to hold short of the Aisne. XIX Corps reported the easy capture of Pontoise and General Hobbs, who is not known as an optimist, remarked during the day that never had he seen such amateurish fighting tactics as those displayed by the enemy.

The General sat up until late in the evening discussing this front and other fronts with General DeWitt.

Thursday, 31 August 1944: General Bradley came to our headquarters this morning to give the latest instructions to the First Army, which were: To continue the drive northeastward at all possible speed. The new note of urgency was added by a plan, Operation LINNET [Linnet I],[36] which calls for a drop of parachute troops, number unknown, in the vicinity of Tournai, just across the French-Belgium frontier. General Hodges promptly informed Corps Commanders of the necessity of everywhere speeding up their troops so that union with these paratroops could be made on the appointed day, scheduled to be September 3rd. During the afternoon the General flew to XIX Corps for a conference with General Corlett. When he returned, most of Master's Rear Echelon had already moved in.

Progress, except in the V Corps sector, was as the General desired. XIX Corps sped ahead against light resistance with the 2nd Armored on the left, 79th in the center, and 30th on the right. In V Corps the 5th Armored advanced to the southwestern edge of Compeigne with its CCB but met heavy resistance in the forest itself. VII Corps, as is not unusual, set the pace. The 3rd Armored Division sent its CCA to Rethel and CCB to Mont Cornet [Montcornet]. During the afternoon, acting on the new instructions given by General Hodges because of the intended parachute drop, the Corps changed its attack from northeast to north. The 1st Division kept its defensive positions on the Corps left flank between Soissons and Laon, while CCB finally reached Verveins [Vervins] and CCA reached coordinate 3841. Rather to our surprise the British for once kept up. The 2nd British Army with the 11th Armored Division captured Amiens during the morning and with the town a prize package in the shape of General Eberfeldt [Heinrich Eberbach],[37]who apparently was not at all dismayed at the prospects of spending the rest of the war in a comfortable British prison camp. The Canadians are continuing to exploit their bridgehead near Rouen while in the Third Army sector the only big news of the day was that 7th Armored Division had established a bridgehead over the Meuse south of Verdun.

Friday, 1 September 1944: The General spent all morning in the War Room in conference with staff officers and on the telephone finding out whether the advance was progressing at required speed. He left at one o'clock for the XIX Corps where in a ceremony before assembled staff officers he pinned a Distinguished Service Medal on General Corlett. This medal was given by the Navy for General Corlett's leadership of the 7th Division in its attack on Kwajalein. He then flew to V Corps for a conference with General Gerow and was picked up by Bill who drove him to the new CP.

The CP, farther forward than that of V Corps (and not for the first time) is in the house of the Count and Countess de Coulombiers, one mile out of Senlis. Reconnaissance for it had proven exceedingly difficult since the Germans had left almost all the chateaus and private houses in the neighborhood in fashionable pig sty German shape. In the house itself are only the General's office, the War Room, and the mess; the rest of the headquarters is scattered throughout the estate.

Both XIX and VII Corps continue their drive to the north being at midnight not many miles from the Belgium border. Resistance everywhere is light although small pockets of Germans, bewildered and lost by the sweep of American armor are being methodically mopped up. General Hodges oriented all but VII Corps (which he was unable to reach by telephone) of his new intended swing to the east once our northern objectives, as set up by Group, have been reached and boundaries (temporary) were drawn tonight and an overlay prepared for presentation to General Bradley.

Saturday, 2 September 1944: The Germans opened the day for us at 5:30 by sending over, at uncomfortably low altitude, five or six of their buzz bombs. The racket woke up at least half of the staff, some of whom got out of bed in time to catch a glimpse of the V-1 streaking across the sky. General Collins also telephoned at six o'clock to report that they had passed over his area and that one had fallen only a few yards away from one of his MP's who was unscratched. A farmer on the estate also reported that one had dropped some three kilometers up the road but falling in the field had done no damage.

The weather being bad, the General had to cancel his plans to fly to Group this morning and left instead by car. A long conference with General Eisenhower, General Bradley and General Patton was held and the results from General Hodges' standpoint were, to say the least, "not altogether satisfactory."

The situation boils down to this:

1. The para-drop [Operation Linnet I] has been cancelled seemingly because of our rapid advance which makes it unnecessary. (The General never was of the impression that Tournai was the best spot in which to drop.)

2. Both the Supreme Commander and General Bradley also apparently are extremely worried over the gasoline situation which is becoming more instead of less critical.

3. General Hodges was, therefore, ordered to curl up both VII and XIX Corps short of Tournai and Mons respectively and to hold the Corps there. It was presented as a possibility that they will both have to turn north with the objectives of Ghent and Antwerp respectively but it is more likely that they will not. V Corps passing through VII Corps will attack to due east.

4. As it has happened before, General Montgomery will have use of the best east-west roads, including this time the highway running east from Tournai. The whole plan is not altogether to the General's satisfaction since he believes he can whip the gasoline problem and that while the Germans are on the run there should be no halt for even a minute.

There have been so many changes in the First Army direction that indeed there seems at times as if those "on top" did not have an altogether clear and consistent conception of [the] direction from which they wish to cross the German frontier.

There was a little trouble tonight over the use of the road running from Ochries [Orchies] to Tournai and General Hodges gave specific instructions to General Corlett that that road was to be left strictly to the British and that if he had any troops on the outskirts or in Tournai he was to withdraw them without delay. He informed all Corps Commanders that their new instructions with an overlay would reach them early Sunday morning.

The big news of the day militarily speaking, of course, was that both the VII and XIX Corps crossed the Belgium border. The XIX Corps claiming to be first with a column of the 2nd Armored reaching the border at 9:30, followed closely with the town of Cernay far to the right by B Reconnaissance Troop of the 9th Division. General Collins' forces were not, however, as he said they would be in Mons.

General DeWitt was again a visitor to the headquarters and stayed up until midnight with General Hodges discussing the new instructions.

Another indication of the quick advance came today when three German prisoners were brought in to the CP, no one knowing where the nearest PW cage was located. The men were given K rations for supper and were ferried southward shortly before midnight. Colonel Slappey and Colonel [Charles F.] Williams[38] also returned at midnight from a reconnaissance north in the direction of St. Quentin, in search of a new CP. They reported that a bridge had been blown a half mile ahead of them at Chauny and that there was still a pocket of some 500 Germans in that vicinity which needed to be cleaned up. However, we will probably move again Monday.

Sunday, 3 September 1944: The General flew this morning to Second British Army Headquarters near Amiens for lunch and a lengthy conference with Generals Montgomery, Bradley, and Dempsey. He returned at four o'clock with news that we are to push on East as settled previously and not drive north to Antwerp or Ghent as was presented as a possibility. Already the 30th Division has withdrawn from Tournai across the inter-army boundary when elements of the British Guards Armored Division entered the town, and the report tonight is that the British are nearing, if not already in, Brussels. V and VII Corps will cross columns, V Corps to be on the right and to drive straight to Germany through Luxembourg.

The air never had so good a day as today. Some 1700 motor transport, some 50 tanks and some 500 plus personnel. Pilots reporting said that it was far better hunting than that afforded in the Falaise pocket. The hunting in the vicinity of Mons was also carried on by the 3rd Armored Division and the 1st Division which came north to meet the enemy. This originally strong pocket of resistance west of Mons was reduced by nightfall to small isolated groups which were being quickly liquidated and VII Corps reported tonight that their bag for the day was an estimated 7,000 prisoners. On the Corps right flank First Army Group [14th Cavalry Group, VII Corps] captured Mezieres [Charleville-Mézières] and established a patrol line along the west bank of the Meuse. One general officer was captured and stated that he had no idea that Americans were anywhere near the vicinity; one by one we have reduced the assembly positions picked out by the Germans, arriving there far before they themselves ran into us. Both Generals Gerow and Collins arrived at the CP before dinner for a brief chat with the General.

It was not definitely established at this conference which Corps was the first to cross the border. XIX Corps claims that a column of 2nd Armored was first while VII Corps has pushed 9th Reconnaissance Squadron as the winner.

The Push to the Siegfried Line, 4–12 September 1944

Monday, 4 September 1944: CP moved today 42 miles northeast near the Village of Villequiet-Aumont [Villequier-Aumont] above Chauny into a large modern chateau building owned by Monsieur and Madame Ternecque. As has been the case now for the past month this house had been previously occupied by the Boche but unlike our other hosts these people seemed unreceptive and cold to our arrival.

The General sat in the War Room from three until 5:30 this afternoon for a portrait by the Marchioness of Queensbury[39] being painted for Life. This portrait along with others of the leading American and British Generals of land and air will be published in three months. Lady Queensbury was the General's guest for drinks and dinner but left before dark to spend the night at a private home in Chauny. The general consensus is that she has done a fairly competent job although the General thinks he has been made to look a little too sad. General Quesada also sat for her during the evening.

The military news is as follows: XIX Corps: The 30th and 79th Divisions mopped up small pockets of enemy resistance south of Tournai. General Hodges tried to obtain definite word from General Bradley whether the 79th would stay with General Corlett or revert to Third Army control but no hard or fast decision was forthcoming. VII CORPS: The 3rd Armored and 1st Divisions continued to squeeze into nothing the enemy pocket trap south of Mons. A total of over 12,000 PWs was claimed and over a thousand vehicles and tanks. 3rd Armored then continued the attack in the direction of Namur and by dark CCB had occupied Charleroi. The 9th Division, on the Corps left flank, continued on to the Meuse where bridges were found blown from Dinant to Givet. One foot bridge was constructed before midnight and two treadway bridges[40] were under construction. V CORPS: 28th Division crossed on the Corps south flank in the vicinity of Le Tour [Le Thour] and the 4th Division and 5th Armored Division were crossing in assembly area Rocroy and preparing to cross the Meuse.

The British continued their astoundingly rapid drive into Belgium completing the occupation of Brussels and sending the 11th Armored Division on to Antwerp. The British bag from this huge pocket now completely closed was expected to amount into huge figures daily.

Tuesday, 5 September 1944: The sky was overcast, the General was not feeling in top form, and so he spent the day in the War Room, after sitting another hour in the morning for Lady Queensbury. She said that the portrait would probably be printed in Life not before December.

The decision on the 79th Division is final and it moves to Third Army starting tomorrow. In the XIX Corps sector there is no other change except that the 113th Cavalry has pushed its reconnaissance well forward in the direction of Wavre. In the VII Corps sector the 1st Division is still cleaning up the pocket of Germans west and south of Mons, and the total of dead and prisoners was estimated today to be 20,000. Hospital arrangements have been made to transfer an Evacuation Hospital into the area in order that medical treatment may be given to the many German wounded. Our wounded remain comparatively infinitesimal in numbers—the total yesterday being less than a hundred. The 39th Infantry which has crossed the Meuse, one of the places where the General expected the Germans to stand if indeed they could stand anywhere, reported tonight encountering small arms, tank, mortar, and flame-thrower fire. CCB of the 3rd Armored has Manur [Namur] well under control. There is nothing new to report from V Corps—as during the last week the supply of gasoline remains a major problem.

Wednesday, 6 September 1944: The bad weather again prevented the General from leaving the CP as he had hoped to do. General Ingalls [Harry C. Ingles],[41] Chief Signal Officer, arrived during the afternoon and was his guest overnight.

The military situation was as follows: The 2nd Armored Division and the 113th Cavalry continued their advance to the east against very light resistance. In V Corps sector the 12th Infantry crossed the Meuse. In the VII Corps sector there was no reported change. This regrouping of V and VII Corps is almost completed and it is expected that the real drive to the Rhine will gather speed tomorrow. The Guards Armored Division is at Louvain [Leuven] and the 11th Armored Division is conducting extensive patrolling to the north and east of Antwerp.

The premature report from Brussels that Hitler was dead and the war was over seems to have excited very few people. Although as the BBC remarks tonight "there was every reason to believe it." The General said tonight that given ten good days of weather he thought the war might well be over as organized resistance was concerned.

The 22nd Infantry combat team which has been helping the 1st Division to mop up the vicinity of Le Cateau is being released from this job tomorrow morning at nine, it being fairly well established that the Boche left are very few in number. The first train arriving in Soissons carried only PX supplies but today three more came in with gasoline and food, and these acute shortages may soon cease to exist.

Thursday, 7 September 1944: General [Ernest N.] Harmon[42] who commanded the 1st Armored Division in North Africa and Italy and only returned to the U.S. a month ago reported for duty into the General this morning. He will shortly assume command of the 2nd Armored Division replacing General Brooks who will take command of V Corps. General Gerow's departure for the U.S. is scheduled for approximately the middle of September.

Military news continues—and this is getting to be a truism—to be good and all on our side. VII Corps with elements of the 3rd Armored Division captured Liege, one of the largest and most important industrial cities of Belgium. V Corps pushed more infantry units of the 4th Division across the Meuse against some small arms and mortar fire. XIX Corps has had gas trouble and has not been able to move the 2nd Armored at the speed to which they are accustomed. The British have planned for tomorrow the first of several paratroop jumps which they hope will further isolate the Germans and establish a bridgehead across the Rhine.

This afternoon the General was interviewed by G. K. Hodenfield,

Lieutenant, star feature writer for the Stars & Stripes.[43] Hodenfield said that he had received orders directly from General Eisenhower to give General Hodges a "build-up" for the troops, who knew him by name but did not know enough about him personally as their own commander. The General spent at least an hour with him.

Friday, 8 September 1944: The General flew with Captain Campbell this morning, visiting all three Corps during the day and arriving back at the new CP at Ham sur Heure about four o'clock. Aside from getting up-to-date information as to the progress of the Corps he said that the visit had particularly impressed him with the nature of the tough terrain over which V Corps was passing. Our new CP is the most luxuriant in which we have yet been housed, located a few miles south of Charleroi. It is famed in Belgian history as the property of a great number of the old and ruling families of the country. It served as an exile to the widow of the Count of Egmont after the latter's execution in 1568. Louis XIV exiled from France lived in the chateau in 1667. In 1689 the chateau was besieged by French troops under the command of General d'Humieres and was pillaged and wrecked. It was restored shortly afterward but again in the 30th Thermidor it was destroyed by French troops. It remained uninhabited from 1791 to 1899, the period in which the Count and Countess John D'Oultremont gave the job of restoration over to the Belgium architect Terredaugerock. The original chateau was constructed in the eleventh century, belonging in 1124 to the family of Morialmé, in 1259 to the famous house of Condé, in 1402 to the house of D'Enghien and from 1456 for three centuries to the house of Mérode. Living in the chateau at the time we arrived was the sister-in-law of the Count D'Oultremont who together with Countess D'Oultremont had been assassinated in the main drawing room about a week before our arrival. The house is a large municipal museum filled with same excellent Flemish masters, fine Empire furniture, and Sears-Roebuck junk, all seemingly piled indiscriminately, top on top, throughout the rooms. It is not known precisely how many bedrooms this chateau has but at least forty of them are occupied tonight by officers and enlisted men.

General Bradley called tonight to urge that V Corps push its armor out as quickly as possible. The reason for this request was that the Boche sent tanks into a Third Army Division CP, capturing an SOI [Signal Operating Instructions] and other valuable documents, and he apparently attributes this success to, at least in part, V Corps' failure to push farther on. The general pointed out to him that V Corps had been suffering from a shortage of gas and naturally the Armored Division was cautious because of that fact and furthermore that the terrain was not easy going but the most difficult yet encountered. Privately the General opined that he did not think the First Army should be held responsible for such errors made by the Third. Also put into motion tonight was a reinforcement of the 99th Battalion now patrolling and cleaning up in the area between Vallenciennes [Valenciennes] and Tournai. We received several reports at this headquarters that there are still anywhere from 1,000 to 2,000 Boche in the vicinity, and the General took prompt action tonight to make sure that any such threats to the rear are quickly and efficiently squelched.

Progress along the front today has not been great. Shortage of gas, terrain, and perhaps also fatigue of the troops has not made possible the singular advances which have gone before. However, there was no ceasing of action and everywhere there were general gains of from five to ten miles recorded.

Saturday, 9 September 1944: The General flew this morning northeast of Brussels for a conference with Field Marshal Montgomery, the subject matter of which was not disclosed. Captain Campbell, the pilot who had been late in arriving, picked the General up there and flew him back but lost his way in returning and spent a half hour cruising until finally the General put him on the right beam. The General fired him that afternoon and Captain Stevens of the Army Artillery Section is arriving tonight to serve as permanent pilot.

The General's lack of enthusiasm for our "museum" was justified today when the Countess protested to Colonel Slappey and then to General Kean that a Swiss watch was missing from her room. All officers and men were at once ordered to move out of the chateau and a check of all baggage was instituted an attempt to find the watch—without results.

This afternoon and tonight the General received detailed reports from liaison officers of the "reported" 2,000 Boche in the woods between Tournai and Vallenciennes. The 99th had checked every one of eight areas susceptible for harboring Boche and at four o'clock that afternoon had neither seen nor captured one single enemy. The extra troops alerted by XIX Corps for today for duty in this area were released again for action. The 99th will continue active patrolling in that sector.

Today's military news was as follows: XIX Corps continued the attack with the 2nd Armored on the left, the 30th Division on the right, and good progress was made against increasing resistance. 113th Cavalry continued to patrol the west bank of the Meuse and the Albert Canal,[44] where all bridges were blown and where the banks on the opposite aide are seemingly well defended. VII Corps did not make spectacular advances although the 83rd Reconnaissance Battalion reached Limbourg only a few miles from the German frontier. The armor pushed up to Viervies [Verviers]. V Corps made the most spectacular advances. 112th Infantry is approximately five miles west of the city of Luxemburg and the 5th Armored, CCA, advanced to Petauge [Petange] after crossing the border of the Duchy of Luxemburg at 1:30. The 4th Division made good progress against stubborn but scattered resistance on the left.

The British airborne drop is indefinitely postponed.

Sunday, 10 September 1944: General Kean travelled to XIX Corps today to give instructions from General Hodges to General Corlett about protecting their left flank as the present British plan is a swing to the north thus leaving the flank comparatively exposed. Since he was absent the General stayed in the CP at the War Room all day. Shortly after noon he received word that the CCA of the 5th Armored had captured the capitol [capital] and city of Luxemburg at 9:45 and that the infantry was advancing rapidly behind.

General Bradley called at four o'clock to say that General Ridgway and Colonel Quill[45] would arrive to discuss future secret operations and General Hodges sent two liaison planes to the Brussels airport to pick them up. A staff conference was held in the War Room during the evening and the supply picture, extremely discouraging, was presented in length by Colonel Wilson [G-4].[46] He said, among other things, that there were no large reserves and that they were scraping together enough for issue every twenty-four hours. Trains are running to Soissons but he can't obtain any accurate information ahead of time as to what they are carrying or when they will arrive. Despite assurances that gasoline was arriving by C-47s at the large field at Juvincourt, none has as yet been flown in. This supply situation will undoubtedly delay slightly at least any concentrated attack on the Siegfried Line[47] although Colonel [Brigadier General] Hart promises five days intensive fire on hand by Friday night. After hearing this picture the General held a secret conference with only General Ridgway, General Quesada, General Kean, and General Thorson present.

The only other military news of the day of importance aside from V Corps excellent advance was the final regrouping of the VII Corps which will be the main spearhead in the Army's drive into fortress Germany.

Monday, 11 September 1944: General Gerow arrived by plane at ten o'clock this morning and for 3½ hours was closeted with the General in the War Room, in an occasionally rather tempestuous discussion of V Corps' tactical approach to the border. The General knowing the importance that General Bradley placed on the strength of the right flank ordered the 112th Infantry to assemble in the area of the 5th Armored and generally laid down to General Gerow the plans he wished to see adopted for the attack on the Siegfried Line. At two o'clock with his new pilot, Captain Stevens, he flew to the new CP, Chateau de la Sarte, three miles southeast of Huy, and belonging to Monsieur Preud'homme-Torkay. The owner presented the General with the History of the French Army written by General [Maxime] Weygand[48] and brought from his cellar a fine 1919 bottle of Chateau la Tour.

General Collins came in by car at three o'clock and for two hours they were closeted in the map trailer discussing VII Corps' approach to the border. Shortly after 8:15 there came news from V Corps that elements of the 5th Armored Division had crossed the frontier approximately at the 42nd horizontal. General Hodges at once called General Gerow who denied the fact, but later in the evening it seemed established beyond a doubt that patrols had crossed the border and had stayed across the border and they had been joined in their respective sectors by patrols of both the 4th and 28th Divisions. No one claimed that the Siegfried Line—or what there is of it—had been pierced; the fact remained that we were in Germany and the first to have that distinction. From the XIX Corps sector the big news was that a Battalion of the 119th had established a bridgehead across the Albert Canal and the Meuse River. The remainder of the regiment crossed during the late afternoon and proceeded to widen the bridgehead. 113th Cavalry crossed the Meuse in the VII Corps sector north of Liege then swung northward. All V Corps is now massed in the appointed assembly areas and ready for its attack across the border at the appointed day and hour set by General Hodges. All G-2 indications are that the Wall [Westwall] as such is manned mainly by service and SOS[49] troops. The air had a good day yesterday and today.

Tuesday, 12 September 1944: The General left at nine o'clock for a conference at Twelfth Army Group headquarters at Doue—a flight of over 1½ hours. There together with General Patton and their respective G-4s he had a lengthy conference as to our attack into Germany and especially the critical supply situation. It seems likely that we shall have to halt at least for a short period once the Rhine is bridged and our troops firmly established on the other side. During his absence General Brooks called on General Kean on his way to V Corps, to acquaint himself with the V Corps situation before assuming command.

General Hodges, General Kean, and a few other staff officers had a short reception with the owner of the house and Mrs. Preud'homme. It is an established fact that they were friendly with the Germans although the Belgian people around here admit that they committed no act which could be called definitely that of collaborationists. However, they sought from the Germans certain small favors such as use of a car, loan of gas, and passes which Colonel Dickson remarked were a sign of their general attitude.

Today's military news, all of which is pleasing, was as follows: XIX Corps: Troops of the XIX Corps or the 117th and 119th Infantry entered Holland, the former advancing as far as Geerteriud [Geertruid]. 2nd Armored and 82nd Recon Bn continued to patrol the Albert Canal and the Army left boundary. General Corlett called during the evening to say that he was rather worried over the strength facing him as a captured map showed the existence of five divisions on his front. However, German divisions now are at best at regimental strength and General Hodges and Colonel Dickson believe that the sum total of German troops facing XIX Corps is not much over twelve to fifteen thousand.

VII Corps: VII Corps became the second Corps to cross the German border. The honor fell to the 1st Battalion, 16th Infantry at 1515. A half-hour later in the 3rd Armored zone CCA also crossed and advanced against light opposition but heavy obstacles to coordinate 874352. In the right portion of the Corps zone the 4th Cavalry Group advanced to the line Weywertz–St Bith [Weverce–St. Vith]. VII Corps reported that all civilians from Eupun [Eupen] to the border displayed white flags and were coldly indifferent to our troops in contrast to the reception given up to that point. Eupen has long been a disputed territory and the occupants are strongly pro-German.

V Corps: In the 4th Division sector the 22nd Infantry also crossed the German border and the 110th and 109th have had at least one battalion into Fortress Germany. First Army now has troops in five countries, France, Belgium, Holland, Luxemburg, and Germany.

Third U.S. Army: The 10th and 11th Infantry have now crossed the Moselle and the 2nd Infantry is now making the crossing. The 80th Division and elements of the 4th are preparing to cross.

The main news from the British front today was that LeHavre has fallen.

Chapter 4

The Battle of Germany,
13 September–15 December 1944

Consolidation, 13 September–1 October 1944

Wednesday, 13 September 1944: General Bradley flew in unannounced this morning and had a long and secret conference with General Hodges in the War Room. General Brooks also was present throughout most of the conference and both stayed for luncheon. Later in the afternoon the General took off for V Corps by plane but the latter had unfortunately forgotten to notify this headquarters that they had changed the location of their field. The General landed in a cow pasture only to be swarmed by thousands of Belgian tots, from whom no information was forthcoming. After searching the area thoroughly from the air the General returned here shortly before dinner, mission unaccomplished.

Today's military news: XIX Corps: The 30th Division today captured Maastricht (all bridges blown) and extended the bridgehead over the Albert Canal and Meuse River. CCA, 2nd Armored cleared the enemy from along the Albert Canal on the Corps right flank had slow progress due to marshy terrain, stubborn enemy resistance, road blocks, and minefields but General Hodges tonight assured General Corlett that he was performing an extremely valuable job in protecting VII Corps push and that there was no reason to be discouraged by the fact that he too had not entered upon German soil. VII Corps: The 1st Division continued to conduct reconnaissance in force inside the perimeter of the Siegfried Line toward Aachen. Some of the line's emplacements were not manned but where manned resistance was determined. 1st Division is generally tonight south and west of the city, some six miles from its center. The 3rd Armored made limited advances during the day over very difficult terrain and extensive road blocks, tank obstacles, dragon's teeth,[1] railroad rails, steel beams, and blown craters. Mines are everywhere. 9th Division occupied the woods south of Eupen after overcoming light enemy resistance. The 4th Cavalry Group maintained contact with V Corps on the south flank and were up to the border encountering many road blocks but few enemy personnel. V Corps: Here the story was practically the same. 4th Division advanced over German soil through heavily mined areas and successive road blocks. Artillery fire here as nowhere else was heavy. 28th Division found a similar situation. Both the 28th and the 4th are from six to seven miles inside the enemy's territory.

The air, hampered by limited visibility, had only a fair day's shooting. Principal results were the hitting of one large fuel dump.

The General's new War Room trailer arrived today and was brought around to and parked next to his living van. It is a superb job, spacious with infinite map board, all in plexi-glass. Maps are being installed tonight and it is contemplated that as we move into Germany it will become the War Room proper.

Thursday, 14 September 1944: General had a bad cold today and consequently remained at the CP during the day. The only visitor was Colonel Kolloch [Parker C. Kalloch][2] who formerly served with the General in the Philippines and is now on duty in this theater with the Corps of Military Police. He stayed for dinner with the General.

Despite the doctor's admonitions the General did not retire early but spent the rest of the evening in the War Room talking to Corps Commanders over the phone and studying the map. Because of his orders that all troops should stay tightly "buttoned up" progress has not been so fast as before but the General believes that this is the only sound way to attack the line proper.

Today's military new was: XIX Corps: The 2nd Armored made good progress throughout the day and generally reached the Canal. In the 30th Division sector the 117th Infantry reported Maastricht clear of the enemy and two battalions went out five miles to the south and east of the town. VII Corps: 1st Division is now within three kilometers of Aachen. The city itself is surrounded on three sides, the 3rd Armored Division being approximately five miles due east. The 9th Division made the best progress of the day, the 47th Infantry smashing well inside the German border and the 4th Cavalry Group patrolling into the forests Monschau and Bucholz [Buchholz]. V Corps: Here resistance is spotty—some pillboxes being defended to death, others are completely unmanned. 4th Division made excellent progress, the 2nd Battalion

12th Infantry reporting that it had passed through all fortifications. In the 28th Division sector the 110th Infantry is six miles inside the border while the 109th is approximately three. 5th Armored Division is patrolling along the Moselle in the vicinity of Grevenmacher.

News from other fronts: CCA of the 4th Armored is now some 15 miles east of the Moselle to the northeast of Nancy. Stiff fighting, however, is still generally in progress in other sectors along the River.

Guests during the evening were Colonel Shellhammer and Major Don Faith,[3] Aide to General Ridgway. Both officers wished to find out from General Hodges if there were any chance of being picked up by First Army trucks and fed by First Army after they completed their latest mission—which will be a jump in the British sector north of our boundary sometime "in the near future." Major Faith said that General Ridgway was naturally particularly anxious to get the troops back in American territory and if possible especially under General Hodges' command. A temporary assembly area was picked out for them around Verviers-Maastricht and General Hodges and General Kean both said that once they arrived in the Army area the food would be forthcoming and trucks probably could be gathered together in an emergency to take them where they had to go.

Friday, 15 September 1944: The General's cold was still bad today and the weather grim so he made no plans for leaving the CP. This turned out for the good as he had as his distinguished visitor on very short notice Archbishop Spellman[4] of New York who drove up from Third Army with the latter's Chaplain [Col. James H.] O'Neill. The General had a chat with him in the War Room. The Archbishop went to Command Echelon at six o'clock to say mass, returning for dinner with the General.

Colonel Dickson stated yesterday that on the basis of the intelligence which he had, the Germans were now resolved to throw in everything on the present line in an attempt to hold the Americans before they could crack the defenses along any broad front. This statement since seems to be being borne out by the slowing down of all Corps. XIX Corps did send CCB across the river at Maastricht and a bridgehead is definitely established there. The 30th Division which is pushing on to the left of VII Corps hoping to relieve the pressure at Aachen captured Valkenburg. VII Corps' 16th Infantry was today east of Aachen successfully bridging the second line of the Siegfried Line and the city is now definitely surrounded on three sides. Resistance against the 3rd Armored which is also advancing northeast of Aachen was heavy. The

V Corps situation continues to worry the General as the three divisions are spread out on an exceedingly wide front and progress made by the XX Corps of Third Army on its right flank is slow and does not appear at the present time to cover V Corps' right very successfully.

Saturday, 16 September 1944: The General intended today to fly to V Corps but so discouraging was the weather throughout the day that he was advised against it. Gains along the entire front were limited. R5 [Combat Command Reserve, CCR] of the 5th Armored did push six miles through the line and the 1st Division is tightening its grip around Aachen, while XIX Corps continues to push its 30th Division further east. However, there were no startling major gains and the Germans are throwing in considerably more artillery fire than before. They also launched minor counterattacks along the entire line all of which were successfully repulsed.

Archbishop Spellman left by car this morning for Charleroi from which place Major Zwink is flying him to Paris. He will probably return next Thursday by which time the General hopes to be able to give him the opportunity to say High Mass in the Aachen Cathedral.

The General spent some time tonight at dinner and after that in the War Room with Richard Tregaskis[5] the six-foot-four star correspondent of the International News Service and author of the best seller, "Guadalcanal Diary." Tregaskis told the General he walked through the first and second lines that afternoon near Aachen and could not see, at least from his observation point, that the opposition was very fierce. He has a commission to do an article for Cosmopolitan Magazine and will return later for more information.

Reports of civilian reaction to our entrance on German soil are varied, and no generalizations should be made from the scattered bits of information thus far received. Some report the younger children as being very friendly and the older people coldly indifferent, but whether this is from fear of allied repression (this having been the official propaganda line) remains to be seen.

No authoritative report has been made tonight as to the cause of the tragedy which took place this morning at Master Command CP, a mile and a half away from ours. Shortly after eleven o'clock there was a terrific explosion and we later learned that a bomb—origin unknown—had exploded near the enlisted men's mess line killing one and injuring more or less seriously seven. Whether it was a time bomb, a German bomb, or an American bomb we do not as yet know.

Sunday, 17 September 1944: General Bradley flew in this morning for a long and for the most part secret conference with General Hodges. The only established facts are that supply both of POL [petroleum, oil, and lubricants], ammunition, and food continues to become more critical and that we are not now even holding our own. General Plank[6] and other officers of the Communications Zone [COMZ][7] were in attendance during a part of the conference but whether we shall see any improvement or not is doubtful. It is not improbable that we shall have to slow up, even altogether halt, our drive into Germany and this in the very near future.

The conference over, the General came on by car to the new CP, a trip of 42 miles to the Chateau de Maison Bois which is south of Verviers owned by the Count and Countess De Pinto. Here for the first time the new trailer was officially set-up as the War Room. The General, however, spent most of the evening with General Kean trying somehow to increase the supply of artillery ammunition to the troops. This was the fifth successive day in which air activity has been to all intents and purposes washed-out by ugly weather, and there is no indication tonight that tomorrow will see any improvement.

However, the great airborne show of the British went off in Holland as planned at one o'clock today.[8] There the skies were blue, the weather fair, and preliminary reports show that the 82nd and 101st American Divisions and the 1st British Airborne Division landed in good order. There was no interference from the air but apparently ground resistance is considerable. Still with us is the driver of Major Don Faith, Aide to General Ridgway, whom the latter hopes to be able to pick up "within the next few days."

There were no advances made on the VII Corps front. The only news of interest is that the first case of sabotage occurred when wire was stretched across a highway near Eupen. This slowed down and damaged a jeep but the shots which were fired at the driver fortunately went wild. General Hodges has again instructed General Collins to meet violence with violence and to have no qualms about taking the most stringent measures possible to avoid recurrence of such incidents. In the XIX Corps sector 2nd Armored pushed out several kilometers east and north of Maastricht and the 120th Infantry approached the 82nd vertical thus coming nearer to sealing off Aachen. A stiff counterattack in the V Corps sector drove CCR 5th Armored back three miles.

Monday, 18 September 1944: For the sixth successive day the weather prevented air activity so the General was required to travel by car to V Corps this morning. This was his first visit inside Luxembourg and he had a long chat and farewell luncheon with General Gerow who leaves by plane Wednesday for the UK and thence to Washington. General Brooks officially assumed command of the Corps at noon yesterday. General Hodges returned here shortly after four o'clock.

There was no important military news of the day. The only two squadrons of aircraft to leave the ground, at five o'clock, got into a fierce dog fight over Aachen. 4 Boche were claimed and one of ours is definitely missing. XIX Corps made some progress especially along its left flank almost encircling the large town of Sittard. Positions in the VII and V Corps remain substantially unchanged. Enemy aircraft activity, however, was considerable throughout the day. VII Corps CP area being bombed twice, once around noon and once at night.

The General's only visitor today was Don Whitehead,[9] chief correspondent in this theater for the Associated Press, who is writing a short piece on the General for one of the national magazines.

Perhaps the most important news of the day is that the 29th Division reverts to First Army control and will be assigned to the XIX Corps probably arriving there four days from now. The General has confidence in the drive and push of the 29th which has set up for itself a fine record of aggressiveness in this war.

Tuesday, 19 September 1944: General remained at the CP all day trying to iron out the supply difficulties with which the Army is now beset. There will be an emergency supply by air of a hoped-for 3,000 tons of ammunition, and in general everything has been said and done during the past forty-eight hours to quicken the pace with which AD-SEC is shipping supplies forward.

The news from the military front was uneventful. Second Armored has now drawn abreast of the 30th Infantry Division but the attack to break the Siegfried Line scheduled for tomorrow has been postponed until favorable weather permits the use on a large scale of medium bombers and fighter bombers. Only two missions were flown during the entire day.

After support and without advance warning a party of five headed by Major General [Milton A.] Reckord,[10] Provost Marshal General of the theater and Colonel Philip McCook[11] of the JA's [Judge Advocate General's] Department came to visit the General. Judge McCook who served in the same division as the General during the first World War and whose greatest hope during this tour was to be able to see the General and talk to him, had a long chat in private. Also a member of the party was Colonel Kolloch who had visited the General at the last CP.

Wednesday, 20 September 1944: General set foot on German territory for the first time today—visiting VII Corps during the afternoon by automobile. He had planned to fly to Verdun to see General Bradley but bad weather kept him grounded. The trip through Germany was uneventful and the General spent almost two hours in secret conference with General Collins, whose headquarters is housed in the [Nazi] party headquarters of a small town five miles inside the border.

(Tuesday, 19 September 1944: The General received tonight from Major Miner, head of the CIC [Counter-Intelligence Corps] Detachments a terra-cotta bust of Adolf himself taken from a Kreis [district] headquarters in Roetgen)

Today's military news did not contain important changes. XIX Corps continued to assemble for its attack; VII Corps continued its bitter house-to-house fight in Stolberg; while in the V Corps sector numerous counterattacks varying from company to battalion plus size were met and repulsed without loss of ground. 5th Armored Division reported the destruction of twenty enemy tanks during the period. Ninth Army reported that all organized positions in Brest had ceased which fact in all probability should give us another division in the near future. From the Second British Army front the news tonight is that the Guards Armored Division reached Nijmegen where the 82nd Airborne had made the major part of its landing. A coordinated attack by the Guards Armored and the 82nd was launched to seize the bridge across the river and to join up with the 1st British Airborne in the vicinity of Arnhem where stiff fighting today is in progress. The Canadians are moving troops rapidly into the Antwerp area preparatory to a drive into Holland on the left of the 2nd British Army. The port of Antwerp is expected to be in operation soon; Le Havre has opened already to limited shipping.

Thursday, 21 September 1944: The General flew to Verdun after lunch today—a flight of 65 minutes—for a conference with General Bradley. The upshot of which appears to be that we will get shortly the 83rd Division under General Macon. Although this has not been announced it is more than likely that it will be put into the V Corps sector.

Tonight the headquarters was thrown into a flurry of excitement by a radio broadcast picked up by G-2 which purported to be a statement by Von Runstedt [Field Marshal Gerd von Rundstedt][12] that he had seized the city of Cologne and that he had called upon all soldiers and civilians to take over power, oust Hitler, and the SS. The General was closeted with Colonel Dickson, General Kean, and General Thorson until after midnight.

Among the guests tonight were Archbishop Spellman, who tomorrow will start his visit of Corps headquarters; General Ridgway who had just returned from a visit to the 82nd Airborne Division and William Stoneman,[13] crack foreign correspondent of the Chicago Daily News.

The General paid a visit this evening to the Count and Countess De Pinto who opened several fine bottles of champagne for him and his Staff officers.

Today's military news was nil. No changes were recorded on any front except that VII Corps has now completed the mopping up of Stolberg. The weather considerably better, allowed General Quesada's aircraft to put on a limited show of power. XIX Corps is scheduled to attack in the morning after preliminary bombardment.

Friday, 22 September 1944: This morning we learned—some to their great disappointment, others not to their surprise—that the story of the "uprising in Cologne" was the product of the P&PW Section [Publicity and Psychological Warfare Section] broadcasting to the German people and not the real thing as had first been thought. Faces were downcast.

A two hour conference between General Hodges and all three Corps Commanders was held in the War Room starting at nine this morning. One of the results was that the attack of the XIX Corps has been postponed until such time as the 29th Division arrives in the line. It seems now probable that when the VIII Corps comes into the line, taking over part of the V Corps sector, that First Army will still be given the responsibility of making the main effort toward Germany. Neither General Collins, nor General Corlett have the slightest doubts as to their ability to smash through provided gas and ammunition are at hand in more plentiful quantities than before. Later in the morning and until three this afternoon the General was closeted with General Ridgway and other staff officers—the subject being the dropping of airborne troops [on] the other side of the Rhine.

In accordance with the now accepted routine of inviting one newspaper correspondent to dinner and a conversation with the General, the guest tonight was Mr. Peterson [Ivan H. "Cy" Peterman] of the Philadelphia Inquirer who has been covering American forces since the early bitter days of Cassarine [Kasserine] Pass.

There were no changes in positions anywhere along the First Army front. Third Army likewise was meeting stiff opposition and have no recorded gains of note. In the British Airborne drop sector the 101st and 82nd Divisions are now completely secured by the joining but the 1st British Airborne is continuing to have a fierce fight with as yet no substantial meeting up with the British ground forces. Late this afternoon the Germans were able to drive an armored wedge between Eindhoven and Nijmegen separating the 82nd and 101st and temporarily cutting off General Dempsey and his tactical staff who had moved in the vicinity of Nijmegen. However, Colonel Harden, liaison officer from British Army, seemed confident that this wedge would be quickly cut off and the gap sealed again.

The air had a somewhat better day although ground haze and bad weather at best prevented full employment, more than 1,000 Forts passed to and from Germany directly over our CP, but it is not yet known what particular German target they were smashing. There was today no reappearance of V-2[14] or V-3[15] in our immediate vicinity, although two explosions nearby during the night were thought to be manifestations of these "secret" weapons.

Saturday, 23 September 1944: Today was a quiet day both on the war front and for the General. Most of it was spent in the War Room in consultation with General Quesada, General Kean, and other members of the general staff. The only guests were Archbishop Spellman who returned this evening from his stay at XIX Corps and two officers from VIII Corps who came to plan details of the movement of the 83rd Division into what is now the V Corps sector. The 83rd Division will not belong to First Army but will take over a great deal of the territory now held by 5th Armored.

There was no change of positions anywhere along the Army front. Minor counterattacks were everywhere repulsed without loss of ground.

General Hodges today published an order addressed to all members of his command and read by Section Chiefs to all headquarters personnel, restricting them to their immediate CP area, and forbidding them to talk to or fraternize with civilians. The primary purpose of this memorandum seems to be to insure greater security—it having been common knowledge among the civilian population in this area that General Hodges was present.

Sunday, 24 September 1944: The Archbishop left by car early this morning for V Corps—not to the General's regret since he had far more important business to do than to entertain guests, however important. The General left by car in the morning for a trip to General Montgomery's headquarters some fifty miles due north of our CP and there Monty, he, and General Bradley were closeted for several hours discussing the new "orientation." Reports of the result of this conference have not yet filtered down to the lower echelons but the gist of it seems to be that First Army will again change direction, if only slightly, and head more northeast in the general direction of the Ruhr. This change apparently is not what the General wished.

Again there was no change in front line dispositions. First Army is to get, in addition to the 29th Division, the 7th Armored Division which will start to move towards our area immediately. It is hoped that it arrives in better shape than the 5th Armored Division which Third Army turned over to us shortly after the fall of Paris, in such run-down and dilapidated shape that it took a whole week to make repairs and replacements.

It was miserable weather all day, bitterly cold, and windy and air activity was almost nil. The weather is now of primary interest to the General since he believes that two solid weeks of good weather and unrestricted bombing would bring, together with infantry action, the enemy to their knees.

Monday, 25 September 1944: General Corlett was an early arrival today to discuss with General Hodges the new XIX Corps plan to protect the British right flank. General Hughes[16] and General Virgil Peterson,[17] The Inspector General, arrived early this afternoon and together with General Hodges paid a trip to VII Corps returning shortly before supper time.

There was no military news of importance from any front. The weather continues abominable. Reconnaissance for a new CP has thus far proved fairly unsuccessful although General Kean will inspect one possible site tomorrow.

Tuesday, 26 September 1944: The General left by car this noon for General Montgomery's headquarters again and this time the results of the conference were entirely to his liking. It will now be necessary only to send one division up to protect the British right flank and the boundary between Second British and First Army has been altered so that upon reaching Maaches [Maashees] the boundary double-tracks down to coordinate K-6270. The shape of the wedge is similar to that which XIX Corps had at Elbeuf although this time its mission will be purely a protective one not an offensive one. In addition, the Belgian Brigade will come under control of First Army (though supplied by 21 Army Group). This new arrangement will again permit VII Corps to strike

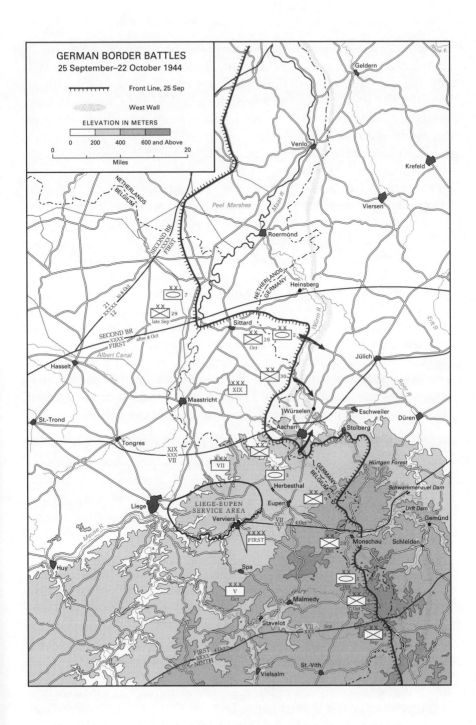

Front Line, 25 Sep

West Wall

ELEVATION IN METERS

0   200   400   600 and Above

0   20
Miles

ahead since XIX Corps will have three divisions which it can employ as an offensive weapon. General Corlett, Colonel West, and Colonel Wilson arrived shortly before dinner to learn with delight, of this change in plans. G-3 is putting out an amendment to the Field Order published yesterday containing the new Army army boundary and new Corps corps boundaries.

The General also had as his guest this evening Hugh Baillie,[18] President of the United Press, and Hank Gorrell,[19] Chief UP correspondent in this theater. Mr. Baillie disclosed that Wright Bryant [William Wright Bryan] the Atlantic Constitution correspondent who was the first to interview the General had been among those captured by the Boche on the Third Army front three days ago.

The General was closeted with General Corlett and his staff until a late hour this evening, a conference of the other two Corps commanders has been called for early tomorrow morning.

General Kean vetoed any change in CP locations and unless G-2 thinks it necessary from a security viewpoint that we move we shall probably stay for several days more in the present chateau.

Wednesday, 27 September 1944: General Collins and General Brooks arrived shortly after nine o'clock this morning for a two hour conference with General Hodges and his staff on the coming attack—target date for which, depending on the weather, is 1 October.

The General is extremely optimistic over the turn of events and believes that given decent break from the air VII Corps with XIX and V Corps pushing hard and protecting the flanks will drive through to Duren [Germany].

Shortly after lunch Lieutenant General [John C. H.] Lee[20] and General Plank arrived for an all afternoon conference with General and General Kean. Major General [Robert McG.] Littlejohn[21] also came in shortly before dinner and spent the night.

The 7th Armored Division closed in the assembly area above Maasstricht at three o'clock today and immediately established patrols with the 113th Cavalry on the east and the 99th Battalion of the Belgian Brigade on the north. Organic vehicles of some of the 29th Division closed in that division's assembly area near Maastricht; the main part of the division is still enroute from the Brittany peninsula. On the VII Corps front active patrolling was conducted while the 39th and 60th Infantry continued their attack to the east against numerous pillboxes and strongpoints making limited gains. From the V Corps sector there was no news of note. Second British Army: After a stand of ten days in the

Arnhem bridgehead, fighting in a narrowing perimeter under continuous fire, the 1st Airborne Division withdrew to the south bank of the Nedder Rhine [Neder Rijn] the night before last. Approximately 2,000 soldiers including two general officers were apparently the only ones from the division to be saved. Around Nijmegen and Eindhoven the bridgehead is secure and is being widened both to the east and to the west, by attacks by the Guards Armored, 7th Armored, 3rd Division, 43rd Division, and 53rd Division.

Thursday, 28 September 1944: General Bradley flew up from Verdun this morning for a long conference with the General and members of his staff in the war trailer. They were joined after lunch time by General Ridgway for a continuation of the conference. General Bradley took with him General Hodges' gift of the terra-cotta bust of Hitler.

General Plank spent most of the day with General Kean and General Hodges discussing the intricacies of the supply problem. General Hodges posed briefly in the morning for the photographers of the War Department. One of the colored shots is due to appear as the cover of a national magazine shortly.

7th Armored Division began to move this morning to a new assembly area in the vicinity of Deuren [Deurne, Holland]. All of the motor elements of the 29th Division have closed in the assembly area east of Maastricht. There was no news of importance in the VII and V Corps sectors. The air favored with good weather for the first time in over ten days went after railroad lines with a vengeance cutting them in more than ninety places behind our [their] lines.

Friday, 29 September 1944: General Eisenhower and General Bradley flew in this afternoon for a meeting with General Hodges to which were called in all three Corps Commanders. The group was closeted in the war trailer for more than an hour. When asked after the conference if it was satisfactory, the General remarked that what apparently tickled everybody the most was General Eisenhower's statement that he was going to "chase the SOS[22] out of Paris and make it a well ordered rest center for combat troops."

Supplies are slowly building up in desired quantities for the coming push although unfortunately the weather reports for the next week are extremely discouraging and the attack may have to be postponed until good weather arrives. There was no military news of note today; the 7th Armored has pushed rapidly into its sector encountering thus far no opposition. 29th Division had almost completed its closing by midnight.

Saturday, 30 September 1944: General Bull who has just been relieved after his ten day stay as Commanding General of the 4th Division arrived shortly before noon to have luncheon and afterward a conference with General Hodges. General Van Fleet had been appointed to succeed General Barton but this appointment has been complicated by the fact known today that General Barton had been declared fit for full field duty and therefore will probably take over command of the division as before. We also learned today that General Gerow is on his way back to Europe but it has not yet been announced that he will again take V Corps replacing General Brooks.

At 5:30 the General held his second large press conference. For almost an hour he briefed correspondents on the operation which, weather permitting, will strike in the XIX Corps sector tomorrow.

Today's military news is limited except in the XIX Corps area where the 7th Armored Division on the Corps left flank advanced from Deuren to forward assembly areas near Oplon [Oploo, Holland] from which they launched an attack at 1530. Heavy resistance was encountered in the woods northwest of Overloon. 115th Infantry relieved CCA of the 2nd Armored in which maintenance work is being conducted; 175th Infantry moved forward to the front. In the V Corps sector a strong enemy counterattack was made against the 39th Infantry at seven o'clock but two hours later the enemy had been thrown back with heavy losses and the original line had been restored.

VIII Corps with the 2nd and 8th Infantry Divisions is enroute from Brittany to take over the zone in the First Army right flank. It should complete relief by morning of 4 October.

Sunday, 1 October 1944: Again bad weather—low scutting [scudding] clouds and occasional rain—prevented the attack from going off as scheduled. Weather reports, however, for tomorrow are favorable. There was little news of note today since the 7th Armored Division was the only one to be making the attack. They advanced and took Overloon against heavy resistance of all types—including nebelwerfers, artillery, road blocks and tanks.

A report from Colonel Patterson, AA Officer, reveals that over 64 of what is now referred to as V-2 have fallen in the Army area. Since the speed of this 46 ton weapon which travels 55 miles into the air before it begins its descent is close to 3600 feet per second, no one has yet seen it in action and one case at least is known of troops within 100 yards of its impact point who although shaken and shocked were completely uninjured. The warhead itself weighs 1600 lbs and the propellant composed of liquid oxygen and ethyl alcohol weighs over 9 tons. It is now established that over one-third of Germany's war potential is being directed to the production of this and other V weapons—for which the General said today that we should be duly thankful. "Machine guns and artillery," he added, "would have infinite number of times the effectiveness if directed as weapons at the front line troops."

The only guest during the day was Drew Middleton,[23] Chief correspondent of the New York Times, who had dinner with the General and then returned about 9:30 to the press headquarter at SPA.

The Aachen Offensive, 2–21 October 1944

Monday, 2 October 1944: XIX Corps started its attack at eleven o'clock this morning following air preparation lasting 1½ hours—mediums, which were fairly successful; and fighter-bombers, which were very successful. The General left after an early lunch for XIX Corps headquarters and spent a good part of the afternoon following the progress of the assault in the War Room with General Corlett. At the day's end leading elements of the 30th Division—represented by the 117 and 119th Infantry had progressed to a point 600 yards east of the main railroad line running south from Geilenkirchen. Opposition from the pillboxes was consistently heavy throughout the day and artillery and mortar fire were strong.

Shortly after his return to the CP the General was visited by Generals Spaatz, Doolittle,[24] Van Denberg [Vandenberg],[25] and Quesada and he spent more than an hour in conference with them in the war trailer.

Other military news of the day: In the 1st Division sector the 116th Engr Group [1106th Engineer Combat Group] with 237th and 238th Engr C Bns [Engineer Combat Battalions] relieved the 18th Infantry south of Aachen—first time that engineer combat battalions have actually occupied front lines positions of infantry under prearranged plan. The enemy is still counterattacking in the sector but all counterattacks have been repulsed. In the V Corps sector relief of the 5th Armored Division by elements of the 8th Infantry Division was completed and the relief of the 28th Division is now going on. There is no news of importance from other Army fronts.

Tuesday, 3 October 1944: Generals Lee and Plank of the SOS flew in this morning from St. Trond [St. Truiden] for a conference with General Hodges and General Kean leaving shortly before lunch to continue their inspection visits of SOS units. Shortly after two o'clock General Bradley arrived by car from Verdun to pay a twenty-four hour call with General Hodges and to visit some of the units formerly under his command. In a driving downpour with General Hodges in the latter's jeep he drove on to VII Corps for a chat with General Collins and other members of the Corps staff returning here shortly before seven o'clock.

News of the XIX Corps attack shows the going to be tough and slow but nevertheless steady. 117th Infantry occupied Ubach and the advance of the 119th reached the east edge of the wooded area south of this town. The 2nd Armored Division began to pass through 30th Division. However, boggy terrain and heavy artillery and anti-tank fire made its progress exceedingly limited. In the Corps sector west of the Maas [Meuse River in Germany and the Netherlands] the 7th Armored Division was held up by the stubborn enemy resistance in the vicinity of Overloon where house to house fighting was in progress. The low marshy terrain was heavily mined, as well as roads, and again the gains could not be measured by a kilometer.

The air today had very little opportunity to support the ground; the sun came out for only brief intervals. There was no news from the VII Corps sector. In the V Corps the relief of the 28th Division by VIII Corps units continued as well as of the 5th Armored Division.

The CP of the Ninth US Army opened at Arlon and it is expected that V Corps will be completely moved into its new boundary of action by six o'clock, the morning of the 5th. In the Second British Army heavy uncoordinated attacks southeast and northeast of Nejmegen [Nijmegen] were repulsed with heavy losses to the enemy. Absolutely no gain was made by these thrusts.

Wednesday, 4 October 1944: General Bradley stayed overnight and was in conference all morning with General Hodges in the war trailer leaving shortly before noon for a trip to the XIX Corps for a conference with General Corlett. Just after they left the CP was visited by 2 ME109s skirting low over the trees to avoid fire from 40s and 50s.[26] Our cavalry outfit opened fire from half-tracks but the two planes disappeared unscathed and arrived over Maastricht just as General Hodges and General Bradley reached there.

The XIX Corps is still having a tough time with the push and Boche; in the north the 7th Armored Division is being held up by strong resistance, double aproned barbwire entanglements and minefields; three strong counterattacks, each supported by considerable artillery were directed against it. The 30th Division continued to attack against very stubborn resistance but were unable to gain much ground. Elements of the 120th infantry, however, on the right did advance nearly three kilometers at one point. The 2nd Armored Division passed through the 30th Division but due to the difficult terrain made little progress.

There were no changes in the VII Corps sector. In the V Corps, units continued to move up to their new assembly areas and it expected that the three divisions will close there early tomorrow.

The VIII Corps has assumed responsibility for the area it was to take over from V Corps.

Bill Walton,[27] correspondent for Time, arrived shortly before dinner and was the guest of the General for drinks and dinner. Time is going to publish a "cover story" on General Hodges, to appear next week.

Thursday, 5 October 1944: General Gerow flew in from 12th Army Group this morning and until 3:30 this afternoon was in conference with General Hodges. He returned by car to V Corps.

The attack of the XIX Corps made some progress to the north and east today against very strong anti-tank, artillery, and nebelwerfer fire. Elements of the 2nd Armored Division advanced up to three miles although the progress of the 30th Infantry Division on their right was much slower, being limited to gains of 500 to 1,000 yards. There is nothing to report from VII Corps. V Corps continued to regroup its troops; 4th Infantry Division completed its move into the area as well as the 5th Armored Division which is now in position in rear of the interval between the two infantry divisions. Enemy aircraft were active yesterday over the XIX and VII Corps fronts; over 70 reported, AA claimed 25 as destroyed or damaged. There was no important news from any of the other fronts.

Friday, 6 October 1944: General Sir Miles Dempsey flew in for a conference and lunch with the General today. The results of their talk are: That the 7th Armored Division will hold its present positions near Overloon until relieved by units of the 8th British Corps after which it will occupy defensive positions from Deuren to Weert and continue to protect the east flank of the Second British Army.

XIX Corps attack is still going slowly although the 2nd Armored Division pushed north to the outskirts of Geilenkerchen [Geilenkirchen] and east to the outskirts of Beggendorff [Beggendorf]. The 30th Division which received a strong counterattack during the day made little advance; the 116th Infantry began to relieve the 120th. In the VII Corps sector the 9th Division attacked to the southeast on limited objectives driving for th [?] over extremely difficult terrain with gains of two or three miles recorded. There was no news of activity from the V Corps front.

Received today were additional copies of the 5 October 1944 issue of Stars & Stripes which carried the story by G. K. Hoddenfeld [Hodenfield] on General Hodges.

Saturday, 7 October 1944: The General spent a busy day today in the field; in the morning he drove to the CP of the 30th Infantry Division for a long talk with General Hobbs whom he had not seen in almost two months, returning here at three o'clock and immediately taking off by Cub plane for a conference with General Gerow and General Brooks, returning here shortly before supper time.

Extremely good progress was made by the 30th Division during the day; the leading elements of 117th Infantry advanced four kilometers, capturing Alsdorf and Merkstein. Resistance increased during the day and our counterattacks launched resulted in heavy losses to the enemy and considerable prisoners for us. The 7th Armored Division has been relieved by the 11th British Armored Division. The former is on route to new positions in the vicinity of Maarheeze [Maashees].

The 9th Division in the VII Corps continued the attack and the 39th and 60th Infantry Regiments made limited gains against organized field fortifications and houses. There was nothing to report from V Corps front.

The air had one of its biggest days over Germany since the beginning of the war—somewhere over 5,000 planes converging on the Nazis from all directions taking part in the attack. For the second consecutive day we were blessed with excellent weather and predictions are that the air will also be able to operate with equal effectiveness tomorrow.

Sunday, 8 October 1944: The General flew to St. Trond early this morning and there met General Marshall and General Bradley. From there they went on to General Montgomery's headquarters for a conference, General Hodges returning here shortly after one o'clock. It is now believed that General Marshall and at least one member of his party will arrive at First Army during the week for a short visit.

The attack continues with success. The 120th Infantry has pushed further south and the attack launched by the 18th Infantry north to join with the 120th Infantry laid a two-mile advance. It is hoped that the circle closing in Aachen will be completed by tomorrow. The 7th Armored Division, the First Belgian Brigade, passed to the control of the Second British Army and a new boundary has been established by the change between the 21 and 12th Army Groups running generally in a straight line from Hasselt to Neuss. There were no changes from other fronts.

Monday, 9 October 1944: The circle around AACHEN needs only two miles more to be closed; the 120th Infantry reached its southernmost objectives this afternoon and halted, waiting for the 18th Infantry, which stood off several brisk counterattacks this morning to advance to it.

CCA 2nd Armored with aid of units of the 30th Division cleaned out the town of STAUFFENBERG [Schaufenberg]. The 9th Division advanced up to a kilometer against exceedingly tough resistance and V Corps front was comparatively quiet.

In the afternoon the General motored onto VII Corps and from there to the 1st Division CP to see General Huebner. The story there told with delight is of the trolley cars which the 1st Division has captured on a hill overlooking AACHEN. They load the trolley cars, which they call V-13, with dynamite and then roll them down the hill into the city.[28] The 1st Division as is usual was full of cockiness and fight, confident that they can take "anything the General wants any time he wants it."

General Kean with G-4, Ordnance, and Ammunition Officer spent the day in conference at Twelfth Army Group and upon his return late this evening he and the General were closeted for a discussion regarding the conclusions reached at the conference.

The General now has the new P-38 pistol,[29] the gift of Brigadier [General] Wyman of the 1st Division who after 3½ years overseas is returning to take command of a division soon to be shipped to an overseas theater.[30]

As expected, bad weather returned today making all air effort useless. Predictions for tomorrow are very discouraging

Tuesday, 10 October 1944: Representatives of VIII Corps, Ninth Army, and XIX Corps—the G-3s and G-4s—had a long conference at the headquarters today apropos of the forthcoming shift of Ninth and First Army. Details of this shift are not yet forthcoming but reconnaissance has again been sent out to look for a possible CP in the vicinity of SPA or MALMEDY as we lose the XIX Corps and thus our axis is shifted. The General left after this conference to the VII Corps for a conference with General Collins.

The military news was as follows: XIX Corps: 30th Division reached its objective along the Corps boundary in the vicinity of WESELEN [Würselen] five miles northeast from the center of AACHEN. VII Corps: The 1st Division continued its attack against very stiff resistance where by midnight house to house fighting was still going on in ARREN [Haaren]. Although there is a gap of almost two miles between the 30th Division and the 1st Division the roads of escape from AACHEN to all intents and purposes have been cut. General Heubner [Huebner] issued a 24 hour ultimatum of surrender to the commander of the German forces which was delivered today at 10:15 and a reply is expected before tomorrow morning. 9th Division made little progress in its attack against a stubborn enemy. First Canadian Army was making some progress in its job of clearing out WALCHEREN ISLAND and through an amphibious attack south of the SCHELDT and gained considerable tactical surprise. DUNKIRK still holds out. From the Second British Army there was no reported change.

Wednesday, 11 October 1944: General Marshall accompanied by General Handy,[31] OPD Head, and Colonel Frank McCarthy,[32] Secretary General Staff, toured the First Army area today. They were met at V Corps headquarters by Colonel Throckmorton[33] who is acting as the General's Aide throughout the trip. After a tour of the 4th, 28th, 1st; and 9th Divisions, and a stop at VII Corps headquarters the party returned to Master TAC shortly after six o'clock where General Hodges met them. After drinks and dinner General Marshal conferred briefly with General Hodges and retired shortly after nine o'clock.

Major Sylvan took a message to General Marshall from Prime Minister Churchill now in Moscow and ran a risk in doing so. Just as he reached the outskirts of VERVIERS, eight P-38s (thus identified at the present writing) circled leisurely over the city and then dove in to dump their bombs damaging one bridge, setting warehouses afire, and demolishing the windows in many a nearby home. As the P-38s passed over Master TAC all the anti-aircraft in the vicinity was firing at them and Colonel Patterson later reported that two had been brought down. IX TAC has no statement to make although some eye-witnesses report that there were enemy markings on the plane. Whether or not these P-38s were friend or enemy, there is no doubt of the fact that enemy air activity was on a scale unsurpassed since D-Day. Shortly after seven o'clock tonight there were over eighty aircraft registered on the warning board, five or six of which reached the VERVIERS area but apparently did not drop any bombs. Colonel Patterson stated in a directive issued to Corps Commanders that this increased activity may very well become routine and that the enemy may be capable of sending out flights of as many as 150 aircraft at one time.

There was no reported change from the XIX Corps sector. In the VII Corps a report was received by noon time that no reply was received by noon to the 24 hour surrender ultimatum issued to the enemy in AACHEN, consequently air bombardment was begun at 12:30 lasting three hours, followed by an intensely heavy artillery barrage which continued until nightfall. 1st Infantry Division continued to exert pressure along its front but there were no changes in the troop dispositions. There were no important changes from the entire Army front.

Thursday, 12 October 1944: Breakfast was scheduled this morning for 7:20 but shortly after seven o'clock General Marshall (who had been awakened at ten minutes to seven) appeared in the dining room and fortunately Corporal DeCaesar was there to serve him. He and General Hodges left in one car, followed by other members of the party, directly to the CP of the 30th Division at Heerlen. There assembled were General Corlett, General Hobbs, General Gerhardt, and General Harmon. General Marshall was in conference with all of them for over a half hour at which time the party left directly for XIX Corps in MAASTRICHT for a brief introduction to the Corps staff and a look at the war room map. General Hodges said good-bye to General Marshall there and he was escorted to the field at St. Trond where two C-47s, General Bradley's and General Hodges', were waiting for him. Since General Bradley was there waiting for him the party took his plane and flew directly to PARIS. Justice Byrnes[34] who was scheduled to arrive there and to pay a visit to the 30th Division decided instead to fly back with the party.

Both our air and enemy air were active during the day. XIX Corps reported that the support given by the air during the day equalled any of the previous "best days" since D-Day and that the damage to enemy vehicles and personnel was exceedingly high. AACHEN was bombed again by five groups but there is no sign of diminishing resistance within the city. In fact, all along the front, especially in the XIX and VII Corps sectors, increased enemy activity and movement behind the lines was noted. As reserve for any possible armored threat coming from the XIX Corps sector, CCA of the 5th Armored Division left V Corps tonight and is expected to close in the vicinity of HEERLEN tomorrow. The 99th Infantry Battalion has also moved up from VII Corps sector to XIX Corps.

The G-2 puzzle of the moment is why lights were burning in COLOGNE and DUSSELDORF. Both cities were entirely "lit-up" and pilots reported that they could see signs of shooting in them. However, it is considered more likely that the lights were kept on in order to facilitate troop movements. The puzzle is by no means considered settled as yet. Enemy air was especially active between seven and nine o'clock this evening striking at some of our important dumps in the vicinity of Eu-PEN. Preliminary reports show little damage.

Friday, 13 October 1944: Today was a day of preparation for the visit tomorrow of His Majesty the King [George VI] and high American military leaders. The General did not leave the CP during the day. General Eisenhower was to have come to spend a night with us but this visit was postponed at the last minute.

The military news: XIX Corps: In the 30th Division zone the 116th Infantry passed through the 119th Infantry and attacked to the south with a mission of closing the 1½ mile gap between the 1st Division and itself. It was extremely difficult due to heavy resistance from both mobile and dug-in tanks. Hard fighting continued throughout the day and an advance of only from 200 to 600 yards was made. Below in the VII Corps sector, 1st Division began to close in on AACHEN and both the 2nd and 3rd Battalions of the 26th Infantry were making slow but steady progress in house-to-house fighting. Relentless air and artillery bombardment was continued of the city. There was no change from the V Corps front and no change of any importance from any other Army front.

The lights were again on last night in several Rhine cities including BONN which was a university town and has no important industrial installations. G-2s are still baffled.

Saturday, 14 October 1944: Today was the big day. At 10:45 General Simpson arrived, followed by General Collins, General Gerow, and General Corlett. Shortly after 11:15 General Eisenhower, General Bradley, and General Allen arrived. The last American General to arrive was General Patton who flew in by Cub shortly before 11:45. Promptly at twelve o'clock noon The King,[35] accompanied by General Hart who had gone to 21 Army Group headquarters the night before to meet His Majesty, drove into the gate. Accompanying the King as members of his official party were Sir Alan Lascelles,[36] his personal secretary, and Sir Lt. Col Piers Leigh [Lt. Col. Sir Piers Legh],[37] his military assistant. Also in the party was the proverbial Scotland Yard "Dick," whom you could spot a mile away by the fact that his right hand was continuously placed inside his coat jacket. The Royal Salute was given His Majesty by the Army band.

After meeting the Generals His Majesty came into the front room to be introduced to members of First Army staff among which Colonel Carter was so embarrassed that he could not get out his name. The only untoward incident in this introduction was furnished by Lt. Col. Cadman [Charles R. Codman],[38] Aide to General Patton, who had not been invited to the ceremony. He unceremoniously joggled a small table and knocked over a vase which fell to the floor with a resounding crash. Following the introduction The King who was dressed in a Field Marshal's uniform was taken to the G-3 room where both General Thorson and Colonel Dickson gave a briefing on the situation.

Following the briefing the party went to General Hodges' office for a glass of sherry, Scotch, or bourbon as befitted his tastes, during which time General Bradley was made a Knight Commander of the Bath by the King.

Shortly after quarter of one they went into the dining room and sat down at the table, for one of Louie Bosi's best meals consisting of Consomme, Steak with Mushroom Sauce, French Fried Potatoes, Salad, Pie and Coffee, all flavored with the finest of wines and port.

Following the dinner General Eisenhower had a conference with General Hodges for ten minutes after which the King reviewed the MP Honor Guard giving the photographers, of whom there were fully a dozen, the opportunity they had wanted to snap His Majesty and other high American Generals together. The King left at 2:15 and General Eisenhower then called all the remaining Generals out on the steps where for the benefit of news reels and still photographers they posed for five minutes.

General Corlett called before dinner to say that the XIX Corps was stopped and requested more troops and ammunition. For not the first time, the General reminded him to obtain more troops and more ammunition was at the present time impossible and that he was doing everything in his power to see that the XIX Corps received more of both. He urged XIX Corps to present whatever alternative or whatever plan they had in mind but surely they were not admitting that they could go no farther or that "as far as you are concerned the war is over."

The military news: Very little progress was recorded during the day by either XIX or VII Corps. The 1st Division was making no errors in its house-to-house progress in AACHEN. Seeking and combing out every one methodically as they pursue their slow march to the center of the city.

The air had another splendid day—more than 2,000 heavies attacking DUISBERG, COLOGNE, and other industrial targets east of the Rhine. Vapor trails could be seen throughout the morning and early afternoon.

Sunday, 15 October 1944: The two most important facts of the day were the extensive conference held with leaders of the Airborne Divisions and also the stiff counterattack launched against the 1st Division by the 8th Regiment of the 3rd Panzer Grenadier Division

Those arriving in the morning for the conference were: Major General Ridgway, Maj General [William M.] Miley,[39] 17th Airborne Division; General Gail [Richard Nelson Gale][40] of the 6th British Airborne Division and Maj General [Paul L.] Williams,[41] IX Air Force Troop Carrier Command. They were accompanied by half dozen British and American staff officers and the conference which began after lunch continued until after four o'clock. What operations were evolved or discussed remained at the present time a secret shared only by those participating. General Simpson arrived at three o'clock and sat in the conference until its close.

The counterattack against the 1st Division—the 16th and 18th Infantries—were repulsed with heavy losses to the enemy. Despite bad weather two groups of General Quesada's forces landing at bases other than their own (which were closed in) managed to give the infantry a helping hand and the 1st was permitted to exceed its ammunition allowances, in order to save lives and beat down the attack. No information has yet been received as to the number of enemy tanks destroyed in the operation. Since the enemy now appears to be massing considerable force in this area with a grim determination to hold on to AACHEN and its escape corridor which is now limited to a few hundred yards, CCB of the 5th Armored Division and the 2nd Bn of the 110th Infantry were this afternoon moved from the V Corps area into VII Corps and put at the disposal of General Collins.

In the 30th Division sector the 116th Infantry continued to advance south against heavy mortar and small arms fire and moderate artillery fire. No counterattacks were reported during the period. In the Second British Army sector the 11th Armored and three divisions continued to attack to the south to clear the OVERLOON area. They made little progress.

Monday, 16 October 1944: It rained hard again all day and the General did not leave the CP area. The biggest military news of the day was that contact between patrols of K Co 18th Inf and the 2nd Bn 119th Inf were made at five o'clock this afternoon. This juncture completed the encirclement of AACHEN. Inside the city 2nd and 3rd Bns of 26th Inf advanced house-to-house through the littered streets. Civilians still continue to emerge, like rats, from the smashed dwellings all of which look like gigantic Swiss cheeses so punctured are they with artillery and mortar shells. The 18th Inf and the 16th Inf are still under heavy pressure and counterattack throughout the day but no ground was lost. There were no reported changes from the V or VII Corps.

Tuesday, 17 October 1944: General Bradley arrived this afternoon, stopping overnight on his way to BRUSSELS for a conference on the use of ANTWERP. Shortly afterward General McLain former commander of the 90th Division who is to replace General Corlett as CG of XIX Corps arrived and not long afterward General Brooks, whom Major Zwink flew to England Monday, for a brief visit came in. General Brooks is leaving tomorrow to assume command of a Corps under Seventh Army. The four generals were in conference until 11:30 this evening—the subject matter of their discussion naturally not being known, although the conference doubtless concerned the employment of the XIX Corps in conjunction with the VII Corps in the final destruction of AACHEN and the drive eastward.

Bad weather again prevented the air from giving any close support to ground troops and aside from inside AACHEN itself where the going was slow but steady, there were no changes made in the front lines. To our north the Third British Division had two companies in VENRAG [Venray] last night and expected to wink out the last Boche tomorrow.

Wednesday, 18 October 1944: General Bradley returned from Brussels this afternoon after what he termed, "a very satisfactory conference." He was joined at the CP by General Simpson. General Hodges was up until midnight discussing the results of the conference as well as the shift of the First and Ninth Armies which is shortly to take place. Ninth Army has already opened an advance CP in MAASTRICHT.

XIX Corps and the VII Corps together continued to draw the noose tighter around AACHEN. The 30th Division and the 1104th Engr Group reduced enemy pillboxes north and northwest of the city, while the 1st Division continued its house-to-house cleanup inside the city and improved its juncture with the 30th. More than one-half of the city is now definitely in our hands and the enemy is making frantic efforts to supply the beleaguered garrison by air.

The Second British Army (VIII Corps) continued to attack south to clear land west of the MEUSE and the 3rd British Division captured VERNAG [Venray] and ST. SERVATUS Monastery. The 7th US Armored Division advanced two miles east in conjunction with this drive.

Thursday, 19 October 1944: After the morning conference in the war trailer General Hodges travelled to VII Corps to bring General Collins "good news." Both generals with General [Richard C.] Partridge[42] and the Corps G-3 were closeted for well over a half hour discussing the new plans. The General then drove up to the 1st Division CP for a chat with General Heubner.

Guests at the chateau tonight were General Middleton, CG of VIII Corps., and General Puechler [Theodore E. Buechler][43], artillery commander of General Ridgway's airborne corps who stayed overnight. General Middleton will shortly come under our command.

Captain Smith made a trip to the 29th Division to obtain the complete story on the general's nephew who was reported missing in action on October 4th. The general had received no detailed report from division headquarters and was naturally anxious to know the complete story. Both his battalion and regimental commander believe that Sam is a PW. Several Boche prisoners have stated that they saw five American officers being taken to the rear following the attack on SCHIERWALDEN-RATH which K Company held.[44]

Task Force "Hogan" of the 3rd Armored Division in conjunction with the 26th Infantry attacked north of AACHEN today and took the high ground bordering the city from the northern flank. Over two-thirds of the city is now firmly in our control.

There was no other news of any importance from any of the other fronts.

It now seems certain that this headquarters will move to SPA intact on Wednesday the 25th.

Friday, 20 October 1944: The General had in for a morning long conference today four Corps Commanders: General Collins, General Gerow, General Middleton, and General McLain, who the day before yesterday took over official command of the XIX Corps from General Corlett. The latter left yesterday for Paris with his two Aides and will shortly fly to the United States.

VII Corps reported tonight that the bulk of AACHEN is now in our hands leaving only a few defenses in the western outskirts yet to be taken. More than four hundred PWs were captured during the day.

The 9th Armored Division closed in the VIII Corps area in the vicinity of MERSCH [Mesch] and the 102nd Division is assembling soon in the vicinity of VALKINBURG [Valkenburg].

Saturday, 21 October 1944: AACHEN fell today at 12:06, some twenty hours after the BBC had announced its capture. Colonel Wilks, commanding the remaining 1500 troops of the city, officially surrendered at that time and all organized resistance has seized [ceased]. AACHEN is the first German city of any size to fall into Allied hands and if its condition is a criterion of future operations there will not remain much of Germany at the end of this war.

This morning at ten o'clock VERVIERS became "on limits" for some 700 troops of VII Corps on rotation for a period of 48 hours. Combat troops of this Corps as well as others will be given freedom of selected towns—to sleep, to drink, to eat, to loaf, and to do whatever they wish within the limits of propriety. VALKINBURG is the rest area center of the XIX Corps and it is believed that MALMEDY will be selected by V Corps. These towns will remain "off limits," however, to all other personnel except those furnished with a pass and badge by the Corps.

Shortly after eleven o'clock tonight one flying bomb scooted over the CP to be followed by others within the next twelve hours. Although no reports have come in as to their destination, Colonel Patterson believes they are aimed at ANTWERP.

Preparations for a New Offensive,
22 October–15 November 1944

Sunday, 22 October 1944: General Collins and General Gerow arrived at 9:30 this morning for a morning long conference with the General, the purpose of which was to draw the new plans for the forthcoming push. They brought their respective G-3s for settlement of details with General Thorson.

The VIII Corps with attached units in present positions came into control of First Army at noon. The new boundary between First and Third Armies is the same as was occupied between the Ninth and Third Armies. General Simpson and his Ninth Army have taken over control of the XIX Corps as well as the XIII Corps which opened yesterday at TONGRES [Tongeren].

The front was quiet today and the only incident was the passage of some eight "buzz-bombs" over the CP during the day. The third day of cloudy weather kept them from view.

The guest of General Hodges tonight for dinner was Col. Tim Mc-Coy,[45] former Hollywood star, who served under the General a long time in the Louisiana maneuver area. Colonel McCoy is shortly on his way to Sixth Army Group[46] where as Chief of Staff to General Royce he will aid in setting up of the First Tactical Air Force (Provisional). General Royce was to have headed the air staff of SHAEF replacing Marshal Leigh-Mallory who has gone to head the Asia command [Southeast

Asia Command, SEAC] but according to Colonel McCoy he decided that he would prefer a more active command.

Monday, 23 October 1944: The General left at ten o'clock this morning for Luxembourg where he had lunch with General Bradley and conferred with the latter until late this afternoon, returning to TAC headquarters at 6:45. In the evening he and his staff poured over air mosaics of the section in which this coming operation will be launched.

More buzz-bombs, an estimated twelve in number, crossed to the left and to the right of the CP during the day. The BBC and British newspapers have announced that the destination of these was the ANTWERP area although their existence is still treated a Top Secret matter in this command. Colonel Patterson has stated that from radar and other reports the launching sites seem to be located in the "L" square at the approximate coordinates 2527. No anti-aircraft measures are being taken against them although requests have been put in for bombing of the sites as soon as the weather permits. A parade of Lancasters[47] and Halifaxes,[48] Germany bound, also passed over the CP shortly after seven o'clock.

The 9th Armored Division is now fully closed in the VIII Corps area, while the 104th Inf Div and 7 Armd Div assigned to Ninth Army have been attached for operations to 21 Army Group. There was no change in the front lines except for relief of units by other battalions and regiments.

Tuesday, 24 October 1944: Today was a quiet day on all fronts and with no changes in any of the Corps front lines.

The General spent the day in continuous conference with General Quesada, General Thorson, General Hart, and other staff specialists. This afternoon General Lee, General Saylor [Henry B. Sayler],[49] and General Plank arrived from Group and spent an hour and a half in session with the General. General Lee brought with him the copy of TIME which features the "cover story" of General Hodges. The drawing on the front cover does not look very much like the General but the article itself is workmanlike and a competent job and the General thought it was "pretty good." It was a considerable change from the article which Bill Walton who interviewed the General several weeks back cabled to New York, The improvements were made by the home office.[50]

There were more flying bombs today, many of them visible.

Wednesday, 25 October 1944: Before representatives of the press and several newspaper photographers, General Bradley at one o'clock today pinned the Bronze Star on General Hodges. The citation read by General Kean was as follows: "For meritorious achievement in connection with military operations against an enemy of the United States at Aachen, Germany. The forces led by Lt. General Hodges first assaulted the strongly held key city 8 October, 1944. On 21 October, nine days after an ultimatum had been presented to the German commander, the surrender of the city was assured. Lt. General Hodges' brilliant victory has upheld the highest tradition of the military service of the United States." Both General Hodges and General Kean when they learned of the presentation laughed a bit but this presentation was in line with a policy General Bradley discussed previously with General Hodges—to increase the value of the Bronze Star award which in the estimation of some does not have its proper significance.

This presentation came after a long morning conference between General Hodges, General Simpson and his staff, General McLain and his Chief of Staff and in this conference General Bradley also participated for an hour.

Most of Command Echelon moved today to the new headquarters at SPA.

There were no changes of any note in the front line positions. A new field order was published late tonight setting up new boundaries, the most important change in which was the regrouping of forces in the V and VII Corps; the 9th Div moving southward to replace the 28th Div which is being moved north to occupy the sectore formerly held by the 9th. This field order which set forth the main objectives of the coming drive is probably the most important order issued by General Hodges to-date. On its successful completion may very well depend the early outcome of this war.

Thursday, 26 October 1944: TAC Headquarters ceased to exist at three o'clock today amalgamating once more with Command into one headquarters at SPA. Master Rear will for the present at least remain separate. The headquarters occupies all of the Hotel Brittanique [Britannique]; General Hodges' spacious office is one formerly occupied in 1918 by Field Marshal Von Hindenburg.[51] As at Bristol the Generals have set up another "Holmes," a new and spacious private home high on a hill overlooking a valley and some two and a half miles from their offices. In this home, the property of a Liege steel man, reside four Generals and Aides. Other officers are billeted in hotels about the town. The town is, however, "Off Limits" to all personnel with the exception of churches and the baths.

After saying good-bye and paying their respects to Count and Countess De Pinto, whose hospitality we had enjoyed for five and a

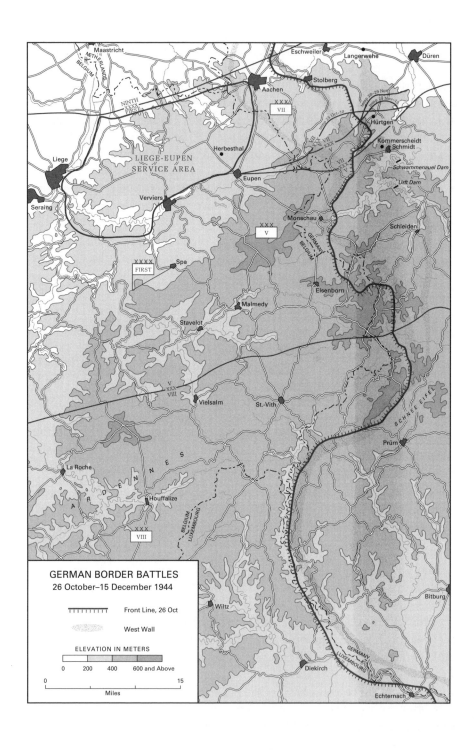

Maastricht
NETHERLANDS
BELGIUM
Eschweiler
Langerwehe
Düren

NINTH
FIRST

Aachen
Stolberg

XXX
VII

Hürtgen

Herbesthal

LIEGE-EUPEN
SERVICE AREA

Liege

Eupen

Kommerscheidt
Schmidt

Schwammenauel Dam

Urft Dam

Verviers

Monschau

Schleiden

Seraing

XXX
V

GERMANY
BELGIUM

XXXX
FIRST
Spa

Elsenborn

Malmedy

Stavelot

Elsenborn

V
XXX
VIII

Vielsalm

St.-Vith

SCHNEE EIFEL

Prüm

La Roche

A R D E N N E S

Houffalize

BELGIUM
LUXEMBOURG

XXX
VIII

GERMAN BORDER BATTLES
26 October–15 December 1944

⊤⊤⊤⊤⊤⊤⊤⊤⊤ Front Line, 26 Oct

West Wall

ELEVATION IN METERS

0   200   400   600 and Above

0   15

Miles

Wiltz

Bitburg

GERMANY
LUXEMBOURG

Diekirch

Echternach

half weeks (the longest occupancy of a CP since D-Day) the General motored to his new home shortly after one. He returned to the office after dinner tonight for a talk with Colonel Dickson and for other planning work.

Friday, 27 October 1944: With bad weather making flying impossible the General motored this afternoon to BASTOGNE for a conference with General Middleton. Also included in the discussions were General Leonard[52] of the 9th Armd Div, General Stroh of the 8th Div and General Hoag [William M. Hoge] who has returned to the 9th Armd to which he was assigned before his work on the Alaska Highway.[53] The gist of the conference was that General Middleton is giving up one of his chemical mortar battalions and receiving one of the two excess TD [tank destroyer] battalions that V Corps now has. Colonel O'Hare[54] was the General's guest for dinner tonight and after dinner at the office the General decorated Colonel Jesse Gibley [Gibney], formerly of the 60th Infantry with the DSC and Lt. Colonel Gurney [Mark Gurnee],[55] Assistant Engineer Officer with the Bronze Star for his work prior to and after D-Day.

The buzz-bomb which shook the buildings in SPA landed, according to Colonel Patterson, three miles north of the city in an open field causing neither damage nor injuries. Radar had clocked the buzz-bomb travelling at 6,000 feet and at 300 miles per hour, and suddenly the motor cut. Colonel Patterson believes some mechanical defect was responsible for the sudden nose-dive.

The 60th and 39th Infantrys closed today in the vicinity of Camp Eisenborn [Camp d'Elsenborn, Belgium] while the 109th and 110th Infantrys have moved into the front line positions which they formerly held. CCB of the 5th Armd Div is beginning to move early tomorrow morning to rejoin the division in the V Corps sector. There was otherwise no change in the front line positions.

Saturday, 28 October 1944: General Gerow arrived for lunch and General Hodges broke to him the news that he was losing one of the TD Bns but obtaining the 86th Chemical [Mortar] Battalion in exchange from VIII Corps. Upon return to the office General Middleton arrived and both Corps Commanders were in conference with the General until 3:30 in the afternoon.

Colonel Throckmorton called twice during the day to inform General Hodges and General Kean of the progress of his negotiations in the UK. Elaborate measures have been taken by stationing officers in Paris and with each regimental combat team—to insure that the 84th Division and the 99th Division will arrive before the big show. The 84th will land on either Omaha or Utah beach on the 31st and the 99th should close in the vicinity of EUPEN on 8 November.

Today was bright, clear, and cold and the air had one of the few opportunities it has had in the last month to do its job. Fighter-bombers, Forts [B-17s], and Liberators [B-24s] were seen over SPA a good part of the day especially in the afternoon. Flying bomb activity ceased at least for about a twenty-four hour period.

Tonight the General opened the bottle of Chateau de la Tour 1919 which Monsieur Preud'homme-Torkay [Proud'homme-Torkay] presented to him when we were at HUY. He said at the time that is was the finest bottle that he had in the cellar and tasting it tonight convinced us he was speaking the truth.

The General returned to the office after dinner for more conferences leaving for his quarters shortly after eleven o'clock.

Sunday, 29 October 1944: General Collins, armed with ample overlays of the VII Corps plan of attack, arrived at eleven o'clock and immediately went into conference with the General. Following the lunch hour he was joined in the General's office by General Simpson, General [James E.] Moore,[56] and Colonel [Armistead D.] Mead[57] and shortly after three o'clock by General [Lucian K.] Truscott[58] and General Carlton [Don E. Carleton],[59] his Chief of Staff. The conference went on until 5:30 in the afternoon.

General Truscott was leaving shortly for the United States for a two weeks leave before returning here to assume command of the Fifteenth Army. He spent the night in the General's home, he and the General discussing before dinner how the Army headquarters should operate and how many Corps it should have under his control. Also discussed was the question of replacements. General Truscott said—and the infantrymen of the 3rd Division have already been replaced four times since the division first saw action—that there was no question that it was far better to work replacements into the line when the battalion or company was out of action. If they were moved directly into action, casualty and straggler rates were uniformly high. General Truscott also said that the battle fatigue casualties most recently had been those of veterans who had served the division since they first saw action, that these men who had seen and done so much had apparently reached the end of their rope. He also added the information that General Patch's[60] son previously wounded in action and sent to General Patch's headquarters to recuperate had been killed the first day that he had rejoined his unit.

Despite clear weather the Germans launched several buzz-bombs today which passed over SPA. An order was distributed putting SPA on limits to troops of this command. Purchases of everything but food may be made; there will be a bed check of enlisted men at eleven o'clock.

There was no change in positions in the front lines of the First Army nor in those of the Ninth Army where regiments of the 102d Division continued to relieve elements of the 2nd Armored and the 30th Division. The British drive to force the enemy north of the MAAS River continued with success, the 53rd and 7th Armored advanced three miles after by-passing LOON-OP-ZAND.

The Polish Armored Division reached the outskirts of BREDA and the 49th Division the outskirts of ROOSENDAAL. On the BEVELAND Peninsula the campaign is progressing very successfully with the 2nd Canadian Division advancing from the mainland and establishing contact with the 52nd Division in the beachhead on the south side of the peninsula. Continued enemy pressure on the 8th British Corps continued today and as a result the 15th Scottish Division and the 6th Guards Tank Brigade have been moved up in rear of the 7th as reserve. No great penetration of our lines has been made there but it does not appear that the enemy intends to call off his offensive tactics on this flank.

Monday, 30 October 1944: It now appears that the 84th Division instead of coming to us will relieve the 101st in the Nijmigen sector. However, there is a good possibility that the 99th Division will still make its appearance on our front. To this may be added the 104th Division under General Terry Allen[61] which is currently operating with the British in the drive to push the Germans north of the MAAS. With this drive having continued success it is thought possible today that the division may be able to close in our area by 8 November. However, headquarters has learned not to count on any division until they actually see it in their own area.

General Truscott left this morning for PARIS and General Hodges after lunch made a quick trip to V Corps for a conference with General Gerow who is now established in EUPEN.

After dinner the General saw four Signal Corps films, two of which told inaccurately the story of the liberation of PARIS, the third of which dealt with the airborne operation in HOLLAND and the fourth of which was a combination of war shots. The photography, especially in the film dealing with the airborne operation, was uniformly good but the commentary was uniformly bad. The FFI, General Patton, and General LeClerc [Leclerc] were given full and complete credit for the freeing of the French capitol [capital]. The General was also amused at the commentary of the airborne landing which said among other things that it would be responsible for bringing the end of the war many months closer.

There was no change in the front line dispositions along the First Army front and although enemy pressure continues, no additional ground has been lost to the Boche counterattack directed against the British 8th Corps around MEIGEL [Meijel] and WEERT. The 7th US Armored Division has been relieved in this area and replaced by the 15th Scottish Division. To the west of the 8th Corps, British and Canadians continued their advance. The 7th Armored Division gained up to six miles in occupying GREVELDUIN KAPELLE and reaching the outskirts of VOSTERHAUT. Resistance in this area has been considerably less than has been anticipated and an early closing of the Corps zone is now foreseen. The BEVELAND peninsula has now been completely cleared by the 2nd Canadian Corps except for small isolated enemy pockets. The 1st Canadian Corps with the Polish Armored Division and the 4th Infantry Division occupied BREDA and ROOSENDAAL and the distance separating forward elements from the MAAS is in some cases not more than five miles.

Tuesday, 31 October 1944: The attack of V Corps which was to inaugurate the new offensive plan of First Army tomorrow morning was this afternoon postponed because of extremely unfavorable weather reports for tomorrow. Regardless of weather, however, it will go off on Thursday morning unless the General orders otherwise at the last minute.

The General this afternoon motored to Ninth Army headquarters at MAASTRICHT where he had a long conference with General Bradley and General Simpson and spent the night. The main subject matter of the conference was whether First Army will or will not get additional divisional reinforcement.

There was no change in front line dispositions of the First Army. The attack being launched by the Germans against the Allies in the area of MEGIEL [Meijel] and OVERLOON appears to be successfully stopped. The 7th Armored Division has withdrawn and is now closing in the vicinity of WEERT while the 53rd British Division relieved of its task in driving the Boche northward towards the MAAS is assembling in the vicinity of BREE to reinforce the Belgian Brigade. A substantial progress was made by the British XII Corps in clearing the enemy from the area south of the MAAS. The 51st and 7th Armored reached the MARK

CANAL AND THE MARK RIVER as far west as TERHEIJDEIT. First Canadian Army likewise made substantial progress with the Polish Armored and the 49th Division gaining as much as 10,000 yards. There still remain a few isolated pockets of resistance on the BEVELAND peninsula but operations against WALCHERAN ISLAND are being made today by a special Commando task force.

Bad weather has prevented aerial observation of the RHINE near COLOGNE where one of the bridges was accidentally hit and demolished on 14 October. It is known that the demolition of this bridge prevented barge traffic for a considerable length of time but whether the Germans succeeded in clearing the River we do not know as yet. General Hodges and General Kean wish that all the bridges could be destroyed either by plan or by accident but the Air Corps is apparently unwilling to take on the job.

Wednesday, 1 November 1944: General Seibert [Edwin L. Sibert],[62] G-2 of the Twelfth Army Group, was the General's guest for luncheon. General Gerow came to see the General after lunch for a final discussion of V Corps' attack tomorrow morning, and with him the General left at three o'clock for a visit to the 28th Division, which is to spearhead the attack. He found the Division in fine fettle, rarin' to go, and optimistic over their chances of giving the Boche a fine drubbing. The General said their plan was excellent; they are feinting to the north in hopes of fooling the Boche into the belief that this is the main effort, and then whacking him with everything in the direction of the town of SCHMIDT. General Davis was chiefly responsible for the plan, and the General said that he had never looked in better shape. Weather reports for tomorrow are still uncertain. Two groups of fighter-bombers are to support the attack with two more groups on ground alert.

The First Army front was quiet with only occasional artillery fire, the customary patrol activities, and very little enemy air action. In the Third Army, the 80th Division made a limited objective attack and cleared ABAUCOURT and LETRICOURT. In the XV Corps, the 2nd French Armored drove three miles to BACCARAT. The VI Corps with the 45th Div leading the way were within a mile of ST. DIE.

Substantial progress was also made along the British and Canadian fronts. The 15th Division, in the VIII Corps sector, recaptured LIESEL and continued on to the canal, wiping out almost all gains previously made by the Boche. In the XII Corps, the 7th British Armored Division reached the MAAS River. The Polish Armored and the 104th have crossed the MARK River but not as yet reached the MAAS.

The WALCHEREN ISLAND campaign is going well. The 2nd Canadian Division forced the causeway between the island and the peninsula, while the Commando landing in the vicinity of FLUSHING has been extended to the outskirts of the city. On the mainland, at the mouth of the SCHELDT ESTUARY, the 2nd Canadian Division reached KNOCKE with an advance of almost four miles. The Boche are here compressed into a tiny pocket some four miles in diameter, and their end is not far off.

Thursday, 2 November 1944: At nine o'clock yesterday morning the 28th Div launched the V Corps attack to the east with the 109th and 112th Infantry, after an artillery preparation in which 25 Bns participated. The attack progressed well during the morning but slowed up in the afternoon as the Battalions met increased fortifications and heavy mine fields. The 1st and 3rd Bns of 109th Regiment reached intermediate objectives advancing over a mile southeast of HURTGEN. 2nd Bn of 112th Inf advanced 1½ miles to the town of VOSSENACK to its initial objective in the vicinity of F 050330. The 110th Inf jumped off at noon but made only a slight advance. 350 prisoners were taken during the day and the General tonight is well satisfied with the progress made. The air had only slight opportunity because of bad weather to aid the attack and on one occasion dropped its bombs in the midst of our troops causing, according to preliminary reports, 15 casualties. All was quiet on the VII and VIII Corps fronts with the exception of heavy shelling throughout the day of the VII Corps CP at KORNLIMUENSTER [Kornelimünster]. One shell—it is thought that an 88[63] or 105 was doing most of the shelling—landed just outside of General Collins' office breaking all the glass in his offices. Other shells also landed in the court-yard of the CP but fortunately no one was injured throughout the day, although as a precautionary measure General Collins has moved his offices and the War Room downstairs to more protective quarters.

General Middleton arrived shortly before noon, apparently worried over the situation on his Corps right flank, and had lunch with the General. He told two amusing stories of the pillboxes which some of his infantry troops are occupying. On one occasion the Boche sent over an aggressive night patrol shooting up the area where they believed one of our OPs to be, since we had moved out they killed no one but perhaps as a prank more than in seriousness they locked the door of one of the pillboxes and threw away the key. 7 GIs were slumbering inside and the next morning there were frantic calls for a locksmith to open the door. In another area where troops were undergoing training in blowing pillboxes' doors, a French farmer excitedly ran up as the demolition charge was being placed in the hinge of the door and yelled, "Don't do that, don't do that! I have the keys! I have the keys!"

In the Second British [Army] lines the situation was as follows: 8th Corps: The 15th Scottish Division has retaken HEITRAK and has advanced one-half mile to the southeast. Further south elements of our 7th Armored Division made an attack which was held up by mine fields. The enemy has taken no offensive action in this area during the last two days and it is considered not likely that he will do so. The First Canadian Army cleared the Island of THOLEN and NORTH BEVELAND of all enemy. On WALCHEREN, Commandos are still fighting in FLUSHING while another Commando landing by the 4 SS [Special Service] Brigade on the westernmost point of the Island has been exploited inland more than three miles.

900 heavy bombers of the RAF passed over the General's house at dinner time tonight. We learned later that the target was DUSSELDORF. Flying bomb activity today over SPA was limited to three or four.

Friday, 3 November 1944: General Simpson and his staff, General Collins, General Quesada, and General McLain were guests of the General at "The Holmes" this morning preliminary to a conference which started at 1:30 in the General's office and did not break up until almost 5:30. In this conference a full discussion and determination of attack plans of the two Armies was made.

General [Henry S.] Aurand,[64] former CG Sixth Service Command,[65] and now on the continent, it is believed to assume an important Ordnance position, saw the General briefly in the mid-afternoon.

The 28th Division this morning resumed the attack with the 110th and 112th Infantry. The 110th on the right met with heavy resistance from pillboxes on which the enemy were placing their own artillery and mortar fire making it difficult for our troops to approach and place demolition charges to them. In addition to pillboxes, there was considerable small arms fire and barbed wire in 8' high concertina rolls.[66] The 3rd Bn of the 112th, however, entered the outskirts of SCHMIDT at four o'clock after advancing about 5,000 yards. This Bn was followed by the 1st which stopped about a mile northwest of Schmidt and the 2nd Bn continued to occupy its objective at VOSSENACK. All buildings there were destroyed by our artillery but the basements themselves were fortified and considerable bayonet and hand-to-hand fighting was necessary to clear the enemy from these points. The General is extremely satisfied tonight of the progress made.

News from other fronts: NINTH US ARMY: The 102nd has received their organic transportation and began to relieve the 29th Division and part of the 2nd Armored Division today. VI CORPS, SEVENTH US ARMY: The 100th Division has been assigned to the VI Corps and will relieve the 45th Division in the near future. The 45th will then pass to control of XV Corps. FIRST CANADIAN ARMY: The Polish Armored, 104th US, and the 49th Divisions established substantial bridgeheads over the MARK River. The WALCHEREN Island campaign is progressing satisfactorily with FLUSHING almost clear and with the bridgehead now expanded on the western side of the Island to include DOMBERG [Domburg]. The Island is almost entirely flooded making progress slow. On the mainland the 3rd Canadian Division has cleared KNOCKE and all resistance south of the SCHELDT has thereby ceased. The total bag for this campaign is 600 Officers and 12,000 EM [enlisted men]. Mine sweeping operations started today in the WEST SCHELDT estuary to open at long last the port of ANTWERP.

Saturday, 4 November 1944: The General did not leave the CP today but spent most of the time in his War Room and also in G-3 following closely the V Corps attack. Things did not go very well. The 3rd Bn of the 112th, counterattacked at ten o'clock, withdrew almost a mile to the vicinity of KOMMERSCHEIT [Kommerscheidt]. Early yesterday afternoon a heavy artillery concentration and air bombardment was placed on SCHMIDT the 3rd Bn attempted to regain the village but this attack was met by enemy counterattack of a Bn of infantry and about a dozen tanks. Our progress towards SCHMIDT was at nightfall only 300 yards and reports from General Gerow to General Hodges this evening were to the effect that the 3rd Bn suffered very heavy casualties. Some progress, however, was made by the 109th Inf, 1st and 2nd Bns in the HURTGEN area. Progress was slow due to numerous mines, dug-in infantry, and accurate artillery fire.

NINTH US ARMY: 102nd Division less the 406th Inf took over the 29th Division sector. 406th Inf is still attached to 30th Division. The area for the employment of the XIII Corps is expected to include the general zone between GEILEKIRCHEN and MAESEYCK [Maaseik] at a date as yet undetermined. Initially the Corps will have the 102nd Division and the 113th Cavalry Group and later on the 7th Armored Division. The area from MAESEYCK to the Army Group boundary now held by 113th Cavalry Group will be taken over by the British. 84th Division is expected to close in the vicinity of GULPEN on the 9th of November. VI CORPS, SEVENTH US ARMY: The 103rd Division is expected to close in the Corps area on 9 November to be followed at the end of the month by the 14th Armored.

SECOND BRITISH ARMY: Some progress was made by the 7th Armored Division in the vicinity of WEERT.

FIRST CANADIAN ARMY: Further gains were made by all three divisions in their bridgeheads across the MARK. They may all reach the MAAS tomorrow. The WALCHEREN Island campaign is going slowly but FLUSHING is now clear of the enemy except for isolated snipers.

Colonel [George P.] Seneff,[67] Assistant Artillery Commander of the 28th Division, was General Kean's guest for dinner tonight. Colonel Seneff has just been made the Commanding Officer of the Army Photo Interpretation Center.

Sunday, 5 November 1944: The General and General Kean had lunch at noon today and started out for an afternoon long tour of the front. General Collins met them out of EUPEN and escorted them through much of the fortified area over which there had been consistently heavy fighting in the early days of the break-through. Using isolated back roads that covered the area from ROTGEN [Roetgen] to JAGERSHAUS [Jägerhaus] (one house only) to JAGERSFAHRT to ZWEIFALL and from there to BUSBACH, CP of the 3rd Armored Division. There General Rose, decked out in pinks and riding boots, met the General. There was heavy artillery fire at the time but all of it a gift from us to the Boche with none returning. The General went to ROTT, CP of the 28th Division, and met General Cota from whom the General learned first hand of the exceedingly tough time that the "Bloody Bucketeers" Division[68] is having. On the way back the General stopped briefly at 7th [VII] Corps headquarters returning to the CP shortly before six o'clock.

Little progress was made by the 28th Division throughout the day. In the morning contact was made by the 1st and 2nd Bns of the 110th and in the afternoon the 1st Bn managed to crack several pillboxes and push through heavily wired defenses to the extent of 300 yards. The 112th Inf has been strengthened by 13 tanks and 14 TD guns but no progress was made in the direction of SCHMIDT. In the area just southwest of HURTGEN the 109th Inf continued to hold positions which they gained two days ago and HURTGEN itself was heavily bombed by bombers in the morning after enemy tanks were spotted in that area.

The 9th Division less the 47th Inf completed the relief of the 4th Division yesterday afternoon. The 4th Division how [now] has its regiments in assembly areas directly in the rear of their former front line positions and will probably start moving tomorrow. The First Canadian Army with the Polish Armored, 104th and the 49th Divisions have now generally reached the MAAS River all along the front, the Boche keeping one important key bridge open for escape of the remnants of his forces. Mine sweeping on the SCHELDT is progressing satisfactorily and the WALCHEREN Island campaign should be over in two days. The force which landed in FLUSHING advanced north to within a mile of MID-DLEBERG [Middelburg] in the center of the Island and the southwest part has been cleared up to the flooded area.

The air had a good day yesterday. The RAF was over again last night in force. Flying bombs were also exceedingly active during the day and Colonel Lowe [Low] reports that damage being done to both BRUSSELS and ANTWERP by V-2 more than by V-1 is becoming increasingly serious.

Monday, 6 November 1944: The General did not leave the CP today, being occupied with the fight which the 28th Division is having. No less than four separate counterattacks were made against the 28th all supported by heavy artillery fire. In the 112th Inf sector the 2nd Bn at Vos-SENACK was forced back 500 yards from the town by an enemy assault of 500 infantry supported by 10 tanks. At 1400 they received a second counterattack which was repulsed without loss of ground. No progress was made in the direction of SCHMIDT, and bad weather coupled with uncertain red smoke markings made air support of little value.

General [Bryant E.] Moore,[69] Assistant Division Commander of the 104th Div, arrived this morning to see General Hodges and General Kean and was promptly dispatched by Cub plane to ANTWERP with a series of instructions to be given to General Allen. For a few minutes this afternoon the General saw Bishop Hobson, Episcopal church leader who is making a tour of the fighting fronts.

There was little news in other Army areas except in the Second British Army front where the area south of the MAAS River has been completely cleared except for one small enemy pocket at S'HURTOENBOSCH ['s Hertogenbosch]. Considerable progress has been made on WALCHEREN ISLAND and there is now a possibility that the enemy will be cleared out within 48 hours.

Tuesday, 7 November 1944: The General motored to LUXEMBOURG this morning to testify before the Joint Chiefs of Staffs Special Committee for the Reorganization of National Defense.[70] This Committee, composed of Admiral J. O. Richardson[71] (a four star Admiral formerly in command of the Pacific Fleet), Major General H. L. George,[72] Major General W. F. Tompkins,[73] Rear Admiral M. F. Schoeffel,[74] and Colonel Truby Davidson [F. Trubee Davison],[75] former Assistant Secretary of War for Air, has been working for the past six months interviewing and evaluating the ideas of those military leaders who have taken part in joint operations against the enemy. On the way down talking with General Quesada, General Hodges indicated that his testimony would be something along this line: That there was no necessity for separating the ground and air forces but that it was imperative that in future years especially at the War College and at Leavenworth, the officer be thoroughly trained in both ground and air operations so that logically by this system an air force officer could command a corps or an army. He said he thought cooperation between air and ground in this war had been of such a high caliber that to split the two into separate forces might be to spoil or tear asunder the present close partnership. Present at the conference in addition to members of the Committee were General Bradley, General Quesada, General Lev Allen, and General [Raymond G.] Moses.[76] After the meeting broke up at 3:30, General Eisenhower arrived and he, General Hodges, and General Bradley had a cup of coffee and talked until 4:30. General Eisenhower will be our guest along with General Bradley sometime before the end of the week.

General Hodges returned to The Holmes at 7:30 to find the 28th Division situation going from bad to worse. 12th Inf has now completely relieved the 109th and the 109th has moved down to assist the 2nd Bn of the 112th in the vicinity of Vossenack where tonight it is learned the enemy is now in possession of it. The remainder of the 112th and the 3rd Bn of the 110th were forced back 500 yards to the high ground northwest of Kommerscheidt by very heavy pressure and continual counterattacks. Reports from the 28th indicate that never has enemy artillery along our front been so heavy but the General insists that the Battalions cannot be properly deployed or dug-in. He said that no matter how heavy enemy artillery was, casualties would not be high nor would ground be lost. He is rather worried tonight over the general situation since full employment of his other divisions in the drive towards the Rhine rested to a certain extent upon the success of the 28th and it is possible that there may be some personnel changes made. General Davis is scheduled to lead a task force in an attempt to recapture Schmidt tomorrow morning.

The 104th Division has closed two infantry regiments below Aachen and they have begun to relieve the 1st Division which will in turn relieve the 3rd Armored. The 4th Division less the 12th Inf has begun to assemble in the VII Corps area in the vicinity of Zweifall. In the Ninth

Army, XIII Corps has become operational; 84th Division on route to GULPEN has been attached to the XIX Corps and the 7th Armored Division is on route to MHEER [Mehr] from the 2nd British Army sector and is being attached to XIII Corps.

The Third Army was scheduled to jump off this morning with a coordinated attack by the XX and XII Corps, but this has been postponed until tomorrow morning.

On WALCHEREN Island, MIDDLEBURG has been occupied and the whole island cleared except for a small area in the northern part of the island. Small ships are using the part of ANTWERP although the SCHELDT has not been entirely cleared of mines. The total bag of prisoners in the SCHELDT Estuary area and the WALCHEREN Island campaign has now reached 25,000.

Wednesday, 8 November 1944: The General had an early lunch and departed for V Corps where in the absence of General Gerow he had a brief chat with Colonel [Orlando C.] Mood,[77] former G-4 of V Corps who is now Chief of Staff. On his way down to Holiday (28th Division) he met General Collins on the roadside and stopped for a brief chat with him. Upon arriving at Holiday he found General Eisenhower, General Bradley, and General Gerow talking the situation over with General Cota and pleasantries were passed until the official party left, then General Hodges drew General Cota aside for a short sharp conference on the lack of progress made by the 28th Division. General's chief complaint seemed to be that the division headquarters had no precise knowledge of the location of their units and were doing nothing to obtain it. Since eight o'clock that morning they had no word of General Davis who with two armored cars had set out for KOMMERSCHEID to lead back and disengage from action the 1st and 3rd Bns of the 112th Inf and 3rd Bn of the 110th. General Hodges, needless to say, is extremely disappointed over the 28th Division's showing and his feelings are shared by General Thorson and General Kean, both of whom served a long time with this division. General Hodges again stopped at V Corps on his return home to tell General Gerow to keep a close watch over the Division's efforts and to recommend any personnel changes he thought necessary. The drive back to The Holmes was through a blinding snow storm, the first of the year, and not welcome to either the General or Major Sylvan.

Later during the evening General Gerow telephoned to say that General Davis had successfully withdrawn three battalions to the assembly area, approximately five kilometers to the rear of KOMMERSCHEID.

There were some 25 walking wounded and 25 litter cases among the three battalions. The 2nd Bn of the 109th continued today to hold Vos-SENACK against strong enemy pressure while the 1st and 2nd Bns of the 110th made small gains in the SIMONSKALL-RAFFETSBARND [Raffelsbrand] area.

There were other changes along the First Army front as regrouping continued for the forthcoming major attack. The 415th Inf of the 104th Div relieved the 26th Inf which assembled in the vicinity of 9737. Relief of the 1st Division will be completed tomorrow. In the VIII Corps area the 83rd Division passed to operational control of the Third Army. The Third Army launched an attack at 7 o'clock today with the 35th, 26th, and 80th Divs abreast and by noon general advances up to 2,000 and 3,000 yards were made along the entire Corps front; the resistance was moderate but failure of the air to operate at full strength because of weather and muddy terrain slowed the advance. However, in the estimate of Army headquarters the attack was progressing on schedule. Tonight at 9 o'clock the XX Corps led off its attack with the 95th Div to establish a bridgehead over the MOSELLE; the 90th Div to attack 6 hours after the 95th.

Thursday, 9 November 1944: A final conference for the "big show" was held today at V Corps headquarters with General Hodges, General Collins, and General Gerow in attendance. Long range weather reports for the period 11–16 November do not look too promising at the present time.

At 5:30 this afternoon General Hodges and General Quesada briefed the press on the attack which in its magnitude exceeds anything that has been thrown at the Boche since D-Day. Almost the entire 8th and 9th Air Forces plus heavy bombers from the RAF will participate in the attack; artillery is using some 75 battalions plus rockets; and AAA [antiaircraft artillery] is using a new method of firing green smoke rockets to mark front line positions. The attack will go off anytime between the 11th and 16th and if by the 16th the weather is still bad the attack will undoubtedly go off without air support although as General Quesada added to the correspondents, his fighter-bombers would back up the attack any time regardless of the weather. Into this attack have gone weeks of careful planning, last minute movement of troops, and unceasing efforts to obtain more ammunition. General Collins, as is customary, is extremely optimistic over its success and General Hodges, although he sees hard fighting ahead, does not think the Boche can long stand up under such a coordinated concentrated blow. The press conference which went off extremely satisfactorily in the General's office lasted more than an hour. General Hodges and his three general officers were the guests of General Quesada at the latter's private home in Spa. The delicacy of the evening being plover.

In the VII Corps, 104th Division completed relief of the 1st Div which is now assembling in the FOREST WENAC [Wenau Forest] in rear of the front line positions of the 3rd Armored and 47th Inf, the latter of which is now attached to the 1st Div. V Corps: The 28th Div with the 12th Inf attached consolidated its present front lines against strong enemy pressure. The 99th Div has been attached to the Corps and is now assembling in the vicinity of WIRTZFELD. CCR of 5th Armored Div passed to control of VII Corps in its present position.

The Third Army attack is progressing extremely satisfactorily despite the unusually serious flood condition of the MOSELLE River. The 90th Div crossed it in two places however, and the bridgehead is now approximately five miles deep and three miles wide. The 10th Armored Div will pass through the 90th Div over this bridgehead. Further south, elements of the 95th Div crossed the river in the vicinity of UCKANGE. In the XII Corps sector, rapid advances have been slowed down more by mud than by the light enemy resistance thus far encountered. Gains up to three miles along almost the entire front have been made by the 26th, 35th, and 80th Divs. The 4th and 6th Armored Divs are passing through the 35th and 80th Divisions respectively.

Friday, 10 November 1944: General Eisenhower completed his tour of Ninth and First Army units today and General Hodges went to V Corps at noon to lunch with him and General Bradley. General Simpson came to his office at four o'clock for a final one hour review of the coordinated two Army attack.

The General's main pre-occupation today has been weather. Up until nine o'clock tonight the forecasts for tomorrow were clear and it appeared that the Air Forces would say they could go ahead. However, before ten o'clock the picture had changed completely and by eleven o'clock the decision was definitely made to postpone the attack in hopes of a better day.

The Twelfth Army Group Artillery Officer, General Heins [John H. Hinds],[78] was General Hart's dinner guest this evening and for over an hour was bombarded with questions about why the shortage of ammunition to which he gave answers in no way satisfactory to the four generals present.

There were no changes in the VII Corps beyond last minute regrouping. 28th Div continued to improve its positions with the 1st and 2nd Bns of 110th Inf making progress against pillboxes in the SIMONSKALL-RAFFETSBARND area. The 109th Inf continued to hold VOSSENACK while the 1st Bn of the 109th moved to the north into the gap between the 2nd Bn of 109th and 3rd Bn of 112th and made astonishing progress to within 1,000 yards of HURTGEN. The 393rd Inf started relief of the 39th Inf while the 395th Inf completed relief of CCB 5 Armored Div. The permanent boundary between VII and V Corps with very slight modifications became effective at 1900.

Continued progress was made today by the Third Army in its coordinated attack. The 26th Div which has advanced up to 7½ miles on a 5 mile front mopped up CHATEAU SALINS and HAMPONT. 35th Div after advances of 9 miles on a 6 mile front cleared up VILLIERS [Viviers] and BACOURT in rear of the 4th Armored which has passed through the 35th and is tearing ahead. The 6th Armored Div which likewise is exploiting the gains made by the infantry division, this time the 80th, shot ahead through BUCHEY [Buchy] to LUPPY, an advance of 10 miles. The XX Corps continued to expand its bridgeheads over the MOSELLE which now having reached the high water stage is causing considerable trouble. In the northern bridgehead the 90th Div now has all three regiments across and the bridgehead 6 miles wide and 3 miles deep includes the towns of KERLING-LES-SIERCK [Koecking and Sierck-les-Bains] and KOENIGSMACHER [Koenigsmacker]. The small bridgehead which the 95th Div established farther south has been reinforced but not substantial expanded. On the Corps south flank the 5th Div continues to gain.

There was no news from the Second British Army which continues to regroup along with the Canadian Army for their offensive advance to the east toward the RHINE. WALCHEREN Island has been definitely cleared with an additional 2,000 prisoners being taken yesterday and the operation south of the MAAS River is complete as the Polish Armored Division finished off the last Germans just north of MOERDIJK.

Saturday, 11 November 1944: General Gerow was closeted in the General's office this afternoon from two until almost 5:30. The General is still far from satisfied with the situation in the 28th Division and it is believed that a large part of the conference was taken up with the discussion of what steps to take in its advance and rehabilitation. The main question of the day, of course, was again the weather. Preliminary reports during the day gave no cause for hope and the final report was telephoned to the General in his quarters shortly before twelve o'clock with the answer being, "no."

Regrouping continued in the First Army. The Third Army with armored spearheads continues to drive well ahead although the MOSELLE River, on a rampage, has already done away with two of the temporary bridges erected.

Leon Degrelle,[79] Belgian Rexist Leader, now in Germany, promised over the radio this morning that Germans would dispatch 1,000 buzzbombs unto Belgium today. As usual the traitor was lying although the number passing over Spa during the day was a bit heavier than usual—some two dozen.

Sunday, 12 November 1944: General Hoyt Van Denberg, Commanding the IX Air Force, and Rear Admiral Richard Byrd[80] who said he brought General Marshall's best wishes to General Hodges were guests at the morning conference. After lunch the General left for VII Corps where General Collins tried, but unsuccessfully, to woo away from General Gerow most of the latter's troops. The conference lasted until after five o'clock thus preventing the General from making a visit to the 104th and 4th Divisions as he had tentatively planned to do.

It started snowing shortly after dinner and the weather man, not unexpectedly, told the General that there was 1 in 1,000 chance of sun tomorrow. This poor Major is the most harrassed, worried, and hard working officer on the continent at the present time and should the present situation last beyond the 16th he would undoubtedly be fair meet [meat] for a Section VIII discharge [mental illness].

General [Royal B.] Lord,[81] General [James H.] Stratton,[82] and General Plank were all visitors to the headquarters today discussing "generalities" to General Kean about supply but unable to answer any of his specific questions on individual items. They reported that 12 Liberty ships[83] are expected to enter Antwerp harbor on November 25th and that the ammunition production in the states is not up to par and that a lot of it is being diverted to the Pacific.

Minor gains were made in the 28th Division sector and two companies of the 2nd Bn of the 12th which were cut off temporarily regained contact with the 1st and 3rd only to lose it later. However, Corps is not worried over the situation. The MOSELLE continues to rise to its worst flood in over fifty years washing away several more of the temporary bridges in the Third Army sector. A new boundary between Twenty-One and Twelfth Army Groups went into effect today putting the XIII Corps and some of its troops, including the 84th Division, under operational control of the British and cramming Ninth Army into a small sliver of land.

It is as yet not known nor are there any signs as yet that the Germans have shifted strength away from the First Army sector to meet the threat of the Third Army and in the G-2 Estimate #35 published today, Colonel Dickson expresses the belief that the enemy is capable of an offensive against the Second British and Ninth U. S. Army and that the implementation of this capability is viewed as of high probability—in the customary G-2 language. This attack, it is G-2's belief, will come down the west bank of the MAAS in the SITTARD-MAASTRICHT sector. "It is a desperate gamble by a desperate foe," says the G-2 summary. It is uncertain how much stock General Hodges and higher headquarters put into this estimate but there is no question but that Germans have had time to build-up his smashed and depleted Armored Divisions which with the exception of a small show by the 116th Panzer in the SCHMIDT area and by the abortive attack of the 9th Panzer and 15th Panzer Grenadier Divisions in the MEIGEL [Meijel] area, these have not been used extensively any place on the front during the past month.

Monday, 13 November 1944: The General made a final tour of his combat divisions today preliminary to the "big show." After stopping at VII Corps briefly, he went on to the 1st Division CP, where on top of a hill in a captured German bunker was the personal headquarters of General Huebner. Aside from telling General Hodges, as of course every one in the 1st Division tells everybody else—that the 1st Division fights differently than the rest of the Army—General Huebner was perturbed about decorations. Although the 1st Div is the most decorated division in First Army, General Huebner still insists that his division should receive more. Since Twelfth Army Group has now put a quota on the number of decorations which may be given out per month per outfit, General Huebner's wishes will not, in all probability, be granted. From the 1st Division the General next went to the 4th Div where in the absence of General Barton he had a brief chat with Colonel Rodwell, Asst. Div. Commander. A long talk at the 28th Division with General Davis followed. General Davis' explanation for the failure of the 28th to hold SCHMIDT and its bad showing afterward was that they could not get armor up forward quickly enough because of the terrain. On the way back to the CP the General stopped in at V Corps.

Again tonight the news from IX Tac's weather expert is that bombers will not be able to take off tomorrow from any bases here or in the UK, and consequently once more the attack is postponed. However, the General said definitely tonight that they would go the 16th whether there were bombers or not.

Our front remained static with no change in positions except that in the V Corps area the 1st Bn of the 110th Inf drew back and assembled in the new area. The Third Army continued to push ahead especially in the XII Corps sector where the 4th and 6th Armored Divs followed closely by the 26th and 25th [35th] Inf Divs made advances up to 3 miles. Leading elements of the 80th Division are now within 5 miles of FALKENBURG [Falkenberg or Faulquemont] which is the Corps objective. In the XX Corps sector the flooded MOSELLE is gradually receding and steady progress is being made in the 90th Div bridgehead as the ferrying of armored vehicles across the river continued. The fort at THIONVILLE has been cleared.

Tuesday, 14 November 1944: General Bradley and General [Charles H.] Bonesteel,[84] who it is reported will act as a personal emissary for General Bradley in important matters, arrived this afternoon at three o'clock for a two-day stay. They were closeted with General Hodges for the rest of the afternoon and after supper at The Holmes returned to hear the weather briefing which—in accordance with our expectations—was again discouraging. At 10:30 the final decision was made not to open the attack tomorrow morning.

The 8th and 28th Divisions began today to exchange positions with the 112th moving to the 8th Division sector. Today the 13th Inf will move up to replace the 2nd Ranger Bn moved in to relieve the 2nd Bn of the 112th. The 99th Division has now taken over complete control of the front lines formerly held by the 9th Division and has already officially assumed full responsibility for the 9th Division sector. Further gains were made by Third Army, most notable being the advance of some two miles west of the fortress of METZ, one fort fell during the advance.

In the First Canadian Army sector the 82nd and 101st Divisions have at long last been relieved. Their area being assumed by the 3rd Canadian Division. ANTWERP, it is now learned, will not be available for shipping of normal size until 22 November. In the Second British Army sector a limited attack was made by the XII Corps with the 51st and 53rd Divisions with the intermediate objective of establishing a bridgehead over the NOORD [Noorder] and WESSEM Canals. In the general area of GRAETHEN the VIII British Corps will attack when this bridgehead is established. The XXX Corps, north flank of the Ninth Army, will attack in conjunction with it.

Wednesday, 15 November 1944: The Generals parted ways after lunch today, General Bradley going to Ninth Army for a conference with General Simpson and General Hodges and General Bonesteel leaving for VII Corps front. At VII Corps General Bonesteel left to visit the 1st and 28th Divisions while General Hodges paid his first call to the 104th. He found Terry Allen cocky and confident of success when the drive finally starts. The General also made his first tour of Aachen and returned via V Corps headquarters where he met General Bonesteel.

The weather conference with Major McCall of IX Tac came as has been the custom for the past week promptly at nine o'clock. The news, for the first time, was encouraging and at 1215 General Quesada called General Hodges to say definitely that the 8th Air Force would "visit sometime between 10:30 and 1300—not before 10:30 and not later than one o'clock." At a later hour in the morning, orders went out from First Army headquarters to the units involved that the attack would begin, first bombers starting at 1115. It is not certain tonight whether General Quesada's fighter-bombers would be able to participate or not but at least the RAF, our heavies, and our mediums can perform their job on which so much depends.

The Third Army had much slower slugging today meeting increased enemy opposition. However, in the XX Corps sector the 10th Armored crossed the MOSELLE in force at THIONVILLE and MALLING and the 95th Div attacking from the northwest closed the pincers tighter around the fortress of METZ.

The British XII Corps attack made gains up to 3 miles establishing a bridgehead over the WESSEM canal and capturing intact the lock gates at PANHEEL. Resistance was chiefly in the form of heavy mine fields. In the British VIII Corps front the 15th Scottish Division retook MEIGEL which for the past month has been occupied on and off by the British, Americans and Boche.

The Drive to the Roer River, 16 November–12 December 1944

Thursday, 16 November 1944: The big attack for which General Hodges has been waiting patiently and which General Bradley believes will be the last big offensive necessary to bring Germany to her knees started at 1245 today with a coordinated attack launched by the 104th, 3rd Armored, 1st, and 4th Divisions.

It started with the use of air power in unprecedented strength; heavy bombers 1100 in number, saturated the area in the vicinity of ESCHWEILER and LANGERWEHE starting at 1115. From 1:30 to 3:30 700 of our mediums struck at eight other selected targets and the RAF wound up the afternoon sending over 1150 Lancasters. Although we could hear the American heavies we could not see them. It was not until the overcast cleared into spotty sunlight in the late afternoon that the individual British Lancasters, flying low over the CP, were clearly visible. Rockets were also used in preparation for the attacks and reports indicated that there were, for the first time, no "shorts." So effective was the counterbattery and the bombing that during the first four hours of the attack only 7 shellreps [shelling reports] were reported. However, the enemy troops which were dug-in close to our lines were not affected by the bombing and they, aided by heavy minefields and barbwire rolls, but [put] up considerable small arms and mortar fire against our troops as they started on the road to the Rhine.

As the General said, you can tell nothing about an attack of this nature until after the passage of 48 hours. At midnight the main progress was made by the 3rd Armd Div which with Task Force "Mills" (1st Bn 33rd Armd Regt) advancing to the outskirts of HUSTENRATH [Hastenrath] and Task Force "Love Lady" [Lovelady] (2nd Bn 33rd Armd Regt) capturing WERTH. The 1st Div advanced the 1st Bn of the 47th Inf to the outskirts of GRESSENICH where bitter house to house fighting was still going on tonight. The 4th Div made very little progress in the dark inpenetrable woods against heavily dug-in and camouflaged positions. The 104th Div made limited gains up to 500 yards. The Ninth Army's gains were made before the enemy had a chance to bring its artillery into action, through an area where considerable minefields and other obstacles were reported as not being unusually heavy. The towns of MARIANDORF [Mariadorf], SEIRSDORF [Siersdorf], IMMENDORF, FLOVERICH, and LOVERICH were all captured and the 119th Inf made almost a mile into the eastern edges of WURSELEN. The Ninth Army captured over 900 prisoners during the afternoon while First Army's bag was approximately 100.

Further to the north the Second British Army with the 51st and 53rd Divs advanced as much as four miles drawing nearer to the MAAS, while the Third U. S. Army with the 10th Armd Div on the north leading the way made gains up to four miles. The noose around METZ is being drawn tighter every hour. Gains were also made by the Seventh U.S. Army and by the First French Army. The Boche are now confronted with a drive along a 400 miles front and while he may be able to plug the gap here and there, it is not thought that he can stop for any length of time the combined weight of seven Armies—4 American, 1 French, 1 British, and 1 Canadian.

Friday, 17 November 1944: Today, the second day of the attack, the 3rd Armd Div continued to show the way occupying its objective which included clearing of HASTENRATH and KOTTENICH. In the 1st Div sector the 1st Bn of the 16th Inf, after repulsing several minor counter-attacks continued in house-to-house fighting in HAMICH, while the 2nd Bn of the 26th veered off to the right and drove through wire and mine defenses for a 1,000 yard advance. The 104th Div, which according to the General, "still has much left to learn," did not make any advances during the day.

During the afternoon the General visited VII Corps where he found General Collins optimistic despite the limited gains thus far recorded. General Collins during the day had told the 104th Div in no uncertain terms to get moving and get moving fast. From the VII Corps the General next visited the 4th Div to see General Barton, with whom he had not talked for a long time, where the terrain, the General said tonight, was the toughest he had seen in a long time but he was under the impression that they were going about the attack in the wrong way—running down roads as far as they could instead of advancing through the woods tightly buttoned up yard by yard. General Barton told him that the resistance there was fanatical; one platoon which had tried to infiltrate into our lines was killed to the last man, the members refusing surrender or retreat. On the way back from the 4th the General stopped briefly at 28th Div and then after clearing their way through a monstrous traffic jam caused by the movement of CCB of the 5th Armd (without reconnaissance) to the vicinity of ROTGEN, he came on home.

The weather, not unexpectedly, turned for the worse today and only three groups of fighter-bombers were able to perform their missions in front of the 104th Div. However, it's clear and cool tonight which perhaps bodes well for tomorrow.

The 9th Panzer has now been definitely identified in front of Ninth Army and CCB of the 2nd Armd today had a strong enemy counterattack near PUFFENDORF consisting of 40 to 50 Mark V and Mark VI tanks. However, this was contained and the 29th and 30th Divs made gains in their sector from 1,000 to 3,000 yards. The fighting tonight was still going on in HONGEN and WURSELEN but NEUSEN, BROICHWEIDEN, SETTERICH and most of SEISDORF [Siersdorf] were in American hands. The Third Army likewise continued to push ahead, especially on the [XX] Corps north flank, where the German border was crossed by our patrols and where the 3rd Cav Group reinforced advanced over three miles to

MANDERIN [Manderen] and RITZING. Both commands of the 10th Armd likewise pushed northeast, east, and southeast for considerable gain.

In the Second British Army the noose is being drawn tighter around ROERMOND.

Saturday, 18 November 1944: It was a brilliant, clear, cool day today and the Air had one its best field days since August at Mortain. The 1st Div was loud in its praises of what the fighter-bombers were able to do in loosening up the stiff opposition in front of them. The 16th Inf finally took HAMMICH [Hamich] and held a strong counterattack which was launched by some 300 infantrymen supported by 15 tanks. 104th Div advanced almost a mile to the left of the 3rd Armd Div sector while on the right flank the 8th Inf made a thousand yards against barb wire and heavy small arms, mortar, and artillery fire. Enemy pressure was strong and fighting was intense over practically the entire VII Corps front with the exception of the lines nearest to AACHEN held by the 104th Div where the enemy seems to be slowly pulling out. Heavy fighting also continued to the north where APWEILER and BETTENDORF were cleared and progress made in the center of WARDEN and BROICHWEIDEN. Some 3,000 prisoners have now been taken by the Ninth Army since the start of the offensive.

Third Army now has METZ completely surrounded except for a two mile escape gap. There are reportedly some 6,000 second grade troops in METZ whose escape or surrender is prevented by the Gestapo,[85] and it is believed that house-to-house fighting will be necessary before the city capitulates. Gains ranging up to six miles were made by the 10th Armd Div and the 90th Div and the two corps objectives, BOULAY [Boulay-Moselle] and FLAKENBERG are within three miles of our front line troops. Gains were also made by the Seventh Army and by the Second British Army.

The General did not leave the CP today but called in General Gerow in the afternoon for a three-hour conference and in the evening received Generals Doolittle, Spaatz, and Quesada for another session.

General Collins today told General Hodges that with one or two more days of good weather he thought that the crust could be smashed. Today, he said, there were signs that it was giving in front of the 1st Div and that strong pressure tomorrow and the day after should bring excellent results.

Sunday, 19 November 1944: The 104th Division, prodded into action by General Hodges and General Collins and helped by the advances of their left flank of the XIX Corps, today made gains up to six kilometers along the Corps north flank to Rohe while other elements west of Stolberg advanced 2,000 yards and into the northern outskirts of the town in heavy house-to-house fighting. Some elements were reported last night on the outskirts of Eschweiler. The 1st Div likewise continued to move ahead against stubborn resistance. The story was told today that General Collins gave General Heubner "hell" when the latter protested that the 1st Div was holding the enemy in check. "Hold the enemy in check!" protested General Collins, "I knew you could do that, I want you to advance. This is an offensive!" The 1st did advance in some places more than a mile while the 1st Bn of the 47th Inf, which led the way, advanced to Hill 187 north of Volkenrath [Scherpenseel]. The 18th Inf entering the line between the 26th and 16th advanced its 3rd Bn to the edge of Wenau. The 4th Div continued to meet extensive wire entanglements and mines and there was little change in the front line. Tonight its 3rd Bn took an enemy strongpoint on their enemy front capturing 40 PWs and inflicting heavy casualties.

Today the 8th Div officially assumed responsibility for the 28th Div sector and the 1st Bn of the 109th, which is the last remaining element of the 28th Div to move into their new sector, began its march.

The General today motored to Korlinmunster for a conference with General Collins especially to settle the new temporary boundary between V and VII Corps which goes into effect at midnight tomorrow. Both the V and VIII Corps are scheduled to attack on the 21st. A warning has gone out from First Army headquarters to all Corps and from there to all troops that they may now expect the appearance of the German Air Force in strength. This notice cautioned them to maintain regular intervals in road convoys and to keep all machine guns manned, but today over Korlinmunster, Aachen, and the whole area which was plainly visible, there were nothing but P-47s and P-51s.[86] Seldom before, the General said, had he seen so many U.S. aircraft in one spot. Visibility was perfect up until five o'clock when the rain started to fall. Weather reports for tomorrow indicate that there will be no flying.

On the way home General Hodges stopped in at Eupen for a settlement of the new boundary with General Gerow and left shortly thereafter for Army headquarters.

Third Army continued to make startling gains. Metz is now completely encircled both on its eastern outskirts and also by another ring eight miles east of the city. The 10th Armd Div in the north was across the border in strength on a 6 mile front. Everywhere facing the Third

Army, enemy resistance is decreasing and Tac R [tactical air reconnaissance] had reported a steady stream of German convoys churning up the roads towards SAARBRUCKEN and SARREGEMUINES [Sarreguemines]. The XIX Corps likewise made general mile advances mopping up SETTIRICH [Setterich] reaching SCHEIDEN [Schleiden] and occupying HONGEN, WARDEN and KINZWEILER. Elements of the 84th Div and the 43rd British Div early today had completed the encirclement of GEILENKERCHEN and by midnight the city was completely cleared of enemy by our troops. In announcing the capture of the city, General Montgomery said that the American troops could take most of the credit for it. Gains up to 2 miles were also recorded in several places along the Seventh Army front. Everywhere the Boche is giving way not in a rout but with the exception of the Third Army front only after hard determined fighting.

Monday, 20 November 1944: Substantial progress was recorded all along the First Army front with the exception of the 4th Div area. The 104th Div occupied ROHE, advanced to HELERTH [Hehlrath], cleared STOLBERG and STEINFURTH [Steinfurt], and generally at midnight were sitting everywhere on the outskirts of ESCHWEILER. The 1st Div had stiffer going against heavy mortar and artillery fire, but the 1st Bn of the 47th (attached) took HILL 187 and the 3rd Bn advanced almost a mile. HEINTERN [Heistern] was cleared by the 18th Inf. 4th Div again made little progress against the rugged terrain stubbornly defended by the enemy. The 1st Bn of the 8th, however, made almost a mile to close the gap between the 2nd Bn of the 26th Inf and the 2nd Bn of the 28th Inf.

The 121st Inf, 8th Div, closed last night and moved into assembly positions preparatory to its attack this morning. General Hodges motored to see General Stroh during the afternoon and came back exceedingly well pleased with the tactical planning which had been evolved. General Hodges especially noted the fact that General Stroh thought he was being supported by a remarkable amount of artillery—18 Bns—and was confident of success. Their attack will jump off at nine o'clock although General Hodges said he could wait until eleven o'clock if it looked as if there would be more favorable weather.

Our neighbors to the north, the XIX Corps, likewise continued their advances. ALDENHOVEN, DURBOSLAR, and FREIALDENHOVEN were cleared of the enemy and two battalions of the 119th pushed beyond ALDENHOVEN. A sharp Boche tank counterattack in the vicinity of GEREONSWEILER was repulsed. North of the XIX Corps the British made no gains. The Third U. S. Army likewise continued to push its armored spearheads ahead. FALKENBERG fell, SAAREBOORG-METZ railroad was cut at NOLRING, and METZ was completely in our hands except for isolated pockets and snipers. The three forts still holding out on the outskirts of METZ will be starved out according to present plan. The BBC announced yesterday that the First French Army had reached the RHINE in the vicinity of BALE [Basel] although there was no official confirmation of this tonight.

The pressure is being relentlessly applied to the Boche all along the front and whereas First Army had not taken many prisoners to date, the number of Boche dead and wounded due to our air and artillery fire is considered exceptionally high.

After two solid weeks of 8 A.M. to midnight schedule, the General tonight left the office at 10:30. Frankly, he admitted that he needed some rest. He was pinning much hope on the success of the 8th Div attack tomorrow. If the attack should fail the advance of VII Corps to the north could be seriously hampered. He has the greatest confidence in General Stroh's tactical ability and believes that with a half-way break in the weather—one that would allow at least the Cubs to function—we should push the Boche back a good piece.

Tuesday, 21 November 1944: Because of duties on the "Home Front," the General did not leave the CP today. He was expecting a visit from Mr. Robert Murphy[87] who will be the American Administrator of that section of Germany which we will control after the war and Colonel John Bottiger [Boettiger],[88] the President's son-in-law. However, they were taken to AACHEN by Colonel [Damon M.] Gunn.[89] The General read a Thanksgiving Day message which was recorded by NBC and will be broadcast to the United States; had some new pictures taken by the Signal Corps; and during the afternoon saw, among other officers, General Kenna [Albert W. Kenner], SHAEF Surgeon General, and Colonel Anding.[90] Of greatest interest to the General today was the attack of the 121st Inf towards HURTGEN. The General had instructed General Stroh to go slowly, buttoned up, and to avoid if possible mine casualties. Consequently, he was not disappointed in the limited advances, 400 yards or so, made by the 3rd Bn and the lesser advances made by the 1st and 2nd Bns.

General Hodges and General Hart worked out an artillery plan whereby fire starts in the enemy rear area and works forward (or backward, whichever way you view it) towards our fronts line troops. In this way they hope to remove many of the mortar nests which on all fronts have been furnishing our troops their most bitter and deadly opposition.

Good progress was made by the 104th Div on the Corps north flank.

The 413th cleared 1/3 of the town of Durwiss on the northern outskirts of Eschweiler while in the southwestern suburbs of Eschweiler the 415th advanced slowly from house-to-house. The 1st Div had a tough day making little or no progress as the enemy continued to defend with the greatest stubbornness the Eschweiler-Langerwehe-Duren road with intense fire of all types.

Flying bomb activity was at a new high throughout the day and during the evening although none were visible due to low clouds which hung over Spa and most of our front throughout the day.

Good gains were recorded by the Third Army which had completely cleared Metz with the exception of 5 forts and to the east, especially in the XII Corps sector, where gains up to 6 miles were made. The front before the XV Corps of the Seventh U. S. Army fell apart and the 44th Div advanced almost 10 miles to Saarburg [Saarbourg] with the enemy reportedly retreating in confusion. Advances up to 2 miles were also made by the VI Corps which was preparing to by-pass St Die. It was definitely confirmed today that the 1st DB Div [Division Blindée, French Armored Division] with FFI troops attached reached the Rhine, Belfort falling on the way, and Mulhause is likewise expected to fall in the near future.

General Hodges reported that he had talked with General Bradley over the telephone today, the latter was exceedingly pleased with our advance. No one but the most optimistic sky-gazers expected that we would crack the line in 24 hours and dash to the Rhine in the manner of St Lo break-through. There has been nothing but the stiffest kind of fighting and opposition all along our front and the gains recorded consequently have satisfied everybody.

Wednesday, 22 November 1944: Today was a day of visitors and conferences, starting with the arrival of Mr. Robert Murphy who was accompanied by General McSherry[91] and Col Bottiger, followed by Lt. Gen. [Edward Kenneth] Smart,[92] Australia's representative to the Imperial War Council,[93] followed by luncheon and an afternoon long conference with General Bradley and General Simpson, and topped off before dinner by a conference with General Gerow. The afternoon conference with General Bradley and General Simpson was naturally the most important of the day, centering around the drive of the two Armies towards the Rhine and the blowing of the Roer dam.[94] The RAF it seems has definitely turned down the project which General Hodges considers to be of the utmost importance and now the time to have it blown. Sufficient pressure may possibly be laid on the RAF so that a "yes" will be forthcoming before it is too late.

Foul weather—and prospects are that it will continue for another week—did not halt the 104th Div which cleared DURWISS, advanced to PUTZEHOLN [Pützlohn], and completely cleared ESCHWEILER which was found to be practically a "ghost city" because of our previous heavy artillery and air bombardment. Enemy resistance, as night fell, decreased as the 414th moved northeast toward WEISWEILER. The 1st Div had stiffer fighting in attacking towards LANGERWEHE; the 1st Bn of the 47th Inf finally took HILL 187 after two days of exceedingly heavy fighting which included massed artillery concentration from 18 Bns of the VII Corps Artillery. The 8th Inf and 22nd Inf made small gains over the worst terrain that perhaps the First Army has even faced, not excluding hedgerow country in Normandy.

Against this same terrain and heavy resistance the 121st Inf likewise made gains which could be measured in terms of yards. There was no activity, as is now usual, on the VIII Corps front. Above us the XIX Corps was temporarily held up and in the southern part of its sector, elements of the 30th Div were forced to withdraw from HOLN [Lohn] because of heavy enemy pressure. Gains on the Third Army front continued to be in terms of two or three miles, and on the XII Corps southern front contact is soon expected with elements of the 44th Div which today cleared SAARBURG. The 79th Div in the XV Corps, Seventh Army sector, is moving on toward STRASBOURG and made a gain of some 10 miles during the day. Enemy withdrawal seems to be constant everywhere along the VI Corps front and BBC announced tonight that the 1st French Armd Div had taken MULHAUS and had completely cleared BELFORT with the exception of some resistance on the eastern approaches to the city.

A new element in today's fighting was the now corroborated news from Colonel Patterson and Colonel Dickson that LIEGE is being subjected to steady V-1 bombardment. 12 of the missiles landed in the town proper causing damage and casualties to U. S. military personnel as well as civilians; others fell in the periphery of the city and in towns nearby. No bombs have been recorded for the last 36 hours having fallen on ANTWERP or BRUSSELS and it now appears that the Boche is going to disconcert whatever defense we wish to place against the bombs by shifting his target area at will. However, if approved by higher headquarters, Colonel Patterson intends to move a battalion of anti-aircraft to the V Corps sector to intercept as many of the V-1s as possible. 111 actually crossed the First Army sector during the day. Colonel Patterson said that experience has shown that if hit, 50% of the ro-bo's will explode in mid-air, the other half will be deflected in uncertain flight to the ground. General Gerow, it is understood, has approved a certain section of his sector as suitable for location of this anti-aircraft battalion. Reasons governing a now active defense against the V-1 weapon are two-fold: 1—The danger to our troops and troop installations now seems greater than before, and 2—we can no longer permit, from a humanitarian point of view, Belgian cities to be thus attacked without taking some steps to prevent it. Thus far there is no indication that the bombs dropping within a few miles of SPA have been directed on it but it would surprise no one if this were to prove to be the case in the next few days.

Thursday, 23 November 1944—"Thanksgiving Day": Thanksgiving Day was celebrated by the General in a long tour of the front accompanied by General Kean. They started early this morning for the 8th Div where they met General Collins and General Gerow in addition to General Stroh. To the latter the General said in emphatic terms that he was not satisfied with the progress being made; that the minefields had not proven to be as much of an obstacle as people feared and that the progress, or rather lack of it, made by the division showed lack of confidence and drive. He made it quite clear that he expected better results on the morrow. As if to prove his point that the division was not going ahead as it should, one battalion went out later that afternoon and captured 90 prisoners. From the 8th Div both generals went to the 4th Div where they joined General Barton for a conference and for a Thanksgiving dinner. They returned to the Army CP shortly before four o'clock. None of the Generals attended the Red Cross party as promised, but Gus and Louie, the two chefs, had put on a magnificent spread at The Holmes, in addition to decorating the house and the table in colorful "A" designs[95] and for each person there was an individual cake on which had been stenciled in pink frosting the name of each officer. Following the dinner the General consented to relax long enough to see the gay movie, "Janie." He, however, returned to the office for a conference with General Kean and Colonel Dickson, leaving shortly before midnight.

The 104th Div had slower going during the day against heavy artillery and mortar fire. Fighting continued in PUTZLOHN and several counterattacks of considerable strength supported by four or five tanks were launched consistently throughout the day. However, we lost no ground and the 3rd Bn of the 414th Inf managed by continuous attack to reach the western outskirts of WEISWEILER. The 1st Div likewise drove ahead despite heavy fighting, approaching LANGERWEHE and WEISWEILER from the south. The effect of our artillery fire was attested by Major Swearingen, Liaison Officer to the VII Corps, who stated that more than twelve truck loads of dead Boche had been taken during the day from Hill 232, one of the toughest spots which the 1st Div has had to crack in its present offensive. In the 4th Div front, the 3rd Bn of the 8th Inf made almost a mile in the Wenau forest. There were no changes of position of any note along the entire V Corps front.

Along other fronts the British drew up within a mile of Venlo and the enemy is now driven almost completely east of the Maas. However, since the ground on the other side of the river dominates the British front, movement can be made only by night. South of us, the Third Army made no progress along the XX Corps front and progress was limited along the XII Corps front. Opposition appears to be stiffening before General Patton's Army. However, the front continues to loosen for the Seventh Army and there were reports last night that American and French troops were fighting within Strasbourg. The 1st French Armd Div is now 8 miles north of Mulhouse and St Die which has been such a hard nut for the VI Corps to crack is reportedly completely in our hands.

V-1 bombardment of Liege continued throughout the day causing, as the communiques say, "casualties and damage." Because of poor visibility Colonel Patterson's anti-aircraft outfits have been unable to effectively combat these flying bombs.

Friday, 24 November 1944: The General did not leave the CP during the day. During the afternoon he interrupted his work long enough to receive M. Joseph Leonard, Burgomeister of Spa, who represented his homages and said how grateful the people were for their liberation. Ten minutes of pleasantries finished off the Burgomeister and a few minutes later the General received M. Dehalge and another gentleman, both high worthies of the town, who presented him with a box made from the old wood of Spa.

Hampered again by bad weather which curtailed flying activities and made even Cub patrols difficult, the Army was not able to chalk up any remarkable gains during the day. However, the 104th Div clear[ed] Putzlohn after two days of hard fighting and pushed deeper into the western part of Weisweiler in stiff fanatical house-to-house fighting. Task Force "Richardson" composed of the 2nd Bn of the 47th Inf plus the 3rd Bn of the 32nd Armd Regt captured Huckeln [Hücheln]. 1st Div made gains of 300 up to 900 yards in heavy fighting. Excellent gains were made by the 8th and 12th Inf in the wooded area west of Gross-

HAU. V Corps front continues to be sticky and the largest gains chalked up by the 121st was 350 yards by the 2nd Bn. There was nothing to report from VIII Corps except for a German broadcast in English to front line troops which artillery of the 83rd Div silenced in practically no time at all.

It is now confirmed that the Second French Armd and 79th Divs have Strasbourg under control and that more important, they have captured intact the three bridges which lead across the Rhine; a small but nonetheless important bridgehead has been established into Kehl across the river. Gains made by the Ninth Army and Third Army were limited as the Boche threw in fresh armor in their counterattacks.

20 Liberty ships are due to arrive in Antwerp tomorrow although the port capacity in [is] considerably greater, V-1 and V-2 bomb interference has limited daily capacity to an estimated 60,000 tons. We have two new Brigadier Generals—Robert W. Wilson, G-4, and John Rogers, Surgeon. Going home tonight and remarking that the sky was unusually clear, the General was optimistic that tomorrow would bring the good weather for which he so long has been anxiously waiting.

Saturday, 25 November 1944: As predicted by the General the weather turned out fine this morning permitting the Air an opportunity to go about its job again. The General did not leave the CP, having a conference with General Lee this morning, but good news of the attack continued to come into him during the day.

414th Inf was fighting three-quarters of the way through Weisweiler and Task Force "Richardson" composed of the 1st Bn of 3rd Armd Div with 2nd Bn of 47th Inf made good progress of over a mile in the direction of its objective, Franzhofen [Frenzerburg]. 1st Div continued to attack against extremely heavy resistance; the 18th Inf is still fighting for Hill 203; 2nd Bn of the 22nd Inf advanced 3/4 of a mile to within a mile of Kleinhau. The attack against Hurtgen in the V Corps area did not go well—CCR of the 5th Armd entered the fray this morning but armored elements were unable to advance beyond the edge of the woods. No gains were recorded by the Ninth Army but the Third Army and the Seventh Army drove ahead; the Third Army against a defense which appears to be again consolidating.

General Plank was guest at The Holmes tonight and corrected the figures originally given that Antwerp would take 60,000 tons a day. He said the present estimate was 40,000 tons, two-thirds of which was going to the American troops. He saw no reason, however, that the port capacity should not be in time considerably greater. The railroad situation, he said, was still not up to par considering the amount of time that we had had to repair it and bring in new rolling stock. However, this is outside of his control.

Sunday, 26 November 1944: The General went to VII Corps at eleven o'clock this morning and after conference and luncheon with General Collins motored to the CP of 104th Div which is in the middle of battered and broken ESCHWEILER. He found Terry Allen not looking particularly well but "cocky," and, said the General when he finds one of his officers like that, he never worries about it. Apparently General Collins feels that the 104th Div after a slow start has performed in excellent manner. General Hart says his whole artillery section functions beautifully according to the book and what the General particularly likes thus far of what he had seen of the 104th is there ability to button up tight and hold the place tight once they have taken it. There is no record yet of the 104th giving ground.

From the 104th Div CP the General motored out a short distance to reach the AUTOBAHNSTRASSE,[96] one of Hitler's fourteen "miracle" roads. This one starts outside of AACHEN and runs to COLOGNE and the General wished to inspect it for the reason that General Quesada would like to have a section of it for a fighter-bomber landing strip. The General came back enthused over the idea.

Upon his return the General said he had seen only one German in the wilderness of these battered and crumpled buildings and this particular German was being given the devil by an MP for blocking traffic with his cart. The General said it gave him pleasure to see destruction thus wrought on Germany for a change instead of on the villages and cities of France and Belgium. Very little enemy artillery, according to the General, had been fired during the day—in fact, he was not sure he had heard any enemy rounds—for the one principal reason that General Hart's Cubs were up and whenever the Cubs are up, the Boche does not dare show his flame.

Progress during the day was as follows: FRENZ was cleared by the 414th; the outskirts of LANGERWEHE were reached; the 121st advanced to the edge of HURTGEN which they report still stoutly defended. This reads perhaps small in type but into these yardage gains went thousands of shells, tons of bombs, and many lives.

Gains were also recorded on the Third and Seventh Army fronts especially in the latter where the link around the Boche west of the RHINE is being thrown constantly tighter.

Monday, 27 November 1944: General Stroh, worn out from two years of steady combat duty, and saddened by the death of his son, a Fortress pilot, requested 20 days leave in the United States. A request, approved by General Gerow who believed that under the existing circumstances General Stroh could not do justice to a divisional command, was put in yesterday and General Hodges recommended to General Bradley at least two months leave in the states. This was approved and the following changes are to take place today: General [William G.] Weaver,[97] Assistant Division Commander of the 90th Div, is to become CG of the 8th Div; Col [Joseph M.] Tully,[98] well known leader of the 4th Cav Group, will replace him with the 90th Div; and Colonel McDonald [John C. MacDonald][99] for whom General Hodges has been trying to find a field command for a long time, has finally been released by Third Army (this is the third try) to take over Colonel Tully's job with the Cavalry Group. General Weaver motored up from the 90th Div this morning and after a short talk with General Hodges left promptly for V Corps.

The other visitors during the day were General Brereton, General Ridgway, and staff. Bas reliefs of the RHINE River were laid out in the General's office and for two hours there was a general discussion as to when, where, and how the airborne army would next make its appearance. However, the 101st and 82nd Divs, the former of which was only withdrawn from the line yesterday, will not be ready for another engagement until February and, of course, it is everybody's hope that by that time employment of the airborne troops will not be necessary.

The biggest news of the day was that HURTGEN, which has caused General Hodges so much worry and which has slowed down our advance in the Corps right sector, finally fell. Although the town was not altogether cleared by nightfall, today the 1st Bn of the 13th Inf was firmly entrenched in the northeast outskirts of the town, while the 2nd Bn of the 121st Inf was in the middle of the town. These two battalions, working from opposite directions, should clean up this strongpoint tomorrow.

Good flying weather enabled our fighter-bombers to deal with several enemy tanks and self-propelled guns which were in this sector.

The news from the VII Corps front was that LANGERWEHE was partially cleared. This town was a major road-center and the Germans brought up additional infantry units to defend it. The fighting was everywhere stiff and the Boche made more than abundant use of mortar fire which now is their principal and most effective weapon. This fire prevented the 104th Div from making any progress towards LAMERS-

DORF. The 4th Div attacking towards GROSSHAU and KLEINHAU reached the outskirts of the first named town.

Buzz-bombs continued to "phhhht" overhead all day long. AA the day before yesterday knocked down seven and today claimed three. Thus far 90mm fire has proven completely ineffective because of the low altitude at which the robos are flying. AW fire has accounted for all of those brought down to-date. One of the robos landed in the Base Echelon but reports of casualties are not in as yet. Another, landing near the airfield at LIEGE, caused six of our Colonels to dive into the dust as they prepared to board Al Zwink's plane for a 72 hour leave in London. More than three thousand people are now homeless in LIEGE and the Germans put forward the theory yesterday in their propaganda that the reason they were subjecting LIEGE to such continuous bombardment was that a higher headquarters was located in the city.

Forts also flew over the CP today at exceptionally high altitude and the General is praying for good weather tomorrow although weather reports indicate the contrary. He still is optimistic over the progress made, and tonight he repeated, the second night in a row, that he believed the war would be over in two months.

Tuesday, 28 November 1944: The big news of the day was that HURTGEN, for so many weeks a thorn in the side of our troops, fell shortly after noon. Surrounded on all four sides the Boche put up terrific resistance from the cellars of the badly battered town but when things started to get too warm, they tried to make a run for it only to be mowed down by our men who were angered at the Boche firing at Red Cross personnel and in general by the hard relentless fighting which had gone before. In the end, some 200 prisoners were taken, and the total German dead was considerably higher. Later in the afternoon the 1st Bn of the 13th Inf moved on almost a mile to cut the KLEINHAU-BRANDENBURG [Brandenberg] road. The 474th [Fighter] Group meanwhile put 67 out of 70 Napalm bombs[100] on KLEINHAU, leveling it by fire to the earth. Troops, however, were unable to take advantage of this bombardment on the town or what was left of it, and were unable to occupy it during the day. In the VII Corps sector, fighting was still going on in INDEN and LAMERSDORF was approximately half cleared against heavy fire. The 1st Bn of the 18th Inf moved, house-by-house, to LANGERWEHE, while the 3rd Bn of the 26th cleared JUNGERSDORF up to the railroad tracks.

Flying weather until fairly late in the day was good. From their side, the Boche put over their customary number of flying bombs, six of which fell in or near VERVIERS. Because of the danger existing at LIEGE, Major Zwink has been ordered to use only the St. TROND field.

Above us, in the XIX Corps sector, KOSLER [Koslar] and KIRCHEBURG [Kirchberg] were cleared and the 29th and 30th Div sectors run almost to the ROER River. XIII Corps regrouped as the 84th and 102nd Divs prepared to attack tomorrow morning. The 78th Div is closing in the XIII Corps area today and the XVI Corps is on route to TONGRES. The 75th and 106th Divs have been earmarked for the Ninth Army and are expected to arrive in December, while the 12th Armd Div, previously assigned to the Ninth Army, is now going to Seventh Army.

There were no reports of any changes in the Second British Army sector but to the south of us Third and Seventh Armies' steady gains from one to three miles were made, especially in the middle of the Third Army sector and north of STRASBOURG.

General [Joseph A.] Holly,[101] who formerly served at Fort Benning in the Motor Maintenance Division when the General was Commandant of the [Infantry] school, was guest at dinner tonight. General Holly is now a tank expert serving with the War Department.

Wednesday, 29 November 1944: The General was busy throughout the day with visitors and army administrative matters. In the morning he saw General Auran [Aurand]; and General [Hugh T.] Mayberry[102] and Colonel Davidson [Paul R. Davison],[103] Assistant Division Commander and Chief of Staff respectively of the 99th Inf Div. Colonel McDonald [MacDonald] who is to assume command of the 4th Cav Group came in for lunch and the General and he had a fine chat. A few words of advice that the General had to give were to the effect that Colonel "Mac" should take his time, become acquainted with the terrain, and the personnel of his "Task Force." Not unexpectedly, General Patton tried to keep Colonel McDonald there by promising him, "but in the future the command of a Cavalry Group or an Infantry Regiment" in the Third Army. Colonel McDonald declined to wait. He is obviously tickled over his assignment and especially over the chance to serve again under General Hodges—both of which sentiments he expressed frequently to Bill who took him to VII Corps in the afternoon. In the afternoon the general received, for a three-quarter hour visit, Leland Stowe[104] of the National Broadcasting System and William Shirer[105] of the Columbia Broadcasting System.

Throughout the day good news continued to come to the General's office of the progress made by the 4th and 8th Divs. Colonel McKee's 8th Regt advanced almost a mile towards HARDTHOF [Hof Hardt] while the 5th Armd Div cleared out KLEINHAU and advanced north to GROSHAU [Grosshau] which later in the day was taken by the 3rd Bn of the 22nd Inf. The air in the afternoon had a fine time over DEREICHSWEILER [Derichweiler] and GEICH, as well as acting in direct support of the 104th Div and the 1st Div.

LANGERWEHE and LAMERSDORF were officially cleared by midnight but north of these towns at INDEN the Boche managed to take possession of the bridge across the INDE River and blow it, which was a surprise blow to the 413th Inf fighting to control the town. The 26th Inf advanced over a mile to enter MERODE. Late today Cos E & F were cut off and the last communication from them was by means of a Sergeant who came through about midnight. Their poor roads make it difficult for our troops to bring up supporting weapons and to keep contact. However, it is expected that contact will be re-established without too much difficulty tomorrow.

A new boundary (temporary) between V and VII Corps became effective at noon today while at the same time the 5th Armd Div less CCR was attached to VII Corps. The move of the 83rd Div to relieve the 4th Div starts tomorrow, and General Hodges, through a telephone call with General Middleton this afternoon, also arranged for the transfer of another TD [tank destroyer] Bn to strengthen VII Corps front. General Collins telephoned the General this evening to say that fighting was exceptionally hard in the 1st Div area and that it was necessary to kill rather than capture members of the 3rd Para [Parachute] Div. This division, which was one of the best faced by our troops early in the Normandy campaign, has been re-established and although the men are not of as high caliber as their predecessors, they are fighting with the same fanatical fervor.

Two buzz-bombs caused minor excitement tonight, one clearing the house by only a few hundred feet and causing such vibration that a mirror was wrenched from a third story wall and hurled across the other side of the room; the second gliding in to a loud three-point landing about a mile away from the house lifting the floors a foot or so before setting them down to rest. The last explosion also took several windows out of the Brittanique [Britannique] Hotel, splattering glass far enough to cut the sergeant sitting at the information desk.

Steady gains were made by the Third Army during the day, especially by the 90th Div. Elements of which reached the SAAR River south of MERZIG. The 95th Div, operating below the 90th, also made substantially larger gains along a three mile front. The Ninth Army, attacking with its XIII Corps in a northeasterly direction, reached the edge of LINDERN and captured the high ground east of BEECK [Beek]. The XIX Corps now controls all of its sector west of the key RUHR [Roer] River.

Precise news is still difficult to obtain from the Seventh Army front where the lines fluctuate from minute to minute. However, the 79th Div pushed north from STRASBOURG to the vicinity of BISCHWEILER [Bischwiller], while good progress was made in clearing the enemy from the general area west of MULHAUS . One sizeable pocket of resistance southwest of MULHAUS with escape to the enemy denied should bring forth a fine bag of prisoners. In the Second British Army there were no changes in the front lines, the 49th British Div began movement to the First Canadian Army sector and it may be that the NIJMEGEN bridgehead will be effectively exploited in strength.

Thursday, 30 November 1944: The big news of the day was that after consistently refusing to tackle the job, the RAF has finally consented to try to blow the ROER dams. They are scheduled to undertake the job sometime about noon tomorrow, weather permitting.

The General left this afternoon for V and VII Corps, arriving back here in time to entertain a group of important industrialists from the United States. They included: Duncan W. Fraser, President of American Locomotive Co.; S. E. Skinner, Vice-President of Oldsmobile Division, General Motors Corp.; Clarence H. Stall, President of Western Electric Company; Charles Kendrick, President of Schlage Lock Co., producing bomb tail fuses and other ordnance products; Stewart W. Cramer, Jr., President of Cramerton Mills, Inc., producing cotton twill and nylon parachute cloth; and Frederick C. Crawford, President of the National Association of Manufacturers; also Brig. Gen. Albert J. Browning,[106] Assistant Director of Materiel Procurement of Army Service Forces. The General entertained the party at drinks in the office adjoining his and he and General Kean were hosts to dinner at the Senior Officers' Mess afterward. Tomorrow they will make a tour of AACHEN and the front line troops.

Tonight it developed that the TAC R and other reports of considerable troop movement, both of infantry and tanks in the lower V Corps and VIII Corps sectors, are not being considered as a serious threat.

Hard fighting continued on all fronts during the day; the 104th is still having a terrific fight in INDEN and in the 1st Div sector the two companies of the 26th Inf which were cut off yesterday in MERODE have still not been contacted; the 4th Div made good progress although forced to go slowly because of heavy minefields; the 47th Inf has finally been relieved and is returning to V Corps sector.

Friday, 1 December 1944: General Hodges motored to MAASTRICHT this morning for a conference with General Eisenhower and General Simpson. Uppermost in which was the question of the dam. General Quesada went along to lend support to the General's arguments and Colonel Carter, Army Engineer, also accompanied the General to answer any technical questions which might arise.

General Simpson's Ninth Army in the XIX Corps sector is now on the west bank of the River ROER and Corps and Division Commanders are urging him to make the crossing now. The opposition against his troops has not been as tough as that against ours. We have suffered some 8,000 casualties since the drive began on the 16th and have taken almost 7,000 prisoners.

Upon the General's arrival back at Army CP he had a short talk with General [George H.] ("Daddy") Weems,[107] Assistant Commandant of the Infantry School, who is touring the front as an observer. Robo Bombs were scarce during the day—they were heavy over MAASTRICHT while the General was there—but shortly after midnight tonight one landed a mile due east of the house and two others cut off above the house landing between SPA and VERVIERS. Overzealous MPs suggested that the house be awakened and its occupants take refuge in the bomb shelter. This suggestion was vetoed.

The attack on the dams was postponed because of bad weather until tomorrow. Meanwhile First Army troops slugged it out along the line. INDEN is not yet clear nor has contact been established with the two companies in MERODE.[108] The 8th Inf was held up by heavy minefields; the 12th and 26th Inf, however, the former from the northwest and the latter from the southwest, made good progress toward GEY through dense forests and over poor roads which were obstructed by many felled trees. 1st Bn of the 12th advanced 800 yards to the high ground overlooking GEY while the 1st Bn of the 22nd advanced almost three-quarters of a mile southwest. The 8th Div with CCR of the 5th Armd attached continued its attack on BRANDENBERG. The 1st Bn of the 13th advanced 700 yards to coordinate 059360 while the 2nd and 3rd Bns made only 400 yards against heavy resistance. The 3rd Bn of the 28th, however, advancing on BRANDENBERG from the southwest made almost a mile. The 60th Inf moved to LAMERSDORF as the 47th closed at CAMP ELSENBORN. The start of the rotation of the 83rd and 4th Divs which was scheduled to begin tomorrow has been postponed until 3 December.

Good gains were made on other Army fronts. LINNICH was reported almost cleared by the 406th Inf in the XIII Corps sector and LINDERN was reported completely cleared. The XX Corps of General Patton's Third Army drew closer to MERZIG and SAARLAUTERN and most of the west bank of the SAAR—some nine miles has been cleared in the 10th Armd Div zone. Today the Third Army reported that since 8 November it had taken 25,000 prisoners. Second British Army is sitting still.

Saturday, 2 December 1944: The General visited VII Corps headquarters this afternoon and 4th Division headquarters where he saw Generals Barton, Gerow, Weaver, and Blakely [Blakeley]. He came back to report that relief of the 4th Div is not going to happen any too soon as its troops are obviously tired and at the end of their rope. He also said that the participation of a combat command of the 3rd Armd in the coordinated night attack planned between 104th Div and 1st Div has been cancelled because of the conviction of General Rose that the ground is too damp and his tanks would be road bound in consequence thereof. The General said that he knew that this coming from General Rose could be considered as an actual fact. The General said he did not think the plans for the night attack were particularly good but under the existing conditions they were probably the best that could be put forward. Combat Team 330 of the 83rd is closing tonight in the VII Corps area and will start to relieve the 22nd Inf tomorrow.

Ample proof was offered of the fatigue of the 22nd Inf this morning when a counterattack in battalion strength over-ran Co K and Co I and reached a point only a few yards away from the Battalion CP, before it stopped. By noon the counterattack was under control but not without loss to us.

Little progress was made by V Corps during the day towards BRAN-DENBERG. CCR attacked along the KLEINHAU-BRANDENBERG road but mines and direct artillery fire, the latter of which destroyed much of their radio equipment, made progress limited. During the day the 413rd cleared INDEN west of the IND [Inde] River.

For the second day running the attack of the RAF on the dams was postponed and although it is supposed to go off tomorrow the time is not yet set.

Sunday, 3 December 1944: The RAF's bombing of the URFT River dams today was a "dud." As a matter of fact, the General was of the impression that no bombs were dropped. General Hart's sound and flash equipment in the V Corps picked up nothing at the time of the bombing and preliminary aerial reconnaissance showed the dam completely undamaged with no craters in the immediate vicinity thereof. Whether no bombs were dropped or whether they all dropped in the water is a question which cannot be answered until a full report comes in. 300 bombers made the effort shortly after 9:45 today and, weather permitting, they will attack it again tomorrow. This failure of the RAF was, of course, a disappointment to the General and to the staff but there were other more encouraging pieces of news.

Attacking during the night, two battalions of the 104th Div successfully crossed the IND River and by six o'clock tonight the 3rd Bn of the 415th Inf had cleared the enemy from LUCHERBERG. In so doing the 104th Div drove south a considerable amount of enemy which fell into the hands of the 1st Bn of the 16th Inf, which this morning advanced almost a mile to occupy LUCHEM. The total bag of prisoners from this operation was over 300. Construction of bridges across the IND River started at once and by midnight tonight one was completed. Some TD's and tanks have already crossed to the other side. However, because of the constant enemy artillery fire zeroed in on the locations of bridge building, it is doubtful whether they will stand without damage for any length of time. Further south in the 4th Div sector the 22nd Inf was relieved during the day by the 330th Inf. The 22nd assembled in the rear area and tomorrow morning early will start to move to the 83rd Div zone.

In the V Corps sector the 8th Div with CCR of 5th Armd Div attached made substantial progress. CCR reached and occupied BRAN-DENBERG and advanced 600 yards further towards BERGSTEIN. 28th and 121st Inf likewise made progress, one company of the 3rd Bn 121st Inf clearing out an enemy pocket which was caught between our forces and capturing a total of 170 PWs.

Perhaps the most interesting news of the day was that as predicted by our headquarters shortly beforehand the Boche Air Force returned in strength today. Some 50 planes being reported over the VII Corps sector; some 60 over the V Corps sector. They were in the main ME-109s and appeared to be piloted by novices or at least inexperienced pilots. General Thorson, on his way back from VII Corps, heard a plane pass 150 feet over his car and got out to take a look. The plane had not strafed him even though he was in a staff car and was not aware of the plane's presence. This plane, along with three others, banked and General Thorson started to dive towards the ditch but the plane without apparent reason veered off the road and proceeded to strafe an empty field 200 yards to the left, kicking up little clods of dirt but doing no damage to anything or anybody. Major Bach, our 1iaison officer to the 8th Div at the present time, jumped into four foxholes on his way back from HURTGEN to EUPEN, but the only damage he saw was one jeep which had been riddled. Two Cubs were lost during the day because of this action but a grand total of 41 destroyed and 10 probables was claimed by AA units at the end of the day. Colonel Patterson said there might be some overlapping and another day's checking would be required before accurate figures could be given. The planes ranged as far deep into our territory as EUPEN and there were no reports of bombs being dropped. Our aircraft were confined to their bases and, therefore, did not engage the enemy aircraft and were unable to attack this "on-slaught" by the GAF [German Air Force].

Another interesting fact is that for the first time today in over two months there were no flying bombs reported directly over SPA. It appears that the Boche have shifted their zones of flight, doubtless having knowledge of the success of our AA in shooting them down. The General also added that it would not be improbable to suspect that sooner or later they would run out of these robos because of the heavy damage which continues to be dealt to their industrial output by our strategic bombing. Tonight Colonel Patterson experimented with "artificial moonlight." The bright lights thrown by a searchlight battalion shooting its beams into a low overcast were seen tonight by Bill while returning to the house before midnight said that it was almost as bright as day. This experimentation is for the purposes of finding out whether such lights can effectively aid a night attack.

Minor gains were recorded all along the Ninth Army, Third Army, and Seventh Army fronts. One of the German commentators remarked today that "it may surprise General Eisenhower to learn" that the First Army is far more aggressive than the Ninth. Our casualties are at the present time higher than our PW total but that, of course, does not take into account the number of German dead and wounded. Major Bach said that along the strip of road near HURTGEN, and without getting out of his car because of the minefields bordering the road, he counted no less than 120 Boche dead. A similar report came in from Major Boyd who had visited LAMERSDORF. It is fighting of an intensity and difficulty equaled perhaps only by that in the hedgerow country and while we are wearing down German manpower the gains to the outsiders may seem measured in yards. However, no one expected a break-through such as occurred at ST LO. The Germans seem to have committed or about to commit west of the RHINE the bulk of all they have left and no matter how slow our advance, if we destroy it, the days of the German Wehrmacht are at an end.

Monday, 4 December 1944: The General and General Kean motored this afternoon to Luxembourg passing on the way the mud covered trucks and unshaven worn faces of the men of the 22nd Inf who had just been relieved in the line. The General said later that he wished that everyone had had a chance to see those men. Upon arrival at Group headquarters shortly after four o'clock they both went into conference with General Bradley and General Simpson. Before the conference was over they learned that the second RAF attempt to blow the dam (at 3:15) had been unsuccessful. Hits were made on the dam but no damage was done. After six o'clock the General came to his quarters at the Alpha Hotel and at 7:30 sat down to a magnificent dinner featured by steak "How would you like it?" and ice cream with melted chocolate sauce. (Group's mess has become much better, according to Major Hansen,[109] since General Bradley and he visited First Army mess at The Holmes). General Bradley has somewhat recovered from his illness of last week but is still suffering from hives which have swollen his face. He is still under doctor's care. Throughout the evening the heavy crack of 90mm guns was heard—for almost the first time since we left the beaches. A later report said that 13 enemy aircraft over the city during the evening on reconnaissance and AA claimed 3 Categories "A."[110] After dinner the General saw a movie and after the movie was over the conference was once again resumed. The results of which are primarily as follows: We will get from the Ninth Army the 78th Div which has just closed in their area as well as the 106th Div which is to be unloading at present at Le Havre. With these two divisions V Corps will be able to put on a large scale attack. The General also learned that, apparently under direction from Washington, the Eighth Air Force will be used more in the future for direct support of troops instead of strategic bombing. Consequently First Army is to submit again and keep submitting a list of its first priority targets which along with those of other Armies will be considered by the Air Force.

There were only minor changes in the front line during the General's absence. The 1st Div regrouped forces and prepared for relief by the 9th Div. No offensive action was scheduled but in the V Corps sector gains were made towards BERGSTEIN and the attack will be resumed tomorrow.

Tuesday, 5 December 1944: The General started back at nine o'clock this morning and against almost continual two-way traffic—tank battalions moving both ways, TD battalions moving both ways, and the 83rd Div and 22nd Inf still finishing off their moves—made Army headquarters by 11:30.

General Thorson informed General Hodges that Colonel Throckmorton had left for Le Havre to supervise the movement of the 106th Div to our area and that relief of the 1st Div was proceeding according to schedule. He also gave the General the unhappy news that once again for the third time the British bombed the ROER dam but without effect. Information coming through later in the day corrected this report and it now appears that the British were unable to drop any bombs because of bad visibility. General Middleton was a visitor during the afternoon and in addition to certain key personnel matters they discussed the transfer of the 2nd Div. General Gerow arrived later in the afternoon and was closeted with the General until after six o'clock discussing plans for the coming V Corps offensive.

After dinner tonight the General saw a ten-minute short made by the Signal Corps the purpose of which is to stimulate war production of critical items especially ammunition back in the states. Both he and General Kean thought the film was a magnificent one.

The news from the front today was as follows:

VII Corps: Minor counterattacks launched against the 104th Div in the LUCHENBERG [Lucherberg] area during the day resulting in destruction of four enemy tanks. 1st Div consolidated positions and prepared for relief by the 9th Div with the 26th Inf already closed in the division's new assembly area in the vicinity of AUBEL. The 39th Inf took its place in the line. The 16th Inf took over the area held by the 60th Inf and the latter is moving north tomorrow into the 1st Div sector. There were some enemy aircraft operating over VII Corps tonight but no damage has been reported.

In the V Corps sector the most important news of the day was the capture of BERGSTEIN by CCR of the 5th Armd Div. BERGSTEIN had already been heavily bombed and shelled and in what was left of the town the resistance was not as stubborn as had been anticipated.

In the Third Army sector the big news of the day was that the 95th Div made a second crossing of the SAAR River and established a bridgehead at LISDORF, striking gains were also made in the XII Corps sector where CCB of the 4th Armd Div advanced almost eight miles to reach BENING [Béning-lès-St. Avold] and SCHMITTVILLE [Schmittviller].

Resistance in the Seventh US Army against the 79th Div was strong and Hagenau was not taken as anticipated. Further south, however, the pocket below Strasbourg is gradually being whittled down.

There are now a thousand and one indications that the Boche has moved Fifteenth Army and most of the divisions therein from Holland where they opposed a crossing of the First Canadian Army and the British Second when the latter was operating in that sector, to our front and two more threatened zones. To replace these troops the enemy has resorted to flooding and there were several breaches in the dikes visible yesterday. It is now believed that he will keep in Holland only a thin shell across the river and special task forces which in the event of Allied or Canadian attack will proceed with the customary German demolitions.

Wednesday, 6 December 1944: The General visited VII and V Corps today for two long conferences. He learned from General Collins that the latter wishes to attack on the 9th, which is an earlier date than anticipated, but which the General approved, agreeing with General Collins that it was wise to keep plugging while the Boche were still being rocked back on its heels and before he had time to build up additional replacements. With General Gerow he went over the proposed V Corps attack and in general found it satisfactory. The main effort, the General insists, should be made towards Gemumd. If this road center is captured the drive is bound to be a success and the General insists that the 8th Division's attack southeastward will clean out that area despite the belief of most people.

The front was generally quiet throughout the day. In the VII Corps sector the only attack was made by the 3rd Bn of the 414th Inf which made a limited objective assault and advanced 450 yards against scattered pockets of resistance taking more than 100 PWs. The 26th Inf prepared to move to Aubel and the 60th Inf moved up and closed in an area northwest of Heistern. Tomorrow the 60th Inf will relieve the 18th and the 331st will relieve the 12th. In the V Corps sector minor gains were made against stubborn resistance in the vicinity of Bergstein. CCR of 5th Armd received what appeared to be a formidable counterattack at 3:30 in the afternoon. It was repulsed without loss of position but the General authorized the movement up of the 2nd Ranger Bn which passed through CCR and tomorrow will attack southwest.

In the Third Army, both XII and XX Corps drove on ahead. In the XX Corps sector the 90th Div crossed the Saar River north Dillingen at four points and established a substantial bridgehead by the end of the day. At SAURLAUTERN [Saarlautern], two regiments of the 95th are already across. Further south in the First French Army sector a coordinated attack by both French Corps on the Colmar pocket[111] west of the RHINE was launched.

For the second successive day no buzz-bombs were reported over the First Army area. There are various interpretations: 1–He has temporarily run out of supply; 2–That his production facilities have been so damaged that he has decided against further output of the weapon; 3–That he is getting ready to shift these blows to a new area; and 4–He is building up a gigantic reserve to let loose at one time. The General is inclined to favor the fourth viewpoint.

Thursday, 7 December 1944: The General did not leave the CP today. General Gerow and Colonel [John G.] Hill,[112] G-3, came for lunch and spent the better part of the afternoon working out with the General V Corps' plan of assault.

The 9th Div tonight assumed responsibility for the 1st Div sector and the 83rd Div assumed responsibility for the 4th Div sector at 1600. Movement of the remaining elements of the 1st and 4th Divs will begin tomorrow. In the V Corps sector the 2nd Ranger Bn made good progress reaching all of its objectives especially Hill 400 east of BERGSTEIN and repulsed two counterattacks directed against this strong point. The 78th Div began to close in the assembly areas east of EUPEN. The remaining elements are expected to close there the day after tomorrow. No great activity is planned on the V Corps front. The Rangers will simply consolidate their position on Hill 400.

There was no news from the Ninth Army front. Steady stiffening resistance along the XX Corps front in the Third Army area slowed up their advance. 90th Div continued to enlarge their bridgehead in the DILLINGEN area. Two more forts in the METZ area surrendered yesterday leaving only FORT DRIANT, the commander of which has steadfastly refused to enter into negotiations of any kind. Further south along the west bank of the RHINE advances were made and our forces now control a stretch of forty miles with STRASBOURG in the middle. The attack of the French on the COLMAR pocket made substantial progress from the north and west.

If weather permits, the British will have their fourth crack at the south dam on the URFT River tomorrow with 200 Lancasters. Bad weather today prevented all air activity of a close support nature. Tonight the General received for a brief interview Major General [A. M.] Cameron,[113] Anti-Aircraft Officer of SHAEF. He also received in the mail an autographed advance copy of Ernie Pyle's[114] new book, "Brave Men." There were again no "robos" reported over our area.

Friday, 8 December 1944: The RAF, 200 Lancasters strong, had their fourth try at the dam shortly before eleven o'clock this morning. Aerial photographs show hits but they are the size of a half dollar. Apparently the small boxes which were noted on the dam two or three weeks ago are not the prepared demolitions anticipated. Tonight it was not known whether the British would take still another try at breaking it.

The General spent most of the day in discussing the future operations; VII Corps jumps off on the 10th and V Corps on the 13th. The General anticipates that General Collins will have no great difficulty in reaching DUREN. There, of course, his Corps must halt until the dam or dams are under our control. It may be slow going for a while in the V Corps sector but the Boche simply has not the reserves to meet this 1-2-3 punch. The third punch being that of the 8th Div which will probably hit southward about the 16th or 17th.

Today was a quiet day on the front. 1st Bn of the 330th Inf made a local attack advancing some 700 yards and seizing Hill 375 at coordinate 072377. The 1st Div finished closing in the vicinity of AUBEL and the CP moved back to its old location at HAUSET. In the V Corps sector the 2nd Ranger Bn attacked, defended, and consolidated its positions and last night was relieved by the 3rd Bn of the 13th Inf. CCR of 5th Armd Div closed at WALHORN and passed to V Corps control from the 8th Div. The 309th Inf of the 78th Div closed in the vicinity of EUPEN and the division set up its CP near RUTGEN [Roetgen]. In the VIII Corps sector the 1st Combat Team of the 106th Div, the 422nd Inf, closed near ST VITH.

Gains on other fronts were limited. Weather during the afternoon prevented all air activity.

After supper the General pinned stars on First Army's two new Brigadiers, G-4 Robert W. Wilson and Surgeon John Rogers. Although they knew their names had been submitted the ceremony caught them both by complete surprise.

Colonel Medaris brought in for the General's inspection a 60mm mortar which factories in France and Belgium are now turning out in mass production. With very small differences it is the same as that produced in the United States although the manufacturers have stamped it (along with the tires which are also being manufactured here) "First U. S. Army" instead of "U. S. Army."

Saturday, 9 December 1944: Today was a day generally without great news or changes in the front line as final preparations were made for the VII Corps attack opening tomorrow morning. Positions were generally consolidated along both Corps fronts and new troops brought up for relief, especially the 311th Inf of the 78th Div which relieved two battalions of the 13th Inf in the front line. In the VIII Corps area the 106th Div continued to assemble in the vicinity of ST VITH and all elements with the exception of some artillery have now closed.

Below us in the Third Army sector, General Patton's forces, especially in the XX Corps area, are meeting heavy enemy resistance and unprecedented artillery fire. House-to-house fighting still continues in SAARLAUTERN and DILLIGEN [Dillingen]. The 87th Div has taken over the METZ area where one fort, Jeanne D'Arc, still holds out.

Because of uncertain weather the RAF scrubbed their plan to attack the south dam today with 150 to 160 heavy bombers. Despite the lack of success which has thus far attended their efforts, the General is emphatic in his belief that 1,000 bombers should be sent over until the dam is broken.

G-2 reports keep putting emphasis on the fact that 6 Panzer Armee is drawing up on the other side of the ROER with at least three of its six armored divisions facing the First Army front. Reports from prisoners indicate that moral[e] is high and that the Boche will soon be ready to stage an all-out counter-offensive. There is also rumor that "pressluft" will be employed by its artillery. The General has acknowledged that there is no question but that a professional is now guiding the German Army in its efforts but he does not appear unduly concerned over the existence of these Panzer Divisions, on his front.

Sunday, 10 December 1944: VII Corps jumped off at 0745 this morning and by nightfall gains of up to 2 miles were made in some areas against resistance which at no time could be considered heavy although in some localities it was determined.

The 1st Bn of the 414th advanced 2,000 yards to the outskirts of PIER and there the Boche are holding. The 3rd Bn of the 414th advanced over a mile in the direction of SCHOPHOVEN. Task Force "K," one of the three Task Forces of CCR, occupied ECHTZ in conjunction with the 1st Bn of the 60th Inf. Task Force "H" advanced to the western edge of GEISCH [Geich] where they were slowed down by heavy anti-tank fire. The 2nd Bn of the 39th and 1st and 2nd Bns of the 60th also attacked but not until this afternoon. OBERGEISCH [Obergeich] and D'HORN were occupied.

Below us the 83rd Div began their attack at 6:30. The 2nd Bn of the 331st reached the center of GEY and continued to fight its way through the town against stiffening resistance. STRASS and SCHAFBERG were taken.

The 5th Armd Div moved up at nightfall and it is scheduled to attack tomorrow. In the V Corps sector the 2nd Div began to move up from VIII Corps; The 9th Inf closing in Camp Elsenborn. They were relieved in the VIII Corps sector by the 422nd Inf of the 106th Div. The 329th Inf will relieve the 8th Inf tomorrow thus completing the transfer of the 4th and 8th Divs.

General Bradley arrived at five o'clock this afternoon for a conference with General Hodges and a conference tomorrow with both him and General Simpson. General Bradley brought two pieces of information, one encouraging and one discouraging. The news from the states is that the ammunition situation is going to improve every day. They have made a thorough canvass of all stocks of it in the United States and have cut down some two weeks in average shipping time. By May the amounts on hand will come very close to what First Army has constantly asked for. Theater and Group will take some of these supplies in order to build-up their respective reserves and so that Army will not have to carry in transport too large a reserve. The discouraging piece of news was that there is as yet no hope in sight for replacements, and when General Kean asked, "Would U. S. divisions have to fight decimated and in half-strength like the German Kampfgruppers?" General Bradley replied, "Yes, I am afraid that is so." He said they had considered breaking up the new divisions now being sent to this area but unfortunately this was not very economical. The replacements needed were riflemen and there was a tremendous wastage in breaking up a division, since you had to re-train such a large percentage of the men in order to furnish you with the desired number of M-1[115] carrying replacements.

After dinner all the Generals saw the new thriller, "Laura" with Clifton Webb and Gene Tierney. Afterward the General returned to the office for a short consultation with Colonel Dickson.

Monday, 11 December 1944: General Simpson arrived shortly before nine o'clock with this Chief of Staff General Moore and G-3 Colonel Mead as well as General Nugent.[116] For the rest of the morning until almost one o'clock, General Hodges and his staff, the Ninth Army staff, and General Bradley were closeted in the General's war room discussing future operations. The only clew that the General gave came at supper tonight when he said that, "We are right where we started from this morning." Apparently, the Ninth Army has more involved tactical ideas than those which General Hodges presented, and there will, undoubtedly, have to be an ironing out of these points of view at a later conference. One of the questions undoubtedly discussed was that of the time element, whether to keep hitting now or to delay until after the first of the year when certain conditions may make an offensive more propitious. However, both General Bradley and General Hodges apparently seemed to believe that the time is now.

The RAF with 230 Lancasters had another crack at the dam between 2:30 and 3:30 this afternoon. Aerial reconnaissance flown directly after the last bombers had passed overhead showed one hit in the center of the dam and apparently some water is spilling over it. However, the dam [can] in no way be considered blown. Two more hits were made on the approaches to the dam, successfully cutting the road across it which the Boche had been using and which they depend upon.

Steady gains, equal to those of the first day, were made by the VII Corps—Confirming the point of view that the Boche is not going to defend too strenuously this side of the ROER. MERKEN was entered and two-thirds cleared; stubborn resistance continued in PIER; MERODE and SCHELICH [Schlich] were cleared by the 1st and 2nd Bns of the 39th Inf. About 150 prisoners were taken in these two towns. The 3rd Bn of the 60th also resumed the attack and advanced to the western edge of KONZENDORF. More than 520 prisoners have been taken by the 9th Div in the last two days of fighting.

Below this sector the 83rd Div had somewhat tougher going. GEY has not as yet fallen. A company of infantry infiltrated into and re-occupied SCHAFBERG and the 2nd Bn of the 330th was rushed down there to re-assume control. CCB of 5th Armd attacked through the 83rd and made advances against light enemy resistance. However, extensive minefields and heavy anti-tank and artillery fire did not make the going fast. CCA moved up to GROSHAU [Grosshau].

Today at seven o'clock the 106th Div officially assumed responsibility for the 2nd Div area; the 2nd Div minus the 23rd Inf is now closed in Camp Elsenborn. The attack of V Corps remains unchanged—scheduled to jump off the morning of the 13th.

General Bradley returned to Group after lunch today. General Hart tonight invited the General to see a demonstration of the new ammunition which has been used so successfully in the Pacific by our aircraft carriers shooting against Jap planes. This new ammunition carries a small radio and by some electro-magnetic "hokus-pokus" the shell explodes not upon impact but upon approach to the object toward which it is aimed.[117] In other words, we can interdict a bridge preventing the enemy from using it and at the same time not destroying it. These shells can be so laid down as to explode a few feet off the ground, a far better and easier substitute for time fire. General Hart said that we are obtaining this ammunition in increasing amounts and although he was lukewarm about its use at the beginning he is now convinced that it will prove one of the most valuable "secret weapons."

Tuesday, 12 December 1944: The General spent a full day in the field, leaving early after lunch. The first stop was at V Corps where he had a brief chat with General Gerow, moving from there on to VII Corps where, in the absence of General Collins, he talked to Colonel [Richard C.] Partridge[118] briefly. The third stop was at the 83rd Div where, in the absence of General Macon and General Ferenbugh [Ferenbaugh], he chatted for a short time with Colonel Krauthoff, the Chief of Staff, who served in the last war as a soldier in the German Army.[119] He then returned to VII Corps where in a brief ceremony he pinned the DSC on General Maurice Rose of the 3rd Armd Div. His fifth stop was at the 78th Div CP in Rotgen where he talked to General [Edwin P.] Parker[120] and General [John K.] Rice[121] and then called the staff of the division together for a brief chat. The General assured them that there was nothing to be nervous about, that it had been proven, time and time again, that our training methods in the United States were not only correct but completely adequate to defeat the Boche, and that he had the utmost confidence that the 78th would tomorrow begin its battle history with a fine showing. His sixth and last stop was at V Corps. There official word came through, not unexpectedly, that General Gerow is to take command of the newly formed Fifteenth U. S. Army. General Heubner will take over V Corps. Probably three or four days from now. It is considered probable that General Andrews [Clift Andrus],[122] Artillery Commander of the 1st Div, will succeed General Heubner [Huebner] in that post.

Fine gains were recorded throughout the day by VII Corps. 104th Div cleared Pier and Merken. More than 200 PWs were captured. CCR of 3rd Armd Div with the 1st Bn of 60th Inf attached drove straight to the east to seize and clear Hoven which is on the Roer. In the 9th Div sector, 2nd Bn of the 60th advanced two miles from Geisch to Mariawieler [Mariaweiler] and at midnight tonight three-quarters of that town was cleared. 3rd Bn of the 39th advanced 1 1/2 miles from Merode to Derichsweiler and now hold one-third of the town. More than 300 PWs were captured by the 9th Div during the day. The General seems to think that, contrary to first expressed views, the Boche did not forsake this territory leaving only a light screen as protection but that he was defending it strenuously and that only the vigor of VII Corps' attack enabled it to make such fine advances. The PW total bears out the General's contention. Further south in the 83rd Div sector HOF HARDT was cleared by the 1st and 2nd Bns of the 329th; SHAFBERG [Schafberg], which was occupied two days ago only to be retaken by the Boche yesterday, was [again] cleared of the enemy. Fighting still continued in GEY. The 83rd Div took 200 PWs.

Final preparations were made in the V Corps for the attack which will jump off with elements of the 78th Div leading at six o'clock tomorrow. The 2nd Div passed to control of V Corps at 10:30 yesterday and its last troops closed at Camp Elsenborn.

The XX Corps of the Third Army continued to have an extremely hard fight in SAARLAUTERN and DILLIGEN. Elements of the XII Corps, however, kept on advancing in some sectors as much as two miles. Four divisions of the Third Army are now out of the line resting and re-equipping: 5th, 80th, 4th Armd, and 10th Armd. These divisions were badly cut up during the present fighting and there have been as yet no replacements for them. Good progress was likewise made by the Seventh US Army whose 44th and 100th Divs took BITSCH [Bitche]. The 45th Div occupied REICHSHOVEN [Reichshoffen] and the 79th Div advanced almost eight miles in a narrow sector running along the RHINE to the outskirts of SUFFLENHAN [Soufflenheim].

Buzz-bombs again made their re-appearance over First Army area. A total of 19 being clocked for the twenty-four hour period ending at midnight. The destination was unknown. The RAF mission for the day against the dams was cancelled because of bad weather but is scheduled to go on tomorrow, weather permitting.

The Roer River Dams Offensive, 13–15 December 1944

Wednesday, 13 December 1944: The V Corps jumped off this morning with a regiment plus of the 78th Div, the 9th Inf of the 2nd Div, and the 393rd Inf of the 99th Div. Surprisingly good progress was made and only 35 to 45 prisoners were captured during the day, leading the General to believe tonight that the attack caught the Boche off-base and that he believed the V Corps sector was merely an extension of the quiet VIII Corps zone. This attack, the real objective of which is to secure the ROER River dams (the RAF thus far having no success) succeeded at day's end in putting the following towns in our hands: ROLLESBROICH, WITZER-ATH, SIMMERETH [Simmerath], BICKERATH and KESTERNICH. All these towns fell to the 309th and 310th Infs of the 78th Div. The General was a little worried tonight that they had over-extended themselves and hoped that the new division would know how to button up well. The 2nd and 99th Divs all reached their initial objectives through the heavy MOND-SCHAU [Monschau] Forest. Artillery fire was at a minimum all day.

Farther north, however, heavy artillery fire was the order the day and CCB of the 5th Armd Div suffered tragically heavy losses, 98 were reported killed and 380 wounded because of this fire. GEY, however, was cleared and the GEY-STRASS road has been cleared of mines. This clearing took longer than usual because of the fact the mines employed were of the wooden-box type and therefore, invulnerable to our mine detectors.[123]

The 83rd Div, in addition to clearing GEY, advanced the 2nd Bn of the 329th almost two miles to GURZNICH [Gürzenich], followed by the lst Bn. The rest of General Collins' troops continued their march up to the banks of the ROER. SCHOPHOVEN was cleared and patrols were extended to the river. The only remaining enemy resistance in the 104th Div sector is a castle strong-point south of this town. The 9th Div also reached its objective clearing HOVEN, MARIAWEILER, and DERICHSWEILER. CCR of the 3rd Armd, its mission accomplished, reassembled at MAUSBACH.

The RAF mission on the dams was scrubbed because of weather. Medium bombers, however, operating by [SCR] 584[124] bombed eight towns in the V Corps area through the overcast. Among the important targets were SCHLEIDEN and GAUMAND [Gemünd]. Results were, of course, unobserved.

General [Cuthbert P.] Stearns [Stearnes],[125] former[ly] a TAC [tactical officer] at West Point with General Hodges, and now a member of the G-5 Section of Comm Z, called to pay his respects to the General and was his guest for luncheon.

The General spent a good part of the afternoon with M. Francotte of the famous gun manufacturing concern at LIEGE bearing his name. The General finally settled on a gun to be made according to his definite specifications, which he believes should be a beauty. About a month's work will be necessary before it is completed. General Quesada also was a purchaser—of two.

Thursday, 14 December 1944: Today it appears that the V Corps attack, which from all accounts started so well yesterday, was stopped cold. It was impossible to get from Corps headquarters any definite positions or locations of troops and it was not until liaison officers from this headquarters returned late in the afternoon that the General was able to find out the approximate facts of the case. Even then the situation of the 78th Div was obscure to say the least. As much as can now be said definitely about its positions it seems that the report last night that they had captured KESTERNICH was over-optimistic or just plain false, for today two battalions were still attacking it and trying to enter; one battalion from the southwest, the other from the north. Because of the confused situation and lack of knowledge as to exact location of troops the General feared that this division, new in battle and untried, was going to get itself smacked hard by the Boche as was the 28th Div in Schmidt, and he told Corps in very definite language to get down there and get the thing straightened out. Summing it up the 78th Div made no visible gains during the day.

The 2nd Div, still attacking with only one regiment, the 9th, was also stopped before the cross-roads at 995132 [Wahlerscheid crossroads] by enemy pillboxes, heavy concertina wire, and exceedingly heavy mine-fields. In the two days of the attack the 9th has already suffered 200 battle casualties, in addition to 200 non-battle casualties. Major Bach, Liaison Officer from this headquarters, described the fighting there as comparable in every way to that in the HURTGEN FOREST although the Boche numerically are probably not strong. To the right of the 2nd Div, the 99th Div also advanced through the Forest against considerably less opposition and were abreast of the 9th in most places. VII Corps continued to do well; the 104th Div cleared the last remaining enemy elements in its sector from the castle directly southwest of SCHOPHOVEN. Only 4 PWs were captured in this attack, the rest were killed. The 60th Inf likewise made progress against an enemy pocket which was north of GURZNICH. The 83rd Div made very substantial progress; the 3rd Bn of the 329th Inf captured BIRGEL, took 100 PWs in so doing, and then re-pelled a counterattack consisting of an estimated company of infantry backed up by six tanks. The pressure continued strongly throughout the day in front of this division as the enemy continued to move south towards KRAUTHAUSEN where the only bridges south of DUREN remain intact across the ROER River. The 5th Armd Div finally started to move in good shape. CCA cleared HORN [D'Horn] and advanced north an-other mile to the outskirts of KUFFERATH; CCB advancing to the south made almost a half-mile and consolidated its positions with the 2nd Bn of the 330th.

Today was the most beautiful day in our immediate front since we have been here but was non-operational most of the day in the rear ar-eas. The medium and heavy efforts were call [all] cancelled, including the proposed RAF's fifth attempt at the dam and it was not until eleven o'clock that the first squadron of fighter-bombers were able to get off their heavily iced fields. From then on until five o'clock the air did have good shooting.

The guest of the General for lunch today was Major General [Leroy H.] Lutes,[126] head trouble shooter for General Somervell. General Lutes told General Hedges that by a requisitioning of all available ammunition in the United States, from every nook and cranny, they were able to assure him that until May 1st this theater would have close to the number of 105 and 155 ammunition which they had been steadily requesting. By that time, he said, the new expansion program in the United States—new factories and enlargement of now operating factories—would probably be able to keep up after a short time lag, this supply. He said he was still trying to trace down the cable which was sent from this theater back to Washington sometime last March stating that we would need no more ammunition than that shot during the Italian campaign. General Lutes did not wish to be publicly quoted (this is a private diary) but he said he felt quite bitter about the fact that ours had now become a two front main effort, instead of one main effort as had been originally planned and as had always been written for strategists to follow. He said that the Navy, which always cloaks its activities in the maximum secrecy, had suddenly appeared on the scene without warning with a Navy far greater in size than even the most optimistic people had thought possible, and that they obviously were going to use that Navy. This not only robbed the Army of much of its potential manpower—and he said General Handy was fully cognizant of the critical replacement problem but saw no immediate solution—but it also made necessary tremendous shipments of both men and materiel to the Pacific front. This was where a lot of our 105 and mortar ammunition was going and where it was now stocked—Since this ammunition is obviously more in demand in jungle fighting than any other kind. He said he hoped ANTWERP would be able shortly to unload 25,000 tons a day. He estimated the total theater necessities as a daily 60,000 tons and said that thus far we had been making about 42,000. Le Havre is now making about 5,000 tons with berths for five to seven ships. General Hodges and General Kean went over, upon his request, the most critical item shortages that the Army thus far had to deal with but said that there had been an improvement in being able to obtain information as to what had been unloaded and as to what could be expected to arrive in the Army area. General Lutes said he was still battling with the problem of tonnage; that the transportation corps thought only in terms of

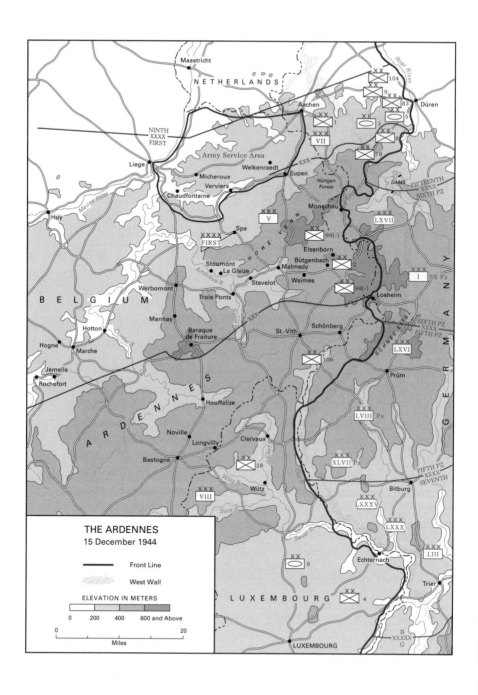

THE ARDENNES
15 December 1944

Front Line

West Wall

ELEVATION IN METERS

0   200   400   600 and Above

0   20
Miles

Maastricht

NETHERLANDS

Roer River

Aachen

Düren

NINTH
XXXX
FIRST

Liege

Army Service Area

Micheroux

Welkenraedt

Eupen

Hürtgen
Forest

DAMS

FIFTEENTH
XXXX
SIXTH PZ

Verviers

Chaudfontaine

Monschau

LXVII

Huy

Meuse River

Spa

HOHE VENN

FIRST

99(-)

Elsenborn

Bütgenbach

Stoumont

La Gleize

Malmedy

Waimes

I   SS Pz

Amblève R.

Stavelot

99(-)

Losheim

BELGIUM

Werbomont

Trois Ponts

Salm R.

SIXTH PZ
XXXX
FIFTH PZ

Manhay

Hotton

Baraque
de Fraiture

St.-Vith

Schönberg

SCHNEE EIFEL

LXVI

Hogne

Ourthe R.

Marche

106

Prüm

Jemelle

Rochefort

ARDENNES

Houffalize

LVIII   Pz

Noville

Longvilly

Clervaux

Clerf R.

XLVII Pz

FIFTH PZ
XXXX
SEVENTH

Bastogne

28

Bitburg

Wiltz R.

Wiltz

Our R.

LXXXV

VIII

Sure R.

LXXX

9

Echternach

LIII

Trier

LUXEMBOURG

4

G E R M A N Y

LUXEMBOURG

B
XXXXX
G

tons and not in terms of items, and that obviously a lot of useless stuff had been shipped ahead of materiel which we needed right away. He offered no explanation for such inexcusable errors in judgment as that which was responsible for providing overshoes, all in the smaller sizes. He said that he would do his very best to solve the critical item shortages that we had mentioned.

Friday, 15 December 1944: The VIII [VII] Corps continued the attack on its southern flank to reach the ROER River. BERZBURY [Berzbuir] was cleared by the 2nd Bn of the 331st Inf while the 3rd Bn advanced 1,000 yards, almost up to the river's edge. The 5th Armd Div less CCR with the 2nd Bn of 330th Inf attached made substantial gains likewise, KUFFERATH was seized and cleared by CCA, while the north column advanced to the high ground overlooking the River. CCB with the 2nd Bn of 330th Inf advanced a mile to BERGHEIM which has now been cleared.

All Corps advances were limited throughout the day as numerous enemy pillboxes, strongly defended and fortified positions, huge rolls of concertina wire, and minefields everywhere made the going slow. KASTERNICH [Kesternich], about which the General was perturbed yesterday, has now been definitely cleared by the 78th Div, while the 310th Inf held and improved its positions north and northeast of ROLLESBROICH. The 2nd Div with the 9th Inf continued to assault but with little success the 11 pillboxes which stand in the vicinity of the road center at 995130. SP-155 guns[127] were being employed against the concrete fortifications and two pillboxes were definitely knocked out. The Boche, however, is fighting determinedly and the prisoner bag is almost nil. In the 99th Div sector little progress was likewise made against the same kind of positions.

There were no changes in the VIII Corps front except that increased artillery fire was generally received.

Today was another fine day for the Air with all fighter-bombers squadrons being aloft. The mediums could not find their targets so laid all their bombs on one town.

During the afternoon the General received for a very brief session the visiting galaxy of ball players including Frankie Frisch, Bucky Walter, Dutch Leonard, and Mel Ott. General Middleton dropped in shortly after the ball players had left for one hour conference with the General. General Thorson is two days overdue from his vacation in England because, it is presumed, of bad weather.

As usual the British front was exceptionally quiet. No startling gains were made by Third Army. Seventh Army, however, drove ahead with the 14th Armd, 45th, 103rd and 100th Divs to reach, along a broad front, the German border. They are now only some eight miles away from the important German city of KARLSRUHE. Resistance along the front was everywhere light although below in the COLMAR POCKET the Boche continues to fight tenaciously and with vicious counterattacks.

Chapter 5

The German Counteroffensive and the Drive to the Roer River, 16 December 1944–22 February 1945

The German Counteroffensive, 16 December 1944–2 January 1945

Saturday, 16 December 1944: Today, exactly one month after we launched our attack towards COLOGNE, the Boche began a counteroffensive, on which, according to a captured order, which was signed by Von Runstedt [Rundstedt], the enemy is gambling its life. According to Von Runstedt the fate of the German nation depends upon the success or failure of this savage blow directed at the VIII Corps. According to PWs captured, who were more precise, the counteroffensive is a pincer movement on AACHEN, and an attack is apparently about to begin in the Ninth Army area to join up with those troops who have attacked to the south.

First word that something was brewing came from VIII Corps sector shortly before seven o'clock this morning when an attack of infantry supported by tanks retook the town of ROTT [Roth]. Simultaneously attacks, some in large patrol strength and others in battalion strength, came all the way down the line starting against the 78th Div at ROLLESBROICH and extending down our front sixty miles to ECHTERNACH [Luxembourg]. Simultaneously came the news that the enemy had shelled MALMEDY, EUPEN, ST VITH, ROTGEN [Roetgen], and other communications centers, with large caliber artillery while at the same time approximately 12 rounds of the heretofore unknown long range projectile were dropped on VERVIERS. The study of the shell fragments indicated tonight that the shell is six inches in diameter and five to six feet long, but it is not known whether it is fired by artillery, heavy mortar or rocket propelled. The effect is similar to any other medium artillery shell. Casualties in MALMEDY included three officers killed, eight civilians killed, and a score of people wounded.

At first it appeared that these counterattacks of the Boche were only what the General called "spoiling attacks"—to take the pressure off the important V Corps drive towards the ROER River dams. But by eleven o'clock it became more evident that the enemy was staking all on this drive and that he was putting his maximum strength against the 106th Div and in the general area bordering the boundary between V and VIII Corps. General Hodges immediately put the 1st Div, resting in AUBEL, on a six hour alert and not long afterward in a call to General Bradley he was given the 7th Armd Div of the Ninth Army and the 10th Armd Div of the 3rd Army. He likewise called General Collins and ordered Combat Command B of the 3rd Armd Div to be placed on a similar alert, ready to move.

Throughout the day the attack continued with heavy shelling interfering materially with communications. In the 106th Div sector the enemy forced the 4th Cav Group, later reinforced by elements of the 9th Armd Div, to withdraw up to three miles to the west where positions were being reorganized and consolidated. In the 28th Div sector on the north flank, strong pressure continued during the day and slight penetrations were increased during the night-time up to 2½ miles. However, the 2nd Bn of the 110th Inf was immediately committed and they in combination with the 112th Inf succeeded in restoring almost all their former positions. In the 4th Div sector, elements of the 12th Inf are isolated but still holding BERDORF, ECHTERNACH, OSWEILER and DICHWEILER.

The following divisions are at nightfall definitely identified on the VIII Corps front: 18 VG [Volksgrenadier][1] Div; 116 Panzer Div; 26 VG Div; 352 VG Div; elements of the 276 VG Div; and 212 VG Div. Further identification at nightfall established the presence of the 62 VG Div and the 560 VG Div. The 560 VG Div was known to be moving south from NORWAY although this is the first definite identification of it. The 62 VG Div has been unlocated for some time; its last known location was in RUSSIA. A document captured in the approximate area in which the 116th Panzer Div is reported, identifies the 2nd Panzer Div and the 11th Panzer Div as being in this same area. The identification of the 2nd Panzer Div is almost definite.

At 5:30 tonight one enemy plane dropped a large caliber bomb and anti-personnel bombs about half a mile north of the CP. Another attack at 9:45 was made with one plane—perhaps jet-propelled—strafing the road in front of the General's house and also dropping bombs in the vicinity of SPA. Before midnight an intercept of a message brought us the news that 70 planes were ready on a field near COLOGNE to drop paratroopers through our area. The guard at the house was alerted and doubled. Reports continued to reach G-3 throughout the night that small groups of paratroopers—the largest being fifteen in number—had been dropped on almost all fronts and in the rear areas where they could interfere with our supply lines. A small group was reported dropped within six miles of SPA according to information received by the Army Provost Marshal.

The General was neither optimistic nor pessimistic during the day; knowing, on the basis of the evidence thus far received, that this is an all-out enemy effort, he believes that we can not only handle them but that this is the quickest way to bring around the decimation of the Wehrmacht. Liaison Officers returning to the CP late in the afternoon reported that although we had lost ground and although our troops were in some cases isolated and without support, that no one thought the situation critical but were continuing to fight hard to crack up the attack before it gained momentum in any one place in the line.

Throughout the day air activity was extremely limited because of bad visibility at the bases. Only two squadrons were able to do their job and other missions were scratched.

A two battalion attack was also launched during the day against the north flank of the Ninth Army. This attack was murdered; one battalion commander was killed, the other taken prisoners and in two hours the enemy was completely in rout.

Word was also received during the day that the VII Corps could expect an attack at night with the employment of a new secret weapon. This attack had not at this writing yet materialized.

It was unfortunate that during this busy evening the General, because of previous commitment, had to entertain Lieut. Gen. Grassett [Arthur Edward Grasett],[2] G-5 of SHAEF, along with Colonel [Cornelius E.] Ryan,[3] G-5, Twelfth Army Group, and Colonel Gunn. The fact that they arrived three-quarters of an hour late did not help matters.

It is probable that all air along the entire front will be diverted for our use tomorrow. Weather report at this writing is, "non-operational."

Sunday, 17 December 1944: The situation developed badly during the day and may be considered tonight to be serious if not yet critical. Captured orders taken from prisoners and signed by every leading

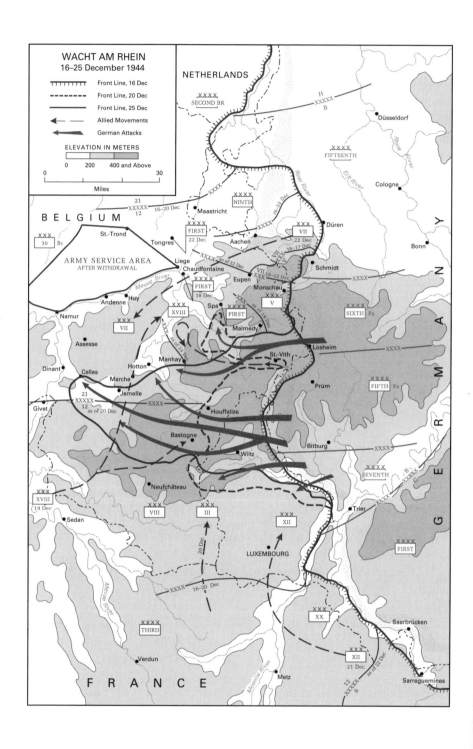

WACHT AM RHEIN
16–25 December 1944

Front Line, 16 Dec
Front Line, 20 Dec
Front Line, 25 Dec
Allied Movements
German Attacks

ELEVATION IN METERS

0   200   400 and Above

0   30

Miles

NETHERLANDS

SECOND BR

Düsseldorf

FIFTEENTH

Rhine River

Erft River

Cologne

NINTH

Maastricht

BELGIUM

St.-Trond

Tongres

FIRST
22 Dec

Aachen

VII

Düren

Bonn

Schmidt

ARMY SERVICE AREA
AFTER WITHDRAWAL

Liege
Chaudfontaine

Eupen

FIRST
18 Dec

Monschau

V

SIXTH Pz

Meuse River

Andenne   Huy

Namur

XVIII

Spa

FIRST

SEVENTH

Assesse

Malmedy

Dinant   Celles

Hotton   Manhay

St.-Vith

Losheim

Marche

Jemelle

Prüm

FIFTH Pz

Givet

Houffalize

Bastogne

Bitburg

Wiltz

Neufchâteau

VIII

III

XII

LUXEMBOURG

Trier

FIRST

XVIII
19 Dec

Sedan

Meuse River

THIRD

Verdun

Metz

Moselle River

FRANCE

XX

XII
21 Dec

Saarbrücken

Sarreguemines

VII

HB

G E R M A N Y

Wehrmacht high commander prove that the Boche is staking his life on this drive. The G-2 Estimate tonight says that the enemy is capable of attempting to exploit his initial gains by driving through our rear areas and seizing bridgeheads over the MEUSE River and that he will move at night as directed in captured documents and probably continue his parachutist operations. Increasing air support of his spearheads can be expected.

As ample witness to the extent to which the Boche are carrying out this bid for victory came a story tonight which measures up to and matches anything thus far published of Boche brutality and atrocity. The story first came from an MP who was brought to this headquarters. He spoke as follows: He was directing traffic at a cross roads in V Corps area and had just let through tanks of the 7th Armd Div. These were followed by trucks carrying more of the same Division. Suddenly there appeared from the woods six or seven tanks and approximately 200 officers and men were taken prisoners. They were herded together into a side field and an SS officer fired two shots from his pistol and immediately there came the crackle of machine gun fire and the whole group was mowed down in cold blood. This MP who was standing with the group realized what was happening and fell to the ground at the first shot and played dead for over forty-five minutes before he was able to rise and make his escape. It is not yet certain on what group of officers and men this atrocity was committed—some say they were trucks of men going to the front as replacements. There is absolutely no question as to its proof—immediate publicity is being given to the story. General Quesada has told every one of his pilots about it during their briefing.[4]

The critical point along the front is still the sector formerly held by the 106th Div, two of whose regiments are completely cut off. Enemy tanks were last night reported as far west as STAVELOT where our biggest POL Dump, some two million gallons, is located. Only one Engr Co and a Co of 562nd [526th] Armd Inf Bn was there. For a time during the day it looked too as if MALMEDY was in enemy hands but these reports proved exaggerated. Colonel Throckmorton, Asst. G-3, was in the town at 9:30 tonight and came back to report that road blocks were well established and that a company of infantry was defending it.

The general situation starting from the north and working to the south is tonight approximately as follows: VII Corps: The 83rd Div continued its attack and the towns of ROLLESDORF [Rölsdorf] and LANDERSDORF [Lendersdorf] have been cleared of the enemy. Rear areas of the Corps were being searched for paratroopers. Enemy air was active tonight over the area with 75 planes reported, 16 of which were claimed to be destroyed. More paratroopers were unquestionably dropped and an intensive search is being conducted for them. V Corps: The 78th Div less 311th Inf and with the 2nd Ranger Bn attached relieved elements of the 309th in SIMMERATH. Two counterattacks against KESTERNICH were thrown back. The 2nd Div defended its present positions with the 9th and 38th Inf and sent its 23rd Inf southward to establish a line of defense along the ridge of ROCHEROTH-KRIMHELT-WERTZFELT [Rocherath-Krinkelt-Wirtzfeld] to the lake east of GUTEBUTGENBACH [Bütgenbach] in support of the 99th Div. Heavy enemy pressured forced 393rd and 394th of the 99th Div to withdraw approximately one and a half miles to the general line 0007–0101. At two o'clock the 28th [26th] Inf attached to the 99th Div attacked southeast and advanced to 928022 approximately two miles southeast of BUTGENBACH against an enemy penetration which had been made yesterday. The enemy likewise attacked through MONSCHAU and got as far as MUNTEZENICH [Mützenich] by [but] the line was later restored to its former position. 99th Inf Bn plus TD elements established defense during the night in the MALMEDY-STAVELOT area. The 18th Inf is located in the area just southeast of EUPEN and the 16th Inf is in Corps reserve at Camp Elsenborn. 47th Inf closed west of MUTEZENICH. 30th Inf [Div] attached to V Corps closed just north of EUPEN. Enemy air forces were again active last night and tonight over the V Corps area and EUPEN was attacked by 12 of them. VIII Corps: The 18th Cav Squadron which during the first two days of the attack lost over 300 of its men or almost one-half of its strength withdrew from the line BORN-WALLERDE [Wallerode] which line was re-established by CCB of 9th Armd Div. 106th Div engaged in heavy fighting throughout the day; little is known as to their exact location. The 28th Div was likewise engaged in a no quarter give and take close combat and although forced to give ground were by no means put into retreat. The pressure seems somewhat lifted off the 4th Div front. 7th Armd continued closing in the VIII Corps area; CCB has been committed in the vicinity of 8688; 10th Armd continued to close in the vicinity of LUXEMBOURG.

Although General Bradley was still in PARIS with General Eisenhower and therefore difficult to reach during the first part of the day, he returned to Group Hq late yesterday and at seven o'clock last night had acceded to General Hodges' request and gave him XVI [XVIII] Airborne Corps. The 82nd and 101st Airborne Divisions will start moving early tomorrow to the VIII Corps area from Reims. General Ridgway will command the Corps and at General Hodges' specific request; it had been suggested that these troops be turned over to the XVI Corps under General [John B.] Anderson.[5]

Although the General spent almost all morning in the G-3 Section, General Van Denberg [Vandenberg], General Quesada, General Simpson, General [Samuel E.] Anderson[6] and five or six other Major and Brigadier Generals of the Air Force gathered in General Hodges' office for a conference as to the targets to be hit now and later.

Although the sun was not out, a high overcast permitted our Air, nine groups in all, to operate actively during the day. We had difficulty in identifying our own columns since the Boche have painted all their vehicles with American insignia and it was necessary for the pilots to go down unto [on to] the deck before they could tell what belonged to whom. Consequently damage because of flak was heavy but the air considered that they had excellent shooting. The Cubs were likewise up and General Hart reported that his artillery had had an excellent day breaking up enemy columns, one of which coming out of Gumend [Gemünd] was at least five miles long.

Although no exact total is as yet available, it is believed tonight that we have rounded up a majority of two companies, 120 men each, of enemy parachutists which were dropped last night. They had the mission of getting up and meeting on the Eupen-Malmedy road and were ordered to hold or block it for two days until they were relieved by two armored divisions.

Enemy air continued to appear in strength throughout the day but Ninth TAC also claimed 45 destroyed, this not counting the AA bag which is as yet not established. V-1s continued to pass over the Army area throughout the day again bound for Liege but there were no reports of the shelling by unknown weapons such as Verviers experienced yesterday.

Casualties when they become known will undoubtedly be extremely heavy. According to one report it was everywhere all along the front a question of no quarter and few prisoners. Our bag for yesterday was 1,059. Our service installations are moving to the rear and what we have to leave in Boche hands we shall have destroyed. Only one battalion of field artillery—the weapons at least, have been over-run and one battery of VIII Corps artillery. The planes were active twice over Spa but no report as yet has been received of bombs dropped or damage caused.

Monday, 18 December 1944: The situation is rapidly deteriorating and the position of the enemy is uncertain. Cheerful news, however, came this morning that we are to get General Ridgway and the two A/B Divs and that they will start moving from REIMS tonight and tomorrow. It is not yet known whether Twelfth Army Group fully appreciates the seriousness of the situation though both General Hodges and General Kean talked with General Bradley half a dozen times during the day.

The biggest danger point this morning was the STAVELOT section where both tanks and infantry are reported in strength. They are from 1st SS Panzer Div. The 30th Div has moved down into the area in an attempt to control it but about three o'clock this afternoon there were reports that tanks were coming up from STAVELOT headed towards SPA. They were definitely identified at LA GLEIZE. Only a small road block and half-tracks stood between them and our headquarters. Shortly before four the whole headquarters with the exception of one officer in each section was sent out to man the road leading into town and Colonel Dickson came to General Hodges to say that he thought he ought to be prepared to leave at once and that a Cub plane was waiting at Maroon Strip to take him away.

By one of the fortunes of war that can never be explained, tanks turned southwest from LA GLEIZE and reports that they were a mile from the outskirts of SPA proved untrue. This was the greatest of good fortune for two reasons: 1–our headquarters with no heavy equipment would have been unable to resist long this armored thrust; and 2–Between us and them was our largest gas dump consisting of some 2,000,000 gallons, enough to keep a Panzer Div rolling for thirty days. Nevertheless, the headquarters continued with its plans made early in the afternoon to move to Master Rear at CHAUDFONTAINE.

The 3rd Armd, which was this morning put on a three-hour alert and a one-hour alert, is beginning to move. General Hodges stayed on at headquarters in hopes of meeting and talking to General Gavin who reported in this morning and was to have returned shortly after nine o'clock tonight. However, he did not appear and shortly after ten, preceded by an armored car and with one following in the rear, the General, General Kean, General Hart, and General Thorson moved on to the new headquarters. It was an active night for German air all along the road with flares being dropped and AA firing. Shortly beforehand a buzz-bomb going down the alley towards LIEGE dropped on the road near PEPIMINSTER [Pepinster] and hit a truck of G-4 Traffic Control Section killing all fourteen occupants. There was no trace of the bodies to be found and what was left of the two-and-a-half ton truck was a small crumbled mass which was thrown into the river. It also killed two more in the truck which was 50 yards to the rear of the one hit.

At midnight we pulled into the new CP. The General is located on the second floor of the Palace Hotel and the offices are across the main VERVIERS-LIEGE highway in the Hotel Des Bains. Buzz-bombs, passing at frequent intervals overhead, made the night not particularly restful.

Tuesday, 19 December 1944: General Ridgway with his two customary hand grenades strapped to his shoulder arrived early this morning for a conference with General Hodges and General Kean. The situation is better in V Corps and VII Corps than in VIII Corps where it is extremely fluid and where apparently the 28th Div has taken a considerable pounding. There are reports that BASTOGNE has fallen and has not fallen; the same applies to HOFFLEIZE [Houffalize].

No gas dumps have as yet been captured by the enemy. We have already moved over a million gallons out of the large dump southwest of SPA and other units are now drawing from it. Service units have almost completed the move to the rear which will prevent any important installations becoming Boche property.

The big question mark right now is the location of the 2 SS Panzer Corps. Is it going to hit V Corps in the MONSCHAU section as suspected or will it move south to exploit the stab made in our lines: MALMEDY-STAVELOT. The 7th Armd which has joined up with the one regiment of the 106th Div not cut off [424th Infantry Regiment] is doing a magnificent job in holding firm at ST VITH against tremendous pressure. This holding has split the German drive and Third Army, it is now learned, is going to swing (the exact date unknown) up to meet the southern stab in the VIII Corps sector.

The Boche has definitely thrown his Sunday punch; already identified in the VIII Corps sector are 116th Panzer, 2nd Panzer, Panzer Lehr, 5th Para, and Fuehrer Brigade [Führer Begleit Brigade][7]; and identified in the STAVELOT area are 1 SS [Panzer] Corps with 1 SS Panzer, 12th SS Panzer, and 3rd Para [Divisions]. Volksgrenadier Divs in large numbers are backing up the enemy armor.

General Rose came in this afternoon at four and made plans to keep moving his division minus CCA, which is backing up V Corps, and minus CCB which is backing up the 30th Div., to the vicinity of WERBONNET [Werbomont] where XVIII Corps headquarters has opened. A mile away from our CP a buzz bomb hit as he passed, knocking his Aide completely out of the car. The bomb landed in an open field but it and one which directly followed it landed close enough to knock out several windows in the headquarters building and causing casualties in the P & PW [Publicity and Psychological Warfare] Section.

We have already captured quite a few number of the parachutists and infiltrators in American uniform who dropped every night since the attack began. The infiltrators travelling in American jeeps with dog-tags, pay-cards, etc., had various assorted missions—several teams to blow bridges; other teams to cut lines and communications; teams to obtain information on our movements and wire back the news; and teams to capture Corps and Army headquarters. Three men who turned into an Ordnance dump by mistake above STAVELOT had the express mission of capturing First Army headquarters. Another group of 50 headed by the notorious [Otto] Skorzeny[8] were supposed to be on their way to PARIS to do the same to SHAEF and General Eisenhower. Question now is: Shall authority be given Army and lower unit commanders to pass judgment on their trials without the papers having to go through numerous headquarters channels. Verbal authority has already come from SHAEF for General Hodges to sit as final judge, but he is waiting for written confirmation.

General Huebner arrived late in the afternoon and is spending the night at our CP. He reports pressure everywhere against V Corps but as usual he's confident that his divisions including the famous 1st can take anything that may come his way. We have word from General Bradley tonight that three divisions to operate under III Corps are coming up from Patton's Army but that General Middleton is not to commit them unless penetration [permission] is given by Group. Shortly before twelve o'clock General Middleton called asking for permission to commit CCB of 4th Armd Div and the call was relayed to General Bradley who said: "Yes, commit it if absolutely necessary but only to hold and not as an offensive weapon."

Wednesday, 20 December 1944: At 2:30 this morning a representative of Field Marshal Montgomery had a bedside conference with General Hodges and General Kean in the former's suite. The Major brought information that Monty had moved his 30th British Corps now consisting of four divisions and later to consist of five, in the general assembly area: HASSELT-LOUVAIN [Leuven]-ST TROND [St. Truiden], prepared to back up any retreat to the MEUSE if such should be necessary. He said that they were also taking charge of the bridges at NAMUR, LIEGE, HUY, and GIVET and were prepared to blow them upon call. Early in the morning General Bradley called to inform General Hodges that Monty would probably take over the First and Ninth Armies. A decision which he shortly afterward confirmed by telephone. The temporary boundary between 21 and 12th Army Groups is fixed as a line running from GIVET on the MEUSE to ST VITH. General Patton, serving under General Bradley's command, will take the section below and Sixth Army Group under General Devers[9] will move north to take over some of the Third Army's sector. Effective at once the VIII Corps is no longer under our control.

At 1:30 this afternoon General Montgomery arrived for his first conference with General Hodges. He believes that it is imperative that the V Corps, as does the General, shoulder be held at all costs. Bridges all along the front and including those in the VIII Corps sector have been prepared for demolition by Colonel Carter's engineers. To the engineers' everlasting credit will go for the exploits of several small detachments at many points, especially that one at Trois Ponts which has been fighting steadily since the offensive began. Details are not now available but it seems that they—and they were only two officers and about twenty enlisted man—blew one bridge and kept on giving the Boche hell despite the overwhelming odds against them. During General Montgomery's stay a Lieutenant Colonel arrived from the 7th Armd Div to report that the 7th and 9th Armd Divs together are holding firm at ST VITH along the approximate line: P-7191–ST VITH–HOLDINGEN. Contact between the 82nd and 7th Armd and between the 82nd A/B and what remains of the 106th was made tonight although not in strength. The two regiments of the 106th are still cut off and there is no word from them. The 112th Inf which has performed magnificently under Colonel Rudder is now attached to the 7th Armd Div.[10] 101st A/B Div below is very heavily engaged but is still holding at BASTOGNE. STAVELOT is definitely in our hands and we are closing the net around STOUMONT where the 1st SS is. G-2, VIII Corps tonight figures that the Boche will drive south from BASTOGNE to WILTZ with its main force; he having been blocked in his drive north towards LIEGE and NAMUR. Tonight General Plank and General Lee arrived for a conference. General Lee was given full responsibility from SHAEF for the MEUSE bridges. Question is: Will this conflict with the responsibility already assumed by Montgomery for these operations? From General Plank's G-3 we learned of the existence of an ADSEC TD Bn and General Hodges had no difficulty in persuading General Lee to reduce the fighting strength of ADSEC and move the TD Bn at once into our zone.

The weather was foul all day and no planes were aloft. Buzz-bombs in countless numbers passed over the CP although none cut off as close as those of yesterday. However, the planes and the continual traffic moving up and down the main road makes it difficult for the General to obtain the quiet which is necessary in the making of these vast decisions. Base moved today back to the vicinity of ST TROND and arrangements are now being made to move our CP to TONGRES [Tongeren]. It is not as close to the front as the General would like but it is necessary to move it because of good communications offered. Colonel Dickson explains the shortage of buzz-bombs by saying that the Boche is too busy bringing up other supplies to bother with them.

Thursday, 21 December 1944: The II [SS] Panzer Corps whose exact whereabouts were unknown has appeared against the 1st Div and further west below MALMEDY in an attempt to exploit the corridor and drive north towards VERVIERS. 30th Div is having a tough fight, likewise the 1st, although the latter as usual is supremely confident in its ability to take anything the Boche can hand out, and this morning wanted to know when they will get their orders to attack. General Gerow has reported that eight enemy tanks have thus far been knocked out and things are holding well. One of the great questions now is where to shift armored strength. The attack in V Corps is anticipated and therefore CCA of 3rd Armd is held in reserve. Is his threat in the VIII Corps sector greater or not?

Early this morning General Collins arrived for a long conference with General Hodges. In yesterday's conference it now appears General Montgomery told General Hodges he wanted the most aggressive fighting Corps Commander with adequate troops to attack from the general area southwest of the XVIII Corps sector. For this attack the 84th Div is moving down from the Ninth Army. 75th Div which has just arrived is being added and what is available of the 3rd Armd Div will likewise be used. This morning Brigadier [Ronald Frederick King] Belchem[11] of Marshal Montgomery's headquarters suggested also the immediate move of the 2nd Armd Div which has been in reserve in the Ninth Army down to add strength to the push. This headquarters heartily approved. At 11 o'clock General [Alexander R.] Bolling[12] called to say that it developed that there was small arms fire and some penetration at MARCHE where he had temporarily set up headquarters with his division. The question he wanted to know was: Should he commit the only combat team which had arrived? He was told, "yes, hold." Now the question is: Does this enemy penetration make the assembly area unsafe for VII Corps. There will be no offensive weapon if it has to be committed piece-meal in defense. Should it move further back?

General Collins is strenuously in favor of moving CCR of 5th Armd Div now at ROTGEN [Roetgen] in the V Corps area down to support the one combat command of General Rose which is trying to block any drive northwest from BASTOGNE towards NAMUR on Route 4. General Collins insists that the Boche cannot attack through the 78th and 9th Div sector with tanks. The area there is high marshy plateau, is still heavily mined, and there are only two roads. He believes any effort there by the enemy would be futile and could be broken with relatively little strength. This headquarters did not make any immediate commitments.

General Collins is full of his usual fighting Irish vigor. He is confident that with the 2nd and 3rd Armd Divs he can beat any collection that the Boche want to throw at him and that the 2nd and 3rd Armd are the two best outfits of its kind in the world, in his opinion.

Colonel Dickson reported today that the group of paratroopers dropped in battalion strength on the EUPEN-MALMEDY road the first night of the drive are now without rations and ammunition and are trying to make their way back through enemy lines. The prisoner bag is thus far small. Our troops know of the atrocities committed by the enemy and know that now is a matter of life or death, we or they. Casualties on both sides are admittedly high but no definite figures are available. There is as yet no word of Colonel Ray,[13] Ammunition Officer. He has not been heard from since the first day of the attack and it is thought he was one of the murdered group.

From captured documents and maps the first objectives of the Boche attacks seem definitely to have been HUY, EUPEN, VERVIERS, and LIEGE with ANTWERP the eventual goal thus splitting our two Armies and making supply impossible. Both Panzer Armie V [5 Panzerarmee] and Panzer Armie VI [6 Panzerarmee] are taking part in the attack along with Seventh Army in the extreme south, TRIER Section, and the Fifteenth Army pitted against the old VII Corps now XIX Corps area. The 47th German Panzer Corps is now definitely identified as being involved in the VIII Corps sector. It is impossible to tell where we stand at this point. One minute things look good and the next minute bad. On the ability of the VII Corps to assemble without being committed and then attack eastward will depend much. General Kean who said on Monday that Wednesday would be the crucial day now says that on Friday we can tell whether we can hold or will have to further withdraw to a defense line such as the MEUSE. We learned tonight that the night we left SPA American flags, pictures of the president, and all other Allied insignia, were taken down and that the Mayor released 20 suspected collaborationists out of jail. Next day Colonel Fisk who was in charge of the local security and task force went back to the town. Some officer again pulled up the American flag on the most prominent pole in the town. Spa is quiet.

G-2 claims that one officer of the infiltrated jeep group has offered to tell all in exchange for a pistol with which he can commit suicide and thus hold fast to his strange out-worn conception of honor. We shall cordially accommodate him although we do not know whether he is playing square or not. We know now that many of the group thus far picked up have been through MPs who dissatisfied with American credentials offered have asked these men such questions as: "What is Sinatra's first name?" "Who won the World Series?" and, "What became of Klem Winkle McSlop?"

Marshal Montgomery arrived against [again] at 1:30 today for a conference with General Simpson and General Hodges. After the conference he asked if things looked better and General Hodges replied in the affirmative. General Ridgway has telephoned frequently during the day to say that he is being attacked in strength all along the line by an estimated two or three armored divisions. 82nd A/B has some TD and some of Colonel Patterson's 90mm guns but his anti-tank strength is, of course, limited. There are as yet still no reports that dumps of any size have fallen into Boche hands. He started the drive with three days' supply of gas and has probably been able to gain an additional day or two through gas drained from captured vehicles.

The third successive day that the weather was bad. With good weather we could stop this. SHAEF has laid on everything: mediums, heavies, and fighter-bombers of all the air forces of US and Great Britain. If only a break should come. On the dark side of the picture is the fact that the Boche has by no means committed all of his reserves as he is obviously waiting to see which of the two corridors he has created is easiest to exploit. After three days it seemed that he was going to throw the weight through BASTOGNE. This still may be the case although the 101st A/B Div is holding it secure. However, this morning's attack in the north corridor towards MALMEDY may indicate he wishes to exploit both breaches to the fullest with LIEGE as the objective of the second.

Friday, 22 December 1944: Two early pieces of good information this morning is: 1—Third Army with 4th Armd, 26th Inf, and 80th Inf Divs jumped off from ARLON this morning at six o'clock and preliminary reports show them to be gaining three to four miles. 2—Colonel Van Der Heidt [von der Heydte],[14] former CO of 6th Para Regt and in command of the special group which dropped behind our lines in strength in the EUPEN–MALMEDY road sector surrendered this morning and was being evacuated through medical channels. He is suffering from pneumonia and trench foot and was disheartened by the failure of the attack to reach him. He heard over the German radio that MON- SCHAU was taken, a fact he knew to be untrue, and he remarked to his captor that the Americans were "too obstinate."

1st Div according to a report from General Huebner who visited it yesterday was never madder. They had called up at least three times to find out when they could attack. Germans switched their buzz-bombs in strength to HUY and a small town named ESURUX. At HUY they are after the bridge and at the latter town they are trying to block the traf- fic which they know is moving down that road. General Collins was a visitor early this morning. He is particularly concerned about any infiltration which may have occurred below or to the west of his Corps assembly area, and he immediately called for Colonel Carter to find out what bridges in that area had been prepared for demolition espe- cially those over the MEUSE and the LESSE. He knows this country, hav- ing come through it on his offensive into Belgium and is convinced that a few well blown bridges and mines can hold up any spearhead for a considerable length of time. There was, however, no need for him to worry about this as Monty arrived shortly after 1:15 and brought the General the good news that an Armored Brigade with 50 tanks at NAMUR, 50 at GIVET, and 50 at a point equi-distant between those two towns, had sent its reconnaissance elements forward to the VII Corps assembly area and would methodically clean up any small pockets of Germans if such existed.

We have no definite information as to the success of the withdrawal of the 7th Armd Div. They were attacked last night in strength and they had to move out of ST VITH early this morning. They were given permis- sion by General Kean to reform their lines slightly to the rear. A good part of one combat command of the 9th operating with the 7th was wiped out in this supreme German drive. There is no attempt to rob from General Hasbrouck the tremendous credit due him and his entire force operating in that area for their magnificent work in splitting the main German blow. By his refusal to give up ST VITH he forced one Pan- zer Corps to take the northern route just south of MALMEDY and leading to STAVELOT where it is receiving a terrific artillery pounding and an- other Corps to take the southern route where it is expected the attack of the Third Army in conjunction with that of VII Corps will successfully block it. The 101st A/B Div still holds BASTOGNE but is cut off and is calling for supply by air. However, it is believed that the escape routes to the west are very lightly held by the enemy and the 101st could fight their way out any time that they felt forced to do so. However, by holding BASTOGNE which is a key road center they are forcing the enemy spearheads off into minor road nets. This, combined with snow and ice which is everywhere in the VIII Corps sector, is going to take much of the punch out of their drive.

Monty was chipper and confident as usual. The employment of this Armored Brigade to screen in back of VII Corps area lifted a tremendous load off the General's mind. Obviously we had no troops to do it. General Kean telephoned Brigadier Belchem after the conference requesting that Monty make overtures to SHAEF for the immediate transport to Belgium of the 17th A/B Div. This division could probably be put into action, if given good weather, five days after it was alerted.

Execution at Master Rear this afternoon of the three infiltrators of the unit STEILAU was postponed. These men have been tried and found guilty and the General had received verbal authority from SHAEF and from Group, General Bradley himself, to pass on the sentences. However, the telegram this morning from Group specifically delegating such authority had not yet arrived by four o'clock and the General was reluctant to go ahead with the execution of these men without it.

We moved at 4:30 this afternoon through LIEGE to TONGRES where the CP now occupies the barracks which were Belgium's West Point before the war. Here the General should have the peace and quiet which are necessary for the momentous decisions which must be made. We arrived shortly after six o'clock to find the ack-ack [antiaircraft artillery] firing away at some planes. Before we went to dinner General Gerow called to say that a strong attack had been launched against the 39th Inf by enemy infantry backed up by self-propelled guns. High ground was lost and General Gerow said that reinforcements must be had. The General immediately decided to switch the 60th Inf which had been scheduled to assist the 7th Armd Div in its offensive back to General Craig. This was done with some difficulty as they had left STOLBERG at three o'clock in the afternoon and we had no communications with VII Corps. He told General Gerow to button up as tight as possible, to make liberal use of mines, blocks, and demolitions, and to hold on until relief should be forthcoming.

The 1st Div had a rough time yesterday but the enemy in front of them had even a rougher time. They reported through Corps that the bodies of the German dead were piled up in front of their positions while their losses were between three and four hundred men. During the day enemy pressure continued on the 82nd A/B Div front. The enemy had been forced to the east back of the SALM River from 6995 to 6701. Elements of the 505th Para held the bridgehead on the east side for a while but withdrew about 7:30 in face of a strong enemy attack. In so doing they blew the bridge killing 30 Germans who were on it at the time. STOUMONT has been recaptured by them and our troops had moved toward LA GLEIZE, which is not yet reported as fallen. There were tonight numerous paratroop scares and occasionally our own men were firing at each other but no serious damage was done. The small enemy force re-entered HOTTON tonight but elements of the 3rd Armd Div will take care of them tomorrow. 75th and 84th and the 2nd Armd are all closed and the attack of VII Corps should begin on Sunday morning.

Again we had almost no air. There were reportedly a few mediums overhead but this was not corroborated. Reports for tomorrow are more encouraging.

G-2 reports that the Boche despite his gains are extremely disappointed at the progress made. They have obviously thus far at least failed to make a wide deep penetration and we have, in the wild mixed fighting that has been going on, forced them to split their forces and attack everywhere instead of along the scheduled routes. The shoulder is still the crux; if we can hold it until the VII Corps drive begins we shall drive them out. If the shoulder weakens the situation may be considerably more serious.

The order of the day arriving from General Eisenhower at five o'clock this afternoon for distribution to every man in the AEF [Allied Expeditionary Force], told them that this was the last supreme effort of the enemy and that should we hold fast we would soon have the power to bring the war quickly to the end [see below].

G-2 is weary [wary?] of any predictions. The Boche still has considerable strength in the Ninth Army sector and if he knows that we have weakened it to the extent that we have done, he may feel that he can very well put on another attack there. Two captured orders have been taken in which the commanding generals of divisions instructed their soldiers to take no prisoners "except a few officers" who were to be brought promptly back to headquarters for questioning. Another prisoner stated that the Boche had learned of our weakness in the VIII Corps sector through interrogation of our prisoners.

LIEGE was bombed heavily tonight by the enemy, damages and casualties are not yet known.

FOR THE EYES OF GENERAL HODGES ONLY

FROM SHAEF MAIN   221400A DEC 44
TO FOR ACTION FIRST UNCLE SUGAR ARMY   URGENT
SUGAR 71980
IN THE RECENT BATTLING YOU AND YOUR ARMY HAVE
PERFORMED IN YOUR USUAL MAGNIFICENT STYLE AND
YOUR GOOD WORK IS HELPING TO CREATE ABLE SITUATION
FROM WHICH WE MAY PROFIT MATERIALLY PD IT IS
ESPECIALLY IMPORTANT NOW THAT EVERYONE BE KEPT ON
THEIR TOES AND THAT ALL OF US LOOK AND PLAN AHEAD
WITH KEEN DETERMINATION CMA AND WITH OPTIMISM
CMA TO TAKING ADVANTAGE OF ALL OPPORTUNITIES PD
NOW THAT YOU HAVE BEEN PLACED UNDER THE FIELD
MARSHALS OPERATIONAL COMMAND ITEM KNOW THAT YOU
WILL RESPOND CHEERFULLY AND EFFICIENTLY TO EVERY
INSTRUCTION HE GIVES PD THE SLOGAN IS QUOTE CHINS UP
QUOTE PD PLEASE MAKE SURE THAT ALL YOUR SUBORDINATE
COMMANDERS EXERT THE MAXIMUM OF LEADERSHIP AND
EXAMPLE IN SUSTAINING MORALE AND CONVINCING EVERY
MAN THAT HE IS IN BETTER CONDITION THAN THE ENEMY PD
GOOD LUCK AND LET US SEEK ABLE REAL VICTORY PD

SIGNED IKE EISENHOWER

Saturday, 23 December 1944: The General left the CP at 11 o'clock this morning to visit General Collins at the new VII Corps headquarters at MARCHE, in an old chateau. He left with an armored car escort. It was bitterly cold, clearing the heavy fog which for three days has cancelled air operations, and over their heads, on passage down and back, fighter-bombers, mediums and heavies flew in steady procession.

The General went over the attack with General Collins, and with General [Brian Gwynne] Horrocks,[15] British XXX Corps Commander and admittedly the most aggressive in the British line-up here. General Horrocks said that the Americans had fought magnificently, that the 82nd was the best division he had ever seen in action, and only regretted that his Corps, standing in reserve behind the MEUSE with five divisions, was not yet able to get into the fray; that it was unfair for the Americans to take the sole brunt of this blow. During the General's stay there, four enemy parachutists were reported to have been dropped a mile or so from the CP, while further down the main road a tank engagement was going on. General Collins was as confident as ever, though it appears that he may have to commit much of his force before the offensive, now postponed until Christmas Day, can start. The 84th is now almost entirely in the line, and there is a tank threat toward the MEUSE at DINANT, which he may have to engage, with elements of the 2nd Armd Div.

During his absence, General de Guigand [Francis de Guingand],[16] who was stranded in England when the offensive started, drove in to see General Kean, and shortly after two o'clock, he was joined by Field Marshal Montgomery, who was returning from a visit to V Corps. The 60th Inf arrived there early today, and one battalion has been committed. Everything, however, is quiet in this sector. The Boche, learning that they cannot break the shoulder against the 2nd and the 1st Divs, are going elsewhere. Right now, the biggest threat appears to be a push between General Ridgway and General Collins, or a drive straight west, which we fear far less. The 7th Armd and the 106th are now disengaged, and are returning through the XVIII Corps sectors to reform. We do not yet know how much of them have been saved.

The extent of enemy espionage came forcibly to our attention this afternoon when nine Bochs planes bombed and strafed our old headquarters at CHAUDFONTAINE. One 500-pounder was dropped directly in front of the Palace Hotel, killing Richard Frankish, UP correspondent, wounding Col [Flynn L.] Andrew, P&PW, and killing and injuring several civilians. They broke every window in the Palace, and left very little of the Hotel des Bains, across the street. AA fire was unsuccessful against them.

It is now certain that the 17th A/B Div is on the way from the UK, as soon as weather permits. They will take up positions behind the MEUSE. The Third Army attack made good progress, one CC of the 4th Armd coming within a few miles of the isolated 101st A/B Div at BASTOGNE, the 26th pushing up well on the right.

Today, the three spies of unit Steilau were executed near EUPEN. The prisoners' last request was to hear Christmas carols, sung by a group of German women prisoners. They were granted it.

A summary of our air activity today shows our planes to have been heavily engaged throughout most of the day in air battle, thus reducing the destruction they were able to give Boche armored columns. The weather prediction for tomorrow is: EXCELLENT.

The General is now well located in a private home, formerly occupied by General Anderson of the XVI Corps. With a chance for rest, and with good food again provided, he is obviously feeling fitter and better able to cope with the constant pressure of this work and strain. Reading of the Stars & Stripes discloses that this threat is not lightly dismissed in the US, that newspaper editors, at least, regard the counteroffensive as an all or nothing attempt by our enemy.

Sunday, 24 December 1944: The big news of the day is that for the first time in a week the sky is completely clear of clouds and our Air as well as that of the Boche is up in strength. We and the RAF are sending heavies, we are sending mediums and three groups of fighter-bombers are going to fly every mission they can before five o'clock. Preliminary reports indicate that they have destroyed 290 motor transports as well as approximately 20 tanks. The day's shooting was everywhere magnificent. Various air battles were fought between here and the German lines with 5 B-17s being knocked down east of LIEGE. AA claimed 33 for the day and the total count of German aircraft claimed to be destroyed by all means available totaled 178. Our total losses are not yet known.

There is an indication of the extent of enemy air activity when four planes, ME109s shot low over the CP shortly after one o'clock today. Whether they were on an offensive mission or simply lost after one of these air battles and trying to regain their lines we don't know but our quadruple mounts in the court-yard and on three sides of the CP went immediately to work. One of the planes burst into a ball of orange fire at an estimated altitude of 1,000 feet and dove to the ground only a half mile from the CP. Later inquiry showed the pilot to be only fifteen years of age. Another plane was seen smoking as he left the area and it is claimed as a probable. Tonight also enemy bombers were over the area and AA fire was heard on three distinct occasions. Another plane appeared shortly after 3:30 in the afternoon passing a few hundred yards to the left of the CP in a dive but our AA fire was without effect. An air raid siren now gives some seconds of notice so that helmets can be put on and exit made to the basement cellar if necessary.

General Montgomery arrived as usual for his afternoon conference with General Hodges and General Kean. The outlook this afternoon is not good. Elements of the 2nd SS Panzer have penetrated as far west as CELLES not too far from DINANT on the MEUSE. They are being met by both our forces and those of the British 29th Armd Brigade. Whether they are there in strength or not we do not know. But this threat if pushed northward could prove seriously embarrassing.

The good news of the day was that the 119th Inf backed by elements of CCB of the 3rd Armd Div cleared the enemy pocket at LA GLEIZE capturing about 150 prisoners and 170 vehicles including 38 tanks, 78 half-tracks, 8 armored cars, and 6 self-propelled guns. Remainder of the Div continued to hold tight at STOUMONT, STAVELOT, and MALMEDY. The 82nd A/B Div likewise held their position during daylight hours against heavy enemy pressure with the strongest push being put against the MANHAY–MALEMPRE area. Tonight the decision was made for the 82nd Div to withdraw to the line P-5492–6797. 7th Armd Div which has closed to the north of this new 82nd area has moved down into the front and was being attacked tonight from MANHAY. CCB of 9th Armd with the 112th Inf attached moved last night to a bivouac area in the vicinity of HERVE, K-5301. CCB of 9th Armd Div is finally out and in fairly good condition in spite of the heavy fighting which occurred when they were cut off from the 7th Armd Div and 106th Inf. The 106th Div likewise bivouacked may be regrouped and re-equipped in their assembly area. The division has made a fervent plea to retain its identity rather than to be merged as replacements for some other division. Radio contact with the two cut-off regiments has now ceased entirely.

The VII Corps, instead of proceeding to the offensive as planned, has now to assume a completely defensive role. 3rd Armd less CCB and with the 2-89th [289th] and 290th RCTs of the 75th Div attached—continued to defend at HOTTON-SOY-MANHAY area against increasing enemy pressure. Task Force Hogan is still isolated at MARCOURAY and attempts to supply them from the air have not been successful. The day before yesterday the gas dropped in enemy hands and today it dropped two miles into our own front lines. No contact is likewise been established with 3rd Bn 35th Inf which was isolated at ROCHEFORT except for one officer and 32 men who worked their way back to our lines. Tonight about 300 enemy infiltrated into VERDENNE and in the 84th Div sector the enemy was reinforced in the town by another 200 infantry but we were engaging them and late tonight still held the town. It appears that tomorrow may be a crucial day in the VII Corps sector with Terrible Ernie Harmon's tank forces getting the chance of a life time to do the work which he loves.

Limited gains were made along a broad front by the III Corps of the Third Army. Although reported early this morning that one Combat Command of 4th Armd had reached BASTOGNE, this now proves to be unconfirmed according to a telephone call from General Bradley to General Hodges.

Two new developments have taken place during the day as a result of conferences. 1—51st Scottish Division under General Remmie [Tom Gordon Rennie][17] 17,800 strong is moving across the river and taking up assembly positions southeast of LIEGE. Another British division is going to move in to back up the line in front of AACHEN. The 11th Armd Div coming from the UK is expected to close in the vicinity of REIMS three or four days from now. 2—General Huebner was General Hodges' visitor before dinner for a long conference which lasted until midnight. They made plans for the movement to the rear of all heavy equipment of V Corps divisions, in order that, if it becomes necessary for these troops to withdraw, the roads would not be clogged with this heavy material and it would [not] be necessary to hand it over to the enemy.

Despite the air's magnificent performance today things tonight look, if anything, worse than before. Indications from G-2 are that the Boche will attempt to drive north with everything he possesses towards VERVIERS and LIEGE. Although it does not appear that as yet the enemy has gained for Hitler any of the Christmas presents which they promised they now have considerably more freedom of movement because of the withdrawal of the 7th and 9th Armd and the withdrawal tomorrow of the 82nd. However, things always look blackest just before the dawn and the weather man promises us an identical flying day tomorrow. Since the Boche is on the offensive he cannot travel by night alone but must use the roads by day to build up necessary POL and supplies, and we can hit him. For the second time in this war time is on our side and not on that of the enemy. Every preparation is being made to lay road blocks, minefields, barbed wire and other impediments wherever it seems that the Boche might be able to create any small indentation. We are doing our best to organize a defense in depth and only time can make that possible.

Monday, 25 December 1944—Xmas: Christmas day opened inauspiciously for the General today when two shots fired in succession shortly before two o'clock up the street from our house awakened everybody. The guard was immediately alerted and five minutes later another series of shots were heard. After fifteen minutes, with the help of two British sergeants, two men, one purporting to be W/O [Warrant Officer] Fleury, French Liaison, attached to this headquarters, and the other a guard at the Motor Pool, were taken into custody. They said that they had been given instructions to fire at any light or signal which was being shown when planes appeared overhead. One of the British sergeants, however, asserted that a bullet had whizzed uncomfortably close to his head. The two men were taken to the Provost Marshal's office for questioning.

This morning the situation looked bad; strong enemy pressure being directed due north from MANHAY and also in the CELLES area against the 2nd Armd. The lines, however, held. At nighttime most of the lost ground at MANHAY, some 2,000 yards, was regained. MANHAY was definitely re-entered by elements of the CCB of 7th Armd but withdrew to the north where they could better control and cover the town and roads with artillery fire. Contact was established with CCB and 3rd Armd on the west. The 82nd A/B completed its withdrawal to the general line: MALEMPRE-SART-VIELSALM to the high ground leading to TROIS PONTS. During the day only light to moderate pressure existed on their front. Shortly before the General went to dinner General Collins called to report a "cracker-jack" day for his Corps. There were bad spots, of course, and Task Force Richardson consisting of one tank company and one infantry company was over-run and forced to destroy their equipment in the vicinity of MALEMPRE, but CCB of the 3rd Armd which reverted to VII Corps control was committed and reduced the enemy penetration, re-entering GRAND MESMIL [Grandmenil] where five dug-in enemy tanks were still holding out. Task Force Hogan surrounded for three days at MARCOURAY was directed to destroy their equipment and attempt to return to our lines by foot. The 84th Div had a field day; one reconnaissance battalion, probably of the 2nd SS, came up towards them in an attempt to establish a line of departure and were whacked hard, the total of 4 tanks and 350 PWs were taken. An enemy pocket has been surrounded in the vicinity of P-3586. The 2nd Armd attacking against scattered to strong resistance cleared CELLES. This was done by CCB. CCA repulsed enemy counterattack and advanced to FRONDEUX [Frandeux] and HAVRENNE, inflicting heavy losses on enemy personnel and equipment. 13 self-propelled guns were captured which were out of gas and 470 PWs were taken. Contact was made along this line with the British and the British now have patrols of their 11th Armd Div on the other side of the MEUSE extending down past the Group boundary.

Everything was quiet on the V Corps front. There was only moderate enemy pressure but no concentrated attack. However, TAC R at 1615 reported extremely heavy traffic moving into the MONSCHAU Forest area and General Hart expects to make their life unhappy tonight with artillery interdiction.

Certainly the best and biggest news of the day was that for the third day running we were blessed with an absolutely cloudless sky. General Quesada called on General Hodges personally after dinner to report that his people had had probably their day's finest shooting since the war began. No accurate total of tanks or motor vehicles destroyed exists although one extremely fine punch they put in was to destroy ten out of twenty tanks and thirty out of sixty motor vehicles in the Man-hay area. Our mediums and our heavies were likewise extremely active, hitting deeper into the Boche supply lines. German air was still on a large scale although not so large as yesterday. There were a few dog fights over Liege and Colonel Patterson reported that ME109s had strafed unsuccessfully our AA positions surrounding that city. His AA units continued to pile up an amazing toll bringing down almost half of the 60 odd planes reported today over the V Corps front.

PW reports received tonight indicate that our artillery has been chewing up a terrific percentage of the attacking forces. Many PWs had not eaten for two days or beyond what they could scrounge from captured American supplies.

Bill met General Bradley at St Trond airfield this afternoon and motored him to Field Marshal Montgomery's headquarters at Zondhoven. General Bradley told him that the 101st A/B Div in the Bastogne area claimed destruction of 150 tanks. They still have not yet been relieved there. He told the story of a Quartermaster Officer who seeking the road to Luxembourg and misdirected by an American MP blithely sailed into Bastogne under nothing more serious than small arms fire. General Bradley had intended to visit General Hodges but because of his later arrival was forced to immediately return to St Trond after spending thirty minutes with the Field Marshal who had divested himself of his usual eight garments and put on for Christmas Day an extremely natty dress uniform.

The day ended inauspiciously also with the arrival of a V-1 which landing some 300 yards west of the CP shattered all but one window in the General's office and breaking windows in The Holmes and injuring, although not seriously, 65 members of the headquarters including Colonel [Peter C.] Hains[18] and Colonel [Rosser L.] Hunter[19] who were hit by flying glass.

Tonight it can be said that the enemy is temporarily at least halted. No more gains were chalked up by him today. This does not mean, as both the General and General Kean realize, that he is going to stop attacking. But we have now had time to dig in and move our troops.

General Kean impressed most forcibly on Field Marshal Montgomery this afternoon in a transfer of troops, in a telephone conversation that he wished to obtain at once an infantry division preferably the 102nd which could be replaced by a British Division. We have the 51st Highlanders backing up our line but the General would prefer to stick in the 102nd to strengthen the front of the XVIII and VII Corps. But they feel there is infiltration, since the front is extremely wide, of small groups of Germans, which infiltration in time could become extremely serious. Field Marshal Montgomery said he would give an answer tomorrow.

The weather prediction for tomorrow is: GOOD.

Tuesday, 26 December 1944: Things continued to look better all day today.

The V Corps front was quiet; all positions are maintained and patrol activities continued. Patrols of the 99th Div destroying 10 enemy tanks which had been abandoned after becoming mired in the mud.

XVIII Corps: Although there was little enemy pressure on the 30th Div front, there were steady attacks against the westernmost part of the Corps sector. During the day CCB of 7th Armd Div continued to attack MANHAY inflicting heavy losses on the enemy but were unable to enter the town.

VII Corps: The heaviest fighting along the front was in this sector. The 3rd Armd Div continued to attack GRANDE MESNIL with CCB and now hold most of the town including the cross roads in the center. 90% of Task Force Hogan which had been isolated in MARCOURAY today successfully infiltrated back to our lines. During the day 4 tanks and 400 infantry penetrated the lines of the 334th Inf but were cut off and mopped up together with other elements previously surrounded at that point—P 335853. An enemy force attacking at 1700 between MESNIL [Ménil] and MARENNE [Verdenne] were repulsed with losses including at least three tanks. There was stiff fighting throughout the day in the 2nd Armd Div sector; both, east and west of CELLES one company alone knocked out 7 Mark Vs, 1 Mark IV, 3 half-tracks, 1 armored car, 10 trucks, and 2 anti-tank guns.

The 83rd Div which we are getting instead of the 102nd as requested started to move this morning to the vicinity of HAVELANGE and closed late tonight. The fourth successive day of good weather brought out almost as much air from the UK and from bases here as had flown the previous day. The Luftwaffe activity dropped off to a mere 70 planes during the day and night. One JU-88[20] flew over TONGRES between 11 and 12 o'clock and there was intermittent AA fire throughout the evening. They also attacked and bombed CHARLEROI with a force of 12 JU-88s.

Below in the Third Army sector contact was finally made between the surrounded 101st A/B Div at BASTOGNE by advancing elements of the 4th Armd Div. General Patton is throwing, in addition, the 35th Div and the 6th Armd Div, and is reputed to have said, "The damn Jerries have stuck their heads in the meat grinder and I've got the handle." Elements of the 11th Armd US Div have already crossed the MEUSE from their CP at CHARLEVILLE and are advancing steadily east towards the HOUFFALIZE area. The 6th British A/B Div has arrived and is taking up positions between, and both east and west of the MEUSE, GIVET and DINANT and other British divisions have moved down closer to the MEUSE as defensive reserves.

We are getting from the British 200 tanks which will be used to replace our losses now estimated at over 250. We are to pay the British back only when it becomes convenient to do so. Both General de Guigand and Marshal Montgomery were at the CP between 1400 and 1430 today for a long conference with General Hodges and General Kean.

Tonight shortly before eight o'clock, prisoners captured asserted that there would be a strong attack in the XVIII Corps sector launched by 9th SS [Panzer] and 26 VG Divs. However, this attack did not materialize and increasing statements from PWs bear evidence that the supply problems is becoming overwhelmingly difficult. Although it is yet too early to be optimistic the picture tonight is certain[ly] far rosier than on any other day since the counteroffensive began.

Wednesday, 27 December 1944: Enemy pressure continued to slow down on all fronts today and G-2 came up with a PW report that 2nd Panzer Div had received orders at midnight last night to destroy everything they could not carry with them and to retreat to the southeast. Reflecting at least temporary lack of offensive spirit on the part of the Boche. General Quesada said at lunch today that his boys were having nowhere near as good shooting as they had had. There were individual groups of motor vehicles but none of the long columns which his men have beat up for the previous three days.

The Corps by Corps front:

V Corps was quiet generally. Tonight General Hart put additional artillery at work in front of 1st and 2nd Divs because of a rumored spoiling attack along their line.

XVIII Corps: 82nd A/B Div continued to improve its defensive positions with only light contact with the enemy. CCB of 7th Armd Div

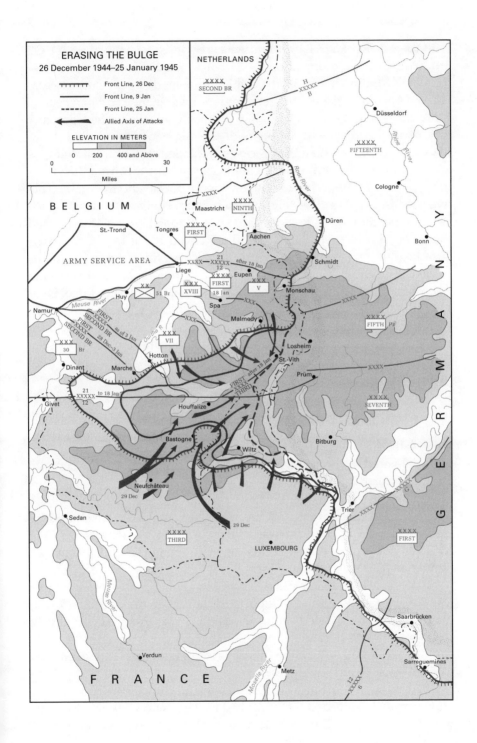

ERASING THE BULGE
26 December 1944–25 January 1945

Front Line, 26 Dec
Front Line, 9 Jan
Front Line, 25 Jan
Allied Axis of Attacks

ELEVATION IN METERS

0   200   400 and Above

0   30
Miles

NETHERLANDS

Düsseldorf

XXXX
SECOND BR

H
XXXXX
B

XXXX
FIFTEENTH

Rhine River

BELGIUM

Roer River

Cologne

St.-Trond

XXXX
Tongres   FIRST
Maastricht   XXXX
NINTH

Düren

Bonn

ARMY SERVICE AREA

Liege

Aachen

Schmidt

21
XXXXX   after 18 Jan
12
XXXX   Eupen   XXX
FIRST   V
XVIII   18 Jan

Monschau

XXXX

Huy   XX   51 Br
Namur   Meuse River   FIRST   as of 3 Jan
SECOND BR
FIRST   28 Dec–3 Jan
SECOND BR

Spa

XXX

Malmedy

XXXX
FIFTH   Pz

XXX
VII   Ourthe R

Losheim

Hotton   XXXX
30   Br

St.-Vith

XXXX

Dinant   Marche

21   to 18 Jan
XXXXX
12
Givet

Houffalize

FIRST   after 18 Jan
XXX
THIRD

Prüm

XXXX
SEVENTH

Bitburg

Bastogne   Wiltz

Neufchâteau
29 Dec

29 Dec

Trier   XXX

G   E   R   M   A   N   Y

Sedan

XXXX
THIRD

LUXEMBOURG

XXXX
FIRST

Saarbrücken

Verdun

Moselle River

Metz

12
XXXXX
6

Sarreguemines

F   R   A   N   C   E

with the 1st Bn of 517 Para Inf attached established contact with CCB 3rd Armd Div and mopped up the MANHAY area. During the night 551st Para Bn operating in the 508th Para Inf zone made a raid toward AMACOUNT [Amcomont] but they encountered an enemy company some 1,000 yards of the town which they promptly attacked. The Company commander and several members of the company were killed and 5 PWs were captured against our losses of 1 killed and 10 wounded.

VII Corps: CCB 3rd Armd cleared GRANDE MESNIL during the morning. 84th Div finished clearing out an enemy pocket and maintained active patrols. 2nd Armd Div eliminated scattered enemy elements which remained in the CELLES–ROCHEFORT area. CCR took HUMAIN. CCB cleared the wooded area east of CELLES and advanced to VERRE. CCA cleared JAMBLINE and extended elements to the HOMME River. Other elements advanced to the outskirts of ROCHEFORT and reports are that there are two enemy battalions who will make a stand as a covering force. Over 1,000 PWs were taken by the 2nd Armd and heavy losses inflicted in both personnel and equipment. The 83rd Div less the 33rd [330th] Inf which is in Corps reserve is now preparing to relieve elements of the 2nd Armd in the line while the 75th Div is taking over that sector held by the 3rd Armd.

Above in the Ninth Army sector the gap left by the withdrawal of the 83rd Div was covered by elements of the 52nd British Div.

In the VIII Corps sector the contact points between III Corps and the isolated BASTOGNE pocket have been connected and 52 trucks of supplies delivered to the 101st. Steady progress although slow was made by the III Corps to the north.

General Anderson, CG of XVI Corps, along with other members of his Corps headquarters and his attached Signal Bn were shifted by General Hodges after a conference this morning to headquarters of the XVIII A/B Corps. General Anderson will act as General Ridgway's deputy and his staff will give the latter whatever assistance he desires.

General Montgomery did not come today but made instead a trip to see General Eisenhower. Reportedly he urged the Supreme Commander to go on a defensive in the Sixth Army Group sector and to shift six divisions here to the north so that the drive towards the ROER could be exploited now to the fullest. It is not known what the reaction of "Ike" was.

Bad weather kept most of the heavies grounded in Great Britain. However, we again had a cloudless day. The enemy air was on a reduced scale and for the first time in several days there were no signs of

Boche aircraft over our immediate CP sector. 61 V-1s were over the area, 24 of which landed in LIEGE.

The general feeling at the CP tonight is one of complete optimism. General Hodges, General Kean, and General Thorson went over at midnight the three possible attack plans submitted by General Collins; two of which have BASTOGNE as the objective, one of which has ST VITH. They are broad and sweeping in their concept of offensive action and General Collins frankly admits in the papers submitted with them that they will require some strength because of the exposed flanks. General Hodges has had enough of exposed flanks for the last two weeks and it is thought that the most conservative of the three plans will be the one finally adopted.

Thursday, 28 December 1944: Today was generally quiet all along the front and a heavy fog prevented all but the heavies from the UK from operating.

There was some increase in pressure along the V Corps front and before noon it was estimated that 21 Bns of Boche artillery were laying shells down on the front lines and especially in the rear areas. However, shortly after four o'clock it died down and no attack materialized.

There was no change in the XVIII Corps. VII Corps consolidated its positions and mopped up most of the enemy which infiltrated through the 290th Inf front to SADZOT, 120 being killed or captured. The 83rd Div relieved elements of the 2nd Armd Div and closed in with 2 Bns at ROCHEFORT. In the Third Army the BASTOGNE pocket was widened and good gains were made especially by the III Corps led by the 26th and 35th Divs.

General Hodges motored to VONDHOVEN [Zondhoven] this morning over an icy slippery road for a long conference with General Montgomery. The general objective of which was to determine when and where we would stage our own counteroffensive. The XXX British Corps is going to take over the responsibility for the general area now occupied by troops of 2nd Armd and will act as a back-stop on the east bank of the MEUSE between NAMUR and GIVET in the event the Boche wishes to get his nose bloody again in that direction.

It is reliably reported from high intelligence channels that the Boche are extremely worried over the advances made by the Russians in the direction of AUSTRIA and that this worry may influence him to withdraw his troops to a strong defensive line enabling him to ship some reinforcements to the threatened Balkan area. Apparent he thought he could get away with this offensive on a quick time schedule, throw us off balance and still keep the situation below in hand. He has been thus far successfully balked and we have every intention of keeping him in this frustrated mood.

Friday, 29 December 1944: General Hodges left at eight o'clock today for stops at both the XVIII and VII Corps to find in both commanders a fine confident spirit of optimism. General Collins is "hell-bent" on attacking and so is General Harmon. However, General Montgomery still believes that the Boche is not yet through trying to push north through these two sectors, probably that of VII Corps, and that the threat has not yet passed. Consequently, the target date is not so immediate as both of these Corps Commanders would wish. General Hodges brought back with him over-lays of the proposed VII Corps attack and these are now being studied. Today the VII and XVIII Corps boundary was changed to give General Ridgway control of the 75th Div.

V Corps front was quiet. Two minor pockets of infantry which had filtered through the front lines of the 75th Div were mopped up in the rear by 509th Para Inf. The 83rd Div continued to attack ROCHEFORT against stiff resistance. Third Army: Roads from BASTOGNE to MART-LANGE [Martelange] have been cleared although still under enemy artillery fire. The VIII Corps with the 11th Armd and 87th Divs assembling in its area today is due to jump off early tomorrow morning.

Heavy bombers were up as usual today but all fighter-bombers and mediums were scratched. Weather prediction for tomorrow is uncertain.

Saturday, 30 December 1944: With an incipient cold the General kept to the house most of the afternoon and this evening; came to the office only after lunch in order to have a conference with Field Marshal Montgomery. In this conference there was further discussion when and where the First Army would reassume the offensive.

It was quiet all along our front. Enemy air was active during the night and EUPEN was bombed but no damages were reported. Enemy appears to have withdrawn considerably, at least in front of the 82nd Div and they were moving their OPL [outpost line] out over a mile on the right flank. The 2nd and 3rd Armd Divs have been withdrawn from the front for refitting and re-equipping; their positions have been taken by the 83rd Div and units of the British XXX Corps, which tonight became responsible for the westernmost sector of the German thrust.

The pressure which was so firmly applied to us up until two days ago appears to have shifted to the Third Army. Strong enemy counterattacks were delivered in the vicinity of SIERET [Sibret] P-5055 and

LUTREBOIS P-5653. Both 1st SS and 2nd SS are now reported on that front, that is, what is left of those divisions after our chewing. The VIII Corps attack advanced on the left flank against light resistance to VESQUEVILLE P-3259 while other elements reached MORICY.

It was revealed today that in reply to the ultimatum which was given to the 101st A/B Div at BASTOGNE by the Germans in giving them two hours to surrender before the town was "destroyed"—the CG of the 101st wired back a one word answer: "NUTS!"

Our air was up part of the day and all our heavies were operating in addition to 1,000 RAF bombers which came over about eight o'clock. There was one or more planes over our CP area during the night and much AA firing, but available reports now are that no bombs were dropped but that simple reconnaissance was being made.

G-2 still officially feels that the enemy may try again to hit in the MANHAY-HOTTON area towards LIEGE and that the attack should come at any moment. However, the G-3s do not share this opinion believing that the Boche has been so severely damaged that he has no other alternative but to draw up a defensive line east of the OURTHE River. Our patrols have everywhere advanced 1,000 yards before our front lines and have found extremely light and in some cases no resistance. It is now estimated that the total number of gallons of American gas seized by the Boche in their offensive was about 50 to 60,000 gallons. More than was originally estimated but that is still insufficient to take him more than two or three days at the very most in any new push by an armored Corps. There are some new identifications in the German lines, not of Panzer Divs but of VG Divs which have moved in. Third Army has found that these outfits are about 25% effective with most of the men having had no more than from 3 to 4 weeks training. The 25% effectiveness comes from experienced non-coms [non-commissioned officers] who had been brought back from the Russian front to form the nucleus of the division.

Sunday, 31 December 1944: General Ridgway and General Collins arrived at noon today for luncheon and a two and a half hour conference with General Hodges, General Kean, and General Thorson for final preparations for the offensive. The VII Corps consisting of the 2nd and 3rd Armd Divs and the 83rd and 84th Inf Divs will attack in the zone of action east of the OURTHE River with the objective being HOUFFALIZE. The ground now occupied by the 84th Div will be taken over by the British XXX Corps on the night 1–2 January and 2–3 January. XVIII A/B Corps will protect the left flank of the VII Corps and be prepared on order from General Hodges to attack in the direction of St Vith. 75th Div now belonging to VII Corps will assemble as Army reserve. The XVIII Corps will shift the mass of this reserve to the east in order to permit concentration of VII Corps directly in the rear through which it is to attack. The positions are not to be weakened during this shift and VII Corps Artillery units should actually replace XVIII Corps units before the latter are moved. D-Day and H-Hour are not yet known and await General Montgomery's word and both General Hodges and General Kean motored to Vondhoven at 3:15 today with the final plans in their pocket.

The Army front was quiet with the exception of an attack against the 2nd Bn of the 112th Inf which started at 5:15 this afternoon. This was first reported as an attack in force but it soon turned out that only some 200 enemy infantry were involved and by 6:30 we had restored our positions.

Our air was active during the day as was that of the Boche who appeared over Tongres on reconnaissance during the evening. By noon AA had claimed 22 Categories I [confirmed kills].

Third Army continued to press northward especially in the VIII Corps area. There was heavy fighting all along that front but General Patton believes the Third Army still had the initiative and will continue to drive them back. The Boche have acknowledged ferocity and strength of the Third Army attack.

The General uncorked tonight the case of champagne given to him by General Collins after the capture of Cherbourg and we had a toast to New Year. At midnight we again assembled in the living room and another toast was made but this time with orange juice. Soldiers were indiscriminately firing their rifles all over Tongres and hasty investigation showed that no attack was going on but that simple exuberance [was] having its day.

Monday, 1 January 1945: Boche celebrated New Year's Day by sending out the largest-number of planes yet recorded on the western front—more than 600. More than 300 of these participated in an early morning sneak raid on British airdromes especially those at Eindhoven and Bruselles [Brussels] and they caught the British with their pants down so badly that last night General Montgomery's G-2 sent a pair of suspenders as present to the G-2 of their Tac Air Force. Observers who were present at the Bruselles field testified that more than 100 planes, closely parked in formation, were shot up and wrecked completely and by tonight the total was over 180.[21]

However, though this loss is considerable, it does not match the loss which the Boche suffered. The British claim more than 160 fighters brought down by their own fighters and AA and Colonel Patterson claims 102 for their AA boys; 76 Cat ls and the rest Cats 2. This added to a first estimate of Air Corps total of 53 brings the total of Boche planes destroyed during the day close to 300. His effort "rocked off" greatly in the afternoon and tonight only 18 reconnaissance planes were reported over the entire First Army area. Colonel Patterson said that the total number of Boche that we have destroyed or claimed destroyed as Cats 1 & 2 since the offensive began has now risen to 471.

The Air likewise had a good day in attacking German supply columns and dumps especially in the LA ROCHE area near which 2 SS is assembling and prisoners continue to speak of the lack of food and of the increasing supply difficulties—statements which are borne out by higher intelligence reports.

Our front was exceedingly quiet during the day. Third Army had a tough fight on its hands with several counterattacks of intensity being launched against their front lines by [but] at the day's end good gains were made especially in the VIII Corps area. There were several attacks made against the Seventh Army front in the vicinity of BITCHE and against the sector held by the 14th Armd Div. These attacks ranged from company to battalion strength and appeared to be of a probing nature. There are reports that the Boche has assembled 3 infantry and 1 Panzer divisions in this general area and will soon put on a large scale attack. However, all Seventh Army lines were regained by night's end with the exception of one small 2,000 yard penetration in the 44th Div sector.[22]

Elements of the 84th Div were relieved by the British today as the British XXX Corps–US VII Corps boundary continues to move to the east preparatory to VII Corps' attack the morning of 3 January 1945. There will be another change in the boundary tomorrow.

The General had as his guests this afternoon General Doolittle, General Spaatz, General Van Denberg, and General Quesada. Final plans were made to saturate the area with all kinds of bombs with all kinds of planes to support the VII Corps attack. The IX Air Force is going to do the principal work.

There were planes over our CP again—one lone ME109 at 9:30 this morning and later this afternoon. All fired but scored no hits.

SHAEF is now deciding whether to disband the 106th Div and give us the 424th Inf Regt as a separate infantry regiment to be used in support of armor, or whether to try to refill it with replacements and reconstitute it. We had urged, naturally, that it be kept with us as a separate infantry regiment but we can't do no more than urge it. General Wilson said today that we have been able to replace in surprisingly large quantity all materiel which was lost in the German counter-offensive. We have now received most of the tanks loaned to us by the British and by stripping the three infantry regiments which belong to SOS we have been able to acquire a good number of necessary infantry weapons.

Tuesday, 2 January 1945: Regrouping continued throughout the day as VII Corps made final preparations for its attack at 8:30 tomorrow.

New inter-Corps boundary between VII and XVIII went into effect and the 75th Div passed to VII Corps control. The 84th Div which was on the British side of the new boundary to go into effect at midnight tonight was relieved by the British 158th Brigade Group and moved to assembly areas northeast of HOTTON. The 83rd Div, 2nd Armd Div, and 3rd Armd Div started yesterday afternoon to roll into their assembly positions from which they will launch their attack. Patrols during the day on both the VII and XVIII Corps front reached out more than a mile in some places without gaining enemy contact.

The weather was operational during the morning but closed in during the afternoon. Predictions for tomorrow are not good.

Third Army continued to receive the weight of the German attack. The Boche is still trying to get BASTOGNE before he re-attempts to push northward toward LIEGE and it is certain that Third Army is not going to let him have that key communications center. Numerous counterattacks were thrown off and in the 11th Armd Div sector gains were made. 17th A/B Div is relieving the 11th Armd while the 28th is taking over the mission of patrolling the MEUSE in place of the Airborne. 17th will go right into the line and attack probably 4 January with the mission of reaching the line of the River OURTHE.

The attack continues against Seventh Army in intensity and ground up to five or six miles has been lost east of BITCHE. It is not known whether Sixth Army Group is extremely worried over the situation or not but two or three new divisions have been identified in the area and the enemy has not yet committed the major part of his armor. It is, therefore, too early to see how serious a threat this attack may become. Despite his cold the General motored after lunch today to VII Corps for a last minute conference with General Collins. Even if it is not good as far as weather is concerned, the attack will go on as planned. We cannot delay the attack any longer because of the pressure being put on Third Army and the hopes of getting at least a few prisoners in the bag if we successfully reach HOUFFALIZE which is the Corps objective.

The Allied Counterattack, 3–27 January 1945

Wednesday, 3 January 1945: This morning at 8:30 the VII Corps launched its coordinated attack toward HOUFFALIZE. 3rd Armd Div plus 330th Inf followed by the 83rd Div minus the 330th Inf and the 2rd Armd followed by the 84th Div minus. Both divisions made what can be considered, in the abominable weather yesterday, excellent gains. Roads were icy and tanks, despite the fact that gravel was laid, slipped off into the sides, destroying communication set-ups and slowing traffic. Cubs were able to operate only part of the day and fighter-bombers none at all. About 180 heavies made a trip from England. MALEMPRE, BEFFE, and FLORET [En Floret] were the most important towns cleared by the Armd Divs during the day. 2nd Armd was engaged, especially in the afternoon, in an extremely heavy fight with 2 Panzer and losses on both sides were heavy. The 2nd Armd Div took a total of some 300 PWs before they buttoned up before dark. On the right flank the 82nd Div pushed out against infantry resistance to record excellent gains. TROIS PONTS was cleared as was REHARMONT and by nightfall the line HIERLOT-AMCOMONT-DAIROMONT-BERGEVAL was reached. 500 PWs were taken by the 82nd Div.

The attack brought no surprise to our G-2. Identified were 2 Panzer, 10 SS, 62, 18, and 12 VG Divs. The surprise identification of the day, however, was the 89th Div, PWs from which were taken at the V Corps bulge. The 89th had been last reported in the JULICH area. Indications are that the enemy has thinned out as much as we have along the ROER.

Demonstrations were also made during the day by V Corps divisions and both 30th Div. Strong elements went out as patrols as far as 2,000 yards and one or two of them were engaged in fast fire fights. By nightfall, however, all returned to their original defensive positions.

General Montgomery, who called on General Hodges at two o'clock, was greatly pleased with the progress made and kept remarking, "Good Show. Good Show." Two brigades of his 53rd Div will attack early tomorrow morning in the extreme west to bring his line up to that of the 2nd Armd.

Heavy pressure continued to be exerted in the BASTOGNE area and one sharp regimental-size attack supported by 40 tanks was launched against the 101st Div. They made some penetration but by seven o'clock were sealed off and the 101st was proceeding to mop up. The VIII Corps did not "play ball" today but will jump off early tomorrow morning with relief of the 11th Armd by the 17th A/B now complete.

Seventh Army troops are withdrawing to the Maginot Line,[23] where they will hold. The G-2 of Seventh Army is not perturbed about the situation despite the penetrations made and believes that it can be driven back. It was halted in most areas today and the 14th Armd is moving up to counterattack, as well as a French Division.

Colonel Dickson's estimate tonight is the most optimistic he has turned out since the 16th of December. He believes that the sole result of the enemy's offensive apart from the losses inflicted on us, will be that of a spoiling attack upsetting our drive for the RHINE and gaining time to prepare his Spring campaign and the calling up of the 1928 Hitler Jugend class.[24] The enemy will continue to launch secondary attacks with limited objectives to hold the shoulder open to withdraw from the ROCHEFORT–BASTOGNE salient but Colonel Dickson believes that eventually he will go back to the SIEGFRIED line in order to economize his depleted forces. Morale in the Army and especially in the VG [Volksgrenadier] Divs is lowering fast. New Divs arriving are greatly pepped up but their morale declines in the face of our artillery. Morale in the SS Divs and the good Panzer Divs continues high but all these Divs are now containing increasing percentage of Volksdeutsche,[25] especially Slovaks, who are not particularly enthusiastic.

Thursday, 4 January 1945: The worst day of weather that those on the fighting front have yet experienced—snow, heavy fog which limited visibility to one hundred yards, and icy roads—everywhere slowed our attack.

XVIII A/B Corps fighting with infantry alone against infantry recorded the best gains, advancing their line on the right flank almost 2,000 yards and taking approximately 600 PWs. 505th Inf was counterattacked at three o'clock by a battalion supported by mortar fire only but our lines were restored after a very slight penetration.

In the VII Corps area, in addition to the weather, minefields were considerable detriment. BEFFE which had been claimed yesterday was finally cleared today by the 2nd Armd. CCB cleared FREYMEUX [Freyneux] and advanced beyond LAMORMENIL. 3rd Armd went half-mile beyond LANSIVAL and finally got through the tough minefield south of MALEMPRE to reach BIFOSSE. There were no changes or action on the V Corps front with the exception of a fine 240 Pozit barrage on DREIBORN some eight or ten mile east of the front lines. The 78th Div reported considerable movement of vehicles and approximately 500 enemy infantry and General Hart promptly put his heavies into action.

Perhaps because enemy communications are bad or perhaps because he does not regard our attack as yet a serious threat, the enemy continued to pound the BASTOGNE area as on previous days. According to G-2, it is now a matter of pride especially to the SS and their continued attacks on this front may prove as disastrous as did their pounding around MORTAIN. Some ten different counterattacks were launched against the 101st Div which destroyed 34 enemy tanks during the period. 17th A/B went into action for the first time after relieving 11th Armd and CCA of 9th [Armd] Div and operating on the left of the 101st advanced along a 3,000 yard front almost a half-mile. The 87th Div likewise continued their attack but made no progress. Gains of up to one mile were recorded on the right of the salient by the 35th Div.

The situation at BURE was obscure. The British had it yesterday and the Boche counterattacked during the night and it was still obscure with stiff fighting going on during the day. The 53rd Div attacked this morning with the 158th Brigade making gains up to one mile to the right of the 2nd Armd along the OURTHE River.

Heavy pressure continued in the XV and VI Corps sectors of the Seventh Army with enemy attacks coming in battalion strength with strong tank support. The heaviest kind of fighting is going on at REDERCHINGEN [Rederching], PHILIPSBERG [Philippsbourg] and WEIPERTSWEILER [Reipertsweiler]. We are counterattacking everywhere along the line and thus far holding the enemy from further penetration.

General Ridgway called twice during the day to urge adoption now of his original plan which called for an attack by the 30th Div as well. It is not yet known what decision will be made. General Montgomery called briefly at this headquarters for a chat with the General after which time the General retired to bed at three o'clock. He has a slight temperature and the cold has become worse.

There was no air of any kind over the First Army front today.

Friday, 5 January 1945: Today was a repetition of yesterday with the First Army making good gains against resistance which was not as heavy while the pressure against the Third Army front continued unabated. The biggest gains of the day were made by the 82nd A/B Div which reached phase line "ITALY" and kept an actively patrolled terrain between the front lines and the SALM River. Tomorrow morning the 30th will launch a limited objective attack with the 117th Inf attached to establish a bridgehead over the river west of STAVELOT over which the 112th Inf will pass through.

Third Armd cleared LAVAUX [La Vau] which advanced under heavy artillery fire toward LIERNEUX. Bad weather and poor visibility again hampered operations. CCB of 2nd Armd cleared ODEIGNE. A new temporary boundary was drawn between 2nd and 3rd Armd Divs in order to permit the latter to use the main north-south roads, the crossroads of which joining the lateral road east and west is one of the prime objectives of the attack.

It was a case of repelling countless counterattacks in the Third Army sector. The 17th A/B withdrawals up to two miles were made on the left flank and the 6th Armd Div was forced to forsake its thumb salient northeast of BASTOGNE and withdrew to a safer defensive position.

This afternoon an enemy force estimated at one battalion crossed the RHINE in barges north of STRASBOURG and there is a reported build-up on the east bank of the RHINE at the site of the crossing. The Seventh Army, however, is on the offensive itself in the hopes of regaining or sealing off the penetrations made earlier in the week.

There were no changes recorded in the XXX Corps sector as the Boche put up stiff resistance in GRUFONT [Grupont] and BURE. A counterattack against the 158th Brigade forced them to withdraw some 1,000 yards although this did not cancel the gains they had made previously in the morning. Marshal Montgomery was a visitor against [again] this afternoon.

There were no fighter-bombers aloft all day although the heavies operated as usual in the rear supply areas of the Fifth and Sixth Panzer Armies mainly to the west of the RHINE between COLOGNE and TRIER. Medium missions were cancelled because of the inability of our fighter groups to get off the field to act as escorts.

Today was the General's 58th birthday and a splendid dinner was served up by Gus and Louie complete with a huge cake with red icing. Picture of the General cutting the cake was snapped by Captain Witscher.

Saturday, 6 January 1945: Resistance generally decreased along the VII and XVIII Corps fronts today but this headquarters thought laughable the suggestion made by General Siebert [Sibert], G-2 of 12th Army Group, that we should be on the alert for any "imminent German collapse." General Collins likewise thought the suggestion fairly ridiculous.

Group apparently was made optimistic by the fact that for the first time in many days the pressure likewise fell off against the BASTOGNE salient, and that the attack made by the enemy a week ago against the Seventh Army front had not been able to record, during the past twenty-four hours, any gains.

30th Div this morning launched a limited objective attack on the east flank of the 82nd with attached 112th Inf which advanced 3,000 yards against very light resistance to the line P-709984–P-702970–P-692958. The 82nd Div continued to send out strong combat patrols in the direction of the SALM.

VII Corps made steady progress. 500 PWs were taken in the town of LA FALISE [La Falize]. LIERNAUX was cleared, as well as FRAITURE and Task Force Hogan after by-passing road blocks advanced 2,000 yards to cut the VIELSALM-LA ROCHE road at coordinate P-752852. In the 2nd Armd sector advances up to 2,000 yards were made by Task Force B of CCA cleared DEVANTAVE. TFC, TFD, and TFA advanced more than a mile towards DOCHAMPS. 84th Div less 335 Inf plus 290 Inf continued in close support of the 2nd Armd. 83rd Div remained in assembly area prepared to support the 3rd Armd when the time should arrive. 75th Div began to move to the XVIII Corps zone tonight.

51st Highland Div reverted back to the Second British Army control and will probably replace the 53rd Div which in turn will move to positions below LIEGE.

The General had three guests today. In the morning, Major General Lord, Chief of Staff to General Lee, with whom he and General Kean discussed supply and resupply matters; General Rennie, commanding the 51st Highland Div; and at four o'clock in the afternoon Field Marshal Montgomery who had just returned from a conference with General Collins and General Ridgway.

There were no fighter-bombers aloft today but 1100 mediums from the UK made the trip and two groups of mediums struck at rail lines in the ST VITH area. Weather predictions for tomorrow are likewise discouraging.

Pressure has by no means ceased in the Seventh Army front but Army Hq remain confident that they will withhold anything thrown against them. A few more enemy crossed the RHINE in boats above STRASSBOURG but not in force.

Sunday, 7 January 1945: Astoundingly good progress was made during the day by the 82nd Div and by VII Corps, but despite the lack of enemy in numbers and the virtual absence of tanks, Colonel Dickson still believes that we may expect or at least should be on the lookout for a counterattack by a Corps consisting of at least two or three divisions.

The 82nd Div gained up to 2½ miles and approached its final objectives taking GRAND SART east along the high ground north of the LA ROCHE-SALM Chateau [Salmchâteau] road to the SALM River thence north along the high ground commanding the River up as far as GRAND-HALLEUX. A small enemy pocket exists north of MONT but is being mopped up. The CCB of the 9th Armd Div reverted to its former command back of 3rd Army area.

Enemy resistance along the VII Corps was exceedingly light during the morning but stiffened during the afternoon particularly in the form of enemy artillery fire. The 3rd Armd: CCA cleared GRAND SART and SART; Task Force M cleared RAGNE [Regné], and Task Force H established a road block on the LA ROCHE–SALM Chateau road after securing the cross-roads at P-576852. 2nd Armd Div also reached the road, its Task Force C advancing to DOCHAMPS where fighting of a minor nature still continues. Along the extreme right flank of the Corps the 84th Div continuing in close support captured MARCOURAY.

The British gained up to a mile on their XXX Corps front. Tomorrow the 51st Highland Div will relieve sections of the 53rd Div.

Enemy pressure decreased somewhat along the Third Army front and the 17th A/B made some good progress left of BASTOGNE taking the town of FLANIERGE [Flamierge] against very heavy resistance. A counterattack by infantry of unknown strength supported by 5 tanks was repelled and all 5 tanks were destroyed. The 87th Div continued in its attempt to clear TILLET P-4259.

Enemy pressure continued unabated in the Seventh Army and First French Army fronts. The RHINE bridgehead east of BISCHWEILER [Bischwiller] was reinforced by armored elements and further gains were made. The original salient pushed in the front lines east of BITCHE was being slowly reduced against heavy resistance with the 45th Div clearing LICHENBERG [Lichtenberg] and mopping up the estimated 500 enemy pocketed in WINGEN.

Col Wall [not identified] said that the original order sent out by Sixth Army Group called for withdrawal of our forces west of STRASS-BOURG but that when the French Army heard of this they were moved to send off a passionate protest to De Gaulle who in turn brought the matter up through high government channels. Apparently this reached the British Cabinet and President Roosevelt and a decision was made to change the boundary so as to give STRASSBOURG to the First French Army which would continue to attempt to hold it. The French now have another division, the 10th, composed of FFI [French Forces of the Interior] troops in the line and they have moved one of their Algerian Divs up from the COLMAR pocket to the vicinity of STRASSBOURG to strengthen the defense in that area.

Monday, 8 January 1945: Despite an all day heavy snowfall which in the battle area by nine o'clock this morning was 8" deep and which naturally prevented all observation and all use of aircraft with the exception of the heavies, VII Corps plowed ahead for remarkably good gains especially on the east flank.

3rd Armd with infantry attachments continued to advance against scattered to moderate resistance with most elements reaching their objectives. Task Force D of CCA advanced almost 3 miles to capture PROVEDEREUX [Provèdroux]; Task Force W of CCB took OTTRE.

The 2nd Armd made little progress against heavy enemy fire, dug-in infantry, AT and SP [self-propelled] guns but Task Force C cleared DOSCHAMPS [Dochamps] and the 84th Div on the extreme Corps right flank cleared CIELLE while the 4th Cav Group with the 1st Bn of the 290th attached cleared MARCOURT. The Cavalry is patrolling OURTHE River.

Tomorrow's main objective is SAMREE which is thought the Boche will defend heavily. Elements of the 9th SS Panzer were identified on the VII Corps front today.

XVIII Corps improved their positions with enemy pockets on the west of the SALM River being cleared up. The 75th Div, 7th Armd, and 106th Div minus, remained in Corps reserve.

The battle in the BASTOGNE salient continued to be a see-saw struggle. Elements of the 17th A/B which yesterday had reached FLAMIERGE were forced to withdraw in the face of 18 infiltrated tanks plus infantry. 9 of the tanks were knocked out but the regiment minus one battalion which remained cut off in the town withdrew below the 50 grid. Tomorrow the III Corps will attack with the 6th Armd and the 90th Div in an attempt to reduce the salient on the east side of BASTOGNE. The XII Corps will likewise attack but probably not before the end of the week with the 80th, 5th, and the 94th Divs going due north towards ST VITH while the 4th Div will have a mission of protecting the Corps right flank.

The XXX British Corps continued to regroup. The enemy were reported withdrawing in front of the Corps throughout the day but British troops were maintaining what was described by one radio commentator rather obscurely, "an offensive-defensive mission."

Heavy enemy pressure continued on Seventh Army front and First French Army front. The VI Corps made some slight progress and the enemy pocket in the vicinity of WINGEN was cleared. In the XV Corps sector the attack across the Rhine of infantry reinforced by tanks now appears held and the situation is officially described as "stabilized." Below Strassbourg the enemy made small extensions in the bridgehead. The Seventh Army still does not appear worried over the situation.

There were no visitors during the day. The General's cold is better.

Tuesday, 9 January 1945: Again despite almost constant snowfall during the day good gains were made but both First and Third Army progressed in trying to close the pocket.

VII Corps made good progress against increased enemy resistance. The most important gain being the capture of the high ground overlooking Samree which the 2nd Armd will go after early tomorrow morning. 334th Inf also seized the high ground northeast of La Roche and another battalion got within 3/4 mile of it. In the XVIII Corps sector 424nd relieved the 112th Inf while the 82 A/B improved defensive positions along the Salm River and patrols which probed up to two miles east of the river made only light contact with the enemy. Tonight the pressure over the area was decreasing and the bridge over the river at Vielsalm was blown by the Boche.

After a long conference with Field Marshal Montgomery at the Army CP the General left with Gen Thorson and Bill at 11:30 for XVIII Corps Hq situated in the old and beautiful chateau d'Herze just east of Harze. General Collins joined them after three o'clock for a long discussion of the XVIII Corps proposed plan of attack using the 30th, 75th, and 7th Armd Divs with the 82nd pulled out of the line as reserve. Both General Ridgway and General Collins advocated bold and immediate attack policy. Gen Ridgway being convinced that no army in the world could push his Corps back off the high ground once it was reached. General Collins feels exactly the same way and Field Marshal Montgomery said tonight that he would come tomorrow for another final going over of the plans with General Hodges.

There is now no question but that the enemy is trying to get out of the pocket. The British found no enemy at all west of the L'Homme River and advanced to towns three miles the other side without gaining any contact whatsoever. They have finally pushed their line from the north down abreast of that of the 2nd Armd likewise without any noticeable opposition.

Today, in conjunction with our attack, the VIII Corps launched a coordinated attack with its three divisions. The 101st made the biggest gains capturing Racogne [Recogne] and advancing as far north as co-ordinate 5665. In the 87th Div sector one Bn of 347th Inf contained Til-

LET while other elements by-passed the town on the east and advanced 10,000 yards to the north. 17th A/B concentrated in the center and did not make any gains. The elements of the 513th Para which had been cut off in FLAMIERGE infiltrated back through the enemy lines to the regiment.

The III Corps likewise attacked this morning on a four division front with the 26th, 9th [90th], 36th [35th], and 9th Armd reading from right to left. Gains up to a mile were generally recorded everywhere. Moderate to strong enemy resistance continued on the Seventh Army front, it being a case of we advancing a few yards and the Boche hitting back in a new place for a few yards. Pressure also continued against the First French Army which was forced to release two small towns south of STRASSBOURG.

The only air aloft today were 30 mediums which bombed the AHR-WEILER RR [railroad] bridge. Cubs were up for a few minutes in the morning only. A long range prediction is bad but the General is confident that after four bad days we should be striking a good one any time now.

Wednesday, 10 January 1945: Only in the VII Corps sector today was there much activity, as all was quiet in the V Corps and XVIII Corps was occupied with the shifting of troops and the relieving of the 82nd A/B Div by the 75th Div which officially assumed responsibility late tonight.

The 3rd Armd Div in the VII Corps occupied present positions without contact while the 83rd Div attacked; advances of 500 to a thousand yards were made and tough house-to-house fighting went on in BIHIAN [Bihain] which was finally cleared at 6:30. The 2nd Armd cleared, without too much trouble, SAMREE and in the afternoon took the high ground a mile southwest and southeast of the town. Patrols on the extreme flank poked wearily [warily] into LA ROCHE without finding evidence of strong enemy forces.

In the Third Army sector TILLET finally fell to the 87th Div while the 101st A/B Div continued its attack to the north along with the 4th Armd Div and made gains up to a half-mile. III Corps likewise continued to attack with the 26th, 90th, and 35th Divs in an effort to make disappear the long but narrow enemy salient coming down in the direction of HARLANGE. This town was cleared during the day by the 6th Cav Group.

The British continued to advance from the west without encountering any enemy opposition other than that of heavy minefields. There is no question now but that the Boche is pulling out all his heavy equipment leaving only light reconnaissance forces in the west in an attempt to slow down the advance. It is an orderly withdrawal and in no sense a rout or retreat and the snow makes doubly difficult the clearing of the minefields as well as any progress along the main roads.

Enemy pressure continued to be strong all along the Seventh Army front and although there were no breakthroughs as such, small penetrations were made and the town of HERSHEIM was contained.

There was bad weather again today restricting even operation of the heavies. The long range prediction remains bad. General Montgomery called at a quarter of three this afternoon and stayed for an hour discussing final plans of the XVIII Corps attack which jumps off in the morning of the 13th.

Thursday, 11 January 1945: The XVIII Corps continued to readjust for the attack on Saturday morning and the 106th Div today assumed responsibility for the right portion of the 30th Div sector. The 82nd has now been completely relieved and has moved in the assembly positions in the vicinity of MALMEDY. The 75th Div is occupying the front line positions held formerly by them.

VII Corps continued the attack although not on a grand scale. Infantry of the 83rd Div advanced a mile south from BIHIAN to its initial objective at P-627823 where two counterattacks were repulsed with considerable loss to the enemy including one tank and 63 PWs. During the afternoon the attack continued along the front against stiff resistance from dug in tanks, infantry, machine gun and artillery fire and only small gains were made. However, good progress was made by the 3rd Bn of the 331st Inf which captured PETITE LANGLIR [Petite Langlire] and took 75 PWs. The 2nd Bn of the 329th Regt reached the vicinity of LANGLIR itself. 2nd Armd Div which moved back into the assembly area for a day's rest will attack tomorrow morning towards CHASBREHES [Chabrehez] and LASTILLES [Tailles].

In the Third Army sector the VIII Corps had little trouble in clearing VISQUEVILLE below ST HUBERT and ST HUBERT itself was entered late in the day by elements of the 4th French Para Bn. The III Corps likewise continued its attack to eliminate the enemy salient to the right of BASTOGNE and made gains everywhere from one to two miles.

The XXX British Corps entered LA ROCHE in the morning without making any contact with the enemy and during the afternoon went as far south as CHAMPION [Champlon] and again without making contact and Colonel Dickson believes that the Boche front lines in this sector will be found at the OURTHE River and along the northwest road there but that there is nothing left between LA ROCHE and ST HUBERT.

Heavy enemy pressure continued in the Seventh Army front where additional penetrations were made in the sector of the 79th and 45th Divs. A strong enemy attack on the First French Division sector forced further withdrawals and two towns ROTHSFIELD [Rohrwiller] and HERB-SHEIN [Herrlisheim] were cut off by the enemy.

Only two squadrons of fighter-bombers were able to get aloft this morning because of fogged-in bases but they had a "field-day" in attacking an ammunition dump at L-2091 deep in the enemy rear and setting it ablaze and then attacking two trains, both apparently loaded with ammunition in the immediate vicinity of the dump and destroying both of them. They sighted much traffic here and west of ST VITH but because they ran out of ammunition destroying the trains they were unable to do any further damage. One PW captured yesterday reported that the roads leading in and out of ST VITH were cratered to such an extent for two or three miles in every direction that you could build a whole underground city in them. Interesting news received today showed that both 3rd and 5th SS Panzer Divs which were estimated to be possible reserve forces on the western front had been identified as late as 8 January trying to push back the Russians outside of BUDAPEST. Since the 2nd Para Div, likewise on the reserve list, has been definitely identified by the 2nd British Army as opposing them across the MAAS, the reserve forces now left to Von Runstedt appear to be only three or four divisions at the most and there seems to be a definite shift of strength of available forces to exploit the gains already made in the SAAR areas and below STRASSBOURG. Where the enemy will attempt to stand on our front we do not yet know although there are indications of strong defensive positions in the vicinity of ST VITH which would be a logical place for them to try to stand.

Friday, 12 January 1945: All was finally settled today for the attack tomorrow with XVIII Corps, while VII Corps kept on its slow but sure drive under the usual foul weather towards HOUFFALIZE.

The 83rd Div continued the attack to secure a bridgehead across the RONCE River in the vicinity of LANGLIR and made considerable gains against heavy resistance from small arms, mortar, artillery, and direct fire from ten enemy tanks. The towns of PETITE LANGLIR and LANGLIR itself have been cleared of all enemy and a firm bridgehead over the river in that area has been secured. The 2nd Armd Div—CCB cleared the town of PETITE TAILLES [Petites Tailles] with the principal opposition being extensive road blocks and mines. One heavy enemy patrol which tonight tried to get through the lines of the 329th Inf lost heavily in killed and we took 50 PWs.

The real news of the day, however, is that there no longer exists a pocket. The British report that there are to the best of their knowledge no enemy west of the 45 vertical grid line and they have made contact with elements of the 87th Div at the cross-road at CHAMPLON. It is now apparent that the Boche has pulled his old trick of evacuating the SS, leaving a shell of Volksgrenadier to hold the shoulders and put up covering opposition until all the heavy equipment is out. In one town which the British went through today they discovered the bodies of 34 murdered Belgian civilians—additional proof, though none is needed, that the Boche are up to their old Polish tricks.

The Third Army on its left flank pushed northward against very little resistance. The 87th Div walked into LAVACHERIE and found nobody. The III Corps finished eliminating the enemy salient southeast of BASTOGNE with the 90th Div coming up from the north to capture BRAS and the 6th Armd Div capturing WARDIN. General Bradley told General Hodges tonight that more than 2500 PWs have been taken by III Corps in this two-day operation.

11 Buzz-bombs exploded in or near TONGRES during the day, several of them apparently in the air. Colonel Dickson believes that they may be "registering in" before they really lay down a good load. Though neither damage nor casualties were reported, the bombs seemed to be falling generally from four to six miles away.

Saturday, 13 January 1945: The attack of the XVIII Corps jumped off this morning at eight o'clock. The first news coming in was all to the good—the 120th, 119th, 424nd, and 517th Infs quickly reached lines two or three thousands yards from their departure. However, this is where they were at the end of the day and General Hodges is not pleased with the results since the 30th Div has pushed patrols out this distance in the past week and General Hodges said it could be considered that they only reached their patrol line and no further. Corps generally described the opposition as from moderate to heavy, with the Boche making full use as usual of towns as strongpoints, namely: THIRIMONT and HENU- MONT. At six o'clock tonight an estimated ten tanks and a battalion of infantry forced the 2nd Bn of the 120th to withdraw from the outskirts of the first town to positions north of it, but the 117th, during the night, came down to reattack at midnight tonight; results of this counterattack are not known. Colonel [Alexander D.] Surles,[26] G-3 of XVIII Corps, came to see the General late in the afternoon with a plea that the 1st Div be allowed to attack now. The General, however, turned this request promptly down saying that the 30th Div with attachments would have to reach its first phase line as previously directed before V Corps would put on any kind of a show.

The real good news of the day was furnished, therefore, not by the XVIII Corps but by the 7th [Armd Div] and this afternoon the 83rd Rcn Bn cut the HOUFFALIZE-ST VITH road about four miles northeast of HOUF-FALIZE and occupied the high ground just west of where the road was cut. Later on, elements of TFK reinforced that road block as other elements contained the enemy which are now pretty well cut off at MONT-LE-BAN [Montleban]. TFL cleared the enemy from LORME [Lomré] and TFW advanced to the edge of BACLAIN. During the day at least four enemy tanks were knocked out and more than 150 PWs taken. The General was naturally greatly pleased by this performance although he was not surprised and he has the greatest confidence in the driving leadership of General Rose.

The 2nd Armd with the 335th Inf attached attacked with CCB at eight o'clock, While CCA followed a little while later. Minefields and moderate resistance were the opposition until they reached the 78 grid line where they were opposed by dug-in infantry and as CCB moved on individual strongpoints along HOUFFALIZE-LIEGE road and west of the road were encountered. The town of PISSEROTTE was occupied by TFY and once this was taken TFX & Y moved more easily south and west of the town. The 84th Div took the town of BERISMENIL [Bérsménil], BORZEE, and MABOGE, all against stubborn delaying action. TFW of 3rd Armd kept on going after dark to take the town of BACLAIN.

Although the weather predictions for the day were bad, both heavies and mediums were out and a small number of fighter-bombers making a total of some 120 sorties. Claims were not extravagant and varied between 15 and 16 motor transports and a few armored vehicles. The RAF caught a huge concentration at coordinates 6590 but how much they banged it up is not known at the present time since our aircraft did not participate in this attack. Boche aircraft made a few brief appearances over the Army area during the day and two RAF Tempests[27] ran into our AA fire over VERVIERS as Boche were there. No Boche were shot down but two Tempests were. However, both pilots parachuted to safety.

General Somervell, General [Levin H.] Campbell,[28] General Lee, and General Sayler were the General's guests for luncheon. Afterward they attended a long conference at which General Wilson was the chief Army representative. Somvervell [Somervell] said he did not understand the shortage of signal equipment as to the best of his knowledge everything was "on hand." General Wilson said after the conference that it appeared that Army Service Forces back in the US never received the real information about what we wanted; that our requests for equipment of all kinds went through so many channels and then worst of all through Army Ground Forces in Washington that by the time the Service Forces received the requests they were totally different from those which we had originally submitted in the combat area. In other words, there was improper delayed liaison. The Generals also protested against the erratic arrival of mail; another thing which General Somervell did not understand as all Xmas packages left the US on the 15th of October, and that there was no excuse for their non-delivery by Christmas time.

The VIII Corps of Third Army likewise continued the attack today against considerably lighter resistance than that encountered by us. The 87th virtually walked into ORTHEUVILLE while the 17th A/B advanced to GIVES and GIVEROULIE [Givroulle]. The 11th Armd Div which took over the eastern part of the 17th A/B sector advanced up to 3,000 yards toward BARTOGNE [Bertogne] while other elements repulsed an enemy counterattack of infantry supported by 25 tanks north of NOMAVILLE [Monaville]. There as here the Boche is sensitive to any push on the extreme eastern part of what is left of the pocket, proving that he has still not had time to take out all of his heavy equipment.

Tonight General Kean called a meeting of all staff officers to tell them that Jack Thompson and Hal Boyle[29] were going to write a book about the German counteroffensive and that they were not going to criticize high levels but were going to write it by taking General Bradley's statement to the press yesterday as the departure point. They were instructed by General Kean to give these two writers all and every information possible—"truth and nothing but the truth."

Sunday, 14 January 1945: The biggest thing of the news today was the fact that the fighter-bombers were able to get aloft again. Squadrons of the IX, XIX and XXIX TAC aided by RAF Tempests accounting for some 200 motor transports during the day, especially in the vicinity of HOUFFALIZE which is now the Boche bottleneck of withdrawal. Heavies and Mediums were also up in strength.

30th Div continued the attack today against stiffening enemy resistance with fighting still going on in THIRIMONT, LIGNEUVILLE was occupied, as well as PONT. In fact, by this evening with the exception of the fight at THIRIMONT, the 30th and 106th were everywhere on the first phase line and General Hodges acting on this certainty in the afternoon sent word to V Corps to start their attack in the morning. The 75th Div CP was bombed tonight about six o'clock, several officers in the mess were killed.

The VII Corps kept on slugging with the 3rd Armd clearing BA-CLAIN, MONT LE BAN, and HALONREUX [Halconreux]. Task Force L continued to fight in CHERAIN but this morning withdrew back and will continue the attack later on. 2nd Armd cleared DINEZ, WILOGNE, and WIBRIN, knocking out six out of 12 enemy tanks at the last named place. The 84th Div advancing against scattered resistance cleared the towns of NADRIN, PETITE MORMONT, GRANDE MORMONT, FILLY [Filli], and OLLO-MONT. Late in the afternoon a patrol from the 24th Cav Squadron joined up with the patrols of 506th Para Inf [101st A/B Div] of the VIII Corps south of LA ROCHE.

News broadcasts to the contrary, it is assured that our troops will reach HOUFFALIZE before those of the Third Army. The 11th Armd reached NOVILLE where fighting is still going on and COMPLOGNE [Compogne] is also being defended. While on the left flank the 17th A/B advanced several kilometers without making any contact with the Boche at all.

General Gerow had a great chat with the General this afternoon. Tomorrow he gives over command of V Corps to General Huebner, to himself take command of the Fifteenth U. S. Army.

Monday, 15 January 1945: The General left at eleven o'clock this morning with Bill for a nasty sleety drive to FRANCOCHAMPS [Francorchamps] where XVIII Corps is now located. General Ridgway who is as usual up with the front line companies did not return to the CP until after two o'clock. The General kept abreast of the situation until then and had a long chat with him after he arrived. According to General Ridgway, resistance is nowhere near as stiff as the soldiers would have people believe. As his Aide remarked, he is accustomed to dealing with parachutists, the toughest breed of all and is inclined to judge performance by their performance.

Despite complete lack of any air support, V Corps jumped off at 6:30 this morning and by tonight were clearing the town of FAYMON-VILLE. 1st Bn of 23rd cleared STEINBERG [Steinbach]. The 1st Div—"cagy fellows" the General calls them, attacked with only three battalions and will keep up throughout the night substituting battalions here and there so that people can get their due amount of rest without giving the

Boche any at all. The 30th Div likewise kept going reaching HOUVEG-NEZ [Honvelez], clearing PONT and THIRIMONT. 75th Div coming across the SALM River at three o'clock in the morning clearing SALMCHATEAU and BECH [Bèche]. Resistance in the area near GRANDE-HALLEUX [Grand-Halleux] was heavy. The most satisfying news of the day came at ten o'clock this evening when we learned that patrols of the 2nd Armd Div TFY had entered HOUFFALIZE without encountering any enemy. TFB after clearing ACHAUFFE [Achouffe] advancing towards HOUFFALIZE was slowed down by destroyed enemy vehicles and equipment which blocked the road into town. STERPIGNY attacked further to the east by TFW of the 3rd Armd was a hard nut to crack being heavily defended by both tanks and anti-tank fire and by tonight our troops were forced to withdraw from its edges. General Collins informed General Hodges over the phone tonight that the fighting along the VII Corps front had everywhere been of an extremely intense nature and that our tank casualties were higher today than on any previous day during the past ten days. The 84th Div has now reached the limit of its sector and will hold tight preparatory to movement out of the area.

The Third Army made some advances during the day but they were not particularly noteworthy. Stars & Stripes tonight carried the story that they had accounted for some 80,000 Germans, which figure is totalled [totaled] in the usual Patton manner, of multiplying PWs captured by ten.

Tuesday, 16 January 1945: This was our last day under command of Marshal Montgomery and he arrived at 2:30 this afternoon for a farewell chat with General Hodges. General Hodges told him what a great honor it had been to serve under the Marshal's command and what great assistance had been given by the cooperation of the British—in the way of tanks, in the way of movement of troops, and tactical decisions. Bill later took up 5 lbs. of coffee to the Marshal's headquarters at ZONDHOVEN.

As a last day, it was a pretty good day. HOUFFALIZE was definitely cleared and the 11th Armd Div reached the southern part of the town in strength. The V Corps attack advanced but against heavy opposition. FAYMONVILLE was cleared and the outskirts of CHOPPEN [Schoppen] were reached. ORDENVAL [Ondenval] was cleared.

The XVIII Corps also continued the attack and the 30th Div made a considerably better penetration, meeting considerably lighter resistance than did the 1st, and by tonight elements of the 119th and the 517th had reached points overlooking the two important road junctions which General Hodges wants to have. The 75th Div likewise continued the scrap against the enemy across the river but made very slow progress. General Hodges believes that offensively the 75th is through for the time being, tired out and exhausted. It appears that the 75th is not going to be one of First Army's better divisions.

VII Corps likewise continued the attack against very stiff resistance. STERPIGNY was cleared after very heavy fighting as was CHERAIN. The indomitable Task Force Hogan attacked toward BRISY, was halted about a mile north of the town by the heaviest kind of fire. Task Force K tried to enter the town from the west but was likewise held up by the enemy including dug-in infantry. In HOUFFALIZE the main bridge over the river has a sixty-foot gap but the foot bridge is intact. Another bridge on the secondary road has been damaged but will carry light vehicles. Bridging operations should be completed tomorrow. The 84th Div now out of contact with the enemy continued to assemble today near DOCHAMPS. The 83rd Div resumed the attack this afternoon but made slow progress. Heavy casualties, however, were inflicted on the enemy at three different times when they attempted to mass in the woods east of HONYELEZ [Honvelez] for an attack on the town itself. It can be expected that there will be a continuing hard fight for the town of BRISY as there is evidence that the enemy is not only digging in but placing tanks and mortars in position. Proof that they do not intend to surrender it lightly.

The very lightest kind of opposition permitted the Third Army to make good advances; 11th Armd took MABOMPRE and WICOURT while the 101st Div advanced to the outskirts of BOURCY. The XII Corps will attack tomorrow with four divisions: 80th, 5th, 4th, and the 87th which was pinched out two days ago on the VIII Corps left flank.

In the Seventh Army the VI Corps is attacking to clear the enemy from the RHINE bridgehead. The town of HATTON around and in which there has been the most confusing and heaviest kind of fighting for over a week is finally again definitely in our hands.

The British XII Corps attacked yesterday morning in an attempt to clean out the German salient in the SITTARD area. Preliminary reports reveal that the 7th Armd Div has made moderate progress against moderate resistance.

The air was up in fairly good strength today but reports tonight indicate that the harvest was not as rich as had been expected, some 100 motor transports were destroyed and buildings and railroad cuts were made.

General Quesada, Col Myer [Dyke F. Meyer],[30] and General Quesada's G-2 were guests of General Hodges today for luncheon and afterward had a conference drawing up preliminary plans for another blanket air attack in the event the First Army push is on for a breakthrough.

Wednesday, 17 January 1945: Contrary to what was stated in yesterday's diary, we did not return to control of Twelfth Army Group until today. The boundary which was announced to us by TWX [teletype message] tonight was LIEGE to EUPEN to GEMUND to EUSKIRCHEN all inclusive to First Army. The boundary between us and Third Army remains the same.

General Hodges motored today through the vilest kind of weather for a conference with General Ridgway at XVIII Corps CP. Advance of the XVIII Corps troops has been uniformly slow due not only to the weather but also in the opinion of General Ridgway to a general lack of aggressiveness and good leadership especially in the case of the 75th Div.

Progress in the VII Corps was also limited due to snow and visibility which was never during the day more than 50 yards. All bomber and fighter-bomber missions were of course cancelled.

In the V Corps sector slow progress was recorded by 1st Div which was having its hands full with last ditch elements of the 3rd Para Div who have reputed themselves for being tough cookies.

XII Corps' attack, scheduled for today, was postponed until tomorrow.

The British attack in the SITTARD salient is going well. For the first time in many a month we have now brought out a map of the Russian front and are following it closely.

Thursday, 18 January 1945: We said good-bye, not regretfully, to TONGRES at 10:30 this morning, arriving at our old SPA CP at 12:30. The General's office was in a frightful mess—no chairs, a small stove, evidence of the map-board being used for kindling wood, dust on the floor, and water on the desk—but things were put in order again by 2:30 although much of G-3 Operations was flooded during the rest of the evening and night by two inches of water which leaked from the snow-laden roof.

General Bradley, taking five hours to come from LUXEMBOURG, arrived at the CP shortly before two o'clock and he and General Hodges went into conference which lasted uninterruptedly until six o'clock. It is now definite that Ninth Army will remain under the command of

Marshal Montgomery. What plans were announced for the First Army beyond the capture of St Vith are not yet known.

Tonight at 8:30 with all Chiefs of Sections present, General Bradley pinned on General Hodges' blouse the Oak Leaf Cluster to the DSM, which was awarded the General for his work as Deputy Commander of First Army and then as Commanding General from the period June 6th to October 14th. Pictures were taken of the ceremony following which General Bradley made a short address congratulating the Army Commander and his staff for their sterling performance in taking the brunt of the German offensive and stopping it.

The day's military news was negligible. The enemy attempted to drive up the road defile between the 1st Bn of the 23rd and the lst Bn of the 18th and the heaviest kind of hand-to-hand fighting went on all during the day. The enemy efforts were contained by [but] little progress was made in clearing the defile itself. The 120th Inf advanced south some 2,000 yards and the 117th consolidated its positions on the high ground north of Racht [Recht]. The 75th Div likewise moved ahead against steadily decreasing opposition to reach the positions generally along the 74 and 75 vertical grid line.

VII Corps continued the attack but they met tough opposition and had to be content with small gains along the Cherain–Gouvey [Gouvy] road. The 2nd Armd Div is being withdrawn to assembly area and refitted while the 84th Div likewise remained out of contact.

In the Third Army the XII Corps launched a coordinated attack toward St Vith with the 4th, 5th, and 80th Divs. Bridgeheads were established over the Sauer and advances up to a mile were made against moderate to heavy resistance. Fighting continued in Diekirch at the end of the period.

There were no important changes in the Seventh Army front although heavy pressure continued unabated. The British attack in clearing the area west of the Roer met with success; advances up to two miles being made and Echt, Susterun [Susteren] and Hongen being the three most important towns to fall during the day.

General Bradley will leave in the morning for General Simpson's headquarters at Maastricht.

Friday, 19 January 1945: General Bradley left for Ninth Army shortly after breakfast this morning and for the rest of the day General Hodges was closeted in conference with General Kean and General Thorson planning the offensive action which the First Army will take, minus two of the divisions it now has, once the present objective of St

VITH is reached. General Ernie Harmon who is to take a Corps in the Fifteenth Army arrived with his two Aides during the afternoon and had a long chat with the General about his division's work in the south bracket and afterward he spent the night at the house and will leave early tomorrow morning for General Gerow's headquarters at SIUPPES.

Although weather permitted the use of only two fighter-bomber squadrons, good gains were made in all three Corps fronts. The enemy withdrew in front of the 1st Div and resistance was light during the day as they cleared MONTENAU, IVELDINGEN, and SCHOPPE [Schoppen]. 30th Div took RECHT and the 75th Div swept the GRAND BOIS eastward and had patrols joined up with the 30th Div. The 83rd Div occupied BOVIGNY and COURTIL without meeting any enemy. TFD, TFR, and TFK of the 3rd Armd Div accounted for the towns of RETIGNY [Rettigny], RENGLEZ and BRISY. The 2nd Armd Div will start moving tomorrow morning for its new positions near SPRIMONT.

A wide-spread transfer of divisions is now in progress along other Army fronts. The 101st is moving to the Seventy [Seventh] Army tomorrow while the 76th is coming up from the beaches into the VIII Corps area. The 28th Div closed in the vicinity of ST DIE in the Seventh Army sector yesterday while the 10th Armd Div minus moved from METZ to DIENGE. One Combat Command of the 8th Armd Div is likewise moving to the METZ area as well as the 35th Div which has been relieved from duty with the Third Army.

The XII Corps attack made moderate progress against moderate to heavy enemy resistance. The Towns of BESTENDORF [Bettendorf] and DIEKIRCH were cleared. The British attack continued to make progress; the biggest capture of the day being the city of BREBEREN.

For the first time in a long while there were no signs or sounds of V-1s over our CP area. Tonight it started to snow again and by midnight there was almost a foot on the ground. Our snow plows are out, however, and doing a great job in keeping the roads clear, although as General Harmon pointed out, it was impossible for his tanks to use anything except main roads; side trails being absolutely impassable because of the softness of the under-snow surface.

Saturday, 20 January 1945: The 7th Armd Div attacked at eight o'clock this morning to secure the high ground north of ST VITH, against the most difficult kind of terrain and hampered by icy roads, but they made what can be considered good progress. CCA advanced a mile to DEIDENBERG which was secured by TFW while TFR moved on another 1,000 yards to its objective. CCB attacking through minefields advanced in three columns unto BORN which was entered from the west late tonight but not cleared. The 30th Div attacking on the right of the 7th Armd pushed down within four miles of ST VITH against light enemy resistance while the 75th Div clearing woods likewise advanced up to two miles against extremely scattered small arms and mortar fire. V Corps did not attack today. VII Corps started to relieve its 3rd Armd from the line with the 4th Cav Group and its only activity during the day was to occupy CIERREUX which was found clear of enemy. 84th Div will tomorrow relieve the 83rd and pursue the attack towards GOUVEY.

The General left the office after eleven o'clock for XVIII Corps for a conference with General Ridgway. It has now been recommended that both the CG [Maj. Gen. Fay B. Prickett] and Arty Commander [Brig. Gen. Albert C. Stanford] of the 75th Div be relieved from their command to revert to the rank of Colonel, although this action has not yet taken place pending approval of higher headquarters.[31] The General then went to General Huebner's headquarters at EUPEN. The General heard a new piece of evidence of the effectiveness of POZIT fuses today when the story was told of one unit advancing this morning being forced to practically sweep out the dead bodies off the roads at one place where a serenade of POZIT had been put down. The dead, it was said, numbered well over 100. The Germans now call this "a terror weapon." As G-2 remarked, "terror weapon" because it is not on their side.

The Third Army likewise continued the attack. VIII Corps occupied several towns southeast of HOUFFALIZE without having any contact with the enemy at all. 90th Div on the III Corps north flank advanced a mile and a half while the XII Corps advanced about a mile on a 4,000 yard front taking the towns of BRANDENBERG and BURDEN. Heavy enemy pressure continued on the XX Corps front against the 95th and 94th Divs. Further north the British continued their advance; the most important capture being that of the town of BOCKET. The Seventh Army, however, continued to take it on the chin. The Boche's bridgehead northeast of STRASBOURG was enlarged; heavy enemy pressure continued in the 45th Div sector with an enemy attack surrounding one battalion. 12th Armd Div it is now learned suffered extremely heavy casualties in the vicinity of HERLISHEIN [Herrlisheim] and was forced to withdraw some two miles west of the ILLE River. 36th Div took over the 12th Armd Div sector and today repulsed a strong attack. Another battalion, this one of the 314th Inf, was cut off in this area near the town of DRUSELHEIM [Drussenheim]. The Seventh Army, however, is getting reinforcements and their general outlook remains unchanged, i.e., they are sure they can hold it.

General Gavin was a guest of the General's house tonight for dinner. General Brereton, head of the Airborne Army, was present at General Ridgway's CP today and apparently discussion is still going on as to the continued employment of these parachutist divisions in a ground role. Although with the present weather there seems little possibility of their being effective, given time for additional replacements and training as trained parachutists. General Gavin said he was enforcing a strict training schedule for members of his division as the best possible way to keep them out of trouble.

Tonight at 8:30 General Hodges pinned the Bronze Star on General Kean and General Thorson for "heroism in the face of the enemy." They both disembarked on OMAHA Beach on D-Day to obtain information for the Army Commander despite the fact that the beach was subject to enemy fire and had not yet been cleared of mines.

Sunday, 21 January 1945: Today was bright and clear. The air was up early and we soon had reports of a tremendous vehicular movement of the Boche, generally east and northeast from out of what remains of the pocket and deeper. The fact that he is moving in broad daylight is considered almost definite evidence of the crisis on the eastern front and his last-minute efforts to regroup his battered armored divisions and move them in that direction. The air went after them with a vengeance destroying several hundred, blowing up an ammunition train, and cutting railroad lines everywhere between here and the RHINE.

On the ground meanwhile XVIII Corps continued the attack; resistance was extremely heavy in BORN which was finally cleared after six o'clock; 165 PWs, 8 SP guns, and 4 tanks were captured and over one hundred dead Boche were found in the town. We lost 8 tanks, 5 of which can be repaired. TF Sugar advanced over a mile against light resistance to the high ground overlooking ST VITH which is now less than 4 kilometers away. VII Corps regrouped, prepared to continue the attack tomorrow. The 84th Div moved into replace the 83rd Div which is extremely tired after its fight in this toughest of all terrain and weather and they will drive tomorrow towards BEHO. To VII Corps' south, VIII Corps kept moving on with the 17th A/B and the 11th Armd. It was a walk. They made some 3 miles reaching the outskirts of OURTHE and WATTERMAL, almost without contact. Substantial progress was likewise made by the III Corps, attacking with the 90th, 26th, and 6 Armd Divs. WILTZ was cleared as were other towns on the Corps north flank. Further to the right, the XII Corps likewise pushed ahead; the resistance on the left flank generally light and strong on the east. It now appears increasingly clear that the Boche intends to make no real fight until he is safely back in what remain of the defenses of the Siegfried Line. There probably he will attempt to hold with fortress battalions and Volksgrenadier outfits, regrouping and transferring his crack units to his other point of crisis.

The British, to our north, continue to attack and occupied three or four more towns against sporadic heavy resistance.

The bad news of the day was that the VI Corps of the Seventh US Army withdrew in the face of heavy enemy pressure and increased build-up in enemy forces from the salient northeast of STRASBOURG to the general line WEYERSHEIM–BISCHWEILER–HAGENOU–Q-7738 [Weyershim–Bischwiller–Haguenau–Q-7738], representing the withdrawal of some six to ten miles along most of the Corps front. This must have been a blow to General Brooks who is a fighting aggressive Corps commander, who has as his opponent this time nobody else but Himmler[32] himself who is apparently determined as before to sacrifice and kill to the limit for what ultimate objective nobody knows. This Corps front is being reinforced by the 101st and probably the 35th and 8th Armd Divs and if necessary General Hodges could dispatch both the 2nd and 3rd Armd Divs which are now out of the line to aid them. The withdrawal was completed without incident and the Corps front is now held by the 36th, 79th, 45th, and 103rd Divs with the 12th Armd and 14th Armd in reserve. Two isolated battalions of infantry are trying to infiltrate back into our lines.

The General had two visitors today: General [Isaac D.] White[33] who will assume command of the 2nd Armd Div in place of General Harmon and General Ridgway who came to headquarters shortly before six o'clock and later to the house for a drink and brief chat with the General. General Ridgway according to his Aide is not satisfied with the progress made by the 7th Armd Div toward ST VITH and will drive them hard tomorrow.

Monday, 22 January 1945: Again the big news outside of the tremendous gains once more being chalked up by the Russians, was the activity of our Air. The withdrawal which commenced yesterday continued today in even larger columns. At first quoted as consisting of 1800 assorted vehicles being spotted near PRUM, others of lesser size being spotted on all roads leading east from ST VITH shortly afterward. All three TAC Commands went out and at one o'clock the British were called in to help. Pilots reporting at six o'clock tonight believe that they scored greater successes than those chalked up in the FALAISE pocket and the total count as read over the BBC tonight was 2700 motor transports and half-tracks destroyed and 112 tanks put out of commission. We shall know perhaps eventually how much of these claims are true when we try an advance along those roads.

At any rate the ground opposition offered to our troops today was generally everywhere light. The 30th Div took KAPELLE [Kapellen], HEINDERHAUSEN [Hinderhausen], RODT, and OBER EMMELS while the 7th Armd attacking to the south captured HUNNINGEN and the high ground just over a mile from ST VITH. The VII Corps made gains up to three miles clearing BEHO and GOUVY and everywhere generally advancing against very light resistance.

The three Corps Commanders were guests of the General for lunch and afterward returned to the office for a two-hour conference on the First Army attack which will start when word is given by Group following the definite capture of ST VITH and the reaching of final objectives of this current drive. The plan as originally drawn up at this headquarters was apparently considerably altered by the conference and General Hodges said afterward that a very more flexible and better plan had been designed. Because of the narrowness of our front it will be a two Corps attack, therefore, leaving a Corps for the first time in reserve. How many divisions we lose is not yet definitely known though it is rumored to be two in number.

The advances made by the VII Corps were paralleled by those made by the VIII Corps with 11th Armd being squeezed out and the 17th A/B advance advancing rapidly towards its final objective at which time the VIII Corps will likewise be squeezed. These gains were paralleled in the III Corps and XII Corps areas and the line in a day or two should almost be a straight one running from ELSENBORN shoulder directly to the south to WILTZ.

For the first time in many days the Seventh US Army front was fairly quiet but the bad news was learned that 51 Sherman tanks from the 12th Armd Div were cut off during the recent fighting and 42 were captured by the Boche. It is believed that the enemy has placed these tanks into operation against us. The 101st Div is now closed in the XV Corps area and will be ready soon to resume its "Bastogne Tradition."

General Kean and General Hart left today for a six-day leave in London. A showing of the "The Conspirators" was held at the house tonight. The audience thought it a very bad film.

Tuesday, 23 January 1945: The Air had another banner day today with the sky clear and the air crisp. They went hunting yesterday and continued hunting today in the Prum area and east of St Vith, and by the end of the day had accumulated a bag of some 1500 Motor Transports, destroyed or damaged plus innumerable railroad cars, roads, and armor. Though flak was in many places heavy, there were but few scrabbles with opposing enemy aircraft and General Quesada, calling the General this afternoon, said "there was so many of the aircraft out, you couldn't see the sun." As is now SOP, XIX and XXIX Tac also contributed their share to the day's total bag.

The big news of the day groundwise was the recapture of St Vith. There were not many enemy putting up a show of resistance but artillery and Nebelwerfers fire was heavy and did cause casualties as CCA of the 7th Armd, which so gallantly defended the town during the first few days of the breakthrough, re-entered the town during the afternoon and by 5:45 this afternoon had cleared it. The 30th Div likewise continuing the attack against moderate resistance advanced almost two miles to capture Neundorf, Krombach [Crombach] and Weistein [Weisten]. 75th Div also advanced, taking Braumlauf [Braunlauf] and Waldingen [Maldingen]. Opposition tonight was still going on in the outskirts of Aldingen [Aldringen]. VII Corps, attacking with only the 84th Div made gains up to two miles against moderate resistance to occupy Ourthe. To all intents and purposes they have reached their final objectives as their high ground positions control all the remaining few yards yet to be cut. The VIII Corps slowed down only by hip deep snow advanced to take Hautbellain. 50 Boche there fired a few shots and then surrendered. Second British Army kept up their advances in the Sittard salient, clearing four towns during the day. For some unknown reason the Boche still feels that he can obtain some kind of a success—for morale purposes, if nothing else—by pushing against Gen Brooks' VI Corps of Seventh Army. There was heavy pressure there all during the day.

Wednesday, 24 January 1945: The General left at nine o'clock this morning with Bill for Luxembourg, using the old route so well known to him before: Remonchamps-Manhay-Houffalize-Bastogne-Arlon. Houffalize he found a complete wreck, similar to the Cherbourg peninsula towns of Valognes and Montebourg; Bastogne a little better. Destroyed enemy tanks and equipment were to be seen periodically on both sides of the road, especially in the Houffalize area. The conference was not a long one. As a matter of fact, General Hodges said that the actual business could probably have been conducted over the telephone in five minutes. General Hodges willingly conceded to General Patton the use of a road net on the Army right flank if he promised to get something up there. General Patton promised that five divisions would attack on our right flank. The Army boundary was changed slightly. The left boundary hits in toward EUSKIRCHEN but farther north, while the right boundary also changes direction to go due east.

General Collins called this morning to give General Hodges the news that his Corps was on its objective; that the 84th Div was passing to control of General Ridgway. General Collins with General Hodges' blessings is going to take a well-earned leave in MONTE CARLO while his Corps staff likewise takes it easy preparatory to future activities.

1st Div attacked at four o'clock this morning with elements of all three infantry regiments. There was some moderate resistance but the attack's principal enemy was deep snow and dense woods. MODER-SCHEID was cleared.

The XVIII A/B Corps with the 7th Armd plus 424th Inf consolidated positions and repulsed three enemy counterattacks which came from the vicinity of WALLERODE against light resistance that pushed south and southeast of ST VITH. 30th Div also consolidated positions as did the 75th Div which likewise cleared ALDERINGEN [Aldringen].

The VII Corps on the right flank kept up with our advance clearing WATTERMAL from which annoying and persistent fire of VII [VIII] Corps units had been coming these last few days. A new boundary for VIII Corps now extends through HASHERVILLE [Hachiville] and STOUBACH [Stubach]—With VIII Corps' objective correspondingly changed. The III and XII Corps made small but beneficial advances during the day. Further north the British cleared HEINSBERG, the largest German city in the SITTARD salient west of the ROER. 300 PWs were taken.

With the sky clearing at noon-time the Air was out in force all during the afternoon. The targets were not so heavy or as lucrative as on the two preceding days but they chalked up a total of almost 500 Motor Transports, damaged or destroyed; shooting on railroad cars and railway targets was likewise lucrative.

Bill came down with the flu and retired before supper tonight to his bed.

Our two Corps attack will definitely now start, the General said tonight, this Sunday. This does not give the 1st Div any time to rest but it is thought necessary to push on while the Boche is withdrawing his major armored forces.

This afternoon at three o'clock Maj Gen Raymond Porter,[34] former

G-3 of the War Department and for the past few weeks acting CG of Fifteenth Army arrived for a conference with General Hodges prior to taking over the 75th Div in place of General Prickett. Both Gen Prickett and his Arty Comdr are being relieved and it is Gen Hodges' recommendation that they both be reduced to permanent grade of colonel.

Thursday, 25 January 1945: Gen Hodges conferred after lunch today with Gen Simpson, Gen McLain of XIX Corps, and Gen Huebner. As a result of the conference Ninth Army is taking over part of our northernmost boundary and has undertaken to clear the IMGENBORICH [Imgenbroich]–EICHERSCHEID area simultaneously with the attack of V Corps. It was, General Hodges said, a most satisfactory conference. Shortly after it was over, Gen Collins who is leaving early tomorrow morning for the RIVIERA called to pay his farewell respects. He will be at CANNES for a week and his Corps staff is dispersing to England and other points for a rest. His Divisions, 2nd and 3rd Armd, and the 83rd are all now in assembly areas and out of contact with the enemy. The Armd Divs regrouping and doing necessary maintenance work while the 83rd simply resting after three straight months of fighting without relief. Tonight Gen Hodges along with his other three present General Officers went to Gen Quesada's house for drinks and dinner.

1st Div made good progress during the day taking AMEL and MIRFELD against moderate resistance. It now puts the 1st Div on their line of departure for Sunday's big attack. Below, the XVIII Corps seized WALLERODE and put 424nd Inf but a few hundred yards from the Corps line of departure. Positions south and east of ST VITH were cleared and consolidated and during the day the 75th Div was relieved by elements of the 84th and the 30th.

With the strategy yet undecipherable the Boche yesterday opened another strong attack on the Seventh Army sector making slight penetrations and seizing MULHAUSEN [Muhlhausen]. Our counterattacks restored most of the penetrations but the heaviest kind of pressure is expected to continue.

The Second British Army now has cleared most of the area between MAAS and ROER Rivers and the 102nd Div will jump off early tomorrow morning to seize the few remaining yards between them and the ROER. Slight resistance was expected.

The Air had a moderately good day—very good by ordinary standards but only moderately good by those set this week—by smashing or damaging an estimated 1,000 vehicles. No concentrations of 200 vehicles were spotted; it was a base of picking up 25 or 50 here and there and giving them the well-known "works."

Friday, 26 January 1945: Final preparations were today underfoot for First Army's smash-attack Sunday. The new boundary between V Corps and XVIII Corps became effective at six o'clock tonight and at the same time the 1st Div passed to the control of General Ridgway. The XVIII A/B Corps continued its operations to strengthen the line between south and west of St Vith in order that a good line of departure could be reached before the attack. 424th Inf did most of the work, reaching all of its objectives by eleven o'clock against slight resistance. The 82nd A/B started to move today to the rear of 7th Armd prior to relieving the latter outfit. The 75th Div assembled and started movement to Seventh US Army.

The VIII Corps which is going to be on our right flank for this attack likewise continued to regroup forces with the 87th and 90th Divs continuing to clear the area west of the Our River. A new boundary between VIII and III Corps which extends the former Corps sector to the south became effective at noon today. The 87th and 90th are now in the front lines; the 17th A/B has been completely relieved and will soon move out of the Corps area; the 11th Armd is to be in reserve. A liaison officer from Corps stated today that General Patton was going to move up the 4th and 95th Divs into the VIII Corps area in order to make, as he promised, a five division drive out of his participation in First Army's offensive.

In the XII Corps the 76th Div was the one to relieve the 87th. They are a new outfit which just arrived and this is their first battle experience. The 102nd Div striking north to help the British clear up the Sittard salient had absolutely no trouble at all in capturing the towns of Brachelen and Hilfarth. Patrols which went out at midnight found no enemy in opposition and there were only seven casualties during the day all caused by mines. In the Seventh Army sector there was considerably less pressure against the VI Corps and we have now regained all but the square kilometer of the ground previously lost.

General Hodges had one of his favorite Generals, Maurice Rose, to lunch today. General Rose is on his way to Brussels for a three-day leave. General Collins was unable to fly to Cannes today because of bad weather but hopes to be able to leave tomorrow.

Almost all air activity was cancelled for today due to snow flurries and bad weather at the bases. There was no medium or heavy effort. Maj Zwink has been grounded in England for the past three successive days and there does not seem to be much chance that he can get off of the ground tomorrow.

At eight o'clock after they had given the password at the gate and Bill had told Sgt Woods to let them in, two men dressed in GI clothing were admitted to the house with a "message" for the Chief of Staff. They refused to give us the message. The General became suspicious and once we were back at headquarters where the men had followed us, an immediate check was made of their credentials and of their story. They said they had come from 49th AAA Brigade from a Major Kalakas, S-2. Colonel Patterson immediately checked with Brigade and they had no knowledge of the existence of any two such men. By this time we had three guards standing over the men; had removed their pistols and were ready to club them over the head should they make a move. After a nervous half hour of checking and double-checking we learned that the thing was merely a stunt of the CIC [Counter-Intelligence Corps] which had set out to test the security control at the General's headquarters and as is now obvious had proved it wanting.

Saturday, 27 January 1945: The General paid a last minute visit to the Corps and Divisions taking part in the new First Army attack. He left at 12:30, stopped at General Ridgway's headquarters and then motored to Camp Elsenborn where he pinned the DSC on the blouse of Maj Gen Robertson of the 2nd Div, also having there a long chat with Gen Huebner on V Corps' plan of attack. Everything is set to go; both commanders confident and in no doubt, with the soldiers' morale fairly high in view of the Russian offensive and despite this abominable weather.

Before the General left, however, one incident occurred which was extremely displeasing to him. General Bradley telephoned at 11:30 to say that Gen Patton had requested the use of the Gouvy-Beho-Crombach road and the Vielsalm–St Vith road, both in First Army area, for the use of his troops. General Hodges said he had no intentions of permitting Gen Patton to use the cover of First Army advances to bring his forces in through the back way, helping to block our traffic and taking advantage of ground which we had gained and which we needed. A call, however, to XVIII Corps disclosed that they didn't need and were not using the lower road and consequently in a call back to Gen Bradley shortly after noon the General did give his permission for use of the lower road. Use of the upper road was absolutely impossible and there the matter was settled.

In the evening after dinner the General saw the compulsory War Department film on non-fraternization[35]—a gory, straight-forward, hard-hitting piece of propaganda reminding soldiers of the German past history and telling them that distrust of the Germans and non-fraternization with them was to be the order of the day once they were on German soil. The General thought the film was an excellent job. He motored down to the office after seeing the film to conduct a briefing of the press on tomorrow's operations. General Quesada also participated. The briefing was probably the most successful held to date with clear expositions being given and good questions asked by the correspondents. Tonight after dinner it started to snow once again and about midnight three inches had fallen with no end of it in sight.

During the day there was little activity on our front as forces continued to change positions and draw up for tomorrow's drive. TFW of 7th Armd did push out on the main road leading southeast of St Vith and reached its objective. The 87th Div although they advanced close to four miles, encountering only road blocks and mines and extremely little small arms fire, are still behind us on the right flank. The General told Gen Bradley this morning that he had no intentions of waiting for Gen Patton's forces to catch up to us and our drive would go off regardless of where they were at the time. On other fronts things were generally quiet. Pressure has been relieved on the VI Corps front in the Seventh Army, while below us on the XII and III Corps fronts good gains were made against stiffening resistance as our forces there have reached the line held on December 16th and are now nearing the outer perimeter of the Siegfried Line.

Air was operational during the afternoon but visibility was limited and only sections of two groups were able to fly. Claims for the day were some 300 motor transports destroyed or damaged with numerous rail cars and cuts claimed. There were no large sightings, 200 being the top figure.

There is considerable discussion tonight as to the genuineness of an order captured on a wounded SS officer who died tonight in a hospital before we could question him. This letter, in draft form and signed by Sepp Dietrich[36] commanding the Sixth Panzer Armee, called for the movement of the 1st and 2nd [SS] Panzer Corps; one Corps to go north to Holland and the other Corps to go south to the LANDAU district. Colonel Dickson is of the opinion that the order is a "plant" since there seems no particular reason for movement of these two Corps to the above named places, although it is known that the Boche for some unknown reasons believe our troop concentrations opposite JULICH to be large and possibly feel a British thrust northward across the MAAS into

Holland. The Russians have now definitely identified three divisions which up until two or three weeks ago were on our front and it is not thought improbable that these two Panzer Corps are likewise to follow suit. The Russians today were reported to have pushed beyond POZNAN to reach the Reich frontier only some ninety miles from BERLIN.

The Drive to the Roer River, 28 January–22 February 1945

Sunday, 28 January 1945: First Army's latest and everybody hopes the last offensive since D-Day cracked open this morning at four o'clock. The 1st Div attacking with the 18th Inf completely caught the enemy by surprise and was in the middle of HEPSCHEID before being discovered. 100 enemy occupied the town and the 1st Bn killed 50 and captured the rest. About the same thing happened at HEPPENBACH where the town was captured early in the morning with about half of the 150 Germans being taken PWs. Both Bns of the 18th continued on and net advances for the day were about 2 miles. The 82nd A/B attacking two hours later than the 1st Div made excellent progress advancing up to 4 miles with the main resistance coming from small arms and mortar fire. The Boche were generally organized as strongpoints of 15 to 30 men in bunkers and gave up bunkers and houses reluctantly because of the cold weather and hip-deep snow—probably the worst conditions under which the First Army has yet had to fight. The 3rd Bn of the 504th went through HERESBACH [Herresbach] and the total count at midnight was as follows: 50 Boche killed, 200 taken PW, 1 Mark V Tank destroyed, 2 destroyed 75mm guns taken, and 2 guns of the same caliber taken intact. All of these PWs are from the 3rd Para Div, once the pride of Marshal Goering's[37] parachute outfits and now probably setting an all-time low for the Wehrmacht for morale. G-2 reports as a result of their testimony that these men, forced to go into combat despite frozen feet and despite lack of hot food for three days, are now finally rebelling. News of the Russian advances has reached all soldiers on the Western Front, mainly in the form of rumors but to this is added a final crowning blow to their already lowered morale and there seems little doubt.

During the day the 7th Armd Div was being steadily relieved by the 82nd A/B and movement of the former to assembly areas in the vicinity of EUPEN and VERVIERS being carried on. The 424nd Inf of 106th Div moved back into the far rear area: The General is exceedingly pleased with the progress made, especially taking into consideration the heavy snow conditions.

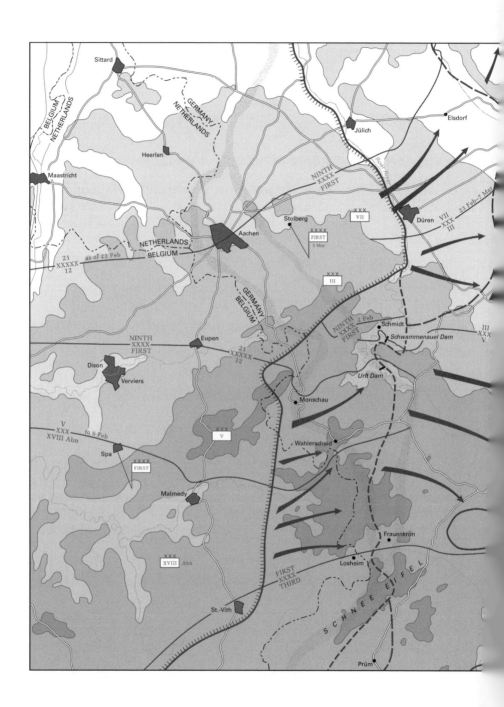

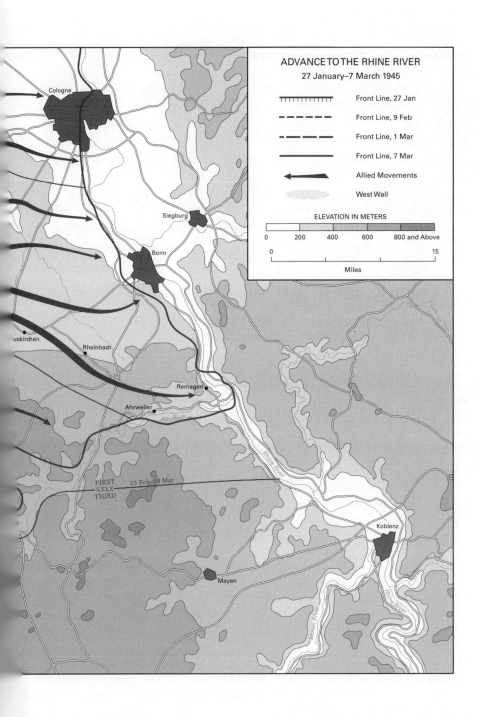

ADVANCE TO THE RHINE RIVER

27 January–7 March 1945

Front Line, 27 Jan	
Front Line, 9 Feb	
Front Line, 1 Mar	
Front Line, 7 Mar	
Allied Movements	
West Wall	

ELEVATION IN METERS

0   200   400   600   800 and Above

0   15

Miles

Cologne

Siegburg

Bonn

uskirchen

Rheinbach

Remagen

Ahrweiler

Ahr River

Rhine River

FIRST
XXXX   23 Feb–20 Mar
THIRD

Koblenz

Mayen

Mosel River

Rhine River

Despite all promises made at the conference in LUXEMBOURG last week, General Patton's Third Army has yet to draw anywhere near abreast of our forward units. The VIII Corps on the right flank now consists of the 87th Div, the 90th Div, and the 4th Div which went into the line late last night but the OUR River has not yet been crossed by any of these units, and our patrols are being met by fire from the other bank.

The Air was operational only one or two hours during the early morning. No great results were obtained.

General Kean and General Hart returned from their six-day leave in England tonight at supper time.

Monday, 29 January 1945: Switching for the time being to night attacks which we have used infrequently and which the Boche certainly do not expect, the 26th Inf jumped off this morning at two o'clock on BULLINGEN. The defenders were caught unawares, house-[to-]house fighting took place but by ten o'clock BULLINGEN was completely in our hands with a total of 234 PWs taken. 82nd A/B followed the example of the 1st, cracking off at 5 AM with both regiments advancing up to 4,000 yds during the day against light to moderate small-arms, artillery, and mortar fire. The 508th Inf cleared MEDENDORF and HOLZHEIM, mopping up also was completed in HERESBACH where—and this is an absolutely true story, they took 201 PWs and counted 67 dead Germans all without the loss of one of our men. Total PWs for yesterday was just under a thousand, adding strength to Col Dickson's argument that perhaps now we shall find Nazi morale on the Western Front completely broken.

General Hodges spent a good part of the morning with General Kean, General Wilson, and Colonel Medaris discussing the percentages of AP [armor-piercing], HE [high-explosive] and SABOT[38] ammunition which should govern our requisitions in the future. They also discussed questions to be brought before General Lee who with General Plank and the latter's Chief of Staff arrived at one o'clock for luncheon. Throughout the luncheon General Lee had paper and pencil by his right hand and for the first time actually appeared to be taking notes on what we needed and why we needed it.

The General left after the departure of General Lee for XVIII Corps headquarters at MALMEDY—a long and tiresome ride because of the movement back to EUPEN of the 7th Armd Div which today was completely relieved by elements of Third Army's 87th Div. The General was disappointed in the fact that V Corps did not attack today as ordered. A night attack was ordered of all divisions along our front. The 1st will start off shortly after midnight to be followed at hourly intervals by the 2nd, 9th, 99th, and 82nd and in the XIX Corps area at 5:30 in the morning by the 78th Div which will come south and southeast to its objectives. This certainly should, on the basis of past performances, completely rock the Boche back on his heels.

Large spottings were made this morning by fighter-bombers—one of 2,000 MTs [motor transports] which were travelling in an easterly and northeasterly direction some ten miles east of St Vith. Early in the afternoon we were able to put effective air coverage on these columns and the toll at seven o'clock tonight was some 300 MTs destroyed and 300 MTs damaged. XIX TAC concentrated on railroad cars in the Euskirchen and Duren areas chalking up 113 for the day.

The VIII Corps made a valiant effort to try to bring its line up to ours, succeeding in crossing the Our River in two places. The good old 4th Div with the 12th Inf made one crossing capturing Hemmeres while below there the 90th Div with elements of the 357th Inf waded across to take Welchenhausen along the entire VIII and III Corps front. They are now abreast of the Our River and standing on the frontier line.

There was no change of any kind in the Seventh Army front. The First French Army continues to attack toward Colmar with our XXI Corps consisting of the 3rd, 28th, and shortly the 75th Divs leading the way. The so-called Colmar pocket has now been cut in two with one French force having shot due east above Colmar to reach the Rhine.

Tuesday, 30 January 1945: First Army smashed ahead on both Corps fronts yesterday making gains as high as six miles. To add to yesterday's bag of 1,000 PWs, we took over one thousand today: 339 coming from the 1st Div, 415 from the 82nd A/B, and 257 from V Corps.

The V Corps attack jumping off at regular hourly intervals from midnight made good progress against initially light resistance which increased as our elements reached near to the first bank of the Siegfried Line. 60th Inf cleared Rohren and went a mile further east. 47th Inf advancing south of the 60th went through the Staats Forest [Staatsforst] for gains of three miles. The 99th Div attacking to protect the north flank of the 2nd Div made small gains with the principal resistance coming from arm-pit deep snow. 38th Inf cleared Wirtzfeld and Klinkelt [Krinkelt] and almost clearing Rocherath.

The 1st Div in the 18th Corp [XVIII Airborne Corps] attacked at 1:30 in the morning and cleared Murrengen [Mürringen] with the 26th Inf. The 18th Inf cleared Hunnigen [Hünningen] and Honsfeld and went a mile farther east to the high round. The 82nd A/B attacking at 5 AM drew close to the outer Siegfried Line clearing LANZERATH after heavy fighting. Much enemy material fell into the hands of the 82nd A/B including one battery of artillery intact. Tomorrow both Corps will continue the attack to the outer ring of the line which they will try to smash the day after tomorrow. The XIX Corps attacking with the 78th Div and the CCA of the 5th Armd Div on our north advanced up to 5 000 yards against generally light resistance. 310th Inf cleared KONZEN and advanced to the outskirts of IMMGENBROICH. 311th Inf cleared KESTERNICH and HUPPENBROICH. CCA of the 5th Armd cleared EISHERSCHEID [Eicherscheid]. It also advanced elements to near a contact point of the Ninth and First Army boundary. If there are any enemy in IMMGENBROICH they are hopelessly cut off. XIX Corps' total of PWs was 528.

Moving the 326th Inf through the 82nd Div and attacking south from HEPPENBACH the VIII Corps was able at the end of the day to claim the capture of ANDLER, LANDERFELD [Laudesfeld] and SCHONBERG [Schoenberg]. Elements of the 245th Inf advanced three miles east to captures NEUEM and SETZ. They have not yet made contact with the 346th. Smaller gains across the OUR River were made by the 4th and 90th Divs.

A stray—or at least we would like to think a stray—V-1 landed 800 yds due south from the center of SPA shortly before the morning conference, apparently causing no casualties but blowing out considerable number of windows in the Brittanique, including one in the General's office. There was sporadic V-1 activity during the day but this was the only one which landed in our vicinity.

The Seventh Army and Second British Army fronts were generally quiet. Very good gains were recorded by the XXI Corps operating under the First French Army which with the 3rd, 28th, and 75th made excellent progress to the east of COLMAR. The 3rd Div alone captured 1200 PWs and claimed they killed 500 of the enemy.

General Kean had a "Top Secret" staff meeting tonight at which a general briefing and discussion of the problems which might arise out of a German collapse was held.

Air was non-operational all day—no heavies, no mediums, no nothing. The weather forecast for tomorrow is equally as dismal. However, late tonight it started to rain and because of high temperature will probably not freeze the roads as was first feared. This rain should hasten our movement along the front and certainly make less miserable the living conditions for front line troops.

Wednesday, 31 January 1945: The XVIII continued to justify the

General's faith in it by making the last day of the month an excellent one. Almost along the entire front they drew abreast of the Siegfried Line, captured 4 enemy tanks, 1 battery of artillery, and an ammunition dump a quarter of a mile long, and continued to prove that their two divisions are about the best that can be found on any fighting front.

The German border was crossed by the XVIII Corps in no less than four places and the only battalion to meet any kind of steady resistance was the 3rd Bn of 26th Inf which, moving up from BULLINGEN encountered 5 tanks and 100 enemy infantry on the 00 vertical grid line near the Corps boundary. These Boche were surrounded without trouble and during the night two of the tanks were knocked cut.

The General was by no means satisfied, however, with the progress of V Corps, the 2nd Div of which continues to irritate him almost as much as it did during the NORMANDY days. From his point of view the 2nd and the 9th Divs have a golden opportunity to push forward to meet at the key cross-roads in the vicinity of 0112 but as of tonight they are both more than two miles way. The General believes that with at least an infantry regiment in reserve in each division and with each division having a supporting tank battalion, and with resistance being admittedly not of heavy nature, they should have pushed forward before now to this cross-roads. As it was, only moderate gains were made during the day by the three attacking divisions. However, over a thousand PWs for the third successive day were claimed by First Army, and PW reports bear out that the morale of the soldiers opposing us is at an all-time low ebb.

Above our sector in XIX Corps there was little news as the 78th consolidated and improved its positions clearing IMMGENBROICH. XIX Corps claimed 700 PWs taken during the last 48 hour period.

Progress again continues to be slow on our south flank as the 87th Div, claiming extreme supply difficulty and road trouble, made practically no gains at all. The 90th Div alone was able to advance some two miles to capture WINTERSBELT [Winterspelt] and HONCKALENFELD [Heckhalenfeld].

For the third successive day the thaw continued reducing the snow level to about six inches and almost clearing the roads. Though this is favorable for moving supplies in the rear areas on firm roads, it has created a minor hell with the front where both Corps had to deal with dirt roads or simply cross-country trails. The heavies, however, were able to be out in force against industrial targets inside Germany.

The Second British front was quiet with no change recorded. The First French Army backed especially by the XXI US Corps made excellent gains both due south and east of COLMAR. The pocket here is being narrowed down in rapid fashion and it would not be surprising to see it completely liquidated within the next week's time.

Thursday, 1 February 1945: Much to the General's disappointment XVIII Corps did not crack the Line today, instead patrols were sent deep into the outer fringes and reports from both the 1st and 82nd Divs were almost identical: pillboxes were almost unoccupied, there was no artillery fire, and small arms fire was the only kind of opposition. One patrol of the 1st Div blew up two pillboxes and occupied another. Patrols of the 504th Inf of the 82nd took intact 12 88mm guns and at last report turned them around and were firing them on the Boche. The Corps will attack early tomorrow morning in an attempt to breach the first of the double switch line.

V Corps, though progress was slow, finally made junction at the key cross-roads which before Von Runstedt's push was the objective of the 2nd Div and which they had just reached when his tremendous blow fell, here today at coordinate 002123 the 9th Inf met elements of the 47th Inf of the 9th Div. This junction pinched out the 99th Div which will not [now] revert to reserve tomorrow.

Weather again restricted all but a few minor fighter-bomber missions. With visibility bad over the target area they went farther on to the RHINE concentrating on barges and railroad cars.

The biggest and most unsatisfactory news of the day is that there will probably be a general regrouping and shifting of forces in order that the British together with the Ninth Army, which will probably be the biggest offensive weapon, may put on its long planned and long wanted "big show" across the ROER in the DUREN area. General Thorson arrived back from Group tonight with this news and tomorrow Gen Bradley and Gen Simpson will arrive for a conference on details. It appears at the present time that we will lose at least one division out of the bargain. We will give the 2nd and 3rd Armd to Ninth Army or at least one of them. Our boundary will be extended to include the area now held by the 78th, 5th Armd, and 104th, and we shall probably hand over the 83rd, 84th and one more infantry division as well. The 7th Armd and 5th Armd will probably stay with us. This news this morning coming at a time when our offensive is just getting under way with less than one-quarter of our real strength actually committed is a blow to the General and to his key staff officers. By the extension of the boundary our offensive power is naturally limited since we will no longer have VII Corps in reserve. However, it still may be possible for the XVIII Corps, composed of excellent fighting troops, to smash through the Siegfried Line and press onward, which will certainly take a good bit of ginger out of any credit which might go to the British or the Ninth Army. Their drive, if British regrouping take its customary time, could not be launched for another ten days or two weeks. In the meantime, we can do much and needless to say the Russians are doing much for us. The General would like to argue this thing out with Gen Bradley tomorrow but how far he feels he is able to go in contesting it, we naturally do not know tonight.

The Seventh Army launched an attack early this morning to cancel the bridgehead which the Germans established across the RHINE in their drive concurrent with that through the HAGENAU Forest. They are meeting barbed wire and minefields but thus far no determined enemy opposition. First French Army continue to make good steady progress in clearing out the COLMAR salient and we have now cut their only supply and escape route directly across the RHINE. If they continue to retreat they will have to cross the River by barges or hastily erected ponton bridges.[39]

Friday, 2 February 1945: This was a steady day of conferences and of gains—General Bradley (accompanied by Generals Allen and [A. Franklin] Kibler),[40] General Patton (accompanied by his DC/S), and General Simpson (accompanied by Col Mead and Gen Nugent) arrived at noon today for luncheon and for a two and a half hour conference on the shape of things to come. The gist of the conference is not different from that outlined in yesterday's diary. To repeat again: we lose the 2nd and 3rd Armd and the 30th, 83rd, and 84th Divs. Two of which start moving tonight to the XIX Corps. In return, we get most of the area now held by the XIX Corps, including the 78th, 8th, and 5th Armd and probably also to arrive in the near future which will be the 9th Armd which has been out of the lines since the early tragic days of the German break-through. Our plan will be approximately as follows: Gen Huebner with his V Corps will take charge of the lower southern flank of our sector. There we shall hold firm. The present drive being made towards the dams and DREIBORN will be continued until the final Corps objective is reached and then there too we shall hold tight. This will permit the VII Corps and a good part of the XVIII Corps as well to strike across the ROER in strength in conjunction with the Ninth Army. This is the third time that one of our offensives had been halted in midstream in order to pursue another plan and in order to regroup forces. There is no sense in not saying that it is an extreme disappointment to General Hodges and to the staff and during the day as the gains rolled in the disappointment took on added meaning for all along the two Corps fronts our divisions were breaking through the Siegfried Line, sometimes without difficulty, sometimes only after fierce fighting, but the fact remains that breaches were being made and that if the 30th and 84th were available as originally planned we could turn our drive into a real smash.

Shortly before the General's first guests left, General Ridgway and General Huebner and later on Colonel Partridge of VII Corps, representing Gen Collins who has not yet returned from the Riviera, discussed the changes made necessary by higher order, the vast troop movements, of course, which are now necessary as well as the fixing of new Corps boundaries. The new boundary between Ninth and First Armies has not definitely been settled as there are numerous points of small dissention regarding use of roads, partial use of Aachen, etc., that must be ironed out.

General Ridgway was forced at 10:30 this morning to notify the 82nd and the 1st Divs of the change in plans and, therefore, of necessity of slowing down and halting when temporary pillbox objectives were reached. The 82nd especially could not go farther since it is now at least 8 miles ahead of advance elements of VIII Corps and without the added strength to protect that flank further advance would be extremely dangerous.

For specific facts, the 325th Inf took NEUHOFF and UDENBRETH, both of which lie inside the first defenses. The 504th Inf moving through one of the holes in the line and attacking due south advanced almost three miles from bunker-to-bunker to coordinate 064990, meanwhile repulsing two enemy counterattacks supported by tanks between two and 4:30.

The 1st Div likewise went ahead against very heavy mortar and machine gun fire; the 18th Inf advancing almost two miles through two lines of dragon's teeth tank barriers to capture SCHIETERT and adjacent high ground. The 1st Div will attack tomorrow with the 26th Inf but the 82nd Div will hold fast. Generally speaking the resistance was not as of desperate a nature as had been anticipated by some but the going was far from easy. Machine gun fire was extremely heavy throughout the day as well as mortar fire. Artillery, however, was sporadic and light. Even better gains were recorded by V Corps. Though it must be taken into consideration that they had broken through the defenses long before this present offensive and that they had only opposition without barriers to deal with. The 9th Inf moving fast and up until eight o'clock last night cleared SCHONSEIFFEN [Schöneseiffen] and HARPERSCHEID had taken over 400 PWs in the process, and for this victory Gen Hodges sent Gen Huebner two bottles of champagne paying him off for a bet which he made previously in the day that this could not be done before midnight. Elements of the 60th Inf, 23rd Inf, and the 47th Inf likewise made excellent gains. The 78th Div which passed to the operational control of V Corps at six o'clock tonight advanced 1 Bn to HAMMER which was found completely clear of enemy.

For the first time in four days we had partial flying weather; some 125 sorties being flown with claims of some 100 MTs destroyed and damaged and a few barges on the RHINE sunk. Mediums and heavies were out in force.

The only other news from other fronts of any importance (outside of the Russian fronts) was that the First French Army had entered COLMAR from two sides and was in the process of clearing it tonight. From captured PWs and orders it now appears that the Boche, unable to reinforce the troops in this pocket, is holding open the big break at BRISACH in order to withdraw its troops which he now has in it. It is increasingly probable that the COLMAR pocket will be completely liquidated in the end of a week's time. The Bridgehead south of STRASBOURG and north of COLMAR has now been completely erased.

Saturday, 3 February 1945: Excellent gains were made by V Corps throughout the day. The 78th Div which was attached yesterday attacked early this morning across the ROER River to occupy DEIDENBORN [Dedenborn], the 47th Inf advancing on the right of the 78th Div captured EINRUHR and pushed its 1st and 2nd Bns forward to occupy strategic high ground. 39th Inf entered HEPHAHN [Herhahn] and continued fighting there throughout the night. DREIBORN was completely cleared by the 60th Inf while the 1st Bn of the 9th cleared ETTELSCHEID and the 1st of the 23rd cleared BRONSFELD. The prisoner bag, not yet tabulated, will run high as Gen Huebner reported that two companies have been captured almost intact in addition to those which they ferreted out of the cellars of DREIBORN.

XVIII Corps was not exceedingly active as they were intent upon proper consolidation of their positions. The 26th Inf did launch a limited objective attack at noon and secured the cross-roads at 0407, mopping up pillboxes in that area against stubborn resistance and numerous mines. During the night, patrols reported that the enemy had withdrawn from MIESCHEID and the town is occupied by elements of the 3rd Bn of the 18th. 99th Div which was pinched out two days ago today attached its 395th Inf to the 1st Div and tomorrow they will drive in a northeasterly direction up the Corps left boundary.

Two of our divisions involved in this big transfer of troops, viz: 30th and 84th, cleared the First Army area today to occupy assembly areas in the Ninth Army and the other two divisions will follow probably tomorrow. In addition the Ninth Army is getting the 8th Armd Div which is assembling near VALKENBURG. 35th Div will relieve the British 52nd Div when it has closed and the XVI US Corps will take over the area now occupied by the British XII Corps.

South of us the 87th put on a burst of speed to come almost abreast of our positions. The towns of LOSHEIM, KREWINKEL, ROTH and BLEIALF were all taken and the only the last named town putting up any kind of organized resistance.

Good progress was also made along the Seventh and First French Army fronts; 36th Div attacking to reduce the bridgehead north of STRASBOURG reached HERLISHEIM against powerful enemy counter-blows. In the First French Army sector, COLMAR was cleared by the 75th Div and [the 3rd and] 28th Divs were pushing south of COLMAR on both sides with steady gains to show for their fighting.

The air was operational during the afternoon and some 150 MTs, 50 railroad cars were their principal booty. Mediums were also out and BERLIN received what is now said to be the heaviest single raid of the war—over 2500 tons of bombs in the time of 45 minutes. Escort fighters, just for the hell of it, went a few miles beyond BERLIN to catch a glimpse of the advancing Russian forces.

General Collins, in fine vigorous mood, after his trip to the Riviera, reported to the General at 9:30 this morning and was closeted with him until after lunch. He is, not unexpectedly, raring to go and anxious to get all his Corps troops back which have been subdivided among the other two attacking Corps during the past two weeks. The General left the office at two o'clock for EUPEN where the V Corps headquarters are located and where he had a long conference with Gen Ridgway, Gen Huebner, Gen Parker and Gen Weaver.

The Generals saw tonight "The Animal Kingdom" an adaptation of the Phillip Barry play and it was received very well by the audience.

Sunday, 4 February 1945: The outstanding news of the day was that elements of the 9th Div reached the western bank of the southernmost URFT River dam and likewise captured ORDENSBURG VOGELSLANG [Ordensburg Vogelsang],[41] the special German school to train "future fuehrers"; a school which we have long looked at with interest as a possible CP site, was found fairly well damaged by our bombs which were not directed at the school itself but against the nearby dam. There was no defense of the school such as perhaps a few people expected because of its significance to Germany. Only four scared and tired soldiers were found in its spacious caverns and cellars. Elements of the 47th Inf did not try to cross the dam; machine-gun fire was pouring across from a pillbox on the other side and there were a succession of rumors starting at five o'clock that the Boche had tried to blow it. However, if they did so try, they did not succeed, although the road across it is badly cratered, whether from our explosives or theirs, we do not yet know.

These were two of the best gains during the day in which we everywhere made good progress. The 311th Inf of 78th Div with CCR of 7th Armd attached cleared RUHRBERG [Rurberg] and occupied the high ground along the ROER River east of the town. Another Bn of the 311th mopped up in the ROER River bend between DEDENBORN and EINRUHR where the bridge was found intact. 3rd Bn of 47th Inf captured WOLLSEIFEN while the elements of the 39th and 60th Inf cleared HEPHAHN [Herhahn] and MORSBACH. For the first time since the clearing out of AACHEN we are again coming across German civilians in strength; approximately one thousand have been evacuated in the last two days to rear areas mainly old men and women, and children, who hid in cellars until the fighting had passed.

1st Div with 395th Inf attached advanced north along the left flank to make a gain of almost three miles against scattered enemy resistance. 26th Inf captured HOLLERATH. Tonight the 82nd will be relieved by elements of the 99th and will move back for a few days' rest to assembly areas at SALM CHATEAU.

2nd Armd completed its movement to the Ninth Army while Col McDonald's [MacDonald] 4th Cav Gp closed near AACHEN as the first of VII Corps troops to move in the new area.

VIII Corps elements on our right flank secured ROTH and secured and captured four or five other small towns to advance generally two miles to the east.

Air was non-operational during the day. The thaw continues; the snow is almost completely melted down.

Monday, 5 February 1945: VII Corps CP opened at the old stamping grounds at KORNELIMUNSTER at four o'clock today and at that time officially assumed responsibility for the 8th and 104th Divs at the present location and for the XIX Corps sector. At the same time new boundary between First and Ninth Armies became effective. The 78th Div with CCR 7th Armd attached continued its attack in the direction of SCHMIDT with elements of 309th advancing to within 2500 yards to that much sought town. CCR cleared STRAUCH and STECKENBORN; resistance was initially light but increased during the day as the attack progressed, especially artillery fire. However, Gen Hodges, checking on this report discovered that the division had only received some 100 rounds in comparison with 20,000 rounds which Corps had shot the previous day. He, therefore, did not consider the shelling particularly heavy and it could have been done entirely by a battery. Our troops are now within a mile or so of both GEMUND and SCHLEIDEN but HELLENTHAL, which was attacked during the day by two battalions of the 38th Inf, was a hard nut to crack. An estimated enemy battalion supported by tanks was in the town and our efforts to clear it continued during the night with no reported success. There is no change in the situation as regards the three dams. We now control the western entrances to two and, of course, the present attack of the 78th Div which will be backed tomorrow by an attack from the 517th Para Inf coming down south from BERGSTEIN aims to secure the third. During the night the 1st Div was relieved by elements of the 99th Div, the former has moved back to assembly areas at STAVELOT for a short recuperation.

Gen Ridgway arrived for a conference with Gen Hodges at two o'clock to discuss extension of VII and XVIII Corps boundaries up to the RHINE. Shortly before six Gen Eisenhower and Gen Bradley, accompanied only by Maj Hanson [Bradley's aide], arrived as Gen Hodges' guests for the night. Dinner was held at the house and after that our Generals came back to the office as usual while Gen Eisenhower and Gen Bradley stayed to see "Saratoga Trunk."

Tomorrow night the VIII and XII Corps of Third Army are putting on an attack to try to secure PRUM and BITBURG. These objectives must be reached by February 10th and beyond those points after they are secured the Third Army will not advance.

Contact between pincer forces has been established between 1st French Army advancing from the south and the XXI US corps advancing from the north at RUFTACH [Rouffach], thus spitting the COLMAR pocket in two. The PW count there is on an average of 2,000 a day and liquidation of the remaining forces should not require more than two or three days' time.

Again Air was non-operational. Thaw with light rain continues; the temperature is that of Spring weather.

The only interesting fact to come out of General Eisenhower's visit was that he had bet $10 to $30 that the Russians would be in BERLIN by the 31st of March. The early thaw which has apparently set upon that front as it has on ours will be the possible deterrent to his winning the bet as he readily admits.

Tuesday, 6 February 1945: Today was a day devoted to "official-dom," out of which the General managed to snatch a few minutes for important conversations with his Corps Commanders.

Without coming down for the morning conference, Gen Eisenhower, Gen Bradley, Gen Hodges, and party left the house at a nine o'clock for V Corps Hq at EUPEN where they met Gen Huebner and Gen Ridgway. The next stop was at the 78th Div for a talk with Gen Parker whose troops are now conducting the vital attack towards the dam, and after that to VII Corps Hq at KORNELIMUNSTER where the party was met by Gen Simpson, Gen Collins, and Gen McLain. After a talk there, Gen Eisenhower and Gen Bradley stayed on for lunch and talks with Gen Collins, Gen McLain, Gen Rose, and Gen Birks of 9th Div. After lunch he motored back to V Corps where he continued his conference with Gen Huebner and Gen Ridgway, in addition to Gen Andrus commanding the 1st Div.

The General was not too well satisfied with the progress made during the day towards SCHMIDT. The area was heavily mined and pill-boxes strongly defended, but the General nevertheless felt with all the strength we had in that area greater gains should have been made. To-night, forward troops had advanced to the 04 vertical grid line, still some 3000 yds away from the western ends of the town. The 517th Para Inf which attacked south early this morning from the vicinity of BERG-STEIN likewise ran into heavy minefields defended by small arms fire and by the end of the day it made only some 800 yards and were not yet up to the KALL River. However, tonight at eight o'clock HELLENTHAL had been cleared by the 38th Inf.

The 1st Div was completely relieved and occupied assembly areas and the Div CP opened at AYWYLIE [Aywaile]. At six o'clock tonight 99th Div reverted from control of XVIII A/B Corps to V Corps and responsibility for XVIII Corps zone was assumed by V Corps at the same time.

VIII Corps' attack towards PRUM made good progress during the day with general advances of over a mile. The XII Corps will attack early tomorrow morning.

The remaining movements of troops in the forward line positions went on today and will continue tomorrow; 83rd Div will move to Ninth Army and 5th Armd and 3rd Armd will move up starting early tomorrow morning.

Substantial progress was made in reducing the two enemy pockets remaining in the COLMAR area. They are now capturing on the average of 1000 PWs a day in that vicinity and the Boche are putting up stubborn resistance only in certain isolated strongpoints.

Air was again non-operational all day as the thaw with intermittent rains continued.

General Stroh and Aide who have returned from two months in the states were the General's guests for dinner tonight. General Stroh tomorrow assumes command of the 106th Div. They are going to receive in the near future two more regiments, one the 3rd separate infantry regiment, the other one as yet unknown and thus come back to complete fighting strength.

Wednesday, 7 February 1945: SCHMIDT, which has been the "bugbear" of First Army, for many a month, was finally entered late this afternoon and although not cleared, by midnight was finally in our control. KOMMERSCHEIDT was cleared by the 309th Inf. The 517th Inf, however, again encountered heavy minefields which although previously breached had apparently been remined by Germans who had slipped back in, consequently no gains in that area were recorded. Evidence of the nature of the resistance was given this afternoon when V Corps reported that 159 pillboxes had been captured west of SCHMIDT in the last three days. Our casualties have not been excessive although the resistance has been of a determined nature despite the fact that the Boche had defended with very few men.

XVIII A/B Corps becomes operational early tomorrow morning having opened its new CP today at ZWEIFALL. Technically, it has under its control at the present time only the 16th Inf which today replaced the 13th Inf of 8th Div which moved northward. As soon as the 82nd and 1st Divs come up from their present assembly areas the XVIII Corps will really go into action. Gen Ridgway was with the General most of the day at this headquarters. It now appears that Gen Brereton is trying to get Gen Ridgway and his Corps back in order that some airborne operation may be planned. Gen Hodges and Gen Kean, of course, are protesting against this suggestion especially as it comes at a date when XVIII Corps is completely ready to assume its important place in our coming action, and when relief would be practically impossible. Gen Ridgway concurred wholeheartedly in a letter which

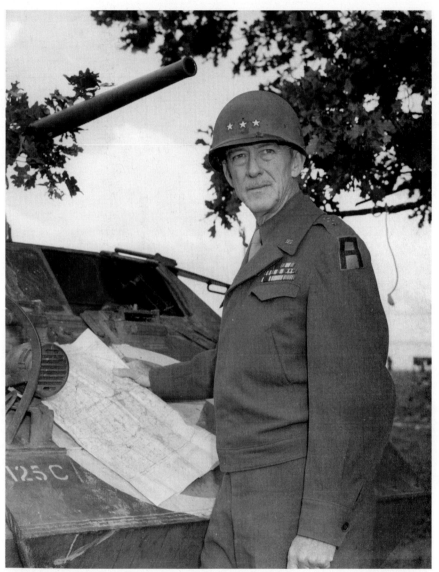

A War Department photo of Lt. Gen. Courtney H. Hodges taken at First U.S. Army headquarters at Verviers, Belgium, for *Collier's* magazine. (U.S. Army photograph; courtesy Dwight D. Eisenhower Presidential Library)

Saturday, 15 July 1944: A GI plays taps at the military funeral of Brig. Gen. Theodore Roosevelt Jr. at the American soldiers' cemetery at Ste-Mère-Église, France. (National Archives and Records Administration)

Thursday, 17 August 1944: Lt. Gens. Courtney H. Hodges, Omar N. Bradley, and George S. Patton Jr. discuss the Third Army's drive through Brittany at Bradley's headquarters. (National Archives and Records Administration)

Tuesday, 25 July 1944: Lt. Gen. Lesley J. McNair, former commanding general, Army Ground Forces, was killed in action in the bombing during Operation Cobra only a few hours after this photo was taken. (National Archives and Records Administration)

Tuesday, 29 August 1944: At the Arc de Triomphe, Maj. Gen. Leonard T. Gerow, commanding general, Fifth Corps; Courtney H. Hodges; Gen. Marie-Pierre Koenig, French army, the French military governor of Paris; and Lt. Gen. Omar N. Bradley, commanding general, Twelfth Army Group, salute during ceremonies marking the liberation of Paris. (National Archives and Records Administration)

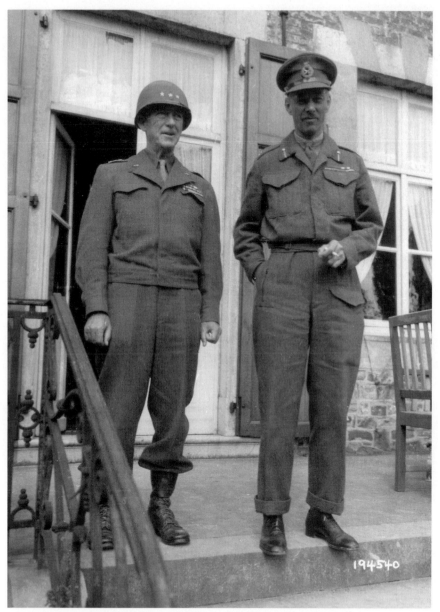

Friday, 15 September 1944: Courtney H. Hodges and Lt. Gen. Sir Miles C. Dempsey, commanding general, British Second Army, pose together leaving Master Tactical headquarters at the Château de la Sarte near Huy, Belgium. (National Archives and Records Administration)

Friday, 15 September 1944: In the map room at First U.S. Army's tactical command post at Château de la Sarte, Maj. Gen. William B. Kean, chief of staff, Army, points to map while discussing operations with Courtney H. Hodges; Col. Benjamin A. Dickson, intelligence (G-2); Brig. Gen. Truman C. Thorson, operations (G-3); and Brig. Gen. Charles E. Hart, army artillery officer. (U.S. Army photograph; courtesy Dwight D. Eisenhower Presidential Library)

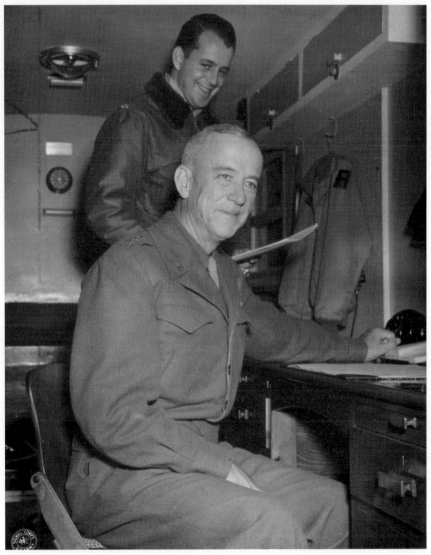

Friday, 15 September 1944: Courtney H. Hodges smiles as he reviews the progress of his forces on their drive toward Berlin. With the general in their field office is his senior aide-de-camp, Maj. William C. Sylvan, one of the coauthors of the First U.S. Army's war diary. (National Archives and Records Administration)

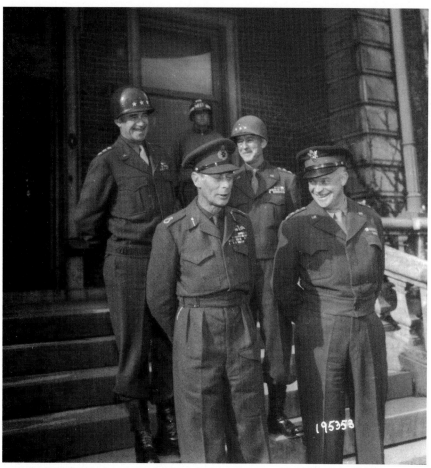

Saturday, 14 October 1944: King George VI, front left, and Gen. Dwight D. Eisenhower, supreme Allied commander, front right, with Omar N. Bradley, rear left, and Courtney H. Hodges, rear right, at First Army Headquarters, near Verviers, Belgium, after presentation of awards. Bradley was named Knight Commander of the Bath. (National Archives and Records Administration)

Wednesday, 22 November 1944: Attending a conference on U.S. operations on the western front at Headquarters, First U.S. Army, Spa, Belgium, are, from left to right: Maj. Gen. Raymond McLain, commander, Nineteenth Corps; Maj. Gen. William B. Kean, chief of staff, First U.S. Army; Omar N. Bradley (pointing at map); Courtney H. Hodges (back to camera); and Maj. Gen. William H. Simpson, commander, Ninth U.S. Army. (U.S. Army photograph; courtesy Dwight D. Eisenhower Presidential Library)

Thursday, 23 November 1944 (Thanksgiving Day): Courtney H. Hodges and William B. Kean visited a number of units of Fifth and Seventh corps. At the headquarters of the Fourth Infantry Division at Zweifall, Germany, Hodges and Kean (fourth and fifth from the left) met with (from left to right) Maj. Gen. J. Lawton Collins, Seventh Corps commander; Maj. Gen. Raymond O. Barton, Fourth Infantry Division commander; and Maj. Gen. Maurice Rose, commanding general of the Third Armored Division, Seventh Corps. General Barton hosted a Thanksgiving dinner following the meeting. (U.S. Army photograph; courtesy Dwight D. Eisenhower Presidential Library)

Thursday, 30 November 1944: Courtney H. Hodges (at the head of the table) dines with Brig. Gen. A. J. Browning and a group of American industrial leaders during their visit to Headquarters, First Army, at Spa, Belgium. (U.S. Army photograph; courtesy Dwight D. Eisenhower Presidential Library)

Friday, 2 February 1945: U.S. Army generals shown on the steps of First U.S. Army Headquarters, where they met with Omar N. Bradley to map plans for the attacks on Germany's western defenses. Left to right: Bradley, Courtney H. Hodges, William H. Simpson, and George S. Patton Jr. (National Archives and Records Administration)

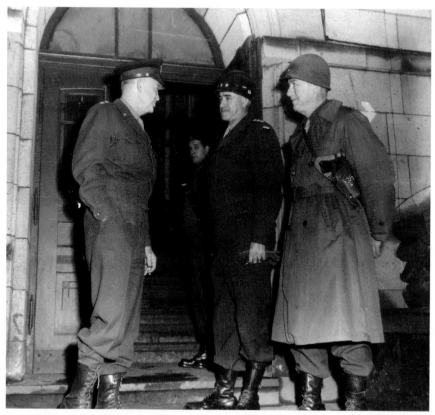

Tuesday, 6 February 1945: Dwight D. Eisenhower with Omar N. Bradley (center) and Courtney H. Hodges leave Fifth Corps headquarters at Eupen, Belgium, after a conference. (National Archives and Records Administration)

Friday, 9 March 1945: Gen. Alphonse Pierre Juin, chief of staff, French armed forces, presents the Grand Officer of the Legion of Honor to Courtney H. Hodges at Namur, Belgium. (National Archives and Records Administration)

Saturday, 24 March 1945: Courtney H. Hodges, left, and Maurice Rose witness distribution of the Distinguished Unit Badge to the Third Armored Division in the Rhine River area, Germany. (National Archives and Records Administration)

Sunday, 25 March 1945: Dwight D. Eisenhower, left, is greeted by George S. Patton Jr. (arm raised), Omar N. Bradley, and Courtney H. Hodges at First Army headquarters' airfield at Euskirchen, Germany. (National Archives and Records Administration)

Monday, 26 March 1945: After their visit to Remagen and various sites along the Rhine River front Dwight D. Eisenhower (looking out of window), Omar N. Bradley, and Courtney H. Hodges stopped at the Kurhotel, Königswinter, Germany, for lunch and a meeting with J. Lawton Collins, commander, Seventh Corps (right). (U.S. Army photograph; courtesy Dwight D. Eisenhower Presidential Library)

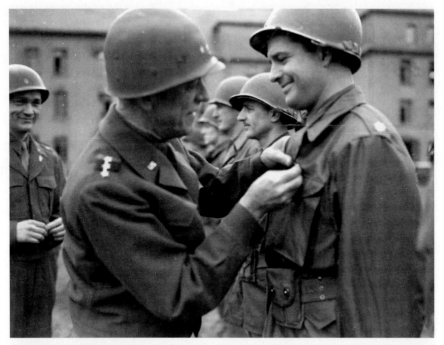

Thursday, 29 March 1945: Courtney Hodges pins a Bronze Star medal on his senior aide and one of the authors of the war diary, Maj. William C. Sylvan, at award ceremonies for thirty-five members of the headquarters at Euskirchen, Germany. (U.S. Army photograph; courtesy Dwight D. Eisenhower Presidential Library)

Friday, 6 April 1945: The Sixty-ninth Infantry Division has the guard of honor at Army Day ceremonies at Fort Ehrenbreitstein overlooking the Rhine River at Koblenz, Germany, where the Stars and Stripes was raised for the first time since the same flag was lowered by the same American infantry units in 1923 at the end of the American occupation after World War I. Omar N. Bradley inspects the guard of honor. (National Archives and Records Administration)

15–24 April 1945: The Fürstenhof Hotel in Bad Wildungen, Germany, was the location of First U.S. Army's headquarters from 15 to 24 April 1945. Hodges' rooms were on the second floor in the right corner of the hotel. (U.S. Army photograph; courtesy Dwight D. Eisenhower Presidential Library)

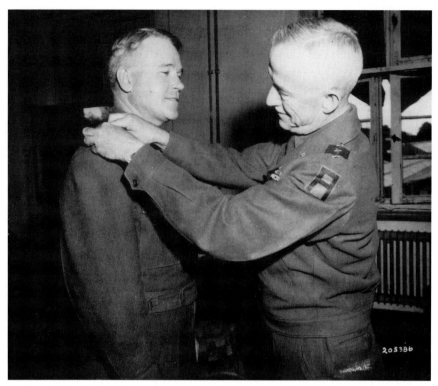

Friday, 27 April 1945: Courtney H. Hodges pins third star on now Lt. Gen. J. Lawton Collins, who commanded the Seventh Corps, First U.S. Army, throughout the war in Europe. (National Archives and Records Administration)

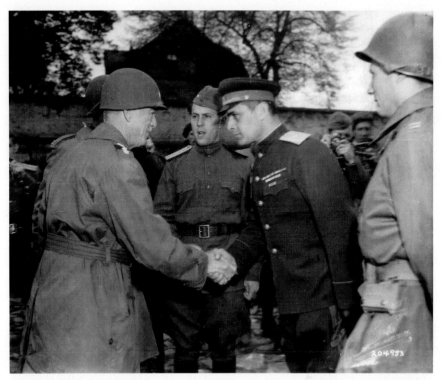

Monday, 30 April 1945: Courtney H. Hodges is met on the bank of the Elbe River at Torgau, Germany, by Maj. Gen. Gleb Vladimirovich Baklanov, commanding general, Soviet Thirty-fourth Corps. (National Archives and Records Administration)

24 April–14 May 1945: While at Weimar, Germany, from 24 April to 14 May 1945, Hodges and First Army headquarters occupied the palatial house of the former Nazi leader Fritz Sauckel. (U.S. Army photograph; courtesy Dwight D. Eisenhower Presidential Library)

Friday, 11 May 1945: American generals who helped pave the way to victory in Europe gather at Twelfth Army Group Headquarters, Bad Wildungen, Germany. Seated in front row are, left to right, William H. Simpson; George S. Patton Jr.; Gen. Carl A. Spaatz, commanding general, U.S. Army Strategic Air Forces; Dwight D. Eisenhower; Omar N. Bradley; Courtney H. Hodges; and Lt. Gen. Leonard T. Gerow, commanding general, Fifteenth U.S. Army. Standing in the rear are, left to right, Brig. Gen. Ralph F. Stearley, commanding general, Ninth Tactical Air Command; Lt. Gen. Hoyt S. Vandenberg, commanding general, Ninth Air Force; Lt. Gen. Walter B. Smith, chief of staff, Supreme Headquarters, Allied Expeditionary Forces; Maj. Gen. Otto P. Weyland, commanding general, Nineteenth Tactical Air Command; and Brig. Gen. Richard E. Nugent, commanding general, Twenty-ninth Tactical Air Command. (National Archives and Records Administration)

Friday, 13 May 1945: Left to right, William B. Kean, Courtney H. Hodges, and Col. Gen. Aleksei Semenovich Zhadov, commanding general, Russian Fifth Guards Army, and Maj. Gen. Clarence R. Huebner (back to camera), commanding general, Fifth Corps, meet in quarters of J. Lawton Collins in Leipzig, Germany, prior to exchange of awards between the Russian and American armies in celebration of the defeat of Germany and the junction of American and Russian armies at the Elbe River. (National Archives and Records Administration)

was signed by Gen Hodges asking that such a move be postponed indefinitely.

Guests of the General tonight for dinner (and Gen Rogers' birthday party incidentally) were Gen [Paul R.] Hawley,[42] Chief Surgeon of the ETO, and Gen [Joseph I.] Martin,[43] Surgeon of Fifth Army.

The British attack scheduled to go to tomorrow morning has been postponed 24 hours—which did not surprise the General as he made a private bet with General Ridgway that Monty would work it somehow that the Ninth Army would attack first.

VIII Corps continued its attack east towards PRUM against heavy enemy artillery fire and increased resistance. Some 500 enemy tried to come back into BASCHEID but they were driven off and 200 were taken PWs. XII Corps made no less than six separate crossings of the OUR River under extremely difficult conditions—the stream being swollen almost to flood size making handling of pontons and rubber boats extremely difficult. However, the 5th and 80th Divs advanced up to a mile across the river to establish substantial and unbreakable bridgeheads. The objective of the XII Corps attack is BITBURG.

The pocket west of COLMAR has now been eliminated while the pocket east of the city has been reduced to half its size. NEU BREISCH [Neu-Brisach] was captured. First French Corps has taken 1500 PWs in the last two days.

Air was again non-operational throughout the day.

Thursday, 8 February 1945: Up to midnight tonight, at which time Gen Hodges left the office, no one was able to explain to him the lack of progress made by the 78th Div in driving towards the dam. Gen Hart has placed some 40 Bns of Arty—780 guns able to fire by the count—in positions to support this attack; casualties reported by the 78th Div have been light; and yet no great progress has been recorded during the day. Lack of gains induced Gen Hodges to order Gen Huebner to the 78th Div to take personal charge of the situation. At noontime Gen Hart sent his own representative to Corps to find out the artillery situation and later this evening the General decided to push the 9th Div on thru the 78th in order that that attack might he pursued with greater success. In his opinion it is just simply a case of "poor management," since with the artillery available we should be able to blast a road from our present front line positions straight to the roads. At midnight last night forward elements of the 78th Div were on the 08 vertical grid line and SCHMIDT in which there was sporadic sniping fire during the day was finally declared clear. The 517th

Para Inf which had been trying unsuccessfully to come down south from BERGSTEIN was withdrawn from the line and the 505th Para Inf took positions in KOMMERSCHEID and then advanced to the northeast. Today they will continue driving straight eastward; the 517th has been removed to assembly areas.

The General had hoped and saw no reason why the hope should not be met, that the dam would he in our hands today. It must be in our hands tomorrow if the Ninth Army attack is to go off without interruption. The General will probably go down to division level tomorrow to add his own personal supervision to the drive. On the other fronts the news was slightly better. The COLMAR pocket was completely erased with the exception of a two mile stretch along the RHINE still held by the last remnants of the Boche trying to flee across the river. In the north the First Canadian Army with the British XXX Corps actually in command of troops launched a four division attack along an eight mile front just south of the RHINE River. Initial objectives were taken with advances up to 6000 yards for more than 1100 PWs were taken. The artillery barrage which opened the attack was of a five-hour duration. Troops were generally on the 82 vertical grid line.

The VIII Corps continued to advance towards PRUM against resistance described as heavy. All pillboxes have not yet been mopped up. In the XII Corps area the bridgeheads made by the 80th and 5th Divs across the OUR River are unfortunately not being strengthened because of the swift flooding water of the river. However, our troops on the other side have successfully beaten off no less than four counterattacks and bridge building is a slow process under the conditions but is under way.

The Air was up in strength today and had great success. Some 330 missions were flown and although not much MT was sighted, fighter-bombers had a field-day this side and the other side of the RHINE. Some 250 RR cars were claimed destroyed, and some 500 damaged, along with some 54 cuts in railroad lines and yards. Fuel dumps, buildings, possible CPs were also among the targets. We lost two aircraft and 28 were damaged due to flak but not a single Boche plane was sighted during the entire day. Most of the mediums were in support of the British attack while our heavies roamed almost at will over the Reich.

It now seems almost certain that we shall lose the XVIII A/B Corps much to our disappointment. It will be replaced by III Corps under Gen Milliken [John Millikin][44] which is now operating in the Third Army. It is not known when this change will take place but it is thought to be imminent.

The assembled multitude saw and enjoyed "Rhapsody in Blue," the life story of George Gershwin.[45]

Friday, 9 February 1945: We have the dam tonight—or at least one-half of it. 1st Bn of 309th Inf is now entrenched in the middle of the dam unable to cross a 50' gap which was blown in the roadway across the top early this morning. Apparently the sluiceways of the dam have been blown open, the practical result of which will be almost the same as actually demolishing the dam. The water is rising rapidly all along the ROER. While there is no danger involved to our troops, it will take some three or four days before it subsides to normal level. No one thought we would be able to capture the dam intact and the damage was no surprise. We have them, damaged or undamaged, and that was the objective. Credit for the final operation should go to both the 78th and 9th Divs. The 60th Inf did its share of the job and more in passing through the 311th late last night and attacking early this morning toward HOSSENFELD [Hasenfeld]. The 309th then came down along the lake line to reach the dam. Not many PWs were taken and those who did surrender testified that the artillery laid down was the heaviest they had ever encountered along our front. It did not, however, they said, and this is subject to verification later on, cause many casualties. Gains during the day were also made by the 505th Inf which relieving the 508th advanced east almost a mile with the principal resistance being furnished by mines and muddy roads.

The General himself had first-hand information of the state of the roads which at first blown into frost blisters over which heavy transportation was passing and then subjected to a steady week of thaw have suddenly collapsed in many places. Practically all roads leading out of EUPEN are in terrible shape and the General was only able to reach ZWEIFALL, CP of the XVIII Corps, by driving several hundred yards on a railroad track with his jeep. The trip from this CP took him 2½ hours. This road condition is something which happened almost over-night and will require a long and steady freeze before any improvement can be noted. How far it will seriously handicap our forthcoming drive, we do not yet know.

The General did not get to V Corps as he planned to do but General Huebner had his own forward CP at the CP of the 78th Div and took an active part in the direction of the capture of the dams. There was constant communication all day between this headquarters and Gen

Simpson and the attack of XIII Corps of Ninth Army is postponed at least 24 hours and probably will be postponed further pending more complete information from our engineers about the state of the dams and the river flood. During the current drive for the dams an estimated 40,000 rounds of artillery have been fired from our guns. The Boche countered last night with some very heavy caliber 280 or 310mm rockets which were fired into BERGSTEIN detonating with terrific blast effect and causing some casualties, which is probably a larger edition of V-1½ which was fired into VERVIERS and other towns upon the start of the Boche December offensive.

Good progress was made by the British XXX Corps in clearing the enemy from the northern area between the RHINE and the MAAS. Elements of the attacking divisions reached the outskirts of CLEVE; more than 2600 PWs have been taken since D-Day of the operation. Way to our south the First French Corps finished clearing its sector up to the RHINE and the entire Corps is now disposed along the RHINE. 1500 PWs were taken yesterday. The 28th Div which has completed its task returns to us and assembles in the LIEGE area. The 9th Armd is also scheduled to close there in the near future. The 69th Div will close tomorrow night in the vicinity of BUTGENBACH. They will relieve the 99th which will assemble in a rear rest area. The VIII Corps tightened the noose around PRUM and now had it fairly well surrounded on three sides; only an escape corridor to the south remaining. The XII Corps and III Corps had less success, being handicapped by the swift current along the OUR River. However, they have succeeded in strengthening their bridgeheads.

Air was operational for a part of the afternoon but no large sightings were made and the day's total bag includes only a few railroad cars and buildings.

Saturday, 10 February 1945: The General spent most of his day today with engineers of this headquarters and V Corps discussing all the available information on the dam. The ROER continued to rise this morning and it reached its peak at nine o'clock. It is now in flood stage and some places are 400 yards wide especially in the JULICH area but in about four days' time the flow should be about normal and the ROER River dams finally are no longer of any value to the German defensive system. Engineers now definitely established that the dams cannot be any further blown than they are at the present time.

It was General Huebner's plan today to pinch out and clean up the high and heavily wooded area which lies between the south dam and the north dam, sending the 2nd Ranger Bn across the river at the south and elements of the 60th Inf across at the north just below the outlet of the Schwahnenauel [Schwammenauel] Dam. The General left at four o'clock in the afternoon for V Corps to discuss this with Gen Huebner and ordered him to postpone it indefinitely. The General's idea is that this will involve a considerable expenditure of men for an objective which has little value and it is far better to conserve our manpower until we put on the main drive at which time that little island of Boche will be forced to disintegrate and retreat. Gen Huebner told Gen Hodges that he thought "he made him another good division," namely the 78th which according to Gen Huebner showed up very well in this fighting which he insisted was of an extremely tenacious nature. Today as proof of the efficacy of artillery fire the bodies of more than 200 dead Boche were found in the vicinity of the dam. Two abandoned tanks were also found in Hessenfeld [Hasenfeld] and it is presumed that these were two of the five encountered in the fight for that little town yesterday. All organized resistance in the bend of the River from the dam north to Bergstein has now ceased with elements of the 60th, 505th and 508th Para Inf everywhere along the river's edge.

Tonight the 69th Div closed in the V Corps area and early tomorrow will start to relieve the 99th which will move into the rear for rest and refitting and afterward come up in the VII Corps area as their reserve.

The British XXX Corps continued to make good progress, getting elements in the north and southwest sections of Cleve, and making good progress in clearing the Reichswald Forest in which the Boche are fighting with old-time vigor. The Third Army's attack still was slowed down by difficulties with high water in the Sauer River as swift current has still prevented construction of any bridges and many boats have been capsized in making the return crossing. VIII Corps, however, drew the noose a little tighter around Prum making four crossings of the Prum River and occupying the high ground only 2000 yds NE of the center of the battered city.

Air was operational after two o'clock today; railroad cars were the principal targets and more than 100 being claimed and some 30 Motor Transports to boot.

Gen Kean, Gen Wilson and Col Miller[46] spent the day at Group. General Bradley will probably come to see us tomorrow.

Sunday, 11 February 1945: The only fighting done during the day was by the 106th and 99th Divs against which the enemy made two small local attacks in an attempt to regain pillboxes. 393rd Inf shot up one of the double-storied ones to capture 35 PWs including couple of officers. No attempt is going to be made to cross the dam and it is doubtful whether the ROER will subside as anticipated because of the heavy rains we have experienced in the last two or three days. Ninth Army has tried to persuade us to somehow block the sluice gates but Col Carter equipped with all the facts and figures has pointed out that to put in the heavy I-beam gate necessary and under small arms fire at the same time would be a fruitless task since by the time it would be completed the dam would be completely empty.

General Bradley arrived at five o'clock for a chat with the General and after they both saw "Lady In The Dark," the General broke all precedent by not returning to the office. He sat and chatted with General Bradley at the house until after eleven o'clock.

VIII Corps has captured one-half of PRUM. British XXX Corps is now half-way thru KLEVE [Cleve] and has driven almost 3/4 of the way through the heavy REICHSWALD Forest. There was no air activity today.

Monday, 12 February 1945: V Corps regrouped forces today and maintained defensive positions along the west bank of the ROER. 78th Div took over the positions held by the 9th Div which reverted back to its old sector near DREIBORN and VOLGENSANG [Vogelsang]. 69th Div completed relief of the 99th and will probably officially resume control tomorrow. 7th Armd continued road repair work—the condition of the roads has materially worsened in the last two days because of heavy rains. There was no report of enemy action on our front during the day. VIII Corps cleared out PRUM while the 6th Cav Gp to the south captured VEINDAN [Vianden]. VIII Corps has taken over the III Corps sector in addition to its own.

British XXX Corps continues to advance despite the fact that Boche reinforcements have been moved up and the fighting has become increasingly intense in nature. More than 4500 PWs have been taken since the drive began.

It rained almost all day and all missions, heavies, medium, and fighter-bombers were cancelled during the day.

Tuesday, 13 February 1945: There were no changes in the front lines today; 69th Div assumed control of the 99th area at ten o'clock; the 78th Div passing to the control of III Corps at 1800 at which time the permanent boundary between III and V Corps became effective. III Corps CP took up at ZWEIFALL where the XVIII left off.

Gen Ridgway arrived at the house at three o'clock to spend the night, tomorrow he will go on to MAASTRICHT and then to his new Hq at

REIMS. Also guests for dinner were Gen [Hugh J.] Morgan,[47] Chief Medical Advisor to the Surgeon General's Office (former head of the Medical School at Vanderbilt University) and Col [William S.] Middleton,[48] Chief Medical Advisor to the ETO.

The General left after lunch today for the new VII Corps CP at ESCH-WEILER where he spent an hour and a half discussing the VII Corps' plan of attack.

There was no substantial change in the water level along the ROER. The Air had a pretty good day; the main targets being railroad trains on both sides of the RHINE especially in the vicinity of BONN and COLOGNE.

Wednesday, 14 February 1945: There was absolutely no change in First Army sector. The General left after lunch for CENTURY[49] at ZWEIFALL where he had a two hour chat with General Milliken. It now appears that there is some build-up especially of artillery along the III and VII Corps fronts. The Boche, having been given a most necessary inconvenient breathing spell because of bad weather and flooding of the dams to regroup his forces, has built-up in this area especially from troops which escaped from the Colmar pocket.

The sun was out today for the first time in almost two weeks and Air had better shooting. 32 marshalling areas were attacked; almost 1,000 railroad cars were claimed destroyed or damaged; over 64 cuts were made in the main lines on both sides of the RHINE between CO-LOGNE and BONN. At the same time 1250 heavies kept up the all-out air assault hitting CHEMNITZ, DRESDEN, and MAGDENBURG [Magdeburg].

Tonight the General's one guest after dinner was Major Gen [Gladeon M.] Barnes,[50] head of the Development Section of the Ordnance Department of War Department who with Colonel Hains came to discuss the present failings of our tanks and the new models which are expected to go into operation shortly.

There were few changes on the other fronts: In the XII Corps, 5th Div enlarged their bridgehead over the SAUR [Sauer] and captured ERN-ZEN. The 95th Div US began to relieve the 52nd British Div in the attack to our north. Pressure was heavy against the British all day, starting with a determined counterattack at nine o'clock near the MAAS town of GENNEP and this did not break off until early in the afternoon with no ground reported lost. The Boche have built up to a great extent in front of the British and from now on it may be expected to become an old-time slugging match until such time as the Ninth Army and our Army will be permitted by weather and road conditions to roll as per schedule.

Thursday, 15 February 1945: There was absolutely no change in the front line positions during the day. The General spent all day in the office getting out of the way a mass of paper work. Although it was fine and sunny here throughout the day, bases in the rear area were closed in until afternoon. However, 125 missions were flown and accounted for more railroad cars, locomotives, and ammunition dumps. The heavies were again out in force in direct support of the Russians.

Bill went to ST TROND this afternoon to pick up Major Gen Hull, who has succeeded Gen Handy as OPD[51] Chief. However, he did not land there as planned and is spending the night at Eagle [12th Army Group] to visit us early tomorrow.

Friday, 16 February 1945: Gen Hull accompanied by Gen Kean and Bill visited VII Corps, 104th Div, 8th Div, and 3rd Armd Div, leaving the office shortly after nine and not arriving back until after six o'clock. Gen Hodges spent the day in the CP cleaning up necessary paper work and discussing before, during, and after lunch V Corps' situation with Gen Huebner.

The Air was generally aloft at eleven o'clock and brought back an amazing total of railroad car and locomotives destroyed and damaged, almost 90 of the former and 70 of the latter.

Before supper tonight, Al brought in the General's new prize possession, a blue roan cocker spaniel of long and distinguished pedigree, age about three months, by name of Jaunty. Although tired, air sick, and a little frightened, Jaunty quickly showed his breeding and established himself at home.

XXI Corps is passing to control of Ninth Army and the 75th and 79th Divs are about to start their trip northward to take over sectors now held by the British. The British made slight gains during the day against very heavy enemy pressure. Tonight at ten o'clock Col Hewitt, G-2 of 21 Army Group called and reported to our G-2 that they had pretty well chewed up, for about the fifth chewing the division had, the 116th Panzer. The British made his best gains on the extreme right south flank and in the middle approached within two miles of GOCH.

Gen Hull spent the night and will leave tomorrow morning for SHAEF.

Saturday, 17 February 1945: Gen Hodges motored to MAASTRICHT this afternoon for a conference at Gen Simpson's Hq which included the following: Gen Bradley, Gen Gillen [Alvin C. Gillem],[52] Gen Anderson, Gen McLain, and Gen Collins, in addition to their respective Chiefs of Staff. The topic discussed naturally was when the attack should start, and although apparently a few were in favor of opening it up right away since they felt the water in the ROER would not substantially go down in the next month, the final decision made was to postpone it at least until the 23rd of this month. Gen Bradley is on a tour of American divisions at the front and after seeing Ninth Army's, tomorrow, will come to us on Monday.

First Army's front was very quiet throughout the day. For the first time since D-Day there was not a single death reported from the front lines and only 40 wounded. We are now definitely going to lose the 82nd A/B Div before the attack starts and the 9th Div is moving up into the III Corps area to replace it.

There was no Air out today because of nasty skies. Gen Hull, however, was able to take off at noon from LIEGE to PARIS.

The British attack made some gains toward GOCH against stiff resistance.

Sunday, 18 February 1945: The 9th Div assumed responsibility for the 82nd A/B Div sector at ten o'clock tonight. 28th Div moved up from the Seventh Army and already has its advance parties in the vicinity of EISCHERHEID [Eicherscheid] and will move probably tomorrow into the zone formerly held by the 9th.

The VIII Corps attacked yesterday with 90th, 11th Armd, and 6th Cav Gp in conjunction with the 80th and 5th Divs of XII Corps. This concerted drive has its purpose to reduce the Boche salient and progress made today was up to a mile generally along the entire front. XV Corps of Seventh Army likewise made gains in the vicinity of FORBACH. Only slight gains were recorded by the British although all but one road leading out of GOCH is now cut.

Again there was no air aloft due to a steady downpour of rain.

Monday, 19 February 1945: Gen Bradley toured the First Army area today but did not come to SPA as was anticipated. Gen Hodges did not meet him during the trip but during the afternoon went to V Corps for a discussion of the possibility of some small-range limited objectives attacks in the V Corps sector to feel out the strength of the enemy. Also there at V Corps headquarters was Gen George Davis, Asst Div Comdr of the 28th Div who had the advance party. The division is coming by rail into AACHEN and will assemble in the 102nd Cav area preparatory to taking over the sector formerly held by the 9th Division.

There were no changes in the First Army front. The river level continues to go down at an estimated rate of one to two inches per day. The British entered GOCH and were clearing the town tonight. The total bag of PWs since the beginning of the operation is 10,100. The VIII and XII Corps continued their attacks and during the course of the day seven or eight German towns were cleared. The salient is being steadily and rapidly reduced. Limited objective attacks on the Seventh Army front brought the 63rd Div into AUERSWETHEN and the 70th Div into FORBACH. Both the 79th and 75th Divs are closing today north of us in the XVI Corps and 30 Br Corps area.

The air was operational this afternoon but did not reap any particularly large rewards; railroad lines were again the principal targets.

Tuesday, 20 February 1945: No changes on our front again today. The 99th Div minus 394th closed in the vicinity of AUBEL and passed to control of VII Corps. 28th Div [minus] one Combat Team continued to assemble in vicinity of ESCHERSCHEID [Eicherscheid]. The level of the lake behind the SCHWAMMANEUL [Schwammenauel] Dam was down to 94.1′ and unless further changes are made the Ninth Army attack will go off on the 23rd.

Third U.S. Army made excellent gains throughout the day with the VIII and XII Corps advancing up to two miles all along the front and XX Corps with 94th Div and 10th Armd Div advanced up to three miles along a ten mile front between the MOSELLE and SAAR Rivers. 2500 PWs were taken by the Army during the day.

Air was up during the afternoon but only a few sorties were flown, and aside from some interesting sightings of tanks and motor transports in the vicinity of BUIR in the VII Corps sector. There was nothing else of great importance.

Wednesday, 21 February 1945: During the General's absence today, getting his back fixed up at the 45th Evac Hosp, General Simpson called to say that the "show" was going as planned—that is, the morning of the 23rd. Apparently typical of the confidence which Ninth Army has in its mission was the phantom[53] which we received tonight from G-3 XIX Corps: "Wherever XIX Corps attacks, it will go through the Boche like shit through a tin horn."

28th Div is now almost completely closed in V Corps area and 9th Armd starts to arrive tomorrow to be attached upon arrival to the III Corps. Air went out this afternoon but found no concentrations or scenes of great enemy activity anywhere along the front on either side of the Rhine. VIII and XX Corps continued to make excellent progress. Elements of the 94th Div reached the SAAR River and elements of the 10th Armd reached SAARBOURG which was reported clear. The VIII and XII Corps advanced up to two miles along the front and the Boche salient has now almost vanished. The British which did not attack in force today are apparently waiting for the Ninth Army show. However, they cleared GOCH and pushed out about a mile south of the town. XV Corps of Seventh Army advanced on a four mile front to within two miles of SAARBRUCKEN which we were forced to cede to the Boche when the great German counteroffensive started.

All Air tomorrow has been turned over to SHAEF which is putting on a "saturation show" in front of the Ninth Army area, apparently with all available aircraft, heavies, mediums, and fighter-bombers. Details are not yet available.

Thursday, 22 February 1945: Over 6,000 aircraft had hit Germany from all sides today to further cripple the transportation system and especially in our front to prevent any possible building-up of reinforcements against the Ninth Army and our Army's attack tomorrow morning. All aircraft were handled by SHAEF for this operation clarion.[54] Weather reports for tomorrow are good and both Armies will jump off at three o'clock to obtain a bridgehead over the ROER. Only our VII Corps will originally participate; III Corps, not attacking until two days from now.

The General made a trip to GREISNACH this afternoon to watch demonstrations of the new T36 [T26E3 or M26] tank,[55] a limited number of which are now being tried out with the 3rd and 9th Armd Divs. Following that he went to the CP of 3rd Armd Div where he had a long chat with Gen Rose and Gen. Collins.

Guests tonight for dinner which featured the General's gifts of lobster and Cherbourg champagne was his old friend, Major General Leonard, who has arrived with the advance elements of his 9th Armd Div. Following the dinner which was in every way a success, the General saw "Strike Up the Band" which he claimed was the best movie yet shown at the house. He returned to the office for a few details preparatory to the attack and stayed until midnight.

The Third Army made excellent progress throughout the day advancing up to three miles and captured over 23 more towns. Over 1,000 PWs were taken by VIII Corps alone. In the 11th Armd Sector 103 pillboxes were captured or destroyed. Third Army's XX Corps occupied the remainder of its sector between the MOSELLE and SAAR Rivers and 94th Div established a bridgehead two miles wide over the SAAR.

Chapter 6

Crossing the Roer River,
23–28 February 1945

Friday, 23 February 1945: This morning at 3:30, preceded by 45 minutes of artillery preparation in which 936 guns were active—the greatest barrage that the Army has yet put on over a small area—the VII Corps launched a coordinated attack with the 8th and 104th Divs. From all accounts this artillery barrage either stunned or killed the enemy so that the enemy reaction to our crossing the stream was extremely light. Mortar fire and machine-gun fire was used principally. However, great difficulty was encountered with the swift current which tore the boats loose, upset them, and prevent cables from being stretched across the river. In the 104th Div all the assault companies, nine in number, were across 50 minutes after the attack was started but the first bridge was not in until almost midnight. During the day especially as daylight came, the enemy zeroed on in the bridge sites with both mortar and artillery fire. At the end of the day Bridge No. 1, a five ton infantry support bridge, was the only one completed in our area. Once across, the assault companies made good progress against light resistance. 415th Inf captured HUCHEM while the 413th cleared BIRKSDORF [Birkesdorf] and the section of DUREN north of the railroad. 8th Div with the exception of the 3rd Bn of the 28th made little progress; the latter advanced to the outskirts of STOCKHEIM, far ahead of the other battalions. Fighting was going on all day in DUREN of a house-to-house nature but most battalions were still waiting for supplies which had to be ferried across the river. At the end of the day no vehicles, tanks, or TDs [tank destroyers] were in support of either division.

Better progress was made by the Ninth Army in its two Corps attack across the ROER since they did not have the swift current to deal with. By dark each Corps constructed an infantry support bridge and Class

40 bridge; heavy equipment including tanks were moved across the river during the night. Elements of the 102nd Div captured BALL [Baal] and KORRENZIG, also to fall to the 102nd Div were BOSLAR, GLIMBACH, and GEVENICH. In the XIX Corps area the 29th and 30th Divs did very well, the former taking BROICH and passing almost completely through JULICH while the 30th Div captured SELGERSDORF and DAUBENRATH. Losses were not as heavy as could be expected with an attack which the enemy has long known would come. They have had plenty of time to zero in their mortars and their artillery and considering that fact with 1,000 casualties suffered by Ninth Army and 400 by First Army, they are not considered heavy. With us the dead only numbered some 90 and of those 90; 60 were of a company which was quartered in a house. The house blew up either because of enemy mines, time-bombs, or because of some failure of equipment on our part. In the main, the majority of casualties were in the Engineers and they will be especially hard to replace. Ninth Army captured over 1,000 PWs during the day; we took over 400. There were no unusual identifications; the units we expected to meet, we did meet.

Generally speaking the attack is considered to have gone well; the General naturally is worried about the lack of bridge facilities but Gen Collins with whom he talked tonight feels confident they would have success during the evening. Artillery fire which had been rigorous during the morning and early afternoon had dropped off considerably as the day wore on. The Army is making extensive use of smoke to shield the bridge sites.

VIII and XII Corps of the Third Army moved ahead rapidly against practically no resistance at all. The 11th Armd has been pinched out; the 6th Armd, 6th Cav Gp and the 90th Div took over 15 towns, suffering almost no casualties. In the XX Corps area the 10th Armd Div continued to mop up the sector between the MOSELLE and the SAAR Rivers while the 94th kept enlarging its bridgehead over the SAAR south of SAARBOURG. Between the 1st and the 21st of February the Third Army has captured almost 14,000 PWs. Yesterday the VIII Corps alone took 700 and at their present rate of advance and considering the present state of disorganization of the enemy they should continue to press eastward without any great difficulty.

It could not have been a better day. It was bright and clear almost until supper time and the Air took advantage of it to the fullest extent. Three groups were in direct support of VII Corps and all small towns in the immediate vicinity of the ROER in front of our advancing troops were thoroughly saturated and several of them were burning at the day's end. Enemy air was more active than usual, featuring jet-propelled planes of which our AA claimed three.

The river is steadily going down and the big SCHWAMMANEUL [Schwammenauel] dam in now almost empty. At its present rate of decrease the river should be completely normal by tomorrow night. Depending on this will rest the General's decision whether III Corps should attack tomorrow or the day after tomorrow.

Saturday, 24 February 1945: Moderately satisfactory progress was made throughout the day; bridge sites continued to receive enemy fire by the artillery and mortars which hampered their construction, but Bridge #6, Class 40 Bridge, was completed at ten o'clock this morning to be the first one finished in the 8th Div area. Over this the remainder of the division moved. Construction of others was hampered tonight by enemy bombers which appeared singly or in pairs and of which AA claimed 18 before the night's end. 104th Div continued to expand its bridgehead likewise and pushed farther on, its section of DUREN was cleared as well as the town of OBERREIZER [Oberzier] and ARNOLDSWEILER was three-fourths clear at the end of the day. 104th Div now has all five bridges including two treadways, two infantry support, and one Bailey[1] in good operating order.

The General tonight, after a long day spent at VII Corps, III Corps, and 1st Div is finally well satisfied with the progress made. During the day he cooked up a scheme whereby the 2 Bns of the 16th Inf will go across the river on the 8th Div bridge and then come down due south to clear KRUZNEAU [Kreuzau] and secure the landing sites on the east bank. This move will immeasurably reduce casualties and was accepted with great favor by the 1st Div. As soon as they secure the eastern bridge sites, the bridges, will of course, be built and the remainder of the division will cross to attack. Casualties on our Corps front remain luckily generally light so far although some of the fighting in DUREN has been described as stiff.

To our north the XIX Corps captured NIEDERZIER and STETTERNICH. 400 plus PWs were taken and in general the situation was going well. Elements of the 102nd Div in the XIII Corps advanced to take MUNTZ and HATTORF [Hottorf]—they were supported by two tank battalions which crossed the river. 84th Div likewise made use of two bridges in LINNICH and pressed on in strength north of BALL.

To our south VIII and XII Corps continued to advance towards the east as high as three miles against resistance which was extremely spotty. Enemy continues to react in a disorganized manner and the VIII Corps alone took over 600 PWs during the day. 6 Bns are now across the river in the XX Corps area as the advance continues toward TRIER. At 10:30 a jet-propelled 262[2] flew up and down the valley causing a brief unsuccessful flurry from our local AAA defense—no bombs were dropped.

Sunday, 25 February 1945: The VII Corps bridgehead now some three miles deep is finally established with nine bridges in all in operation. The Corps bridgehead phase line has been reached and in some cases passed. STOCKHEIM, ROMMELSCHEIM [Rommelsheim], FRAURULLESHEIM [Frauwüllesheim], GIRBELSRATH, BINSFELD and ESCHWEILER have all been cleared. Col McDowell's [MacDonald's] 4th Cav Group passing through on the north edge of the 104th Div sector has gone some one and half miles through the woods north of OBERZIER and established contact with patrols of the 30th Div. Enemy resistance in the woods was negligible. Tonight the 104th Div, using its favorite tactics of attacking [in] the dark, shot on ahead to clear GOLZHEIM and MERSCHENICH [Merzenich]. Captured this morning was a whole battalion complete in the CASTLE RATH. The battalion commander said that he was unable to get artillery support, he saw his position was untenable, and after we had pumped a few shells into the castle, out came the white flag and the troops. The 3rd Armd Div is crossing the river tonight over the four treadway bridges and will attack early tomorrow morning in five columns.

The General's big scheme of the crossing of the 1st Div on the 8th Div bridges went well today. 16th Inf attacked at noon and advanced some 4,000 yards against scattered resistance to clear KREAUXAU [Kreuzau] and DROVE. Immediately after the sites were secured, they put in a Class 5 Infantry Support bridge and two foot-bridges.

The Boche air was active over the front this morning but apparently only in a recon capacity with jet-propelled planes furnishing most of the excitement. AA claimed four.

Gen Huebner is anxious to get into the battle with V Corps and just to keep them on their toes, he sent a patrol into SCHLEIDEN tonight and they came back with 20 PWs with no losses to our side.

Our gains were paralleled by those of the Ninth Army. 30th Div advanced up to 5,000 yards and cleared STEINSTROSS [Steinstrass] and RODINGEN. Aside from heavy minefields and scattered 88 and AT [anti-tank] fire, the resistance cannot be classified as heavy. XIX Corps alone took 1200 PWs. XIII Corps with the 102nd and 84th Divs captured KAT-

ZEM, LOVENICH, GRANTERATH, HONVERATH, and repulsed several enemy counterattacks thrown against DOBEREN [Doveren] this morning.

The Third Army continued to make startling advances, clearing out most of the pocket remaining west of the PRUM River and in some cases advancing over it. XII Corps which went into the town of RITTERSDORF took 1,000 PWs alone in the vicinity of that town—the total bag for the day being over 2200.

Monday, 26 February 1945: Perhaps it is too early to be optimistic but everyone from the General down feels tonight that resistance is on the point of crumbling and that this time we are going to the RHINE quickly without being slowed down. In a 10,000 yard advance today fifteen German towns were captured and we were within two miles of the ERFT River. Except for moderate anti-tank and self-propelled gun fire in the towns themselves, the resistance was generally light and our casualties were almost nil. As an example, the 104th Div took the town of BLOTZHEIM [Blatzheim] and lost only two men killed and seven wounded. In this town, another German battalion was taken intact, also from the Panzer Grenadier Div which has steadily opposed us in the sector.

It was an armored show throughout most of the day. 3rd Armd twice changed its CP to keep up with its rapidly pressing forces. The following towns were taken: BLOTZHEIM, BERGERHAUSEN, BUIR, MONHEIM [Manheim]; while TFW, making the farthest advance reached ELSDORF. 24th Cav Squadron cleared the ELSDORF Forest with very little contact until they reached the north edge of the woods where they encountered some dug-in infantry. The 8th Div minus 13th Inf regrouped and continued the attack. 121st Inf cleared ESCHWEILER; 28th Inf cleared FRAU-WULLESHEIM. The total bag of PWs for the Corps during the day was 1500.

The 1st Div established its firm bridgehead over the ROER completing during the day 1 Bailey and 1 Class 40 Treadway Bridge and capturing six towns. The 18th Inf took over STOCKHEIM from VII Corps—a change in the boundary having been made the previous night by General Collins—and advanced a mile during the night to take over JOKOL-WULLESHEIM [Jakobwüllesheim]. 16th Inf also advancing during the night took SOLLER and FORGENHEIM. The 39th Inf poured across the river during the night and will attack tomorrow morning south of BOICH which was likewise cleared today in order to clear its own bridge sites. 1st Div took over 300 PWs today, raising the Army total to almost 1800.

What follows next was the subject of considerable discussion today since Army Group orders only cover our advance up to the ERFT. The General is worried less his Army be turned over to the control of General Montgomery—he wishes to make it clear to Group that we are having a "helluva" battle up here in order to proceed in accordance with his tactical operations plan which is superb, that of advancing to COLOGNE, and then from there fanning out north and south once the railroad lines and communications running north and south are cut by the VII Corps drive. General Hodges tried to reach Gen Bradley during the day and finally did by telephone reach him this evening. He probably will visit this headquarters tomorrow. Some decision is needed at once on the direction and objectives of this drive which appears to be smashing ahead in unbeatable fashion.

All other Armies, with the exception of the Seventh and the First French, were likewise on the attack yesterday. The [British] 30th and 2nd Canadian Corps started their drive early this morning and late tonight respectively; the XIX Corps and XIII Corps advanced up to 4,000 yards, the latter Corps clearing the key-town of ERKLENZ [Erkelenz]. The XVI Corps likewise went on the attack with the 35th Div which crossing through the bridgehead of the 84th advanced 4,000 yards to capture BRUCK. In the XII Corps the 4th Armd Div advanced two miles to ELS-DORF where fighting is now in progress. 5th Div reached the edges of BITBURG; 76th Div crossed the NIMS River in two spots. In the XX Corps the 10th Armd advanced over 1½ miles to the town of NEIDERZERF which is a few miles south of TRIER.

The Air was non-operational all day on our front although an all-time record attack was made by the 8th Air Force on BERLIN. Mediums also hit in front of us but through blind-bombing. Tomorrow's weather does not look much better.

The total of PWs for the day from all Armies should hit the 10,000 mark.

Tuesday, 27 February 1945: Resistance increased early today all along the VII Corps front but by mid-afternoon the artillery, anti-tank, and tank fire had been so effectively silenced that elements of three Task Forces of the 3rd Armd were sitting on the ERFT River. Task Force Hogan clearing GLICH [Glesch] captured a small bridge of one ton capacity intact and by midnight two companies of its infantry were already across the river. Task Force Richardson had cleared BERRENDORF and Task Force Yeomans reached the ERFT at coordinate 2263. They also placed patrols across the river without difficulty. The 104th Div, following up behind the 3rd Armd, continued to mop up the towns which had been so quickly passed through in the rapid advance of Gen Rose's troops. Good gains, despite a slow start, were also made by 1st Div and elements of the 9th Div. 1st Div, 18th Inf cleared KELZ and reached HOCHKIERCHEN [Hochkirchen], while the 2nd Bn crossed the NEFFEL River and are now mopping up the large forest at 2450. Considerable mines were encountered and some dug-in infantry but the resistance was not of an extremely formidable nature. The 16th Inf further southwest of the 18th Inf cleared VETTWEISS while the 39th Inf passing through the 1st Div bridgehead attacked south from BOICH and cleared THUM and NI-DEGGEN. By midnight tonight three bridges had been put in for the use of the 9th Div including a class 40 Bailey. Tomorrow the 78th will begin passing through 9th Division's bridges to clear its own bridge sites—a duplication of the maneuver ordered by Gen Hodges which proved so successful with the 1st Div.

For the first time in over two weeks there was activity on the V Corps front as elements of the 69th Div pushed out over a mile against very light resistance to clear five small villages. PW count for the day should be slightly over 1,000.

Gen Bradley arrived alone by jeep at nine o'clock for a one hour discussion of the moves to be taken as the pursuit goes on. The plan which he presented was apparently that which Gen Hodges had previously drawn up and which had previously been rejected by Group. It has not yet been published and the details are not available but the General is extremely happy that it conforms with his original estimate of the situation.

A blackout has been imposed on the news of the Ninth Army since they have apparently, at least with elements of the 5th Armd Div, scored a complete break-through. They were last reported on the outskirts of MUNCHEN-GLADBACH [Mönchen-Gladbach]. Elements of the 84th were following up close behind them making gains of up to 15,000 yards. 29th Div gained up to 10,000 yards and the enemy were reported as surrendering without much opposition. 30th Div advanced 10,000 yards also against light opposition [to] GERSCH and the division has almost reached their limited sector where they will be pinched out and go into Corps reserve. The 35th Div of the XVI Corps made advances up to 5,000 yards; resistance was very strong. 8th Armd Div will attack in force tomorrow morning.

Good gains were likewise recorded all along the Third Army front with all elements approaching rapidly to the KYLL River. BITBURG was entered and it is now being cleared. Only in the XX Corps where the

10th Armd and 94th Divs are now completely across the SAAR did resistance stiffen. However, over 500 PWs were taken by the 10th Armd alone.

There was no Air yesterday but estimates are that it will improve tomorrow. The general consensus everywhere is now that the Boche, although not in any sense getting up and surrendering in mass, are fighting a disorganized defensive battle. Stiff resistance where it has been encountered has been centered in the small towns and usually after an hour or so of fighting, the soldiers have come out with their hands up. According to Col Dickson, all divisions that were in reserve on the western front have now been committed and unless the Germans are able to quickly switch divisions from the south, which is unlikely because of the present state of their railway communications and their lack of gas, they can throw into the battle only hastily organized Volkstrum [Volkssturm][3] or Strum [Sturm] battalions.

We are still hunting a CP location, thus far without luck. It is probable that one or two steps will have to be taken: a—split again into TAC and Command or into Command and Supply, or, b—move back into the woods under tents. Col Myers and Bill are going out tomorrow to investigate the possibility of taking over Gen Rose's former chateau headquarters near STOLBERG.

The guests at the General's home tonight were three members of the Army Nurses Corps [Army Nurse Corps], Major [Esther R.] McCafferty,[4] Chief Nurse of this headquarters, Captain McLin and Lieut Hoover. Following the dinner they attended a showing of "Irish [Eyes] Are Smiling" which every one thought was a splendid film. The General came down to the office and worked until after one o'clock on the new Field Order which should be published tomorrow.

Wednesday, 28 February 1945: After being "soireed" into a breakfast at which his guests were General Lee, General Plank, and the two G-1s of ADSEC and COMM Z, the General left at 10:45 with General Kean for his longest tour of the battle-front in many a week. Making his first stop at ZWEIFALL, Gen Hodges had lunch with Gen Milliken [Millikin] and Gen Leonard whose CCB under General Hoag [Hoge] is on its way to attack this afternoon towards ZULPICH. He went to Gen Milliken's office following the meal for a full discussion of the new Field Order and general Army strategy. He left at 2:30 and went to Gen Collins' headquarters, passing over Bridge #6, the treadway, with which the 8th Div had so much difficulty and up the hill through the pile of rubble and bomb craters to an old regimental barracks in which General Collins had set up his headquarters. The barracks were riddled with shrapnel and the shells of SP guns but contrary to outside appearances there were a few rooms still left intact and in these the General had set up his own quarters. After a discussion about the next moves to be taken, the General got in his jeep with General Kean and General Collins and they went from there to the front—through BUIR, GELBERSRATH [Girbelsrath], up through the woods which Col McDonald's [MacDonald's] Cav Gp had cleared and then turning right just before ELSDORF drove into the fine farmhouse chateau residence now belonging to Gen Rose. As is customary, General Rose has the best place east of the ROER. Although his Aide said it was very warm around there the day he moved in, yesterday, now most of the action is across the ERFT and the only noise we heard was the constant pounding of VII Corps artillery, much of which is banked along the road leading to Gen Rose's place. While there, the General had a good chat with Col McDonald whose Cav Gp is being attached to 3rd Armd Div for operations and shortly afterward while coffee was being served, General Rose himself returned after a tour to the very front lines. We did not leave the CP until 5:15 but the General remarked, "I don't care what time I leave; for the first time in a month I heard a gun." We got back to General Collins' CP at six and then we drove in the dark passing Combat Command B of 9th Armd coming up to the front through AACHEN, reaching home shortly after eight o'clock.

Progress made during the day was not perhaps as much as had been expected. The 1st Div reported they received extremely heavy artillery fire throughout the day while VII Corps in establishing its bridgehead across the ERFT was having trouble also from heavy mortar and anti-tank fire. However, the 18th Inf did clear five towns and generally made advances of over a mile. 9th Div continued to move across the River with 60th and 47th Inf; while in the 78th Div sector, 311th crossed the ROER River on the 9th Div sector and attacked south through its elements. All three division CPs of III Corps changed during the day; two of them moving across the ROER itself.

MODRATH and KERPEN have now been cleared by the 121st Inf. A class 40 bridge has been constructed and finished in the vicinity of GLESCH, another class 40 bridge was completed at PEFFENDORF [Paffendorf], and tonight tanks were moved across the river and canal to the edge of the woods. Bulldozers were forced to fill an anti-tank ditch before this could be done. The 395th Inf of the 99th Div closed in the forward areas this afternoon and will lead off the attack tomorrow morning along with elements of the 104th.

Above us the Ninth Army had considerably less trouble in advancing in some cases up to 8 miles during the day. The 2nd Armd Div was not many miles away from NEUSS, the large city opposite DUSSELDORF while the 29th Div kept apace with it to reach RHEIDT-ODENKIRCHEN [Rheydt-Odenkirchen] which is a large suburb of MUNCHEN-GLADBACH. In the XIII Corps the 102nd Div also advanced over 3 miles west of MUNCHEN-GLADBACH thus cutting the principal roads, entering the city from the west, and completing the encirclement of the city on three sides. The XVI Corps attacking with the 35th and CCA of the 8th Armd Div advanced 8,000 yards to MERBACK [Merbach] and the enemy appeared to be withdrawing as fast as they can from the ROERMOND pocket. To our south the VIII, XII, and XX Corps made gains up to 2 miles with the 10th Armd Div drawing closer to TRIER by making gains of 1½ miles to GEIZENBURG.

The air was aloft part of the day but visibility was uniformly bad and all bombing done—137 tons dropped in all—was done blind.

Chapter 7

Crossing the Rhine River, 1–24 March 1945

The Advance Across the Erft River and the Capture of the Remagen Bridge over the Rhine River, 1–7 March 1945

Thursday, 1 March 1945: The main Boche opposition came, not during the day, but at night, when over 100 planes, flying singly or in twosomes, attacked the VII and III Corps front areas and bridges. The final count according to Colonel Patterson was 34 downed with another 10 probable. Losses to personnel are believed light.

The ground opposition during the day did not seem to be very heavy although the artillery fire on the bridgehead of VII Corps was more intense than usual. The VII Corps did not push very far out in this direction, although the 414th cleared HORREN [Horrem], and the 413th cleared QUADRATH and ICHENDORF. 395th Inf cleared BERGHEIM against stiff opposition and KENTEN. Thus at day's end making pretty nearly a continuous front east of the ERFT. Early tomorrow morning, Task Forces R and H will attack. 393rd Inf which has been moved, will follow Task Force H to exploit its gains.

The III Corps kept moving in good shape. The 60th Inf cleared three towns advancing up to 4,000 yards while the 78th Div continued to attack with 311th Inf to clear the east side of the river in the vicinity of its bridgeheads. The town of HAUSEN was captured. We received very little definite news about the progress of the 2 Combat Commands of the 9th Armd until late tonight when we learned that CCB had captured SIEVERNICH, including a bridge intact, while CCA, attacking south, made up to about 1500 yards in the vicinity of VLATTEN. The 1st Div, moving straight east, approached the ERFT River on its front, reaching the towns of WISSERSHEIM, PINGSHEIM, and GLADBACH.

Perhaps more exciting, though not necessarily as important, news was furnished by the XIX Corps which cleared Munchen-Gladbach [Mönchen-Gladbach] and with the 83rd Div attacking on the extreme right of the sector, advanced 6½ miles to the edge of Neuss, which is the western suburb of Dusseldorf on this side of the Rhine. The XVI Corps likewise made excellent progress, advancing 16 miles to enter Venlo. Almost all the Boche have pulled out of this pocket but many civilians remain. Roermond was reported clear. XIII Corps, advancing 5 miles, cleared Dulken and Viersen

The General made a recording this afternoon of a short speech which will be broadcast to all the soldiers of the Army over the First Army radio which officially started operating this morning. The General's guests today were Stephen Early,[1] Presidential Secretary, who is now on a special mission to iron out censor difficulties at SHAEF, and Captain [Harry C.] Butcher,[2] PRO [Public Relations Officer] at SHAEF. During the day we received the sad news that Colonel [George A.] Smith[3] who had just joined the 104th Div as Asst Div Comdr had been killed, along with a regimental and battalion commander at a 104th OP.[4] An artillery shell landed in their midst.

The Third Army's greatest advance during the day was made towards Trier on the southern outskirts of which 10th Armd Div was fighting tonight.

The PW count for the day will be about 1200. Our air was active throughout the morning and most of the afternoon but due to bad visibility was forced to do most of the work blind.

Friday, 2 March 1945: General Bradley arrived from Ninth Army during the morning conference and he and General Hodges sat in the latter's War Room until lunch time receiving the good news from the front and discussing the future moves of the Army. The news from the Corps was as follows: V Corps: The Rangers advanced 3,000 yards through the wooded area lying between the dams against almost no resistance except that encountered from mines. Civilians said that the Boche had pulled out the night before and the only two enemy found were deserters. 102nd Cav Group later crossed the bridge at Ruhrberg [Rurberg] and forward elements joined the Rangers in thoroughly reconnoitering that section. III Corps: 78th Div less the 1st and 2nd Bns of the 310th Inf continued the attack and cleared its sector west of Ober River. 311th Inf cleared four towns including Vlatten and Burvenich. Stiff resistance was encountered by CCA of 9th Armd Div at Wellersheim [Wollersheim] but the dug-in tanks were finally knocked out and they advanced on to clear Langendorf. CCB, General Hoge's command, advanced 6,000 yards to capture BORR and FRIESHEIM. 1st Bn of 310th which is attached, crossed the bridge found intact at FRIESHEIM and mopped up the woods at 3540. The 9th Div cleared more than five towns including ROVENICH while the 1st Div advanced up to 3 miles to clear ERP, GYMMICH [Gymnich], and LECHENICH. III Corps took almost 1300 PWs. VII Corps: MODRATH was cleared after a stubborn fight from both tanks and infantry by the 28th Inf. The factories south of BOLSDORF [Elsdorf] were also cleared after the same kind of fighting. The biggest scraps of the day were at NEIDERSAUSSEM and OBERAUSSEM. The Task Forces of the 3rd Armd Div fought against enemy tanks, anti-tank fire, and dug-in infantry and only succeeded in clearing the towns at night after a rugged fight. The VII Corps reported 1500 PWs for the day and at midnight tonight, Col McDonald's [MacDonald's] 4th Cav Group was making good progress along the Corps left flank.

In front of our troops, only 6 miles away, the RAF dropped over 3500 tons of bombs on COLOGNE, starting the attack by 780 aircraft before ten o'clock this morning and following it up with an additional 125 at four o'clock this afternoon. Our fighter-bombers, despite intermittent snow flurries, were active most of the day.

The Ninth Army was tonight on the banks of the RHINE in several places. 83rd Div has cleared most of NEUSS opposite the river from DUS-SELDORF. XIII Corps advanced straight north to take KREFELD and VORST. 79th Div has now been assigned to it and is assembling at ERKELEN [Erkelenz]. XVI Corps cleared VENLO and other towns in that vicinity and the distance separating the Ninth and First Canadian Armies is now less than 16 miles in some places.

The bridge situation along the RHINE is a little obscure but the HO-HENZOLLERAN [Hohenzollern] combination railroad and road bridge at COLOGNE was definitely destroyed by our air attack this morning. This leaves only one bridge in good shape there. North at DUSSELDORF, four large bridges are still reported intact but whether we will be able to seize them or not, of course, is conjectural.

The Third Army likewise made good progress. Opposition to the VIII Corps' drive from pillboxes is still heavy but the XII Corps advanced to within a mile and a half of TRIER, clearing most of the pocket west of the MOSELLE. They took 1,000 PWs and the 10th Armd Div which cleared three-quarters of TRIER and the adjacent area captured more than 3,000, many of whom were VOLKSTRUM [Volkssturm].

In the morning a SHAEF unit tried to record the morning conference of the General and his staff but the arrival of General Bradley and matters of higher importance caused cancellation of this recording. At dinner tonight, however, we heard the recording made by General Hodges of his speech to First Army troops, over the radio. General Pless [Pleas B.] Rogers[5] came from Paris to spend the night with the General and will leave tomorrow morning for the front lines.

Saturday, 3 March 1945: The General made another long tour of the battle front today starting with III Corps first for a conference with General Milliken [Millikin] and later in the afternoon stopping in at DUREN (which was shelled last night by heavy long range German artillery) for a conference with General Collins. On the way back to Master he stopped in again at III Corps where General Heubner [Huebner] met him and he did not return to the home until 8:30 tonight.

Everything is going along with clock-like precision. The VII Corps, taking almost 2,000 PWs, were tonight looking at the spires of COLOGNE from a distance of not more than six miles. The 8th Div took the FURST-ENBERG coal quarry against rugged resistance and advanced on to occupy FRECHEN where there were many civilians but little show of enemy. 3rd Armd with 13th Inf continued an advance up to six miles against moderate resistance from self-propelled and anti-tank guns. TFY commanded by Lt. Col [Prentice] "Mike" Yeomans[6] cleared ROGGENSDORF and patrols reached the RHINE at 0420 this morning, thus claiming the honor of being the first troops of General Hodges' Army to reach the great river. In so doing, they captured complete, a tractor drawn artillery battery. Other elements of the 3rd Armd in this great swing northeast of the Rhineland capital, took STOMMELN, SINNERSDORF, and PULHEIM. To their left the 99th Div plus the 4th Cav Group advanced within spitting distance of the RHINE at WEBELINGHOVEN [Wevelinghoven].

Excellent progress was also made by III Corps which now seems to have struck its stride. In two places tonight, elements of the 9th Armd were across the ERFT, at WEILERSWIST and another small community further north. A bridge over the ERFT River was captured intact at the latter town. 9th Inf Div advanced up to two miles to clear eight villages on the flank of the 9th Armd. Several small counterattacks with tanks and infantry were directed against Gen Craig's men but they threw them off without trouble. Treadway bridges tonight were completed in three spots over the ERFT in the 1st Div sector. The III Corps took about 1200 PWs.

V Corps is now passing its troops over the 78th Div bridgehead at HEIMBACH and will soon attack in strength. 102nd Cav Group plus the Rangers cleared the KERMETER peninsula against practically no opposition but that furnished by minefields.

Gains on other Army fronts were of a similar nature. Organized resistance has collapsed completely north of us and it is impossible to keep any semblance of a front line on a map so fluid is the situation. Generally, we are along the RHINE from NEUSS, 20 miles up; in front of the British and Canadians the resistance, which was at first so rugged, has now perceptibly softened.

It is impossible not to be elated tonight, even if Ninth Army troops did leave [reach] the Rhine before we did. COLOGNE, the prize city of the RHINE, so much in the news for the past four years, is within our grasp and shortly will be ours. The First Army will be repaid for many of its efforts in the publicity which will attend its capture.

Sunday, 4 March 1945: Master Tac was set up again today for the first time in four months. The new CP is in the house of Mr. Prim, a large chateau high on the hill overlooking STOLBERG, which was formerly occupied by General Rose of the 3rd Armd Div. The General has his bedroom adjoining his office, an arrangement which pleases him greatly, also the map room being in his office. Although the grounds surrounding the chateau are a mud field, it is not thought that we will be here long. For present purposes—to bring the General closer to the front—it is almost perfect, despite the crowded condition. The General did not go out today but left SPA regretfully at two o'clock, arriving here to find that the attack was everywhere progressing according to plan.

99th Div of VII Corps captured 32 towns, advancing against extremely spotty resistance towards the RHINE. The 3rd Armd Div regrouped preparatory to an early morning attack tomorrow. The 104th Div advanced up to three miles to capture the sizeable towns of WEIDEN and LOVENICH, while the 8th Div consolidated its previous gains at FRECHEN and advanced on to GLEUEL. VII Corps kept its record of capturing more than 2,000 PWs a day. They will move their CP tomorrow across the ERFT, leaving us the barracks at DUREN, in the event that it is decided to set up Command and Tac together again there.

III Corps has now cleared the west bark of the ERFT from EUSKIRCHEN to the VII Corps boundary. The 9th Armd Div less CCB with the 60th and 310th Infs attached attacked towards EUSKIRCHEN at two o'clock this afternoon and by eight o'clock had it firmly in their hands.

After all the countless medium efforts directed against EUSKIRCHEN, the town was found in surprising good shape. Most of the bombs, if they did fall where directed, hit the marshalling yards but very few hit the civilian part of the village. It will make some one an excellent CP. III Corps took almost a thousand PWs.

GEMUND and SCHLEIDEN, two names which loomed large in the Boche December offensive were captured today by V Corps troops. The 2nd Div took the first named and the 110th Inf the second. Stiffer fighting was encountered along V Corps than on the other two Corps fronts, and the prisoner bag for the day was less than 300.

For the third successive day the weather was foul and fighter-bomber activity was limited in the main to blind bombing.

The XIX Corps to our north, having cleared the west bank of the RHINE from DUSSELDORF to KREFELD has now completed its present mission. NEUSS was definitely declared cleared by the 83rd Div. All the bridges across the RHINE in the DUSSELDORF area are now blown and the Boche is desperately trying to salvage what little he can through use of ferries, all of which are under Allied artillery fire. In the XIII Corps area the 102nd cleared KREFELD and advanced to MORS [Moers] and HOMBERG. Four bridges in the DUISSBERG [Duisberg] area were reported still in operation. Firm contact has now been established between elements of XVI Corps and the First Canadian Army at GELDERN. It is thought now that this entire sector will be completely cleared up to the RHINE within the next three days. There is no resistance to speak of; the Boche is fleeing madly in what may be properly described as a rout, not a retreat. PWs are coming in so fast there is no official count.

Gains up to 3,000 yards were made almost everywhere along the Third Army front, except in the XX Corps sector where mopping up around TRIER and in the bend between the rivers is still going on.

Monday, 5 March 1945: The General took a long "look-see" today at the V Corps sector. His route to MONSCHAU was down through ROTT and ROETGEN over some of the world's worst roads. It was his first look at MONSCHAU, the tiny village at the bottom of the river, which had the reputation before the war, of being a German honeymoon paradise. He had lunch there with Gen Heubner, V Corps having taken over their finest hotel. From there he motored with the General to "Heartbreak Corner" [Wahlerscheid crossroads], the cross-roads so heavily fortified with pillboxes and obstacles which the 2nd Div had succeeded in taking just before the Boche counter-offensive was launched. He stopped there briefly to chat with General Cota whose 28th Div CP is there in the woods and inspected one of the pillboxes which had proven so hard to crack. From there he motored down to BULLINGEN to pay his first visit to General [Emil F.] Reinhardt, [7] commanding the 69th Div. He was greeted there by Captain Louie Rogers, Aide to General Reinhardt, formerly General Hodges' Aide back in the states. General Reinhardt had found one of the very few buildings in Bullingen, not completely destroyed, and although drafty it still managed to serve the purpose. All along this route, over which we could not exceed a speed of five to six miles per hour, so deep were the ruts and craters, lay smashed and crushed German tanks and half-tracks. Some of the most bitter fighting of the war went on in this area where the Boche tried to break through the shoulder and the battered landscape is full testimony of it. From there he went on to Muringen [Mürringen] for a chat with General Stroh whose 106th Div—really consisting of one regiment plus—he found in fine morale and great condition. He then motored back to V Corps CP for a tactical discussion with General Heubner and we left there about 4:30. A bull-dozer unfortunately impaled itself on the Bailey bridge leading out of Monschau so that we had to come back the long way over the Eupen–Monschau road, from there to Aachen and Stolberg. We arrived home shortly after six.

No sooner had the General arrived than General Collins was on the phone to tell him that street fighting was going on in the outskirts of Cologne. General Collins requested a change in Corps boundary which would swing the VII Corps area further south of Cologne. This was approved by the General, as the 1st Div is now definitely going to stay with the III Corps and not be switched to the VII Corps. The 1st Div will now continue to advance straight towards the river just above Bonn.

Cologne tonight definitely seems almost within our grasp. The houses were being cleared one by one but the opposition is not particularly formidable. Some of the AA defenses, and they were heavy when the city was being bombed, have been turned into a ground role. Aside from the opposition being furnished by these dual purpose guns, the enemy does not seem prepared to force any long siege of the city. At last count 2600 PWs have been taken during the day and spirits are running high everywhere along the front.

The huge airfield southeast of Euskirchen which General Quesada so much wants for his fighter-bombers is tonight in our hands as the 47th and 39th Infs made excellent gains during the day, driving in the general direction of Bonn across the Erft. The 9th Armd Div advanced up to three miles to the southeast as well and our troops are generally on the 41 vertical grid tonight. III Corps captured 1200 PWs.

V Corps captured some 15 towns and are continuing their advance to the south and southeast. Never before perhaps, has an operation been so beautifully timed and worked so to schedule. The General said tonight he did not believe the Boche knew what we were up to in this

V Corps area and this was attested to by the fact that they were running into our troops in all directions, seemingly bewildered by our advance and not knowing from what direction it was coming. However, the fighting in this neighborhood still remains perhaps stiffer than any place else. Only 160 PWs were taken by the Corps. Tonight General Hart turned his 8" guns for interdiction of the approaches to the BONN bridge. He has, for the last two days, kept his Pozit on the one remaining bridge of COLOGNE and he hopes tomorrow to be able to interdict the bridge further to the south of BONN.

All bridges over the RHINE in the vicinity of DUISSBERG are now reported blown. All Corps of the Ninth Army and the First Canadian Army continued to make sweeping advances and there now appears a chance that by tomorrow night all resistance of any kind west of the river will cease. The VIII and XII Corps advances were likewise expansive and there are now no enemy west of the PRUM River.

For the fourth consecutive day air operations were hampered by low murky clouds and intermittent rain and snow. There was some blind bombing done but only in one case in the attack of MUNSTEREIFEL were the results observed.

In celebration of the arrival of his troops on the RHINE, or as the General put it another way, to take the curse off the roast pork, he ordered champagne to be served during the dinner and Bill proposed a toast "to an early crossing" of the Rhine.

Tuesday, 6 March 1945: Tonight COLOGNE, before the war, the Reich's third largest city, belongs to the First US Army, and tomorrow morning's newspapers will so state. Against light resistance and with only a few troops still holding out, General Terry Allen's 104th Div cleared the city while the 3rd Armd Div continued the attack to clear the enemy from the division sector north and west of the Rhine. There hasn't been as yet no official estimate made as to the number of civilians still remaining in COLOGNE but it will total more than 100,000, many of whom came out today out of their dugouts and wrecked houses to watch our troops roll in.

VII Corps took a total of 1200 PWs during the day. Tomorrow the 8th Div will clean out the sector south of the city up to its boundary. There are not estimated to be many enemy in that vicinity.

If this was big news, the progress made by the III and V Corps was almost as good. 9th Armd Div advanced up to 10 miles to come within 8 miles of the Rhine. They are shooting ahead against light and scattered opposition and it is possible that we may be able to seize bridges across the Rhine River before the enemy has a chance to blow them. Army Group's latest field order to arrive only today did not give boundaries for the First and Third Army beyond that previously given a month ago, past which point, of courses, we have progressed many miles. Because of the fluidity of the situation, First Army may continue on across the river.

V Corps pushed up to 8 miles along the entire front, almost without contact with the enemy which appeared to be either in confusion or making a quick withdrawal across the river. Almost 30 towns fell to the 2nd, 28th, and 69th Divs and casualties were numbered in tens. Very few PWs were taken during the day; additional proof that the enemy has decided to beat it.

There was little change from other Army fronts. The news is solidly ours. General Collins tonight urged General Hodges to come and take a look at his city tomorrow and the General may do so. It has not yet been decided whether civilians will be evacuated to areas west of COLOGNE, because of the security and possible epidemic danger involved. At the present time no public utilities are functioning in COLOGNE and it is not likely that our engineers and G-5 Sections[8] will be able to fix them for quite a period. As the General remarked today: Our problems are only beginning with occupation and they will continue to mount as we continue to advance.

For the fifth day running air was inactive with the exception of the heavies. There is as yet no sign of it clearing.

Wednesday, 7 March 1945: General Hodges motored to KOLLEGE FORTUNA, CP of VII Corps, where he found General Collins undoubtedly tired by his magnificent efforts of last week in bed with a bad cold. From there the General motored on to the CP of the 3rd Armd Div in COLOGNE itself and then, accompanied by Colonel Bradley, VII Corps' PM [Provost Marshal], went on a tour of the city and actually stepped through an opening in the rubble, and entered the inside of the famous COLOGNE Cathedral. Only the walls of it still remain. There is no roof and no glass. The General said that except for the northwest section of the city, COLOGNE bore resemblance to all the other wrecked towns in Germany through which he has passed and especially near the railroad yards, great blocks of houses are completely flat. While there, two of our Piper Cubs were leisurely cruising over the town despite AA fire from the other bank. This was the only sign of enemy activity seen or heard. General Collins said General [Walter F.] Lauer[9] had implored him last night for permission to send across two battalions of infantry but he naturally had to refuse. However, he told General Hodges he hoped the Army would not make the mistake of waiting long enough to permit the Boche to pull back their strength. General Collins said he would put across his Corps any time General Hodges gave him necessary engineer equipment. As is always the case, he is raring to go, and does not want to stop. The General returned here shortly before six o'clock to find the biggest piece of news of the day right on his desk:

CCB of 9th Armd had captured intact the plank railway bridge at Remagen.[10]

All Corps Commanders were under instructions that if they found such a bridge, to exploit its use to the fullest, and establish a bridgehead on the other side. General Milliken who had called General Kean an hour previously was reminded of this fact and steps have already been taken to transfer additional infantry forces to him so that we can make this bridgehead secure. From six until almost half past eight, the General was in his office with his staff making quick-action decisions, setting into motion the necessary troop movements, so that full advantage could be taken of this great opportunity. A change in boundary was made between V and III Corps, giving the 78th Div to V Corps, as well as an additional slice of territory—thus relieving General Milliken of some responsibility in area and permitting him to devote his full energies to the bridgehead attack.

The other Combat Command of the 9th Armd had seized intact at least two bridges across the Ahr River and had crossed the river to protect them. We have as yet not made contact with elements of the 4th Armd Div which tonight also had reached the Rhine at approximately 1800; but General Hart and General Thorson were in contact with Third Army all day, establishing and changing the no-fire line so that there would be no artillery damage done to friendly troops.

General Bradley who called frequently during the day still had no news of future plans but said that General Bull was arriving at Group tonight from SHAEF and perhaps he would be able to tell us more tomorrow. SHAEF knows about the crossing and for some absolutely inexplicable reason asked permission from First Army to release the fact to the press. This request was turned down instantly and emphatically; we do not know why they even asked for it. As General Thorson said, "How about asking the guy who is establishing the bridgehead whether he wants it released?"

Truck loads of prisoners are reported on their way back to the rear as V Corps during the day completed its present assignment. Advancing against light opposition and in almost all places reaching the Ahr, they established contact with the 6th Cavalry Group of VIII Corps. There is absolutely no PW count for the day that can be considered accurate; the latest report gave us more than 4,000.

Colonel Carter said this evening that it was almost as exciting as the breakthrough and, indeed, it is in a different way. No one anticipated we would be able to secure intact a bridge. It is too early to tell, of course, whether we shall be able to hold it. What the Boche Air is capable of and how many troops he has in the vicinity, is still problematic. Latest reports tonight were that opposition on the other bank was light and the Boche has no longer naturally the mobility he once possessed in being able to rush troops to dangerous spots. However, no one anticipates any push-over. Net companies to protect the bridge against floating mines, truck companies, Duck [DUKW] companies,[11] and two AA Gun Bns are being rushed into the area tonight and for once we hope that bad weather will prevent the Boche as well as us from flying. Aside from the tremendous gains made by CCB of 4th Armd Div which was sending prisoners back without guard because of its inability to take care of them, there was very little news recorded on other fronts.

The First Canadian Army and Ninth Army have not been able to make any substantial progress in clearing out the enemy pocket at Wessel [Wesel].

Tonight the whole show is ours. Cologne is ours. A bridgehead is ours. We have taken more PWs today than any other Army. Whether we shall be able to say the same tomorrow night, Lord only knows. But certainly every effort has been made by this headquarters to insure success for this latest First Army exploit.

Build-up of the Remagen Bridgehead, 8–24 March 1945

Thursday, 8 March 1945: —The General returned from III Corps and 9th Armd Div at 8:30 tonight to find on his desk the following message from General Eisenhower which was read over the phone by the General himself to General Kean shortly after 7:30 tonight: "The whole Allied force is delighted to cheer the First U. S. Army whose speed and boldness have won the race to establish our first bridgehead over the Rhine. Please tell all ranks how proud I am of them. Signed: Eisenhower, Supreme Commander."

This message pleased the General but he does not feel tonight, after a day spent in discussions with General Milliken and General Leonard,

very satisfied with the situation. Apparently there has not been sufficient control applied by the Corps over the troops on the other side;
there is a lack of accurate information; and the transfer across the other
side of the 9th Div as has been desired has not been sufficiently expedit-
ed. However, tonight the combined strength of the various units across
the river is approximately that of one division, including the 47th RCT,
311th Inf complete, two armored infantry battalions, one tank battalion,
and portions of other outfits. As expected, the Boche threw a portion
of the Luftwaffe at the bridge tonight just as it was getting dusk. 3 of
the 4 planes were JU-87s,[12] out of the Luftwaffe scrap heap. They were
all shot down as was the fourth which was an ME-109. Artillery fire
continues to strike on and near the bridge but thus far traffic across the
bridge has not been stopped for any period longer than 15 minutes.
Some PWs have already been captured on the other side of the River. Resistance is characterized as being thus far, "light," although reports came
in late this evening that columns of German vehicles with lights on were
reported approaching the bridge site from both the north and the south
and opposition is expected to increase substantially tomorrow.

In the VII Corps sector above, the 1st Div, which today was attached
to VII Corps, continued to fight in Bonn against stubborn resistance.
Three-quarters of the town is clear but as of midnight tonight we do
not yet know whether the ponton bridge is intact. VII Corps captured
over a thousand PWs yesterday. The most distinguished one to fall into
our net was Lieutenant General Schimpf,[13] famed commander of the 3rd
Para Div who apparently was perturbed about the orders given him
to fight to the last man. He said something to the effect that, "Damn it,
he was the last man." The 7th Armd Div is clearing the sector lying between Bonn and the bridgehead site. It has been attached to III Corps.

V Corps captured the total of six bridges over the Ahr, all of them
intact. They are being protected by patrols. Crossings in force will not
be made until tomorrow morning when a coordinated attack will be
launched. V Corps, however, in sending its troops everywhere up to
the river took over 1,000 PWs. Colonel Carter has been likewise busy all
day worrying about bridges. One ferry service is expected to start tomorrow and the treadway bridge may be finished by tomorrow night.

To what extent our crossing will be permitted to become a major one
remains to be seen. Apparently no decision as yet [has] been reached in
SHAEF or Twelfth Army Group whether full exploitation will be made
of this bridgehead or whether Corps will simply make the bridgehead
secure and then halt. The show of Monty's up north opposite the Ruhr

is still apparently the big thing, and this afternoon General Hart was asked to surrender seven of his artillery battalions, including one of the 155 SP, to the British for their attack.

The news of our bridgehead though hinted at throughout the day by the radio was not officially announced until this evening. Bill said that he had never seen such traffic moving along the roads. Bottlenecks were at ZULPICH which is a walled town and through which on most of the streets only one way traffic can pass. At EUSKIRCHEN the roads have been cratered and smashed by our previous bomb attacks and at one place 2 tanks of the 7th Armd trying to cross a Bailey (against orders as the bridge will only take one tank) broke it in two. On the road are Ducks, LCVPs, heavy ponton equipment, AA, Tanks, supply vehicles, etc. The result is that there is an almost continuous column from EUS-KIRCHEN headed southeast.

General [James G.] Christianson [Christiansen],[14] Chief of Staff Army Ground Forces, was a brief visitor at the headquarters this morning. General Hodges did his best to try and persuade him not to go to III Corps, which is up to its neck with the bridgehead problem, but he nevertheless headed that way. For the seventh consecutive day air activity was practically nil because of low scutty [scudding] clouds. The prediction for tomorrow and the day after tomorrow is no more favorable.

General Hodges was in touch with General Bradley four or five times during the day. From their conversations no clues were received as to our future directions.

Friday, 9 March 1945: The General motored to NAMUR at noon today, and returned at nine o'clock—with two very handsome decorations from the French Government. The General is now a Grand Officer of the Legion of Honor (the highest award the French can make) and likewise possessor of the Croix de Guerre avec Palmes. Decorated along with him, by General [Alphonse Pierre] Juin,[15] Chief of Staff of the French Army, were Generals Bradley, Doolittle and Patton. General Brereton, Simpson, and Vandenberg received the Officer of the Legion of Honor— and did not seem to be pleased to be placed in a lesser category.

The General remarked to General Patton, whose 4th and 11th Armd Divs are rolling in all directions through the Eifel, that his front-line "looked like an intestinal tract." General Patton was hugely amused by this comment.

The General forsook his plans to stay in NAMUR overnight because the situation at the REMAGEN bridgehead, which does not look too promising. Today, as before, the greatest difficulty the headquarters had was in obtaining correct and speedy information on the disposition of troops, what had crossed and what had not crossed. Colonel Russell Finn,[16] Executive Officer of an FA [Field Artillery] Brigade; flew in at five o'clock fresh from a talk with General Craig, who is now commanding all troops on the eastern bank. General Craig is confident that things are going as well as can be expected. The bridge was knocked out this afternoon when a shell hit an ammunition truck, and the treadway bridge is making slow progress because of artillery fire. However, General Craig had the highest praise for the anti-aircraft, thought he was going to get good artillery support, and said that the biggest problem was in the bottleneck of traffic around the western approaches to the bridge. There still does not seem to be a sufficient control by Corps of the whole situation, although General Milliken telephoned the General tonight that General Leonard had been placed in command of the western bridgehead site, and that his Corps Engineer had set up his CP at the river to supervise the bridge-building. There is no attempt made to hide the fact that everybody here wishes the bridgehead command had fallen to General Collins. The main worry here is that the troops have not pushed sufficiently far east to deny the Boche observation of his artillery fire; the bridgehead is still too narrow, furthermore, for proper employment of the forces now across—almost 20,000 men, it was estimated tonight.

BONN is now officially clear, as well as Bad GODESBERG. The 1st Div had a tough fight at the first place, and are gradually rounding up an estimated 2,000 PWs. The main bridge and the ponton bridge have both been blown. V Corps is pushing down rapidly toward the Rhine where its artillery can lend support to the bridgehead forces. The VIII Corps, on our south, continues to mop up its area—and at last count had taken some 7,000 PWs, a field hospital complete. The disorganization of the enemy is complete.

Saturday, 10 March 1945: We moved again today, this time to the regimental barracks outside DUREN, recently vacated by the VII Corps. The barracks, looking like nothing so much as one gigantic sieve or piece of rat cheese, are without heat or water; but coal stoves have been installed and though there is often more smoke than fire, we shall manage to be fairly comfortable. The barracks was occupied, in its balmier days, by Field Marshal [Walther] Model[17]—we should like to give him an escorted visit of it now.

The General came here for a quick visit and a quick lunch and then afterward motored to RHEINBACH, the new CP location of the III Corps.

On the way down—a 2½ hour trip—he had to stop for one full hour on the road, so cluttered was the traffic. Coming back he needed only one. In general, the situation is better tonight.

The 60th Inf has pushed farther south, and the 39th Inf is now in the process of crossing. The 78th Div CP is crossing tonight. The Boche have counterattacked several times, with infantry supported by a few tanks, but these have been repulsed. Artillery fire, which yesterday was at the rate of one every two minutes, has now fallen off to four or five rounds an hour—and the bridge has been in operation throughout the day. Progress on the treadway is slow—but it is believed it can be completed by early tomorrow morning.

The 99th Div is now assembled close to the bridge, and has started to cross this evening. A change in boundary made between us and the Ninth Army relieved General Collins today of the responsibility of patrolling far to the north with his 4th Cavalry Group. This sector has been taken over by the 113th Cav Group of XIX Corps.

Guest tonight of the General was Henry J. Taylor,[18] newspaper correspondent of Scripps-Howard Newspaper Alliance, and one of the biggest bores and most inconsiderate people the General has been forced to entertain. Coming with letters of introduction from General Eisenhower (and everybody else, with the possible exception of Stalin), Mr. Taylor was graciously received by the General who chatted with him at length before and after dinner.

Sunday, 11 March 1945: The General paid his first trip today to the eastern bank of the RHINE. Although both Corps and Division Commanders were opposed to his crossing, the General insisted. Finally on Corps order the treadway bridge was cleared of traffic and his jeep sped across; fortunately at a time when shelling of the site was not in progress. However, no sooner had he stepped inside the door of the house containing General Craig's CP than three shells landed around in quick succession. One demolished the latrine right outside the building; another landed a few yards away, injuring General Craig's Aide; however, the General was fortunately by this time in the cellar.

This treadway was only completed at seven o'clock this morning. A heavy ponton bridge was completed at five o'clock but was damaged soon afterward when an LCVP, out of control, crashed into the trestle at the east end. However, it was repaired and ready for operation at eleven o'clock. Enemy artillery generally in the bridge area was lower than yesterday, and between six o'clock and 11:30 tonight only two rounds of fire fell in the vicinity. By midnight tonight, all three regiments of the

99th Div were across the RHINE and they will become operational as a division probably tomorrow.

Advances up to a thousand yards have been made generally by the 9th and 78th Divs although these advances were not anywhere near as much as the General had hoped for. Aside from the 11th Panzer and the 106th Brigade and elements of Panzer Lehr, no additional division has shown up as yet in strength. The main opposition to the three named are hastily assembled march battalions of assorted groups.

The capture of two enemy artillery installations provided an interesting sidelight to the day. Air OP Liaison officer made a bracket adjustment on a four gun battery and immediately after fire for affect began, white panels were displayed. He flew over the enemy battery position, radioed his report to his battalion, and immediately went out to collect the four guns and the gun sections as prisoners. Another battery surrendered intact when the artillery liaison officer with the 39th Inf arranged for a TOT [time on target] on the enemy CP consisting of four 88mm guns and 100 men. The Liaison Officer then delivered an ultimatum to the enemy CP demanding their surrender which they complied with at once.

Although we are not out as far as the General would wish, the bridgehead does look secure now. We have three infantry divisions plus across and two battalions of artillery, and with the help which the artillery of V Corps and VII Corps are lending, we are as rich in heavy fire-power as ever before. No word has yet come from Group whether this bridgehead is to be expanded and made a main effort, or whether SHAEF is still placing its money on the yet to be won bridgehead north of us in Monty's sector.

Up there the enemy pockets west of the WESSEL [Wesel] were cleared and the last organized resistance along the west bank of the Rhine between NIJMEGEN and SINZIG was crushed. The VIII Corps and XII Corps to our south continued to mop up isolated enemy pockets west of the river with the VIII Corps, for the third successive day, taking over 3,000 PWs.

Monday, 12 March 1945: General [Marie-Louis] Koeltz,[19] former commander of the French XIX Corps, in North Africa, who arrived last night too late for dinner with the General, from VIII Corps, today decorated members of the First Army staff and VII Corps staff and divisional staffs from VII Corps. Altogether 137 officers and enlisted men, headed by General Kean, General Collins, and General Rose were decorated by the French General. The high ranking officers were "knighted" and "kissed" by General Koeltz upon receiving the order of the Officier of the Legion of Honor, while the others including most section heads of this headquarters received the Croix de Guerre with Palm. The ceremony itself was made impressive by the background—one of the shattered wrecked barracks buildings in which we are now located. General Koeltz afterward had coffee with General Hodges and General Collins and then left for VII Corps and a trip to COLOGNE.

General Collins stayed on with General Hodges for a discussion of how VII Corps is going to come into the present bridgehead enlargement. Present plans are for the 1st Div to cross the 15th, 16th, or 17th on the bridges already established by III Corps and then to strike out north to obtain ground which can be used for a fourth bridge. General Collins remarked upon entering the General's room, "What a shame it was that VII Corps had not been the people to establish the bridgehead," remarking that, "at the end of the first day, he would have been out at the Autobahn."

The General did not leave the CP during the afternoon but remained home to clean up some paper work and direct progress of the bridgehead operations from headquarters. Enemy resistance was moderate on the north and south but stiff towards the east in the rugged high ground which commands the area between the bridge sites and the Autobahn. 310th Inf did occupy HILL 448 and advanced one thousand yards to the road at coordinates 699240. The road was also cut further south by the 60th Inf which entered HARGERGEN [Hargarten] against heavy resistance. About 360 PWs were taken by the Corps, all from the east bank, and their morale was generally low. Several small counterattacks were launched in the middle of the line during the day by the Boche, but in every case these were repelled and no ground lost. They were supported by two or more tanks in every instance.

Tuesday, 13 March 1945: General "Beetle" [Bedell] Smith, General Eisenhower's Chief of Staff, paid us his first visit since last August, arriving from Ninth Army shortly after ten. Apparently he had no news to give General Hodges or General Kean about the bridgehead or about future plans in general. General Collins was there during his visit straightening out details of his Corps attacks and did not leave until shortly before noon. General Hodges then left by jeep after a quick lunch for III Corps headquarters at BAD NEUENAHR, the attractive watering resort only a few miles from the RHINE.

Advances in the north up to 2400 yards were made today while the 2nd Bn of 60th Inf crossed the north-south road in the vicinity of ST KATHARINEN. Elements of the 9th Div encountered 15 or 20 tanks during the day and destroyed 7. 355 PWs were captured. There are now 9 Bns of artillery on the other side.

It was a good day for the first time in twelve and both our Air and Boche Air were active throughout the day. By six o'clock Colonel Patterson had claimed for his anti-aircraft units—4 Gun Bns and 13 AW Bns—18 cat 1's and 6 cat 2's. General Quesada's pilots were in constant dog-fights throughout the day from Cologne south to Koblenz and areas 20 to 30 miles deep across the Rhine. We lost 6 aircraft and they claim 13 shot down in fighter battles. No damage whatsoever was done to any of the three bridges. We have now ceased to use the railway bridge as repairs and work are being done to strengthen it and to make it two-way. Both the treadway and the heavy ponton are in good shape and they are supplemented by constant ferry service and use of LCVPs. The General returned shortly before six o'clock to the new Master TAC CP which is located in a large barracks just west of Euskirchen. These barracks were not shot up as badly as were those at Duren and will constitute a more than adequate quarters for our estimated one month stay here. Master Command will follow us in four days.

The General then went to the residence which is a handsome home at Kessenich, one mile north of Euskirchen. This house was left a wreck by the field artillery battalion which occupied it, but after three day's work, Bill Smith and his crew have it in fairly good shape and by tomorrow we should have adequate heat as well as running water.

A message came through by radio last night from the Germans requesting a two hour armistice of our artillery fire so that evacuation of some 300 German children could be made from a monastery located just north of the area now held by the 311th Inf. It was hard to know what to do. Is any German's word of any value? Finally, the General decided that artillery fire would cease between the hours of eleven and one and this message was so communicated to the German authorities. However, this action, General Hodges said, will not be repeated. It could be used so many times, even this time, for any number of infamous purposes and we have been dealing with the Boche too long to trust his motives.

Wednesday, 14 March 1945: The bridgehead continued to expand against light to heavy resistance. The resistance was heaviest, as has been the case since the beginning, against the 9th Div. The 60th Inf, however, was fighting in the outskirts of Lorscheid at the end of the day, after knocking out 8 out of the approximate number of 35 tanks which opposed them.

Further north the 78th Div with the 60th Armd Inf Bn attached, made advances up to 1½ miles, reaching the outskirts of AGIDIENBERG [Aegidienberg] which is only 1½ miles away from the Autobahn. General Quesada's 5 groups which were operating throughout the day picked up several heavy concentrations of motor vehicles and infantry in the periphery of the bridgehead area, and attacking them, claimed at least 25 armored vehicles and tanks destroyed and 22 damaged. The Corps took 256 prisoners during the day.

One of the best surprise acts of the war was pulled by IX Tac this morning when they zoomed down to strafe and bomb the enemy airfield at LIPPE which is some thirty miles due east of the bridgehead area. Apparently the Boche have been using this extensively for their excursions against the bridge and General Quesada's people, after five hours of almost continuous attack, reported 58 planes destroyed on the ground with a possible 48 additional also rendered useless.

General Hodges is extremely interested in the Third Army drive which opened this morning at two o'clock. Both the 5th and 90th Divs of XII Corps crossed the MOSELLE at four points establishing a consolidated bridgehead and within six hours had erected four treadway bridges across the river. They advanced up to three miles on a four-mile front against light to moderate resistance. Meanwhile, the XX Corps continued to attack to the east along the south bank of the MOSELLE, advancing anywhere up to three miles. General Hodges hopes "George" is able to swing north one of his armored spearheads into action. This will not only relieve pressure from the bridgehead area but will hasten the capture of the SAAR area, which the Germans can ill afford to lose. This attack will become three way tomorrow when the Seventh Army launches its coordinated attack to clear the area running west of the RHINE in conjunction with the Third Army.

General Heubner, anxious to get into the scrap once again, called on the General at ten o'clock this morning and stayed for lunch. He told the General a wonderful story of a GI who engaged in a brisk fight outside of GEMUND, refuged underneath a Boche tank which had been "knocked out." During the course of the fighting, firing constantly with his carbine, he accounted for 9 Boche. Suddenly the tank moved on, leaving a bewildered and flabbergasted GI lying in the middle of the road. In General Heubner's words "he flagged it the hell out of there." General Heubner also told General Hodges about the great number of supplies of all kinds, including trucks, ammunition, and tanks, which V Corps had seized back of the GEMUND-SCHLEIDEN area where the Boche apparently intended to make a real stand.

Thursday, 15 March 1945: General Bradley, still wearing three stars although his fourth was given to him yesterday, flew in by Cub at noon time along with his Chief of Staff General Allen. He and General Hodges and the others were closeted in the office for an hour and a half after going to the house for lunch. General Bradley said he still clung to the view held officially by SHAEF that there should be no major effort made on the eastern bank of the Rhine until all resistance is cleared from the west bank; a viewpoint in which General Hodges does not agree. They told the amusing story of a telephone call made by 21 Army Group requesting that SHAEF put on some "diversion" before the big crossing up north takes place. Five minutes later news came through that First Army had established a bridgehead, putting an end to all talk about "diversion." General Allen also told a good story about a telegram sent to General Patton by General Patch. These two apparently take great delight in kidding each other. The telegram read: "Congratulations on your being the last Army to reach the Rhine. Knew you would make it some time," to which General Patton wired back "Appreciate your telegram so much, especially coming from the one who was the first one to leave the Rhine." General Bradley added his bit to the merriment by relating the story of the three German Generals who searching everywhere for a GI to whom to surrender, finally found a group guarding a AA gun. Their testimony of good faith and their willingness to give themselves up was shown when they threw three Luger pistols at the GIs and immediately there was a free-for-all and the officers still had no one to whom to surrender.

To go from the sublime to the ridiculous—we learned pretty definitely that SHAEF does not wish the bridgehead expanded and as a matter of fact were almost disappointed when they learned the news that we were across the river, since it upset their previously made calculations. They still are placing all their money on the assault crossing to the north and have no intentions at least so far of making our crossing any kind of a major effort. General Hodges also discussed with General Bradley the possibility of replacing General Milliken with another Corps Commander. Both agree that General Milliken was a good officer but that in a pinch he was too timid and in general the bridgehead control had been almost non-existent until General Hodges personally took charge. Apparently General Milliken was involved in some disagreements with General Patton, which fact was the primary reason for his transfer to the First Army. Among possibilities mentioned for replacement were Generals Harmon, Van Fleet, or Gaffey. General

Hodges would like to have General Harmon but General Bradley was not sure that his transfer from the Fifteenth Army could be made.

Although our troops did not reach the Autobahn, as the General had hoped, they did approach within a half mile of it. Excellent gains were made during the day by the 99th Div especially in the south. The 60th Inf captured LORSCHEID and the 47th took a stubborn quarry strongpoint, capturing two officers and over 100 enlisted men. In general gains up to 2,000 yards were made almost everywhere along the front. The General is still disappointed with the performance of the 9th Div, which he believes is not doing its usual good job. As the General said this evening, "Mind you, I have only the greatest admiration and respect for the GIs doing the fighting out there, but I think they have had bad leadership in this bridgehead battle."

Perhaps not unexpectedly, in view of the pounding that IX TAC gave the field at LIPPE, Boche aircraft made no appearance over the bridge until dusk. During the night 7 planes were over, of which AA claims 2 cat 1s and 1 cat 2s. Our Air had a field day roaming wide and deep to get some 320 MTs destroyed and 250 damaged; 418 railroad cars destroyed and 399 damaged; hangars, dumps, marshalling yards, highway cuts, town, barracks, etc. It seemed that there was almost nothing they did not go after during the course of a beautiful flying day. HAGEN was found to be crammed with all kinds of rolling stock, etc., and there, both XIX and XXIX TAC had fine shooting.

The 1st Div moved its 26th Inf completely across the river this morning; they will be followed by the 18th Inf tomorrow. 1st Div has likewise moved its CP to the other side of the river. VII Corps opened its CP today in a handsome new barracks just southwest of BRUHL. When 1st Div has pushed sufficiently far north to guard the site, a fourth bridge will be built.

During the afternoon the General was interviewed for almost an hour by Gladman [Gladwin A.] Hill, one of the chief Paris correspondents of the New York Times.

Friday, 16 March 1945: The General paid another visit to the bridgehead today, stopping for the longest period of time at the Div CP of General Andrus, which is located in the labyrinth cellar of a fine old home almost on the bank of the Rhine. The 1st Div, he reports, is raring to go and should push forward north without great difficulty to secure a bridge site.

Just five minutes before the 78th Div officially passed to control of VII Corps—noon—we learned that the AUTOBAHN had been cut by the

1st Bn of the 309th Inf. This cut apparently had not reached the ears of the Germans, for late in the afternoon trucks careened down the Autobahn to meet our withering fire. A tremendous toll of enemy was taken. Against steady advances and pressure in all directions, the Boche appeared to be fighting with somewhat less determination than on previous days, as the total of PWs taken on the eastern bank amounted to over 1,000. 78th Div likewise captured an underground aircraft factory at coordinates 633300.

It was learned today that General Bradley is now trying to convince SHAEF to push the Third Army across the river in our bridgehead area and then to swing south; they to go in the direction of FRANKFURT and we toward GEISSEN [Giessen]. Third Army today was going "great guns" with the 4th Armd Div off on one of its now famous "end-runs"; they have reached BAD KREUZNACH representing a gain of over 25 miles, and capturing intact an entire divisional headquarters and staff. The VIII Corps likewise went across the MOSELLE and they are now pushing north toward COBLENZ [Koblenz]. General Hodges is convinced that this Third Army drive has doomed the Boche on the western front, and after this, if we take full advantage of his present weakness and drive ahead with everything we have, that the end of all organized resistance will be soon in view.

To exploit the gains made by the XII Corps and its 4th Armd Div, Twelfth Army Group this afternoon through General Bradley ordered 28th Division to leave our area and to join XII Corps. Motorized, it will exploit the gains made by General Gaffey's troops and mop up the area. General Bradley also announced that General Van Fleet would arrive at Army Group tomorrow and would be on his way to us. General Van Fleet's rise in this war has been spectacular. He landed on D-Day as a regimental commander in the 4th Division.

General Ben Lear[20] paid the General a brief half hour visit this morning on his way back to Paris from the bridgehead area. He left us with no information.

Saturday, 17 March 1945: The General stayed at the CP today to welcome General Van Fleet who arrived at two o'clock and with whom he had an hour talk. The General is extremely pleased that General Bradley was able to get him to succeed General Milliken.

About 2:50 General Hodges called General Milliken to say "I have some bad news for you" and then told him that he was going to relieve him and that if he wished he should drop by this headquarters tomorrow. When the General had finished, General Milliken said, "Sir, I have some bad news for you too. The railroad bridge has just collapsed." The story as we obtained it later from witnesses during the day was that without warning the huge center span suddenly crumbled and slid into the water. We have as yet no complete total casualty figures but it is thought that they will be over a hundred as the engineers were busy repairing the bridge when the accident occurred and had absolutely no inkling of the impending disaster. Everybody knew that the bridge had been weakened, first by the demolition charges and secondly by artillery shells and by the constant flow of tanks and materiel across it. For three days the engineers had been working hard to get [the] bridge into shape.

The General is not particularly dismayed about its loss. We now have three other bridges across the river, constant ferries, and we have sites for more. The bridge served its purpose well while it lasted.

Two other incidents around the bridge were noteworthy today. One V-2 fell some 500 yards away on the east bark shortly before noon hitting a building and killing some 15 soldiers. Two other V-2s fell in the back area, not near the bridge, before the day was up. During the night a special team of six or twelve swimming saboteurs, especially flown to the bridgehead from Vienna, tried to swim downstream with the mission of blowing up the ponton bridge. Our precautions against these teams have been elaborate and our searchlights quickly picked them up. One detonation was fired off by our bullets and at last count we had three of the saboteurs including one SS lieutenant who led the party.

Good progress was made during the day all along the front and we now control some 7 miles of the Autobahn which has been crossed in none less than seven places. The stiffest resistance was against [again] encountered in the center part by the 9th Div, which nonetheless cleared STRODE [Strodt], HALLERBACH, and FROHNEN. The 39th Inf cleared the landing strip on the west side of the Autobahn and continued on across it. The III Corps took 916 PWs as a total. In the VII Corps area the 1st Div continued the attack with the 18th and 26th Inf which passed through the 309th Inf. Advances up to 1500 yards were made. The 78th Division cleared ITTENBACH, capturing the new CG of the remnants of the 3rd Para Div and 110 of his men. Considering the small number of troops involved, the total of 641 PWs is considered quite remarkable.

The General's attention is almost equally divided these days on the attack of the Third Army which is a beautiful thing to watch. Spearheads of the 4th Armd Div are everywhere striking south, with the motorized infantry following close behind. Third Army likewise had bridge trouble when one at BRATTZENHEIM [Bretzenheim] collapsed under our tanks and were fortunate in that they were still able to ford the stream at a narrow place. The 87th Division continued house-to-house fighting in COBLENZ and should clear it tomorrow. The XX Corps, coming straight east in the middle of this three-quarter moon-shaped area, has advanced up to six miles, and one combat command of the 10th Armd Div is within two miles of BIRKENFELD. In the Seventh Army sector, resistance is somewhat stiffer and mainly in the form of mines which are laid across the entire front in density never before encountered.

Sunday, 18 March 1945: The General left the CP briefly today to witness a demonstration of a flame-throwing mortar, flung from an M-7 chassis. This demonstration was held in an open field about five miles from the CP and was witnessed by artillery and tank officers representing all troops in the Army. The mortar shell travels very high and has a range of some 1200 yards. Though the targets were well plastered with its burning materials, the General still said he preferred a little white phosphorous used by a 4.2 [inch] mortar. This equipment is heavy and hard to handle and the General does not see where it has any particular advantages over the equipment already possessed by us.

He had two visitors during the afternoon: General Milliken who came for a ten minute chat before proceeding on to Twelfth Army Group; then General Heubner who came at four o'clock and stayed for an hour and a half. General Heubner is itching to get into this present scrap and is letting no opportunity pass to present his case.

Good gains were made in the center and northern sector of the bridgehead area today but the General's attention for once seems to be centered on another Army than his own. He kept saying throughout the day, looking at the unbelievable front of the Third and Seventh Armies, "The war is over, I tell you—the war is over." Six Armd Divisions are now in play. The 11th Armd, joining the 4th Armd yesterday afternoon, has come down to its right and is now engaged in a tough fight in KIRN which is on the NAHE River. The 4th Armd withstood a very stiff counterattack at HACKENHEIM this morning and then kept moving on about 10 miles to reach BATTENHEIM [Badenheim]. The 87th Div cleared Co-BLENZ except for one fort on the Rhine River edge, and the Rhine bank is now completely clear except for very small isolated pockets all the way from COBLENZ down to BINGEN. The XX Corps, employing the 12th Armd Div, today for the first time advanced up to GUMBACH 7416 which puts it within 15 miles of joining up with elements of the 11th Armored.

Good gains were also recorded by the 94th, 80th, and 26th Divisions both to the north and south of this 12th Armd spearhead.

Resistance on the Seventh Army front varied from light to moderate but there is as yet no evidence of mass withdrawal from the Siegfried Line defenses. Each division has had over one thousand men engaged in mine removal alone and the majority of casualties have been caused them [by] mines today. However, on the right flank in the VI Corps sector the 103rd and 36th Divs and elements of the 14th Armd Div advanced ten to twelve miles on a combined sixteen mile front, to reach WEISSENBURG [Wissembourg] which they were on the point of entering in December before they were forced to withdraw. To their right the 5th DB Div [Division Blindée, Armored Division] of the First French Army kept pace with them.

Air was limited operationally all day; visibility in the target area was bad and the claims tonight are low. We had an attempted showing this evening of "A Tree Grows in Brooklyn," but since the sound track in the machine broke down at an average of once in every ten minutes, the performance was not considered a success.

During the afternoon the General also pinned assorted medals on 58 members of this headquarters staff.

Monday, 19 March 1945: Something is in the air and that something may be an armistice. Major Dempsey of PRO [Public Relations Office] came in this morning to find out if we had any information about the 18 C-47s that flew eastward over the bridgehead area late yesterday afternoon. He said everyone in the bridgehead area was excited about it, and that furthermore—which is more important—the three correspondents that are stationed at "Muckraker" [codename of the press camp for war correspondents attached to the First Army] who had been previously picked to represent their newspapers and magazines in Berlin when our troops should enter, had been alerted last night by SHAEF and ordered to report to Paris at once with full field equipment.

We received more hints of something brewing at noon when General Bradley telephoned General Hodges and told him to fly at once LUXEMBOURG to meet him and General Patton. General Bradley had just finished a conference with General Eisenhower. The General flew by Cub, arriving there at 2:30 and returning here at 5:30. He was not particularly communicative except [to] say that he now had permission to send at least nine divisions across the Rhine; five more than we now have, and that the "Big Show" would be Friday. Whether the "Big Show" means the opening of a tremendous new drive by our Army in collaboration with Third Army or whether it means an impending armistice, we do not yet know but certainly from the way things are now going in the SAAR-PALATINATE sections, a collapse of the German Reich is not far off, although it may not end in another month or so.

Our new plan, which is now understood to go into effect as soon as the troops can be assembled, calls for the complete crossing of all three Corps to the other bank of the Rhine and for a drive straight toward GIESSEN. The Corps Commanders will confer with General Hodges early tomorrow morning here regarding details.

It was an unprecedented day for the Air. With clear cool weather, fighter bombers, mediums, and heavies were aloft from dawn to dusk. IX TAC—to mention a few of the results—destroyed 310 MTs [motor transports] and damaged 194; destroyed 608 railroad cars and damaged 370; destroyed 67 locomotives and damaged 17; knocked out 23 tanks and damaged 31. The combined report of IX, XIX, and XXIX TAC who flew in all 1795 sorties was as follows: MT–1007 destroyed, 519 damaged; Railroad Cars–1229 destroyed, 1001 damaged; Locomotives–117 destroyed, 41 damaged; enemy aircraft–22 destroyed on the ground; and Horse-drawn Vehicles–265 destroyed and 98 damaged.

With this kind of support and with its armored columns ranging "free, wide, and handsome" through the SAAR, Third Army chalked up today an estimated 18,000 PWs. The 12th and 11th Armd Divisions made contact at L-8719, closing a pocket about 30 miles long and 12 miles wide, and from this pocket many thousand Boche will come. The two Comds [commands] of 4th Armd Division joined their separate spearheads after capturing BAD KREUZNACH and advanced 13 miles along a 17 mile front further east towards the Rhine. The 10th Armd Division, operating on the right of the 12th, advanced about 15 miles to approach the key SAAR basin town of KAISERLAUTERN [Kaiserslautern]. Stiff fighting in the pillbox area in the Seventh Army sector was still going on, although penetrations have been made and the 36th Div captured WEISENBURG [Wissembourg] which they were on the point of entering when Von Rundstedt's December offensive broke loose. Perhaps most remarkable of all was the fact that in the fighting in the bridgehead area on a narrow front, First Army alone took almost 1700 PWs. Boche artillery fire was heavy throughout the day but the 1st and 78th Divisions advanced north to make gains up to two and a half miles, while in the south, the 99th Division captured ROCKENFELD, HAMMERSTEIN, and RHEINBROHL. There is no sign yet that resistance is beginning to crumble in our sectors; the fighting still remains of a stiff nature, but our advance nevertheless is not being checked. Rugged terrain is adding to our difficulties.

Tuesday, 20 March 1945: General Hodges' three Corps Commanders appeared at the office at nine o'clock this morning for a hastily-called conference in which the Army Commander gave them full details of his previous day's talk with General Bradley and the steps to be taken at once to move other divisions across the river preparatory to an all-out drive to begin Friday the 23rd. He conferred with them for two hours and then hopped a Cub to MUNCHEN-GLADBACH, Ninth Army's head-quarters, where at an impressive ceremony the General was the first to be decorated by Field Marshal Montgomery as CB, Commander of the Bath. General Kean who flew up with him likewise received the same decoration. Other officers of General Hodges' Army received the DSO [Distinguished Service Order], OBE [Order of the British Empire], and the MM [Military Medal]. General Rogers, Army Surgeon, was one of those to be given an OBE. The General flew back here at four o'clock to resume his conferences and talks.

The main effort in the bridgehead today was made by the VII Corps which with the 1st Division continued the attack to the north against extremely heavy enemy artillery and nebelwerfer fire. Advances up to 2500 yards were made. 78th Division on the left marched along the east bank of the Rhine, advancing up to three miles or within 1,000 yards of the SIEG River, the present limit of our advance, against light to medium resistance. CCR of the 3rd Armd Division which will go into action to-morrow morning, crossing in the 1st Division sector tonight.

During the day's operations the VII Corps captured the remark-able number of 1171 PWs. III Corps which was static most of the day, took 110. Everyone was on the alert tonight for an all-out effort by the Boche against the bridges, and our aircraft was forbidden to fly over the bridgehead sector as we wished to have full authority to deal with all enemy planes and parachutists. However, the threat did not material-ize. Although some 23 enemy planes did put in an appearance, we shot down three of them. For the second successive day we had magnificent flying weather and although today's results were not as high as those registered on the previous day, IX TAC did destroy 159 MTs, 13 Tanks, and 348 RR cars. IX [XIX] and XXIX TAC had equally as good days.

The General continued to follow, with the most tremendous inter-est, the breakthrough of the Third Army which continued to drive to-wards the east against disorganized enemy resistance and the enemy was trying to escape from our heavy air attacks. The XII Corps today entered WORMS and has now cleared most of the area west of WORMS and MAINZ. Another pocket was cleared today when 11th Armd Division, advancing on WORMS from the southwest made contact with the 4th Armd Division in that vicinity. In the XX Corps sector the 12th Armd advanced 15 miles to within 7 miles of MANNHEIM, while the 10th Armd Division, by-passing KAISERSLAUTERN, advanced 15 miles to the south. The 80th, 26th, and 65th Divisions were mopping up behind. Third Army is unable to give even an estimate of the number of PWs taken. In the Seventh Army, SAARBRUCKEN fell to the 70th Division while the 6th Armd Division, cutting straight north through the 63rd, advanced to HOMBURG and thus created the third pocket. Over three-quarters of the area west of the Rhine which existed at the beginning of the campaign on 15 March has now been captured by the two US Armies.

Wednesday, 21 March 1945: Today the V Corps regrouped its forces and took over the sector from the III Corps along the east bank of the Rhine as new Corps boundaries became effective at midnight last night. 69th Division took over the 2nd Division sector west of the River and the 2nd Division took over the sector from the 99th Division with its 38th Infantry, which relieved elements of the 393rd and 394th. The 9th Armd Division was attached to V Corps and assumed command of the sector along the east bank with CCB. V Corps will attack tomorrow.

III Corps was inactive today but moved its CP to LINZ [Linz am Rhein] to thus become the first Corps to establish headquarters east of the Rhine.

In the VII Corps area the 78th Division cleared the area south of the SIEG River from its junction with the Rhine due east to the Autobahn. The 4th Cav Squadron relieved elements of the 310th and 311th Infantry and outposted the river. The 1st Division with CCR of 3rd Armd attached made good gains to the north although the enemy still remains sensitive to any attempts to push out to the east and General Collins who flew in this afternoon to confer with General Hodges did not minimize the fact that the fighting was hard and the Fighting First had plenty of fighting, with Boche artillery fire continuing to be unusually heavy. Meanwhile the 8th Division relieved the 104th and took over the latter's sector along the west bank of the Rhine from BONN all the way up to the First and Ninth Army boundary. The job of patrolling the River will be shared shortly by the 86th Division which will cross in the next three or four days. A Class 40 Treadway Bridge—the sixth now over the river—was completed this afternoon in a record time of ten hours and fifty-five minutes, and General Collins, losing his bet, must provide beer for every member of the Engineer Battalion which constructed it.[21]

The 104th Division is now in the process of moving across the River. One RCT is already across.1116 PWs were captured by the Corps during the day.

General Collins also told General Hodges of two Americans captured in the fighting in the Hurtgen Forest in October, who re-appeared into our lines this morning. They had served as orderlies in a German hospital in SIEGBURG when the Boche pulled out two days ago—at which time they pulled out in the opposite direction and for two days they were quartered and fed by German civilians who helped them escape to our lines.

The Boche tried for the second time, this time unsuccessfully, for a short armistice in order to evacuate, so they said, 80 young kids and some aged people from two small towns opposite the front of the 9th Division. General Hodges ordered the German Captain who came with this message to be told bluntly this "you get out of the town and we will take care of the people when we come in."

Again the Air was up in strength all during the day. Claims ran about as yesterday. Good weather is promised for tomorrow.

The rout of the Germans in the SAAR-PALATINATE area has now become a true catastrophe for their First and Seventh Armies. The XII Corps is along the Rhine in an area from LUDWIGSHOFEN [Ludwigshafen] to WORMS and only in the area around MAINZ where some SS troops are still holding out is the resistance of a stubborn and coordinated nature. Everywhere else Germans are surrendering in mass. In the estimate of PWs taken yesterday by both Armies the total is almost 30,000. Over seven-eighths of the area has been cleared and it is expected tomorrow will see both armies drawn up along the west bank with only the laborious process of marching back PWs remaining. In addition to General Collins, General Hodges also had as his guest during the day General Quesada, General [Thomas] North[22] of OPD in Washington and Colonel [Dan] Gilmer, OPD.[23]

Thursday, 22 March 1945: The Army initial bridgehead line was everywhere secure today and Corps are now consolidating preparatory to the all-out attack which the General decided should be the 25th instead of the 26th. Marshal Montgomery is to hit on the 24th, the day after tomorrow, and the word from Third Army is that they are now going to cross at the first available moment without air-drop and without giving the Boche a chance to recover from the pounding he has taken in their sector. General Heubner's V Corps, which today cleared the area west of the WEID [Wied] River meeting little enemy resistance except in the town, wished to push on further today but the General denied him that request, saying it was better to hold up until all three Corps hit at once.

At noon today the 28th Division was attached in its present position to V Corps, at which time the First Army boundary was extended south to the north edge of COBLENZ. The First Army bridgehead was at midnight tonight 31 miles wide extending from the SEIG [Sieg] to the WEID River.

In the VII Corps sector the 78th Division continued to advance north to take HENNEF while the 3rd Armd moved up close to the river preparatory to crossing tomorrow. IX TAC had an excellent day accounting for over 200 MTs with an additional 200 damaged. 35 Tanks and armored vehicles and 753 railroad cars were also destroyed or damaged. The Third Army sector reported MAINZ cleared while the 12th Armd Division is advancing south of LUDWIGSHOFEN to reduce the remaining small pocket west of the Rhine. Yesterday the Third Army took 12,000 PWs, building their total since the present attack began to over 35,000.

General Kenna [Albert W. Kenner], and Colonel Eckelles [Marion P. Echols],[24] and Major Zwing were guests of the General for dinner tonight.

Friday, 23 March 1945: The big news of the day came shortly after twelve o'clock when General Bradley called to tell General Hodges that the Third Army had crossed the river with over five battalions south of MAINZ. Complete secrecy has been placed on this operation and it will not be released to the press or to anybody else for quite a few hours. Tonight also, the British started crossing the Rhine, although the air drop will not take place until tomorrow morning.

All the Corps in building up their equipment for the attack, continued to probe out in all directions, taking some 1500 PWs in so doing. Gains up to 2 miles were made. 3rd Armd crossed in the VII Corps sector and the 7th Armd Division crossed in the III Corps sector.

News of the Third Army's attack with the 5th Division and the 90th Division is good. The Treadway was completed today near OPPENHEIM and the bridgehead is now three miles deep and some seven miles wide. Meanwhile to the south, fighting continued in LUDWIGSHOFEN and SPEYER. Additional information received tonight shows that the Ninth Army has crossed almost ten infantry battalions against light resistance south of WESEL, while the 1st Commando Brigade of the Second British Army entered WESEL itself, a total wreck from a month's consolidated bombing.

Saturday, 24 March 1945: General Hodges and General Kean spent the day in the field making last minute inspections of the forces scheduled for tomorrow's big show. They stopped first at V Corps for luncheon where General Hodges pinned the Legion of Merit on General Robertson. From there they went to III Corps and then to the CP of the 3rd Armd Division, located in a beautiful house belonging to Herr Mauser, maker of the famed guns. There two colonels of the division were decorated for past meritorious service. Following drinks with General Rose, the party returned to EUSKIRCHEN. General Quesada was the guest for dinner tonight.

In the VII Corps sector opposition against the 104th Division and the 1st Division still continues to be heavy with numerous small counterattacks being thrown in with infantry, tank, and SP guns. It is estimated that 20 tanks and SP guns were destroyed by the 1st Division alone.

III Corps maintained defenses and regrouped in preparation for the coming assault, while the V Corps continued to probe out against practically no resistance, setting up its lines for the 9th Division to pass through on the offensive.

In the British sector the 17th Airborne, making it first drop, and the 6th Airborne British [Division] descended on top of the Boche at ten o'clock this morning six miles southeast of WESEL [Operation Varsity].[25] The Boche had brought in a tremendous amount of flak and our losses in C-47s (35) are considered heavy. However, the drop was extremely successful and it is expected to loosen the front considerably. Second British Army today took over 6,000 PWs. XVI Corps of the Ninth Army advanced up to four miles entering the town of DINKSLAKEN [Dinslaken]. Three bridges have now been built across the Rhine. At midnight tonight the VIII Corps will join the XII Corps in crossing the river, they are to make an assault crossing in the BOPPARD area. The XII Corps bridgehead was strengthened and enlarged today. Tonight it was about eight miles deep and twelve miles wide, while a column of the famed 4th Armd Division had advanced 18 miles, by-passing DARMSTAD [Darmstadt], to reach several miles east of the town. CCA has cut the Autobahn between MANNHEIM and FRANKFURT.

Further to the south the once large pocket between the two armies has been whittled down to an area some eight miles square in the vicinity of WORTH [Worth am Rhein].

Chapter 8

Exploitation of the Remagen Bridgehead, 25 March–18 April 1945

Encirclement of Army Group B, 25 March–5 April 1945

Sunday, 25 March 1945: The General is today showing the public that when it comes to using armor he is second to no one. The 9th Armd Division of V Corps advanced eight miles to clear BENDORF. The 3rd Armd of VII Corps advanced to ROTT, ERSFELD and RETTERSEN, making an advance of some ten miles against opposition which was extremely heavy in spots. The 104th Division, mopping up in rear of their advance, took over 450 PWs as against the armored 850. To the north of them, the 1st Division continued to meet the strongest enemy pressure all day and progress along the low ground south of the river was slowed down by enemy fire from the high ground on the northern bank. At least four counterattacks were repulsed by them but late tonight the enemy resistance was reported to be decreasing. It is reported that General Collins tonight twitted General Rose on the lack of 20 to 30 mile advances such as the press has reported the 4th Armd to be making. General Rose's reply was that every time the 3rd Armd wanted to make a dash they found all the German available armor against them. However, the gains made during the day are considered by everyone to be good and an excellent omen for tomorrow and the forthcoming week.

The British continued to ferry more troops across the river while the XVI Corps of the Ninth Army completed more bridges and advanced, especially with the 30th division, up to three miles. About one-third of each of the 75th and 35th Divisions have now crossed into the bridgehead area. Third Army's XII Corps continued to rapidly expand its bridgehead to the north and northeast. Elements of the 90th Division cleared DARMSTADT while the 4th Armd Division, continuing its lightning advances, reached the MAIN River at HANAU where bridges were

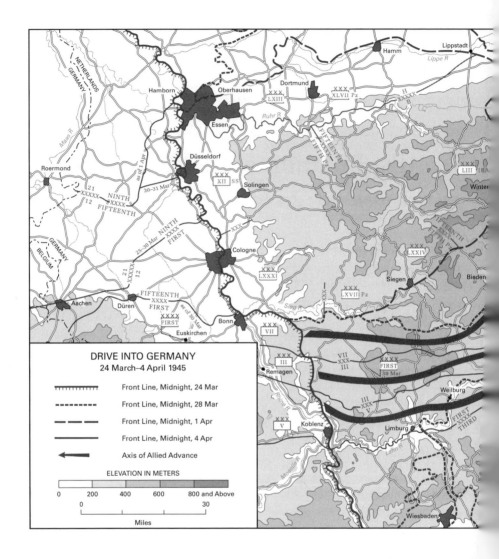

DRIVE INTO GERMANY
24 March–4 April 1945

⊥⊥⊥⊥⊥⊥⊥⊥⊥	Front Line, Midnight, 24 Mar
- - - - - - -	Front Line, Midnight, 28 Mar
— — — —	Front Line, Midnight, 1 Apr
———————	Front Line, Midnight, 4 Apr
◄——	Axis of Allied Advance

ELEVATION IN METERS

0	200	400	600	800 and Above

0   30

Miles

seized intact and elements continued on across. The VIII Corps' crossing of the Rhine met solid resistance and the bridgehead is only about one mile deep. Seventh Army announced today that all organized resistance west of the Rhine has now ceased.

Monday, 26 March 1945: Today our front really exploded. The 9th Armd Division advanced about 20 miles against light and scattered resistance. CCB was in Limburg at 3:30 and three or four tanks succeeded in crossing the river before the bridge was blown. Infantry elements crossed soon afterward and cleared the town. CCA reached Diez. The

9th Armd, released from long captivity some 1,000 Allied PWs in making this advance, among them was Major General [Victor Morven] Fortune,[1] Commanding General of the 51st Highland Division, who was captured by the Boche near St Valarie in June 1940 just before [after] Dunkirk. In turn V Corps took almost 1300 PWs.

To the north, the 3rd Armd Division spearheaded the VII Corps attack and advanced about seven miles against heavy resistance from tanks, mines, dug-in infantry, mortar, rocket, SP, and artillery fire. Altenkirchen was cleared by CCR. CCA had less resistance and advanced about 15 miles reaching HACHENBURG. The 1st and 104th Divisions continued to mop up behind the armor, making gains up to three miles. About 1700 PWs were taken.

The 7th Armd Division kept up the good work by travelling up to 30 miles, the greatest gains of the day. CCA reached OBERTIEFENBACH and CCR reached HASSENBACH [Hasselbach]. Reports now indicate that from five to ten thousand PWs were taken by the division and that the Germans were marching back along our advancing columns, automatically raising their hands as our vehicles approached, and were motioned back by our tankers who could not stop for such petty game. As is the case in the other two Corps, infantry is following rapidly, being motorized as much as possible, coming behind the armor.

The news obviously elated the General as well as the General's guests, General Eisenhower and General Bradley, who flew in to Y-60 [a forward airfield] near EUSKIRCHEN this morning and went from there to the III and VII Corps. General Collins moved his entire kitchen and part of his headquarters to the PETERSBERGERHOF, the great hotel overlooking the Rhine near KONIGSWETTER [Königswinter]. The soldiers were as pleased with the presence of the Supreme Commander as he was with the news. The only change to come from the conference which General Bradley had with General Hodges was that part of V Corps should now cut south to NIEDERHAUSEN [Niedernhausen] in order to join up with the Third Army and help collect what should be a sizeable bag of PWs. They are resisting the VIII Corps advance with tenacity.

There were good gains made in other Corps sectors today, but the outstanding was that recorded by the 6th Armd Division, which committed in the bridgehead, has reached the MAIN River south of FRANK-FORT [Frankfurt] and a damaged bridge over the river has been secured. A new bridgehead over the Rhine which has crumbled as a defense line everywhere was established by the Seventh Army which pushed both the 3rd and 45th across. Resistance was only moderate.

Tuesday, 27 March 1945: The General had his usual number of guests today. General Lee, General Plank, General Collins, General Quesada, and Colonel Partridge were at our house for lunch and in the afternoon Judge [Samuel I.] Rosenman,[2] Special Adviser and ghost writer to the President, now making a survey of Military Government set-ups, visited him at the headquarters. Contrary to expectations and plans, and much to everyone's obvious relief, the Judge left after a half hour, permitting the headquarters to spend its full time waging the war.

The gains reported continued to be startling and for the first time since the march on Paris and on Belgium, we are almost unable to keep up communications with the advancing elements. CCA of 3rd Armd advanced almost 25 miles in two columns to reach HERBORN [Herbern] and BURG. CCB moved along the routes taken by CCR were last reported about 5 miles west of town. Leading elements of the 104th Division were about 14 miles in rear of the advance elements of the 3rd Armd. 1st Division, having completed clearing the area south of the SIEG River, west of the bend, jumped off to attack to the east and made about three miles during the day. To the south, 7th Armd Division made 15 miles against light and scattered resistance, captured bridges intact across the DILL River at three places. The 9th Division advanced approximately 28 miles and it now appears that General Hodges is going to win the bet he made with General Patton that his forces would be the first to reach GIESSEN. The bet is a box of cigars.

In the V Corps, the 9th Armd Division gained up to ten miles in the morning while in the afternoon CCR crossed the LAHN River at LIMBURG and advanced 18 miles southeast along the Autobahn towards its objective of NIEDERHAUSEN. The PW total continues to mount; 4100 were taken by V Corps, 1,000 by VII Corps, and 3,000 by III Corps. No material changes were reported from Third Army as heavy fighting continues in FRANKFORT and in HANAU. This will have to be cleared before the Army can move on ahead. In the Ninth US Army area gains up to three miles were made and the 79th Div was tonight in the outskirts of DIUSBERG.

Wednesday, 28 March 1945: We continued to push in all directions with great speed. 7th Armd advanced up to 18 miles to reach the southeastern outskirts of MARBURG. CCA cleared GIESSEN against moderate resistance; behind the armor's advance, came the 9th and 99th Divisions, mopping up against light resistance, thus winning the bet for General Hodges. 2600 PWs fell to III Corps. 3rd Armd Division continued to deal in "20's" by advancing 22 miles to MARBURG which was entered without opposition. CCR continued to advance along the left flank to the DILL River. VII Corps took approximately 3,000 PWs and over-ran German hospitals where over 6,000 German soldiers were patients. V Corps continued to mop up small by-passed pockets of resistance and relieved the 9th Armd Division with the 2nd in LIMBURG. CCR of the 9th Armd defended strongpoints along the LIMBURG–FRANKFORT Autobahn from LIMBURG to a point about 20 miles southeast and captured IDSTEIN. They will be relieved by VIII Corps elements tonight and start back for LIMBURG tomorrow morning. 28th Division passed to control of III Corps and tonight will commence movement across the Rhine

while the 69th Division completed its movement and crossed near BAD
EMS. EHRENBREITSTEIN fell to V Corps and a great ceremony is planned at
which the American flag will again be lifted to the top of the fortress.
It was there in 1923 that the last American Occupation flag to fly over
Germany was taken down.

Above us the British and the US Ninth Army have yet to swing
loose any armor and consequently the gains are to be measured in
terms of less than five miles. However, resistance crumbled in DUISBERG
and that part of the town north of the RUHR [River] was cleared. In the
Third Army sector the VIII Corps advanced rapidly against scattered
resistance and established contact with the 9th Armd Division along
the Autobahn and with V Corps at DIEZ. XII Corps bridgehead was consolidated and strengthened with the 80th Division on the left establishing contact with elements of the VIII Corps thus linking the two Third
Army bridgeheads. FRANKFURT is now almost clear, while the 4th Armd
Div, breaking out again after three days of constriction, advanced 25
miles to the vicinity of the Autobahn east of GIESSEN.

The Seventh Army extended its bridgehead and put in the 12th
Armd Division which passing through the 3rd [Infantry Division], advanced 10 miles towards MOSSAU. In addition, the XXI Corps became
another Corps to establish a bridgehead with the 44th Division which
drove three miles inland.

Thursday, 29 March 1945: Bill today received the Bronze Star from
the General at a ceremony held on the parade ground at two o'clock.
He was among 35 officers of the headquarters to receive either the Legion of Merit or the Bronze Star for their work. Shortly before dinner,
General Gerow and General Harmon arrived for an evening's conference with General Hodges and General Kean. Fifteenth Army will take
over a good part of our area west of the Rhine on April 1st and there
were many points, especially as to security and military government,
which had to be straightened out between the two commanders. Colonel Williams likewise returned from a reconnaissance for a new CP and
reported, much to everybody's horror and disgust, that the only place
he could find was a large open field near FREILINGEN. We were supposed
to move to BAD GODSBERG [Bad Godesberg] but the General has felt in
the last three days that this was too far to the rear and consequently he
decided last night that we must move farther on.

Our gains continued to tear apart Germany. The 9th Armd Division
with 38th Inf attached advanced approximately 40 miles as CCB captured SCHWEINSBERG. 69th Division was engaged in mopping up opera-

tions in its zone to the LAHN River generally east of NASSAU. The Corps took 3200 PWs. 7th Armd Division advanced northeast from MARBURG but met increasing resistance and made only eight miles. Enemy tanks and heavy bazooka fire from infantry slowed them up and during the day the Luftwaffe put in its first appearance in over a week with 10 ME-109s. Nevertheless, the III Corps had likewise totalled 3200 PWs for the end of the day.

VII Corps now has the mission, given by Army Group, of extending and swinging almost due north in the direction of PADERBORN where it is intended contact will be made with advance elements of the Ninth Army, thus creating a huge pocket and sealing off the RUHR. The VII Corps set about its task today with enthusiasm and advanced up to 45 miles. An unconfirmed report placed TFW only ten miles south of PADERBORN which would make the advance, if true, almost fifty miles. In this dash, 3rd Armd Division captured two trains, one airplane factory, twelve airplanes on the ground and destroyed and captured [a] large amount of enemy equipment and as yet an uncountable number of PWs. We are now out of communication with the advance elements and have only hazy reports on which to make decisions.

Our gains were almost rivalled by that of XII Corps. The 4th Armd Division broke loose again making gains up to 30 miles, while the 2nd Armd Division attacked to the southeast yesterday in the XIX Corps area, going straight for PADERBORN. Tomorrow the 86th Division passes from First Army to Fifteenth Army control, at which time the XXII Corps of General Harmon will take over responsibility of the defense of the west bank of the Rhine between UDORF and Twenty-One Army Group boundary.

Friday, 30 March 1945: The General's remark when he moved into our forest CP at FLIELINGEN [Freilingen] tonight was, "I am reminded of an old remark the sergeant in the Mexican War used to make, 'Somebody has a taste for—.'" The mess is located in a small beer stuba [*Stube*] 150 yards down the road but the rest of the headquarters is either in caravan, in tents, or in foxholes—and it is very cold. Because of convoys and road difficulties, none of the vans, the generators, or the telephone people arrived at the CP until 4:30. Consequently, things were not at all ready for proper operation.

However, the General was considerably assuaged by the gains which were made by his armor. The 9th Armd Division, swinging northeast to protect the VII Corps flank, advanced from HAMBURG [Homburg] to the EDER River, a distance of 28 miles. Contact during the advance was established at TREYSA between the 9th and 6th Armd Divisions of the Third Army. The 7th Armd, attacking north, from REMSCHENBURG [Rauschenberg], advanced 20 miles to secure the important dam over the EDER River which was the objective for the Corps. The dam was secured intact without trouble at four o'clock. 2,000 PWs were taken.

The 3rd Armd Division with 414th Inf attached continued to advance towards PADERBORN against scattered resistance and at five o'clock tonight elements of CCR were reported within two miles of the town. Unconfirmed reports, especially those from BBC, said the town was taken. The 1st Division will begin to move tomorrow to assembly areas in the vicinity of BERNE [Buren], to protect VII Corps left flank. We still are fairly well out of touch with what is going on in the forward zone but we do know that VII Corps took more than 6,000 PWs. To our north, the 2nd Armd Division, breaking loose, advanced 20 miles to HERBORN and ASCHEBURG [Ascheberg]. To our south, 11th Armored also broke loose, advancing 20 miles to BERKSTEINHUT. The VIII Corps' units generally cleared most of the area west of the Corps boundary which extended along the north and south line through GIESSEN, while the 4th Armd Division took HIRSCHFELD [Bad Hersfeld] and NDR JOSSA [Niederjossa]. In the Seventh Army sector armor also stole the show with the 10th and 12th Armd Divisions advancing up to 20 miles due east.

So fast is our advance and so difficult to trace our front lines that we do not particularly complain, or at least not as much as usual, because of the lack of air support. The weather has been spotty for the past four days with visibility generally bad.

Saturday, 31 March 1945: This morning, shortly after ten o'clock, General Hodges received word that there was an unconfirmed report that General Maurice Rose had been killed in action last night. The Artillery Officer, G-1, and G-3 of the Division are likewise missing. We have no details as yet but it is believed that this tragedy took place with Task Force Welborn which was moving toward PADERBORN and was cut in two by several Boche tanks which crossed the column.

General Hodges flew to the III Corps and met General Collins there for a conference concerning the build-up of infantry behind the armor to stop any attempted break-through by the Boche now almost pocketed between us and the Rhine.

General Collins remarked today, speaking of the General's open-air CP, that he was on historic ground, that Napoleon had spent the night near FLIELINGEN either to or on his way to [from] Russia. "Must have been on the way from Russia," snorted the General.

Later in the day he received confirmation of General Rose's death and immediately phoned General Bradley in an effort to get General Harmon on loan from the Corps. He got an affirmative reply late to-night and General Harmon is scheduled to arrive, if not tomorrow, at least the day after.

A new arrival at the CP tonight was General Ridgway whose XVIII A/B Corps, relieved from assignment in the British sector, will join us in a very few days. Available to him will be the 86th and 97th divisions, now belonging to the XXII Corps. He hopes, as does General Hodges, that they will be able to shake loose from SHAEF the 82nd and 101st A/B Divisions which are now waiting in reserve. However, the chances of getting this done are considered slim. General Ridgway's Corps will take over a sector approximately from SIEGEN to the Rhine and will have the mission of clearing out the pocket which soon will be closed. This will permit General Hodges to swing most of his strength due east and continue the advance. He is as delighted to see General Ridgway again as the latter is delighted to serve under him.

Sunday, 1 April 1945: Today, Easter Sunday, we again hit the road, making a sixty mile trip from our open-field CP to the quaint old city of MARBURG which remains practically untouched by the war. Our of-fices are in a former convalescent home for Boche officers. More than 5,000 German wounded remain in the town under our guard and it is reported that the town is still solidly Nazi—principally, we believe, because it had not been beaten up enough.

The General stayed in the trailer until almost noon in constant consultation with General Ridgway and his staff and flew up here this afternoon to be joined by General Harmon who is scheduled to take command of the 3rd Armd. Shortly after four o'clock he received defi-nite word that the 2nd and 3rd Armd Divisions had joined forces in the southwest section of LIPPSTADT, just a few miles northwest of PADERBORN. Thus, in a classic maneuver—and most of the maneuvering was done by the First Army—an approximate 100,000 Boche are pocketed and doomed. In addition, the RUHR industrial area on which Germany has depended so much throughout the war, is closed to communication with the rest of the nation. It is a big day for the First Army and also for the progress of this war.

This, of course, was the big news of the day—but in addition, we pocketed some 6,000 PWs and the 9th Armd Division advanced some nine miles to the east and northeast to take four or five more towns. The General is obviously concerned about the weakness of our line in the north where only armored spearheads exist; if the Boche were not confused, dismayed, and short of gas, they could obviously put on a dangerous attack from either the east or the west. As it is, the General is going to make every effort to push infantry units up in support and button up tight. To the east the 6th Armd Division is on the outskirts of Kassel, while the 4th Armd Division made another long thrust on the Autobahn to a location just north of Eisenach. To the south, the 12th Armd Division was on the outskirts of Wurzburg and in so doing, captured the commanding general of the Fifteenth Corps.

Monday, 2 April 1945: The General flew back today to a cemetery just west of the Rhine and not far from Bad Godesberg for the funeral of General Rose. Before leaving, shortly after noon, General Collins, General Harmon, and General Ridgway were here for consultation. It now appears certain that General Harmon will not take over the 2nd [3rd] Armd Division but that General [Doyle O.] Hickey, who has been with the division for over three years, will assume command. The situation now appears under control at Paderborn and it has been decided that he should at least have a trial as Commanding General.

Pressure was strong against the 9th and 104th Divisions throughout the day. Wintersburg [Winterberg] was cleared only after fierce fighting while enemy counterattack drove us out of a small town to the south. The 104th went about its business of clearing the heavy woods to the north and everywhere establishing road blocks and laying mines across a possible Boche effort to escape. The 4th Cavalry Group likewise cleared a few small villages and set-up road blocks but only against the most bitter resistance. As an added precaution the General ordered CCA of 7th Armd to be attached to VII Corps and the 104th Division tonight. In this fighting VII Corps rounded up 2700 PWs.

XVIII Airborne Corps, becoming operational today, continued to fight its 8th Division in Siegen where some progress was made. 8th Division alone took 1110 prisoners. The only other changes which took place in the V Corps sector was where the 69th Division moved up from the rear to Maunburg [Naumberg]. There were numerous small counterattacks launched against the 9th Division in the north during the morning but they were all beaten off without loss of ground. The SS Westphalian Division which is really only two regiments in strength has made an appearance there against the 9th. General Heubner [Huebner] today moved his CP into the middle of the fighting and consequently was forced to call on the 2nd Rangers and the 102nd Cavalry Group for a perimeter CP defense.

The British, wanting to show they can use armor too, made a 25 mile thrust with the Guards Armd Division to clear ENSCHEDE. The Boche are trying to pull everything out through the few remaining miles which are open to them as an escape route from HOLLAND and the British Tactical Air Force planes are having a field day. In the Ninth US Army sector the 17th Airborne was fighting in MUNSTER against moderate resistance while the 2nd Armd Division continues to fan out due east to in two columns. The 8th Armd Division is moving in west and northwest of PADERBORN and will probably make juncture with our forces tonight or early tomorrow. KASSEL still remains a hard nut for the Third Army to crack and reports tonight indicate that they only reached the perimeter of the city. There were no important changes in the Seventh Army front—by important, we mean gains of more than ten miles.

Tuesday, 3 April 1945: General Van Fleet and General Ridgway arrived early this morning for a one and a half hour conference with General Hodges at which time boundaries between the XVIII and III Corps were settled. III Corps will take over the sector between the XVIII and VII and will attack in a northeast direction toward the RUHR River with the 99th, 9th, and 7th Armd Divisions. General Ridgway will have the two new divisions, the 86th and 97th, neither of which have yet fired a shot and the 8th and 78th. The 78th will go into reserve as he will employ only three of them originally. General Collins meanwhile will curl up in the north and prepare along with General Heubner to continue the attack due east. This afternoon we received a proposed tentative outline of Army boundaries which carry us up to our juncture with the Russians. The general objective of the First Army is LEIPZIG; Ninth Army gets BERLIN; Seventh Army will get MUNICH. We also, incidentally, get most of the HARZ Mountains to clear and as both General Hodges and General Kean remarked as the boundary was put on a map, "We get no Autobahns to travel on." The general road net of the First Army is definitely inferior to that which the other armies will possess. Third Army will continue to clear KASSEL, at which time the city will come under our control to be taken over by V Corps.

There is one important boundary difference, however, from that previously agreed to by the Ninth and First Armies. The Ninth, according to joint agreement, was to clear south from their present positions to the RUHR River. According to the boundary set by Twelfth Army Group we got a large stretch north of the RUHR to clear. Everyone here hopes to have this inexplicable change by Group re-changed back to the original line.

The only change which was made in the XVIII Corps sector today was the clearing of SIEGEN. The 9th Division of the VII Corps continued the attack against decreased enemy resistance and it now appears that the enemy are everywhere on the defensive instead of on the offensive. Many tanks in groups of three and four made their appearance throughout the day and we knocked out an estimated half-dozen. Elements of the 8th Armd Division of XIX Corps made contact with the 1st Division tonight in the vicinity of OSTRIDEN [Oestereiden]. There was no news of any importance from V Corps sector. Today there fell into our hands the choice plum of 9 V-2's intact together with complete directions on how to assemble them, disassemble them, and fire them. This is the first known capture of this highly vaunted Boche weapon.

Wednesday, 4 April 1945: General Hodges flew this morning by Cub, despite low scudding clouds, to Y-60 on the other side of the Rhine where he met General Bradley and General Simpson (also General Kibler) for a discussion of boundaries and objectives. He returned here shortly after one o'clock and tonight after additional telephone calls between Group and here, it appears that the boundary between Ninth and First Armies will revert to that originally made between the two armies. Our immediate mission as given by Group is to establish a firm bridgehead over the WESER River, and then be prepared to attack upon Group order to the east.

Elements of the 97th Division started relief of the 78th Division in the sector immediately east of the Rhine this afternoon. The 86th Division will start to close tomorrow. 78th Division continued to attack with two RCTs but no material progress was made due to increasing enemy pressure and extremely difficult terrain. As is customary when they are on the defensive the Boche continued to counterattack in platoon and company size, always supported by two or three tanks.

In the III Corps sector the 99th Division took up positions on the Corps left flank and started relief of the 47th Inf. Further north the 9th Division with CCA of the 7th Armd attached made an attack to the northeast and made some two miles to clear NIEDERSFELD.

Further north the VII Corps with the 104th Division continued to sweep its area and regroup forces. Nothing has been found as yet in the large woods southwest of PADERBORN. The 1st Division consolidated its positions and took hold more solidly by making firmer contact with elements of the 8th Armd pushing down from the north. Second British Army continued to make excellent advances to the north and northeast reaching the town of LINGEN, clearing RHEINE, and approaching the western edges of

OSNABRUCK. CCB of the 5th Armd Division reached the EMS–WESER Canal just west of MINDEN. The 2nd Armd Division likewise pulled up to the WESER River opposite HAMELIN [Hameln]. The biggest news from other fronts today, however, was the announcement that KASSEL had definitely been cleared by all three regiments of the 80th Division. CCB of the 6th Armd continued to push a finger out to the east to reach MULHAUSEN [Mühlhausen]. Below them the 11th Armd and the 14th Armd made similar 20 mile advances followed closely by the infantry elements.

This afternoon we moved to our new quarters; a fine modern hotel on the other side of the River, some two miles from the CP.

Thursday, 5 April 1945: Today the Army started to go in two directions in earnest. Both V and VII Corps attacked to the east and made good gains against sporadic resistance.

In the V Corps, the 69th relieved the 80th Division of Third Army in KASSEL and tonight has leading elements of one regiment along the Autobahn northwest of the city. Another regiment entered HANN MUNDEN [Hannoversch Münden]. The 2nd Division gained up to four miles to high ground overlooking the WESER. There was an early report that one bridge had been captured intact but this was later found to be untrue and it is now almost certain that every bridge has been blown.

The VII Corps attacked east from the PADERBORN area with 3rd Armd Division and advanced up to 22 miles. Its Task Force B reached BRUCHHAUSEN which is four miles west of the river. There late tonight they were encountering stiffer resistance in the form of tanks and infantry. 1st Division continued to mop up scattered resistance in the rear and assembled forces as they were by-passed by elements of the XIX Corps who were driving straight south.

The III Corps made only moderate gains during the day. This is mainly an infantry show as terrain is exceptionally rugged and a few well placed machine guns can hold up the advance for hours. Opposition in this area still remains stiff and in General Ridgway's Corps the 97th Division closed in the assembly area and relieved the 78th. Limited objective attacks were made by the 8th Division which advanced up to two miles.

To our north as well, gains were made by the British 11th Division and by our 2nd Armd Division. The 11th Armd Division was driving north and northeast in the direction of BREMEN while the 2nd Armd Division, having crossed the WESER, now have a substantial bridgehead six kilometers deep. To our south, the Third Army continued to mop up around GOTHA their furthermost point of advance, while the 6th Armd

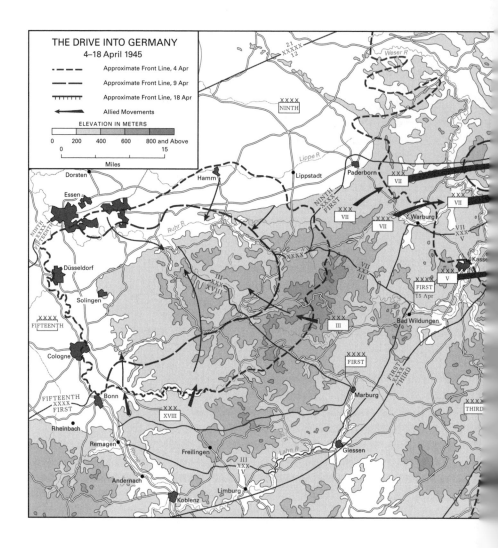

THE DRIVE INTO GERMANY
4–18 April 1945

- – – – Approximate Front Line, 4 Apr
- – – – Approximate Front Line, 9 Apr
- ⊤⊤⊤⊤⊤ Approximate Front Line, 18 Apr
- ◄——— Allied Movements

ELEVATION IN METERS

0   200   400   600   800 and Above

0   15

Miles

cleared MUEHLHAUSEN on our boundary line and then went over into our area to capture SCHLICHTHEIM [Schlotheim]. The biggest city to fall in the Allied hands during the day was KARLSRUHE which was cleared by a French Division.

The General did not leave the CP today but was here nevertheless almost to one o'clock in constant conference with General Kean and General Thorson. The General has been extremely disappointed all day in the progress made by III Corps especially in the important road net area in the north part of our sector and did some very plain speaking over the telephone tonight.

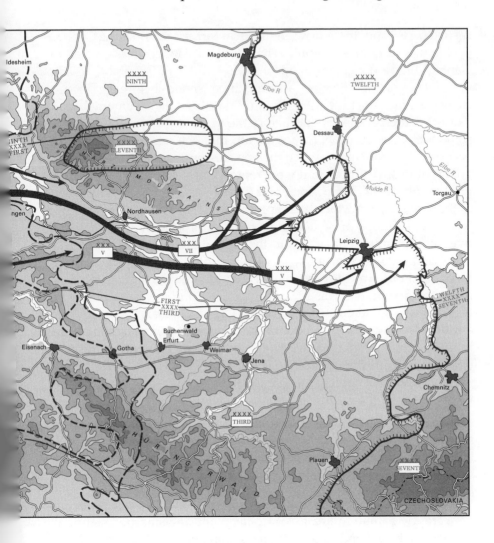

**The Drive to the East and Clearing the Ruhr Pocket,
6–18 April 1945**

Friday, 6 April 1945: Today was the day for the raising of the flag at Fort EHRENBREITSTEIN and the General stayed here in the CP until 12:15 in hopes that the weather would clear, thus permitting him to fly. However, hope vanished at that point and preceded by motorcycle escort and followed by machine-gun jeep we sped down the road with hopes of making the ceremony by three o'clock. We went down the Autobahn so fast that we lost both the motorcycle escort and the radio jeep but proceeded on without them to reach the great fortress overlooking COBLENZ [Koblenz] at a quarter to three. There General Hodges was greeted by General Bradley, General Simpson, General Allen, General Quesada, General Gerow, and later on (arriving three seconds before the ceremony began) by General Patton. Promptly at three the ceremony began. Going up the parade ground before the stand on which the Generals stood were Cos D and N [M] of the 8th Inf—the same companies that occupied EHRENBREITSTEIN when the flag was pulled down in 1923. Also going up in smart formation were representatives of every division in the Twelfth Army Group. The Color Guard was composed of members of the 69th Division which had captured EHRENBREITSTEIN—less than two weeks ago. Troops presented arms to General Bradley who then in a five minute address broadcast to the United States told of the significance of this day to him and to all members of the Allied forces. April 6, he pointed out, was the day on which we entered the war against Germany the first time. It was Army Day as well; and it was peculiarly fitting that we should once more raise the flag on German soil, not only as a tribute to the courage and discipline of our troops, but as a reminder to the German people that we would tolerate no longer their ruthless desire to conquer the world.

Following the speech, the giant American flag—the same one that had flown over the fortress in 1923, was slowly pulled to the top. General Bradley, followed by General Hodges and other General Officers, filed down the ranks to personally shake hands with and congratulate almost all of the soldiers present. One of those in the first row was Sergeant [Junior J.] Spurrier[3] of the 35th Division, the only enlisted man in this theater to wear every medal from the Medal of Honor on down. It was a bitter cold day and the Generals were without overcoats. Below us were the battered remains of Coblenz and the smashed statute of Bismarck which stood so proudly for so long on the Deutscheseck, the point where the Moselle joins the Rhine. The Rhine itself was a graveyard of smashed and broken barge hulls. The Generals did not stay long after the ceremony, and General Hodges left a little before four o'clock being joined by Mr. McCloy,[4] Major General Craig[5] of OPD in Washington, and two others. They are going to spend the night with us and tomorrow go to the front lines.

The General returned home to find fairly good progress made during the day especially in the V Corps where the 69th Division made up to seven miles and the 2nd Division crossed the river. At midnight tonight all except two companies of the 23rd were or the other side and a class 40 Treadway bridge is now under way. Opposition against the 3rd Armd of the VII Corps increased during the day, becoming in spots extremely heavy. The 3rd Armd has not yet crossed the river in any place. The III Corps made moderate gains. The 99th Division being outstanding, reaching FLECKENBURG, four miles from its line of departure. WINGHAUSEN [Wingeshausen], which the Boche elected to defend ferociously the day before, was cleared. In the XVIII sector the 8th Division cleared the barracks in the western outskirts of SIEGEN against stiff resistance, while the 78th advanced up to five miles north of the river over extremely difficult terrain.

Outstanding gains were again recorded to our north by the 2nd Armd Division which expanded their bridgehead east of the WESER to capture HAMELIN and SALZHEM [Hildesheim]. The 8th Armd Division with the 104th Glider Inf Regt [194th Glider Infantry Regiment, 17th Airborne Division] attached crossed the MOHNE River and entered the town of KALLENBERG [Kallenhardt].

Mr. McCloy and his party attended the evening conference; not leaving the General alone to his work until after eleven o'clock.

Saturday, 7 April 1945: General Hodges and his guests arose at 6:30 this morning and left at eight o'clock for CENTURY CP [III Corps]. There the parties split into two; General Hodges proceeding with Fran [Capt. Francis Smith, aide] to the VII Corps, while Bill [Maj. William Sylvan, senior aide] led Mr McCloy and his group on a merry chase to VICTOR [V Corps] and from there to the 69th Division where, satisfying their desire for the smell of powder, they were taken to a battalion CP. During the day, unknown to them, the Assistant Division Commander of the 69th was killed when his jeep ran over a mine.[6]

The General returned after lunch at JAYHAWK [VII Corps]—a two hour drive through the beautiful German countryside—to find good news awaiting him. General Bradley had telephoned during the day to say that we were getting the 5th Infantry and the 13th and 20th Armd Divisions. The 20th Armd, being still in SHAEF reserve, cannot be committed to offensive action but will probably be placed in the rear area as security guard of various bridges and installations. The 5th and 13th, however, can be committed where and when we want and the General, General Kean, and General Thorson were in conference until almost midnight tonight on a plan of action.

Tomorrow the Corps Commanders and the newly arrived Division Commanders will confer with the General here on the steps to be taken.

The 69th Division has now crossed the WESER in strength and the 2nd Bn of the 273rd cleared HANN MUNDEN where highway bridges over the WERRA and FULDA Rivers were captured intact. 2nd Division expanded its bridgehead with the 9th and 23rd Inf to a depth of five miles while a Class 40 Treadway bridge was completed in the vicinity of VAAKE. The 9th Armd Division remained in Corps reserve.

415th Inf of the 104th Division passed through the 2nd Division bridgehead and advancing north behind elements of the 23rd Inf reached BURSFELDA [Bursfelde] where the 1st Bn crossed the river in boats under darkness. 413th Inf will attempt to make a crossing late tonight. The 3rd Armd Division cleared practically all of its sector up to the river against increasingly heavy artillery fire.

The III Corps made better progress during the day in its efforts to reduce the enemy pockets. The 9th Division advanced up to three miles to clear several towns while the 60th Inf on the division's left flank made about four miles. Armored infantry elements of 7th Armd were also employed in the attack. The Boche kept up with their counterattacks, supported by tanks, but all of these were beaten off without loss of ground. Good gains were likewise recorded by the 8th and 78th Divisions while the 97th Division making its initial bow in action crossed the SIEG River with three battalions and advanced up to one mile.

Elements of the Second British Army advancing to the northeast made approximately 25 miles to reach a cross-roads with [within] easy artillery range of HANNOVER. To our immediate north, the 83rd Division crossed the WESER with one regiment, clearing the town of HOLZEN [Holzminden]. The 8th Armd Division cleared SOEST where, according to G-2 estimates, the enemy was reported to be forming up. Elements of the 35th Division and 75th Division were across the LIPPE River and the DORTMUND–EMS Canal and were in the northwest outskirts of DORTMUND late tonight. Further to the west the 79th Division was in the northern suburbs of ESSEN.

The only startling advances made in the Second British Army sector were recorded by the 10th Armd Division which sent one column spinning southeast for a gain of 25 miles towards GRAILSHEIM.

Despite the fact that it was a beautiful day with operations in the air unlimited, IX TAC found practically no targets and some 20 MTs and 12 buildings were attacked and destroyed. That was all.

Mr. McCloy and party changed their plans (not for the first time) and decided to spend the night with us. They will, it is hoped, leave tomorrow morning for Third Army.

Sunday, 8 April 1945: Mr. McCloy and his party finally departed this morning by Cub plane for Third Army and the General was in conference most of the morning with General Van Fleet, General Ridgway, and the Commanders of the two divisions just given us. General Wogen [John B. Wogan][7] of the yet untried 13th Armd Division and General Irwin of the tried and tested 5th Division. General Bradley called this afternoon to inquire whether the First Army would be on the bridgehead line by the night of the 10th. General Hodges assured him that they would be. He admitted to General Kean and General Thorson that he was stretching his optimism a bit but from the present look of things there was a good chance that we could reach that goal. Bearing out his words, both V and VII Corps made good progress in establishing bridgeheads across the WESER and WERA [Werra] Rivers against light resistance. 2nd Division cleared GOTTINGEN, finding no opposition, but 15,000 wounded Boche prisoners in the town. A Class 70 highway bridge over the LEINE River was captured intact. Elements of the 2nd Div continued on four or five miles yesterday to make a total advance of 15 miles during the day. The 9th Armd Division crossed a Class 40 Treadway bridge near HANN MUNDEN and closed in assembly areas about half-way between the WESER and the LEINE Rivers.

In the VII Corps sector the 104th Division advanced up to five miles east of the WESER and completed two bridges. 1st Division likewise established a bridgehead over the river and moved on up to four miles yesterday. 3rd Armd will jump off tomorrow morning across the River.

The pocket continued to shrink yesterday under hard blows delivered by the III and XVIII Corps. The 9th Division which is almost squeezed out advanced up to three miles against moderate resistance and took MESCHEDE. The hardest opposition was given to 7th Armd Division in the center of the III Corps sector but they went on to clear FREDEBURG. 99th Division made up to three and a half miles. 5th Division minus the 11th Inf closed tonight and is now moving forward to assembly areas in rear of the 9th Division through which it will attack tomorrow morning. The 8th Division in General Ridgway's Corps made up to seven miles to clear HEINSBERG.

There was another parachute drop in the British sector and elements of the 4th Canadian Armd Division operating in conjunction with these landings which were made by the 2nd French Airborne Battalion in the area northeast of MEPPEL advanced northwest across three canals to the outskirts of the town. This maneuver lacks only four miles of cutting off completely the German troops in the Netherlands, estimated to consist of some 50,000 combat troops.

To our north, the XIX and XVI Corps continued to advance against stiff resistance through the industrial area of the Ruhr. Dortmund is now half clear and the center of Essen has been reached. The giant Krupp Works[8] have already fallen into our hands.

Monday, 9 April 1945: Bill went to VIII Corps early this morning to pick up General Lear who along with hundreds of others is making the accustomed sightseeing tour of the front. He arrived shortly after one o'clock and the General chatted with him until 2:30. During the meal, General Heubner called to say that he had already reached the bridge-head line established by Twelfth Army Group and that he wished to proceed without further ado. After considerable telephoning this permission was given him by General Hodges. General Heubner's V Corps made startling gains during the day. 69th Division advanced 12 miles to put patrols at Dingelstadt. Contact with elements of Third Army's II [XX] Corps was established at three places. The 2nd Division advanced 12 miles to take Dudderstadt [Duderstadt] while the 9th Armd Division moved on forward to assembly areas near the front lines from which point they will attack tomorrow. In General Collins' Corps 3rd Armd Division advanced to Leine River against moderate to heavy resistance from bazooka and Anti-tank fire. Wehrmacht surrendered easily but the SS were still putting up fanatical resistance. Incomparable Task Force Hogan entered Northeim while the 1st Division continued to expand its bridgeheads over the Weser to capture four towns including a rather large one of Uslar. The III Corps continued west over very rugged terrain to reduce the Rose Pocket.[9] 10th Inf in attacking through the 47th made three and a half miles to capture Kalle [Katle]. Gains up to four to five miles were recorded by the other divisions of the Corps.

During the afternoon Colonel Dickson brought in evidence that armor was concentrating in the vicinity of Olpe, the large town which is reported to be serving as headquarters for Field Marshal Model, and it is rumored that another breakthrough will be attempted by Panzer Lehr reinforced. However, the 8th Division, paying no attention to these rumors, made gains of six miles to capture and clear Olpe by eight o'clock tonight. The Boche armor has disappeared, that is temporarily. The 86th Division assumed control of the sector along the Corps right flank and made new gains up to four miles as it made its initial debut in battle. By ten o'clock tonight 70% of the 13th Armd Division had crossed in the vicinity of the Rhine and during the night elements moved forward to Siegburg from where they will launch their attack up the Autobahn tomorrow morning.

9,712 PWs were taken by the Army today, broken down as follows: V Corps, 2,826; VII Corps, 939; III Corps, 2,356; XVIII Corps, 3,591. The most encouraging fact of these figures is that almost 6,000 of the total came from the pocket itself, and XVI Corps to our north are gathering prisoners in at the rate of over 10,000 a day.

The biggest news from other fronts was that Hanover [Hannover] is now practically encircled as the 84th Division is around it from the north and west and the 5th Armd Division is a few miles south of it. The 84th will move directly into the city tomorrow. Task Force Twaddle consisting of the 8th Armd Division and the 95th Division have now cleared a large part of the Ninth Army portion of the Rose Pocket up to the Ruhr River, while 75th Division cleared Dortmund and the 79th and 17th A/B Divisions kept plugging away through the battered streets of Essen. The 6th Armd Division has now withdrawn its forces from the large sector of our territory it held northeast of Muhlhausen. In general, their forces are regrouping for the attack scheduled to jump off on the 11th.

Tuesday, 10 April 1945: Our armor broke loose again today. The 9th Armd Division led by CCB made advances up to 33 miles against light resistance skirting south of the Hartz [Harz] Mountains. To the north the 3rd Armd Division made gains up to 35 miles and were reported tonight to have patrols in Nordhausen and Herzberg; With Both Corps infantry following up rapidly behind the armor mopping up the scattered resistance which remained. Colonel McDonald's [MacDonald's] 4th Cavalry Group covered the left flank of General Collins' Corps, being especially watchful for any movement coming out of the Hartz area. The III and XVIII Corps continued to slice away at the pocket, making gains up to four miles. The 9th Division is now picked [pinched] out in its zone and will have a few days rest before being again committed possibly with General Collins' Corps. 13th Armd made its initial debut in battle and although it had considerable difficulty with bridging at Siegburg, elements of CCA and CCB crossed the river and made two miles north of Siegburg along the Autobahn. 20th Armd Division closed in the southern part of our Army area and will assume its security duties shortly.

To our north the 2nd Armd Division pushed forward some 20 miles in the direction of Braunschweig. The 84th Div cleared half of Hanover. The 5th Armd Division was 10 miles past Hanover, having cut the Autobahn and captured a bridge across the WESER–ELBE Canal. Advances up to 10 miles were made by the Third Army employing its infantry only while a column of the 11th Armd advanced 13 miles in an attack southeast and cleared COBURG.

The most interesting report of the day was furnished by Twelfth Army Group to the effect that great columns of vehicles had been seen by TAC/R to be entering the "Redoubt" area in the vicinity of Berchtesgaden.[10] Although this has been the fourth successive day of good flying weather, the air results were not impressive. There are not many more Boche targets left. A five group medium-bomber attack on NORDHAUSEN was cancelled in the afternoon because of fear that our troops would be in the town by the time they hit—5:30 in the afternoon.

Wednesday, 11 April 1945: The General's guests today were General Orlando Ward[11] whose 20th Armd Division is now closed in our rear area acting as security guard and patrol. Later in the afternoon, General Lee and General Plank arrived by plane for an hour's conference.

Today's news was excellent. VII Corps advanced to the outskirts of Hartz Mountains while CCB [3rd Armd] cleared NORDHAUSEN where a terrific fight had been expected but did not materialize, and CCR moved on ahead to KLETTENBERG. Tonight General Collins called in a justifiable rage to tell General Kean that his troops had discovered at NORDHAUSEN, the home of the V-1 and V-2 factories, a concentration slave labor camp over the grounds of which were still spread hundreds of bodies of workers who had been literally starved to death. Only some 300 were alive in the camp and in such condition as to make medical care an almost useless thing. III Corps continued west, advancing up to 8 miles in the reduction of the pocket. XVIII and III Corps between them took 9,000 prisoners as resistance everywhere is light and seems about to collapse. To our north XVI Corps made rapid progress in the area north of the Ruhr. ESSEN was cleared; BOCHUM was cleared; and troops were slowly advancing into DORTMUND. 2nd Armd Division in a startling dash reached the outskirts of MAGDEBURG and freed an estimated 40,000 Allied PWs. 5th Armd Div even made a greater gain reaching EHRA, while the 30th Division cleared 1/3 of BRUNSWICK. The XII Corps' 11th Armd Division reached COBURG where the entire town surrendered formally without a fight.

General Hodges is still trying to "nickel out" another infantry division to help General Collins to clear the HARTZ Mountains. The 9th Division is on the way now but this is strictly an infantry job and General Collins wishes to have one more, in which opinion the General concurs.

Thursday, 12 April 1945: General Hodges left by Cub this afternoon for XVIII and III Corps. On landing at the III Corps field which is situated on a side hill, the plane skidded and broke one of the wings. The General was not even shaken up. General Ridgway has drawn a "stop line" beyond which his troops will not advance except on Corps order. By the time this stop line is reached it is hoped that the situation will permit the release of one of the four infantry divisions he is now employing.

Both V and VII Corps continued to strike east in startling fashion and although we are not closest to Berlin of any Allied troops, we are further east than any of the other armored spearheads. The 9th Armd Division advanced 35 miles today and CCR reached WEISSE [Weisse Elster] River, two miles north of ZEITZ. CCA and CCB advanced along the north part of the Corps sector to the SALLE [Saale] River turned south to close in at WEISSENFELS and continued to advance on LEIPZIG from the south. Enemy resistance except in WEISSENFELS which was being mopped up by the 69th Division was generally light. To the north, the 3rd Armd Division made 25 miles while the 104th, following along in its wake, established road blocks on all roads leading north into the Hartz Mountains. The tough job of clearing them was begun by Col McDonalds Cavalry and the 1st Division. III and XVIII Corps continued to reduce the pocket, taking over 12,000 PWs in so doing. Gains up to 10 miles were made by the 8th Division, while other divisions made from four to six miles.

CCA of the 5th Armd Division advanced 54 miles to reach the ELBE, at TANGERMUND [Tangermünde] which is a little more than 50 miles from BERLIN. 2nd Armd Division reached MAGDEBURG while the 83rd Division mopping up in support of it also reached the ELBE at BARBY. To our immediate north the 17th A/B Division finding a bridge intact over the RUHR crossed and were five miles south into our sector. To our south, the 6th Armd and 4th Armd Divisions continued to strike due east. The 4th cleared JENA while other elements reached the 80 north grid after a bridge was constructed over the SALLE River, along the CHEMNITZ Autobahn. There were no great advances recorded by the Seventh US Army except that SCHWEINFURT, home of the ball-bearing industry, was captured after a stiff fight by the 42nd Division.

Our PW count for the day was over 18,000. The Air had one of its best days, claiming over 400 MTs and armored vehicles and the damaging of an additional 400. Boche transport was milling around vigorously in all directions in what remains of the pocket, and there was practically no flak opposition. C-47s continued to speed over MARBURG at the rate of 300 a day to bring the much needed POL [petroleum, oil, and lubricants]. As far as can be determined, we still have sufficient gas to keep rolling, although the amount of gas consumed yesterday by the First Army was almost 1,000,000 gallons.

Friday, 13 April 1945: General Eisenhower and General Bradley drove in this morning from Third Army and one-half [hour] later left on a long tour of the front. General Eisenhower as well as General Hodges and everybody else was greatly grieved by news of the President's death which arrived at our headquarters at one o'clock, and General Eisenhower said that this was probably the worst blow he had received in many a month and just when victory was in sight.

The party went first to XVIII A/B Corps where General Ridgway served them lunch and then to the 86th Division where for some unknown reason General Melasky[12] was absent, consequently the party only stayed there about five minutes to move on over dusty roads which painted everyone a coal black to the 99th Division. There General Eisenhower was photographed by some 200 amateur cameramen all using, as he learned upon query, "liberated equipment." They had planned to go from there to III Corps but so late was their schedule and uncertain their guiding (although General Van Fleet was with the party) that they cut east some 6 miles away from Corps headquarters to visit the trainload of V-2's still guarded in a tunnel some 50 miles southeast of our headquarters. Both General Eisenhower and General Bradley were especially pleased to have a long chat with General Van Fleet whose ability as a soldier they very much admire.

When the party did not return to the headquarters at 7:15 some frantic telephone calls were made to III Corps which also uninformed was awaiting their arrival. Recon patrols were promptly sent out from Corps headquarters but by quarter to eight we had found out that they were on their way direct to us and they pulled in shortly after eight o'clock. General Eisenhower spent the evening at the house talking with his son[13] who three days ago joined the newly established SIAM [Signal Intelligence and Monitoring] Company, while General Hodges and General Bradley went to a large party given by General Quesada who is leaving in a few days to take up new duties in the Pacific, probably with the heavy bombardment section.

Saturday, 14 April 1945: First Army continued to push rapidly on in two directions to become the first army in history to have forces on the ELBE and also on the RHINE. The 2nd Division of V Corps continued to attack to the east towards LEIPZIG against increasing resistance. They cleared the town of MERSEBURG, the last large synthetic oil refinery in Germany, while another group took LEUNA and the 38th Inf crossing the SAALE River moved on northeast.

1st Division continued to attack slowly through the Hartz Mountains, principal opposition coming from road blocks and terrain. The 3rd Armd Division, attacking to the northeast, made excellent progress especially Task Force W, which taking to the back roads, advanced almost 25 miles to within four miles of DESSAU on the ELBE River. 9th Division which is now joining the 1st Division in the Hartz area made up to 6,000 yards without receiving any particular opposition.

The III Corps with its 5th Division advanced up to the RUHR River. The 99th Division made 6,000 yards and the 7th Armd cleared HEMER. The XVIII A/B Corps has now succeeded in splitting what is left of the pocket in two. The 8th Division did the job, advancing due north to make contact with the 75th Division of the XIX Corps at six o'clock tonight.

General Bradley and General Eisenhower left at 9:30 this morning by plane and were going to General Bradley's headquarters. It now seems probable that Third Army will swing to the south down into the "Redoubt" and towards LINZ to make contact with the Russians, although Churchill is extremely anxious for our forces to continue due east to BERLIN. Present plans call for us to hold a bridgehead over the MULDE River but not to advance further except on Group order. Ours will have to be primarily a blocking mission. General Eisenhower it seems feels that quick advance into the Russian sphere of influence will present difficulties not easily solved and that for the present time it is better to push in a southeasterly direction.

Sunday, 15 April 1945: The CP moved late today to the handsome resort town of BAD WILDUNGEN, for whose population our arrival is their first war experience. General Hodges and General Kean stayed on at MARBURG until late in the afternoon arranging details with General Ridgway for a reported surrender of many of the remaining troops in the pocket. Although this surrender did not finally take place, Panzer Lehr, which has given us some of our toughest and most consistent opposition since the original Normandy landings, surrendered to the 395th Inf of the 99th Division tonight. The staff included 3 major generals and between four and five thousand men. Tonight we trust that their good example will be followed by others.

The war continued to move swiftly on in our area. The 9th Armd

Division advancing against moderate resistance which came principally from lowered flak guns reached the MULDE River to the vicinity of COLDITZ and captured two bridges intact. We are particularly anxious to obtain intact a PW camp there as one of the cousins of the King is reported to be imprisoned in that enclosure, as well as other high personalities.[14] CCA and CCB, following CCR, likewise made advances up to 10 to 12 miles while the 69th Division now re-assembled continued mopping up scattered resistance which was by-passed by the armor.

To the north the 3rd Armored Division continued the attack against resistance which was everywhere stiffening. TFW also reached the MULDE River southeast of DESSAU but the Autobahn bridge was destroyed. However, two battalions of armored infantry crossed the river and the bridge was under construction. TFY, advancing to BITTERFELD, found it strongly defended. Contact was established with elements of Ninth Army at 3:30 at a point about four miles northwest of KOTHEN. This contact cuts off from any escape the remaining forces now being engaged by us in the Hartz Mountain area. The 104th Division which is closing in on HELLA [Halle] from both the west and the east was encountering house-to-house fighting. Telephone contact with a German Major General [Generalleutnant Anton Rathke] in command of this area was established through the commercial telephone system in HELLA but the old fool refused to surrender. The 1st and 9th Divisions continued their slow progress through the Hartz Mountains. The General is not particularly satisfied with the progress being made there but very likely the fatigue of both the 1st and 9th Divisions which have had no rest for so long a time has something to do with it.

The III Corps cleared MINDEN with its 5th Division thus reaching the RUHR River along the entire division front. 7th Armd continued its attack to the west and southwest with advances of about four miles being chalked up. 99th Division found resistance tough only in EISERLOHN [Iserlohn].

In the XVIII A/B Corps area the 86th Division advanced 10 miles along the western [bank] of LENN [Lenne] River to its junction with the RUHR River. 78th Division reached the edge of the large industrial town of WUPPERTAL. The 97th Division advanced six miles to BURSCHEID. Our count of PWs for the day was [again] perfectly fabulous, estimated 45,000. It now appears that G-2 was way off key in estimating the 125,000 troops in the pocket. This has already been passed by 50,000.

There were no material changes on the other fronts except in the XIII Corps zone where the 2nd Armd Division was forced back of the

ELBE by a stiff and determined tank-infantry counterattack. They are now going to use the bridgehead, more securely held by the 83rd Division to the south. The British continued to sweep north and northwest reaching the North Sea at three points, clearing ARNHEM, scene of the airborne disaster last Fall, and definitely, once and for all, cutting off the German divisions in HOLLAND, estimated at over 100,000 men.

Among the General's guests tonight was General Milliken [Millikin], former CG of III Corps, who has spent the last month with the 1st and 104th Divisions. It was established tonight that he will take command tomorrow of the 13th Armd Division whose commander General Wogan was injured the day before yesterday by enemy action. Also leaving us and elated over the prospect is Colonel Hains, who will take over one of their Combat Commands. General Hodges had as his dinner guest General [Ralph McT.] Pennell,[15] Commandant of the Field Artillery School. Brigadier General [Benjamin O.] Davis[16] of the IG's [Inspector General's] Office was also here at the headquarters and paid his respects to the General tonight.

Monday, 16 April 1945: General Hodges and General Thorson flew to General Bradley's headquarters this morning where they were joined by General Patton and General Devers. Returning here at 5:30, the General told his story, which is roughly this: In the major regrouping to take place at once, III Corps returns to Third Army and we receive our old favorite General Middleton in return. Fifteenth Army will take over the control and administration of much of our present rear area. The new boundaries which are difficult to trace on the map follow the regular province boundaries of Germany. This was brought about by the obvious importance now being attached to Military Government and to the control of Germany proper once the war is definitely over. We will have thirteen divisions; ten infantry and three armored. We lost the 86th, 99th, 13th Armd, and will lose the 20th Armd, the 5th Division, and the 97th. 7th Armored Division will go into Army Group reserve. We pick up the 87th, 89th, 6th Armd, 76th, and the 29th Division from XIX Corps. These new boundaries and this new set-up will become effective upon agreement of the respective Army Commanders. General Patton must move out his XX Corps, which is on our right flank and move up the VIII Corps prior to our taking over. We must move out of the pocket, once it is definitely cleared, the troops now engaged. This regrouping, probably our last, is the largest we have yet made and General Kean said tonight he intends to take every use of the estimated 600 enemy trucks which have been captured intact today. As hinted at a few days ago, our job will merely be to hold a bridgehead across the MULDE and block for Third Army. We will probably not move into a TAC CP for a few days because of the magnitude of these troop changes and command will not move into GOTTINGEN because of the fact that this now falls into Ninth Army's sector. General Ridgway's Corps will go into Group reserve.

Colonel Dickson tonight is a happy man; he has General Baierlein [Bayerlein] and the latter is being escorted to Bad Wildungen for the Colonel's questioning. This came about when all German units in front of III Corps surrendered. The count of Generals is not yet complete, nor that of the PWs either, but it is estimated that they number over 80,000 and that includes Admiral Scheer,[17] the reason for his existence in the pocket is not yet known. The pocket itself dwindled during the day to a few miles separating our forward troops and the Rhine River. DUSSEL-DORF was in sight. The 7th Armd cleared the III Corps area and the 99th will start leaving the area tomorrow. The 5th Division which will revert to Third Army will stay in its present location. Some few Boche die-hards continue to give sporadic tough resistance to the XVIII Corps and some in front of the III Corps late yesterday refused to pay heed to the surrender orders given by their commanders. We now have definitely, however, the CGs of Panzer Lehr, 116th Panzer, 3rd Panzer Grenadier, 9th Panzer, and the 180th Division.[18]

In our front to the east, CCA of the 9th Armd cleared their objec-tives. They advanced north about 14 miles to the MULDE River opposite WURSEN [Wurzen]. Infantry elements of CCR captured COBLITZ [Cold-itz]. Other elements captured GRIMMA. The 2nd Division advancing due east is now about to tackle LEIPZIG itself. The city is surrounded and cut off but the garrison is apparently preparing to make a last-ditch stand for LEIPZIG, consequently will be in shambles, a week or two from now. The 3rd Armd Division of VII Corps continued mopping up operations along the MULDE River. TFR occupied BERNBURG which was the contact point arranged with Ninth Army. House-to-house fighting continued in HELLA. Slow gains were recorded in the Hartz Mountains.

Tuesday, 17 April 1945: After a morning conference with General Quesada and the latter's guests among which was Dr. Bowls [Edward L. Bowles],[19] Special Aeronautical and Air-Ground Advisor to the Secre-tary of War, the General flew by Cub this afternoon to V and VII Corps. Testimony to the great space which now separates us from the front line was the time of flight—almost an hour and fifteen minutes. General Heubner did not tell General Hodges this, but it was brought out later on, that V Corps is using in its seizure of LEIPZIG exactly the same plan of attack employed by Napoleon in 1813. After they had drawn up the attack and had gone ahead with it, some military student discovered the exact similarity of the plans.

The new directive of ECLIPSE[20] arrived today and it is now confirmed that upon completion of its present mission, or rather the end of the war, First Army headquarters will be immediately withdrawn to NANCY. What comes after that, of course, we do not know, although the General surmises that we may be placed in charge of the NORWAY expedition. Likewise coming from Twelfth Army Group this afternoon was news that we are not getting the 29th Division as had been originally planned.

Tonight over the radio came news that everyone had long been wanting and waiting to hear; General Hodges' nomination for full General went to the Senate. Official confirmation should be forthcoming within a week's time.

News from the military front remained satisfactory. The 9th Armd continued to consolidate its positions all along the MULDE River while the 69th Division advanced north about 8 miles to positions two or three miles due east of LEIPZIG. Meanwhile 2nd Division, attacking the city from the west, reached its outskirts. The VII Corps whose 3rd [Armd] Division was encountering stiff opposition in all the small towns near the river, and especially in AKEN which was partially cleared by tonight, made slow progress. Negotiations for the surrender of HALLE failed early this morning and the 414th Inf resumed the attack. Advances up to 8 miles were made in the Hartz Mountains against dug-in infantry and tanks. III Corps continued to mop up enemy resistance, gathering up PWs, and a tremendous quantity of equipment. XVIII Corps occupied DUSSELDORF not only without opposition but to the sound of actual applause and cheers from the population. PWs taken yesterday—an informal count—numbered almost 50,000. They include so many Generals that we have not yet been able to count them, although Field Marshal Model was conspicuous by his absence.[21]

The only important news from any other front was that three divisions of XV Corps are closing in on NURNBERG and should enter the city tomorrow.

Important news reaching the General tonight was to the effect that VII Corps had come across valuable stored records of the German Foreign Office.

Wednesday, 18 April 1945: The General stayed in the CP all day.

We received the unfortunate word that Colonel Yeomans, former Army Provost Marshal, who had done such an outstanding job as commander of Task Force Y of the 3rd Armd Division was killed in action this morning. At the dinner table tonight just as we were discussing his latest book and writings we received word that Ernie Pyle had been killed by a sniper's bullet.

General Heubner called during the afternoon to say that he was about to conduct negotiations for the surrender of LEIPZIG. General Hodges told him that the only terms were "unconditional." However, word came through in the evening that the gentleman asking for peace was only a minor police official with no authority and consequently the offer was rejected. In the city, however, the 2nd Division cleared its zone of all resistance. 69th Division advancing near the center of the city from the east encountered light resistance except for three strongpoints: The City Hall, the railroad station, and a monument near the center of the town.

The city of HALLE was three-quarters cleared tonight by the 104th Division. The 1st and 9th Divisions continue to cut into the few remaining miles of the Hartz held by the Boche.

The 5th Division passed to [First Army] control and assumed responsibility for the III Corps area as General Van Fleet leaves for Third Army. General Ridgway called early this morning to say that all organized resistance in the RUHR Pocket had stopped. 13th Armd Division moved south, the 8th Division assumed responsibility for the eastern part of the Corps sector, and the 97th the northwestern part. The 86th Division left for Third Army while another RCT of the 78th Division which will take over duties as Army security guard moved into rear areas. First Army's total bag from the pocket is now over 300,000, although G-2 estimates never went higher than 125,000, including all troops and arms. 22,951 PWs were taken today.[22]

Another boundary was crossed this morning by the 90th Division which advanced 8 miles to capture the town of ROSBACH, four miles inside of the Czech border. The other major gain of the day was recorded by the British Guards Armd Division which breaking loose due north, approached within 20 miles of HAMBURG. The 1st Canadian Army pushed on in several spots to reach the English Channel in northern Holland.

Generals Milliken, Moses, [Frank S.] Ross,[23] and Plank arrived this evening for conferences with our G-4 section.

Chapter 9

Final Operations, 19 April–7 May 1945

Consolidation on the Mulde River, 19–24 April 1945

Thursday, 19 April 1945: The headquarters today was filled with representatives of the Ninth and Fifteenth Armies and Twelfth Army Group as negotiations went under way for settlement of the new boundary turn overs. Ninth Army will assume responsibility for the area now held by us on noon of the 22nd, but Fifteenth Army whose motto is "speed" refuses to give any definite date, arguing that they cannot assume responsibility so early. Third Army is anxiously awaiting news that we will take over VIII Corps on the 22nd also, but whether we can establish communications and supply installations by that date remains uncertain. General Middleton called General Kean twice today to say that there were no troops at all in his rear area; that everything had been withdrawn by Third Army and he requested that the shift to First Army control be made as quickly as possible to avoid further mishap.

The news of the day from the military front was that the 69th Division cleared LEIPZIG. 6,000 PWs were taken in the city and it is reported that the Mayor, who wished to surrender the city when we first appeared but was refused authority by the military commander, tonight committed suicide. HALLE was likewise cleared during the day by the 104th Division. The 3rd Armd Division was advancing towards the river attempting to clear a succession of small towns, but progress was slow as fanatical resistance was put up, especially in BOBBAU-STEINFURTH. General Collins has told General Hodges for the last few days that there were appearances of a build-up of strength on the east facing the 3rd Armd and this appears to be conclusive evidence of his suspicions. In the Hartz [Harz] Mountains, QUEDLINBURG and BALLENSTADT [Ballenstedt] were cleared and half a thousand PWs were taken from each town.

26th Inf took the hill on the Ninth and First Army boundary which is 1142 meters high, probably the highest point taken by First Army troops. More than 7500 PWs were taken today out of the Hartz Mts. Tonight a tank of the 4th Cavalry Group fired one round into WARMSTADT [Warnstedt] which resulted in an explosion of unknown nature, which destroyed the town, killed some civilians, and some of our own troops—generally wrecking the place. What the one round hit we do not yet know.

13th Armd started to move to Third Army and 97th will move tomorrow. 78th Division passed to Army control. The total number of PWs taken today was 20,822 with the VII Corps catching the major bag of 9,303.

Friday, 20 April 1945: V Corps sector was generally quiet today with local reliefs taking place but the VII Corps still had a major job on its hands, clearing the small towns west of the MULDE. BITTERFELD was reported about half cleared about midnight tonight. All organized resistance, however, in the Hartz Mts definitely ceased today with General Collins' Corps taking over 16,500 PWs from the woods and small towns. It is expected that the PW count from the Hartz will be more than 50,000 when mopping up operations are complete.

The 8th Division assumed responsibility of the 29th Division area in the XVIII A/B Corps as the latter prepared to leave tomorrow. Both 13th and 20th Armd cleared our area, moving to Third Army.

Saturday, 21 April 1945: General Hodges spent the better part of the day on the telephone trying to obtain instructions from Group as to the procedure to be used in making contact with and greeting our Allies now fast approaching from the east. Although surely SHAEF must have envisioned such a meeting in the near future, they were apparently caught completely off base and the instructions were finally received which consisted of "treat them nicely." Instructions about mutual recognition signals will follow, General Bradley said, if we can get the Russians to agree or to settle on any satisfactory procedure. If necessary, General Bradley added, the small bridgehead which we now have over the MULDE can be pulled back.

Although reports as to actual Russian progress were conflicting, the air picked up several interesting movements today. Generally in our direction, they consisted of motor transports and civilians but since our air craft were in several cases fired at, it is presumed, although not proven, that the approaching columns were those of the Boche trying to get out of the way of the Red Army.

Today the 2nd and 69th Divisions completed relief of the 9th Armd Division which has moved back south of LEIPZIG to reserve and for necessary maintenance. To the north the 104th Division advancing 11 miles cleared its sector up to the MULDE River including the town of BITTERFELD where opposition was heavy. Three Task Forces of the 3rd Armd continued their attack against DESSAU to clear one half of it. The VII Corps kept on in its sweep of the Hartz Mts and out of them today took almost 10,000 PWs. The 5th and 78th Divisions continued their present security mission in the Army area.

Above us to the north the 84th Division and 5th Armd Division attacked due north advancing 12 miles on a 35 mile front. To their south near BRUNSWICK and south of KLOTZE, two apparently independently working groups of Boche with tanks, half-tracks, and plenty of ammunition, are causing trouble. However, the 2nd Armd is after the southern pocket now and has already taken 200 PWs.

Excellent progress is being made by both Third and Seventh Armies in their drive southeast and south. STUTTGART is now almost completely surrounded and one armored column pushed 12 miles south of NURNBERG.

Sunday, 22 April 1945: Although we were hourly expecting news of contact with the [Soviet?] Third Army, no definite word was given to the General today. First Army correspondents have been informed through the General that the first announcement of the Armies meeting will be made in a joint communique to be issued from Washington, London, and Moscow, and that no word will be passed by the censor here until that announcement has been made.

All the sector west of the MULDE River with the exception of the town of EILENBERG has been cleared. There tonight a stiff counterattack by infantry forced a battalion of the 69th to withdraw but the counterattack was stopped by 1900 and by midnight positions were completely restored with 170 PWs taken.

CCA of the 3rd Armd cleared DESSAU late this afternoon and during the night continued to mop up resistance north of the town between the MULDE and ELBE Rivers. General Collins spent the afternoon aloft in a Cub plane trying to spot his Allies and later reported to General Hodges that he had seen artillery, presumably Russian, fall into the German town some six miles east of the ELBE, almost on the boundary between the Ninth and First Armies. At noon today VIII Corps with the 76th, 87th, 89th, and 6th Armd Divisions passed in place to First Army control. The divisions of VIII Corps will continue to maintain their present defensive and patrol positions. The rear area security is now being taken care of by elements of General [Edward W.] Timbertake's[1] Brigade with six gun battalions attached. These gun battalions have not fired a shot at a Boche airplane for two months and it was General Hodges and General Kean's conclusion that they could be well used for this security mission.

Also becoming effective today was the new boundary between the Ninth and the First Army. Elements of the Ninth Army's XIX Corps began relief this morning of the 1st Division and the division will probably be completely re-assembled in our area by midnight tomorrow. Meanwhile, the VII Corps continued to mop up in the Hartz and had a total bag of PWs for the day of 18,000 of which 11,000 were hospital cases. For the fourth successive day our count was over 20,000.

Fifteenth Army whose motto is "speed," was not ready today as originally planned to take over its new area east of the Rhine, and we must therefore with the 8th Division be responsible for that large section of the RUHR until General Gerow's men can make up their minds as to the date of relief.

General Ridgway's Corps is going to assemble within the next few days under General Dempsey, and will be employed at the extreme right flank of 21 Army Group sector. It will consist of the 82nd A/B, the 8th, and the 7th Armd Divisions which is at the present time in our area in SHAEF Reserve. Very likely another infantry division will be added to it.

The day's most startling gains were reported by the French who not only entered STUTTGART but attacking due south captured several bridges intact over the Danube River, reached the west border near Lake Constance, and cut off all Boche between the Black Forest and the Rhine. STUTTGART itself was entered but not cleared. To our north the British Second Army were in the outskirts of BREMEN and dickered with the German Commander there for the surrender of the city. The 12th Armd Division sent a 30 mile spearhead south from DINKLEBUHL [Dinkelsbühl] to reach a point only 60 miles from MUNICH. The entire front in the south seems to have collapsed with startling rapidity.

The 2nd Armd Division cleared the enemy pocket east of BRUNSWICK which has been causing some worry to the General. In so doing, they took almost 3,000 PWs knocked out 21 tanks and over two dozen half-tracks. This, to the General's way of thinking, was a sizeable place and pocket to by-pass and not bother to clean up until it had attempted to break loose.

Monday, 23 April 1945: Our front was generally quiet today as the expected contact with the Russians did not materialize. All organized resistance in EILENBURG ceased and at seven o'clock tonight this was reported to us, but V Corps continued to generally mop up and clear its front and rear areas taking 2,000 PWs. VII Corps reports no enemy resistance remaining west of the MULDE River. The 9th Division continued to sweep the woods in the eastern part of the Hartz Mountains and came up with over 4,000 PWs. Everything is now ready to give the Russians a royal welcome. We have a jeep, similar to that which the General possesses, cigarettes, and a flight bag—these will be presented to the first Russian commander, probably division commander, whom we encounter.

The Third and Seventh Army fronts continued to crumble. 12th Armd Division of XXI Corps crossed the Danube as well as the 10th Armd Division of VI Corps. Troops are on the outskirts of ULM and less than 60 miles from MUNICH. Advance elements of the First French Army reached Lake Constance and another division was within 20 miles of BASLE. Our Allies, the Russians, were fighting in the outskirts of BERLIN.

Tuesday, 24 April 1945: The headquarters moved today to the huge regimental barracks on the outskirts of WEIMAR, celebrated as the home of Goethe. The trip from Bad Wildungen was a distance of 132 miles. The longest single move made by this headquarters in changing CPs. The General's home is the unbelievably handsome and rich modern dwelling owned by Fritz Saukel [Sauckel],[2] Gauletier [Gauleiter][3] of Thuringia. This is unquestionably the finest home we have yet used in Germany and estimates of its cost complete with furnishings run anywhere between one million and two million dollars. There is a swimming pool, a motion picture theater, and an elaborate air raid shelter which is fifty feet under ground, underneath the garden. Saukel, who has been Gauletier [Gauleiter] of this area since the earliest days of the Hitler movement—and "Saukel" [Sauckel] means in German "suckling pig"—was a man high in party circles. Where he got the money for this house is anybody's guess. The library is furnished with magnificent first editions of the best German works, and yet not a page of them had been turned or opened. On the second story alone there are twelve bedrooms and there are no less than four dining rooms in the entire house. With certain exceptions, notably in the field of art—statues and paintings—the house is furnished in the best of modern German-Swedish taste. The house was originally occupied by XX Corps who emptied a good part of Herr Saukel's excellent cellar but left some 100 bottles of real white wine which we will consume without remorse.

Saukel—who had eight children, or as some report, twelve—declared WEIMAR a fortress city twenty-four hours before our troops arrived, but was quick to make his own personal get-away before a shot was fired. Many Germans have reported to the sentry at the gate in the past few days seeking admission for the first time feeling themselves free to find out in what magnificent luxury their local leader lived. General Hodges is having Colonel Dickson for lunch tomorrow and the CIC will go through the house with a fine tooth comb.

The General stayed on at Bad Wildungen until one o'clock to have a talk with General Ridgway who flew in. He then left with Captain Stephenson for both V and VII Corps. There are reportedly a large number of Allied PWs, German soldiers, and German civilians trying to cross the MULDE into our area. General Hodges returned and clearly made it understood that it was his order to accept only the German soldiers and the Allied soldiers, we were going to have nothing to do with taking the thousands of civilians. Four Russian planes were spotted deep over our area today, but as yet there is no reported physical contact with our ground forces.

WEIMAR itself remains the Mecca of all tourists, interested in what General Hodges calls the "peep show," the concentration camp at Buchenwald. The prisoners themselves, some of whom can be seen walking through the towns in striped convict garb, call Buchenwald the recreation center; actually believing that in comparison with others run in Germany the conditions were far better. There have been reported some 100 cases of typhus and numerous cases of tuberculosis in the camp but these are being carefully segregated and looked after by our doctors and medical department. There is some possibility of saving a few of the estimated 1,000 people dying from malnutrition; how many, of course, we do not yet know. Until the prisoners are properly screened, very few are being let out. WEIMAR also is full of German soldiers in uniform; those of the Medical Corps who under General Rogers' supervision are taking care of the thousands of German wounded here in the city.

Tonight orders were received to withdraw all our units west of the MULDE and to keep only light patrols on the other side to make contact with the Russians. This order means the withdrawal of some 15 miles by the 6th Armd and 76th Division who will draw up west of the railroad line leading from CHEMNITZ to ROSSELITZ [Rochlitz].

Despite the fact that there was very little action or fighting on the front today, practically none, V and VIII Corps took a total of over 4,000

PWs. The 1st Division, its job in the Hartz finally done, closed for a rest in assembly areas in the rear. The 3rd Armd will also move to the rear upon relief by the 9th Division.

Contact with the Russian Army and the End of the War in Europe, 25 April–7 May 1945

Wednesday, 25 April 1945: The big news of the day was the definitely confirmed contact made at two points this afternoon with members of the Russian forces. The I & R [Intelligence and Reconnaissance] Platoons of the 271st Infantry, 69th Division patrolling far to the east to REISA [Riesa] from the ELBE made contact at 3:30 with elements of the 15th Russian Division. Elements of the 273rd Inf made contact with the 173rd Regiment of the 58th Guards Russian Division at Torgau. During the day 10,000 Germans knowing the situation lost and as usual expecting better treatment from us than from our Allies, came across into V Corps zone to surrender. An estimated 3,000 also came in to General Collins' zone and 3,000 more are expected. VIII Corps also took well over a thousand. Tomorrow formal meetings between regimental commanders will be held and General Reinhart [Reinhardt], CG of the 69th Division, will meet the CG of the 58th Division at Torgau at four o'clock. The news will probably be announced to the world in a United Nations communique early tomorrow.

Although we thought we were going to have a rest, it happens that a new mission may be given us after all—that of protecting the left flank of the Third Army which continues to race into BAVARIA against extremely sporadic opposition. The three points General Bradley gave General Hodges today on the map were COBURG, AMBERG, and REGEN. A line joining these three points will be our right boundary. Our left would be the Czech-German frontier, which we would patrol and guard. Just when this mission will be definitely given to us and in what form, we do not yet know for sure.

General Hodges visited General Middleton at VIII Corps this afternoon. Apparently their main problem is taking care of thousands of displaced persons so they can have some control over those that are wandering around the area and not yet have been channeled into proper camps. The French Government, however, reported to First Army a few days ago that over half of the French soldiers that expected to return from captivity were already back on French soil, which is an amazing and extremely pleasant piece of news to learn.

Thursday, 26 April 1945: The Russian Contact: At 1640 on the 25th of April, a patrol consisting of one First Lieutenant and three men of the I and R platoon of the 273rd Infantry Regiment, 69th Division, contacted elements of the 173rd Regiment of the 58th Guards Division (Russian) at Torgau. This division is a part of the 34th Russian Corps, Fifth Russian Army. This Corps has the 118th Division on the right (north of the 58th Guard Division) and the 15th Russian Division on the left (south) All three divisions are reported in fair strength along the ELBE River. It was reported that they have orders not to cross the ELBE River. After contact was made three Russian officers headed by Major Lexionou went to the CP of the 273rd Infantry Regiment and later to the CP of the 69th Division. Arrangements were made for a meeting of the Regimental Commanders of the 273rd Regiment and the 173rd Russian Regiment at Torgau at 1000, 26 April. The Division Commanders of the 69th Division and the 58th Russian Division will meet at Torgau at 1600. At this meeting arrangements will be made for General Heubner [Huebner] to meet the Corps Commander of the 34th Russian Corps, Major General [G. V.] Baklanov,[4] sometime on the 27th of April. The 272nd RCT is sweeping the road running between Eilenburg and Torgau. This regiment will remain in position while all visits are being made. A bridge over the MULDE has been constructed in the vicinity of Eilenburg to take Class 40 traffic. The 271st and 273rd Infantry will continue to patrol to their front east of the Mulde River to assist 272nd in protecting the route between Eilenburg and Torgau.

The above paragraph was today's biggest piece of news. Captain Hutton-Williams of our Phantom Section[5] who went along with the party reported that throughout the contact was extremely friendly but that military information was difficult to obtain because of the "language difficulties and the general merriment," leading us to believe that the Russians had not been slow in pulling out the bottles of Vodka.

Aside from this news and the addition to our PW total of 7200 taken by V Corps and 9,200 taken by VII Corps, our front was quiet. To our south the Third and Seventh Armies continued their sweeping gains. 97th Division of Third Army's XII Corps captured the large Czech town of EGER, while the 71st and 65th Divisions of XX Corps cleared REGENSBURG and advanced 10 miles south. Gains up to 10 miles were recorded by all three Corps of the Seventh US Army.

Friday, 27 April 1945: The latest visitors to BUCHENWALD were Generals Doolittle, Sterling [unidentified], and Air Marshal Bottomley,[6] who paid a brief call on the General, coming in before visiting the camp. The

General had as his luncheon guest today Emil Ludwig,[7] the noted German biographer and writer. Following lunch, General Collins flew in from Monarch [VIII Corps] and General Hodges personally pinned on him the three stars which came to him today. General Hodges did not wear the four stars until the evening meal when he put on his new jacket.

This evening General Heubner called to give an account of his meeting with the Russians which was extremely friendly—flowers, drinks, music, girls, in all, it was quite a party. The traditional Russian silence, however, of giving us any piece of military information still exists. General Heubner seeing a tank of a size and gun power not matched at present by our equipment, asked his host the weight of the tank. Without a moment's hesitation the Russian said, "We have bridges that will hold it." Later in the evening General Bradley called to give fuller details of V Corps' new mission which is to protect the left flank of the Third Army. This plan entails simply an extension of First Army's already broad front. 1st Division will move south of VIII Corps while the 2nd Division will swing even further south.

The VII Corps took almost 14,000 PWs today and contact has been established with the Russians by the 104th Division near PRETZOCH [Pretzsch]. General Allen will go out to meet the CG of the 118th Division today and General Collins will meet the Russian Corps Commander also, neither of the meeting places has yet been determined. Third Army's 11th Armd Division consolidated its positions across the Austrian border while the 26th Division mopped up behind. The 99th Division advanced within three miles of NEUSTADT. Seventh Army advanced generally up to 15 miles with the 12th Armd Division approaching LANDSBURG. Enemy resistance along the Seventh Army front appeared to be generally collapsing.

Saturday, 28 April 1945: The General this morning attended the ceremony at this headquarters in which General Craig, General Burks [Birks], General Groh [Robert W. Grow],[8] and numerous section chiefs of this headquarters were decorated by General Koeltz of the French Army. The members of the party were guests of the General at lunch today. The General's guests this evening were General Bonesteel, General Hughes, and General Parker. The parade of guests continues without cessation. During the afternoon the General inspected a collection of HOHENZOLLERN Dynasty [crown jewels] including the scepter and orb which were found in a salt mine not far from here by a First Army Ordnance unit. The whole collection is being sent to a vault in Frankfurt for safe-keeping until final disposition is decided upon.

Elements of VIII Corps maintained present defensive positions while the 1st Division was in the process of relieving the 97th Division of Third Army. They have already assumed responsibility for the left and middle portions of the division sector. The 2nd and 69th Divisions were detached from V Corps zone. The 9th Armd Division remains assembled under V Corps until midnight tonight at which time it will pass to Army control. The total Army PW count today was 10,000. Astounding gains were recorded by XXI, XVI [VI] Corps of Seventh Army. The XXI Corps's 3rd Division moved approximately 20 miles southeast to capture AUGSBURG, practically without firing a shot, CCA & CCB of VI Corps 10th Armd Division moved 25 miles and 40 miles respectively, to put them south of LANDSBURG. The First French Army continued to advance southeast along the southwest border.

Sunday, 29 April 1945: The General spent the entire day in the office arranging final details for the meeting with the Russians which will take place tomorrow near TORGAU.

At noon today the new temporary boundary between the First and Third Armies became effective as the 1st Division completed relief of the 97th Division. V Corps continued to move to the new area on the right of VIII Corps. In the VII Corps the 3rd Armd Division took over occupation of the former V Corps rear area and the 9th Armd Division was attached to VII Corps when they took over the V Corps sector at six o'clock. Despite any lack of offensive move on our part, the PWs continue to roll in today to the tune of 4,000. The Seventh Army continued to chalk up spectacular gains and there are reports tonight that the 3rd Division has occupied MUNICH in collaboration with the 45th Division which was approaching the city from the northwest. The 10th Armd Division captured OBER AMMERGAU [Oberammergau], famed center of the celebrated German Passion Play.

It becomes increasingly apparent tonight that the National Redoubt will be quickly overrun, so swift is the pace of our advance against negligible opposition.

Monday, 30 April 1945: The General accompanied by General Kean, General Hart, Major Sylvan, Captain Smith, and four interpreters, together with General Sterling, and Colonel Myers of IX TAC left in a C-47 today at 10:40 with an escort of six P-38s to meet the Russians. They were escorted all the way and landed at Brandis where they were met by General Reinhardt, CG of 69th Division, who accompanied the party in jeeps to Eilenburg. From there the convoy, accompanied by a careful screen, moved across "no man's land" to Torgau. There they were met, at the river's edge, by a 34 year old Russian Major General, a Corps Commander, who promptly put General Hodges in his car, a captured black German sedan, and without further adieu, whisked him across the bridge over which flew a banner welcoming "Our Victorious Allies." The rest of the party followed as the Corps Commander's car sped at 50 miles per hour down the road passing Russian women MPs and Red Army soldiers standing rigidly at attention. Four miles down the road they turned off into a beautiful estate which had apparently been especially commandeered and prepared for the ceremony. Waiting for General Hodges at the chateau was General Jardov [Colonel-General A. S. Zhadov],[9] CG of the 5th Russian Guards Army, a fifty year old, heavy set, handsome man. After the National Anthems were played, the party went upstairs to a small room where wine was served and introductions were made. Following this the entire party retired to the dining room where the festivities started—vodka, cognac, huge loaves of black Russian bread, whole roasted pigs, geese, caviar, a clear broth with a whole fish floating in it—considered by the Russians as a delicacy—and the whole spirit of the occasion was one of complete joviality and freedom of action—with back-patting, smiles and great exuberation. The toasts were many to Truman, to Stalin, to Roosevelt, to the Red Army, to the American Army. There were "bottoms up." General Hodges' toast to the Marshal of the Red Army was as follows: "I am greatly honored to be here with you on this historic occasion which marks the meeting of our two Allied Armies on the Elbe. We have long looked forward to this meeting as we watched the rapid succession of victories of your brave Soviet soldiers. We have the greatest admiration for their gallantry, their courage, and their stout fighting hearts. You have swept across Germany with the speed and power of an avalanche to cross the Oder and deliver the blow which has brought our enemy staggering to his knees. I know your great leader Marshal Stalin is proud of the prowess of his Armies. His pride and confidence in them has been more than justified by the greatest series of decisive victories in the annals of military history. I am sure that he has reason to be particularly proud of you of the mighty Fifth Guards Army. We of America will long remember what you and your gallant commander have accomplished." The many other toasts that followed could be expected, and as usual the Russians did their best to outdo the Americans in drinking and succeeded in doing so. Correspondents were flat on the floor before the ceremony had broken up at 4:30. General Hodges presented two gifts to the Russians consisting of the First Army Standard and a jeep especially constructed similar to that of General Hodges with plexi-glass windows and square bumpers, which gifts he presented with these words: "This standard has been carried by the First Army from our home station in the United States, across the Atlantic to England. Then across the Normandy beaches, across France, Belgium, and into the heart of Germany to our meeting point here on the Elbe. I wish to present this standard to you, sir, in the name of the officers and men of the First U. S. Army as a token of respect, esteem, and admiration for you and your magnificent Fifth Guards Army. Outside I have an American quarter-ton or jeep which I take pleasure in presenting to you personally as a memento of this occasion. I hope that it may be of service to you in covering difficult roads and perhaps afford you pleasure in sport when peace returns." The Russians presented the General with a marble plaque to which are attached various attractively designed and cut shell cases which can be used for Vodka drinking. The second was the large commemorative medal struck off by the Russian Government when they officially designated General Jardov's [Zhadov] Army as the Fifth Guards Army. At 4:30, with everyone friendly disposed toward everyone else, the party took off, back by jeep and then by plane for Master headquarters.

The V Corps became operational in its new zone at 11:30 at which time the 1st and 99th Divisions were attached and the new permanent boundary between the First and Third Armies became effective. There was no particular news from either VII or VIII Corps. The XVIII A/B Corps which will soon become operational under the British cleared the First Army area today with both the 8th and 7th Armd Divisions.

Tuesday, 1 May 1945: General Bradley came for lunch today and the news which had been suspected but not definitely established became generally known: First Army was going to clear the European theater shortly and has been accepted by General MacArthur[10] for action in the near future in the Pacific theater. This news, although it is a matter of pride to most members of First Army, strikes in very few a particularly enthusiastic or responsive chord. However, if furloughs and leaves in the United States are possible, the new decision to move to another theater will be accepted by most with enthusiasm. General Hodges is naturally pleased at the news, as is General Kean. General Hodges' old friend, General John Leonard, was also a guest at luncheon today. In the afternoon General Hodges made a recording of a speech which will be re-broadcast whenever V-E Day [Victory in Europe] is officially announced by General Eisenhower.

Today we had the great news that the Arch-enemy of all civilization, the man against whom we have been personally fighting for over three and one-half years, is dead. The German radio announced that Hitler had died "at the front" in Berlin. There are not a few who regard this announcement with considerable suspicion, believing that far more likely, that he with a few of his trusted henchmen, has taken off a-foot to less warmer places than Berlin, which now is almost completely cleared by the Russians.

V Corps generally reported a quiet day with the 97th Division moving out some 10,000 yards against light to no resistance. The same was reported by VIII Corps. VII Corps maintained patrolling in the area east of the Mulde River and maintained its contact with Russian forces. Only 2800 PWs were taken today, an all-time low count for the last month.

Third Army's XII Corps crossed all along the border of Czechoslovakia and Austria and pushed several spearheads for a distance of five miles into both countries. The 13th Armd Division gaining up to 45 miles reach Braunau, the Austrian frontier town in which Hitler was born. Equally broad penetrations were recorded by the III Corps' 14th Armd and 86th Divisions. The Seventh Army pushed its 3rd Division fifteen miles beyond the city of Munich in the direction of the Italian border.

Wednesday, 2 May 1945: General Kean left today for a conference with the Russians regarding the transfer of displaced persons and liberated Russian PWs. For some reason—the most charitable and reasonable explanation is that the local commanders require orders from Moscow before they can proceed—the Russians do not appear to be either interested or anxious to facilitate the return of these many thousands of people, and likewise have not been too co-operative as yet in the return of the many American PWs liberated by their advance. However, with patience on our side, the problem will work itself out, without too much difficulty.

General Hodges held an informal briefing for the press tonight. He reviewed the whole campaign from the original Remagen bridgehead on to the present time, and told the correspondents frankly that he considered First Army's mission was now finished, that our front line positions were only defensive in nature and would remain so. The correspondents were particularly interested for two reasons: 1–some of them, at least twenty, wished to follow us wherever we go, and, 2–those unable to do so, wished to be transferred or re-assigned to more active fronts. Without giving away any secrets, the General said that he thought covering the First Army front would not be very productive, in the weeks to come.

36th Division today captured First Army's greatest opponent, General Von Runstedt [Rundstedt], who was found at a castle in Bad Tols [Tolz] with his wife and son, also an army officer. The General was in good health and unusually talkative. The biggest news of the day, however, was from Italy where the unconditional surrender of all enemy units in both North Italy and Western Austria were reported last night on the radio. This report is now confirmed and the Seventh Army has almost completed its mission since they are now in the western part of Austria itself. Tremendous gains were also made by the Second British Army which almost cut off the Danish peninsula by advancing 20 miles to reach LUBECK. It appears that this front would likewise collapse shortly as in the Ninth Army sector the German V-2 Division surrendered with 10,000 men and 1,500 vehicles.

Thursday, 3 May 1945: All leaves, passes, and furloughs as far as Officers and enlisted men of First Army were concerned were cancelled at noon today. It has now been learned that General Hodges had presented to General Eisenhower his very strong hope and plea that First Army personnel be given some rest and relaxation, preferably for thirty days in the United States, before they undertake their next mission. The cancellation of these leaves is interpreted naturally as a sign of early departure from Germany, probably to some staging area in France, or to an immediate port where transportation may be ready.

General Middleton was the guest of the General for lunch today and Colonel "Buck" Lanham one of the General's oldest and best friends dropped in for a few minutes upon his return from a Riviera rest.

In the Second British Army sector HAMBURG surrendered today and was occupied by the 7th Armd Division. In the eastern part of the Army sector, the 82nd A/B Div contacted the Russians at GRABOW thus splitting the northern sector in two. The XIII Corps of the Ninth Army captured 15,000 PWs including five generals and contact with the Russians was being maintained at two points, north and east of WITTENBERG. XIX Corps also were maintaining contact with the Russians on the southern edge of their sector. The Third Army's XII Corps advanced to within seven miles of LINZ over 30 miles inside of the Austrian border. The 71st and 65th Divisions advanced up to 10 miles on a 30 mile front to occupy the remainder of the Austrian frontier from PASAU [Passau] to ERING [Aigen]. 20th Armd Div and 42nd Division of Seventh Army made 25 miles in the area east of MUNICH while the 10th Armd Division approached INNSBRUCK.

Friday, 4 May 1945: General Hodges accompanied by G-1, G-3, G-4, and G-5 flew to Bad Wildungen today for a long conference with General Bradley and staff concerning departure from this theater by First Army. He brought back with him a copy of a telegram sent by General Marshall to General Eisenhower which read as follows: "Comments your SW-20360 are appreciated. Please release the Headquarters and Headquarters Company First Army for sailing to this country as soon as practicable and let us know when it will be ready and estimated strength at which it will move. It may be moved without screening and with sufficient overage of low-score personnel who are trained and experienced in work now done by corresponding high-score individuals to replace the latter after arrival here. The announcement of the arrival in this country soon after cessation of hostilities in Europe of a battle-tried United States Army headquarters en route to the Pacific will have a profound effect on the Japanese."

In the evening a full staff meeting was held at which time all Section Chiefs were informed of the new development and told that they could inform their personnel.

V Corps passed to operational control of Third Army at 7:30 tonight.

The XVIII A/B Corps of the Second British Army reported that PWs were coming in such large numbers that it was impossible to count them. The Corps were making all effort to prevent the enemy troops and civilians from moving westward into our lines. The front there has completely collapsed. In the south the 11th Armd Div captured LINZ while further to the south the 103rd Div neared and cleared INNSBRUCK and advanced on to make contacts with elements of the 88th Division, II Corps, Fifth Army at VIPITEN about seven miles south of the Brenner Pass on the Italian border.

Saturday, 5 May 1945: General Hodges had as his guest tonight Under-Secretary of War Patterson and staff. All German forces in Holland, Denmark, and northwest Germany surrendered to Twenty-One Army Group at eight o'clock this morning, while the Nineteenth German Army and Army Group G surrendered effective six o'clock tonight and noon tomorrow, respectively. Army Group G controls the enemy in the area from INNSBRUCK east and northeast to LEIPZIG thus left fighting the Allies are Army Group S which is fighting on the Russian front and the forces in Norway.

It now appears certain that we will move from WEIMAR on the 15th. General Kean and other representatives will fly to PARIS on next Tuesday to find out details of the movement, the port to which we shall go, and how we shall be redistributed in the states prior to re-assembling.

Sunday, 6 May 1945: The VII and VIII Corps passed to the operational control of Ninth Army at six o'clock today. Assignment and attachment of these units under Ninth Army and complete control of the area now occupied by these Corps will not be effective, however, until six o'clock on the 11th. Tactical control of the Corps is now under General Simpson but we still have supply and administrative problems for the next four days. However, for the second time since we landed on the beaches, the General felt free enough of problems and worries to stay at the house during the evening and to witness an extremely amusing show, "Bring On The Girls."

The General spent the day at the dentist, writing letters in answer to the many congratulatory telegrams and notes which came to him upon his elevation to Full General and in staff conferences relative to our impending move. Exactly who will go on the two C-54s which they are setting up for transport to the United States is not yet known.

Monday, 7 May 1945: General Hodges said this morning at breakfast that General Bradley had called him at five o'clock in the morning to announce that a representative of the German High Command had signed the unconditional surrender of all German land, air, and sea forces in Europe to the Allied Expeditionary Force and simultaneously to the Soviet High Command at 0410 hours Central European Time May 7th under which terms all forces will cease active operations at 0001B [local time] hours 9th of May. In a telegram received at this headquarters shortly afterward General Eisenhower ordered that effective at once all offensive operations by our troops would cease and that present positions would be maintained. He added that because of difficulty with communications there might be some delay in the orders reaching all German troops so that full defensive precautions would necessarily be taken.

Apparently through some error the Associated Press was allowed to release this story and transmission of it was made to the United States, before the three governments could make their simultaneous declaration. Although there was no confirmation therefor coming from President Truman, Churchill, or Stalin, New York and all cities in the United States went crazy mad as expected. Official declarations on the Armistice should be forthcoming tomorrow.

General Hodges left after a session with the dentist to visit and say good-by to General Middleton and General Heubner. Tomorrow he will go to see General Collins. For the second night running the General stayed home throughout the evening, this time to see "Christmas in Connecticut."

URGENT
070410B May 45

FROM: SHAEF FORWARD
SIGNED: EISENHOWER

REPRESENTATIVE OF THE GERMAN HIGH COMMAND SIGNED THE UNCONDITIONAL SURRENDER OF ALL GERMAN LAND, SEA, AND AIR FORCES IN EUROPE TO THE ALLIED EXPEDITIONARY FORCE AND SIMULTANEOUSLY TO THE SOVIET HIGH COMMAND AT 0141 HOURS CENTRAL EUROPEAN TIME, 7 MAY UNDER WHICH ALL FORCES WILL CEASE ACTIVE OPERATIONS AT 0001B HOURS 9 MAY.

EFFECTIVE IMMEDIATELY ALL OFFENSIVE OPERATIONS BY ALLIED EXPEDITIONARY FORCE WILL CEASE AND TROOPS WIIL REMAIN IN PRESENT POSITIONS. MOVES INVOLVED IN OCCUPATIONAL DUTIES WILL CONTINUE. DUE TO DIFFICULTIES OF COMMUNICATION THERE MAY BE SOME DELAY IN SIMILAR ORDERS REACHING ENEMY TROOPS SO FULL DEFENSIVE PRECAUTIONS WILL BE TAKEN.

ALL INFORMED DOWN TO AND INCLUDING DIVISIONS, TACTICAL AIR COMMANDS AND GROUPS, BASE SECTIONS, AND EQUIVALENT. NO RELEASE WILL BE MADE TO THE PRESS PENDING AN ANNOUNCEMENT BY THE HEADS OF THE THREE GOVERNMENTS.

Appendix

Locations of First U.S. Army Command Posts, 9 June 1944–14 May 1945

Locations of the Command Echelon

France

Grandcamp-les-Bains	9 June–2 July 1944
Haute Chemin, near Vouilly	2 July–2 August 1944
Canisy	2–12 August 1944
Coulouvray, Boisbenstre	12–23 August 1944
Haleine	23–27 August 1944
Blevy	27 August–2 September 1944
Versailles	2–6 September 1944
Villequier-Aumont	6–10 September 1944

Belgium

Ham-sur-Heure	10–14 September 1944
Château de la Sarte, near Huy	14–19 September 1944
Château de Maison-Bois, Fays, near Verviers	19 September–25 October 1944
Hotel Britannique, Spa	26 October–18 December 1944
Chaudfontaine	18–22 December 1944
Tongeren	22 December 1944–18 January 1945
Hotel Britannique, Spa	18 January–9 March 1945

Germany

Düren	9–16 March 1945
Euskirchen	16–30 March 1945
Bad Godesberg	30 March–5 April 1945

Marburg	5–15 April 1945
Bad Wildungen	15–24 April 1945
Weimar	24 April–14 May 1945*

*Thereafter en route to the United States

Locations of Tactical Echelon

France

Sept Frères	4–14 August 1944
Le Teilleul	14–15 August 1944
Domfront	15–21 August 1944
Château de Chantepie, Couterne	21–23 August 1944
Maillebois, near Blevy	23–27 August 1944
Auffargis, near Rambouillet	27 August–1 September 1944
Senlis	1–4 September 1944
Villequier-Aumont, near Chauny	4–8 September 1944

Belgium

Ham-sur-Heure	8–11 September 1944
Château de la Sarte, near Huy	11–17 September 1944
Château de Maison-Bois, Fays, near Verviers	17 September–26 October 1944
Hotel Britannique, Spa	26 October–18 December 1944
Chaudfontaine (with Command Echelon)	18–22 December 1944
Tongeren (with Command Echelon)	22 December 1944–15 January 1945
Hotel Britannique, Spa (with Command Echelon)	18 January–3 March 1945

Germany

Stolberg	3–9 March 1945
Düren (with Command Echelon)	9–16 March 1945
Euskirchen (with Command Echelon)	16–30 March 1945
Freilingen	30 March–1 April 1945
Marburg (joined by Command Echelon)	1–15 April 1945

Sources: U. S. Congress, Senate, Col. Elbridge Colby, The First Army in Europe, 1943–1945, Senate Document No. 91-25, 91st Congress, 1st Session, 189; Hogan, *A Command Post at War,* 302–3.

Notes

Courtney Hicks Hodges: A Biographical Sketch

1. Omar N. Bradley, *A Soldier's Story* (New York: Henry Holt, 1951), 226.

1. The Invasion of France and the Lodgment in Normandy, 2 June–24 July 1944

1. Maj. William C. Sylvan was Courtney Hodges's senior aide de camp and one of the primary compilers of this First U.S. Army war diary along with Capt. (later Maj.) Francis G. Smith Jr. and Capt. William E. Smith, Hodges's third aide during the war in Europe.

2. Exercise Brass Hat was the First Army's code name for its final command post exercise prior to the execution of Operation Neptune, the amphibious assault phase of Operation Overlord, the Allied invasion of France. It included the movement and reestablishment of the First Army's command post and communications network to its staging location before it loaded and moved to France. See David W. Hogan Jr., *A Command Post at War: First Army Headquarters in Europe, 1943–1945* (Washington, DC: U.S. Army Center of Military History, 2000), 66.

3. The USS *Achernar* was the headquarters or First Army command ship for the invasion. The *Achernar* (AKA-53) was an attack cargo ship of the Andromeda class (AKA-15) launched on 3 December 1943 and commissioned on 31 January 1944. U.S. Naval Historical Division, *American Naval Fighting Ships*, vol. 1 (Washington, DC: U.S. Government Printing Office, 1959), 7; vol. 4, 1969.

4. Jonas Howard Ingram (15 October 1886–10 September 1952). U.S. Naval Academy, 1907. Ingram was commander of the South Atlantic Force from February 1942 to November 1944, when he was promoted to admiral and assumed command of the Atlantic Fleet, a position he retained until his retirement in April 1947. See Mark M. Boatner III, *The Biographical Dictionary of World War II* (Novato, CA: Presidio Press, 1996), 250.

5. Alan G. Kirk (30 October 1888–15 October 1963). U.S. Naval Academy, 1909. Kirk was the naval attaché in London from June 1939 to March 1941 and

then director of naval intelligence in Washington from March to November 1941, when he took command of a destroyer division operating in the North Atlantic and was promoted to rear admiral. In March 1942 he went to London as chief of staff to Adm. Harold R. Stark, commander of U.S. naval forces in Europe. In February 1943 he took over as commander, Amphibious Forces, Atlantic Fleet, and commanded the Central Task Force for Operation Husky, the invasion of Sicily, in July. In February 1944, Kirk became commander of Task Force 122, the Western Naval Task Force, which was responsible for the naval support of the American landings at Omaha and Utah beaches on 6 June 1944. Kirk retired as a full admiral in February 1946. He later served as U.S. ambassador to Belgium and Luxembourg (1946–1949), Moscow (1949–1951), and the Republic of China (Taiwan) (1962–1963). See Boatner, *Biographical Dictionary*, 280.

6. Roger Lowell Putnam (19 December 1893–24 November 1972). Harvard University, 1915. Putnam served in the U.S. Navy during World War I on board the battleship USS *Mississippi* under then Cdr. Alan G. Kirk. He worked for the Package Machinery Company in Springfield, Massachusetts, as vice president and president from 1921 to 1942. He was elected mayor of Springfield in 1937, 1939, and 1941. At the personal request of Kirk, then a rear admiral, he reentered the U.S. Navy in January 1943 as a lieutenant commander to work with Kirk on special projects associated with the invasion of France and was soon sent to England with him. With Putnam's work largely accomplished after the successful invasion, at President Roosevelt's personal request Kirk released Putnam from active duty to assume a position with the Office of Contract Settlement. Putnam returned to Springfield in 1945 and became deeply involved in his company and local business and civic activities. He later served as the director, Economic Stabilization Administration, under President Truman in 1951–1952. As a member of the Lowell family, he was a trustee of the Lowell Observatory (1927–1967). See William Lowell Putnam, *A Yankee Image: The Life and Times of Roger Lowell Putnam* (West Kennebunk, ME: Phoenix Publishing for the Lowell Observatory, 1991).

7. Oren Root Jr. (13 June 1911–14 January 1995). Princeton, AB, 1933; University of Virginia, LL.B., 1936. Lawyer. Root was a lawyer and principal with various New York City law firms from 1938 to 1995. He was chairman of the Association of Willkie Clubs of America in 1940 that supported Wendell Willkie in the 1940 presidential campaign. He served in the U.S. Naval Reserve as a lieutenant commander on the commander's staff of the Fourth Fleet and then Kirk's Task Force 122 during the Normandy landings. See *Who Was Who in America with World Notables* (hereafter *World Notables*), vol. 9 (1993–1996) (New Providence, NJ: Marquis Who's Who, 1996), 236.

8. First Army's headquarters staff was composed of Omar Bradley, commanding general, Hodges as deputy commanding general, two deputy chiefs of staff (one for administration and one for operations), and the four assistant

chiefs of staff (ACSs) or general staff positions, and the subordinate special staff officers and section chiefs. The ACSs, or the four Gs, as they were called, were ACS G-1 (Personnel), ACS G-2 (Intelligence), ACS G-3 (Operations), and ACS G-4 (Supply), normally called G-1, G-2, G-3, and G-4. At the time of the Normandy landings, the First Army's four Gs were Col. Joseph J. O'Hare, G-1; Col. Benjamin A. Dickson, G-2; Col. Truman C. Thorson, G-3; and Col. Robert W. Wilson, G-4. The chief of staff was Maj. Gen. William B. Kean, and the two deputy chiefs of staff were Colonels Charles F. Williams (administration) and Samuel L. Myers (operations). See First U.S. Army, *Report of Operations, 20 October 1943–1 August 1944,* 1:15–16; Hogan, *Command Post at War,* 21–35.

9. Charles Christian Wertenbaker (11 February 1901–8 January 1995). Correspondent and author. Wertenbaker was *Time* magazine's war editor from 1941 to 1943, at which time he became its chief military correspondent and later the Paris bureau chief (1944–1945). He wrote a book titled *Invasion!* (New York: D. Appleton-Century, 1944), which described his experiences during the Normandy invasion and ensuing operations. See *Who Was Who in America,* vol. 3 (1951–1960) (Chicago: A. N. Marquis, 1963), 904–5.

10. Edwin Lynds Johnson (9 April 1901–10 October 1980). U.S. Military Academy, 1925. Infantry and Field Artillery. Johnson was assistant chief of staff, G-3 (G-3 Air), headquarters, Army Ground Forces, in Washington, D.C., before moving in May 1944 to the same capacity in headquarters, First Army, for the remainder of the war. Johnson retired as a brigadier general in June 1956. See also Association of Graduates, U.S. Military Academy, *Register of Graduates and Former Cadets of the United States Military Academy West Point, New York, 2000.* (West Point, NY: Association of Graduates, 1999), 4-134.

11. Army Ground Forces, under Lt. Gen. Lesley J. McNair, was one of the three major zone of interior (continental United States) commands into which the War Department was divided in the reorganization of March 1942. The other two were the Army Air Forces, under Lt. Gen. Henry H. Arnold, and the Services of Supply (renamed Army Service Forces in March 1943), under Lt. Gen. Brehon B. Somervell.

12. Russell Franklin Akers Jr. (17 December 1911–6 February 1976). U.S. Military Academy, 1933. Infantry. From October 1943 to July 1945 he was assistant G-3, First Army. Akers retired as a colonel in 1961. See *Register of Graduates, USMA, 2000,* 4-167.

13. Omar Nelson Bradley (12 February 1893–8 April 1981). U.S. Military Academy, 1915. Infantry. After commanding Second Corps in North Africa and Sicily, Bradley moved to England in September 1943 to take over the provisional First U.S. Army Group (FUSAG), which was then involved in planning the cross-Channel invasion, Operation Overlord. In addition, Bradley also became commander of First U.S. Army, which was charged with the assault landing and then exploitation of the beachheads on the western flank of the invasion. Dwight Eisenhower, who was appointed supreme commander, Allied Expedi-

tionary Force in January 1944, designated Bradley to command the American Twelfth Army Group as soon as the Third U.S. Army became operational on the Continent. After heading the Veterans Administration from August 1945 to December 1947, Bradley succeeded Eisenhower as army chief of staff in February 1948 and then became the first chairman of the U.S. Joint Chiefs of Staff in August 1949. He was promoted to General of the Army in September 1950 and retired in August 1953. See also Boatner, *Biographical Dictionary*, 57–58.

14. William B. Kean Jr. (July 1897–10 March 1981). U.S. Military Academy, 1919. Infantry. In March 1943, Kean became chief of staff, Twenty-eighth Infantry Division, and a month later was promoted to brigadier general and sent to North Africa as chief of staff, Second Corps, under Omar Bradley. He moved to England with Bradley in September 1943 and became chief of staff, First Army. He remained as Hodges's chief of staff through the rest of the war and until October 1947. He was promoted to major general in June 1944. Kean retired in September 1954 as a lieutenant general.

15. Bradley, Kean, Colonels Thorson, Dickson, and Wilson, a signal officer from the Signals Section, and some enlisted clerks were on board the USS *Augusta* with Admiral Kirk and his staff. The remainder of First Army headquarters, minus the administrative elements, was on the *Achernar*, the army command ship, with Hodges. This was done intentionally so that First Army could still operate if either of the command ships was lost or damaged. Those with Hodges were Col. E. L. Johnson, deputy chief of staff, operations; Col. R. F. Akers Jr., G-3; Col. W. A. Carter, engineer; Col. C. E. Hart, artillery; Lt. Col. W. A. Huntsberry, G-4; Col. C. G. Patterson, Antiaircraft Artillery Section; Col. R. C. Thompson, air officer, Ninth Tactical Air Command; Lt. Col. W. C. Roberson, G-2; Lt. Col. R. E. Conrath, signal officer; and the British liaison officers, Lt. Col. Berenger Bradford, British Second Army; and Maj. R. Bigland, Twenty-first Army Group. See also Hogan, *Command Post at War*, 67–68, 77; Bradley, *A Soldier's Story*, 251–52.

16. USS *Bayfield* (APA-33) was the flagship of Rear Adm. Don P. Moon, who commanded Task Force 125, Assault Force "U" for Utah Beach. The *Bayfield* was also the command post for Maj. Gen. J. Lawton Collins, commander of Seventh Corps, whose Fourth Infantry Division under Maj. Gen. Raymond O. Barton was assigned to take Utah Beach. See Gordon A. Harrison, *Cross-Channel Attack* (Washington, DC: Office of the Chief of Military History, 1951), 190, 301; Vice Adm. B. B. Schofield, *Operation Neptune* (Annapolis, MD: Naval Institute Press, 1974), 42, 79–82; Bradley, *A Soldier's Story*, 253–54.

17. W. C. Roberson (born 20 November 1898). Roberson served in the New York National Guard from 1923 until January 1941 when he was called to federal service. He was an assistant to the assistant chief of staff, G-2, Intelligence, First Army, from May 1941 to July 1945. He returned to the New York National Guard following the war and retired with the rank of brigadier general.

18. Dwight D. Eisenhower (4 October 1890–28 March 1969). U.S. Military

Academy, 1915. Infantry. In the War Department reorganization of March 1942, Eisenhower became the assistant chief of staff, Operations Division, who was charged with overall strategic planning. In June 1942, he assumed the post of commanding general, U.S. Army Forces in the British Isles, shortly to be renamed European theater of operations, U.S. Army (ETOUSA), and was responsible for planning American involvement in the Allied invasion of the Continent. He was named Allied commander in chief for the North African invasion (Operation Torch), which took place in November 1942, and remained in the Mediterranean as Allied commander during 1943. In December he was named commander of the planning for the invasion of France (Operation Overlord), then scheduled for 1944, and a month later became supreme commander, Allied Expeditionary Force, and commander, Supreme Headquarters Allied Expeditionary Force (SHAEF), for operations in Europe. He was also the commanding general, European theater of operations, U.S. Army, and as such commanded all U.S. Army forces in Europe. He was promoted to General of the Army in December 1944. He served as War Department and army chief of staff from November 1945 until he retired in February 1948. Eisenhower was elected to two terms as president of the United States (1953–1957 and 1957–1961). See also Boatner, *Biographical Dictionary*, 152–55.

19. Eisenhower's headquarters, the Supreme Headquarters Allied Expeditionary Force (SHAEF), had a fully integrated, combined U.S. and British Commonwealth staff.

20. Truman C. Thorson (23 January 1895–10 December 1966). Infantry. Thorson was the assistant chief of staff, G-3, Operations, Second Corps, after the Sicilian campaign of July–August 1943. He moved to England and joined First Army, where he remained throughout the war. Thorson retired as a major general in January 1953.

21. Benjamin A. Dickson (18 December 1897–14 February 1974). U.S. Military Academy, November 1918. Infantry. A reservist, he was recalled to active duty and became G-2 of Second Corps in 1943 and then was G-2 for First Army from 1943 on. He retired as a colonel in 1945. See *Register of Graduates, USMA, 2000*, 4-110.

22. Ralph Royce (28 June 1890–7 August 1965). U.S. Military Academy, 1914. Air Corps. In preparation for the invasion, he was appointed deputy commanding general, Ninth U.S. Air Force, charged with coordinating the air support for Operation Overlord. Royce was with Bradley's operational staff on the *Augusta*. He retired as a major general in June 1946.

23. Don P. Moon (18 April 1894–5 August 1944). U.S. Naval Academy, 1916. After serving on the staff of Adm. Ernest J. King, chief of naval operations, from November 1942 to January 1944, Moon was promoted to rear admiral and took command of the amphibious task group responsible for the landings on Utah Beach. He was then assigned to command the amphibious force for the invasion of southern France in August but committed suicide while suffering

from mental exhaustion. See "Rear Admiral Don P. Moon, USN, (1894–1944),"
U.S. Naval Historical Center Online Library, www.history.navy.mil.

24. The Short Sunderland was a four-engine, long-range reconnaissance and anti-submarine-warfare flying boat patrol plane used by the Royal Air Force's Coastal Command throughout the war. The Sunderland was such a successful aircraft that it remained in use in the RAF until 1959. John W. R. Taylor, ed., *Combat Aircraft of the World from 1909 to the Present* (New York: G. P. Putnam's Sons, 1969), 412–13.

25. The Republic P-47 single-engine fighter-bomber was officially nick-named the Thunderbolt but was known more familiarly by its pilots as the Jug. The heavily armed P-47 was an exceptionally durable aircraft that was able to absorb significant damage and still fly, which made it an ideal ground-attack aircraft. Taylor, *Combat Aircraft of the World*, 550–51.

26. The Martin B-26 Marauder was a twin-engine medium bomber. Taylor, *Combat Aircraft of the World*, 529–30.

27. William A. Carter Jr. (27 June 1907–18 May 1996). U.S. Military Academy, 1930. Corps of Engineers. Carter was engineer for Second Corps in North Africa and Sicily (1942–43) and accompanied the component from Second Corps that moved to England in September 1944 to join the First Army. He became engineer for First Army early in 1944 and remained in that post throughout the war in Europe and until October 1945. He was promoted to brigadier general in July 1953. He was appointed as the division engineer, Lower Mississippi Valley Division, U.S. Corps of Engineers, and promoted to major general in 1957. He later served as governor of the Panama Canal from July 1960 until he retired as a major general in January 1962.

28. Omaha Beach was the easternmost of the invasion beaches assigned to First Army. The landings here were the mission of Maj. Gen. Leonard T. Gerow's Fifth Corps and were specifically assigned to the First and Twenty-ninth Infantry Divisions. The units that landed on heavily defended Omaha Beach had by far the toughest assignment, and it was not until late in the evening that the beach was secured and movement began inland to expand the initial foothold.

29. It was not uncommon for American veterans of World War I to use the derogatory French slang for a German or German soldier, *Boche* (German blockhead or chump), when referring to the Germans. See also Paul Dickson, *War Slang: American Fighting Words and Phrases from the Civil War to the Gulf War* (New York: Pocket Books, 1994), 44.

30. Utah Beach was the western invasion beach on the eastern shore of the Cotentin Peninsula on the Bay of the Seine, north of the mouth of the Douve River and south of the town of Les Dunes-de-Varreville. The easier of the two American landing beaches, Utah was assigned to the Fourth Infantry Division of Maj. Gen. J. Lawton Collins's Seventh Corps.

31. Walter A. Huntsberry (6 November 1906–16 October 1967). U.S. Military

Academy, 1933. Infantry and Quartermaster Corps. Huntsberry became assistant to the assistant chief of staff, G-4, in July 1943 and in September moved to England with Headquarters, First Army, and remained an assistant ACS, G-4. He retired in July 1963 as a brigadier general. See *Register of Graduates, USMA, 2000,* 4-167.

32. Charles G. Patterson (2 September 1908–22 September 1991). U.S. Military Academy, 1933. Artillery. Patterson served as the antiaircraft artillery officer, First Army, from December 1943 to 1947. He retired in 1960 as a colonel. See *Register of Graduates, USMA, 2000,* 4-165.

33. Omaha Beach was divided into sectors designated D Dog, E Easy, and F Fox. Each of these was further subdivided into sections that were designated by color, Red, Green, and White. These beach sections were then assigned to the various assaulting units. Hence, units were assigned to beaches Easy Red, Easy Green, Dog Red, Fox Green, and so on. Easy Red beach was assigned to the First Battalion, Sixteenth Regimental Combat Team, First Infantry Division, and was in the area called the St. Laurent Draw, actually the entrance of the Puquet River into the Bay of the Seine. The draws provided the easiest access routes off the invasion beaches and up through the overlooking bluffs. Easy Red was cleared relatively early on D-day and thus attracted many of the units pinned down along the beach and those arriving in the second wave. However, the unit originally assigned to clear it was pushed eastward by the strong currents and landed at Fox Green beach. See Harrison, *Cross-Channel Attack.*

34. William M. Hoge (13 January 1894–29 October 1979). U S. Military Academy, 1916. Corps of Engineers. Then a brigadier general, Hoge commanded the First Provisional Engineer Special Brigade Group, consisting of the Fifth and Sixth Engineer Special Brigades, that was responsible for supporting American troops landing on Omaha Beach. Hoge later commanded Combat Command B, Ninth Armored Division, in the critical fighting at St. Vith, Belgium, during the German Ardennes offensive in December and during the capture of the Ludendorff railway bridge over the Rhine River at Remagen in March 1945. He retired in January 1955 as a full general.

35. J. [Joseph] Lawton Collins (1 May 1894–12 September 1987). U.S. Military Academy, 1917. Infantry. After commanding the Twenty-fifth Infantry Division in the South Pacific, Collins transferred to the European theater of operations (ETO) and was appointed commanding general, Seventh Corps, First Army, in March 1944. Collins's mission on D-day was to secure a beachhead on Utah Beach and drive inland to link up with the paratroopers of the Eighty-second and 101st Airborne Divisions who were to be dropped behind the beaches in the early morning hours. Nicknamed "Lightning Joe" because of his driving style of leadership, Collins emerged from the fighting in Europe as one of the finest corps commanders in army history. He succeeded Bradley as army chief of staff from August 1949 to August 1953. He retired as a full general in 1956. See also Boatner, *Biographical Dictionary,* 101–02;

J. Lawton Collins, *Lightning Joe: An Autobiography* (Baton Rouge: Louisiana State University Press, 1979).

36. Charles H. Gerhardt (6 June 1895–9 October 1976). U.S. Military Academy, April 1917. Cavalry. Gerhardt was promoted to major general in 1942 and commanded the Twenty-ninth Infantry Division from July 1943 until its inactivation in January 1946. He retired in September 1952 as a major general. See also See *Register of Graduates, USMA, 2000*, 4-104.

37. Mulberry was the code name for the artificial harbors to be built for use in Operation Overlord. Because the Normandy invasion area lacked natural deepwater ports through which to supply the Allied forces and it would take some time to capture and rehabilitate major ports such as Cherbourg and Le Havre, two of these artificial harbors were to be built, one in the American area off Omaha Beach and the other in the British area off Arromanches. A severe Channel storm pounded the invasion areas from 19 to 22 June and so seriously damaged the American Mulberry harbor that it was abandoned. After this the First Army had to supply its forces over the beaches until sufficient harbor capacity could be created in the minor and major Channel ports. See Roland G. Ruppenthal, *Logistical Support of the Armies*, vol. 1, *May 1941–September 1944* (Washington, DC: Office of the Chief of Military History, 1953), 269–327, 402–15.

38. Rhino ferry was a modular pontoon barge 42 feet by 174 feet that carried vehicles and cargo from LSTs (Landing Ship, Tank) and transports to invasion beaches whose shallow slopes prevented the larger landing ships from beaching and unloading directly on to the beach. They proved most useful at the Normandy landing beaches, especially after the June storms knocked out the American Mulberry harbor. See Ruppenthal, *Logistical Support,* 1:394.

39. Charles H. Corlett (31 July 1889–14 October 1971). U.S. Military Academy, 1913. Infantry. Corlett commanded the Seventh Infantry Division in the Pacific from April 1943 to February 1944, when he was transferred to the European theater. There he commanded Nineteenth Corps of First Army from March to October 1944, when he was ostensibly relieved for reasons of ill health. Corlett retired as a major general in May 1946.

40. Leland S. Hobbs (24 February 1892–6 March 1966). U.S. Military Academy, 1915. Infantry. Hobbs was commanding general, Thirtieth Infantry Division, from September 1942 to September 1945. He retired in January 1953 as a major general.

41. Gen. (later Field Marshal) Sir Bernard Law Montgomery (17 November 1887–25 March 1976). Sandhurst, 1908. Infantry. Montgomery served in World War I and was seriously wounded. He commanded the Third Division in the British Expeditionary Force (BEF) in England and France in 1939–1940 and Second Corps during May–June 1940. He later commanded several corps and South-Eastern Army in England before going to the Western Desert to take over Eighth Army in August 1942. He won the battle at El Alamein in October–November 1942 against the Africa Corps and was promoted to full general.

He commanded British forces in North Africa and later Sicily and Italy before moving to England to command Twenty-first Army Group for the invasion and operations in Northwest Europe. He commanded British Twenty-first Army Group for Operation Overlord and was the overall field commander of the land forces under Eisenhower during the opening phase of the invasion. He commanded the Twenty-first Army Group throughout the war. After the war he served as chief of the Imperial General Staff (CIGS) (1946–1948) and as Eisenhower's deputy supreme commander, Supreme Headquarters Allied Powers Europe (SHAPE), the military component of the North Atlantic Treaty Organization (NATO), in 1951–1952. He retired in September 1958. See Boatner, *Biographical Dictionary*, 373–75.

42. Brig. Gen. John T. Thompson originally designed the U.S. Army's M1A1 .45 caliber machine pistol or submachine gun for use in World War I, hence its nickname "tommy gun." During the interwar years, U.S. law enforcement officers as well as bootleggers and gangsters adopted the tommy gun because of its volume of fire, large magazine capacity in drums to a hundred rounds and clips of twenty to thirty, and stopping power. The military tommy gun was a favorite weapon of paratroopers for the same reasons. It was replaced in 1944 with the M3 "grease gun." See Alexander Lüdeke, *Weapons of World War II* (New York: Parragon, 2007), 32.

43. Anthony C. McAuliffe (2 July 1898–11 August 1975). U.S. Military Academy, November 1918. Field Artillery. McAuliffe commanded the divisional artillery, 101st Airborne Division, from September 1943 to February 1945 and participated in the D-day airborne operations. He later gained instant fame during the Battle of the Bulge when as acting division commander at Bastogne he responded to the German surrender demand with an abrupt "Nuts!" McAuliffe retired a full general in May 1956. See also Boatner, *Biographical Dictionary*, 351.

44. The antiaircraft artillery (AAA) of the U.S. Army was divided into two basic types of units determined by the weapons assigned to them. The automatic weapons (AW) batteries usually were equipped with multiple .50 caliber machine guns (either two or four .50s, the latter known as "quad 50s") mounted on an M2 half-track or towed and the twin 40-mm "American Bofors" gun of Swedish design. The AW batteries were effective only against low-flying aircraft. The heavier antiaircraft (AA) batteries had the 90-mm M1 or M2 guns, the three-inch M3, or the 120-mm guns, which were mostly used to equip units in the United States. Lüdeke, *Weapons of World War II*, 170, 175; George Forty, *US Army Handbook 1939–1945* (New York: Barnes & Noble Books, 1995), 154–57.

45. George C. Marshall (31 December 1880–16 October 1959). Virginia Military Institute, 1901. Infantry. Marshall became War Department chief of staff in September 1939 and the principal military adviser to President Franklin D. Roosevelt with American entry into World War II in December 1941. He was a member of the U.S. Joint Chiefs of Staff and Allied Combined Chiefs of Staff,

which mapped Allied strategy throughout the war. Many historians consider Marshall to have been the major organizer of the American military victory in the war. Marshall was promoted to General of the Army in December 1944 and retired in November 1945. During his tenure as secretary of state (February 1947–January 1949) he formulated the Marshall Plan for western Europe; he later served as secretary of defense (September 1950–September 1951). See also Boatner, *Biographical Dictionary,* 345–48.

46. Henry H. Arnold (25 June 1886–15 January 1950). U.S. Military Academy, 1907. Air Corps. Arnold became chief of the air corps in September 1938. He became chief of the Army Air Forces in June 1941 and commanding general, U.S. Army Air Forces (USAAF), in March 1942. A member of the U.S. Joint Chiefs of Staff, he was also the U.S. air member of the Allied Combined Chiefs of Staff and participated fully in the U.S. and Allied planning and conduct of the war. Arnold was promoted to General of the Army in December 1944 and retired in February 1946. He received the rank of General of the Air Force in 1949. See also Boatner, *Biographical Dictionary,* 14–15; Col. Flint O. DuPre, *U.S. Air Force Biographical Dictionary* (New York: Franklin Watts, 1965), 8–10; "General Henry H. Arnold" at Air Force Link Biographies at http://www.af.mil/bios.

47. Ernest J. King (23 November 1878–25 June 1951). U.S. Naval Academy, 1901. King became commander in chief. Atlantic Fleet, in February 1941. Shortly after Pearl Harbor, he became commander in chief, U.S. Fleet. In March 1942, he was appointed chief of naval operations and became the first man ever to combine the posts of chief of naval operations and commander in chief, U.S. Fleet. He was the U.S. Navy member of the U.S. Joint Chiefs of Staff and of the Allied Combined Chiefs of Staff. He was promoted to fleet admiral in December 1944 and retired in October 1945. See also Boatner, *Biographical Dictionary,* 376–78.

48. CCA, or Combat Command A. In World War II, all the U.S. Army armored divisions after September 1943 except the Second and Third were organized as "light armored" divisions on a triangular basis of three combat commands, A, B, and C (or R for Reserve). Each combat command had approximately a battalion of tanks, armored infantry, and armored field artillery plus an armored engineer company. The Second and Third Armored Divisions remained "heavy armored divisions," each with two tank regiments and an armored infantry regiment, and were not reorganized like these light armored divisions. See Forty, *US Army Handbook 1941–1945,* 76–79.

49. Samuel L. Myers (31 January 1905–20 March 1987). U.S. Military Academy, 1928. Cavalry. Myers served as deputy chief of staff, Second Corps, from April to September 1943. He accompanied Bradley to England and was made deputy chief of staff, Administration, First Army, in October 1943, a post he retained until June 1946. Myers later commanded the Third Armored Cavalry Regiment (1949–1951). He was promoted to major general in 1952 and served

as assistant deputy chief of staff, Logistics, Department of the Army (1958–61). He was promoted to lieutenant general in 1961 and was deputy commanding general, Eighth U.S. Army, Korea, until he retired in 1963.

50. Willard G. Wyman (21 March 1898–29 March 1969). U.S. Military Academy, 1919. Cavalry. Wyman was assigned as chief, Plans Subsection, G-3 Section, at Allied Forces Headquarters (AFHQ) under Eisenhower in December 1942. He became assistant division commander, First Infantry Division, on 7 August 1943 and served in that capacity through the division's landing at Omaha Beach and subsequent operations in France, Belgium, and Germany. He returned to the United States to assume command of the Seventy-first Infantry Division, which he then led to Europe and commanded in combat from February 1945 to the end of the war. He retired as a full general in July 1958.

51. Clarence R. Huebner (24 November 1888–23 September 1972). Infantry. Huebner served as an enlisted soldier in the infantry from 1910 to 1916 when he was commissioned. During World War I, he received two Distinguished Service Crosses for heroism in action while serving with the First Division. In March 1943 he was assigned to the North African theater of operations and Eisenhower's staff in preparation for the invasion of Sicily (Operation Husky). He later replaced Terry Allen as commanding general, First Infantry Division, on 7 August 1943 and commanded the "Big Red One" until 10 December 1944. During the period, the First Division completed mopping-up operations on Sicily, moved to England to prepare for the invasion of France, landed at Omaha Beach, and fought its way across France and Belgium and into Germany. Huebner succeeded Leonard Gerow as commander of Fifth Corps on 15 January 1945 and held that post until November 1945. He retired as a lieutenant general in November 1950.

52. Leonard T. Gerow (13 July 1888–12 October 1972). Virginia Military Institute, 1911. Infantry. Gerow took command of the Twenty-ninth Infantry Division at Fort George Meade, Maryland, and moved the division to England in October 1942. On 1 July 1943, he became commanding general, Fifth Corps, ETOUSA. As commander of Fifth Corps, Gerow was responsible for the detailed planning, preparation, and conduct of the assault on Omaha Beach and subsequent operations in France in 1944. Except for a brief period in September and October 1944, he commanded Fifth Corps until January 1945, when he was appointed commanding general, Fifteenth U.S. Army. Gerow retired as a lieutenant general in July 1950. See also Boatner, *Biographical Dictionary*, 180.

53. Charles D. Palmer (20 February 1902–7 June 1999). U.S. Military Academy, 1924. Field Artillery. Palmer was chief of staff, Eleventh Armored Division, in the U.S. and Europe until March 1944 when he assumed the same post with the Second Armored Division under Edward Brooks. He then moved with Brooks to Fifth Corps, where he was chief of staff from 25 September to 18 October 1944. He then was transferred to the same post under Brooks at Headquarters, VI Corps, Seventh U.S. Army. He commanded the First Cavalry Di-

vision artillery and then the division itself in the Korean War (1950–1951). He later served as Deputy commanding general, Eighth U.S. Army, in Korea and commanding general, U.S. Army Japan (1957–58) and was promoted to lieutenant general. He was promoted to full general in 1959 and served as Deputy commander in chief, U.S. European Command from 1959 until his retirement in 1962.

54. Edward H. Brooks (25 April 1893–19 October 1978). Norwich University, 1916. Field Artillery. Brooks was artillery officer, Armored Force, until July 1942 when he was promoted to brigadier general and took command of the Eleventh Armored Division. He commanded the Second Armored Division from March to September 1944, leading it through the tough fighting in Normandy and the period of breakout and pursuit across France. After promotion to major general in August, in September–October 1944 he temporarily replaced Gerow as Fifth Corps's commander before moving to Seventh U.S. Army where he commanded Sixth Corps from October 1944 to May 1945. He retired as a lieutenant general in April 1953.

55. Walter M. Robertson (15 June 1888–22 November 1954). U.S. Military Academy, 1912. Infantry. Robertson served as assistant division commander, Second Infantry Division, from December 1941 until May 1942, when he became the division's commander. He commanded the Second Division for the rest of the war, moving the division to England in October 1943 and then leading it throughout the European campaign until June 1945. He retired as a major general in June 1950.

56. Leroy H. Watson (3 November 1893–12 February 1975), U.S. Military Academy, 1915. Infantry. Watson commanded the Fourth Armored Regiment until his promotion to brigadier general in February 1942 and reassignment to command of a combat command of the Third Armored Division. He commanded the Third Armored Division from August 1942 through its early months in France (June–August 1944). He was promoted to major general in September 1942. He was relieved of command in August 1944, reduced to his permanent rank of colonel, and transferred to headquarters, Twelfth Army Group. He later served as assistant division commander of the Twenty-ninth Infantry Division from 31 August 1944 to August 1945, at which time he was appointed commanding general, Seventy-ninth Infantry Division. He retired as a major general in November 1953.

57. Norman D. Cota (30 May 1893–4 October 1971). U.S. Military Academy, April 1917. Infantry. Cota served as the chief of staff, First Infantry Division, from August 1942 until February 1943 and participated in the landings in North Africa in early November of that year. In February 1943 Cota was promoted to brigadier general and was assigned as U.S. adviser to the British Combined Operations Headquarters in England. He remained there until September 1943 when he became assistant division commander, Twenty-ninth Infantry Division. He landed at 0730 on Omaha Beach with the Twenty-ninth's 116th

Regimental Combat Team (RCT) and helped organize the troops to secure a foothold on the beach. For his heroism that day, he received the Distinguished Service Cross. He then commanded the Twenty-eighth Infantry Division from 14 August 1944 until its inactivation in December 1945 following its return to the United States. Cota received his second star in September 1944 and retired as a major general on 30 June 1946.

58. Doyle O. Hickey (27 July 1892–20 October 1961). Hendrix College (Arkansas), 1913. Field Artillery. From April to September 1942, Hickey was with Headquarters, the Armored Force, and then Eighth Armored Division, at Fort Knox. He joined the Third Armored Division in 1942 as commander of Combat Command A. He was named commander of the division after Maurice Rose's death in March 1945 and remained commander until June 1945. He retired in July 1953 as a lieutenant general.

59. Raymond S. McLain (4 April 1890–14 December 1954). Field Artillery. A successful banker in Oklahoma City, McLain was an enlisted man and officer in the Oklahoma National Guard from 1912 to 1940. When the Oklahoma National Guard was federalized in 1940, he was artillery commander of the Forty-fifth Infantry Division. He served with the division under Maj. Gen. Troy Middleton in North Africa, Sicily, and Italy and joined the Thirtieth Division as artillery commander on 10 May 1944. He assumed command of the Ninetieth Infantry Division on 30 July 1944 and then Nineteenth Corps in October 1944, replacing Charles Corlett. He commanded Nineteenth Corps through July 1945 and was promoted to lieutenant general on 6 June 1945. McLain was the only National Guard officer to command a corps in Europe during the war, and there has been speculation that Eisenhower promoted McLain to this position in response to political pressures from the United States. McLain remained on active duty after the war and retired on 30 April 1952 as a lieutenant general.

60. *Nebelgranat.* The diarist means *Nebelwerfer,* the six-barrel German rocket launchers that were either 150-mm. or 210-mm. Because the rockets when fired made a screaming or screeching sound the American soldiers nicknamed them "screaming meemies," not "Minnies," as the writer called them. However, British solders did call them "Moaning Minnies." See Lüdeke, *Weapons of World War II,* 179; Thomas Parrish, ed., *The Simon and Schuster Encyclopedia of World War II* (New York: Simon & Schuster, 1978), 430.

61. Hammond D. Birks (b. 5 February 1896). Infantry. Birks was assistant chief of staff, G-3, G-1, and then antitank officer with Second Corps and then Eleventh Corps until August 1942, when he was given command of the 120th Infantry Regiment, Thirtieth Infantry Division. He commanded the 120th until 7 October 1944, when he was made assistant division commander, Ninth Infantry Division. He was promoted to brigadier general on 7 January 1945 and remained with Ninth Division until June 1945. He retired on 30 November 1946 as a brigadier general. R. Manning Ancell with Christine M. Miller, *The*

Biographical Dictionary of World War II Generals and Flag Officers: The U.S. Armed Forces (Westport, CT: Greenwood Press, 1996), 21–22.

62. Troy H. Middleton (12 October 1889–9 October 1976). Mississippi A & M College, 1909. Infantry. After a distinguished record in World War I, Middleton remained in the army. He served as the professor of military science and tactics at Louisiana State University (LSU) in Baton Rouge from February 1930 until September 1936. He retired upon his own request as a colonel on 31 October 1937. From November 1937 to January 1941, he was dean of administration at Louisiana State University. Recalled to active duty in January 1941, he was promoted to brigadier general in June 1942 and to major general in October 1942, when he became commander of the Forty-fifth Infantry Division. He took the division to the North Africa theater in June 1943, in time to see action in the Sicilian and Salerno campaigns. He left the Forty-fifth Infantry Division in December 1943 and was briefly at Headquarters, Army Ground Forces, before taking command of Eighth Corps, ETO, in March 1944. He commanded Eighth Corps throughout the remainder of the war in Europe. He was promoted to lieutenant general on 5 June 1945 and retired on 10 August to return to LSU as dean and comptroller. From 1951 to 1962, he was president of LSU. See also Boatner, *Biographical Dictionary*, 365–66.

63. Richard G. McKee (2 August 1896–16 September 1986). U.S. Military Academy, June 1918. Infantry. After serving at the Infantry School at Fort Benning, Georgia, until July 1943, McKee became assistant chief of staff, G-3, Third U.S. Army, at Fort Sam Houston, Texas. That December he moved to the ETO as assistant chief of staff, G-3, Seventh Corps, and took part in the invasion and subsequent fighting. He then assumed command of the Eighth Infantry Regiment, Fourth Division, from September 1944 to the end of the war. He retired as a brigadier general in August 1954. See also *Register of Graduates, USMA, 2000*, 4-108.

64. Ira T. Wyche (16 October 1887–8 July 1981). U.S. Military Academy, 1911. Infantry and Field Artillery. After serving as chief, Training Section, Office, Chief of Field Artillery, until April 1941, he was promoted to brigadier general and given command of the Seventy-fourth Field Artillery Brigade. He was promoted to major general and became commanding general, Seventy-ninth Infantry Division, in June 1942. Wyche led the division through its training in the United States, movement to the United Kingdom in April 1944, and into combat in June 1944. He commanded the division until May 1945. He retired as a lieutenant general on 30 June 1948.

65. Jesse L. Gibney (15 January 1895–23 December 1967). U.S. Military Academy, November 1918. Infantry. Gibney commanded the 424th Infantry Regiment, 106th Infantry Division, from October 1942 to May 1944. He then moved to the Ninth Infantry Division as commander of the Sixtieth Infantry Regiment and briefly acted as the division's chief of staff in late June 1944. In December 1944 he became chief of staff, Twenty-eighth Infantry Division, and

served in that post until October 1945. He retired as a colonel in 1953. See also *Register of Graduates, USMA, 2000,* 4-112.

66. Eugene M. Landrum (6 February 1891–24 July 1967). Landrum commanded the Seventh Infantry Division in the Attu operation (May–June 1943) and eventually commanded the force that occupied Kiska in the Aleutians. From October 1943 to April 1944, he commanded the Eighty-seventh Infantry Division in the United States and then was sent to Europe without a specific assignment. Bradley used him to replace Jay MacKelvie as commander of the Ninetieth Infantry Division on 13 June after the division's performance failed to live up to expectation. Landrum himself was relieved of command during August 1944 when Hodges, Bradley, and Eisenhower decided that the Ninetieth's performance was still unacceptable. He returned to the United States and assumed command of the Seventy-first Infantry Division, then completing its training prior to movement to the ETO in October–November 1944. Willard G. Wyman replaced Landrum as commander before departure at the personal request of Eisenhower, who did not want Landrum to return to the ETO. Landrum retired as a major general in February 1951. See also Alfred D. Chandler Jr. and Stephen E. Ambrose, eds., *The Papers of Dwight David Eisenhower: The War Years: IV* (Baltimore: Johns Hopkins University Press, 1970), 2196–97; Ancell, *Biographical Dictionary,* 181.

67. Jay W. MacKelvie (8 September 1890–5 December 1985). Field Artillery. MacKelvie enlisted in the cavalry in 1913 and was commissioned in June 1917. From February 1941 to April 1942 he was a member of the Plans Group, War Plans Division, War Department General Staff. He was promoted to brigadier general in March 1942. He then commanded the artillery of the Eighty-fifth Division until September 1943 when he became commanding general, Twelfth Corps Artillery. In January 1944 he received command of the Ninetieth Division. He was relieved of command "without prejudice" on 13 June 1944. He subsequently served in ETOUSA headquarters and in September became the commander of divisional artillery, Eightieth Infantry Division, in Italy. MacKelvie then commanded V Corps Artillery from June 1945 until his retirement on 30 September 1946 as a brigadier general. Ancell, *Biographical Dictionary,* 198.

68. Matthew B. Ridgway (3 March 1895–26 July 1993). U.S. Military Academy, April 1917. Infantry. From 1937 to January 1942, Ridgway served in the War Plans Division, War Department General Staff. He was then promoted to brigadier general and in February became assistant division commander, Eighty-second Infantry Division, under Omar N. Bradley and assumed command in June. He completed the reorganization and training of the division as the first U.S. airborne division and then led it in the first American combat jump of the war in the Sicilian operation of July 1943. Along with the 101st Airborne Division, the Eighty-second played an important role in Operation Overlord by landing behind the Normandy beaches on the night of 5–6 June 1944. Ridgway jumped with his division that night and remained in command until August,

when he took over the Eighteenth Airborne Corps. He commanded this corps through August 1945. After a number of important commands after the war, including replacing Eisenhower as supreme commander Europe in 1952–1953, he served as army chief of staff (1953–55) and retired as a full general in June 1955. See also Boatner, *Biographical Dictionary*, 456–57.

69. James M. Gavin (2 March 1907–23 February 1990). U.S. Military Academy, 1929. Infantry. Gavin completed parachute training and was assigned to the Provisional Parachute Group at Fort Benning, Georgia, from October 1941 to early 1942. In August 1942, he assumed command of the 505th Parachute Infantry Regiment, Eighty-second Airborne Division, which made the first American combat airborne assault on 9–10 July 1943 at Gela, Sicily, at the beginning of Operation Husky. He became deputy division commander under Ridgway in February 1944. He jumped into Normandy on the night of 5–6 June 1944. He succeeded Ridgway as commander of the Eighty-second in August 1944, becoming the youngest division commander in the U.S. Army since the Civil War. He led the division through the tough fighting in Operation Market in September–October in Holland and then during the Battle of the Bulge. He retired as a lieutenant general in March 1958. See also Boatner, *Biographical Dictionary*, 177–78.

70. Crossbow was the Allied code name for operations against the launching sites for the German V-weapons, the V-1 flying bombs and V-2 rockets. The Germans built numerous launching facilities for the V-1 flying bombs along the occupied Channel coast in 1943–44. Numerous air attacks were directed against these sites from late 1943 onward in an effort to neutralize them before they became operational. The first V-1 was launched toward London from a site in the area of Pas de Calais on the night of 12 June 1944. Within twenty-four hours, three hundred more V-1 "buzz bombs" were launched against England in a V-1 blitz that would continue until March 1945. Numerous V-1s and V-2s were also launched against Antwerp and Liège in Belgium and The Hague in Holland from launching sites in Holland and Germany itself. See Parrish, *Encyclopedia of World War II*, 144; Lüdeke, *Weapons of World War II*, 182–83.

71. Walter C. Stanton (12 November 1902–28 January 1986). U.S. Military Academy, 1926. Field Artillery. Stanton served as assistant artillery officer, Seventh Corps, and G-3, Seventy-ninth Infantry Division, and Thirteenth Corps until departing for duty in the ETO. Stanton was Deputy chief of staff, Eighth Corps, during 1944–1945. He retired as a colonel in 1956. See *Register of Graduates, USMA, 2000*, 4–137.

72. Raymond O. Barton (22 August 1889–27 February 1963). U.S. Military Academy, 1912. Infantry. Barton served from July 1940 to August 1941 as chief of staff, Fourth Infantry Division, and then added duties as chief of staff, Fourth Corps, to these until April 1942. He commanded the Eighty-fifth Infantry Division from April to June 1942 and then became commanding general, Fourth Infantry Division. He was promoted to major general in August 1942. He took

the division to Europe in February 1944 and led it from its D-day landing at Utah Beach on 6 June 1944 through the hard fighting in France, Belgium, and Germany. In December 1944 Eisenhower released Barton for return to the United States because of his failing health and Marshall's request for experienced division commanders who could train additional divisions. He retired on 28 February 1946 as a major general.

73. Theodore Roosevelt Jr. (13 September 1887–12 July 1944). Harvard University, 1908. The son of President Theodore Roosevelt, he had a distinguished record with the Twenty-sixth Infantry, First Division, in World War I. After the war, Roosevelt was involved in politics and government until he rejoined the Twenty-sixth Infantry Regiment as its commander in April 1941. In December he was promoted to brigadier general, and in August 1942 he became assistant division commander, First Infantry Division, under Terry Allen. He served in this capacity in North Africa and Sicily (August 1942–August 1943) when Bradley, commanding Second Corps, relieved both Roosevelt and Terry Allen due to an increasingly serious lack of discipline in the division's conduct and operations. Roosevelt was assigned as liaison officer to the Second French Corps on Corsica until early 1944, when he joined the Fourth Infantry Division as an additional assistant division commander with the specific duty of leading the assault units on the beach on D-day. He was the only general officer to land on Utah Beach with the first assault waves on the morning of 6 June. He played a critical part in establishing control of the beach despite coming under heavy enemy fire. Subsequently he became the military governor of Cherbourg after its capture. Bradley had decided to give him command of the Ninetieth Infantry Division in place of Landrum when he received news that Roosevelt had died in his sleep of a heart attack on the night of 12 July. On 28 September 1944, he was posthumously awarded the Medal of Honor for his courageous leadership on Utah Beach. See also Bradley, *A Soldier's Story*, 332–33; Boatner, *Biographical Dictionary*, 472.

74. The regimental combat team, or RCT, formed the basis for the "triangular" American infantry division of 1940, which was built around three infantry regiments. An infantry regiment, augmented with field artillery, engineers, and often tank support, formed such an RCT, combat team, or task force according to wartime army doctrine and could fight as a separate unit, independently of the division to which it was organic, and attached to other divisions or even corps for specific missions. A number of separate RCTs were formed during the war and saw action around the world. See John B. Wilson, *Maneuver and Firepower: The Evolution of Divisions and Separate Brigades* (Washington, DC: U.S. Army Center of Military History, 1998); War Department, Field Manual 100–5 (FM 100–5), *Field Service Regulations, Operations*, 22 May 1941, 3–4; and 15 June 1944, 5.

75. Henry J. Matchett (7 January 1891–18 February 1982). Infantry. Matchett served in World War I and remained in the army after the war. From August

1942 to October 1943, he was chief, Training Branch, Organization and Training Division, War Department General Staff. He was transferred to the ETO as chief of staff, Fifth Corps, under Leonard Gerow, in October 1943. He was promoted to brigadier general in September 1944 and became commanding general, Ground Forces Replacement System, in the United Kingdom and chief, Replacement Section, Headquarters, ETOUSA. The Ground Forces Replacement System was critical to the success of American forces in the field because it funneled replacements to the combat battalions. In May 1945 Matchett joined Headquarters, Fifteenth Army, in Germany. He retired on 28 February 1950 as a brigadier general.

76. Karl E. Henion (2 June 1895–19 August 1983). Infantry. Henion was commissioned in World War I. He served as deputy chief of staff, Fifth Corps, from 1943 to January 1945, when he moved with Gerow to the Fifteenth Army in the same capacity.

77. Hurley E. Fuller (27 November 1894–29 April 1975). Infantry. Fuller served in the Texas National Guard from 1914 to 1917, when he was commissioned. He commanded the Twenty-third Infantry Regiment, Second Infantry Division, from 14 January 1942 to 16 June 1944, when he was relieved of command. He then served with Headquarters, Twelfth Army Group, and Eighth Corps until he took command of the 110th Infantry Regiment, Twenty-eighth Infantry Division, on 24 November 1944 in Luxembourg. The German Ardennes offensive beginning on 16 December smashed the 110th in Luxembourg, but Fuller led a spirited defense centered around the town of Clervaux, from which he was forced to withdraw on 17 December. Fuller was captured on 18 December and remained a prisoner of war until liberated by the Russians in February 1945. He retired as a colonel in October 1958. See Robert F. Phillips, *To Save Bastogne* (Burke, VA: Borodino Books, 1996); John C. McManus, *Alamo in the Ardennes: The Untold Story of the American Soldiers Who Made the Defense of Bastogne Possible* (New York: John Wiley & Sons, 2007); Hugh M. Cole, *The Ardennes: Battle of the Bulge* (Washington, DC: U.S. Army Center of Military History, 1988).

78. Carl A. Spaatz (28 June 1891–14 July 1974). U.S. Military Academy, 1914. Air Corps. After serving in France in World War I, Spaatz filled a number of important posts in the air corps between the wars. After serving as chief of the Air Staff under Henry H. Arnold in 1941, in January 1942 he became commanding general of the Air Force Combat Command. He was made commander of the Eighth Air Force in May 1942 and assigned the mission of preparing the U.S. Army Air Forces in England for the strategic bombing of Germany. Eisenhower appointed Spaatz as the American air commander for Operation Torch in November 1942. He remained in North Africa and the Mediterranean until December 1943. After his selection as supreme Allied commander, Eisenhower appointed Spaatz as commander of U.S. air forces in Europe in January 1944 and commanding general, U.S. Strategic Air Forces Europe, and placed him

in charge of the strategic air offensive against Germany for the rest of the war in Europe. He succeeded Arnold as commanding general, Army Air Forces, in March 1946. Spaatz guided the Army Air Forces through the period of unification and its transformation into the U.S. Air Force in September 1947. He served as the first chief of staff of the air force and retired in July 1948 as a full general. See also Boatner, *Biographical Dictionary*, 518–19; DuPre, *U.S. Air Force Biographical Dictionary*, 219–20.

79. Robert A. Lovett (14 September 1895–7 May 1986). Yale University, 1918. After a successful banking career, Lovett became assistant secretary of war for air under Secretary of War Henry Stimson on 22 April 1941. He held the post until 8 December 1945, when he returned to private life. On 4 October 1950, he was appointed deputy secretary of defense under George C. Marshall and then succeeded him as secretary of defense on 16 September 1951. He remained secretary throughout the rest of the second Truman administration, leaving office on 20 January 1953.

80. James E. Rudder (6 May 1910–23 March 1970). During World War II, he rose from first lieutenant to colonel. He commanded the Second Ranger Battalion and the Provisional Ranger Force, which was responsible for assaulting and seizing Pointe du Hoc on D-day. During this action, Rudder was wounded twice but still retained command. He received a Distinguished Service Cross for his gallantry. He later commanded the 109th Infantry Regiment, Twenty-eighth Division, from early December 1944 through the end of the war. After the war, he was president of Texas A & M University from 1959 to 1970 and president of the Texas A & M University system from 1965 to 1970. Rudder remained in the U.S. Army Reserve after the war, reaching the rank of major general and commanding the Ninetieth Infantry Division from 1955 to 1965.

81. Max F. Schneider (8 September 1912–25 March 1959). Infantry. Schneider served as an enlisted man in the infantry of the Iowa National Guard during the 1930s and was commissioned a second lieutenant in the National Guard in September 1939. He was called to active duty in February 1941. On 3 April 1944 he was made commander of the Fifth Ranger Battalion in England and was promoted to lieutenant colonel on 30 May. His battalion was assigned to back up James E. Rudder's Second Ranger Battalion that was to take the German defenses at the Pointe du Hoc, overlooking Omaha Beach. If the Second carried out its mission, then the Fifth Ranger Battalion would land with the 116th Infantry, Twenty-ninth Infantry Division, on Omaha Beach. Schneider eventually led the Fifth ashore under heavy German fire on the morning of 6 June. Pinned down on the beach, Norman Cota, assistant division commander, Twenty-ninth Infantry Division, gave the Army Rangers much of their legend when he told Schneider and the Fifth Rangers, "If you're Rangers, get up and lead the way!" Schneider and the Fifth then led the American soldiers off the beaches, up the Les Moulins draw to high ground, and on to take Vierville-sur-Mer. He commanded the Fifth Rangers for the rest of the war in Europe

and remained in the army after the war. He was promoted to full colonel in April 1953. Schneider died while on active duty in March 1959. See Robert W. Black, *Rangers in World War II* (New York: Ballantine Books, 1992), 206; Harrison, *Cross-Channel Attack*.

82. The German *Soldatenbuch* (Soldier's Book) was much prized by Allied intelligence because it provided detailed information on the soldier and his personal military history, including his current unit. It contained a photograph of the soldier and was used for personal identification and pay purposes.

83. Godwin Ordway Jr. (11 April 1901–25 November 1966). U.S. Military Academy, 1925. Infantry. From January 1942 to April 1944, Ordway served as assistant executive officer, Operations Division, War Department General Staff. He then was chief of staff, Twenty-ninth Infantry Division, from 28 April to 13 June 1944, when he succeeded Eugene Slappey as commanding officer, 115th Infantry Regiment, Twenty-ninth Infantry Division. On 18 July 1944, he moved to the staff of assistant chief of staff , G-3, Twelfth U.S. Army Group, where he remained through the end of the war. Ordway retired in 1955 as a colonel. See also *Register of Graduates, USMA, 2000,* 4-134.

84. Eugene N. Slappey (b. 2 October 1894). Infantry. Slappey served in the Georgia National Guard before World War I and joined the Regular Army in 1920. He commanded the 115th Infantry Regiment, Twenty-ninth Infantry Division, from 11 October 1942 to 13 June 1944, when he assumed command of a Ranger group.

85. The Consolidated B-24 Liberator was a shoulder-wing, four-engine heavy bomber that shared strategic bombing duties with the Boeing B-17 Flying Fortress. Easily recognizable because of its twin rear stabilizers, the B-24 was used in most theaters during the war. It had a maximum range of 2,850 miles at a cruising speed of 200 miles per hour with a bomb load of 8,800 pounds. The Liberator was best known for the low-level attack against the Romanian oil fields at Ploesti on 1 August 1943. See Taylor, *Combat Aircraft of the World,* 462–64.

86. Generalleutnant Karl-Wilhelm von Schlieben (1894–1964) was a veteran German army officer who had commanded both the Eighteenth Panzer Division (1943) and the 709th Infantry Division (1943–44). He took command of the Cherbourg garrison on 23 June 1944 and was captured on 26 June. See also "Biography of Lieutenant-General Karl Wilheim von Schlieben" at www.generals.dk.

87. The Douglas C-47 Skytrain was the military version of the famous DC-3 two-engine commercial transport and airliner. Skytrains were used for all major U.S. Army Air Forces' air transport and parachute operations during the war. In British Commonwealth service, the C-47 was called the Dakota. See Len Cacutt, ed., "Douglas DC-3/C-47/Dakota: World Workhorses," in *The World's Greatest Aircraft* (New York: Exeter Books, 1988), 37–45.

88. Unit of fire was a unit of measure for ammunition supply. It was intend-

ed for tactical purposes only to indicate stock levels or specify the expenditure of ammunition in an operation. The specific numbers of rounds of ammunition allotted per weapon varied with the weapons. For example, for the 105-mm howitzer, one unit of fire was 125 rounds, but for the 155-mm howitzer, it was 75 rounds. See Ruppenthal, *Logistical Support*, 1:306–7, esp. fn 77.

89. Maxwell D. Taylor (24 August 1901–19 April 1987). U.S. Military Academy, 1922. Field Artillery. Taylor served as assistant secretary of the War Department General Staff from July 1941 to July 1942 when he became chief of staff, Eighty-second Division. He was instrumental in helping Matthew Ridgway convert the Eighty-second into an airborne division. He became commander of the divisional artillery and was promoted to brigadier general in December 1942. Taylor participated in the landings in Sicily in July and Italy in September 1943. He was given command of the 101st Airborne Division in March and was promoted to major general in May. He jumped into Normandy with his division on the morning of 6 June 1944 and commanded it through September 1945. The division gained great fame for its defense of Bastogne, but Taylor was on leave in the United States during this time and only rejoined the division late in December. In June 1956 he succeeded Ridgway as chief of staff of the army and retired in July 1959. He returned to active duty in July 1961 as President John F. Kennedy's military adviser and then chairman of the Joint Chiefs of Staff from October 1962 to July 1964. He retired in July 1959 and again in July 1964 as a full general. See also Boatner, *Biographical Dictionary*, 555–56.

90. Howard R. Johnson (18 June 1903–6 October 1944). Infantry. Johnson served as an enlisted man and flying cadet in the Air Services in 1926 and was then commissioned in the infantry. He was promoted to colonel and became commanding officer, 501st Parachute Infantry Regiment, 101st Airborne Division, in November 1942. He led his regiment in the D-day airborne operation on 5–6 June 1944 and remained in command during subsequent ground combat operations until the 101st was relieved. He jumped into Holland with his regiment in the air-assault phase of Operation Market on 16 September 1944. He died of wounds received from German artillery fire in Holland on 6 October.

91. "Long Tom" was the nickname for the U.S. Army's M1A1 155-mm gun that was standardized by the Ordnance Department in 1938. It could fire a fixed high-explosive (HE) or armor-piercing (AP) shell a range of 25,715 yards at a rate of fire of one round per minute. See Lüdeke, *Weapons of World War II*, 172; Parrish, *Encyclopedia of World War II*, 372.

92. Charles Bowler King (28 May 1906–22 June 1944). U.S. Military Academy, 1928. Infantry. Assistant chief of staff, Intelligence (G-2), Seventh Corps, 1944. King was killed in action after accidentally crossing into German-held territory.

93. James S. Rodwell (7 March 1896–27 December 1962). Infantry. Rodwell served as an enlisted man and officer in and after World War I. In July 1940, he

was assigned to the Fourth Motorized Division as assistant chief of staff, G-2, and later became chief of staff when the division became the Fourth Infantry Division. From 2 July to 17 September 1944 he commanded the Fourth Infantry Division's Eighth Infantry Regiment. He then was assistant division commander, Ninth Division, from 17 September to 8 October 1944. He rejoined the Fourth Infantry Division as assistant division commander on 10 October and was promoted to brigadier general on 7 December. He remained in this post until he retired as a brigadier general on 31 August 1946. Ancell, *Biographical Dictionary*, 277–78.

94. William K. Harrison Jr. (7 September 1895–25 May 1987). U.S. Military Academy, April 1917. Cavalry. Harrison was the assistant division commander, Seventy-eighth Infantry Division, from July to December 1942. On 1 January 1943, he became assistant division commander, Thirtieth Division, under Leland Hobbs, where he remained throughout the war and until December 1946. He retired in February 1957 as a lieutenant general.

95. John A. Smith Jr. (b. 6 June 1895). Field Artillery. Smith served as chief of staff, Third Armored Division, from 15 September 1943 to end of the war. He retired a colonel in March 1949.

96. Francis B. Wilby (4 April 1883–20 November 1965). U.S. Military Academy, 1905. Corps of Engineers. Wilby was appointed chief of staff, First Army, and promoted to brigadier general in October 1940. In July 1941 he moved to Boston as commanding general, First Coast Artillery District. In September he was promoted to major general and then appointed superintendent, U.S. Military Academy, in January 1942, a post he held until September 1945. He retired in January 1946 as a major general.

97. Mars was the code name designation for the Headquarters, Provisional Engineer Special Brigade Group, under Brig. Gen. William Hoge, which controlled all access to and from, and activities on, the American beaches for the Normandy operation. Such code names were assigned to all American units to protect signal, radio, and telephone communications from German interception.

98. Robert C. Macon (12 July 1890–20 October 1980). Virginia Polytechnic Institute, 1912. Infantry. Macon commanded the Seventh Infantry Regiment, Third Division, from April 1942 to April 1943. He led his regiment in the seizure of Casablanca in Operation Torch in November 1942 and throughout its fighting in French Morocco. He was promoted to brigadier general in February 1943 and became the assistant division commander, Eighty-third Infantry Division, in April. In January 1944, he was made commanding general of the division and held that post until April 1946. He was promoted to major general on 1 June 1944. He retired as a major general in July 1952.

99. Claude B. Ferenbaugh (16 March 1897–10 September 1975). U.S. Military Academy, 1919. Infantry. Ferenbaugh served as assistant chief of staff, G-3, Operations, Second Corps, from the United States and the invasion of North

Africa from February to December 1942. In December he was assigned as chief, North African Section and Theater Group, Operations Division, War Department General Staff. He became the assistant division commander, Eighty-third Infantry Division, on 1 January 1944 and remained in that post until 13 May 1945. He was promoted to brigadier general in May 1944. He retired in September 1955 as a lieutenant general.

100. Samuel L. Krauthoff (18 December 1902–1 February 1945). U.S. Military Academy, 1924. Field Artillery. Krauthoff was the Eighty-third's chief of staff from 1944 to 1 February 1945, when he was killed in an accident at Hamoir, Belgium. See also *Register of Graduates, USMA, 2000,* 4-127.

101. John C. Whitcomb (17 July 1894–31 January 1974). U.S. Military Academy, August 1917. Infantry. From July 1942 to August 1943, Whitcomb was commander of the 310th Infantry Regiment, Seventy-eighth Division. He was director, Tennessee Maneuver Area, until March 1944 when he was assigned briefly to Headquarters, Fourth Army, as G-2 before going to Europe in May. He was assigned to the Eighty-third Infantry Division's staff until he was appointed chief of staff, Ninetieth Division, in July. He remained in this post until May 1945. He retired in 1951 as a colonel. See also See *Register of Graduates, USMA, 2000,* 4-104.

102. Konteradmiral Walther Hennecke (23 May 1897–1 January 1984), the German naval commander, Normandy, from 2 April 1943 to 26 June 1944, was penned up in the Cherbourg garrison with General von Schlieben. He oversaw the massive destruction of port facilities at Cherbourg before he and von Schlieben surrendered to Gen. Manton Eddy, Ninth Division, on 26 June 1944. On 26 June, Adolf Hitler awarded him the Knights Cross of the Iron Cross for his efforts to demolish the port. See also "Konteradmiral Walter Hennecke," at www.deutsche-marinesoldaten.de.

103. Hobart R. Gay (16 May 1894–19 August 1983). B.S., Knox College (Illinois), 1917. Cavalry. He became commander, Fourteenth Quartermaster Battalion, and division quartermaster, Second Armored Division, under George S. Patton, in January 1941. From February to July 1942, he was quartermaster for Patton's First Armored Corps as it prepared for the invasion of North Africa. In July he became Patton's chief of staff of First Armored Corps in North Africa and then chief of staff of Seventh Army prior to Operation Husky, the invasion of Sicily. He was deputy chief of staff for Patton's Third Army from March to December 1944, when he became chief of staff until October 1945. He was promoted to major general on 28 March 1945. He retired in August 1955 as a lieutenant general.

104. Task force. According to U.S. Army doctrine and practice in World War II, task forces or "temporary tactical groupings" were often formed or "tailored" from an infantry or armored division for a specific mission or task, normally of short duration. They were usually composed of tank, tank destroyer, infantry, armored infantry, armored field artillery, engineers, etc., units of

varying size, often from different organizations, depending on the assigned mission, and the "unity of tactical organizations [was] preserved as far as practicable." A task force was either designated with a distinct letter, such as Task Force X, or with the name of the commander, such as Task Force Barber, which came under Brig. Gen. Henry A. Barber, Fourth Infantry Division, soon after the landing on Utah Beach. In an infantry division, the term "combat team" was usually applied to such a task force. See War Department, Field Manual 100–5 (FM 100–5), *Field Service Regulations, Operations*, 22 May 1941, 3–4; and 15 June 1944, 5.

105. Edward H. McDaniel (4 November 1903–17 March 1997). U.S. Military Academy, 1926. Infantry. McDaniel served in the Strategy Section, Operations Division, War Department General Staff, from March 1942 to January 1943 and then moved to the Joint War Plans Committee of the Joint Chiefs of Staff until 1 April 1944. He was sent to Europe, where he was assigned first as chief of staff, Fifth Infantry Division, and then as chief of staff, Twenty-ninth Division, from 15 June to 5 October 1944. He was then commanding officer of the 115th Infantry Regiment (October 1944) and of the 175th Infantry Regiment (March–May 1945), Twenty-ninth Infantry Division. He retired as a major general in November 1963.

106. The Ninety-ninth Infantry Battalion (Separate) was originally formed in July 1942 of Norwegian-American soldiers from Minnesota and North Dakota and Norwegian refugees in the United States and intended for special operations in Norway. It was trained for winter and mountain warfare, but its Norwegian mission was canceled. The Ninety-ninth spent most of the war in Europe in a variety of ground-combat and rear-area security missions from Normandy through the Battle of the Bulge. It became part of the 474th Infantry Regiment (Separate) in January 1945 and had rear-area security missions for Twelfth Army Group for the rest of the war. After helping demobilize German forces in Norway from June to October 1945, it returned to the United States and was inactivated on 2 November. See Douglas Bekke, "Norwegian-Americans and the Ninety-ninth Infantry Battalion (Separate)," Military Historical Society of Minnesota, Minnesota National Guard (www .minnesotanationalguard.org).

107. Cyrus H. Searcy (12 August 1895–8 May 1963). Georgia Military Academy. Infantry. Searcy served in World War I and remained in the army afterward. In August 1942 he became commander of the 362nd Infantry Regiment, Ninety-first Division. From August to December 1943 he was chief of staff, Eighth Corps, in the United States and then accompanied it to the ETO in the same capacity. Searcy was promoted to brigadier general in February 1945. He remained chief of staff until December 1945 when he was assigned to Headquarters, Army Ground Forces. He retired on 31 July 1947.

108. Andrew R. Reeves (b. 31 March 1893). Field Artillery. Reeves served in the Mississippi National Guard from before World War I until June 1919.

He joined the Regular Army in 1920. He was assigned to the General Staff Corps in 1941 and was a member of the Eighth Corps staff in 1944–1945.

109. Frigidaire was the brand name of the first electric, self-contained refrigerator manufactured and sold in the United States. For many Americans of the prewar generation, "Frigidaire" was synonymous with "refrigerator."

110. Frank U. Greer (24 September 1895–17 May 1949). Infantry. Greer served in World War I and remained in the army. He commanded the Eighteenth Infantry Regiment, First Division, from November 1941 through May 1943, earning a reputation as a tough and skilled combat commander for his leadership in Algeria and Tunisia. Eisenhower personally recommended him to Marshall for promotion due to his outstanding performance in North Africa. Promoted to brigadier general in June 1943, Greer was appointed assistant division commander, Seventy-ninth Division, in July and held that post until January 1945, when he went to the War Department for duty with the Bureau of Public Relations. He retired in August 1946.

111. The Field Ration K (K-ration) was originally developed for parachute troops, but it was soon used by almost all American soldiers. The basic ration was one meal packed in a water-proofed cardboard box and marked either "breakfast" or "dinner and supper." The breakfast ration was a fruit bar, Nescafe for coffee, sugar, a tin of ham and eggs, and crackers. The dinner and supper meal was a can of cheese or meat, orange or lemon powder to be mixed with water, crackers, sugar, chocolate or sweets, and chewing gum. There were four other basic rations, A, B, C, and D. The K-ration could be eaten hot or cold. Each soldier normally carried one or two meals with him, and all vehicles usually carried more meals. The GIs carried pocket heaters, and small gasoline stoves were used by many soldiers to heat their ration. See Forty, *U.S. Army Handbook 1939–1945*, 91–92.

112. Robert H. Wienecke (18 December 1903–5 February 1975). Northwestern University, 1925. A reservist, Wienecke was called to active duty in June 1941. In March 1942, he joined the Eighty-second Infantry Division as assistant G-4 and participated in the division's conversion into an airborne division. From August 1942 until February 1944, he was G-3 of the Eighty-second and then served as chief of staff until May 1946. He remained in the army after the war, rose to the rank of major general, and retired in September 1965.

113. Each infantry division in the U.S. Army in World War II had a medical battalion of four companies. Companies A, B, and C were attached to support the line infantry regiments with the collection and evacuation of sick and wounded soldiers to the divisional clearing station, which Company D, the clearing company, ran. At the clearing station patients were evaluated, bandaged, given medications and blood, and either readied for movement to a corps or army hospital or returned to duty with their units. Armored divisions had an armored medical battalion of three companies, one of which supported each combat command. The company's clearing platoon cared for and evacu-

ated casualties to the nearest evacuation hospital but had little holding capacity due to the tactical missions assigned to the mobile armored units. See U.S. War Department, Technical Manual 8–5, *Medical Department Units of a Theater of Operations*, May 1945, 106–20, 128–35.

114. John A. Rogers (7 February 1889–11 December 1966). M.D., Tufts College, 1914. Medical Corps. Rogers served in World War I. From July 1941 to September 1943, he was executive officer, Office of the Surgeon General, U.S. Army. He was surgeon, First Army, from September 1943 until September 1945. He was promoted to brigadier general in 1944 and retired in 1946.

115. Albert W. Kenner (15 December 1889–12 November 1959). Ph.D. (1910) and M.D. (1915), George Washington University. Kenner served as regimental surgeon with the Twenty-sixth Infantry, First Division, in France during World War I. From 1937 to 1941, he was chief surgeon of the Armored Force at Fort Knox, Kentucky. In 1942, he became George Patton's chief surgeon and served in the Western Task Force during Operation Torch. In December 1942, he was promoted to brigadier general and assumed the post of chief surgeon, North African theater of operations, under Eisenhower. In February 1944, he became chief surgeon, SHAEF, in England and remained in Europe until 1946. He retired as a major general in 1949.

116. George S. Patton Jr. (11 November 1885–21 December 1945). U.S. Military Academy, 1909. Cavalry. Patton served in World War I, during which he was involved with tank operations, and became a leading proponent of armored forces in the U.S. Army during the 1930s. After commanding the Western Task Force in Operation Torch in November 1942, he took command of the Second Corps in Tunisia in March 1943. He was promoted to lieutenant general in April and was responsible for planning the American ground campaign for Operation Husky, the invasion of Sicily, in July, and he commanded the Seventh U.S. Army during Husky. He was reprimanded by Eisenhower for slapping a hospitalized soldier in Sicily and languished in the Mediterranean until ordered to England early in 1944 to take command of the Third U.S. Army in preparation for operations on the continent. Third Army became operational on 1 August 1944 when Bradley moved up to the Twelfth Army Group under Eisenhower and Hodges assumed command of First Army. Always an audacious commander, Patton immediately took the offensive and led the American drive across France to the German border, where the lack of logistical support stalled his offensive. After tough fighting in Lorraine, Patton turned his Third Army northward to relieve Bastogne during the Battle of the Bulge and helped blunt the Germans' Ardennes offensive. His army pushed across the Rhine in March 1945 and ended the war in Czechoslovakia, Bavaria, and Austria. He was promoted to full general in April 1945 and remained in command of Third Army and was military governor of Bavaria until October 1945, when he was transferred to the Fifteenth Army, a largely paper organization. On 11 November, he succeeded Eisenhower as commanding general, U.S.

Forces European Theater and was himself succeeded by Joseph McNarney on 26 November. Patton died in Heidelberg, Germany, on 21 December 1945 following a collision between his staff car and an army truck. See also Boatner, *Biographical Dictionary*, 412–16.

117. Hugh J. Gaffey (18 November 1895–16 June 1946). Field Artillery. Gaffey served in World War I. After duty as assistant plans and training officer, G-3, First Armored Corps, under Patton, Gaffey became the G-3 in April 1941. From July 1942 to April 1943, he was chief of staff, First Armored Corps and later Western Task Force, in the United States and North Africa. Following his promotion to major general in April 1943, he commanded the Second Armored Division until April 1944, when he became chief of staff of Patton's Third Army in England. He remained chief of staff during the drive across France, commanded the Fourth Armored Division from December 1944 to March 1945, and then took over the Twenty-third Corps until August 1945. He was appointed commanding general, the Armor Center, and commandant, the Armored School, at Fort Knox, Kentucky, on 2 September 1945 and died in an air crash there in June 1946.

118. George B. Barth (19 December 1897–16 August 1969). U.S. Military Academy, June 1918. Infantry and Field Artillery. Barth was appointed deputy chief of staff for the Services of Supply, Western Task Force, in French Morocco. In March 1943, he became chief of staff, Ninth Infantry Division, and served in that capacity through the Tunisian and Sicilian campaigns, in England, and in Normandy. In June 1944 he was made commander of the 357th Infantry Regiment, Ninetieth Infantry Division. From October 1944 to May 1946 he was professor of military science and tactics at the New York Military Academy. He was promoted to brigadier general in 1949 and later major general before retiring in December 1957.

119. Harold P. Bull (6 January 1893–1 November 1976).U.S. Military Academy, 1914. Infantry. Bull saw considerable action in World War I. In July 1941 he was promoted to brigadier general and made assistant division commander, Fourth Motorized Division. He was recalled to Washington in December to be the assistant chief of staff, G-3 and then G-3, War Department General Staff. He was promoted to major general in May 1942 and made commanding general, Replacement and Training School Command, Army Ground Forces, until February 1943. He went to North Africa as a special observer for George Marshall from April to June 1943. Upon returning to the United States, he was made commanding general, Third Corps. In October 1943, he was sent to London where he became deputy G-3, COSSAC (chief of staff Supreme Allied Commander) and was involved in the planning for Operation Overlord. In February 1944, he assumed the post of G-3 SHAEF and ETOUSA under Eisenhower. From July 1945 to September 1946, he was deputy chief of staff and then chief of staff, U.S. Forces, European Theater, in Germany. He retired as a lieutenant general in July 1952.

120. William C. McMahon (10 January 1895–23 March 1990). U.S. Military Academy, April 1917. Infantry. McMahon served in World War I. From June 1941 to September 1941 he was assistant chief of staff, G-4, and then G-3, Fourth Motorized Division at Fort Benning. Following duty as ACS, G-3, and then chief of staff, Second Corps, he was promoted to brigadier general in June 1942 and made assistant division commander, Eighty-third Division, until December 1942. McMahon was promoted to major general and assumed command of the Eighth Division in February 1943. In December 1943, the Eighth Division was shipped to England for final preparations for combat operation on the Continent. On 12 July 1944, Middleton relieved McMahon of command and replaced him with Brig. Gen. Donald A. Stroh. McMahon became ACS; G-1, Personnel, Fifth U.S. Army, in Italy under Gen. Mark Clark from August to September 1944, and then was Clark's G-1, Fifteenth Army Group, in Italy until August 1945. He remained with Clark as G-1 and chief of staff, U.S. Forces Austria, from September 1945 to November 1946. He retired as a major general in September 1949.

121. Donald A. Stroh (3 November 1892–20 December 1953). Michigan Agricultural College (Michigan State University), 1915. Infantry. Stroh served in World War I. In February 1942, he was made commander of the 339th Infantry, Eighty-fifth Infantry Division. He became assistant division commander, Ninth Infantry Division, in July 1942 and replaced William C. McMahon as commanding general, Eighth Infantry Division, on 12 July 1944. Stroh was promoted to major general in August 1944. He commanded the Eighth Infantry Division until 28 November 1944, when Eisenhower sent him back to the United States for detached service. In addition to the normal strain on a division commander, Stroh was emotionally drained because his only son, Harry, who was a pilot with the Eighth Air Force, had been killed in August. He returned to Europe and on 7 February 1945 assumed command of the 106th Division, which had lost two of its three infantry regiments during the German attack in the Ardennes in December. He commanded the 106th until August 1945. Stroh retired in November 1947 as a major general.

122. Reese M. Howell (9 October 1889–5 March 1967). U.S. Military Academy, 1915. Cavalry and Field Artillery. Howell served in World War I. He commanded the Thirteenth Field Artillery Brigade during the campaign in North Africa (1942–1943) before being appointed commander of the Division Artillery, Ninth Infantry Division, in June 1943 and receiving the promotion to brigadier general. He remained the Ninth's artillery commander until December 1945. He retired as a colonel in June 1946 and was made brigadier general, retired, in 1948. See also *Register of Graduates, USMA, 2000*, 4-100; Ancell, *Biographical Dictionary*, 158.

123. Manton S. Eddy (16 May 1892–10 April 1962). Eddy served in France during World War I. From October 1941 to June 1942 he commanded regiments of the Forty-fourth Infantry Division. He was then made assistant di-

vision commander, Ninth Infantry Division, before becoming the division's commanding general. He was promoted to brigadier general in August 1942 and later to major general. He commanded the Ninth in Tunisia, Sicily, and Normandy and was given command of Twelfth Corps in Patton's Third Army in August 1944. He commanded Twelfth Corps through April 1945. After the war he was promoted to lieutenant general in January 1948. He completed his army career as commanding general, U.S. Army, Europe, from August 1950 to March 1953, when he retired. See also Boatner, *Biographical Dictionary*, 146–47.

124. Mark VI tank. The *Panzerkampfwagen VI (Pzkw VI)*, nicknamed the Tiger, was the heaviest German tank, weighing more than fifty-five tons in the Tiger I model and close to seventy tons in the Tiger II, or King (Royal) Tiger. The Tigers were specifically built for the rugged tank fighting on the eastern front and mounted high-velocity 88-mm guns and two machine guns. The Tiger II had 185 mm. of sloped frontal armor but was underpowered and lacked range and employment flexibility due to its weight. Although a total of only 1,350 Tiger Is and 485 Tiger IIs were built from 1942 through 1945, they achieved an awesome reputation on the battlefield that was well deserved. See Lüdeke, *Weapons of World War II*, 74, 76.

125. John H. Stokes Jr. (27 October 1895–9 November 1968). U.S. Military Academy, November 1918. Infantry. Stokes was assigned as G-4, Second Infantry Division, at Fort Sam Houston, Texas, from January to June 1942. He was made chief of staff, Second Division, in July 1942 and held that post until 15 October 1944, when he became assistant division commander. Stokes received his promotion to brigadier general in March 1945. From June 1945 to February 1946, he was chief of staff, Fifteenth Corps, in Germany, and then became Assistant chief of staff, G-1, and Deputy chief of staff, Sixth Army, until May 1946. He was promoted to major general in 1953, commanded the Military District of Washington from 1954 to 1956, and was chief of military history before retiring as a major general in November 1956.

126. George P. Hays (27 September 1892–7 September 1978). Oklahoma A & M College (Oklahoma State University), 1920. Field Artillery. Hays served in the Tenth Field Artillery in France and received a Medal of Honor for heroism at Greves Farm on 14–15 July 1918. He was Artillery Commander, Second Division, from July 1942 to November 1944 when he became commanding general, Tenth Mountain Division, at Camp Hale, Colorado, and was promoted to major general. In January 1945, he took the division to Italy, where it participated in the Appenines and Po Valley campaigns as part of the Fifth Army. In 1948, he was made deputy military governor of Germany under Gen. Lucius Clay and was commanding general, Office of Military Government for Germany, U.S. He was promoted to lieutenant general in July 1952 and retired in April 1953.

127. Nelson M. Walker (27 September 1891–9 July 1944). Infantry. Walker served in World War I. In August 1942, he was assigned to the Eighty-fourth

Infantry Division until he was ordered to England, where he was assistant division commander, Eighth Infantry Division, from 15 February 1944 until he died of wounds, 9 July 1944.

128. Mark IV tank. The German *Panzerkampfwagen IV* (*Pzkw IV*) was the principal medium tank of the Panzer divisions from 1939 to 1944. During the period, over seven thousand of these versatile vehicles were built. Model G was the latest model introduced, and it weighed twenty-four tons, mounted a long-barreled 75-mm. L-43 gun with two machine guns, and had a top speed of twenty-five miles per hour. See Lüdeke, *Weapons of World War II*, 71.

129. Mark V tank. The *Panzerkampfwagen V* (*Pzkw V*), nicknamed the Panther, was designed as the German answer to the Soviet T-34 medium tank. Introduced in 1943, the Panther carried a long-barreled 75-mm. gun, had thick (120-mm.) sloped and welded armor, and weighed forty-seven tons. The Mark V was superior to any Allied medium tank except the later model T-34 with the 85-mm. gun. See Lüdeke, *Weapons of World War II*, 72.

130. Charles T. Lanham (14 September 1902–20 July 1978). U.S. Military Academy, 1924. Infantry. Lanham commanded a company of the Eighth Infantry until June 1941, when he was assigned to the Training Division, Office of the Chief of Infantry. In 1942–1943, he was at Headquarters, Army Ground Forces, and then commanded the 272nd Infantry Regiment, Sixty-ninth Infantry Division. He was then reassigned to the ETO and given command of the Twenty-second Infantry, Fourth Infantry Division, from July 1944 to March 1945 when he became assistant division commander, 104th Infantry Division, under Terry Allen. He was promoted to major general in January 1953 and commanded the First Infantry Division until July 1954. He retired in December 1954 as a major general.

131. The Second SS Panzer Division ("Das Reich") was initially established in late 1940 from elements of the SS Verfügungstruppe Division—the Deutschland, Germania, and Der Führer. The original division saw action in Holland and northern France in 1940, and the new division was used in Yugoslavia in 1941. From 1941 to 1944 it was involved in heavy fighting in Russia and gained a justified reputation for brutality. Das Reich was reformed and reequipped as a panzer division in early 1944 and was shipped to France in March. It took part in the fighting in Normandy, at Falaise and Rouen, and in the Ardennes before returning to the eastern front in 1945. See K-G Kleitmann, *Die Waffen-SS: Eine Documentation* (The Waffen-SS: A Documentation) (Osnabrück, Germany: Verlag "Der Freiwillige," 1965), 87–105; Samuel W. Mitcham Jr., *German Order of Battle*, vol. 3, *Panzer, Panzer Grenadier, and Waffen SS Divisions in World War II* (Mechanicsburg, PA: Stackpole Books, 2007), 136–39.

132. The Panzer Lehr Division, actually designated as the 130th Panzer Division, was organized in France in January 1944 around the armored demonstration units from the various German army tank schools and training grounds. Under Gen. Fritz Bayerlein, formerly Field Marshal Erwin Rommel's chief of

staff, the Panzer Lehr suffered heavily in the fighting in Normandy. The division gained a reputation as a tough and decent foe that the Allied soldiers learned to respect. It later fought at Bastogne, in Holland, and on the Rhine before being encircled in the Ruhr Pocket and surrendering to the Ninety-ninth Infantry Division on 15 April 1945. See Mitcham, *German Order of Battle*, 3:76–79; Martin Blumenson, *Breakout and Pursuit* (Washington, DC: Office of the Chief of Military History, 1961).

133. Brigadier H. N. Foster commanded a brigade of the Third Canadian Division in the Normandy landing. He was made commander of the Fourth Canadian Armored Division on 22 August 1944 and commanding general, First Canadian Division, on 30 November 1944.

134. Henry A. Barber Jr. (31 July 1896–29 April 1956). U.S. Military Academy, August 1917. Infantry. Barber served with the Third Division in the United States and France and received a Distinguished Service Cross for extraordinary heroism at Moulins, France, on 14–15 July 1918. From August 1940 to April 1942, he was chief, Latin American Theater, Operations Division, War Department General Staff, and then chief, North American Theater Group until May 1943. He was named assistant division commander, Forty-fifth Infantry Division, in May 1943 and moved to the same post with the Fourth Infantry Division in November 1943. He was promoted to brigadier general in September 1943. On 6 June 1944, Barber landed with the Fourth Infantry Division's second assault wave on Utah Beach. He was removed from his post on 2 July 1944 and reassigned to the Office of the Secretary of War until December 1944. After several postwar assignments, he retired as a brigadier general in December 1949.

135. Thomas L. Martin (18 May 1891–24 April 1984). U.S. Military Academy, 1914. Infantry. Martin commanded the Nineteenth Machine Gun Battalion, Seventh Division, in France. He was promoted to brigadier general in June 1942 and made assistant division commander, Second Infantry Division. He arrived in England with the division in October 1943 and saw action in the Normandy fighting. On 4 July 1944 he was relieved and assigned as assistant chief of staff, G-4, United Kingdom Base Section, Services of Supply, and reverted to the rank of colonel. He was chief, Organization and Training Group, National Guard Bureau, from April 1946 until retirement as a brigadier general in April 1951. See also *Register of Graduates, USMA, 2000*, 4-102.

136. John J. Bohn (3 April 1889–21 April 1983). Cavalry and Armor. Bohn served as enlisted man and officer from 1914 to 1919 and remained in the postwar army. From December 1941 to January 1942 he was assigned to the Armored Force School and then was chief of staff, Second Armored Corps, until June. He was promoted to brigadier general in July and was the commander of Combat Command B, Third Armored Division, until 15 July 1944. He was relieved from command on 9 July by Leland Hobbs, whose Thirtieth Division his command was ineffectively trying to support. Eisenhower later requested Bohn's relief because he was too old (fifty-five) for active command in the the-

ater. He was reassigned in the theater as a colonel. Bohn retired as a brigadier general in February 1945. See also Ancell, *Biographical Dictionary,* 26.

137. V-1. The *Vergeltungswaffen,* retaliation or revenge weapons, were developed to strike back at the Allies for the bombing attacks on the German homeland. Among them was the Vergeltungswaffe 1, or V-1, a pilotless flying bomb, powered by a pulse-jet engine that produced a characteristic throbbing or buzzing sound; hence they were called "buzz bombs." The first V-1s, carrying 1,875-pound warheads, were launched against England on 13 June 1944. These robot bombs were also called "robos" by the Allies, and they are often referred to as robos in this diary. A U.S. Army historical study based on German sources placed the total number of V-1s launched at 21,755, of which approximately 2,445 crashed at launch or en route. Of these, 9,767 were launched at targets in England, 8,696 at Antwerp, 3,141 at Liège, and 151 at Brussels. Of those launched against England, only 3,531 actually reached the general target area; the rest were shot down. See I. C. B. Dear, ed., *The Oxford Guide to World War II* (Oxford: Oxford University Press, 1995), 978–79; Lüdeke, *Weapons of World War II,* 182; M. C. Helfers, "The Employment of V-Weapons by the Germans during World War II," U.S. Army Center of Military History, Washington, DC, 91–92.

138. John B. Medaris (12 May 1902–1990). Ohio State University, 1921. Ordnance Corps. From 1938 to 1942, Medaris was executive officer of the Contract Distribution Section, Office of the Undersecretary of War. In 1942–1943, he was named commander of the Ordnance Battalion, Second Corps , and participated in the North African invasion and subsequent operations. From 1943 to 1945, he was chief, Ordnance Section, First U.S. Army. From 1955 to 1958, he was commanding general, Army Ballistic Missile Agency, until it was absorbed into the National Aeronautics and Space Administration (NASA), at which time Medaris became commanding general, U.S. Army Ordnance Missile Command (1958–1960). He retired in 1960 as a major general.

139. "Rhinoceros" hedgerow penetrator. The hedgerows of Normandy and Brittany were very densely intertwined growths of shrubbery, trees, and bushes on earthen mounds that separated the individual fields. The Germans used these easily defended natural field fortifications to slow the Allied movement in the area. In trying to break through the hedgerows, tanks were dangerously exposed to German antitank fire while they could not bring their own weapons to bear on the enemy. Sgt. Curtis G. Culin Jr., of Troop F, 102nd Cavalry Reconnaissance Squadron, devised the "hedgerow cutter" at the request of Captain Person, his squadron commander, who then had the motor officer, Capt. Stephen M. Litton, build the device. Called the Rhinoceros and later just Rhino, Culin's hedgerow penetrator consisted of three vertical blades or knives formed from German antitank "hedgehogs," or metal tetrahedrons, salvaged from the invasion beaches, with three other blades interposed horizontally. When welded to the front of the armored vehicle, these blades allowed

the tank to penetrate hedgerows of six to seven feet deep at about twelve to fifteen miles per hour while not exposing their unprotected bellies to German antitank guns. As soon as he saw them demonstrated, Bradley ordered the Rhinos mass-produced so that by the time Operation Cobra was executed about 60 percent of all American tanks had Culin's device attached. See Blumenson, *Breakout and Pursuit,* 205–7.

140. Harold W. Blakeley (29 December 1893–10 May 1966). Boston University. Artillery. Blakeley served in the United States Army during World War I. He was assigned to the First Armored Division in October 1941 and became the commander of the divisional artillery, Fifth Armored Division, in January 1942. He commanded Combat Command A, Fifth Armored Division, until August 1943, when he became division artillery commander, Fourth Infantry Division. He replaced Barton as division commander on 27 December 1944 when Barton was reassigned due to his failing health. Blakeley was promoted to major general in April 1945 and retired in April 1946.

141. Maddrey A. Solomon (24 September 1908–22 August 1977). U.S. Military Academy, 1933. Infantry and Field Artillery. Solomon was assigned as G-3, Operations, for the Puerto Rican Mobile Group Forces from January 1942 to February 1943, when he became assistant chief of staff, G-3, Thirty-fifth Division, in the United States. In March 1944 he became the division's chief of staff and remained in that post throughout the campaign in Western Europe. He retired as brigadier general in 1957.

142. James E. Wharton (2 December 1894–12 August 1944). New Mexico Agriculture and Mining College (New Mexico State University), 1917. Infantry. Wharton served in World War I. He was chief, Military Personnel Division, Services of Supply, from March to September 1942, when he was named assistant division commander, Eightieth Infantry Division. In the fall of 1943, he was made commanding officer, First Engineer Special Brigade, which was assigned to support the American landing on Utah Beach. He was named commanding general, Twenty-eighth Infantry Division, on 12 August 1944 and was killed in action the same day.

143. "Bazooka" was the nickname for the U.S. Army's 2.36-inch rocket launcher for employment against tanks and fortified positions. It provided the infantryman with a significant antitank capability and was easily carried. The initial models (M1 and M1A1) were a single 54.7-inch tube, but the M9 of 1944 came in two parts and was much easier to carry and use. The 2.36-inch bazooka provided the infantryman with a weapon against armored vehicles, but it lacked the penetrating power to kill the heavier German Panthers and Tigers unless they were attacked from the side or rear. The nickname "bazooka" came from the ungainly musical instrument made famous by Bob Burns, a radio comedian of the period. See Lüdeke, *Weapons of World War II,* 35.

144. Henry L. Stimson (21 September 1867–20 October 1950). Yale University (AB, 1888), Harvard (AM, 1889), and Harvard Law School (1890). Stimson

served twice as secretary of war—under President William H. Taft from May 1911 to March 1913 and under President Franklin D. Roosevelt from July 1940 to September 1945—and as secretary of state for President Herbert Hoover (March 1929–March 1933). He was a member of the law firm of Root and Clarke after 1893. Stimson was a major in the army judge advocate general's reserve but in World War I chose active duty with the field artillery. He was a lieutenant colonel with the 305th Field Artillery in August 1917 and a colonel with the Thirty-first Field Artillery in 1918. He served in France from December 1917 to August 1918. See also Boatner, *Biographical Dictionary*, 540–41.

145. Hamilton E. Maguire (24 November 1891–20 February 1971). U.S. Military Academy, 1916. Field Artillery. Maguire served with the assistant chief of staff, G-2, Intelligence, War Department General Staff, from August 1937 to December 1943. He was then chief of staff , Nineteenth Corps, in Europe until August 1945. He was promoted to brigadier general in September 1944 and retired as a brigadier general in July 1948. See also *Register of Graduates, USMA, 2000*, 4-101.

146. Gustavus W. West (14 March 1902–10 November 1972). U.S. Military Academy, 1925. Cavalry. In January 1942, West was made acting G-1 and commanding officer, Eighty-fifth Armored Battalion, Fifth Armored Division, at Camp Cooke, California. From May to November 1943, he was liaison officer with Headquarters, Third Army. In November 1943, he was shipped to the European theater, where he first served as assistant chief of staff, G-3, Operations, Nineteenth Corps (November 1943–30 December 1944), and then as chief of staff, Second Armored Division (30 December 1944–1 November 1945). He retired as a colonel in December 1949. See also *Register of Graduates, USMA, 2000*, 4-134.

147. James A. Van Fleet (19 March 1892–23 September 1992). U.S. Military Academy, 1915. Infantry. Van Fleet served with the Sixth Division in the United States and France in World War I. He commanded the Eighth Infantry Regiment, Fourth Infantry Division from July 1941 to July 1944. He landed on Utah Beach on 6 June 1944 and participated in operations through the capture of Cherbourg. He became assistant division commander, Second Infantry Division, on 4 July. After briefly commanding the Fourth Infantry Division, he commanded the Ninetieth Infantry Division from 15 October until 22 January 1945. He then commanded the Twenty-third Corps to 16 March and thereafter the Third Corps until February 1946. He was promoted to lieutenant general in February 1948. He commanded the Eighth Army in Korea from June 1951, was promoted to full general in August, and retired in March 1953. See also Boatner, *Biographical Dictionary*, 583.

148. Stafford L. Irwin (23 March 1893–23 November 1955). U.S. Military Academy, 1915. Cavalry and Field Artillery. Irwin commanded the Seventy-second Field Artillery to September 1941 when he was made commander, Divisional Artillery, Ninth Infantry Division. He was promoted to brigadier

general in March 1942. In February 1943, he led the Ninth's artillery on a forced march from Oran to Tunisia, where it played an important part in blunting the German drive at Kasserine Pass. He assumed command of the Fifth Infantry Division in June 1943 and of Twelfth Corps in April 1945. He was promoted to lieutenant general in October 1952 and appointed commanding general, U.S. Forces in Austria, until his retirement in May 1952.

149. William H. Simpson (19 May 1888–15 August 1980). U.S. Military Academy, 1909. Infantry. Simpson served in France during World War I. In August 1940, he became commander of the Ninth Infantry Regiment, Second Infantry Division. Promoted to brigadier general on 1 October 1940, he served as assistant to the division commander, Second Division, until 5 April 1941, when he was made commander of Camp Wolters, Texas. He then commanded the Thirty-fifth Infantry Division from October 1941 to April 1942 and the Thirtieth Infantry Division from April to August 1943, when he took over the Twelfth Corps. He assumed command of the Fourth Army in September 1943 and was promoted to lieutenant general on 13 October 1943. Simpson and his staff moved to England in May 1944, and there they formed the cadre for Headquarters, Ninth U.S. Army, which became operational as part of Twelfth Army Group on 5 September 1944. From November 1945 to April 1946, he was president of the War Department Reorganization Board, also called the Simpson Board, which was charged with completing the postwar restructuring of the War Department. He retired in November 1946 as a full general. See also Boatner, *Biographical Dictionary*, 504.

150. Operation Cobra was the code name for the American breakout from the Normandy beachhead. In Cobra, Seventh Corps was to break through the German front west of St. Lô after American strategic bombers obliterated the defenses in a massed bombing mission. See Blumenson, *Breakout and Pursuit*, 197–246.

151. Maj. Alvin E. Robinson was the pilot of Bradley's aircraft.

152. Air Chief Marshal Trafford Leigh-Mallory (11 July 1892–14 November 1944). Royal Air Force. Leigh-Mallory was commander of the Allied Expeditionary Air Force (AEAF) under Eisenhower. He commanded both U.S. and British tactical air forces assigned to support the Allied land operations on the Continent. He was a member of the Flying Corps and Royal Air Force during World War I. He commanded No. 11 and then No 12 Group of Fighter Command during the Battle of Britain (1940–1941). From November 1942 to December 1943, he was air officer commander in chief, Fighter Command, before being appointed commander in chief, Allied Expeditionary Air Forces. Leigh-Mallory was killed in an air crash in November 1944 while en route to the Southeast Asia Command to become air commander in chief. See also Boatner, *Biographical Dictionary*, 315.

153. Noah M. Brinson (12 March 1900–17 June 1974). U.S. Military Academy, 1924. Air Corps and Infantry. In March 1941, Brinson was made secretary of the

General Staff, Fourth Army, and then was assistant chief of staff, G-1, Personnel, Fourth Army, from February 1942 to September 1943. He was chief of staff, Ninth Infantry Division, from June to October 1944, when he transferred to SHAEF as a member of the U.S. Group Control Council for Germany. He was assigned as military attaché at the U.S. Embassy in Paris from February 1945 to January 1947. He retired in November 1947 as a colonel. See also *Register of Graduates, USMA, 2000*, 4-131.

154. Me 109. The Messerschmitt 109, the Me 109 or Bf 109 for its manufacturer, the Bayerische Flugzeugwerke A. G., was the mainstay of the Luftwaffe's single-engine fighter force during the war. More than twenty thousand of these aircraft were produced through its final model, the 109K. See Taylor, *Combat Aircraft of the World*, 182–84.

155. Lewis H. Brereton (1 June 1890–15 July 1967). U.S. Naval Academy, 1911. After graduation Brereton exchanged his ensign's commission for that of a second lieutenant in the coast artillery. He was a pioneer army flyer, qualifying as an army aviator in 1913. He saw combat in France in 1918. In November 1941 he joined Douglas MacArthur in the Philippines as the commander of the Far East Air Forces. After leaving the Philippines, he commanded U.S. air forces in the East Indies and then moved to India as commanding general, Tenth Air Force, from March to June 1942. He was then transferred to the Middle East, where he became commanding general, Ninth Air Force, in June 1942 and also became commanding general, U.S. Army Forces in the Middle East in January 1943. He was responsible for much of the planning of the Ninth Air Force's raid on the Romanian oil fields at Ploesti on 1 August 1943. He moved to England in September 1943 as commander, Ninth Air Force, which would be the American tactical air component to support the Allied invasion of France in 1944. Promoted to lieutenant general in April 1944, he was given command of the First Allied Airborne Army, which controlled all Allied airborne operations in September 1944, just before Operation Market Garden, the unsuccessful Allied airborne-ground operation to seize the bridges over the lower Rhine River. He retired as a lieutenant general in September 1948. See also Boatner, *Biographical Dictionary*, 61–62; DuPre, *U.S. Air Force Biographical Dictionary*, 25–26; Lt. Gen. Lewis Hyde Brereton at Air Force Link Biographies at http://www.af.mil/bios/.

156. Elwood R. Quesada (13 April 1904–9 February 1993). Quesada enlisted in the army as a flying cadet in 1924. In 1943, he was assigned to command the Twelfth Fighter Command and serve as deputy commander of the Northwest African Coastal Air Force, under the overall command of Carl Spaatz. In October 1943, he moved to England to command the Ninth Fighter Command, Ninth Air Force, which was to provide the fighter support for Operation Overlord. In April 1944, he was promoted to major general and given command of Ninth Tactical Air Command, which was assigned to support the First Army on the Continent. In April 1945, he returned to Washington as assistant chief

of the Air Staff, Intelligence. Early in 1946, he became commanding general, Tactical Air Command. He was promoted to lieutenant general in October 1947 and held a number of important air force and joint posts before retiring in October 1951. He later served as administrator, Federal Aviation Administration, from January 1959 to January 1961. See also Boatner, *Biographical Dictionary,* 440; DuPre, *U.S. Air Force Biographical Dictionary,* 194–95; and Lt. Gen. Elwood R. Quesada at Air Force Link Biographies at http://www.af.mil/bios/.

157. ADSEC. The Advanced Section, Communications Zone (COMZ), or ADSEC, was responsible for all logistical support of the U.S. ground armies on the Continent in the immediate rear of the frontline army zones. The ADSEC was organized to follow the armies; repair, rehabilitate, and operate the lines of communications; assume control of rear area supply problems; and coordinate activities with Communications Zone headquarters (Services of Supply). The ADSEC was established in December 1943 under command of Col. Ewart G. Plank and activated in February 1944. ADSEC's initial mission was to accompany First Army to France and establish control over army supply dumps, roads, ports, beach maintenance areas, railways, and rear area installations. Once the First Army rear area boundary was drawn, ADSEC took over responsibility for all supply and administration until the Communications Zone was established on the Continent under Lt. Gen. J. C. H. Lee on 1 August 1944, at which time it became the most forward of the COMZ's regional base sections. See Ruppenthal, *Logistical Support,* 1:211–16.

158. Lesley J. McNair (25 May 1883–25 July 1944). U.S. Military Academy, 1904. Artillery and Ordnance. McNair served with the First Division and on the staff of General Headquarters, American Expeditionary Force, in World War I. He was promoted to brigadier general in March 1937 and took command of the Second Field Artillery Brigade until April 1939, when he became commandant of the Command and General Staff School at Fort Leavenworth, Kansas. In this post he worked closely with the chief of staff, George Marshall, and virtually ran the General Headquarters (GHQ) that was to be the main theater command for any future war. As a result of the War Department's reorganization in March 1942, McNair became commanding general, Army Ground Forces, which was responsible for the organization and training of all army ground forces in the United States, and was the architect of the U.S. ground forces that fought the war. He was ordered to England in June 1944 to command the First U.S. Army Group (FUSAG), a diversionary command just vacated by George Patton. McNair was in Normandy to observe Operation Cobra in July 1944 and was killed on 25 July when some American bombers accidentally dropped their bomb loads short of the intended target area of the saturation bombing. See also Boatner, *Biographical Dictionary,* 353.

159. Guy V. Henry Jr. (28 January 1875–29 November 1947). U.S. Military Academy, 1898. Infantry and Cavalry. Henry served in the Philippine insurrection. He was chief of cavalry from March 1930 to March 1934 with the rank

of major general and then was commandant of the Cavalry School until his retirement in January 1939. He was recalled to active duty in September 1941. He was appointed chairman, Joint Mexican-U.S. Defense Commission, in April 1942 and served in that post until October 1947, when he again retired. He then served as chairman, Permanent Joint Board on Defense, Canada–United States, from 1948 to 1954.

160. "Pinks" was the nickname for the army class A uniform during World War II and for some time thereafter. The officers' service dress uniform consisted of blouse (tunic) of "forest green" and pants of a light olive drab that looked pinkish tan or beige, with brown shoes, tan shirt, and black (later tan) tie. Hence the term "pink and greens," or just "pinks," for this service dress uniform. See Forty, *U.S. Army Handbook 1941–1945*, 100, 102; Gordon L. Rottman, *FUBAR: Soldier Slang of World War II* (New York: Osprey, 2007), 84.

161. Harold Denny (11 March 1889–3 July 1945). Denny was a reporter for several newspapers in the Midwest before becoming the *Chicago Tribune*'s correspondent in Paris (1913–1922). He served in the American Expeditionary Forces as an enlisted man and was wounded in the Argonne offensive (1918). During the 1920s and 1930s, Denny became a well-known war correspondent. He was with the Finnish army during the Winter War in 1939–1940 and then joined the British Expeditionary Force in France in 1941. Later in 1941 he was in the Middle East and was captured by Rommel's Afrika Korps in November and returned to the United States. He wrote two books on his adventures: *Dollars for Bullets* (1929) and *Behind Both Lines* (1942). See *Who Was Who in America*, vol. 2, 1943–1950 (Chicago: A. N. Marquis, 1963), 153.

162. Hanson W. Baldwin (22 March 1903–13 November 1991). U.S. Naval Academy, 1924. Baldwin resigned his commission in 1927 to become a military and naval correspondent for the *New York Times* in 1929. From 1937 to 1942 he was military editor and critic of the *Times* and then military editor from 1942 to 1945. Baldwin was one of the nation's leading military journalists during the war and spent several lengthy tours overseas. He won the Pulitzer Prize in 1943 for his reporting from the Pacific. Baldwin published extensively on military and naval affairs and history. He retired from the *Times* in 1968. See *World Notables*, vol. 10, 1989–1993 (New Providence, NJ: Marquis Who's Who, 1993), 17.

163. "Foursomes" refers to the standard tactical fighter formation of Army Air Forces in the ETO. American fighter units adopted the German and British fighter formation based on the two-aircraft element with a leader and wingman. Two elements formed a flight of four aircraft. which was determined to be the best combat formation for both attack and defense because of its flexibility. Early in the war, squadrons of twelve aircraft were standard and flew in a formation of three flights of four aircraft each. By the end of the war, two flights, eight aircraft, formed a section, and two sections formed the normal squadron of sixteen aircraft. See Roger A. Freeman, *Mighty Eighth War Manual* (New York: Jane's, 1984), 75–78.

164. The losses in the Thirtieth Infantry Division in the accidental bombing on 24 July totaled 25 killed and 131 wounded. Of these, 14 killed and 65 wounded were from the 120th Infantry alone. See Blumenson, *Breakout and Pursuit*, 229; James Jay Carafano, *After D-Day: Operation Cobra and the Normandy Breakout* (Boulder, CO: Lynne Rienner, 2000), 17.

2. Operation Cobra and the Breakthrough at St. Lô, 25–31 July 1944

1. "Flying in twelves." The standard combat formation for the heavy bombers of the Eighth U.S. Air Force was the combat box of twelve aircraft (usually of the same squadron) flying in four elements or Vs of three aircraft each. The elements were staggered in altitude and distance to provide maximum defensive firepower against attacking German fighters and the most concentrated bombing pattern on the target. See Freeman, *Mighty Eighth War Manual*, 43.

2. James M. Bevans (12 October 1899–1 May 1977). Air Corps. Bevans was commissioned in the field artillery in 1920 after attending the U.S. Military Academy (1917–1918). He completed flight training in 1926 and transferred to the air corps in 1927. He was assistant executive officer, Office, Chief of the Air Corps, from January 1940 to June 1941. He was director of personnel, Headquarters, Army Air Forces, from January 1942 to March 1943 when the Air Staff was reorganized and he became assistant chief of the Air Staff, Personnel (ACAS, A-1), until February 1945. He was promoted to major general in February 1944. From February to June 1945, he was deputy for administration, U.S. Army Air Forces, Mediterranean theater of operations, and then he became commanding general until August. He later served in the U.S. European Command and Air Materiel Command. See also Maj. Gen. James M. Bevans at Air Force Link Biographies at http://www.af.mil/bios/.

3. The general staff structure of Headquarters, U.S. Army Air Forces, was similar to that of the War Department itself. The Air Staff, as it was called, was organized in 1941 to provide an air general staff for the commanding general, AAF. Although during the war its organization changed on several occasions, it basically consisted of the same kinds of general staff functions as any army command: an assistant chief of the Air Staff, Personnel (ACAS, Personnel, or A-1); ACAS, Intelligence (A-2); ACAS, Operations, Commitments, and Requirements (A-3); ACAS, Material Services (A-4). Late in the war, ACAS, Plans (A-5) was added. The theater air forces had similar air staffs, using the A-1 through A-4 (and later A-5) rather than the G-1 through G-4 used in the ground army. See Herman S. Wolk, *Planning and Organizing the Postwar Air Force, 1943–1947* (Washington, DC: Office of Air Force History, 1984), 20–44.

4. "Forts" was the nickname of the Boeing B-17 Flying Fortress, the four-engine heavy bomber that was the mainstay of the Eighth Air Force and the U.S. strategic air offensive against Germany. The B-17E, F, and G models carried the daylight effort of the Allied air war against Germany from 1942 through

1945. The latest model, the B-17G, cruised at 187 miles per hour, had a range of 2,000 miles with a bomb load of 6,000 pounds, and was armed with thirteen .50 caliber machine guns. The earlier versions were so heavily armed for the time (six .50 caliber and one .30 caliber guns) that they received the nickname Flying Fortress. See Taylor, *Combat Aircraft of the World*, 454–55.

5. The Lockheed P-38 Lightning was a twin-engine, twin-boom, single-seat fighter. Although heavily armed (one .20-mm cannon and four .50 caliber machine guns in the H through M models), the P-38s did not have the range for long-range fighter duties. When the P-51 Mustang became available in quantities in late 1943 and early 1944, most fighter units in Europe were equipped with them. See Taylor, *Combat Aircraft of the World*, 511–13, 536–38.

6. German machine pistols were commonly called "Schmeissers," although few of them were designed and built by that arms firm. The major types were the MP 38 and MP 40 machine pistols that were originally designed by Heinrich Vollmer for use by parachute troops but were in general use by the beginning of the war. Both the MP 38 and the MP 40 were 9-mm. weapons, never issued in quantity, known for their high rates of fire (four hundred rounds per minute). Hugo Schmeisser's MP 43 and MP 44 assault rifles (later renamed the Stürmgewehr 44) were mass-produced 7.92-mm weapons developed to meet the needs of the Russian campaign for high volumes of fire. All German machine pistols had a very high rate of fire and emitted the distinct sound of all such "burp guns." See Lüdeke, *Weapons of World War II*, 11–12.

7. Thomas A. Roberts Jr. (5 December 1899–4 August 1944). U.S. Military Academy, 1920. Field Artillery. Roberts commanded the Thirteenth Field Artillery Brigade from July to October 1941, when he was assigned to First Army headquarters until July 1942. Roberts commanded the Second Armored Division's divisional artillery from August 1942 until he was killed in action on 4 August 1944 while moving forward to adjust artillery fire near St. Lô. See also *Register of Graduates, USMA*, 2000, 4–117.

8. Lt. Gen. Lesley J. McNair was the most senior U.S. Army general ever killed in action. He was posthumously promoted to the rank of full general (four stars) in 1945.

9. The bombings on the twenty-fifth killed 111 and wounded 490, all of them in the Seventh Corps. The Thirtieth Infantry Division was hard-hit once again, losing 61 killed and 374 wounded in addition to the 25 killed and 131 wounded it suffered on the twenty-fourth. A total of 136 were killed and 621 wounded in the accidental bombings on 24 and 25 July. See Blumenson, *Breakout and Pursuit*, 229, 236.

10. Harry A. Flint (12 February 1888–25 July 1944). U.S. Military Academy, 1912. Cavalry. Flint served in France and later with the Army of Occupation in Germany to December 1920. He joined the Second Armored Division in 1941 and served with the Second in the North African campaign and also acted as liaison officer between Gen. Henri Giraud, the French high commissioner for

North Africa and army commander, and Allied Forces headquarters in Algiers. On 27 July 1943, he assumed command of the Thirty-ninth Infantry Regiment, Ninth Infantry Division, then operating in Sicily. He commanded the Thirty-ninth Infantry until 24 July 1944, when he was wounded during the hedgerow fighting following the abortive bombing attempt. He died of his wounds the next day. See also *Register of Graduates, USMA, 2000*, 4–95.

11. Van H. Bond (30 April 1908–27 October 1987). U.S. Military Academy, 1931. Infantry. Bond served as an infantry company commander in the Fifth Division from July 1940 to November 1941. He became assistant G-3, Ninth Infantry Division, in June 1942 and participated in the North African fighting until late December, when he was made the division's G-3. Bond commanded the Third Battalion, Thirty-ninth Infantry Regiment, Ninth Infantry Division, from April to October 1943, when he became executive officer. He replaced Flint as commander on 25 July and remained the regimental commander until 25 August 1946. He was assistant division commander, First Infantry Division, from 1954 to 1958 and promoted to brigadier general in December 1956. Promoted to major general in 1963, Bond commanded Twenty-first Corps until his retirement in 1966.

12. Erwin Rommel (15 November 1891–14 October 1944). A highly decorated World War I combat veteran, Erwin Rommel commanded the Seventh Panzer Division in the German drive across France in May 1940. His style of leadership was dynamic and exploitative. Always in or near the front, he frequently took personal charge of the battle to make the most of opportunities presented on the battlefield. In 1941, Rommel was ordered to North Africa, where he took command of the Afrika Korps in support of the faltering Italians. His daring style of fighting and leadership earned him great respect among the British, who called him the "Desert Fox." He achieved his greatest successes during the ensuing fighting in the deserts of Libya, Egypt, and Tunisia until his Panzerarmee Afrika was finally destroyed in May 1943. He lost the critical Battle of El Alamein to Field Marshal B. L. Montgomery in October–November 1942 and then was caught between the British Eighth Army in the east and the Anglo-American forces under Eisenhower in Algeria and Tunisia. In January 1944, he was assigned to command of Army Group B in France and given the mission of meeting the anticipated Allied invasion. He changed the basic German approach and strongly favored trying to defeat the Allies on the beaches. In the few months remaining before D-day, he significantly strengthened the German defenses along the Channel. By the time the Allies landed, Rommel was remotely linked to the plot to kill Hitler. On 17 July, three days before the attempt to kill Hitler miscarried in East Prussia, Rommel suffered a severely fractured skull after his staff car was strafed by Allied aircraft and crashed. During the recuperation, Hitler learned of Rommel's possible involvement in the plot against him. Rommel, given the option of a trial or suicide, chose the latter course to prevent any trouble for his family. He died on 14 October

1944 and was given a solemn state funeral. See Boatner, *Biographical Dictionary*, 461–66.

13. Thomas L. Crystal Jr. (30 September 1912–21 August 1971). U.S. Military Academy, 1934. Field Artillery and Air Force. Crystal was an assistant foreign liaison officer, War Department General Staff, from August 1940 to January 1942, when he was made chief, Andean and Hemisphere Studies Group, G-2. He was assigned as assistant chief of staff, G-2, Intelligence, at Headquarters, U.S. Army Forces, South Atlantic, from February to November 1943. In February 1944, he was appointed assistant G-2, Nineteenth Corps. He served with the Nineteenth Corps in England and Europe until January 1945, when he became ACS, G-2, for Twenty-second Corps. He was an instructor at the U.S. Military Academy after the war until 1950. He transferred to the U.S. Air Force in April 1948 and later served at NATO in Paris (1952–1955). After retiring as a colonel in 1963, he was on the faculty of Stanford University until 1970. See *Register of Graduates, USMA, 2000*, 4-170.

14. Lloyd D. Brown (28 July 1892–17 February 1950). University of Georgia, 1912. Infantry. Brown served in World War I. In September 1940, he was assigned to the War Department General Staff and in June 1941 became assistant to the ACS, G-1, Personnel. From October 1941 to February 1942, he was assistant to the ACS, G-3, and then moved to Army Ground Forces as ACS, G-3, until June 1942. Promoted to brigadier general in May 1942, he became assistant division commander, 102nd Infantry Division, until February 1943, when he assumed command of the Twenty-eighth Infantry Division. Brown was promoted to major general in March 1943. He took the division to the United Kingdom in October 1943 and prepared it for combat in France. Brown was relieved of command on 11 August 1944 and reverted to his permanent rank of colonel on 19 August. He retired as a colonel in December 1948 and made major general, retired, on 1 January 1949.

15. Grant A. Williams (b. 30 June 1902). Williams served as an enlisted man in the cavalry from 1922 to 1926, when he was commissioned a second lieutenant of cavalry. He completed the Signal School Communications Officers' Course in 1929–1930. Williams was signal officer of First Army from October 1943 to the end of the war. He retired as a colonel in November 1948.

16. Paul W. Baade (14 April 1889–9 October 1959). U.S. Military Academy, 1911. Infantry. Baade served in France in World War I. In July 1941, he was promoted to brigadier general and made commanding general, Puerto Rico General Depot and the Post of Fort Buchanan, and in December became commanding general, Puerto Rico Mobile Force. In August 1942, he became assistant division commander, Thirty-fifth Infantry Division, and Southern California Defense Sector with headquarters at Pasadena. He was made commander of the Thirty-fifth Infantry Division in January 1943 and promoted to major general in February. He completed the division's training in the United States and then took the division to England in May 1944. He commanded the

division throughout the war in Europe and until September 1945. He retired as a major general in September 1946.

17. Edmund B. Sebree (7 January 1898–25 June 1966). U.S. Military Academy, 1919. Infantry. Sebree was with the Personnel Division, War Department General Staff, until January 1942, when he became chief of staff, Force 6814, in the South Pacific. Promoted to brigadier general in August 1942, he was assistant division commander and then commanding general, Americal Division, from September 1942 to April 1943. Returning to the United States in September, he was assigned as assistant division commander, Thirty-fifth Division, under Paul Baade. He remained with the division during its deployment to England and combat operations on the Continent until he moved to the Twenty-eighth Infantry Division as assistant division commander in March 1945. After the war he commanded the Fifth Armored Division (1952–1953) and the Seventh Infantry Division in Korea (1954–1955) before becoming chief of staff, Continental Army Command from 1955 until his retirement in 1957 as a major general.

18. Master was the code name for Headquarters, First U.S. Army. Similar code designations were assigned to all American headquarters down to the battalion level to protect signal, radio, and telephone communications from providing the Germans with usable intelligence on units and their locations. The Third Army was called Lucky, Ninth Army was Conquer, Eagle was Twelfth Army Group, Lion was British Twenty-first Army Group, and Shellburst was the advanced SHAEF headquarters in Normandy. Each of the headquarters was divided into several different operational groupings. Master TAC was a small tactical headquarters, usually van mounted during periods of fluid operations, with a skeleton staff from G-2, G-3, G-4, and the Engineer Section accompanying the commander and his personal staff. Master Main (Command Echelon), Master Rear (Rear Echelon), and the Supply Echelon were the main command and support echelons that had the organizational, administrative, and logistical staff of the army and were located in more-permanent facilities in the rear areas. Only rarely were all elements located together in a single headquarters during the war in Europe. See app. 4, "1st Army Headquarters Echelons and Their Movements," in Elbridge Colby, *The First Army in Europe, 1943–1945*, Senate Document No. 91–25, 91st Congress, First Session, 185–89.

19. Fritz Bayerlein (14 January 1899–30 January 1970). After serving as operations officer for Gen. Heinz Guderian's Panzer Corps in France in 1940 and in Russia in the summer of 1941, Bayerlein was transferred in September 1941 to Rommel's Afrika Korps as chief of staff. Bayerlein remained in Africa until the final defeat of the German-Italian forces in the spring of 1943, when he left due to illness. He assumed command of the Panzer Lehr Division, formerly the armored school division, in 1943 and led it through the fighting in Normandy and back across France. The Panzer Lehr was known for its toughness and ex-

cellence in combat. Bayerlein later commanded Fifty-third Corps. See Boatner, *Biographical Dictionary*, 30.

20. The Schutzstaffeln (SS), "Protective Squads" or "Elite Guard," was the Nazi Party's police and military arm. Under Heinrich Himmler, the SS controlled the German secret police (Gestapo) and civilian police, the concentration camp system, and many facets of Nazi power. The SS also built a large, well-armed military force, the Waffen-SS (armed SS), to wage ideological warfare and be the party's safeguard against the professional army. Composed of infantry and armored divisions, corps, and even armies, the Waffen-SS grew into an ideological armed force that rivaled the German army by 1944. SS units were tough opponents who were known for their brutality as well as their discipline and fighting skills. See Dear, *Oxford Guide to World War II*, 814–18.

3. Exploitation of the St. Lô Breakthrough, 1 August–12 September 1944

1. Each corps in the First Army as well as the other U.S. armies in the ETO had a mechanized cavalry group assigned to maintain contact with the neighboring corps, provide reconnaissance and security, and often screen advances and movements. See War Department Field Manual 100–5, 15 June 1944, 9–11.

2. Walter Bedell Smith (5 October 1895–9 August 1961). Bedell Smith entered the army during World War I and served in France. After attending the Army War College in 1937–1938, he was assigned to the Infantry School at Fort Benning. A protégé of George Marshall, he became assistant to the secretary of the General Staff in October 1939, shortly after Marshall's appointment as chief of staff. In September 1941, he was made secretary of the General Staff and in February 1942 was appointed secretary of the Combined Chiefs of Staff. Marshall dispatched Smith to England as Eisenhower's chief of staff just before Operation Torch, and he remained with Eisenhower until the German surrender in May 1945. From November 1942 to January 1944, he was Eisenhower's chief of staff at Allied Forces headquarters, and he was given the same post when Eisenhower was appointed supreme commander, Allied Expeditionary Forces, and commanding general, ETOUSA. In these positions, Smith played a critical role in the planning and execution of Allied operations in northwestern Europe. After the war, President Truman appointed him ambassador to the Soviet Union (February 1946–March 1949). He was then commanding general, First Army, from March 1949 to September 1950, when he became director of the Central Intelligence Agency. From February 1953 to October 1954, he was undersecretary of state to John Foster Dulles in Eisenhower's first administration.

3. Gen. Sir Miles Christopher Dempsey (15 December 1896–5 June 1969). Dempsey was educated at Shrewsbury and then the Royal Military College at Sandhurst. He served in World War I and remained in the army after the war. He commanded the Thirteenth Infantry Brigade of the British Expeditionary

Force in France in 1940 and covered the Dunkirk evacuation of May 1940. After returning to the United Kingdom, he became brigadier general staff (chief of staff) with the Canadian forces under Gen. A. G. L. McNaughton. He assumed command of Thirteenth Corps, Eighth Army, under Montgomery shortly after El Alamein and commanded the corps through the fighting in North Africa, Sicily, and Italy. In January 1944, he returned to England and assumed command of the British Second Army, which, along with First Canadian Army, was part of Twenty-first Army Group under Montgomery. He led Second Army through the rest of the war in Europe and was highly respected as an extremely able but unassuming leader. He commanded Fourteenth Army in Southeast Asia Command in 1945 and then became commander in chief, Allied Land Forces, Southeast Asia, in 1945–1946. Dempsey completed his career as commander in chief, Middle East, and retired in 1947. See also Boatner, *Biographical Dictionary*, 128–29.

4. Louis A. Craig (26 July 1891–3 January 1984). U.S. Military Academy, 1913. Cavalry, Coast Artillery Corps, and Field Artillery. Craig served in France in World War I. From July 1941 to February 1942, he commanded the Eighteenth Field Artillery. Following his promotion to brigadier general in February 1942, he was commander of the Seventy-second Field Artillery Brigade until becoming commanding general, Ninety-seventh Infantry Division, in February 1943, and receiving his second star. In January 1944, he assumed command of the recently activated Twenty-third Corps in the United States. He was transferred to the European theater in July 1944 preparatory to the movement of the Twenty-third Corps headquarters to the ETO. When Manton Eddy was moved up to command Twelfth Corps in Third Army, Craig was given command of the Ninth Division, which he held until May 1945 when he took over Twentieth Corps, Third Army. After several assignments in the United States, he returned to Germany in July 1947 as inspector general, European Command. He was the inspector general of the army from July 1948 until his retirement in May 1952.

5. Teller and Schuh mines. Teller mines were the basic series of German antitank mines. They were circular metal containers, usually about 12 1/2 inches in diameter and 3–4 inches deep with 10–18 pounds of TNT as the charge. These mines were powerful enough to destroy or disable any American armored and motor vehicles. The *Schuhmine* was a German antipersonnel mine with a 1/2-pound explosive charge in a wooden box. See U.S. War Department, Technical Manual TM-E 30–451, *Handbook on German Military Forces*, 15 March 1945 (Washington, DC: U.S. Government Printing Office, 1945).

6. Leven C. Allen (29 March 1894–27 September 1979). Infantry. Allen served in France during World War I. He commanded the Ninety-fourth Antitank Battalion from January 1940 to May 1941 when he returned to the War Plans Division, War Department General Staff, until February 1942. From February 1942 to October 1943, he was commandant, the Infantry School, at Fort Benning, Georgia, and was promoted to major general in September 1942. In October 1943, he was sent to the ETO where he was chief of staff, First U.S.

Army Group, under Omar Bradley. He remained in this post until 1 August 1944, when Twelfth Army Group was activated, with Allen as its chief of staff. When Twelfth Army Group was inactivated on 31 July 1945, he became deputy commanding general, Fifteenth Army, in Germany and deputy president, General Board of the ETO, until April 1946. He was chief of staff, Eighth Army, in Korea under Walton Walker and then Matt Ridgway until August 1951. He retired as a major general in December 1951.

7. Henry Morgenthau Jr. (1891–1967). Morgenthau was a close friend and adviser of President Franklin D. Roosevelt. He served as secretary of the treasury from 1934 to 1945. During the war years, he was intimately involved in developing the financing of the war effort. He also became involved in foreign-policy matters and was best known for his "Morgenthau Plan" to reduce Germany to an agrarian economy after the war. FDR soundly rejected this idea, and President Truman asked Morgenthau to resign some months after he became president upon Roosevelt's death on 12 April 1945. See Michael Beschloss, *The Conquerors: Roosevelt, Truman and the Destruction of Hitler's Germany, 1941–1945* (New York: Simon & Schuster, 2002).

8. John L. DeWitt (9 January 1882–20 June 1962). Infantry and Quartermaster Corps. Commissioned in November 1898, DeWitt served in the infantry and Quartermaster Corps before and during World War I. He served as quartermaster general of the army from February 1930 to February 1934 and was promoted to temporary major general. He then reverted to brigadier general and commanded the First Brigade, First Infantry Division, until he was transferred to the Philippines as commander of the Twenty-third Brigade, Philippine Division. He became the commanding general of division in December 1936 and was reappointed as a major general. He returned to the United States in June 1937 as commandant of the Army War College. In December 1939, he was promoted to lieutenant general and placed in command of Ninth Corps Area with headquarters at the Presidio of San Francisco. In 1940 he assumed command of the Fourth Army, which was charged with the defense of the West Coast from Puget Sound, Washington, to San Diego. In March 1941, DeWitt added the post of commanding general, Western Defense Command, and was responsible for all the western United States, including Alaska. He is perhaps best known for his conduct of the relocation of the Japanese from the West Coast in early 1942. When the Fourth Army and Western Defense Command were separated in September 1943, he was appointed commandant of the Army-Navy Staff College and promoted to full general on 31 January 1944. He held this post until November 1945, when he was assigned to the office of the chief of staff until April 1947. After McNair's death, DeWitt was sent to Europe temporarily to maintain the validity of the fictitious First U.S. Army Group, which was supposed to decoy the Germans into believing the major Allied threat lurked across the Pas de Calais. DeWitt retired in June 1947. See Boatner, *Biographical Dictionary*, 131–32.

9. IX Tac, or Ninth Tactical Air Command. The Ninth Air Force's fighter and fighter-bomber units were divided into three tactical air commands to support the three U.S. armies of the Twelfth Army Group operating on the continent. The Ninth Tactical Air Command under Maj. Gen. Elwood R. "Pete" Quesada supported the First Army, the Nineteenth Tactical Air Command under Maj. Gen. Otto P. Weyland supported Third Army, and the Twenty-ninth Tactical Air Command under Brig. Gen. Richard E. Nugent supported Ninth Army when it was established. In addition, the Ninth Bomber Command under Maj. Gen. Samuel E. Anderson provided bombardment support for all American ground forces and had the medium bombers. The First Tactical Air Force (Provisional) supported the Sixth Army Group after August 1944. See U.S. Air Force, Ninth U.S. Air Force. *Condensed Analysis of the Ninth Air Force in the European Theater of Operations* (Washington, DC: Office of Air Force History, 1984), 66–72.

10. Robert W. Hasbrouck (2 February 1896–19 August 1985). U.S. Military Academy, August 1917. Coast Artillery Corps and Field Artillery. Hasbrouck served in France during World War I. From September 1937 to February 1941, he was assigned to the War Department General Staff. He was then commander of the Twenty-second Field Artillery from March 1941 to February 1942. In April 1942, he became chief of staff, First Armored Division, in Northern Ireland. In September 1942 he was made commander of Combat Command B, Eighth Armored Division, and remained in that post until August 1943. From September 1943 to September 1944, he was deputy chief of staff, First U.S. Army Group and then Twelfth Army Group, under Omar Bradley. In November 1944, he assumed command of the Seventh Armored Division and remained with the division until August 1945. Hasbrouck was promoted to major general in January 1945 and retired with that rank in September 1947.

11. George A. Davis (19 December 1892–10 January 1969). Davis served in the army as an enlisted man from 1912 to 1915 and was commissioned in 1917 and served in France. He was assigned to the Office, Chief of Infantry, under Hodges, from July 1941 to February 1942. After the War Department reorganization of March, he served as chief, Operations and Training Division, Headquarters, Replacement and Training Command until May 1942. He was then chief of staff, Tenth Corps, until January 1943, when he was assigned as chief of staff, Third Army. Davis was promoted to brigadier general in March 1943. He was assistant division commander, Twenty-eighth Division, from August 1944 to March 1945 when he became commanding general, 6960th Reinforcement Depot, Ground Forces Replacement Command, in France. He retired in February 1946. See also Ancell, *Biographical Dictionary*, 79.

12. Kenneth Buchanan (30 August 1892–12 April 1967). University of Illinois, 1917. Buchanan was commissioned a second lieutenant in the Coast Artillery Corps in 1917 and served in France. In December 1920, he joined the Illinois National Guard as a captain, and in April 1934 he was recalled to active duty with the Supply Division, G-4, War Department. In August 1937 he be-

came aide to George Marshall and remained with him until July 1940. Buchanan served in the National Guard bureau from July to September 1940 and then was transferred to general headquarters. In May he was promoted to brigadier general and made assistant division commander, Twenty-eighth Infantry Division. He remained in this position until August 1944, when he was relieved. In September 1944, he reverted to the rank of colonel after serving as assistant division commander, Ninth Infantry Division, in August–September 1944. He served as colonel until March 1947, when he returned to the Illinois National Guard as a brigadier general and adjutant general. He retired in July 1951.

13. William Wright Bryan (d. 13 February 1991). Clemson University. Bryan was a correspondent for the *Atlanta Journal* who covered the war in Europe and broadcast an eyewitness account of the D-day landings as he saw them from a C-47 during the airborne operations. While covering Third Army in September, he and several colleagues were captured by the Germans and he was wounded. Bryan was in German hospitals and then prisoner of war camps in Poland until liberated in January 1945 by advancing Soviet forces. From 1946 to 1954, he was managing editor of the *Atlanta Journal* before moving to be managing editor of the *Cleveland Plain Dealer* from 1954 to 1963. From 1963 to 1970, he was vice president for development at Clemson University. See obituary, "William W. Bryan, 85, Ex-Newspaper Editor," *New York Times,* 15 February 1991.

14. Maurice Rose (24 November 1899–30 March 1945). Infantry, Cavalry, and Armor. Rose was an enlisted man in the Colorado National Guard in 1916 and was commissioned in 1917 and served in France during World War I. From June 1940 to July 1941, he commanded the Third Battalion, Thirteenth Armored Regiment, and was then executive officer, First Armored Regiment. Rose served as chief of staff, Second Armored Division, from January 1942 to June 1943, taking part in operations in North Africa from November 1942 to May 1943. He then took over Combat Command B of the division and commanded it until early August 1944. On 7 August Rose replaced Leroy Watson as commanding general, Third Armored Division. An energetic and aggressive commander who was always at the front with his armored task forces, Rose was killed on the night of 30–31 March 1945 while trying to surrender to armored SS troops who were attempting to break out of the Ruhr pocket near Paderborn, Germany. See also Boatner, *Biographical Dictionary,* 472–73.

15. Jayhawk was the code name for Headquarters, Seventh Corps.

16. Jacques Philippe Leclerc (1902–1947). Leclerc was a career French army officer who was captured by the Germans in 1940, escaped and rejoined the French army, was recaptured, and escaped again. This time he made his way to England and joined Charles DeGaulle's Free French Forces. He was sent to Chad as military governor and commanding general of French Equatorial Africa. In January 1943, he marched 1,500 miles across the Sahara, destroying Italian posts as he went, to join the British Eighth Army at Tripoli, Libya. Later he

was given command of the Second French Armored Division, which fought in Normandy and at Argentan. Leclerc officially accepted the German surrender of Paris. He then led his division through the fighting to liberate France and then into Germany. Later he commanded French forces in Indochina. Leclerc was a pseudonym he adopted during the war to protect his family living in France from possible German reprisals; his real name was Jacques Philippe de Hauteclocque. See Boatner, *Biographical Dictionary,* 310–12.

17. Generalleutnant Otto Elfeldt (10 October 1895–23 October 1982). Elfeldt served in World War I in the artillery . He remained in the postwar Reichswehr and in the German army under Hitler. He commanded the 302nd Infantry Division in France and Russia from November 1942 to November 1943 and then the 157th Reserve Division in Belgium (December 1943–February 1944) and the Forty-seventh Infantry Division in France (February–July 1944). He was given command of the Eighty-sixth Corps, which was trapped in the Falaise pocket, and he and his staff were captured by the First Polish Armoured Division early on 20 August while trying to infiltrate back into German lines. See "Generalleutnant Otto Elfeldt," in "Some of the Prisoners Held at Special Camp 11," at www.specialcamp11.fsnet.co.uk.

18. Sosthenes Behn (30 January 1882–6 June 1957). Behn was educated on Corsica and in Paris. He was commissioned a captain in the Signal Corps in June 1917. He served with the AEF as a major and lieutenant colonel until February 1919 and received a Distinguished Service Medal for his command of the 332nd Field Signal Battalion at Château-Thierry, St. Mihiel, and the Meuse-Argonne. Behn was involved in a number of international telephone and communications companies. He was chairman of International Telephone and Telegraph for many years and was involved in numerous other telephone, cable, and telegraph companies around the world. See *Who Was Who in America,* vol. 3 (1951–1960), 63.

19. William S. Rumbough (2 November 1892–December 1980). Rumbough enlisted in the Maryland National Guard in 1916 and served in France and Germany through 1920, when he transferred to the Signal Corps. He was signal officer, Ninth Corps, in 1941 and then commanding officer, Camp Crowder, Missouri, in 1941–1942. From June 1942 to July 1945, he was chief signal officer, ETO. He was promoted to major general in May 1944. He retired in May 1946 and returned to George Washington University, where he obtained a master's and a doctorate in education (1949). He then taught mathematics at Falls Church High School, Virginia, from 1949 to 1956 and was later principal of McLean (Virginia) High School from 1956 to 1963.

20. Roberts Commission. President Roosevelt established this commission under Associate Justice of the Supreme Court Owen J. Roberts to investigate accusations about the lack of readiness at Pearl Harbor on 7 December 1941. The commission was composed of Roberts, Adms. Joseph M. Reeves and William H. Standley, and Gens. Frank R. McCoy and Joseph T. McNarney. In its

January 1942 report the commission cited both Adm. Husband E. Kimmel and Gen. Walter Short for lack of coordination and dereliction of duty. In the summer and fall of 1944, separate army and navy boards held secret hearings on the Pearl Harbor attack. It was for these hearings that Gerow returned and not for the Roberts Commission, which completed its work in January 1942. See Forrest C. Pogue, *George C. Marshall: Ordeal and Hope, 1939–1942* (New York: Viking Press, 1965), 429–38.

21. Brehon B. Somervell (9 May 1892–13 February 1955). U.S. Military Academy, 1914. Corps of Engineers. Somervell served as a lieutenant colonel on the Engineer Construction Staff, AEF, in 1917–1918. From November 1918 to May 1919, he was with the Eighty-ninth Division, American Forces in Germany (AFG) , and then served as an assistant chief of staff, AFG, until October 1920. From August 1936 to November 1940, he was administrator of the Works Progress Administration program in New York City. In November 1940, he was given charge of the national defense construction program when he was appointed chief, Construction Division, Office of the Quartermaster General. In November 1941, Somervell became G-4, War Department General Staff. On 9 March 1942, he was promoted to lieutenant general and made commanding general, Services of Supply (SOS), one of the three major interior commands of the army. The SOS, redesignated Army Service Forces (ASF) in March 1943, controlled the entire research and development, procurement, production, supply, logistics, medical, communications, and administrative apparatus of the War Department. Somervell's empire was huge, and only an administrator of his abilities could have directed these wide-ranging, vital activities. He was promoted to full general on 6 March 1945 and retired on 30 April 1946, several months after ASF was disbanded. From 1946 until his death in February 1955, he was president and chairman of the board of Koppers Corporation. See also Boatner, *Biographical Dictionary*, 515.

22. Robert P. Patterson (12 February 1891–22 January 1952). Patterson received his AB from Union College in 1912 and then attended Harvard Law School, from which he received his LLB in 1915. That same year he was admitted to the New York bar and practiced law in New York City thereafter. In 1916 he enlisted as a private in the Seventh Regiment, New York National Guard, and saw duty on the Mexican border. During World War I, he was commissioned and rose to the rank of major in the 306th Infantry and was awarded the Distinguished Service Cross for heroism in action on 14 August 1918. Patterson was appointed as a judge, U.S. District Court, Southern New York District, in 1930. In 1939, he moved to the U.S. Circuit Court of Appeals. On 31 July 1940, Secretary of War Henry Stimson appointed Patterson as assistant secretary of war with specific responsibility to direct the army procurement program. On 16 December 1940, the assistant secretary's position was redesignated as the undersecretary of war. Patterson served in this post throughout the war, and on 27 September 1945 President Truman appointed him secretary of war. He

resigned on 18 July 1947, with the completion of the unification of the armed forces and establishment of the Department of National Defense (later redesignated Department of Defense). He died in an airliner crash at Newark, New Jersey. See also Boatner, *Biographical Dictionary,* 412.

23. Cub (L-4) was the liaison aircraft used for artillery spotting, reconnaissance, and light transportation of men and materials. Built by Piper Aircraft Company, the military version (O-59 Grasshopper) of the civilian Piper Cub was a standard spotter and liaison aircraft assigned to the American ground armies. It was a light, single-engine, high-wing aircraft. See Bill Gunston, *American Warplanes* (New York: Salamander Books, 1986), 75.

24. French Forces of the Interior (Forces françaises de l'intérieur, or FFI) were the armed, military part of the French resistance during the war. The FFI was established under the Committee of National Resistance on 1 February 1944 and theoretically unified all armed resistance groups—the Secret Army of the Gaullists, the Francs-tireurs et partisans français (FTPF) of the French Communist Party, and the Army Resistance Organization (ORA)—under Gen. Henri Giraud. However, the FTPF remained separate in reality. The FFI appreciably assisted the preparations for Operation Overlord through sabotage and intelligence gathering and continued to assist until France was entirely liberated. See Dear, *Oxford Guide to World War II,* 317; Parrish, *Encyclopedia of World War II,* 212.

25. Gen. Sir Harold English Pyman (12 March 1908–9 October 1971) was educated at Fettes College and then Clare College, Cambridge. He was commissioned in the Royal Tank Corps in 1929. In the Western Desert from 1941 to 1943, Pyman was general staff officer 1 (GSO 1) for the Seventh Armoured Division and then commander of the Third Royal Tank Regiment. In 1943–1944 he was brigadier general staff (chief of staff), Home Forces. He was then brigadier general staff for Thirtieth Corps, British Second Army, from early 1944 until 23 January 1945, when he became chief of staff for Sir Miles Dempsey at Second Army headquarters. He accompanied Dempsey to Southeast Asia after victory in Europe and was chief of staff, Allied Land Forces, Southeast Asia, and acting major general in 1945–1946. Pyman was director-general of fighting vehicles, Ministry of Supply, from 1951 to 1953, when he took command of the Eleventh Armoured Division, British Army of the Rhine. From April 1955 to May 1956 he was director, weapons and development, War Office before becoming general officer commanding, First Corps. He was promoted to lieutenant general in 1957 and made deputy chief of the Imperial General Staff in 1958. Promoted to general in 1961, he was appointed commander in chief, Allied Forces, Northern Europe. He retired in 1964. See "General Sir Harold English Pyman (1908–1971)" at www.generals.dk.

26. George D. Shea (b. 11 January 1894). Shea served as an enlisted man before World War I and was commissioned in the field artillery in June 1917. He served in France during the war. He was assistant chief of staff, G-4, Eighth

Infantry Division, from July 1938 to October 1941, when he became chief of staff. Promoted to brigadier general in July 1942, he was assigned in August to the Ninetieth Infantry Division as commander of the divisional artillery. In October 1943 he was assigned to command the 141st Field Artillery Brigade, which became the Nineteenth Corps Artillery in January 1944. He remained commanding general, Nineteenth Corps Artillery, until June 1945, when he became commander, War Department personnel center at Jefferson Barracks, Missouri. He retired as a major general in January 1953.

27. Eagle was the signal and telephone communications code name for Bradley's Twelfth Army Group headquarters throughout the war in Europe.

28. Charles G. Helmick (7 July 1892–December 1991). U.S. Naval Academy, 1913. Helmick transferred to the army field artillery in August 1913. He served in France during the war. He was assigned to the Budget and Liaison Planning Branch, War Department General Staff, from March 1941 until the March 1942 reorganization shifted him to the Services of Supply in the same capacity. Helmick was promoted to brigadier general on 16 April 1942 and assigned as commander of divisional artillery, Thirty-fifth Infantry Division in July. From July 1943 to March 1944, he commanded the Seventy-sixth Field Artillery Brigade, which was redesignated Fifth Corps Artillery in March 1944. He then commanded Fifth Corps Artillery through June 1945, when he was made commander of Fort Meade, Maryland, and the War Department personnel center located there. From October 1946 to August 1948, he was deputy military governor, U.S. Military Government of Korea. He was promoted to major general on 24 January 1948, and in August 1948, he became chief, Civil Affairs Office, U.S. Army Forces in Korea. After a brief assignment in the Office of the Assistant Chief of Staff, Logistics, in June 1949 he was made commanding general, New England District, Army Air Defense Command. He retired on 31 July 1952 as a major general.

29. Marie-Pierre Koenig (10 October 1898–2 September 1970). Koenig volunteered for the French army in 1917. After the war, he joined the French foreign legion and saw extensive duty in French North Africa. He commanded the foreign legion units at Narvik, Norway, in May–June 1940, then returned to France and escaped to England with the collapse of French resistance in June 1940. He joined Charles DeGaulle's Free French movement and was sent to North Africa, where he commanded the Free French brigade attached to the British Eighth Army in the Western Desert. In May 1942 he directed the French brigade's fierce defense of Bir Hacheim against Rommel's Afrika Korps during the Gazala battles. Only after losing over 50 percent of his men did Koenig's brigade evacuate the position on 10 June. In August 1943 he was made assistant chief of staff of French ground forces in North Africa. In March 1944 he was appointed the French Committee of National Liberation's delegate to SHAEF and commander of the French Forces of the Interior in England. He assumed command of the FFI in June 1944 and was then appointed military gov-

ernor of Paris and commander of the military region of Paris in August 1944. He commanded the French occupation forces in Germany in July 1945. During the 1950s Koenig served briefly as minister of national defense. See Boatner, *Biographical Dictionary*, 286–87.

30. Charles De Gaulle (22 November 1890–9 November 1970). As a young French army officer in World War I, De Gaulle was captured during the fighting at Verdun and remained a prisoner of war for thirty-two months. After the war, he was an active thinker on French military affairs and wrote several books of importance. *Vers l'Armée de métier* (The Army of the Future), published in 1932, advocated offensive warfare based on an armored force. De Gaulle's concepts never penetrated the defensive thinking of the French military leadership during the 1930s. Despite this, in 1940, at the age of forty-nine, De Gaulle was the youngest general in the French army. However, he only assumed command of the Fourth Armored Division in early May 1940, far too late to do anything to prevent the coming German armored onslaught. On 6 June, he became undersecretary of state to Minister of National Defense and War Paul Reynaud but could do little to delay the final German victory. In mid-June, he flew to London and began his personal war to keep France in the fight on 18 June when Marshal Pétain sued for peace. He headed the Free French movement from 1940 to 1944, when he organized the provisional French government in May. He became president of the Committee of National Liberation in June 1944 and returned to Paris on 26 August 1944. In January 1946, he resigned as provisional president of the Third Republic after he failed to gain sufficient support for a strong executive branch in the elections of October 1945. De Gaulle remained out of government until 1958, when he returned as premier and developed the new constitution of the Fifth Republic. He was elected president in 1959 and resigned in April 1969 after what he considered an unsatisfactory vote in an unimportant election. See Boatner, *Biographical Dictionary*, 122–27.

31. Wade H. Haislip (9 July 1889–23 December 1971). U.S. Military Academy, 1912. Infantry. Haislip saw duty with the AEF in 1917–1918 and then with the occupation forces in Germany (1917–1921). From 1938 to 1941, he was assigned to the Budget and Legislative Planning Branch, War Department General Staff. After serving in the Office of the Assistant Chief of Staff, G-1, Personnel, from 19 February 1941 to 19 January 1942, Haislip was made commanding general, Eighty-fifth Infantry Division, in April 1942. In February 1943, he became commander of the Fifteenth Corps. From July to November 1943, he commanded the Desert Training Center in California in addition to Fifteenth Corps. In December 1943 Haislip and Headquarters Fifteenth Corps moved to England preparatory to the invasion of France. He commanded Fifteenth Corps during the fighting in France and Germany and was promoted to lieutenant general on 15 April 1945. He became commanding general, Seventh Army, and the Western Military District in Germany in June 1945. In November 1948, he became deputy chief of staff for administration, and on 23 August 1949 he was appointed

the army's vice chief of staff. Promoted to full general in October 1949, Haislip served as vice chief until his retirement in July 1951.

32. Dietrich von Choltitz (1894–1966). Von Choltitz came from a Prussian military family and received his early military education in Saxon cadet schools. He saw duty as a regimental commander during the siege of Sevastopol (1942) and later with Army Group Center in Russia. On 18 June 1944, now a lieutenant general, he was made commander of the Eighty-fourth Corps on the Contentin Peninsula. Operation Cobra smashed through his corps's sector of the German lines on 25 July, and Choltitz was replaced three days later. On 7 August, he was named commanding general and military commander of Greater Paris. Rather than burn Paris as Hitler ordered, Choltitz tried to defend outside the city. He was captured in Paris on 25 August. See Boatner, *Biographical Dictionary*, 89–90.

33. Charles Edward Hart (17 June 1900–9 December 1991). U.S. Military Academy, 1924. Field Artillery. Hart was as an instructor at the Field Artillery School (July 1940–June 1942). From June 1942 to August 1943, he was assistant artillery officer with Second Corps in North Africa and Sicily. In August 1943 he became artillery officer, Second Corps , and then artillery officer, First Army, when most of the corps staff moved to England with Bradley in October 1943. Promoted to brigadier general on 26 August 1944, Hart remained artillery officer, First Army, until 1946. In 1949, he became commander of the First Infantry Division's divisional artillery. In 1950–1951, he was commanding general, Seventh Army Artillery, in Germany. He was promoted to major general in 1951. In 1953–1954, he was commanding general, Artillery Center and commandant, Field Artillery School. Hart was promoted to lieutenant general in 1954 and made commander of Fifth Corps, Seventh Army, in Germany. In 1956–1957 he commanded Second Army and ended his career as commanding general, U.S. Army Air Defense Command. Hart retired in 1960.

34. During the interwar years, Amiot's aircraft company, Société d'emboutissage et de constructions mécaniques, built a number of aircraft for the French air force. The most numerous were the Amiot 143 and 351/354 series of twin-engine bombers produced in the 1930s. The former performed very poorly during the 1940 fighting and few of the latter were then available for use. See Taylor, *Combat Aircraft of the World*, 67–68.

35. Lunsford E. Oliver (17 March 1889–13 October 1978). U.S. Military Academy, 1913. Corps of Engineers and Armor. Oliver served in World War I. He was assigned as the engineer for the Armored Force at Fort Knox, Kentucky, in November 1940. He commanded Combat Command B, First Armored Division, from December 1941 to January 1943, taking it to Northern Ireland, England, and North Africa. He was promoted to brigadier general in February and major general in November 1942. Oliver was then returned to the United States and placed in command of the Fifth Armored Division at Camp Cooke, California, in March 1943. He directed the division's training and then deploy-

ment to England in February 1944. He commanded the Fifth Armored through the fighting in western Europe until July 1945. He returned to Washington as assistant chief of staff, G-4, Army Ground Forces, in August 1946. In May 1948 he retired as a major general.

36. Operation Linnet I was First Allied Airborne Army's plan for an airborne landing in the area of Tournai in support of Montgomery's Twenty-first Army Group. Bad weather and delay forced this operation to be canceled on 2 September 1944. The next day Linnet II, an airborne operation aimed at the Aachen-Maastricht gap, was authorized by Eisenhower, but it also was canceled due to the speed with which the Allied ground forces were advancing. See Forrest C. Pogue, *The Supreme Command* (Washington, DC: Office of the Chief of Military History, 1954), 280–81.

37. General der Panzertruppen Heinrich (Hans) Eberbach (1895–1993). Eberbach, an experienced corps commander and armor officer with extensive combat duty in Russia, was appointed commander of Panzer Group West under Rommel's Army Group B early in July 1944. He commanded the group, redesignated Fifth Panzer Army on 5 August, through the ensuing battles in the hedgerows and then the disastrous fighting in the Argentan-Falaise pocket and the escape to the east. In late August, he replaced Gen. Paul Hausser, who was wounded in the Argentan-Falaise fighting, as commander, Seventh Army, and was captured in his pajamas by the British Eleventh Armoured Division on the night of 30–31 August 1944. See Boatner, *Biographical Dictionary,* 145–46.

38. Charles F. Williams (24 February 1891–22 January 1966). U.S. Military Academy, 1913. Corps of Engineers. Williams served in France in World War I. After serving as an instructor at the Command and General Staff School, he joined Headquarters, First Army, at Governors Island, New York, as Deputy chief of staff in September 1940. In October 1943, he moved to England with the headquarters. He remained with First Army as Deputy chief of staff (Administration) throughout the war in Europe and in the United States in the capacity until January 1948. He served as the district engineer at the New York Engineer District from February to November 1948 when he retired as a colonel. See also *Register of Graduates, USMA, 2000,* 4–96.

39. Catherine Mann (31 December 1896–8 September 1959), the Marchioness of Queensbury, was an artist as well as costume designer for a number of movies.

40. The Treadway bridge was the standard U.S. Army assault bridge for river-crossing operations. Designed specifically for use by American armored forces, the Treadway consisted of sections of steel treadway that could be easily connected and laid on pneumatic floats to permit vehicles to cross almost any water obstacle. Engineer units built Treadway bridges up to class 40 (forty-ton loads) from 10 feet for bridging simple culverts to more than 1,800 feet for crossing the Rhine and the Elbe rivers. See Blanche D. Coll, Jean E. Keith, and

Herbert H. Rosenthal, *The Corps of Engineers: Troops and Equipment* (Washington, DC: Office of the Chief of Military History, 1958), 42–49, 483–97.

41. Harry C. Ingles (12 March 1888–14 August 1976). U.S. Military Academy, 1914. Infantry and Signal Corps. Although commissioned in the infantry, Ingles was detailed to the Signal Corps during World War I. He transferred to the Signal Corps in 1920. He was signal officer, Third Army, from September 1940 to April 1941. Promoted to brigadier general in April 1941, he moved to Headquarters, Panama Canal Department as assistant chief of staff, G-3, Operations, from May 1941 to January 1942, when he became chief of staff, Caribbean Defense Command. He was promoted to major general in December 1942, when he became commander, Panama Mobile Force. From February to June 1943, he was deputy commanding general, ETO, under Lt. Gen. Frank M. Andrews, his former commander in Panama, who died in an air crash in Iceland early in May 1943. Ingles returned to Washington and on 1 July 1943 became chief signal officer, a post he retained until his retirement on 31 March 1947.

42. Ernest N. Harmon (24 February 1894–13 November 1979). U.S. Military Academy, April 1917. Cavalry and Armor. Harmon served with the Second Cavalry in the United States and France during World War I. He was assistant chief of staff for supply, First Mechanized Cavalry Corps, and then chief of staff, First Armored Corps, Armored Force, from 1939 to 1941. Harmon became chief of staff, Armored Force, in 1941. In March 1942 was promoted to brigadier general and given command of a combat command of the Ninth Armored Division. In July he became commanding general, Second Armored Division, and was promoted to major general in August. He participated in Operation Torch in November 1942 and fought in the campaign in North Africa. In February 1943, he went to Second Corps as deputy corps commander to George Patton after the Battle of Kasserine Pass and then took over First Armored Division in Tunisia in April. He commanded the division in the Italian campaign through the fighting at Cassino, Anzio and Rome and to the Arno River. He briefly commanded Twenty-third Corps from July to September and then replaced Brooks as commanding general, Second Armored Division from 12 September 1944 to 18 January 1945. He then commanded Twenty-second Corps and in May became the military governor of the Rhine province as well. Harmon commanded Sixth Corps in Germany from January to May 1946, when it was redesignated the U.S. Constabulary Force in Germany. He retired in February 1948 as a major general. From 1950 to 1965 he was president of Norwich University in Vermont. See also Boatner, *Biographical Dictionary*, 204–05.

43. *Stars and Stripes* was the soldier's newspaper of World War II. The name *Stars and Stripes* was originally used in the AEF in World War I and was used again when the army began publishing the newspaper for American troops in England in April 1942. The intention was to provide the soldiers with news from the United States. In November 1942, *Stars and Stripes* became a daily

newspaper. American forces in other theaters soon had their own *Stars and Stripes*, but they had different editorial policies and varied greatly in quality. The newspaper was very popular with soldiers of all ranks and still remains the official newspaper of the U.S. Armed Forces outside the United States. See Parrish, *Encyclopedia of World War II*, 600–601.

44. Albert Canal. The Belgian government built the Albert Canal prior to World War II both to promote waterborne commerce and to serve as a defense against possible German attack. The canal ran parallel to the Meuse River from Liège to near Maastricht, the Netherlands, where it turned west and continued on to the port of Antwerp. Thus, it linked the interior industrial town of Liège with Antwerp and also joined the Maastricht and Juliana Canal, facilitating connections into the Netherlands and to the Lower Rhine. At the junction of the Albert and Juliana Canals and overlooking the Meuse south of Maastricht, the Belgians completed the modern fort of Eben Emael, which, although supposedly impregnable, fell to German airborne troops on 11 May 1940. The Albert Canal was a significant obstacle to military operations, with its numerous deep cuts and concrete-reinforced banks at places 160 feet above the waterway. See Charles B. MacDonald, *The Siegfried Line Campaign* (Washington, DC: Office of the Chief of Military History, 1963), 96; Dear, *Oxford Guide to World War II*, 248.

45. James B. Quill (15 May 1905–27 March 1986). U.S. Military Academy, 1929. Cavalry. From March 1942 to July 1943, Quill commanded with the Eighty-sixth Armored Reconnaissance Battalion, Sixth Armored Division, at the Desert Training Center and Camp Cooke, California. He was then assigned as deputy chief of staff, Second Armored Corps, which was redesignated Eighteenth Corps (Airborne) in October 1943 and shipped to the ETO in August 1944. He served with the corps in Europe from August 1944 to September 1945. He was promoted to major general in January 1952 and commanded the First Armored Division in Germany in 1953–1954. He retired in 1962 as a major general.

46. Robert W. Wilson (24 August 1893–12 February 1975). Yale University, 1914. Field Artillery. Wilson served in the field artillery during World War I. He resigned from the Regular Army in October 1922 and remained active in the Officers' Reserve Corps while he pursued his civilian career in the sale of pharmaceuticals. He was recalled to active duty in June 1941 and assigned as assistant to the assistant chief of staff, G-4, Headquarters, Second Corps, in Wilmington, Delaware. From July 1942 to September 1943 he was assistant to and then acting assistant chief of staff, G-4; Supply, for Second Corps. He served as G-4 throughout the North African and Sicilian campaigns and in September 1943 moved to England with Bradley. From October 1943 to the end of the war, Wilson was G-4 of First Army. After the war he returned to civilian pursuits. In 1949 he was promoted to major general in the Army of the United States.

47. Siegfried Line. The Siegfried Line was the Allies' name for the German Westwall, a belt of fortifications running along the German border with France, Luxembourg, Belgium, and the Netherlands. Although begun primarily to

counter the French Maginot Line in the Saar area, the defenses were as much as three miles deep and contained more than twelve thousand mutually supporting fighting positions. Built from 1938 to 1940, when work mostly ceased due to the changed strategic situation, the positions were mostly reinforced-concrete command posts, observation cupolas, machine gun pillboxes, infantry bunkers, and bands of steel and concrete antitank obstacles, the latter called "dragon's teeth" due to their pyramidal shape. None of the fortifications could be outfitted with any weapon larger than a heavy machine gun. They were intended to be used as strong points to hinder the enemy's advance and allow the Germans to bring up reinforcements and maneuver their forces to counter any penetration of the defenses. By the fall of 1944 most of the weapons, mines, communications, and barbed wire had been stripped from the fortifications for use elsewhere. The name "Siegfried Line" was apparently derived from the World War I German defensive position called the "Siegfriedstellung" and the Wagnerian opera of the Siegfried legend. A British music hall song, "We're Going to Hang Out the Washing on the Siegfried Line," which appeared during the phony war of September 1939–9 May 1940, popularized the name. See Neil Short, *Germany's West Wall: The Siegfried Line* (Oxford, UK: Osprey Publishing, 2004); Neil Short, *Hitler's Siegfried Line* (Stroud, UK: Sutton Publishing , 2002).

48. Maxime Weygand (21 January 1867–1965). Weygand was a French army officer who served as chief of staff to Marshal Ferdinand Foch during World War I. Weygand was chief of the general staff in 1930–1931 and then commander of the army to 1935. He was recalled from retirement in 1939 and on 20 May 1940 became the Allied ground commander in France. In June he pressed for an armistice with the Germans and allied himself with Marshal Pétain. He was briefly minister of defense of the Vichy government until September 1940, when he was sent to North Africa. However, there he lost out to Admiral Darlan in the struggle for influence. He was arrested in France in November 1942 following the Allied invasion of French North Africa and remained a German prisoner until 1945. He was tried for treason after the war but was exonerated in 1948. See Boatner, *Biographical Dictionary,* 606–8.

49. SOS. The diarist here is referring to the soldiers of the German version of the ETO's Services of Supply, or SOS, which was the rear-echelon logistical and administrative organization that supported the ground armies.

4. The Battle of Germany, 13 September–15 December 1944

1. Dragon's teeth, or *Höckerhindernisse,* were pyramidal reinforced-concrete projections that the Germans used in belts as antitank obstacles along the Siegfried Line. Usually two to four feet high and randomly spaced in rows of zigzagging belts, the dragon's teeth were intended to prevent the passage of tanks or armored vehicles or impale them if they tried to pass over the projections. Such antitank obstacles deprived the Allied infantry of supporting heavy

weapons and made them more vulnerable to German counterattacks and less likely to penetrate the fortifications that overlooked and covered the obstacles. See Neil Short, *Hitler's Siegfried Line*, 20–23.

2. Parker C. Kalloch Jr. (2 October 1888–12 November 1967). U.S. Military Academy, 1910. Infantry. Kalloch served on the general staff of the Thirty-fifth Division in World War I. He resigned in 1923 and worked at the Citadel in Charleston, South Carolina, in various posts. He remained in the reserves and was recalled to active duty with the military police in Washington in April 1942. In June 1942 he was placed in charge of the officer candidate school of the provost marshal general. In November 1942 he was made commandant of the provost marshal general schools. He went to the ETO in December 1943 and was assigned as commander, Headquarter Troops, Paris, in December 1944. He retired in August 1945. See also *Register of Graduates, USMA, 2000*, 4-92.

3. Don C. Faith Jr. (26 August 1918–1 December 1950). Son of a career army officer, Faith was commissioned in February 1942. He was later assigned to the Eighty-second Airborne Division, first as an aide to Brig. Gen. Ridgway and later as a division staff officer. He participated in the Eighty-second's combat jumps in Europe and rose to the rank of lieutenant colonel. After the war he served in the Far East and became commander of First Battalion, Thirty-second Infantry Regiment, Seventh Infantry Division, then on occupation duty in Japan. The Seventh moved to Korea as part of the Tenth Corps in the Inchon invasion and was then moved to northeastern North Korea around the Changjin (Chosin) Reservoir. Faith's battalion was hit by the overwhelming Chinese Communist Forces' offensive late in November, and he led his unit under incessant attack until he was finally killed in action on 1 December 1950. He was posthumously awarded a Medal of Honor on 2 August 1951 for his bravery. See also Billy C. Mossman, *Ebb and Flow, November 1950–July 1951* (Washington, DC: U.S. Army Center of Military History, 1990).

4. Archbishop Francis Joseph Spellman (4 May 1889–2 December 1967). Fordham College, 1911. Spellman was the senior Roman Catholic clergyman for the U.S. Armed Forces. He was archbishop of New York from 1939 to 1946 and then was elevated to cardinal from 1949 until his death in 1967. See *World Notables*, vol. 4: 1961–1968 (Chicago: Marquis Who's Who, 1969), 889.

5. Richard Tregaskis (28 November 1916–15 August 1973). Harvard, 1938. Tregaskis became a leading foreign correspondent during the war. He covered the Pacific Fleet and the operations at Guadalcanal in 1942–1943, and then moved to the Mediterranean and European theaters before returning to the Pacific in 1945. His book *Guadalcanal Diary*, published in 1943, made him a leading war correspondent and is a classic of combat reporting. In 1944, he published *Invasion Diary* on his experiences in Europe. He remained a leading foreign and war correspondent until his death. See *World Notables*, vol. 6: 1974–1976 (Chicago: Marquis Who's Who, 1976), 410.

6. Ewart G. Plank (4 November 1897–2 September 1982). U.S. Military

Academy, 1920. Coast Artillery Corps and Corps of Engineers. Plank served in the Kansas National Guard in 1916–1918 and then entered the U.S. Military Academy on 17 June 1918 and was commissioned upon graduation in June 1920. In May 1942 he was sent to England, where he served in various positions with the Services of Supply, ETOUSA, until September, when he became commander of the Eastern Base Section, Services of Supply. He was appointed commanding general, Advanced Section (ADSEC), SOS, and promoted to brigadier general in February 1944 and assigned to First Army in England and France until July. He was then assigned to the Communications Zone as commanding general, ADSEC, until June 1945. He retired as a major general in June 1949.

7. Communications Zone (COMZ). On 17 January 1944, the European Theater of Operations and Services of Supply (SOS) headquarters in England were consolidated and the SOS commanding general, Lt. Gen. John C. H. Lee, became deputy theater commander under Eisenhower. At the same time, he also became commanding general, Communications Zone, which would be responsible for all logistical support and services for Bradley's Twelfth Army Group once it landed on the Continent. COMZ, however, would not come into existence until the American forces were sufficiently consolidated to allow activation of Patton's Third Army. When established, the COMZ would replace the Services of Supply. The COMZ included ADSEC, immediately supporting the ground armies at the front, and the base sections. It was activated on 1 August 1944 under the command of Lt. Gen. John C. H. Lee and controlled port rehabilitation and operations, transportation, depots, supplies, rail and truck units and movement, rebuilding of the lines of communication, rear-area defense, housing, procurement of supplies and services on the Continent, hospitals, construction, and so on. At its peak, the COMZ had more than 1.4 million officers and men assigned to it—more than were in Bradley's Twelfth Army Group. See Ruppenthal, *Logistical Support,* vol. 1, *May 1941–September 1944,* and vol. 2, *September 1944–May 1945.*

8. Operation Market Garden. Devised by Montgomery as a way of opening a quick road into the German industrial heartland and of shortening the war, Market Garden was a two-phase operation. The first phase, the airborne operation, called for the First Allied Airborne Army to seize key waterways and bridges in advance of the second phase, ground operations by Monty's Second British Army. The airborne phase was conducted on 17 September and took a number of the designated bridges, including the bridge at Arnhem. However, the ground units could not reach the bridge before a strong German counterattack knocked the British First Airborne Division from Arnhem with heavy losses. Overall, the operation failed to achieve its primary objective of propelling the Allied forces across the Lower Rhine River and shortening the war, while the First Allied Airborne Army suffered heavy casualties. See Dear, *Oxford Guide to World War II,* 562.

9. Don Whitehead (8 April 1908–12 January 1981). After stints as a reporter for several Kentucky newspapers, Whitehead joined Associated Press in 1935. In 1941–1942, he was an AP feature writer in New York. From 1942 to 1945, he was a war correspondent in Europe and the Mediterranean. After the war, he was bureau chief in Hawaii (1945–1948), a special correspondent and political writer in Washington (1948–1956), and chief of the *New York Herald Tribune*'s Washington bureau (1956–57). Beginning in 1957, he became a freelance writer and published a number of books. See *World Notables,* vol. 7, 1977–1981 (Chicago: Marquis Who's Who, 1981), 611.

10. Milton A. Reckord (28 December 1879–8 September 1975). Reckord enlisted in the Maryland National Guard in 1901 and was commissioned a captain in 1903. He entered U.S. service as a major in the 115th Infantry Regiment, Twenty-ninth Division, in 1917 and rose to the rank of colonel in command of the regiment by the end of World War I. He was appointed a colonel in the Maryland adjutant general's office (National Guard) in 1921 and was promoted to major general in 1934 and was commanding general, Twenty-ninth Division. From February 1941 to January 1942, Reckord commanded the Twenty-ninth following its call to federal service. He commanded the Third Corps Area, which became the Third Service Command, in Baltimore until December 1943. He was then sent to the European theater where he was provost marshal general until June 1945. Prior to returning to inactive status with the Maryland National Guard in November 1945, he served in the Office of the Chief of Staff. He was then Maryland adjutant general from April 1946 to 1965, when he was promoted to lieutenant general.

11. Philip McCook (b. 1 May 1873). Lawyer and judge. Trinity College, Connecticut, AB, 1895. McCook had enlisted service as a volunteer in the Spanish-American War (1898). He completed Harvard Law School in 1899 and practiced in New York City. During World War I, he served as a major in France and was seriously wounded in the Meuse-Argonne offensive, during which he received the Distinguished Service Cross for heroism. From 1920 to 1943, he was a justice of the Supreme Court of New York, First Judicial District. He resigned his judgeship in February 1943 to join the Office of the Judge Advocate General. He spent much of 1943 and 1944 traveling throughout the American theaters of operation reviewing courts-martial, sentences, and prison conditions for the judge advocate general's office.

12. Field Marshal Karl Rudolf Gerd von Rundstedt (1875–1953). Von Rundstedt was the son of a general officer in the Prussian army. When World War I began, he was commanding an infantry regiment. Later he served as a chief of staff on the eastern and western fronts and with the Turkish general staff. He remained on active duty in the army of the Weimar Republic. During the 1920s, he was commander of Third Army headquarters and also helped to develop infantry doctrine. From 1933 to 1938, he commanded the First Army Group. Von Rundstedt retired in 1938 but was recalled in 1939 and given command of

the southern armies in the Polish campaign. In the spring of 1940 he had Army Group A in the center. He was promoted to field marshal in 1940 and then in 1941 commanded Army Group South in the attack against the Ukraine. In December 1941–January 1942, Army Group South was defeated at Rostov-on-Don, prompting Hitler to remove Von Rundstedt and transfer him to France to be in charge of the coast defenses. He was supreme commander in the west (OB-West) in June 1944 when the Allies invaded Normandy. On 6 July, Hitler again removed him for suggesting that the war be terminated. He was reinstated again in September 1944 because his superior talents were greatly needed to stem the German retreat from France. Although he opposed the Ardennes offensive of December, Von Rundstedt was at least nominally in charge of the entire operation. He retired on 13 March 1945 and was captured by American forces on 1 May 1945. He never came to trial for war crimes because of his failing health, and he was released in May 1949. Boatner, *Biographical Dictionary*, 476–79.

13. William H. Stoneman (15 May 1904–11 April 1987). University of Michigan, 1925. Stoneman was a correspondent for the *Chicago Daily News* for over forty years. His assignments included Rome, Moscow, Paris, and London. During the war he covered the British forces in France in 1940 and their evacuation from Dunkirk and later the fighting in Tunisia in 1942–1943. He later covered the Allied invasion of Europe and combat operations in Europe through May 1945. After the war he was the *Daily News*'s chief European correspondent for a number of years. Obituary, *New York Times*, 14 April 1987.

14. V-2. The V-2 was the German *Vergeltungswaffe 2*—a liquid-fueled, ballistic missile with a range of more than two hundred miles and a payload of 2,150 pounds. The V-2 was undetectable due to its ballistic path and was used primarily against London and other parts of England, Liège, Brussels, Paris, and the port of Antwerp. The exact number of V-2s that were actually launched from 8 September 1944 to 27 March 1945 is unclear, but a postwar U.S. Army historical study places the number at 3,255 successful launches and at least 169 launch failures based on German records, while other estimates range as high as 5,500 launches. See Helfers, "The Employment of V-Weapons by the Germans during World War II," 92; Lüdeke, *Weapons of World War II*, 183; Dear, *Oxford Guide to World War II*, 978–79.

15. V-3. In this instance the diarist must have meant the V-1 or V-2 rather than the V-3. Although the V-1 and V-2 are the best known of the Germans' secret V-weapons, there was a third one. V-3 was the Allied designation for the German Super Gun, or *Hochdruckpumpe* (HDP), which was designed to fire an Arrow projectile on London from a firing location at Mimoyecques near Calais, France. The HDP was a 15-cm (6-inch) gun "made up of forty sections with twenty-eight powder chambers distributed along the bore, so as to give successive explosions to boost the projectile as it progressed along the tube." It had a muzzle velocity of 4,500–5,000 feet per second, was 416 feet long, and could fire

a 165-pound, spin-stabilized, finned Arrow approximately 80 miles. However, at more than 3,300 feet per second the projectile became unstable and tumbled, making it unreliable. The long, slender, fin-stabilized Arrow projectile was developed to provide "a larger payload of explosives from a weapon of a given diameter" and had been in use, primarily in the east, since 1940. The HDP Super Gun was itself unreliable because the barrel exploded approximately every three firings, but the blown-out sections could easily be replaced. The five-tube battery at Mimoyecques was heavily bombed prior to reaching operational status and never fired against London. However, the Germans used a smaller, 197-foot version to fire into American rear areas during the opening phases of the Ardennes offensive in mid-December 1944. See Leslie E. Simon, *Secret Weapons of the Third Reich: German Research in World War II* (Old Greenwich, CT: WE, 1971), 191, 193; R. V. Jones, *The Wizard War: British Scientific Intelligence, 1939–1945* (New York: Coward, McCann, and Geoghegan, 1978), 462–63; Parrish, *Encyclopedia of World War II*, 653.

16. Everett S. Hughes. (21 October 1885–5 September 1957). U.S. Military Academy, 1908. Field Artillery and Ordnance. Hughes transferred to the Ordnance Department in 1916 and served in France until March 1919. He was assistant to the chief, field service, Office, Chief of Ordnance, from May 1939 to March 1940 and then chief, Equipment Division, until May 1942. From July to October 1942, he was the deputy chief of staff, Services of Supply, before transferring to the ETO as deputy chief of staff. From February 1943 to February 1944, he was Eisenhower's deputy theater commander, North African Theater, and then moved back to the ETOUSA as deputy to Eisenhower. He returned to Washington early in 1946 as acting chief of ordnance and then chief of ordnance until he retired as a major general in October 1949.

17. Virgil L. Peterson (22 September 1882–15 February 1956). U.S. Military Academy, 1908. Corps of Engineers. Peterson served at the Engineer School during World War I. He was chief of staff, Headquarters, Sixth Corps Area, in Chicago, from March 1938 to February 1940. He was promoted to major general in December 1940 and appointed inspector general of the army the following February. Peterson served as the inspector general of the army from February 1940 to June 1945, when he was assigned as director of personnel, Army Service Forces. He retired as a major general in February 1946.

18. Hugh Baillie (23 October 1890–1 March 1966). Newspaperman. Baillie attended the University of Southern California from 1907 to 1910 and then joined the *Los Angeles Herald* as a reporter. From 1910 to 1915 he was a reporter for the *Los Angeles Record*. He then became manager of the United Press International offices in Los Angeles, San Francisco, Portland, and New York through 1920. He was UPI's general news manager from 1920 to 1924 and then sales manager until 1927, when he became vice president and general manager. From 1931 to 1935, he was executive vice president and was president from 1935 to 1955. Baillie reported on World War II for UPI, serving as a war correspondent in

North Africa, Sicily, Normandy, and in other parts of Europe. He later reported from Japan during the occupation and from Korea in 1950. See *World Notables*, vol. 4, 1961–1968, 48.

19. Henry "Hank" Gorrell (1911–6 January 1958). Gorrell began his career as a reporter for the *Kansas City (MO) Journal-Post* in 1929. He joined United Press International as a correspondent in 1930. He was assigned to UPI's Rome bureau in the mid-1930s and soon was ordered out of Italy for his reporting. He then covered military operations in the Spanish civil war and barely escaped death several times while covering the fighting. He was soon UPI's leading foreign and military correspondent and covered military operations in Africa and Europe from 1939 through 1945. He became the UPI's chief correspondent with American forces after the United States entered the war. Gorrell was the first correspondent to be decorated during the war when he was recognized for his actions during an air mission in the Mediterranean in 1943. He landed with the Allies at Normandy in June 1944 and was the first correspondent to file a report from the beachhead area and to enter Cherbourg. He left UPI after the war and established the *Veterans' Report*, which he edited from 1946 until his death. See "Hank Gorrell, Reporter of War, Dies," *Editor & Publisher*, 18 January 1958.

20. John C. H. Lee (1 August 1887–30 August 1958). U.S. Military Academy, 1909. Corps of Engineers. During World War I, Lee served as G-3, Eighty-second Division, and chief of staff, Eighty-ninth Division, under Leonard Wood. In France, he was with the Eighty-ninth Division during the St. Mihiel and Meuse-Argonne offensives. In May 1938, Lee was made division engineer, North Pacific Division, Corps of Engineers, covering Idaho, Washington, Oregon, northern California, and western Montana, as well as Alaska. Promoted to brigadier general in October 1940, he was assigned that month to command of all ports of embarkation on the West Coast. In November 1941, he became commanding general, Second Infantry Division, and was made a major general in February 1942. That May he was sent to England to assume command of the Services of Supply in the European theater. Lee was promoted to lieutenant general in February 1944, appointed deputy theater commander for administration, ETOUSA, and charged with mounting the invasion of France from February to July 1944. In August, he moved to Paris and established the Communications Zone, which supported the American forces in Europe for the rest of the war. In August 1945, his command was redesignated Theater Service Forces, U.S. Forces European Theater, and controlled all redeployment of personnel and disposal of surplus property and supplies in France, Belgium, Holland, the United Kingdom, and Germany. In December 1945, he was appointed commanding general, U.S. Army Mediterranean Theater of Operations and deputy Allied commander, Mediterranean, at Caserta, Italy. Following a bitter dispute in the newspapers over his excessive lifestyle, Lee retired on 17 September 1947. He was always a colorful and flamboyant character, extremely

controversial but also exceptionally able. See also Boatner, *Biographical Dictionary*, 311–12.

21. Robert McG. Littlejohn (23 October 1890–6 May 1982). U.S. Military Academy, 1912. Cavalry and Quartermaster Corps. Littlejohn served in World War I and transferred to the Quartermaster Corps in 1920. From June 1940 to May 1942, he was assigned to the Office of the Quartermaster General as chief, Clothing and Equipage Division. Promoted to brigadier general in January 1942, he was assigned as chief quartermaster, ETOUSA, in May 1942 and remained in that post until May 1946. He was made a major general in November 1943 and retired with that rank in July 1946.

22. SOS. The Services of Supply, or SOS, was the logistical and administrative organization that supported the ground armies and air forces engaged in combat operations in the European theater of operations. The same term was used during the World War I to designate rear-area services that supported the fighting troops. In March 1942, all production, supply, administrative, and logistical organizations of the army were lumped into the SOS when the War Department was reorganized (SOS was redesignated the Army Service Forces, ASF, in March 1943). The same pattern was followed in all American theaters, so in the ETO a Services of Supply was established in 1942 under Lt. Gen. John C. H. Lee. The SOS, ETOUSA, included all services, troops, installations, maintenance of equipment and supplies, communications, and transportation needed to support the conduct of the war. After the Allied landings were successful, the SOS on the Continent was designated the Communications Zone (COMZ), whose Advanced Section handled all of the SOS responsibilities in the immediate rear of the armies. Frontline commanders often criticized the COMZ for its inefficiency and showed little understanding of the immense logistical problems that COMZ confronted. Naturally, frontline combat soldiers also considered the SOS soldiers as rear-area layabouts, and tensions between SOS and combat troops were often serious. See also John D. Millett, *The Organization and Role of the Army Service Forces* (Washington, DC: Office of the Chief of Military History, 1954), 11–56, 73–92; Ruppenthal, *Logistical Support*, 2:348–63; Bradley, *A Soldier's Story*, 405–6, 428.

23. Drew Middleton (14 October 1913–10 January 1990). Syracuse University, 1935. In 1938 he joined the New York City office of the Associated Press. With the outbreak of war in Europe, he was assigned as a war correspondent with the British Expeditionary Force in France and Belgium in 1939–1940. After Dunkirk, he moved to England, where he was correspondent with the Royal Air Force during the Battle of Britain and into 1941. When American forces moved into Iceland in 1941, Middleton was assigned to cover them. In 1942 he returned to London attached to Allied forces headquarters and joined the *New York Times* London bureau. In 1942 he won the International News Service Medal for his coverage of the disastrous British raid at Dieppe. He was the *New York Times* war correspondent in North Africa, the Mediterranean, and Allied Forces headquarters in Algiers in 1942–1943. In 1943 he once again was

back in England, this time covering the operations of the Eighth Air Force and RAF Bomber Command. With the invasion of France, he joined First Army and SHAEF as a correspondent until the end of the war. After the war, he was chief correspondent in Germany until 1953. From 1953 to 1963, he headed the London bureau and then moved to Paris until 1965. He was the author of numerous books on military affairs and foreign relations. See *World Notables,* vol. 10, 1989–1993, 245–46.

24. James H. Doolittle (14 December 1896–27 September 1993). Doolittle joined the army in October 1917 and served as a flying instructor with the Aviation Section of the Signal Corps during World War I. In July 1920, he was commissioned in the Air Service and spent most of the next ten years pioneering the development of military aviation. He resigned from the air corps in February 1930 and worked in aeronautics as a civilian, winning a number of trophies and setting world records for speed. Doolittle was recalled to active duty in July 1940 as a major and studied the possible conversion of automobile-assembly plants to production of aircraft. After Pearl Harbor, Doolittle planned and led the famous air raid on Tokyo from the carrier USS *Hornet* on 18 April 1942. For this feat, he was awarded the Medal of Honor. He was promoted to brigadier general following the raid and was then sent to England to the Eighth Air Force under Carl Spaatz. He was given command of Twelfth Air Force in Operation Torch and later commanded Northwest African Strategic Air Force. In January 1944 he moved to England with Spaatz as commanding general, Eighth Air Force, and commanded the strategic bombing offensive against Germany during 1944–1945. In May 1946 he reverted to inactive service and returned to his civilian career as vice president and later director of Shell Oil Company. In March 1951 he was appointed special assistant to the chief of staff of the air force and was an important figure in the development of the air force's ballistic missile and space program in the mid-1950s. He retired finally from the air force as a lieutenant general in February 1959. Congress advanced him to the rank of full general on the retired list in 1985. See also Boatner, *Biographical Dictionary,* 139.

25. Hoyt S. Vandenberg (24 January 1899–2 April 1954). U.S. Military Academy, 1923. Air Corps. Vandenberg completed flight training in 1924. From July 1939 to July 1941, he was assigned to the Plans Division, Office of the Chief of the Air Corps and was then on Arnold's personal planning staff until January 1942. From January to September 1942 he was assistant chief of the Air Staff, Operations and Training. From September 1942 to August 1943, he was chief of staff for Doolittle's Twelfth Air Force and then Northwest African Strategic Air Force. After serving once again on the Air Staff, he went to England as the deputy commanding general, Allied Expeditionary Air Forces, from March to August 1944, when he replaced Brereton as commanding general, Ninth Air Force, which was supporting the American ground armies in France. Promoted to lieutenant general in May 1945, after the war he was assigned to the War

Department General Staff as assistant chief of staff, G-2, Intelligence, and in June 1946 became the first director of the Central Intelligence Group, the predecessor of the Central Intelligence Agency. From April to September 1947 he was deputy commanding general and chief of staff, Army Air Forces. In September he became the vice chief of staff of the air force under Carl Spaatz and in July 1948 became chief of staff upon Spaatz's retirement. He saw the air force through its early formative years before retiring in June 1953. See also Boatner, *Biographical Dictionary*, 584–85.

26. 40s and 50s. The diarist is referring to the standard armament of the automatic weapons antiaircraft batteries assigned to the American ground forces, the multiple .50 caliber machine guns and the 40-mm American Bofors guns. See n 44, 11 June 1944, chap. 1.

27. William "Bill" Walton (1909–1994). University of Wisconsin. Journalist and artist. Walton worked for Associated Press and then for Time-Life as a war correspondent in World War II. He jumped into France with the Eighty-second Airborne Division on 6 June 1944 to cover the story and then covered military operations in Europe. He moved to Washington in 1945 and gave up journalism to pursue a successful career as a painter. He was involved with John F. Kennedy's run for the Democratic nomination and presidency in 1960. For his support, Kennedy named him chair of the Washington Fine Arts Commission (1961–1971). During his tenure, he was involved in historic preservation and the expansion of the National Gallery of Art as well as the design of Dulles International Airport and the Washington Area Metropolitan Transit system (Metro). See Obituary, "William Walton Dies at Age 85," *Washington Post*, 20 December 1994; Barney Oldfield, *Never a Shot in Anger* (Santa Barbara, CA: Capra Press, 1989), 77–79.

28. V-13. The 1106th Engineer Combat Group apparently did not savor being excluded from the general artillery bombardment of Aachen. From their defensive positions overlooking the city from the south, they devised their own revenge weapon, the V-13. They found several streetcars at the top of the hill above the city, crammed one of them with captured German explosives, and set a time fuse. This car was then dispatched down the tracks into the city. Unfortunately, the first V-13 exploded before it reached the target. A second was tried, but it collided with the wreckage of the first and did not go off. Both failures were cleared from the tracks, and the men of the 1106th tried again. This time the V-13 reached the city before exploding, but it was not known what, if any, damage it did to Aachen's defenders. See Beck et al., *The Corps of Engineers: The War against Germany* (Washington, DC: U.S. Army Center of Military History, 1985), 422–23; MacDonald, *The Siegfried Line Campaign*, 310, fn 4.

29. The Walther Model P 38 semiautomatic 9-mm pistol became a standard sidearm in the German military in 1938 to replace the Luger Model 08, which eventually ended production in 1942. Lüdeke, *Weapons of World War II*, 10.

30. Wyman's divisional command was to be the Seventy-first Infantry Divi-

sion, which was then finishing training in the United States. Wyman had been the assistant division commander, First Division, from August 1943 to 7 October 1944. He received the division not only because of his previous command and combat experience but also because Eisenhower refused to accept the commander, Eugene Landrum, back in the European theater after relieving him of command in August and sending him home. See n 66, chap. 1.

31. Thomas T. Handy (11 March 1892–14 April 1982). Virginia Military Institute, 1914. Field Artillery. During World War I, Handy served with the Fifth and 151st Field Artillery in France. From 1936 to 1940, he was in the War Plans Division, War Department General Staff. He then commanded the Seventy-eighth Field Artillery Brigade at Fort Benning, Georgia, in 1940–1941, before rejoining the War Plans Division in 1941. In February 1942 Handy became chief, Strategy and Policy Group, under Eisenhower. When Eisenhower left for England in June Handy became assistant chief of staff, Operations Division, and was promoted to major general. In October 1944, he was promoted to lieutenant general and became deputy chief of staff to Marshall and remained in that post until August 1947. In September 1949, he became commander in chief, U.S. European Command at Heidelberg, Germany, and in February 1952 added the role of deputy commander, Supreme Headquarters Allied Powers Europe. Handy retired as a full general in March 1954.

32. Frank McCarthy (8 June 1912–1 December 1986). Virginia Military Institute, 1933. Field Artillery. In 1937 he became a press agent in New York City. He was recalled to active duty from the reserves in 1941 and served as assistant secretary, War Department General Staff, and then as military secretary to the chief of staff. On 15 January 1944, he was made secretary of the General Staff and held that post until August 1945, when he left active duty. He then went to the State Department as an assistant secretary in 1945 but left there in 1946 to be the assistant to the vice president of the Motion Picture Association of America. He spent 1947–1949 in Europe for the Motion Picture Association and then became an executive and producer at 20th Century Fox Studios from 1949 to 1962 and 1965 to 1972. He was also a producer at Universal Studios from 1963 to 1965 and 1973 to 1975. Among the pictures he produced are *Decision before Dawn, Sailor of the King, A Guide for the Married Man, Patton* (which won seven Oscars, including Best Picture and Best Actor, 1970), *Fireball Forward*, and *MacArthur*. McCarthy remained in the Army Reserve after the war and reached the rank of brigadier general in 1957. See *World Notables*, vol. 9, 1985–1989 (New Providence, NJ: Marquis Who's Who, 1989), 238.

33. John L. Throckmorton (28 February 1913–13 February 1986). U.S. Military Academy, 1935. Infantry. Throckmorton was assigned to Replacement and School Command from September 1942 to January 1943, when he became assistant chief of staff, G-3, Operations, with the Seventy-fifth Infantry Division. In November 1943 he was ordered to First Army in England as assistant to the assistant chief of staff, G-3, and remained with G-3, First Army, throughout

the war in Europe and its redeployment to the United States. He commanded the Second Battalion, Fifth Infantry, in Hawaii and Korea from 1949 to 1951. In 1959–1960, he was assistant division commander, 101st Airborne Division, and then commanding general, Eighty-second Airborne Division from 1962 to 1944. He was deputy commander, U.S. Military Assistance Command, Vietnam in 1964–65 and commanding general, Eighteenth Airborne Corps, 1966–67, before becoming commanding general, Third Army, in 1967–1969, and commander in chief, U.S. Strike Command, and a full general from 1969 to 1973.

34. James F. Byrnes (1879–1972). Byrnes was a U.S. senator from South Carolina who played an important role on the Senate Foreign Relations Committee in the passage of the Selective Service Act, Lend-Lease, and other American preparations for World War II. In 1941 President Roosevelt appointed him to the Supreme Court. In October 1942, the president asked Byrnes to leave the Court and become the director of the Office of Economic Stabilization and chairman of the Economic Stabilization Board. In these posts, Byrnes was the principal person responsible for controlling the American wartime economy. In 1943 Byrnes's office was redesignated the Office of War Mobilization. Byrnes remained one of FDR's principal diplomatic and political advisers and accompanied him to the Yalta Conference in February 1945. After Roosevelt's death in April, Byrnes resigned his positions, but President Truman asked him to remain as his adviser in foreign policy matters. In July, Byrne succeeded Edward Stettinius as secretary of state and attended the Potsdam Conference with Truman. Byrnes remained secretary of state until January 1947 when George Marshall replaced him. See Boatner, *Biographical Dictionary*, 71–72.

35. King George VI (1895–1952). Son of George V, he served in World War I and succeeded to the throne as king of Great Britain and Northern Ireland and emperor of India upon the abdication of his brother Edward VIII on 11 December 1936. See *Webster's Biographical Dictionary* (Springfield, MA: G. & C. Merriam, 1972), s.v. George VI.

36. Right Honorable Sir Alan Frederick Lascelles (b. 11 April 1877) was educated at Marlborough College, Trinity College, Oxford. He served in France during World War I with the Bedfordshire Yeomanry. He was the assistant private secretary to the Prince of Wales from 1920 to 1929. In 1935 he became the assistant private secretary to King George V, then assistant private secretary to King George VI (1936–1943), and private secretary until the king's death in 1952.

37. Sir Piers (Walter) Legh (12 December 1890–14 October 1955). Legh was appointed an officer in the Grenadier Guards in 1910. In 1914–1915 he was aide-de-camp to the Duke of Connaught, governor general of Canada, and then served in Europe until the end of the war. From 1919 to 1934 Legh was equerry to the Prince of Wales and remained in the same post with King George VI until 1946. From 1941 to 1952 he was master of His Majesty's Household.

38. Charles R. Codman (22 February 1893–25 August 1956). Harvard Col-

lege, 1915. Codman was George Patton's aide from early 1943 through Patton's death in December 1945. During World War I, Codman served in the Air Service, AEF, in a day-bombing squadron. After being shot down over German territory, he was captured but later escaped with James Norman Hall and reached Allied lines. He returned to Boston to resume his civilian career as banker and real estate developer. He volunteered once again for duty in 1940 and was commissioned a major in Intelligence due to his fluency in French and knowledge of the country. He served as an interpreter at the Casablanca Conference, and after meeting him there, Patton had Codman assigned to his staff. See also Charles R. Codman, *Drive* (Boston: Little, Brown, 1957).

39. William M. Miley (26 December 1897–24 September 1997). U.S. Military Academy, November 1918. Infantry. Miley commanded the 501st Parachute Infantry Battalion from October 1940 to March 1942 and the 502nd Parachute Infantry Battalion to June 1942. With his promotion to brigadier general in June 1942, he was made assistant division commander, Ninety-sixth Division, and then held the same post with the Eighty-second Airborne Division from September 1942 to February 1943, when he became commander of the Seventeenth Airborne Division. He was promoted to major general in April 1943. He took the division to Europe, where it was in combat in 1944–1945, including the Battle of the Bulge and Operation Varsity, the airborne landing across the Rhine River in March 1945. From May 1952 to July 1954, he was commanding general, U.S. Army Alaska. He retired as a major general in July 1955.

40. Gen. Sir Richard Nelson Gale (25 July 1896–29 July 1982) was educated at the Royal Military Academy, Sandhurst, and fought in World War I. He was promoted to brigadier in 1941 and major general in 1943. In 1943–1944 he raised and commanded the First Parachute Brigade, Sixth Airborne Division. In 1944 he became commander of the Sixth Airborne Division and led it through the airborne operations in Normandy. In December 1944 he became commander of the First British Airborne Corps, and in 1945 he was promoted to lieutenant general and became deputy commander, First Allied Airborne Army. He retired in 1957 but was recalled in 1958 as deputy supreme allied commander, Europe. He retired again in 1960. See "General Sir Richard Nelson Gale" in "The Generals of WWII" at http://www.generals.dk.

41. Paul L. Williams (16 April 1894–1 March 1968). Stanford University, 1917. Williams served in the Aviation Section, Signal Corps, during World War I. He went to England with Spaatz in June 1942 and served in the Eighth Air Force. From November 1942 to January 1943, he commanded the Fifty-first Troop Carrier Wing in England. From June 1943 to February 1944 he commanded the Twelfth Troop Carrier Command (Provisional) of the Twelfth Air Force in North Africa and the Mediterranean and was involved in planning and execution of major airborne operations. He then returned to England and commanded the Ninth Troop Carrier Command, Ninth Air Force, until July

1945. His command provided all the air transport aircraft that lifted the U.S. airborne divisions for their drops on D-day and later in operations Market Garden and Varsity (the crossing of the Rhine River in March 1945). He was promoted to major general in August 1944. He retired in April 1950 as a major general. See also "Major General Paul L. Williams" at Air Force Link, http://www.af.mil/bios/.

42. Richard C. Partridge (15 February 1899–23 July 1976). Harvard College, 1918; U.S. Military Academy, 1920. Field Artillery. After service as a military attaché in Berlin and Hungary from February 1940 until December 1941, Partridge joined the Second Corps in England as assistant G-3 in June. From August 1942 to February 1943, he was assistant G-3 with Allied Forces headquarters in England and North Africa. He was then assistant G-3 with Headquarters Fifteenth Army Group in the Mediterranean until November 1943, when he was made assistant to the G-3 of First Army Group. From April to June 1944 he was G-3 for Seventh Corps and was then commander of the 358th Infantry Regiment, Ninetieth Infantry Division until August. He was the chief of staff, Seventh Corps, until September 1945. He was promoted to brigadier general in March 1945. He retired in 1959 as a major general.

43. Theodore E. Buechler (26 October 1893–6 November 1980). U.S. Military Academy, August 1917. Field Artillery. Buechler was assigned to the War Department General Staff from January 1941 to August 1942. In October he was promoted to brigadier general and made commander, Divisional Artillery, One Hundredth Infantry Division. In October 1943 he became commanding general, Eighteenth Corps Artillery, and moved to Europe with the corps in the summer of 1944. From January to June 1945, he was artillery officer for SHAEF and ETO. He retired as a brigadier general in July 1953.

44. Samuel N. Hodges Jr., was captured on 4 October 1944 and spent the remainder of the war as a prisoner of war. He was repatriated at the end of the war. See record for Samuel N. Hodges Jr., at "World War II Prisoners of War Data File, 12/7/1941–11/19/1946," in online Access to Archival Databases (AAD), National Archives and Records Administration, http://aad.archives.gov/aad/.

45. Tim McCoy (10 April 1891–29 January 1978). McCoy joined the cavalry as a captain in 1917. In 1919, he was appointed the adjutant general of Wyoming as a brigadier general. From 1922 on, McCoy was both a film star and a movie director, appearing in numerous films and later television shows. He remained in the reserves and was promoted to the rank of colonel in 1943 after being recalled to active duty. See *World Notables,* vol. 8, 1977–1981, 387.

46. Sixth Army Group. The Sixth U.S. Army Group was activated on Corsica on 1 August 1944 to control the operations of the Seventh U.S. Army and First French Army after the landings in southern France (Operation Anvil/Dragoon in August 1944). Lt. Gen. Jacob L. Devers was placed in command. Sixth Army Group became operational on 15 September 1944, after Seventh

Army made contact with Twelfth Army Group forces. Eisenhower always saw Sixth Army Group as a force supporting the main Allied drive by the Twelfth and Twenty-first Army Groups, and thus it played a secondary role throughout the war. It was inactivated on 20 July 1945. See Jeffrey J. Clarke and Robert Ross Smith, *Riviera to the Rhine* (Washington, DC: U.S. Army Center of Military History, 1993).

47. Lancaster. The Lancaster was the most successful of the British heavy bombers of World War II. Designed and built by AVRO, the Lancaster had four Rolls-Royce liquid-cooled engines and could carry 14,000 pounds of bombs a range of 1,600 miles or a single 22,000-pound Grand Slam. The Lancaster, a midwing monoplane with a twin tail, entered service in March 1942. Modified Lancasters were used for numerous special missions, including the famous dams mission of 17 May 1943 and later to sink the German battleship *Tirpitz* in November 1944. The Lancaster was arguably the best heavy bomber of the war. See Taylor, *Combat Aircraft of the World*, 314–15.

48. Halifax. Handley Page designed and built the four-engine Halifax heavy bomber for the RAF. This midwing, twin-tail monoplane first flew in 1939 and used four Rolls-Royce Merlin engines. The Halifax carried a crew of seven and 13,000 pounds of bombs. See Taylor, *Combat Aircraft of the World*, 377–78.

49. Henry B. Sayler (4 November 1893–7 May 1970). U.S. Military Academy, 1915. Coast Artillery Corps and Ordnance Department. Sayler transferred to the Ordnance Department in March 1921. He was ordnance officer for First Army and Eastern Defense Command from January to June 1942, when he was sent to the European theater as ordnance officer. He was promoted to brigadier general in April 1943 and major general in June 1944. From August 1945 to February 1946, he was deputy chief of ordnance. He was then chief, research and development, Department of the Army, from August 1946 to November 1949. He retired in December 1949 as a major general.

50. The article on Hodges appeared in the 16 October 1944 issue of *Time* magazine with his portrait on the cover. See issue and article on Hodges, "Precise Puncher," at http://www.time.com/time.

51. Field Marshal Paul von Hindenburg (1847–1934). Hindenburg was a Prussian Army officer who fought in the Austro-Prussian War of 1866 and then the Franco-Prussian War (1870–1871). He later served on the German general staff and was head of the infantry bureau. He was promoted to lieutenant general in 1900 and commanded the Fourth Corps from 1903 to 1911, when he retired. In August 1914 he was recalled to active service to command the East Prussian campaign and directed the crushing victory over the Russians at Tannenberg. He was promoted to field marshal and given command of the German forces facing the Russians in 1915. In 1916 he replaced General von Falkenhayn as chief of the German general staff and took over the direction of the German war effort. In his operational planning, he was heavily influenced by Erich Ludendorff, who had been his chief of staff since 1914 and was the

architect of his victories. Hindenburg retired in 1919 but reentered public life when elected president of the Weimar Republic in 1925. He was reelected in 1932 after a hard-fought election campaign against Adolf Hitler and the Nazi Party, which finally gained power in Germany in January 1933 when Hindenburg was convinced by his conservative friends that Hitler could be controlled if allowed into the chancellor's office. Hindenburg died on 2 August 1934, and the final barrier to Hitler's total control of the German army and government disappeared with him. See Boatner, *Biographical Dictionary*, 219.

52. John W. Leonard (25 January 1890–26 October 1974). U.S. Military Academy, 1915. Infantry. Leonard served in France in World War I. In 1940–1941, he was on the General Staff of the Second Infantry Division and then commanded the Sixth Armored Infantry Regiment from October 1941 to March 1942, when he became commander of Combat Command B, Fourth Armored Division. He was promoted to brigadier general in June and given command of Combat Command B, Ninth Armored Division, in September 1942. The next month he became the Ninth's commanding general and was promoted to major general. He led the division during the war in Europe and through its inactivation in August 1945. He was promoted lieutenant general in February 1951 and commanded Eighteenth Airborne Corps until his retirement in January 1952.

53. Alaska Highway. After the Japanese attack at Pearl Harbor, American military planners feared that the sea lanes to Alaska, their only way to supply troops and equipment, were vulnerable to interdiction. In February 1942, President Roosevelt decided to build a Canadian-Alaskan military highway, later called the Alcan Highway and now the Alaska Highway, across largely unmapped and impenetrable territory in cooperation with the Canadian government. Running from Dawson Creek, British Columbia, to Fairbanks, Alaska, the road would be a secure inland link between the central United States and Alaska that could be used to reinforce and resupply Alaska in case of Japanese attack. The road was also intended to connect the air bases built along the Northwest Staging Route to Alaska for aircraft being transferred to the Soviet Union under the Lend-Lease Act. Initially the road was under the overall direction of Brig. Gen. William M. Hoge, but in May 1942 the road was split into two sectors to facilitate completion. By November 1942 the basic highway was completed and the first army truck convoys made their runs from Dawson Creek to Fairbanks. The Alaska Highway was kept in operation throughout the war, and then the section in Canada was turned over to the Canadian government in 1946. See John T. Greenwood, "Building the Road to Alaska," in *Builders and Fighters: U.S. Army Engineers in World War II*, ed. Barry W. Fowle (Fort Belvoir, VA: Office of History, U.S. Army Corps of Engineers, 1992), 117–35.

54. Joseph J. O'Hare (19 February 1893–2 April 1961). U.S. Military Academy, 1916. Coast Artillery Corps and Infantry. O'Hare served in France during World War I. He was assigned to Headquarters, First Army, as assistant chief of staff, G-1, Personnel, in New York from October 1940 to September 1943,

when the headquarters moved to England. He remained G-1 until August 1944, when he moved to Twelfth Army Group as G-1 for Omar Bradley. He was promoted to brigadier general in November 1944 and became G-1, Service Forces, U.S. Forces European Theater, in July 1945. He was later assigned to Washington as assistant G-1, War Department General Staff, from March 1945 to January 1949. He was American military attaché from May 1949 until his retirement in February 1953.

55. Mark S. Gurnee served with the U.S. Army Corps of Engineers as a junior engineer in the New York, Vicksburg, and Providence engineer districts from 1934 to 1941, when he moved to the Office, Chief of Engineers, in Washington, D.C. He was called to active duty in 1941 and served as S-2, engineer intelligence officer, Engineer Section, First Army, in the United States, European Theater, and Pacific from October 1942 to May 1946. He returned to his civilian work with the Office, Chief of Engineers, after the war. From 1958 to 1972 he was chief, Operations Division, Directorate of Civil Works, for the Corps of Engineers. Biographical Files, Office of History, Headquarters, U.S. Army Corps of Engineers, Fort Belvoir, Virginia.

56. James E. Moore (29 November 1902–28 January 1986). U.S. Military Academy, 1924. Infantry. From April 1941 to March 1942, he was assigned to the Budget and Legislative Liaison Branch, War Department General Staff. He then served as chief of staff, Thirty-fifth Infantry Division (March–May 1942) and of the Thirtieth Infantry Division (May 1942–August 1943) before joining Twelfth Corps as its chief of staff in August 1943. In October he moved to Fourth Army as chief of staff to Lt. Gen. William H. Simpson and was promoted to brigadier general in January 1944. He went to England in May with Headquarters, Fourth Army, which became Headquarters, Ninth Army in the ETO, and remained as chief of staff until September 1945. He was promoted to major general in April 1945. From April 1953 to February 1955, he was commandant, Army War College, and then commanding general, Ryukyus Command, and high commissioner, until 1958. He was promoted to lieutenant general in February 1954. He was chief of staff, Supreme Headquarters Allied Powers Europe, from 1959 until his retirement in 1963.

57. Armistead D. Mead Jr. (16 October 1901–20 February 1980). U.S. Military Academy, 1924. Infantry. Mead became assistant chief, war plans, Headquarters, South Pacific Area and South Pacific Force, in May 1942. He was chief of staff, First Island Command, from November 1942 to April 1943 and then returned to the United States as chief of staff, Airborne Command, from July to October. In December 1943 he was made assistant chief of staff, G-3, Operations, Fourth Army, under General Simpson. In May he moved to England and became G-3, Ninth Army. He was promoted to brigadier general in June 1945. He was promoted to major general as commanding general, First Cavalry Division, in Japan (1953–1954). Mead retired from active duty in June 1961.

58. Lucian K. Truscott Jr. (9 January 1895–12 September 1965). Cavalry.

Truscott commanded the Thirteenth Armored Regiment from September 1940 to July 1941, at which time he was assigned to the staff of the Ninth Corps Area at Fort Lewis, Washington. In May 1942 he joined the Allied Combined Staff under Lord Louis Mountbatten. He recruited, trained, and led the American Rangers who took part in the Dieppe raid on 19 August 1942. In Operation Torch that November he commanded the task force that took Port Lyautey in French Morocco, and then he served as field deputy to Eisenhower. In March 1943 he took command of the Third Infantry Division in Tunisia and made it into one of the best infantry divisions in the theater. The Third played important roles in the Sicilian operation, then landed at Salerno on 18 September 1943 and at Anzio on 22 January 1944. In February 1944 Truscott replaced John Lucas as commanding general, Sixth Corps, and led it through the breakout from Anzio to beyond Rome and then into southern France in Operation Anvil. He was promoted to lieutenant general in September 1944 and selected to command Fifteenth Army when it became operational in January 1945. However, before that could take place, Mark Clark, commanding the Fifteenth Army Group in Italy, requested Truscott as commanding general, Fifth Army. In December 1944, Truscott assumed command of Fifth Army and led it through the final campaigns of the war, including the final assault on northern Italy and the Po River crossing. From October 1945 to May 1946, he commanded Third Army in Bavaria. He retired in 1947 and in 1951 was appointed U.S. high commissioner for Germany. He was promoted to full general on the retired list in 1954. Truscott had an outstanding reputation as a field commander and a soldier's soldier. See also Boatner, *Biographical Dictionary*, 574.

59. Don E. Carleton (22 October 1899–19 August 1977). Carleton commanded the Provisional Squadron, Eighth Cavalry, from August 1940 to March 1941, when he became the S-3, plans and training officer. In May he took over the Antitank Troop, First Cavalry Division. In February 1942 he was assigned as executive officer, Fifth Cavalry, until October 1942. Carleton then served as secretary of the General Staff, Allied Forces Headquarters, from October 1942 to March 1943, when he became chief of staff at Third Infantry Division under Truscott. He moved with Truscott to Sixth Corps as its chief of staff in February 1944 and then to Fifth Army in December. He was promoted to brigadier general in September 1944 and retired on 31 August 1954.

60. Alexander McC. Patch (23 November 1889–21 November 1945). U.S. Military Academy, 1913. Infantry. Patch served with the First Division in France during World War I. After commanding the Forty-seventh Infantry Regiment from August 1940 to August 1941, he was promoted to brigadier general and went to Camp Croft, South Carolina, as commanding general, Infantry Replacement Training Center. He was sent to the Pacific theater in January 1942 and assumed command of the Task Force and Americal Division in New Caledonia in February. He was promoted to major general in March and commanded the division until January 1943, when he was made commanding

general, Fourteenth Corps, South Pacific Theater. In May 1943 he returned to the United States and took command of the Fourth Corps at Fort Lewis, Washington. In February 1944 he took the Fourth Corps to Africa and Sicily, and he then became commander of Seventh Army in March. He prepared Seventh Army for the amphibious landing in southern France, successfully executed Operation Anvil/Dragoon, and commanded the Seventh Army's drive up the Rhone River valley and into southern Germany and Austria by the end of the war. He was promoted to lieutenant general in August 1944. From August to October 1945 he headed a special War Department board of officers, known as "the Patch Board," investigating the postwar reorganization of the War Department. Patch died suddenly at Fort Sam Houston on 21 November 1945. Many of his close friends attributed his untimely death to his depression at the death of his only son, Alexander McC. Patch Jr., U.S. Military Academy, 1942, who was killed in action at Luneville, France, on 22 October 1945 while commanding Company C, 315th Infantry, Seventy-ninth Infantry Division. See also Boatner, *Biographical Dictionary*, 411–12.

61. Terry de la Mesa Allen (1 April 1888–12 September 1969). Catholic University, 1912. Allen attended the U.S. Military Academy from June 1907 to May 1911 but did not graduate. He served with the 358th Infantry, Ninetieth Division, in France during World War I. He was promoted to brigadier general in October 1940 and given command of the Third Cavalry Brigade at Fort Riley, Kansas. In April 1941 he assumed command of the Second Cavalry Division and then took over the Fourth Infantry Division in December 1941. Allen was promoted to major general in June 1942 and became commanding general, First Infantry Division, in August. During the fighting in North Africa and Tunisia, Allen established a solid reputation as an excellent combat commander and also as a hardheaded, frequently insubordinate division commander. The situation grew so bad that in August in Sicily, Bradley relieved both Allen and his assistant division commander, Teddy Roosevelt. Allen was sent home but in October 1943 was given command of the 104th Infantry Division, which was then in training. When Allen landed with the 104th in France in September 1944, he became the only general officer to train and command two divisions in combat during the war. He remained as commander of the 104th through the war. He retired in August 1946 as a major general. See also Boatner, *Biographical Dictionary*, 6; Gerald Astor, *Terrible Terry Allen: Combat General of World War II; The Life of an American Soldier* (New York: Ballantine Books, 2003).

62. Edwin L. Sibert (2 March 1897–16 December 1977). U.S. Military Academy, June 1918. Field Artillery. From July 1940 to December 1941, he was military attaché in Rio de Janeiro, Brazil, and then assistant secretary, Combined Chiefs of Staff, until March. After a brief tour at the Field Artillery School, he was made chief of staff, Seventh Infantry Division, in May 1942. In August, he became commander of divisional artillery, Ninety-ninth Infantry Division, and was promoted to brigadier general in October 1942. In August 1943 he

was sent to the European theater, where he became assistant chief of staff, G-2, from September 1943 to March 1944, when he assumed the same duties with Twelfth Army Group. He remained Bradley's intelligence chief until July 1945, when he became G-2 for U.S. Forces European Theater in Germany until 1946. After several commands in the Caribbean and Panama, he was promoted to major general in 1953 and became deputy chief of staff, acting chief of staff, and chief of staff, Headquarters, U.S. Army Forces Far East until his retirement in January 1954.

63. The German 88-mm gun was one of the most famous and feared of all World War II weapons. Originally designed as an antiaircraft gun, the 88 proved to be especially effective as an antitank gun due to its high muzzle velocity and hence the greater penetrating power of its round. Erwin Rommel was particularly deadly in his innovative use of trailer-mounted 88s in anti-tank screens against British armor in the Western Desert. The gun was so effective that it was used as the main gun on the Tiger tanks (Mark VI), on heavy self-propelled assault guns, and as an antitank gun. In addition to its frontline use, the 88 was still the predominant antiaircraft defense weapon employed against the American and British bombers by the German air defenses. See Lüdeke, *Weapons of World War II*, 150–51.

64. Henry S. Aurand (21 April 1894–18 June 1980). U.S. Military Academy, 1915. Coast Artillery Corps and Ordnance Department. Aurand had several routine Coast Artillery assignments before attending the Ordnance School from October 1916 to November 1917. In June 1940, he was made chief, Requirements and Distribution Branch, G-4 Division, War Department General Staff. From October 1941 to July 1942, he was chief, International Division, G-4, and later Services of Supply after March 1942. He was promoted to brigadier general in January 1942 and to major general in September. From September 1942 to October 1944, he commanded the Sixth Service Command in Chicago. From October to December 1944 he was deputy chief ordnance officer, Communications Zone, ETO. Then he commanded the Normandy Base Section, COMZ, until May 1945, when he was transferred to China as commanding general, Services of Supply, China Theater, until November 1945. Aurand was promoted to lieutenant general in January 1948 and in March 1949 became commanding general, U.S. Army, Pacific, and remained in that position until he retired in August 1952. See also Boatner, *Biographical Dictionary*, 20.

65. Sixth Service Command. After the War Department was reorganized in March 1942, the Services of Supply (later Army Service Forces) created nine service commands and the military district of Washington to replace the former corps areas. These commands were responsible for all production, procurement, SOS personnel, military training, technical services organizations and functions, etc., in their respective areas. As such, they were exceptionally important to the successful prosecution of the war effort. The service commands were abolished and their duties absorbed by the six armies of the Army

Ground Forces in June 1946 as part of the postwar reorganization of the War Department. See John D. Millett, *The Organization and Role of the Army Service Forces* (Washington, DC: Office of the Chief of Military History, 1954), 312–37, 425–26.

66. Concertina wire. Barbed wire was normally spooled into coils for ease of handling and shipment. For use on the battlefield, the wire was uncoiled much like a concertina, or hand organ, was extended for playing. The wire was frequently used from the rolls like this rather than being staked into carefully prepared entanglements.

67. George P. Seneff (b. 24 August 1891). Infantry and Field Artillery. Seneff served in World War I as an infantry officer and transferred to the field artillery in 1924. Seneff was assistant divisional artillery commander of the Twenty-eighth Division until November 1944, when he took command of the First Army Photographic Interpretation Center. He ended the war in Europe as executive officer, G-5 Section, First Army. He retired in November 1945.

68. "Bloody Bucketeers" Division. The Twenty-eighth Infantry Division, the National Guard Division of Pennsylvania, was nicknamed the "Bloody Bucket Division" by the Germans who fought against it during the Normandy campaign. The division's toughness and determination in combat won the admiration of its opponents, who based their nickname on the division's tenacity and its shoulder sleeve insignia, which was the keystone symbol of Pennsylvania done completely in blood red, so that it looked exactly like a full bucket of blood. Hence, the nicknames "Bloody Bucketeers" and "Bloody Bucket Division." During the brutal fighting in the Hürtgen Forest in October and November 1944 in which the division suffered very heavy casualties, the GIs attached a more personal and morbid definition to their newly acquired nickname, seeing it as representing buckets of their blood. The division was also known as the "Keystone Division" because it came from the Keystone State, Pennsylvania, and during World War I, Gen. John Pershing, the American commander in France, called the Twenty-eighth the "Iron Division."

69. Bryant E. Moore (6 June 1894–24 February 1951). U.S. Military Academy, August 1917. Infantry. In January 1942, Moore was sent to the South Pacific Theater as G-2 for the American forces in New Caledonia and in October 1942 became commander of the 144th Infantry Regiment, Americal Division, on Guadalcanal. In February 1943 he returned to the United States and was assigned as assistant division commander, 104th Infantry Division, with a promotion to brigadier general. He accompanied the division to the ETO in the fall of 1944 and remained with it in this capacity through February 1945, when he became commanding general, Eighth Infantry Division, until October. From November 1945 to September 1947 he commanded the 88th Division in Italy and then became commanding general, U.S. Troops in Trieste (TRUST), until June 1948, when he was named Superintendent of the U.S. Military Academy and was promoted to major general. In February 1951 he was assigned to

the Far East Command and then was commanding general, IX Corps, Eighth Army, in Korea. On 24 February 1951, Moore died of a heart attack after the helicopter he was riding in crashed into the Han River.

70. In May 1944, the Joint Chiefs of Staff created the Special Joint Chiefs of Staff Committee on Reorganization of National Defense, chaired by retired Adm. James O. Richardson, to investigate the problem of a unified postwar military establishment for the United States. Called the "Richardson Committee" after its chairman, this group of two officers from the army (one of these from the Army Air Forces) and two officers from the navy made extensive studies of reorganization. As part of their work, the committee members visited the European, Mediterranean, and Pacific theaters of operation in November and December 1944 to interview the principal commanders and their staffs. In April 1945 the committee, except for its chairman, reported in favor of a single department of national defense for all the armed forces. Because of the navy's opposition to the findings of the Richardson Committee, the JCS never agreed on the report's recommendations, and four separate recommendations on defense reorganization were forwarded to President Truman in October 1945. Demetrios Caraley, *The Politics of Military Unification: A Study of Conflict and the Policy Process* (New York: Columbia University Press, 1966).

71. James O. Richardson (18 September 1879–2 May 1974). U.S. Naval Academy, 1902. From June 1938 to June 1939 he was chief, Bureau of Navigation, and then became commander, Battle Force and full admiral. In January 1940 he was made commander in chief, U.S. Fleet. He completed his tour in 1941 and was a member of the General Board until May 1942, when he was assigned to the Office of the Secretary of the Navy. He retired in October 1942 and was recalled to head the JCS's special study on defense reorganization in 1944–1945. He was released from active duty in January 1947. See also "Admiral James O. Richardson, USN, (1878–1974)," Naval Historical Center Online Library, at http://www.history.navy.mil.

72. Harold L. George (19 July 1893–24 February 1986). Air Corps. George was commissioned a second lieutenant in the cavalry in May 1917 but soon resigned to enter flight training, which he completed in March 1918, in time to serve in France. In the late 1930s he commanded the Ninety-sixth Bomb Squadron and then the Second Bomb Group, the first unit to be equipped with the new Boeing B-17s. In June 1941 he became Assistant chief of staff, war plans, on the Air Staff. He and his staff prepared the critical Air War Plans Division study no. 1 (AWPD-1), which outlined the basic strategic air plan for the war against Germany. In April 1942 he was promoted to brigadier general and took command of the Air Corps Ferrying Command, which was redesignated Air Transport Command (ATC) in June 1942. He remained in command of ATC's worldwide air operations until he retired from active duty as a lieutenant general in December 1946. See DuPre, *U.S. Air Force Biographical Dictionary,* 84–85; "Lieutenant General Harold L. George," at Air Force Link, http://www.af.mil/bios/.

73. William F. Tompkins (22 September 1892–26 October 1969). U.S. Military Academy, 1915. Corps of Engineers. Tompkins served in France in World War I. In July 1940 he became executive assistant to the chief of engineers, and in July 1941 he was made engineer of General Headquarters. From February 1942 to May 1943 he was the assistant executive, Munitions Assignment Board, Combined Chiefs of Staff, and was promoted to brigadier general in July 1942. Two months later he was appointed director, Special Planning Division, War Department Special Staff. He was promoted to major general in August 1944. In July 1945 he went to the Philippines as deputy commander and chief of staff, Service Command. He returned to the United States in November 1945 and retired in June 1946.

74. Malcolm F. Schoeffel (3 April 1898–1991). U.S. Naval Academy, 1918. Schoeffel was a naval aviator from 1921 to 1954. He was promoted to rear admiral in 1943 and commanded the light carrier USS *Cabot* in 1943–1944. He later commanded Carrier Division 6 and Task Force 26 of the Atlantic Fleet in 1949–1950 before commanding the Naval Air Test Center at Patuxent, Maryland, until 1951. He was chief, Bureau of Ordnance until 1954, and he retired in February 1955.

75. F. Trubee Davison (7 February 1896–14 November 1974). Yale University, 1918. Davison served as a naval aviator in World War I. After the war he obtained his law degree from Columbia University in 1922 and was admitted to the New York bar. He served in the New York State Assembly from 1922 to 1926. On 16 July 1926 he was appointed assistant secretary of war for air and held that position until 2 March 1933. From 1933 to 1951 he was president, American Museum of Natural History, in New York City. He was recalled to active duty from the reserves in January 1941 as a colonel in the Army Air Forces. After serving as deputy chief of staff, Air Force Combat Command, from June to December 1941, Davison became assistant chief of the Air Staff, Personnel, in December 1941. Later in the war, he assumed control of all Army Air Forces postwar planning as head of the Special Projects Office from April 1943 to September 1945. He was promoted to brigadier general in June 1945.

76. Raymond G. Moses (26 December 1891–14 July 1974). U.S. Military Academy, 1916. Corps of Engineers. Moses served in France in World War I. From June to December 1941 he was chief, Supply Division, Office, Chief of Engineers, and then assistant chief of staff, Communications Zone, Eastern Defense Command, at Governors Island, New York, in January and February 1942. He became assistant chief of staff, G-4, War Department, and was promoted to brigadier general in March 1942. In September 1943, Moses went to the ETO as assistant chief of staff, G-4, for First U.S. Army Group and then Twelfth Army Group. He served briefly as chief U.S. administrative staff officer with the British Twenty-first Army Group from January to August 1944. From August 1945 to January 1946 he was assistant chief of staff, G-4, for the theater general board. From October 1946 to November 1948 he served as divi-

sion engineer, New England Division, in Boston. He retired at his own request on 31 May 1949 as a colonel and was promoted to brigadier general, retired, the following day.

77. Orlando C. Mood (1 December 1899–2 May 1953). The Citadel, 1921. Infantry. From June 1940 to July 1942, Mood was assistant, Equipment Unit, Requirements and Distribution Branch, G-4, War Department General Staff. In July 1942, he became deputy assistant chief of staff, G-4, Headquarters, Services of Supply, ETO, until June 1943, when he joined headquarters, Fifth Corps, in the same capacity. He landed on Omaha Beach on D-day. In October 1944 he became chief of staff, Fifth Corps, and in January 1945 he moved up to Fifteenth Army as chief of staff. Mood became a brigadier general on 12 June 1945. From July 1945 to April 1946 he was chief of staff, Theater Service Forces, U.S. Forces, European Theater. He was promoted to major general in May 1950. In October 1951 he was assigned to Eighth Army in Korea as deputy chief of staff and then chief of staff. He died on 2 May 1953 while on active duty.

78. John H. Hinds (9 February 1898–18 January 1993). U.S. Military Academy, November 1918. Field Artillery. Hinds was assigned to the War Department General Staff from June 1939 to January 1942, when he was transferred to Sixth Corps as assistant artillery officer. He served with Sixth Corps in the United States and then North Africa until June 1943, becoming artillery officer. He returned to the United States in July 1943 as division artillery commander, Seventy-first Infantry Division, and was promoted to brigadier general in September. In October he became artillery commander, Twelfth Corps and Twenty-first Corps, and moved to Europe in April 1944 as artillery officer, First U.S. Army Group. In August, he moved to Twelfth Army Group as artillery officer. From November 1944 to March 1946, he was commander, division artillery, Second Infantry Division, in Europe and the United States. In January 1951 he was promoted to major general and given command of the First Cavalry Division in Korea. From 1954 to 1956, he was chief, doctrine and training, Army Field Forces, and retired in March 1956.

79. Léon Degrelle (15 June 1906–1 March 1994). Degrelle was a Belgian lawyer and political activist. In 1935 he organized and then was the leader of the Belgian Fascist "Rexist" movement in the Catholic party. The Rex (from *Christus Rex*) movement gained twenty-one seats in the 1934 general election with the support of the German Nazi Party. Degrelle ran for the premiership in 1937 and was badly beaten. After the Germans conquered Belgium in 1940, he worked for them and later joined the Waffen-SS and organized the SS Volunteer Brigade Wallonia in 1943. Never very large, it became the Twenty-eighth SS Panzer Grenadier Division Wallonia late in 1944 and was primarily engaged in fighting in the east. Degrelle made his way to Norway in May 1945 and escaped to Spain, where he was interned and remained under the protection of Francisco Franco. Degrelle was condemned to death in absentia for treason in Belgium after the war but was never extradited or imprisoned.

See "Léon Degrelle," at Encyclopaedia Britannica Online, http://britannica. com/ed/.

80. Richard E. Byrd (25 October 1888–11 March 1957). U.S. Naval Academy, 1912. Byrd entered the naval air service in 1917 and became a naval aviator in 1918. After the war, he was active in promoting naval aviation and helped create the Bureau of Aeronautics. In 1924 he commanded the naval flyers assigned to the MacMillan Arctic expedition, from which he returned in 1925. In May 1924 he and Floyd Bennett, his copilot, made the first flight over the North Pole from Spitsbergen, for which both of them received the Medal of Honor. In 1930, Byrd headed an expedition to Antarctica and established a base, Little America, on the Bay of Whales. On 29 November 1929, Byrd and three others made the first flight over the South Pole. This won him promotion to rear admiral (retired). He led other expeditions to Antarctica in the 1930s. Byrd joined Admiral King's staff during the war and renewed his Antarctic operations with a U.S. Navy–backed expedition in 1946–1947. In 1955 he was given command of Operation Deep Freeze, which the navy sponsored as part of the International Geophysical Year (1957–1958).

81. Royal B. Lord (19 September 1899–21 October 1963). U.S. Military Academy, 1923. Corps of Engineers. From November 1938 to July 1940, Lord commanded a company and then a battalion of the Third Engineers at Schofield Barracks, Hawaii. He then commanded the Ninth Engineer Squadron at Fort Riley, Kansas, from August to December 1940 before becoming the assistant director, Bureau of Public Relations, War Department, in January 1941. From September 1941 to August 1942 he was chief of operations, director, Board of Economic Warfare. He went to England in September 1942 as deputy chief engineer, War Requirements Board, and in February 1943 became deputy commander, Services of Supply (later Communications Zone), ETO. He was promoted to brigadier general in February 1944 and major general in November 1944. He also served as deputy chief of staff, ETOUSA, from April to August 1945. He retired in April 1946.

82. James H. Stratton (7 June 1898–16 March 1984). U.S. Military Academy, 1920. Corps of Engineers. Stratton enlisted in the New Jersey National Guard in 1917 and saw service in World War I. He was commissioned in the field artillery in July 1920 and transferred to the Corps of Engineers in September. In December 1941 he was assigned to the Office, Chief of Engineers, as chief of engineering. From September 1943 to March 1945 he was in the ETO as assistant chief of staff, G-4, Communications Zone. He was promoted to brigadier general in May 1944. Stratton returned to Washington as assistant chief of engineers, civil works, and special assistant to the chief of engineers, until May 1946. He served as division engineer, New England Engineer Division, from November 1948 until he retired in August 1949.

83. Liberty ships: The U.S. Maritime Commission designed these merchant cargo vessels so that they could be built easily and swiftly in large numbers. The purpose was to provide sufficient ships to overcome any losses that might

be suffered to U-boat activity. Of the 5,777 ships built by the Maritime Commission from 1939 to 1945, 2,770 were Liberty ships, most of which were operated by civilian shipping firms. See Parrish, *Encyclopedia of World War II*, 367.

84. Charles H. Bonesteel (9 April 1885–5 June 1964). U.S. Military Academy, 1908. Infantry. Bonesteel served with the Seventh Division, AEF, during World War I. In June 1940 he was made chief of staff, Sixth Corps Area, and Second Army, at Chicago. He was promoted to brigadier general in September 1940 and became commanding general, Sixth Corps Area, in December 1940. In April 1941 he was made a major general and given command of the Fifth Infantry Division in July. In September he was made commanding general, Iceland Base Command, with the Fifth Infantry Division as his principal force defending the island. In June 1943 he became commandant, the Infantry School, and in July 1944 he moved to San Francisco to replace John DeWitt as commanding general, Western Defense Command. In November-December 1944 he was assistant to Bradley in Luxembourg and then moved to Versailles, where he organized and commanded the G-1 Section of SHAEF headquarters until May 1945. After serving as inspector general, ETO, and then U.S. Forces European Theater (USFET), he was president of the War Department Manpower Board in the Office of the Chief of Staff until his retirement in January 1947.

85. Gestapo. *Gestapo* was the German term for Geheime Staatspolizei (Secret State Police), which was created after the Nazis came to power in 1933. The Gestapo began operating in Prussia in April 1933 under the control of Hermann Göring, the Prussian minister of interior, who was charged with all criminal and political police matters. Göring placed Nazis in all key posts in the Gestapo, but it was Heinrich Himmler, who took over the Gestapo in April 1934, who made it into the lethal weapon of terror that it later became throughout Europe. In 1939 the Gestapo became part of the Reichssicherheitshauptamt (RSHA), the Reich Main Security Office, or SS headquarters, and was fully integrated into the SS. See Parrish, *Encyclopedia of World War II*, 229–30; Dear, *Oxford Guide to World War II*, 385, 814–15.

86. The P-51 Mustang was designed and built by North America Aviation and became one of the finest fighter aircraft of the war. Originally proposed to the Royal Air Force, the plane had serious problems with the high-altitude performance of its 1,200-horsepower Allison engine. Only when the British installed the 1,400-horsepower Rolls-Royce Merlin engine, built in the United States under license by Packard Motors, was the aircraft's real potential realized. The later-model Mustangs, principally the P-51D with the bubble canopy, were superior fighters that allowed the U.S. Army Air Forces in Europe to achieve total air supremacy over the Luftwaffe by mid-1944. The P-51D had a top speed of 427 miles per hour and an operational ceiling of 42,000 feet and was armed with eight .50 caliber machine guns. The more advanced P-51H had a top speed over 480 miles per hour at 25,000 feet. See Taylor, *Combat Aircraft of the World*, 536–38.

87. Robert D. Murphy (1894–1978) was a career American diplomat who was intimately involved in military-political matters in the Mediterranean and Europe throughout the war. From 1940 to 1943 he was the senior State Department official who worked with the French in North Africa to prepare for the Allied invasion of November 1942. President Roosevelt made Murphy his personal representative to the French in North Africa. Murphy was also the chief civil affairs officer on the supreme commander's staff at Allied Forces Headquarters (AFHQ). Along with Harold MacMillan, Murphy played a key role in arranging the Italian surrender in September 1943. That month he was appointed a member of the Mediterranean Advisory Commission, and the following month he became the political advisor to AFHQ and General Eisenhower. In September 1944 he was made the U.S. political adviser for Germany. He was later the director of the Office of German and Austrian Affairs and U.S. ambassador to Belgium and then Japan. See Boatner, *Biographical Dictionary*, 381–82.

88. John Boettiger (25 March 1900–29 October 1950). Boettiger ran the City News Bureau of Chicago in 1921–1922 and then joined the *Chicago Evening News*. From 1922 to 1934 he was on the staff of the *Chicago Tribune*. In 1933–1934 he was the *Tribune*'s assistant Washington correspondent. On 18 January 1935 he married the president's daughter, Anna Roosevelt Dall. Boettiger was assistant to the president, Motion Picture Producers and Distributors of America in 1935–1936. From 1936 to June 1945, he was publisher of the *Seattle Post-Intelligencer*. After the war, he was editor and publisher of the *Arizona Times* in Phoenix. Boettiger had served in the navy during the First World War and was a lieutenant colonel in the army during the Second World War. In that capacity he participated in the landings in Sicily and at Salerno. See *Who Was Who in America*, vol. 3 (1951–1960), 86.

89. Damon M. Gunn (27 May 1899–5 November 1983). U.S. Military Academy, 1923. Infantry and Judge Advocate General Corps. After serving at a number of posts, Gunn attended Yale University Law School from August 1934 to June 1937, when he received his law degree and then joined the First Division at Governors Island, New York, as an assistant to the judge advocate. In June 1940 he was transferred to the Sixth Corps Area in Chicago. From January to July 1942 he was judge advocate of Second Corps with which he moved to England. He remained with Second Corps through the subsequent campaigns in North Africa and Sicily as judge advocate and civil affairs officer. From October 1943 to May 1944 he was chief, civil affairs, and assistant chief of staff, G-5, First Army, in England. Gunn remained with First Army throughout the rest of the war in Europe. In October 1945 he returned to Washington to be acting director, war crimes, Office of the Judge Advocate General. In April 1949 he was appointed judge advocate for U.S. European Command. He retired in 1953 as a colonel. See also *Register of Graduates, USMA, 2000*, 4–123.

90. James G. Anding (28 April 1903–25 June 1983). U.S. Military Academy,

1924. Field Artillery. Anding was assigned as the commander of the headquarters battery, Twentieth Field Artillery Battalion, Fourth Infantry Division, from June 1940 to January 1941, when he became the assistant chief of staff, G-4, Headquarters, Fourth Corps. He was then G-4, Third Army, from February 1942 to March 1944. Transferred to Europe, Anding served as G-4, Seventh Corps, until early May 1945, when he became G-4 at First Army. He remained with Headquarters, First Army, during its redeployment to the United States and the Philippines and in October 1945 joined Headquarters, Army Ground Forces as assistant G-4. From 1953 to 1954 he was military assistant in the Office, Secretary of Defense. He retired in 1954 as a colonel. See also *Register of Graduates, USMA, 2000*, 4–129.

91. Frank J. McSherry (18 October 1892–1 August 1980). University of Arizona, 1916. Coastal Artillery Corps. McSherry served in World War I. He was made special assistant to the Secretary of War for the training of aviation mechanics from November 1938 to July 1940. He then became the War Department liaison officer with the Labor Department Advisory Commission to the Council of National Defense and later administrative assistant to the director, defense training, Federal Security Agency, and chief, Defense Training Branch, Office of Production Management. During 1942–1944, he served as deputy director, labor supply and training, Labor Division, and then director of operations, War Manpower Administration, War Production Board. In May 1943 he was appointed deputy chief, Allied Military Government in Italy. From January 1944 to June 1945 he was deputy assistant chief of staff, G-5 (civil affairs), SHAEF, and was deeply involved in developing the American military government for occupied Germany. From July 1945 to October 1946 he was head, Manpower Division, Office of Military Government, U.S. (OMGUS), Germany. See also Ancell, *Biographical Dictionary*, 220–21.

92. Lt. Gen. Edward Kenneth Smart (1891–1961). Smart served in France and Flanders from 1915 to 1918, winning both the Military Cross and the Distinguished Service Order. In 1936–1939 he was the military liaison officer, High Commissioner's Office, London, representing the Australian army. He returned to Australia in 1939–1940 to serve as quartermaster general, Australian Military Forces. In 1940–1941 he was general officer commanding, Southern Command. After Pearl Harbor, Smart became head of the Australian military mission to the United States. From 1942 to 1946 he was the Australian army representative to the Imperial Defense Committee and Imperial Chiefs of Staff. He was consul-general in San Francisco (1946–1950) and New York (1950–1954). See "Lieutenant-General Edward Kenneth Smart (1891–1961)" at "The Generals of WWII," http://www.generals.dk.

93. Although there had been an Imperial War Cabinet briefly during World War I and the Committee of Imperial Defence (CID) functioned between the wars to formulate defense strategy and requirements, no such organization of the British dominions existed in World War II. As prime minister both Cham-

berlain and Churchill had a personal war cabinet. Churchill acted as both prime minister and minister of defense during his tenure from May 1940 to July 1945. There was also a special committee of the representatives of the chiefs of staff of the various dominions. See Dear, *Oxford Guide to World War II*, 893.

94. The Roer River dams consisted of two main and several lesser dams on the Roer and Urft Rivers. The main dams were the Urft Dam on the Urft River upstream of the junction with the Roer River and the larger Schwammenauel Dam on the Roer River downstream of the junction near the town of Schmidt. These dams were intended to impound water to control the Roer River and its tributaries and to provide hydroelectric power for Düren and other cities downstream. The lesser dams were Paulushof, Heimbach, and Obermaubach. The large volume of water in the impoundments behind the dams presented grave problems for any American or British crossings of the Roer River downstream and all the way to the confluence with the Meuse River at Roermond, Holland. If the Germans destroyed the dams or released the waters during or after an assault crossing, the attacking forces were in jeopardy of being isolated and surrounded on the east bank. Hence, by November the possession or destruction of these dams loomed large in both German and Allied planning and operations. See MacDonald, *The Siegfried Line Campaign*, 324–28.

95. The "A" designs were renditions of the First Army's shoulder sleeve insignia (patch), which was a large black Gothic A on a horizontally divided white and red background. White and red were the distinguishing colors for armies, and "A" signified Army. John B. Wilson, *Armies, Corps, Divisions and Separate Brigades* (Washington, DC: U.S. Army Center of Military History, 1987), 9.

96. The *Autobahnen* (motorways) were German superhighways built during the 1930s to link key sections of Germany and to provide work for many of the unemployed as part of Hitler's economic policies. The roads were all concrete, with two lanes in each direction, and usually separated by a median strip. When built, they were considered the most modern highways in the world and were the model for the American Interstate Highway System of the 1950s. A total of 3,500 kilometers were completed between 1933 and 1938, but only 500 additional kilometers were added from 1938 to 1945 due to wartime demands. See Richard J. Evans, *The Third Reich in Power* (New York: Penguin Books, 2006), 322–25.

97. William G. Weaver (24 November 1888–25 November 1970). U.S. Military Academy, 1912. Infantry. Weaver saw extensive action during World War I and was wounded in October 1918 in an action that won him a Distinguished Service Cross. He commanded the Fourteenth and Seventeenth Infantry Training Regiments, Infantry Replacement Training Center, from April to December 1941, when he was made commander of the Thirty-eighth Infantry, Second Infantry Division. He moved to England in September 1942 and became chief of staff and field deputy commanding general, Services of Supply, ETO. He was

promoted to brigadier general in April 1943. In July 1944 he became assistant division commander, Ninetieth Infantry Division, and in November took over the Eighth Infantry Division. He received his second star in January 1945 and returned to the United States in February 1945. He retired in February 1946.

98. Joseph M. Tully (4 October 1893–1 May 1970). U.S. Military Academy, 1916. Cavalry. From September 1938 to December 1940, Tully was on the Headquarters Staff at the U.S. Military Academy, West Point. He was then assigned as executive officer, Third Cavalry Brigade and Assistant chief of staff, Second Cavalry Division, until July 1941. He commanded the Fourth Cavalry Group in the U.S. and in France from November 1941 to November 1944 when he became assistant division commander, Ninetieth Infantry Division. He was promoted to brigadier general in March 1945. From October to December 1945 he was assistant division commander, Ninety-fourth Infantry Division, and then commanded the Eightieth Infantry Division until January 1946. From November 1948 to 1950 he was chief of staff, Second Infantry Division, at Fort Lewis, Washington, and in Korea. He retired in 1951.

99. John C. MacDonald (b. 23 July 1895). Norwich University, 1917. He served with the Seventy-fourth Division in the United States and in France in World War I. MacDonald was then secretary of the Cavalry School from June 1939 until August 1942, when he became assistant commandant of the school. From May 1943 to March 1944 he was assistant chief of staff, G-3, Operations, Headquarters, Third Army. When the Third Army moved to England, he became provost marshal and held that post until November 1944, when he became commander of the Fourth Cavalry Group. From June 1945 to May 1946 he was assistant division commander, Seventy-eighth Infantry Division, on occupation duty in Berlin and later deputy commander, Berlin Command. In July 1947 MacDonald became chief of staff, the Armored Center, and was promoted to brigadier general on 12 February 1951. He was promoted to major general in July 1954. From June 1955 until his retirement in January 1957, he served in the Office of the Chief of Staff.

100. Napalm bombs were special containers of napalm, thickened or jellied gasoline, that scattered the burning fluid over wide areas when dropped. Napalm was a powdered gasoline thickener composed of metallic salts derived from naphtha. The earliest of the napalm bombs were made from auxiliary gasoline tanks, but by the end of the war there were two standard types, the M-47 for the 100-pound bomb and the M-74 for the 500-pound bomb with an explosive charge. The napalm bomb was a particularly deadly weapon and was used against the most difficult, dug-in targets. See Parrish, *Encyclopedia of World War II*, 425–26.

101. Joseph A. Holly (25 September 1896–19 August 1987). U.S. Military Academy, 1919. Infantry. Holly was an instructor at the Infantry School from August 1939 to October 1940, when he became director, tank tactics, at the Armored School. In December 1941 he was made chief, Tank Section, the Ar-

mored School. From February 1942 to March 1943 he was chief, Material and Test Section, the Armored School. Upon his promotion to brigadier general in March 1943, he became commandant, the Armored School. In February 1944 he was assigned to Headquarters, SHAEF, as chief, armored fighting vehicles and weapons. He retired in January 1951 as a brigadier general. See *Register of Graduates, USMA, 2000,* 4–114.

102. Hugh T. Mayberry (1 December 1892–28 April 1970). William Jewell College, 1914. Infantry. In February 1942, Mayberry became assistant commandant, Tank Destroyer School, and was then commandant from May 1942 to February 1944. He was promoted to brigadier general in October 1942. He served as assistant division commander, Ninety-ninth Infantry Division, from February 1944 until June 1945, when he became commander of the War Department Personnel Center at Camp Shelby, Mississippi. He retired as a brigadier general in December 1952. See also Ancell, *Biographical Dictionary,* 209.

103. Paul R. Davison (b. 31 March 1890). Cavalry. Davison was commissioned as second lieutenant in the cavalry in March 1912. During World War I, he served in the National Army. He remained in the army after the war and completed the Cavalry School in 1923, the Command and General Staff School in 1924, and the Army War College in 1936. He was chief of staff, Ninety-ninth Infantry Division, until 18 January 1945.

104. Leland Stowe (10 November 1899–16 January 1994). Wesleyan University, 1921. Stowe began working as a reporter for the *New York Herald Tribune* in 1922 and became its Paris correspondent in 1926. He won a Pulitzer Prize in 1930 for his stories on the Paris Reparations Conference. He was one of the first correspondents in Europe to warn about the threat of Nazi Germany. With the outbreak of World War II in Europe, he became a war correspondent for the *Chicago Daily News* and *New York Post* and covered much of the war from Europe to China. After the war, he worked for Radio Free Europe. He joined the University of Michigan as a professor of journalism in 1955 and remained until he retired in 1970, while at the same time working for *Reader's Digest* as an editor. See obituary, University of Michigan, *University Record,* 24 January 1994, at http://www.ur.umich.edu.

105. William L. Shirer (23 February 1904–28 December 1993). Coe College, Iowa, 1925. Shirer was an American foreign correspondent, news commentator, and writer who worked for Universal News Service and CBS in Berlin for a number of years prior to the American entry into the war in December 1941. He published his experiences in Berlin as *Berlin Diary* (1941) and then served as a war reporter for the remainder of the war. He was best known for his award-winning account of Nazi Germany, *The Rise and Fall of the Third Reich: A History of Nazi Germany* (1960). See *World Notables,* vol. 9 (1993–1996), 252.

106. Albert J. Browning (27 September 1899–3 July 1948). Massachusetts Institute of Technology, 1922. Coast Artillery Corps Reserve. Browning held various industrial and management positions until he became an executive

with Montgomery Ward & Company in 1934. From 1938 to January 1942 he was president, United Wallpaper Factories, in Chicago. From October 1940 to January 1942 he served as assistant coordinator of purchases and adviser to the Council of National Defense; deputy director, Division of Purchases; and then special adviser to Donald Nelson, director, Office of Production Management (later the War Production Board). In January 1942 he was recalled to active duty with the Purchases Branch, Procurement and Distribution Division, Services of Supply, with the rank of colonel. In October 1942, Somervell made Browning the director, Purchases Division, so that his experience could be fully tapped for directing the huge production and procurement effort then under way. In June 1943 Browning was promoted to brigadier general. From September 1944 to February 1945, when he returned to inactive status, he was assistant director of material, Headquarters, Army Service Forces. See also Ancell, *Biographical Dictionary*, 37.

107. George H. Weems (27 September 1891–25 February 1957). U.S. Military Academy, April 1917. Infantry. Weems served with the Ninth Infantry, Second Division, in World War I and saw heavy action during the summer of 1918. He commanded the Twenty-second Infantry Regiment, Fourth Infantry Division, at Fort Benning from December 1941 to September 1942, when he was promoted to brigadier general and assigned as assistant commandant, the Infantry School. From November 1944 to January 1945 he was in the ETO on a special mission. He retired in September 1951 as a brigadier general.

108. The Twenty-sixth Infantry was not able to reach these two companies, already badly depleted, and the regiment listed 165 men missing after the Merode attack. See MacDonald, *The Siegfried Line Campaign*, 490–92.

109. Chester B. Hanson was aide to General Omar N. Bradley from 1943 until 1952. He later worked as editor for the internal news magazine of International Business Machines (IBM).

110. The antiaircraft artillery had two general categories for their hits on enemy aircraft, category I or A for confirmed kills and category II or B for probable but as yet unconfirmed kills. See First U.S. Army, *Report of Operations, 1 August 1944–22 February 1945*, vol. 1, *Commanding General First U.S. Army and Headquarters Staff Sections* (Washington, DC: U.S. Government Printing Office, 1946), 173.

111. Colmar pocket. The name refers to the area on the west bank of the Rhine River around the Alsatian city of Colmar that the Germans held from November 1944 through February 1945. The pocket was created in November when the First French Army was stopped in its drive through the Belfort Gap to the Rhine. A bitter stalemate developed around Colmar as the Germans reinforced their hold on the area, thereby threatening the Allied forces both north and south of the pocket. At the end of December the Germans launched Operation Nordwind from Colmar in an attempt to retake Strasbourg and disrupt Allied operations against the Ardennes offensive. The First French Army and

U.S. Twenty-first Corps, Seventh Army, eliminated the Colmar pocket by early February 1945. See Jeffrey J. Clarke and Robert Ross Smith, *Riviera to the Rhine* (Washington, DC: U.S. Army Center of Military History, 1993).

112. John G. Hill (19 December 1899–21 October 1980). U.S. Military Academy, 1924. Infantry. Hill served as an enlisted man in the Kansas National Guard during World War I. He was assigned as adjutant general and general staff officer, Headquarters, Alaskan Department, from May 1940 to July 1943. He went to the ETO in December 1943 as assistant to the assistant chief of staff, G-3, First U.S. Army Group. In February 1944 he moved to Fifth Corps as assistant chief of staff, G-3, and remained there until July 1945. He retired as a brigadier general in August 1954.

113. Alexander Maurice Cameron (30 May 1898–1986) was the British Army officer who served as antiaircraft officer on the staff at Headquarters, SHAEF, during 1944–1945. He was educated at Wellington College and served with the Royal Engineers in France and Belgium during World War I. In 1940 he was promoted to brigadier and assigned to AA Command headquarters and later received command of an antiaircraft artillery brigade and group on England's south coast along with his promotion to major general. He was made AA officer at SHAEF in May 1944 and remained throughout the war. After the war, he was deputy quartermaster general of the army (1945–1948) and then served as officer in charge of administration, Middle East Land Forces (1948–1951). He was general officer in command, East African Command, during the Mau-Mau problem in Kenya. Cameron retired in 1954. See "Lieutenant-General Sir Alexander Maurice Cameron" at "The Generals of WWII," at http://www.generals.dk.

114. Ernie T. Pyle (3 August 1900–18 April 1945) was probably the best-known American journalist of World War II. He was particularly adept at telling the GI's story of the war in his numerous columns. He won the Pulitzer Prize in 1943. He joined the American troops in North Africa as a war correspondent and stayed with them throughout Italy and into France. With the war drawing to a close early in 1945, he went to the Pacific and took part in the landings at Okinawa. He was killed by Japanese sniper fire on the island of Ie Shima, near Okinawa, on 18 April 1945. Before the war, Pyle had served as managing editor of the *Washington Daily News* (1932–1935) and then as a correspondent for the Scripps-Howard newspapers. See Boatner, *Biographical Dictionary*, 439.

115. The M1 rifle was the standard American infantry small arm of World War II. Designed by John C. Garand (1888–1974) of the army's Springfield Arsenal in Massachusetts, the .30 caliber (7.62-mm) M1 (also called the M1 Garand) was adopted by the army in 1936 and entered production. The Garand was a semiautomatic weapon that operated on the blowback system. It weighed over nine pounds and carried eight rounds of .30 caliber ammunition in a clip that loaded directly into the rifle. See Lüdeke, *Weapons of World War II*, 36; Boatner, *Biographical Dictionary*, 176.

116. Richard E. Nugent (12 December 1902–5 November 1979). U.S. Military Academy, 1924. Infantry and Air Corps. Nugent transferred to the air corps in 1930. In 1939–1940 he was in the Officer Personnel Division, Office of the Chief of the Air Corps. After serving as an assistant military attaché in London from January to June 1941, he was chief, Planning Section, and later Operations Section, Headquarters, Army Air Forces, until March 1942. He was assigned to the War Department General Staff until April 1943 and was promoted to brigadier general in June 1943. From November 1943 to September 1944, he was assistant chief of staff, A-3, Operations, Ninth Air Force, in England. In September he became commanding general, Twenty-ninth Tactical Air Command, Ninth Air Force, with the mission of supporting Ninth Army. From the creation of the Department of the Air Force in 1947, Nugent served in various personnel positions in Headquarters, USAF, the last being deputy chief of staff, personnel. He was promoted to major general in February 1948 and to lieutenant general in April 1951. He retired in August 1951.

117. The "hokus-pokus" referred to was really the proximity (POZIT) or "variable time" (VT) fuse, which was developed by British and American scientists during the war. The proximity fuse used a tiny radio receiver-transmitter to send radio waves after the shell was fired. As the projectile came within range of an object (usually the target), waves of sufficient strength were reflected back to the receiver to trigger the fuse and detonate the projectile. The primary use of the VT or POZIT fuse was for air defense, and it was heavily used by the navy in the Pacific. The VT was withheld from use in Europe until late 1944 because of the fear that unexploded fuses would fall to the Germans, who would copy them for use against the Allies. See James Phinney Baxter III, *Scientists against Time* (Boston: Little, Brown, 1946), esp. 221–42; Parrish, *Encyclopedia of World War II*, 508.

118. Richard C. Partridge (15 February 1899–23 July 1976). U.S. Military Academy, 1920. Field Artillery. Partridge graduated from Harvard University and then enrolled in the U.S. Military Academy and graduated in June 1920. From November 1938 to February 1940 he was a student at the German General Staff Academy and then a military attaché in Berlin. He then went to Hungary as the military attaché until he was interned in December 1941. After his repatriation Partridge went directly to England as assistant G-3, Second Corps, which was there preparing for the North African landings, and then was moved to assistant G-3 at Allied Forces Headquarters from August 1942 to February 1943. In November 1943 he moved to England as assistant G-3 at First U.S. Army Group headquarters. In April 1944 he became assistant chief of staff, Seventh Corps, and then commanded 358th Infantry Regiment, Ninetieth Infantry Division, in June and July before being assigned as chief of staff, Seventh Corps, in early August 1944. He was promoted to brigadier general in March 1945 and remained with Seventh Corps until September of that year. After the war he held several intelligence posts in Europe and Washington,

and commanded the Fifth Infantry Division (1954–1955). He retired as a major general in 1959. See also Ancell, *Biographical Dictionary,* 250.

119. There is nothing in Col. Samuel V. Krauthoff's listing in the *Official Army Register* to indicate that he ever served in the German army in World War I. He is listed as being born in Missouri on 18 December 1902 and appointed to the U.S. Military Academy from Missouri on 1 July 1920. See the Adjutant General's Office, *Official Army Register, 1 January 1938* (Washington, DC: U.S. Government Printing Office, 1938), 418.

120. Edwin P. Parker (27 July 1891–7 June 1983). Field Artillery. Parker was commander of the Field Artillery Replacement Training Center at Fort Bragg, North Carolina, from January 1941 to May 1942. He was made a brigadier general in October 1941. From May 1942 to September 1945 he was commanding general, Seventy-eighth Infantry Division, and led it through its training, deployment to the ETO, and heavy fighting in Belgium and Germany. Parker was promoted to major general on 21 June 1942. He commanded Twenty-third Corps and then Third Army in Germany in 1945–1946. Parker served as provost marshal general of the army from 1 April 1948 until his retirement on 31 January 1953.

121. John K. Rice (16 May 1896–19 July 1990). Infantry. Rice served in World War I. From June 1939 to June 1941 he commanded a battalion of the Twenty-seventh Infantry at Schofield Barracks, Hawaii. He returned to the Infantry School as executive officer, Department of Tactics, until May 1942, when he became chief of staff, Thirty-eighth Infantry Division. From January to September 1943 he was assistant division commander, Thirty-fifth Infantry Division, and then became assistant division commander, Seventy-eighth Division. He was promoted to brigadier general in February 1943. He remained with Seventy-eighth until June 1945, when he became commanding general, War Department Personnel Center, Camp McCoy, Wisconsin, until June 1946. Rice retired as a major general in January 1953. See also Ancell, *Biographical Dictionary,* 271.

122. Clift Andrus (12 October 1890–September 1968). Cornell University, 1912. Field Artillery. Andrus served in World War I. He was assigned to the Hawaiian Department and 11th Field Artillery from August to November 1941 and then commanded the 24th Infantry Division's artillery to March 1942. Andrus became commanding general, Divisional Artillery, First Infantry Division, in May 1942. He served with the division through North Africa, Sicily, and Europe, becoming the commanding general on 11 December 1944. After the war, he was commandant, the Field Artillery School, from June 1946 to April 1949. From June 1949 to February 1950 he was director, organization and training, Department of the Army. He retired as a major general in October 1952.

123. The Germans used the *Holzmine* (wooden box mine) containing 11½ pounds of high explosive to avoid the metallic mine detectors used by army engineers to locate and remove mines.

124. SCR 584 was the Army Signal Corps Radio [SCR] microwave gun-directing radar that was first used with antiaircraft batteries at Anzio in February 1944. When employed with the M-9 director and proximity fuses (see 487n117 above), the SCR-584 radar was especially effective for the direction of antiaircraft artillery batteries against hostile aircraft and V-1s. It was also used to direct aircraft to fixed ground targets. See Baxter, *Scientists against Time,* 214–16, 234–36.

125. Cuthbert P. Stearnes (14 August 1885–6 June 1969). U.S. Military Academy, 1909. Cavalry. Stearnes served with the cavalry and as an instructor at the Military Academy before World War I and served with the Spruce Production Division in Portland, Oregon, from 1917 to 1920. From December 1938 to June 1941, he commanded the Fifth Cavalry Regiment. In November 1941 he was assigned to Charlottesville, Virginia, as an instructor at the Military Government School. He remained there until August 1943, when he was attached to the Civil Affairs Division in North Africa. In November he moved to England, where he organized and commanded the European Civil Affairs Division and Training Center until June 1944, when he became assistant chief of staff, G-5, Civil Affairs, ETOUSA and COMZ. Stearnes was promoted to brigadier general in September 1944 and remained in Europe until July 1945. He retired in February 1946.

126. Leroy H. Lutes (4 October 1890–30 January 1980). Infantry and Coast Artillery Corps. Lutes served in the National Guard from 1908 until March 1917, when he joined the Regular Army. In January 1940, he became assistant chief of staff, G-4. Third Army, and in October took over all supply planning for it. In February 1942 he was assigned to the War Department General Staff, and in the March 1942 reorganization of the War Department, Lutes became director of operations, Services of Supply (SOS), under Somervell. In January 1943 he was made director of planning and operations, SOS, and later Army Service Forces. He served two special tours in the ETO, from April to June 1944 prior to D-day, and from December 1944 to January 1945, as Somervell's personal representative on munitions supply. In April 1945 he became chief of staff and deputy commanding general, Army Service Forces (ASF), and was promoted to lieutenant general on 5 June 1945. He was commanding general, ASF, from January to June 1946, when ASF was abolished. Lutes then became director, Services, Supply and Procurement Division, War Department General Staff, until January 1947. He commanded Fourth Army from October 1949 until he retired as a lieutenant general in January 1952.

127. SP-155 (M12). The U.S. Army used several different models of the self-propelled 155-mm gun in Europe. The basic version was the M1918 gun mounted on a modified M3 chassis and was designated the GMC M12. The M1 or M1A1 155-mm gun was mounted in a pedestal at the back of the chassis, was lightly armored, and had a rear spade that acted as a shock absorber upon firing. A subsequent version of the SP-155 was the M40, which had a new 155-mm gun

on an M4 chassis. In addition to the 155-mm guns, 8-inch howitzers, 8-inch guns, and 240-mm howitzers were also built as self-propelled artillery in addition to the smaller-caliber 75-mm and 105-mm howitzers. Forty, *U.S. Army Handbook 1939–1945*, 111; Lüdeke, *Weapons of World War II*, 131.

5. The German Counteroffensive and the Drive to the Roer River, 16 December 1944–22 February 1945

1. Volksgrenadier (VG). In the summer and fall of 1944, the German army suffered heavy losses of experienced infantry and armored divisions on both the eastern and western fronts. This forced the Wehrmacht to obtain as many personnel as possible from the navy and Luftwaffe, the elderly and youths, the unfit, the recovering wounded and sick from military hospitals, and nonessential rear-area troops to build new divisions. These units were smaller (six rather than nine infantry battalions), armed with more automatic weapons, such as the Sturmgewehr 44, and intended mainly for defensive missions. A new name was given to these divisions, *Volksgrenadier*, "People's Grenadier," which emphasized the nationalism of the German people (*Volk*) and military traditions (*Grenadier*) in an effort to enhance morale. These units were hastily trained and thrown into battles where they generally performed without distinction, although some performed at an acceptable level. See U.S. War Department, Technical Manual TM-E 30–451, *Handbook on German Military Forces*, 15 March 1945 (Washington, DC: U.S. Government Printing Office, 1945), 90, 92, 116–20; Cole, *The Ardennes*; Charles B. MacDonald, *A Time for Trumpets: The Untold Story of the Battle of the Bulge* (New York: William Morrow, 1985), 43–44; Matthew Cooper, *The German Army 1933–1945: Its Political and Military Failure* (Lanham, MD: Scarborough House, 1990), 489, 522.

2. Lt. Gen. Sir Arthur Edward Grasett (1888–1971). Born and educated in Canada at the Royal Military College at Kingston, Grasett joined the Royal Engineers in 1909 and served with distinction during World War I. In 1937–1938 he was brigadier general staff, Northern Command, and then was general officer in command, China. In 1941 Grasett was made a division commander and soon moved up to command a corps until 1943. In 1943–1944 he was assigned to the War Office as chief, Liaison Branch, and then chief, European Allied Contact Section, when SHAEF was established. In April he was appointed chief, G-5, Civil Affairs Division, SHAEF. From 1945 to 1953 he was lieutenant governor and commander in chief, Jersey. He retired from active duty in 1947. See "Lieutenant-General Sir Arthur Edward Grasett (1888–1971)" at "The Generals of WWII" at http://www.generals.dk.

3. Cornelius E. Ryan (12 May 1896–6 June 1972). University of Connecticut, 1917. Infantry. Ryan served with the 304th Infantry, Seventy-sixth Division, and with the Forty-ninth Infantry, Eighty-third Division, in the AEF until July 1919. From June 1939 to January 1943, he was first an instructor in the Tank Sec-

tion, the Infantry School, and later chief, Automotive Section. He was assistant chief of staff, Third Army, in the United States until June 1943, when he went to Headquarters, ETOUSA, as chief, civil affairs, and was later assistant chief of staff, G-5, First Army, and then Twelfth Army Group. He was promoted to brigadier general in January 1945. From August 1945 to January 1946 he was assigned to Headquarters, Fifteenth Army, in Germany and then commanded the U.S. garrison in Berlin in 1946–1947. He later commanded the 101st Airborne Division in 1950–1951 and was chief, Korean Military Advisory Group, from June 1951 to June 1953. Ryan received his second star in November 1952. See *World Notables*, vol. 5 (1969–1973) (Chicago: Marquis Who's Who, 1973), 628; Ancell, *Biographical Dictionary*, 286.

4. Malmédy massacre. On 17 December 1944, at the Baugnez crossroads near the Belgian town of Malmédy, Obersturmbannführer (Lt. Col.) Jochen Peiper's First SS Panzer Regiment, First Panzer Division, captured elements of Battery B, 285th Field Artillery Observation Battalion, that were attached to the Ninth Armored Division, then on its way to St. Vith, and other miscellaneous American vehicles and troops. Over one hundred Americans were herded on to a snow-covered field. After some delay the Germans opened fire on the unarmed captives, eighty-six of whom were murdered in the worst atrocity of the war in Europe for the U.S. Army. News of the massacre spread quickly among American troops, who thereafter fought hard and often to their deaths against the German attackers rather than surrender. After the war Peiper and seventy-three other SS men were tried, convicted, and sentenced for their part in the massacre. None of them were executed or served their full prison terms. Peiper was killed in 1976 in his French home under mysterious circumstances. See Cole, *The Ardennes*, 260–64; Dear, *Oxford Guide to World War II*, 558; and James J. Weingartner, *Crossroads of Death: The Story of the Malmedy Massacre and Trial* (Berkeley: University of California Press, 1979).

5. John B. Anderson (10 March 1891–1 September 1976). U.S. Military Academy, 1914. Field Artillery. Anderson served in Belgium and France in 1917–1918. He was promoted to brigadier general in October 1941 and became commanding general, Second Infantry Division Artillery in November. He commanded the 102nd Infantry Division, from June 1942 to December 1943 and was promoted to major general in August 1942. In January 1944 he became commanding general, Sixteenth Corps, at Fort Riley, Kansas, and took the corps headquarters to Europe in September. He commanded Sixteenth Corps throughout the remainder of the war in Europe and returned to the United States with it in October 1945. He retired on 30 June 1946.

6. Samuel E. Anderson (6 January 1906–12 September 1982). U.S. Military Academy, 1928. Air Corps. Anderson was the operations officer with the Second and then the First Bombardment Wing at Langley Field, Virginia, from July 1940 to October 1941. After serving in the Office, Assistant Chief of the Air Staff until March 1942, he was assigned to the Operations Division, War Depart-

ment General Staff, until June 1943. He then went to England, where he took command of the Third Bomb Wing (Medium), Eighth Composite Command, Eighth Air Force, in July. In October 1943, his command was redesignated the Ninth Air Force Bomber Command (Medium) and reassigned to the Ninth Air Force. He was promoted to brigadier general in November. Anderson's three combat wings had all the medium bombers of Ninth Air Force that supported the ground forces on the Continent. He was promoted to major general in August 1944. He was the director, plans and operations, Headquarters, U.S. Air Force, from February 1948 to August 1950, when he became commanding general, Eighth Air Force, Strategic Air Command. In May 1953 he was promoted to lieutenant general and made commanding general, Fifth Air Force, in Korea. He was promoted to full general in March 1959 and named commanding general, Air Materiel Command. In the Air Force reorganization of 1961, he became commander, Air Force Logistics Command. He retired in July 1963. See also DuPre, *U.S. Air Force Biographical Dictionary*, 5–6; "General Samuel E. Anderson," at Air Force Link at http://www.af.mil/bios.

7. Führer Begleit Brigade derived from the elite Führer Begleit Bataillon, which was organized originally under then Oberst (Colonel) Erwin Rommel in 1939–1940 to act as a personal military escort for Adolf Hitler when necessary. When the army's elite Grossdeutschland Infantry Regiment was expanded into a division, one of the new elements was a Führer Begleit Abteilung (detachment), which was continually expanded thereafter. It eventually reached brigade size before the Ardennes offensive and was assigned to the Fifth Panzer Army and placed under the command of Oberst Otto Remer, a loyal Nazi who had played a major role in putting down the 20 July 1944 uprising against Hitler in Berlin. The brigade became a division and Remer a major general before the end of the war. The division was destroyed in April 1945. See Cole, *The Ardennes*; Boatner, *Biographical Dictionary*, 450; and Samuel W. Mitcham Jr., *German Order of Battle*, 2: 210–11.

8. Otto Skorzeny (1908–1975) was a Waffen-SS officer who achieved fame for rescuing Benito Mussolini from his mountaintop prison on 12 September 1943. Skorzeny had fought with the Waffen-SS in France, Yugoslavia, and Russia before being assigned to the Reichssicherheitshauptamt, SS headquarters, to work under Walter Schellenberg on organizing espionage activities. It was Skorzeny who developed the concept of Operation Greif which used English-speaking Germans in American uniforms and with American equipment to disrupt the American rear areas during the early days of the Ardennes offensive of December 1944. Skorzeny's men achieved far greater notoriety than effect and gained him a reputation beyond his actual achievements. He was tried by a U.S. Army court in 1947 but was acquitted of war crimes. He later escaped internment in Germany and lived for a number of years in Spain. See Boatner, *Biographical Dictionary*, 505–7.

9. Jacob L. Devers (8 September 1887–15 October 1979). U.S. Military Acad-

emy, 1909. Field Artillery. Devers became chief of staff, Panama Canal Department, in August 1939 and was promoted to brigadier general in May 1940. He returned to Washington in July 1940 as commanding general, Washington Provisional Brigade, and a member of the president's board to select air and naval bases in the Caribbean and Atlantic. In October 1940 he was made a major general and given command of Fort Bragg and the Ninth Infantry Division. From July 1941 to May 1943 he was chief of the Armored Force at Fort Knox. Devers was promoted to lieutenant general in September 1942. In May 1943 he became commanding general, European Theater of Operations, U.S. Army, with overall responsibility for planning American involvement in the invasion of France in 1944. In December 1943, with Eisenhower's selection to become supreme Allied commander, Devers was transferred to the post of commanding general, North African Theater of Operations, U.S. Army, and deputy supreme Allied commander, Allied Forces Headquarters and Mediterranean Theater of Operations. After the successful Allied invasion of southern France in August 1944, he became commanding general, Sixth Army Group, and commanded the Allied armies in the southern sector of the European front. Promoted to full general in March 1945, Devers returned to the United States in July 1945 as commanding general, Army Ground Forces, and later of its successor, Office of the Chief, Army Field Forces. He retired on 30 September 1949. See also Boatner, *Biographical Dictionary*, 129–30.

10. Col. James E. Rudder then commanded the 109th Infantry Regiment, Twenty-eighth Infantry Division, on the division's south flank opposing the Fifth Panzer Army's breakthrough, while Col. Gustin M. Nelson commanded the Twenty-eighth's 112th Infantry Regiment on the division's north flank.

11. Brigadier Ronald Frederick King Belchem (1911–1981). A British Army officer who was educated at Guildford and Sandhurst, Belchem was commissioned in the Royal Tank Regiment in 1931. From 1936 to 1939 he was in Egypt and Palestine. During World War II he served in Egypt, Greece, the Western Desert (including as commander, First Royal Tank Regiment, in 1943), Sicily, Italy, and northwest Europe. In 1944–1945 he was brigadier general staff, operations and training, for Montgomery's Twenty-first Army Group. He was Monty's chief of staff at Supreme Headquarters, Allied Powers Europe (SHAPE) from 1948 to 1950 and then commanded the Thirty-third Armoured Brigade before retiring in 1953 as a major general. See "Major-General Ronald Frederick King Belchem (1911–1981)" at www.generals.dk.

12. Alexander R. Bolling (28 August 1895–4 June 1964). Infantry. Bolling served with the Fourth Infantry, AEF, in France and saw action in the Aisne-Marne, Champagne-Marne, St. Mihiel, and Meuse-Argonne operations. From June 1938 to March 1942 he was chief of staff, First Corps Area. He then became assistant chief of staff, G-1, Personnel, Headquarters, Army Ground Forces, until November 1943, when he was appointed assistant division commander, Eighth Infantry Division. He was promoted to brigadier general in August

1942. The same month, he moved to the same position with the Eighty-fourth Infantry Division. In June 1944 he became commanding general, Eighty-fourth Infantry Division, and moved to Europe with the division in September and became a major general in January 1945. After the war, he remained in Germany as chief, Special Services, U.S. Forces, European Theater. He served in various intelligence posts on the Army Staff from December 1947 to August 1952. He was promoted to lieutenant general in July 1952 and commanded the Third Army from August 1952 until his retirement in July 1955. See also *World Notables*, vol. 4 (1961–1968), 100.

13. Lt. Col. John Ray was the ammunition officer in the Ordnance Section. He was not killed or captured and served with Headquarters, First U.S. Army, throughout the rest of the war in Europe.

14. Baron Friedrich August von der Heydte (30 March 1907–7 July 1994). Von der Heydte was a veteran of the German airborne invasion of Crete in 1941 and commander of the German army's parachute training school. On 8 December 1944, he was directed to organize a unit for a special operation as part of the Ardennes offensive. The unit was to be dropped at night in an area north of Malmédy to seize roads for use by advancing armored forces and to block enemy movements. The objectives of this difficult mission were not accomplished due to the scattering of the small force in dense woods and the injuries that von der Heydte sustained upon landing. Although the paratroopers were taken prisoner by 23 December, their presence did cause a great deal of confusion among the Allies. After the war, Baron von der Heydte had a successful career in the law before returning to serve in the West German Bundeswehr, in which he rose to the rank of general of paratroops before his retirement. See Boatner, *Biographical Dictionary*, 217; "The Rosary Paratrooper of World War II: The Baron von der Heydte," http://www.geocities.com/josephcrisp2/heydte.html.

15. Lt. Gen. Sir Brian Gwynne Horrocks (7 September 1895–4 January 1985). Horrocks was graduated from the Royal Military College, Sandhurst. He served with the Middlesex Regiment in France and Belgium during World War I and was captured by the Germans. During World War II, he commanded the Forty-fourth (Household Cavalry) Division, the Ninth Armoured Division, Thirteenth Corps at El Alamein, Tenth Corps in Egypt and North Africa, and Thirtieth Corps in Twenty-first Army Group in northwest Europe in 1944–1945. From 1944 to 1948 he was general officer in charge (GOC), Western Command, and then GOC, British Army of the Rhine, in 1948–1949. Horrocks retired in 1949. See Boatner, *Biographical Dictionary*, 238.

16. Francis Wilfred de Guingand (28 February 1900–29 June 1979). A graduate of the Royal Military College at Sandhurst, de Guingand was military assistant to the secretary of state for war in 1939–1940. He later moved to Egypt, where he served as director of military intelligence before becoming chief of staff, Eighth Army, in July 1942. He remained in this post when Bernard L.

Montgomery assumed command in August and remained with Montgomery throughout the rest of the war. He planned the invasion of Sicily and later moved to England with Monty as chief of staff, Twenty-first Army Group. "Freddy" de Guingand frequently had to employ his considerable personality and diplomatic skills to extricate Monty from his numerous scrapes with Eisenhower and the American commanders. He retired as major general in 1946 and went on to have a very successful business career. See Boatner, *Biographical Dictionary*, 127.

17. Tom Gordon Rennie (3 January 1900–24 March 1945). Rennie was educated at Loretto and the Royal Military College, Sandhurst. In 1919 he joined the Black Watch (Fifty-first Highlanders) as adjutant of the Second Battalion. He served as a staff officer with the Fifty-first Highland Division in France in 1939–1940. In 1941–1942 he was commander of the Fifth Battalion, Black Watch, and then became commander of the 154th Brigade, Fifty-first Highland Division, in 1942–1943 and was promoted to brigadier. He led the brigade during the fighting in North Africa and Sicily. In December 1943 he assumed command of the Third Division and was promoted to major general. He directed it during the early days of the fighting in France, and in July 1944 he became commander of the Fifty-first Highland Division. He was killed on 24 March 1945 while directing his division's crossing of the Rhine. See "Major-General Tom Gordon Rennie (1900–1945)" at www.generals.dk.

18. Peter C. Hains III (11 May 1901–3 July 1998). U.S. Military Academy, 1924. Cavalry. Hains commanded a battalion in the Thirteenth Armored Regiment from December 1941 to May 1942 and then commanded the First Armored Regiment, First Armored Division, in the United States, North Africa, and Tunisia until July 1943. After serving as assistant chief of staff, G-3, Tank Destroyer Command, until March 1944, he became ACS, G-3, at Headquarters, Army Ground Forces. He was sent to the ETO in April 1944 and briefly commanded a combat command of the Second Armored Division before becoming armored officer, Headquarters, First Army, in May. He remained in this position until October 1945. He was deputy director, Office of Military Assistance, Office of the Secretary of Defense, from September 1950 to February 1953, when he became chief of staff, Second Army, and was promoted to brigadier general. Promoted to major general in 1955, he later was chief, Joint U.S. Military Advisory Group, Thailand (1956–1959), and deputy chief of staff, plans and operations, Headquarters, U.S. Army Pacific (1959–1961), before retiring in 1961.

19. Rosser L. Hunter (4 September 1891–28 February 1956). George Washington University, 1916. Infantry. He served as an enlisted man in the District of Columbia National Guard and as an officer in World War I and remained in the army after the war. Hunter transferred to the Inspector General's Department in August 1939. He was the inspector general, Headquarters, First Army, from October 1943 through the end of the war.

20. The Junkers Ju 88 was probably the Luftwaffe's most versatile aircraft. The twin-engine Junkers began service in 1938 as a medium bomber. The model A-4 had a top speed of nearly 300 miles per hour at over 17,000 feet and a range of 1,500 miles with 5,000 pounds of bombs. The Ju 88C was used as a night fighter, primarily against the RAF Bomber Command, and an improved Ju 88G night fighter also saw considerable service. More than 9,000 of the bomber models were built during the war, but the large number of the other versions brought total output to more than 15,000 aircraft. See Lüdeke, *Weapons of World War II*, 202–3; Parrish, *Encyclopedia of World War II*, 325; Taylor, *Combat Aircraft of the World*, 178–80.

21. The Luftwaffe devised one last gamble to strike a surprise blow against the Allies on their home airfields in Belgium and Holland to regain some measure of control in the air. Codenamed *Bodenplatte* (Baseplate), the Luftwaffe gathered more than 700 of its remaining combat aircraft for this operation, which took place against seventeen American and British airfields on 1 January 1945. The Germans lost 270 aircraft destroyed and 40 damaged and 214 irreplaceable pilots, while the Allies lost more than 150 aircraft destroyed (36 American) and 111 more seriously damaged and approximately 50 killed, only a few of them pilots. These losses largely marked the operational end of the Luftwaffe. See John Terraine, *A Time for Courage: The Royal Air Force in the European War, 1939–1945* (New York: Macmillan, 1985), 675–76; Norman L. Franks, *The Battle of the Airfields, 1st January 1945* (London: Grub Street, 2000); Wesley Frank Craven and James Lea Cate, *The Army Air Forces in World War II*, vol. 3, *Europe: Argument to V-E Day January 1944 to May 1945* (Washington, DC: Office of Air Force History, 1983), 665.

22. These German attacks were the beginning of Operation Nordwind (North Wind), which German First Army launched against the Sixth Army Group's Seventh U.S. Army and First French Army in Alsace and the Vosges on 31 December 1944. Combined with an attack by the German Nineteenth Army out of the Colmar pocket toward Strasbourg, this counteroffensive pushed back the Allies some miles and was a serious threat for the Sixth Army Group, which was stretched thin due to taking over part of the Third Army's front so that Patton could shift some of his forces north to relieve Bastogne. The offensive was contained by the end of January, and the Germans suffered additional heavy losses in men and equipment that might have been better used in the main Ardennes counteroffensive to the north. See Clarke and Smith, *Riviera to the Rhine*, 492–532.

23. Named for the French minister of war, André Maginot, the Maginot Line was an interlocking series of reinforced concrete, underground forts that stretched along the French-German border from Switzerland to the French-Belgian border but not to the English Channel. Built between 1930 and 1935, the line was to protect France from any German attack while the French mobilized. In May 1940, German armored divisions attacked through Luxembourg

and Belgium and spun around the open end of the Maginot Line, which would later fall without much of a fight in June 1940. See Parrish, *Encyclopedia of World War II*, 384.

24. Hitlerjugend (Hitler Youth) was the Nazi youth organization that came under Baldur von Shirach. By 1936 the Hitler Youth had replaced all other youth organizations, which were now outlawed. In 1939 all German children were conscripted into the Hitler Youth, which was an important part of the Nazi Party's program for complete domination of all aspects of German life. The party used the activities of the Hitler Youth to indoctrinate the children in the party's ideology, identify potential leaders and members of the party, and prepare them for military service and to fight for the Third Reich during its dying days as part of the *Volkssturm* (see note 3, chap. 6). See Dear, *Oxford Guide to World War II*, 425.

25. *Volksdeutsche,* or foreign-born Germans, was the Nazi Party's definition for those of German blood born and living in areas other than Germany or the Greater German Reich. Among these Aryans were the Sudeten Germans, Alsatians, and Germans in Poland, the Baltic States, Russia, Romania, and so on who could be claimed as ethnically, linguistically, and culturally of German descent. The Volksdeutsche formed an important fifth column in many countries of Eastern Europe, but more than anything they were an important pretext for the aggressive foreign policy of Nazi Germany. After the war, these German populations were ruthlessly expelled by the countries in which they had resided for many years. The Slovaks, as a Slavic people, were not Volksdeutsche, although they were allied with Hitler during the war and had taken part in the partition of Czechoslovakia in 1939. See Robert Cecil, *The Myth of the Master Race: Alfred Rosenberg and Nazi Ideology* (New York: Dodd Mead, 1972), 7, 70, 190; Wolfgang Benz, *A Concise History of the Third Reich* (Berkeley: University of California Press, 2006), 173–74; Franz Neumann, *Behemoth: The Structure and Practice of National Socialism, 1933–1944* (New York: Harper Torchbooks, 1963).

26. Alexander D. Surles Jr. (15 January 1914–12 December 1995). U.S. Military Academy, 1937. Cavalry and Armor. Surles served as a company commander with the Armored Force at Fort Knox from August 1940 to January 1942, when he became regimental S-3 (operations officer) and assistant G-3 of the Sixth Armored Division. From July 1942 to May 1943 he was G-3 of the division and then G-3 of Second Armored Corps, later the Eighteenth Corps, until July 1944. He went to the ETO with the corps, which was redesignated the Eighteenth Airborne Corps and assigned to First Allied Airborne Army in August 1944. He retired as a lieutenant general in 1972.

27. The Hawker Tempest was a British fighter-bomber. Armed with four 20-mm cannon, its primary mission was ground attack and to knock down V-1s headed for England. Tempests eventually claimed more than six hundred "buzz bombs" destroyed. See Taylor, *Combat Aircraft of the World*, 390–91.

28. Levin H. Campbell Jr. (23 November 1886–1 November 1976). U.S. Naval Academy, 1909. Coast Artillery Corps and Ordnance Department. Campbell transferred to the Coast Artillery Corps in 1911 and in 1921 to the Ordnance Department. He was assistant chief for facilities, Industrial Service, Office of the Chief of Ordnance, from June 1940 to April 1942. He was promoted to brigadier general in October 1940 and made assistant chief of industrial services for production. On 1 April 1942 he was promoted to major general and on 1 June 1942 he was appointed chief of ordnance. On 16 April 1945 he was promoted to lieutenant general. Campbell retired in May 1946. See also Ancell, *Biographical Dictionary*, 45.

29. Harold V. "Hal" Boyle (21 February 1911–1 April 1974). A reporter and columnist for the Associated Press, Boyle was a war correspondent who covered the North African, European, and Pacific theaters during World War II. He received a Pulitzer Prize for his war reporting in 1944. He and Thompson never produced a book on the Bulge. See *World Notables*, vol. 6, 1874–1976, 47.

30. Dyke F. Meyer (b. 28 May 1905). Washington University, St. Louis, 1927. Air Corps. Meyer completed flight training in February 1930. He commanded the 366th Fighter Group, Ninth Air Force, in 1943–1944 and the Eighty-fourth Fighter Wing, Ninth Air Force, September 1944–1945.

31. Maj. Gen. Fay B. Prickett, commanding general, Seventy-fifth Infantry Division, and Brig. Gen. Albert C. Stanford, artillery commander, were relieved on 23 January 1945 because the division, which was experiencing its initial combat, was not performing up to Hodges's expectations.

Fay B. Prickett (29 April 1893–18 December 1982). U.S. Military Academy, 1914. Cavalry and Field Artillery. Prickett served with the Tenth Cavalry in 1916–1917 and in August 1917 joined the Thirteenth Field Artillery. He later served in France. After commanding a field artillery brigade, he was First Army artillery officer from November 1941 to February 1942. He was then commanding general, Fourth Infantry Division Artillery, until August 1943. He was promoted to brigadier general in March 1942. From August 1943 to 23 January 1945, he commanded the Seventy-fifth Infantry Division in the United States and the ETO. Prickett received his second star in January 1944. After being relieved by Hodges, he became deputy commanding general, Twenty-first Corps, until May 1945, when he assumed command of Tenth Armored Division in Germany. From September 1945 to March 1946 he commanded the Fourth Infantry Division and then the First Constabulary Brigade until December 1947. He was deputy inspector general of the army from July 1948 until his retirement in 1953.

Albert C. Stanford (25 March 1895–7 November 1952). U.S. Military Academy, April 1917. Cavalry, Signal Corps, and Field Artillery. Stanford served in the United States during World War I. After serving at Fort Jackson, South Carolina, he was assigned to the Thirty-fourth Infantry Division as artillery commander in May 1942 and was promoted to brigadier general in July. He served with the Thirty-fourth in Northern Ireland, North Africa, and Italy, including at Cassino and Anzio, until May 1944. He returned to the United States as artillery commander of the Seventy-fifth Infantry Division, which was then preparing for deployment to the ETO later in 1944. He served with the division in Europe from November 1944 until 5 March 1945. After his relief, he returned to the United States. He retired in January 1946 as a colonel. He was promoted to brigadier general on the retired list in 1948.

32. Heinrich Himmler (7 October 1900–23 May 1945). Himmler served as an officer cadet in the German army in 1917–1918 and then in one of the numerous Freikorps after the war. (Freikorps, or "Free Corps," were groups composed largely of former German army soldiers and dedicated to extremely conservative leaders who harshly put down socialist and Communist uprisings in 1918–1920 in Germany and the Baltic States.) He joined the Nazi Party in August 1923 due to his friendship with Ernst Röhm and played a minor part in the Beer Hall Putsch of November 1923. He joined the SS in 1925 and was made deputy head of party propaganda by Hitler in 1926. Hitler promoted him to chief of the SS, Reichsführer SS, in 1929. Himmler was a firm believer in the concept of Aryan and Nordic supremacy and fully indoctrinated his SS officers and men in the ideas of Germanic racial superiority and Nazi dogma. Himmler's SS was the watchdog for Hitler both in and out of the party. After the Nazi seizure of power in 1933, the SS dominated all police functions, exterminated the Sturmabteilung (Brown Shirts) leadership of Röhm in June 1934, and organized and ran the concentration camps. During the war, Himmler's SS became an immense undertaking, fielding its own Waffen-SS, running an industrial empire that was largely based on the concentration camps and forced labor, controlling police and security functions, and taking over army command functions. After the 20 July 1944 attempt on Hitler's life, Himmler became chief of the Replacement Army and was appointed commander of Army Group Oberrhein (Upper Rhine), which he commanded until Hitler shifted him to command of Army Group Vistula late in January 1945 to stiffen the defenses against a massive Soviet breakthrough. His commands were undistinguished, and he gave up in March 1945, when he became involved in peace initiatives on his own. When word of Himmler's activities leaked out, Hitler fired him on 28 April 1945. He was captured by British troops on 23 May while masquerading as a German army corporal. As soon as his identity was discovered, he committed suicide with a cyanide capsule concealed in his teeth. See John Keegan, ed., *Who Was Who in World War II* (New York: Bison Books, 1978), 102–5; Robert Wistrich, *Who's Who in Nazi Germany* (New York: Bonanza Books, 1982), 138–42; Joachim C. Fest, *The Face of the Third Reich: Portraits of the Nazi Leadership* (New York: Ace Books, 1970), 166–85.

33. Isaac D. White (4 March 1901–11 June 1990). Norwich University, 1922. Cavalry and Armor. In July 1942 White took command of the Second Reconnaissance Battalion, Second Armored Division, first under Charles Scott and

then under Patton. From June 1942 to April 1943, he commanded the Forty-seventh Armored Reconnaissance Regiment, Second Armored Division at Fort Benning and then as part of the Western Task Force in Operation Torch and subsequent operations in Morocco,. He then commanded Combat Command B, Second Armored Division, in North Africa and Europe until January 1945. He was promoted to brigadier general in May 1944. He became commanding general, Second Armored Division, in January 1945, when Harmon took over Twenty-second Corps, Third Army. White was promoted to major general in March 1945 and commanded the Second Armored until July. After the war he commanded the U.S. Constabulary in Germany from May 1948 to November 1950, when he became deputy commanding general, Seventh Army. He served as commanding general, the Armor Center and School, from August 1951 to August 1952, when he took over Tenth Corps, Far East Command, where he served until September 1953, receiving his third star in November 1952. In June 1955 he was promoted to full general and assigned as commanding general, Headquarters, U.S. Army Forces, Far East, and Eighth Army. From July 1957 until his retirement in March 1961 he was commander in chief, U.S. Army Pacific.

34. Ray E. Porter (29 July 1891–10 August 1963). Infantry. Commissioned in August 1917, Porter served with the Thirty-fourth Infantry Regiment in France and received a Distinguished Service Cross for heroism in November 1918. After serving as plans and training officer G-3, Fifth Corps, from November 1940 until December 1941, he was chief of staff, Thirty-eighth Infantry Division, until May 1942 and then commanded the 349th Infantry, Eighty-eighth Infantry Division, until July 1942. He was assistant division commander, Thirty-fourth Infantry Division, until November 1942, and deputy commander, Eastern Task Force in Operation Torch, landing at Algiers in November 1942. He then was deputy commanding general, Second Corps, and deputy chief of staff, Allied Forces, and responsible for Eisenhower's advanced command post. From May 1943 to December 1944, he was assistant chief of staff, G-3, War Department General Staff. He was promoted to major general in October 1943. After briefly commanding Fifteenth Army in December 1944–January 1945, he replaced Prickett as commanding general, Seventy-fifth Infantry Division, on 23 January 1945. In June 1945 he returned to Washington as director, Planning Division, Special Staff, War Department. After the war he commanded the Panama Canal Department (1946–1948) and U.S. Army forces in the Antilles (1948), and the Caribbean (1948–1951). He was commanding general, 101st Airborne Division, from June 1951 until he retired as a major general in June 1953. See also Ancell, *Biographical Dictionary*, 261.

35. On 12 September 1944, the day that Allied troops first crossed the German border in the west, Eisenhower proclaimed a policy of "nonfraternization" between all Allied soldiers and all German civilians. Eisenhower was now enforcing the Combined Chiefs of Staff's CCS 551, "Directive for Military Government in Germany Prior to Defeat or Surrender." Eisenhower's direc-

tive defined nonfraternization as "the avoidance of mingling with Germans upon terms of friendliness, familiarity, or intimacy, individually or in groups in official or unofficial dealings." This policy and the guidelines put in place to enforce nonfraternization with German civilians, spelled out in pocket guides, lectures, and films such as the one mentioned by the diarist, were to no avail as human nature prevailed. With some minor exceptions in the area of lodging and marriage, the policy was officially ended on 1 October 1945. See Joseph R. Starr, *Fraternization with Germans in World War II*, Occupation Forces in Europe Series, 1945–1946. (Frankfurt-am-Main, Germany: Office of the Chief Historian, U.S. European Command, 1947). Copy in U.S. Army Center of Military History, Washington, DC.

36. Josef "Sepp" Dietrich (28 May 1892–21 April 1966) joined the German army in 1911 and rose to the rank of sergeant during World War I. In the early 1920s he joined Ernst Röhm's Nazi Party SA and became a party member in 1928. He helped organize the SS in Bavaria in the early 1930s, and when Hitler became chancellor in January 1933, Dietrich took over responsibility for Hitler's SS bodyguard, the Liebstandarte Adolf Hitler. In 1938 the Liebstandarte became an active field force of the Waffen-SS. It later became a panzer division and saw considerable action in Russia, where Dietrich gained a notorious reputation for effectiveness. Late in 1944 Dietrich was promoted to colonel general and given command of the Sixth Panzer Army for the Ardennes offensive. His forces carried out a brutal campaign in the Ardennes, including the murder of over one hundred Americans in the Malmédy massacre and many Belgian civilians. He was arrested in 1946, tried for his was crimes, convicted, and sentenced to life imprisonment. He was pardoned and released in 1955 only to be rearrested in 1957 and convicted for his part in the June 1934 murder of Ernst Röhm and his colleagues. He was released from prison due to health reasons in 1959. See Boatner, *Biographical Dictionary*, 133–34; Wistrich, *Who's Who in Nazi Germany*, 50–52.

37. Hermann Göring (12 January 1893–15 October 1946) was a distinguished German flyer and ace of World War I who succeeded Baron Manfred von Richthofen as commander of the "Flying Circus" in July 1918. He joined Hitler's Nazi movement in 1923 and took charge of the SA, or Brown Shirts. He played a prominent part in the abortive putsch of November 1923, during which he was wounded. Afterward he went into exile to escape trial, returning to Bavaria in 1927. After the Nazi's election gains of July 1932, he became president of the Reichstag. In 1933 he became commissioner of aviation and minister of the interior in Prussia. In March 1935 he became head of the Luftwaffe (air force) and second in command after Hitler and later received the grandiose rank of Reichsmarschall. Göring had a significant role in the development of German air power prior to the war, but his personal excesses and habits (drug addiction) gradually diverted him from a meaningful involvement in the Luftwaffe's daily operations. His political fortunes eroded as the Luftwaffe faltered

and eventually cracked under the Allies' aerial onslaught. By 1945 he no longer had any influence in the higher councils of Hitler's Germany. He committed suicide just hours before his execution after his conviction in the Nuremberg trials of 1945–1946. See Keegan, *Who Was Who in World War II*, 93; Wistrich, *Who's Who in Nazi Germany*, 101–5; Fest, *Face of the Third Reich*, 109–25.

38. A *sabot* was normally a lightweight carrier that allowed the firing of a subcaliber projectile in a larger-caliber weapon. Sabots were especially used for hypervelocity antitank projectiles that contained a tungsten-carbide core which was the subcaliber projectile. John Quick, *Dictionary of Weapons and Military Terms* (New York: McGraw-Hill, 1973), 363.

39. Borrowing from their original French instructors, U.S. Army engineers have always used the term *pontons*, not *pontoons*, to describe the boats and later the inflatable pneumatic rubber floats that supported their tactical floating bridges for crossing water obstacles. These floating bridges came in a variety of types and weight-carrying capacities to support the range of American ground forces. Late in the war, bridges could support standard loads of twenty-five to fifty tons, normally with one-way traffic. The lighter Treadway bridges used the pneumatic rubber floats, while the heavy pontoon bridges used the larger ponton boats. See Blanche D. Coll, Jean E. Keith, and Herbert H. Rosenthal, *The Corps of Engineers: Troops and Equipment* (Washington, DC: Office of the Chief of Military History, U.S. Army, 1958), 37–53, 483–97.

40. A. Franklin Kibler (10 July 1891–24 January 1955).Virginia Military Institute, 1912. Field Artillery. Kibler served in the Virginia National Guard before joining the army during World War I. In March 1939 he joined the War Plans Division, War Department General Staff. From June 1942 to September 1943 he commanded the divisional artillery of the Seventy-eighth Infantry Division and then became commanding general, Thirteenth Corps Artillery. He was promoted to brigadier general in June 1942. From October 1943 to August 1945 he was assistant chief of staff, G-3, Twelfth Army Group, under Bradley. Kibler received his promotion to major general in November 1944. In September 1945 he was appointed director of operations, ETO General Board. He was the U.S. Army representative on the UN Military Staff Committee and a member of the Joint Chiefs of Staff staff from August 1946 until February 1949, when he became chief, U.S. Delegation, Military Committee of the Five Powers (Brussels Pact), in London. He retired as a major general in June 1952.

41. *Ordensburg Vogelsang.* Overlooking the lake formed by the Urft River dam in the Eifel hills, Vogelsang was one of four *Ordensburgen,* or Order Castles, developed by Robert Ley (1890–1945), the Nazi labor leader, based on a mystic view of the castles of the Teutonic Order. The Order Castles were to train future Nazi Party leaders and administrators in racial mythology, physical fitness, and leadership prior to their entering the SS, army, party bureaucracy, or government. The Order Castles at Falkenburg in Pomerania, Sonthofen in Bavaria, and the Eifel (Vogelsang) were completed and fully operational prior to the

outbreak of the war in 1939, but the fourth castle, at Marienburg, East Prussia, which was to instruct the future rulers of the Lebensraum to be conquered in the East, was never finished. See David Schoenbaum, *Hitler's Social Revolution: Class and Status in Nazi Germany, 1933–1939* (Garden City, NY: Anchor Books, 1966), 269–72; William L. Shirer, *The Rise and Fall of the Third Reich: A History of Nazi Germany* (New York: Simon and Schuster, 1960), 255–56; Evans, *The Third Reich in Power*, 286–89.

42. Paul R. Hawley (13 January 1891–24 November 1965). Indiana University, 1912; Cincinnati University, MD, 1914. Hawley was commissioned in the Regular Army Medical Corps in 1917 and served in France in World War I. From January to May 1941, he was commanding general, Medical Department Replacement Training Center, and then from May to September was commandant, Medical Field Service School. In September 1941 he went to England as chief surgeon, Special Observer Group, which was coordinating American-British military planning. From January to July 1942 he was chief surgeon, U.S. Army Forces, British Isles, and remained as chief surgeon, European Theater of Operations, when it was established. He held the dual posts of chief surgeon, ETO, and chief surgeon, Headquarters, Services of Supply, ETO, until August 1945. He was promoted to major general in February 1944. From August 1945 until his retirement in June 1946, he was medical adviser to Omar Bradley at the Veterans Administration and chief medical director until 1947. He was director, American College of Surgeons, from 1950 to 1961. See also *World Notables*, vol. 4 (1961–1968), 420.

43. Joseph I. Martin (1 February 1894–13 April 1957). Chicago Hospital College of Medicine, MD, 1918. He was commissioned in the Medical Reserve Corps in July 1918. From June to December 1940 he was medical inspector, Sixth Corps Area, and then commanded the Medical Department Replacement Training Center at Camp Grant, Illinois, until March 1943. His next assignment was as chief surgeon, Fifth Army, in the Mediterranean. Martin was promoted to brigadier general in February 1944. He remained there until July 1945 when he returned to Headquarters, Army Service Forces, briefly before moving to Headquarters, Army Forces Western Pacific and Army Forces Pacific as chief surgeon, until August 1946. He received his second star in September 1945. From August 1953 to August 1955 he was assigned to the Office of the Surgeon General. He retired on 30 November 1955 as a major general.

44. John Millikin (7 January 1888–6 November 1970). U.S. Military Academy, 1910. Cavalry. Millikin served in France in World War I. In October 1940 he was promoted to brigadier general and given command of the First Cavalry Brigade. In June 1941 he assumed command of the Second Cavalry Division and was promoted to major general. After briefly commanding the Eighty-third Infantry Division from May to August 1942, he commanded the Thirty-third Infantry Division in the United States and the Pacific (September 1942 to October 1943). From October 1943 to March 1945 he commanded Third Corps

in the United States and the ETO but was relieved of command by Hodges for lack of action after the Remagen bridgehead was secured. He was commander of the Thirteenth Armored Division from April to September 1945. In February 1948 he retired as a major general.

45. George Gershwin (1898–1937) was an American composer who specialized in musical comedy and orchestral works. His most famous works were *Rhapsody in Blue* (1923), Piano Concerto in F (1925), "Lady Be Good" (1924), "Funny Face" (1927), "Girl Crazy" (1930), "Of Thee I Sing" (1931), and the opera *Porgy and Bess*.

46. George A. Miller (8 September 1891–20 June 1978). See also Infantry and Adjutant General Corps. Miller served as an enlisted man and officer in World War I. He was detailed to the Adjutant General's Department in February 1939 and then transferred to it in July 1941. In November 1943 he transferred back to the infantry. After serving as an assistant ACS, G-1, in Headquarters, First Army, he became G-1 when Colonel O'Hare moved to Twelfth Army Group with Bradley in August 1944. He remained G-1 throughout the rest of the war. He was promoted to brigadier general in June 1945 and retired in February 1948. Ancell, *Biographical Dictionary*, 227.

47. Hugh J. Morgan (25 January 1893–24 December 1961). Vanderbilt University, 1914; Johns Hopkins University, MD, 1918. He served in the Medical Corps with the AEF during World War I. He was professor of clinical medicine at Vanderbilt from 1924 to 1928 and then physician in chief, Vanderbilt University Hospital, until 1958. Morgan was recalled to active duty with the Medical Department in 1942 and served as chief consultant in internal medicine, Office of the Surgeon General, U.S. Army, from 1942 to 1946. He was promoted to brigadier general in December 1942. He served as a member of the Medical Advisory Committee to the secretary of war from 1946 to 1948.

48. William S. Middleton (7 January 1890–9 September 1975). University of Pennsylvania, MD, 1911. Middleton joined the University of Wisconsin Medical School in 1912 and remained with it through 1955, serving as dean and professor of medicine from 1935 to 1955. He served in the Medical Reserve Corps in World War I. He was chief medical director for the Veterans Administration from 1955 to 1963. From 1964 to 1970, he was a consultant to the VA hospital at Madison, Wisconsin, which is now named in his honor. He was recalled to active duty in 1942 and was chief consultant in medicine, ETO, from July 1942 until July 1945.

49. Century was the communications code name for the headquarters of the U.S. Third Corps.

50. Gladeon M. Barnes (15 November 1887–15 November 1961). University of Michigan, 1910. Coast Artillery Corps and Ordnance Corps. Barnes was commissioned in the Coast Artillery but joined the Ordnance Corps in 1914. He was chief, Technical Staff, Office of the Chief of Ordnance, in 1939–1940. He then moved to the post of assistant chief for engineering, Industrial Service,

Office, Chief of Ordnance. In 1941 he became assistant chief for research and development, Industrial Service, and remained in charge of ordnance research and development throughout the rest of the war. Barnes was the dominant personality in ordnance research and development from 1938 through 1946. He was promoted to major general in March 1943 and retired in August 1946.

51. OPD was the Operations Division, War Department General Staff, that conducted the strategic and logistical planning for the War Department during World War II. It acted as George Marshall's brain trust and was largely responsible for the American successes in ground and air operations.

52. Alvin C. Gillem (8 August 1888–13 February 1973). Gillem began his service as an enlisted man (1910–1911) and was commissioned in 1911. From January 1940 to January 1941, he commanded the Sixty-sixth Infantry (Light Tanks). Following his promotion to brigadier general in January 1941 he served with the Second Armored Division and was promoted to major general in July 1941. In January 1942 he took command of the Second Armored Corps. From May to November 1943, he was commanding general, the Armored Force (later Armored Command), and then was made commander of Thirteenth Corps, which deployed to the ETO in July 1944. Gillem was promoted to lieutenant general in June 1945 and commanded the Seventh Corps from August 1945 to July 1946. From June 1947 until his retirement in August 1950, he was commanding general, Third Army.

53. The diarist here is referring to a message received through the "phantom intelligence network." The British developed this sophisticated system of information and intelligence gathering and reporting centers that were established at units below the level of army headquarters. The personnel assigned to these centers relayed information by radio directly to the army headquarters, so that valuable time was saved in collecting and assessing data at army level. With the Eighth British Army in North Africa, Montgomery and his chief of staff, Francis de Guingand, set up a system of specially trained liaison officers who were assigned or dispatched to various critical places along the front to report their impressions directly to Monty. This system was continued in northwest Europe and was combined with a radio intercept intelligence system, the "Y Service," to become the "phantom intelligence network," which included sections in various American headquarters and fed intelligence information back to Monty on a daily basis. The American command eventually established signal intelligence and monitoring (SIAM) units to provide the same services. However, "Phantom Section" was also sometimes used as the cover for the Ultra representatives with the Special Liaison Unit (SLU) attached to G-2 Section First Army headquarters to provide intelligence information obtained from German military, naval, air, and diplomatic communications. These British liaison officers and communications sections, and their American counterparts, were responsible for feeding intelligence information and analyses based on Ultra from the British intelligence service at Bletchley Park, England, to Allied

field commanders. Each American army in Europe had such an SLU attached to it. Because Ultra was such a closely held secret, only a few top officers at each headquarters knew what the "phantom section" or "the special Limeys," as they were called at Twelfth Army Group headquarters, actually did. Thus, the shadowy "phantom network" was a convenient cover for the SLU and Ultra. It is interesting to note that the American Ultra representative at First Army, Lt. Col. Adolph G. Rosengarten, while assigned to G-2 Section, never showed up in its personnel list. At First Army, only Hodges, Kean, Thorson, Dickson, Rosengarten, and several others in the G-2 Section actually had knowledge of and access to Ultra intelligence. Francis de Guingand, *Operation Victory* (New York: Charles Scribner's Sons, 1947), 144, 147; Omar Bradley and Clay Blair Jr., *A General's Life* (New York: Simon and Schuster, 1983), 399; Ronald Lewin, *Ultra Goes to War* (New York: Pocket Books, 1978), 147–74; Dear, *Oxford Guide to World War II,* 684; Hogan, *A Command Post at War,* 49, 84–85, 220–21, 262–63, 286.

54. Operation Clarion was the carefully planned Allied air operation against German communications and transportation that was intended to paralyze German economic life and support for the fighting front. American and British aircraft were to strike all possible transportation targets, many of them located in small towns that had not yet been air targets. Anglo-American strategic and tactical air forces executed Clarion on 22 February with what were believed to have been such excellent results that a second Clarion operation was mounted the following day. Although the principal airmen such as Spaatz and Doolittle thought the Clarion strikes were effective, no additional Clarion operations were flown, and postwar analysis indicated that they were less effective than was first thought. See Dear, *Oxford Guide to World War II,* 190; Craven and Cate, *Europe: Argument to V-E Day,* 732–35.

55. The T26E3 (M26) was a 45-ton heavy tank, nicknamed the Pershing, that mounted a 90-mm gun and was developed in response to the German Panther, Tiger, and King Tiger heavy tanks, which were far superior to the standard American M4 Sherman medium tank. The initial production versions were delivered in November 1944 with only fifty built before the end of the year. A small number of M26s were sent to Europe and assigned to the Third and Ninth Armored Divisions for combat evaluation. These tanks performed very well in their first tank-to-tank combats, in which they proved that they could take on and kill Panthers. See Lüdeke, *Weapons of World War II,* 134; Constance McL. Green, Harry C. Thomson, and Peter C. Roots, *The Ordnance Department: Planning Munitions for War* (Washington, DC: Office of the Chief of Military History, 1955), 237–38.

6. Crossing the Roer River, 23–28 February 1945

1. The Bailey Bridge was the standard "all-purpose" tactical bridge used by the Allies during World War II. Designed by Sir Donald Coleman Bailey of

the Royal Engineer School prior to the war, the Bailey bridge consisted of individual panels that could be combined in a variety of ways to produce fixed or floating semipermanent bridges of varying weight-carrying capacities. Bailey panels were easy to transport and assemble and proved to be extremely valuable in allowing the American and British armies to cross virtually any water obstacle. See Coll et al., *Corps of Engineers*, 50–51, 483–97.

2. The Messerschmitt 262 (Me 262) was the first operational combat jet aircraft. Designed and built by Willy Messerschmitt, the Me 262 was powered by twin Daimler Jumo jet engines mounted in pods underneath the wings. Hitler's personal intervention after the plane's initial test flights in 1942 led to redesigning the aircraft from a fighter to a "Revenge bomber," something that was not successful but delayed the Me 262's combat appearance for over two years. By the time the Me 262 entered aerial combat in 1944, it was too late for the Luftwaffe to regain any measure of air superiority despite the technical excellence of the first jet fighter. See Lüdeke, *Weapons of World War II*, 195; Len Cacutt, ed., "Messerschmitt 262," in *The World's Greatest Aircraft* (New York: Exeter Books, 1988), 100–106; Taylor, *Combat Aircraft of the World*, 187–88.

3. The Volkssturm, or People's Militia, was created by Hitler in September 1944. Made up principally of men up to and over sixty and boys of the Hitler Youth under sixteen, these units were inadequately armed and led. Although they engaged in some significant fighting in both east and west, the Volkssturm and its Sturm battalions were largely a last-gasp effort that produced little in the way of effective military operations or resistance. See Dear, *Oxford Guide to World War II*, 368–69.

4. Esther Reese McCafferty joined the Army Nurse Corps in April 1931 and served at Walter Reed General Hospital, in Hawaii, and at the U.S. Military Academy hospital through February 1941, when she returned to Walter Reed. In June 1942, she went to England and was assigned to Headquarters, Services of Supply, where she was assigned to the Nursing Division, Office of the Chief Surgeon, to oversee nursing in the ETO. She was promoted to major in January 1944 and became chief nurse, First Army. In July 1945, she returned to Valley Forge General Hospital in Phoenixville, Pennsylvania. She resigned her commission in December 1945 upon marrying John J. Moran. At the time no army nurses were allowed to remain on active duty if married. See Mary T. Sarnecky, *A History of the U.S. Army Nurse Corps* (Philadelphia: University of Pennsylvania Press, 1999), 229, 232, 239; Personnel Card, Esther Reese McCafferty, Army Nurse Corps Collection, Office of Medical History, U.S. Army Medical Command, Falls Church, Virginia.

7. Crossing the Rhine River, 1–24 March 1945

1. Stephen T. Early (27 August 1889–11 August 1951). Early began his career as a member of the United Press International staff in Washington, DC, from

1906 to 1913. He was then with Associated Press from 1913 to 1917 and 1920 to 1927. During World War I he served as an infantry captain in the AEF and won the Silver Star for heroism. He briefly worked for Franklin D. Roosevelt as an advance representative in 1920 before returning to AP. From 1927 to 1933 he was the Washington representative for Paramount News. With Roosevelt's election, Early became assistant to the president on 4 March 1933. On 1 July 1937 he became FDR's secretary and remained in that post until the president's death on 12 April 1945. He remained with Harry Truman as special assistant for a short period and then joined Pullman, Inc., as vice president from 1945 to April 1949. Early served as deputy secretary of defense from August 1949 to September 1950 and then returned to his vice presidency at Pullman. See *Who Was Who in America*, vol. 3 (1951–1960), 248.

2. Harry C. Butcher (15 November 1901–22 April 1985). Iowa State College (University), 1924. Butcher received a degree in agricultural journalism from Iowa State College in 1924 and first met Dwight Eisenhower in 1926. After managing an agricultural journal for several years, Butcher joined Columbia Broadcasting System in 1929 in its newly opened Washington office. In 1939 he was commissioned a lieutenant commander, and he volunteered for service in the navy in 1942. Shortly thereafter, Eisenhower, who was then Allied commander for the impending invasion of North Africa, requested Butcher as his naval aide. Butcher served in this post from 1942 to 1945 and was also chief, Public Relations Office, Headquarters, SHAEF, in 1944–1945. During the years he spent with Eisenhower, Butcher was intimately involved in Eisenhower's daily activities and kept a detailed diary. After the war, a shortened version of this diary was published as *My Three Years with Eisenhower: The Personal Diary of Captain Harry C. Butcher, USNR, Naval Aide to General Eisenhower 1942 to 1945* (New York: Simon and Schuster, 1946). After 1946 Butcher owned a radio and cable television system in Santa Barbara, California. See *World Notables*, vol. 8 (1982–1985) (Chicago: Marquis Who's Who, 1985), 64; Boatner, *Biographical Dictionary*, 71.

3. George A. Smith Jr. (29 March 1902–1 March 1945). U.S. Military Academy, 1926. Infantry. From May to August 1941, Smith was successively group plans and training officer, group adjutant, and battalion executive officer in the Infantry Replacement Training Center, Camp Wheeler, Georgia. He then went to England with the Special Observers Group until December 1941, when he returned to Washington as assistant to the assistant chief of staff, General Headquarters. As a result of the March 1942 reorganization of the War Department, Smith became a member of the Future Operations Section, Strategy and Policy Group, Operations Division, War Department General Staff. In August 1942 he was sent to England as assistant to ACS, G-3, Allied Forces Headquarters, and moved to North Africa in November. He remained in this post until May 1943, when he was made commander, Eighteenth Infantry Regiment, First Infantry Division. He commanded the Eighteenth Infantry in Sicily, the Normandy

invasion, across northern France, and into Germany. On 26 February 1945 he was made assistant division commander, 104th Infantry Division, under Terry Allen. He was killed in action at Sindorf, Germany, on 1 March 1945.

4. At 0300, 1 March 1945, an artillery shell demolished the CP of the Second Battalion, 414th Infantry Regiment, in Sindorf and killed Brig. Gen. George A. Smith Jr.; Col. Anthony J. Touart, commander, 414th Infantry; and Lt. Col. Joseph M. Cummins Jr., commanding the Second Battalion. See Leo A. Hoegh and Howard J. Doyle, *Timberwolf Tracks: The History of the 104th Infantry Division, 1942–1945* (Washington, DC: Infantry Journal Press, 1946), 257.

5. Pleas B. Rogers (14 November 1895–25 December 1974). Infantry. Rogers served in the Texas National Guard in 1916–1917 as an enlisted man and as an officer in the AEF in France in 1918–1919. From April 1942 to August 1944, Rogers commanded the Central (London) Base Section, Services of Supply, ETOUSA. He was promoted to brigadier general in March 1943. In August 1944, with the creation of the Communications Zone on the Continent, he became commander of the Seine Base Section, a post he held until November 1945. He retired in January 1948 as a brigadier general.

6. Prentice E. Yeomans (26 July 1902–18 April 1945). U.S. Military Academy, 1926. Air Corps and Cavalry. Originally in the air corps, Yeomans transferred to the cavalry in 1927. After serving with the Fourteenth Cavalry (May 1938–May 1940), he was assigned to the Thirteenth Armored Regiment at Fort Knox as the supply officer and then company and battalion commander until April 1941. He was then regimental S-3 and intelligence officer, Third Armored Cavalry Regiment (redesignated Thirty-third Armored Cavalry Regiment in May 1941), to December 1941. From January 1942 to December 1943, he commanded the 703rd Tank Destroyer Battalion in the United States and England. He was then provost marshal, Headquarters, First Army, until July 1944, when he became executive officer and unit commander in the Thirty-third Armored Cavalry Regiment. After recovering from wounds suffered early in August, he commanded the Eighty-third Reconnaissance Battalion, Third Armored Division, from September 1944 until he was killed in action at Thalheim, Germany, on 18 April 1945. See also *Register of Graduates, USMA, 2000*, 4–137.

7. Emil F. Reinhardt (27 October 1888–24 July 1969). U.S. Military Academy, 1910. Infantry. Reinhardt served in the United States during World War I and then in the occupation of Germany. Promoted to brigadier general in April 1941, he was assistant division commander, Seventh Infantry Division, until November. He then was commanding general, Infantry Replacement Training Center, Camp Wolters, Texas, until April 1942, when he was promoted to major general. From May to November 1942 he was commanding general, Seventy-sixth Infantry Division, and then became commanding general, Thirteenth Corps. He was sent to the European theater in November 1943 and commanded Eighth Corps until March 1944, when he returned to the United States to command Ninth Corps. In September 1944 he was made command-

ing general, Sixty-ninth Infantry Division, and took the division to the ETO in December. His division later made the initial American contact with the Russians at Torgau, Germany, on 25 April 1945. He returned to the United States in August 1945 and commanded the Infantry Replacement Training Center at Camp Robinson, Arkansas, from October 1945 until June 1946. He retired as a major general in September 1946.

8. The assistant chief of staff, G-5, Civil Affairs, was added to the First Army General Staff on 18 July 1944 under Colonel Damon M. Gunn. The section was first established as the Civil Affairs Section, Special Staff, First Army, under Gunn on 1 March 1944 due to the impending responsibilities for establishing military government in areas of Germany that might be occupied and for reestablishing civilian control in those areas liberated from German occupation.

9. Walter F. Lauer (29 June 1893–13 October 1966). Lauer was commissioned in the infantry in 1917 and served with the AEF from June 1918 to May 1919 and then in the American occupation of Germany until April 1923. After being assistant chief of staff, G-4, and plans and training officer, Third Infantry Division, from December 1939 to February 1942, he became the chief of staff. He went overseas with the division and participated in the North African operations before returning to the United States to become assistant division commander, Ninety-third Infantry Division, in January 1943 and received his first star. In July 1943 he moved to the Ninety-ninth Infantry Division as the commanding general. Lauer was promoted to major general in January 1944 and brought the division to Europe in September 1944. He commanded the Ninety-ninth Infantry Division through the difficult fighting in the Bulge and until 18 August 1945. He retired as a major general in March 1946.

10. In 1916, the Germans built a 1,069-foot, three-span, dual-track railroad bridge over the Rhine River at Remagen. After World War I the bridge was named in honor of Gen. Erich Ludendorff, chief of staff to Field Marshal Hindenberg during the later part of the war. The bridge's formal name was the Ludendorff Railway Bridge, but it was commonly known as the Remagen Bridge. In March 1945, the railroad tracks were being boarded over to convert the railroad into a road bridge so that it could be used to push reinforcements, supplies, and equipment to the Fifteenth Army on the Rhine's west bank. Although prepared for demolition to prevent it falling into American hands, advance elements of Brig. Gen. William Hoge's Combat Command B, Ninth Armored Division, took the bridge on 7 March after the Germans blew the charges but failed to drop the bridge into the river. See MacDonald, *The Last Offensive*, 195, 213–17.

11. The DUKW, pronounced "duck," and derived from army nomenclature was the army's amphibious truck. It could carry up to 5,000 pounds of general cargo or twenty-five men on land or fifty men afloat. The 7,000-pound DUKW was a 2½-ton 6x6 truck chassis modified for amphibious operation. It had a

speed of 50 miles per hour. The DUKW's principal use was in amphibious truck companies that acted as lighters (small watercraft or barges used to move cargo to shore from ships anchored in deep water) to move supplies, equipment, and men from transports and cargo ships to landing beaches or across water obstacles. During the war twenty-one thousand of these useful trucks were built. See Lüdeke, *Weapons of World War II*, 57; Baxter, *Scientists against Time*, 243–51.

12. Junkers designed and built the Ju 87 for the Luftwaffe as a *Sturzkampf-flugzeuge*, or dive-bomber, better known as the terrifying "Stuka" of the blitzkrieg's early years. Renowned for pinpoint bombing in Poland and France, the Stuka was slow and vulnerable to fighter attack and ground fire. It labored on in the Luftwaffe as its major ground-attack aircraft, especially on the eastern front, where it developed into an effective "tank-buster" when armed with dual 37-mm antitank guns. See Taylor, *Combat Aircraft of the World*, 177–78.

13. Generalleutnant Richard Schimpf (16 May 1897–30 December 1972). Schimpf served as an infantry officer in the German army in World War I and remained in the Reichswehr. He transferred to the Luftwaffe when it was established in 1935. He commanded the Twenty-first Luftwaffe Field Division in Russia in 1942–1943. In February 1944, he took command of the Third Parachute Division, which was assigned to the Seventh Army in France. He was severely wounded at Falaise in August 1944 and upon recovery reassumed command of the division in January 1945. He was captured on 8 March 1945 and remained a prisoner of war until December 1945. He joined the Luftwaffe of the new German Bundeswehr (armed forces) in October 1957 and commanded Military District III until his retirement in July 1962. See "Generalleutnant Richard Schimpf (Luftwaffe)" at www.islandfarm.fsnet.co.uk.

14. James G. Christiansen (27 September 1897–6 July 1982). U.S. Military Academy, 1918. Corps of Engineers. Christiansen was assigned to general headquarters (GHQ) of the army in August 1940 and in July 1941 was made assistant to the engineer, GHQ. From March to June 1942, he served in the Training Division, Headquarters, Army Ground Forces (AGF, formerly GHQ), and then was appointed deputy chief of staff, AGF. He became chief of staff, AGF, in February 1943 and was promoted to brigadier general the next month. He was promoted to major general in August 1944 and briefly served as commanding general, AGF, from May to July 1945, when he reverted to chief of staff. From September 1945 to October 1946 he was assigned to Army Forces Western Pacific, serving as chief of staff and then commander from March to October 1946. He commanded the Second Armored Division from September 1947 until August 1949, when he became engineer, General Headquarters, Far East Command, in Tokyo. From November 1951 to March 1952 he was assigned to the Office, Chief of Engineers, and then commanded the Sixth Armored Division until March 1953. He retired in September 1954.

15. Alphonse Pierre Juin (16 December 1888–27 January 1967). Born in Al-

geria, Juin graduated from St. Cyr in 1912 and fought throughout World War I with Moroccan units. He commanded the Fifteenth Motorized Infantry Division during the German offensive of May 1940 and fought stubbornly until captured. He was repatriated in 1941 and sent to command French troops in Morocco, later becoming commander of French land forces in North Africa. He joined the Allies at the beginning of Operation Torch in November 1942 and commanded French forces in Tunisia until December, when he began building French forces for operations outside North Africa. He later commanded French forces in Italy until he became chief of staff for national defense under Charles De Gaulle in August 1944. Juin served as commander in chief, Land Forces, Central Europe, in the North Atlantic Treaty Organization (NATO), from 1951 to October 1956, when he retired. He was promoted to marshal of France in May 1952. See Boatner, *Biographical Dictionary*, 262–64.

16. Russell T. Finn (28 September 1903–29 November 1996). U.S. Military Academy, 1925. Field Artillery. Finn was transferred from the air corps to the field artillery in 1926. He commanded the Thirty-fourth Field Artillery's 609th Tank Destroyer Battalion from August 1940 to March 1942. In June 1942 he became a battalion commander in the 190th Field Artillery Regiment, which deployed to the United Kingdom in August. He served as executive officer of the regiment until August 1943 and then moved to the Assault Training Center as artillery officer. From May 1944 to May 1946 he was executive officer, Thirty-second Field Artillery Brigade, which saw action across Europe. In May 1946 he was assigned to Headquarters U.S. Forces European Theater and its successor, U.S. European Command. He served in Headquarters, Eighth Army, in Korea, and then was promoted to brigadier general in July 1954 and was chief of staff, Fifth Army, until his retirement in June 1956.

17. Field Marshal Walther Model (24 January 1891–21 April 1945) was an infantry officer in the German Army during World War I. In 1939–1940 he was chief of staff, Fourth Corps, and then Sixteenth Army in the Polish and French campaigns. He later served as commander of the Third Infantry Division in the opening days of the Russian campaign and then commanded corps, armies, and army groups. He gained a reputation as an excellent defensive fighter and was known as "the Führer's fireman" because of Hitler's confidence in him to restore deteriorating situations and his frequent transfers to critical fronts. In August 1944 he moved to France to take command of Army Group B and replaced von Kluge as commander in chief, West. A month later von Rundstedt was restored to the commander in chief, West, and Model kept Army Group B. He was instrumental in defeating the Anglo-American airborne operation Market Garden and later was deeply involved in the Ardennes operation. In March and April 1945 he was trapped in the Ruhr pocket with Army Group B. After trying to break out of the encirclement, he shot himself on 21 April 1945 because he believed that a field marshal should not surrender. See Wistrich, *Who's Who in Nazi Germany*, 210–11; Boatner, *Biographical Dictionary*, 369–71;

Charles B. MacDonald, *The Last Offensive* (Washington, DC: Office of the Chief of Military History, 1973), 372.

18. Henry J. Taylor (2 September 1902–24 February 1984). University of Virginia, 1924. Foreign correspondent for the Scripps-Howard Newspaper Syndicate in Europe, the Middle East, and the Far East from 1941 to 1945. U.S. ambassador to Switzerland, 1957–1961. Taylor was also columnist and radio commentator during 1945–1956 and 1961–1981. See *World Notables*, vol. 8, 1982–1985, 392.

19. Lt. Gen. Marie-Louis Koeltz (1884–1970) served in the French army's intelligence section during and after World War I. In 1939 he was chief of staff, Eighth Army, in France. He moved up to General Headquarters in 1940 to become deputy chief of staff for operations. After the armistice of June 1940 he was appointed director, Armistice Services (1940–1941) before going to French North Africa as commander, Algeria (Nineteenth) Military District. In 1942 he joined the Allies and led the French forces (French Nineteenth Corps) against the Germans in Tunisia. After the invasion of France, he headed the French military mission for German affairs, was senior French liaison officer to the Allied forces, and briefly commanded French forces in occupied Berlin before becoming assistant commanding general, French Forces in Germany, in 1945–1946. He retired in 1946. See Parrish, *Encyclopedia of World War II*, 342.

20. Ben Lear (12 May 1879–1 November 1968). Cavalry. Lear served as a sergeant and lieutenant in the First Colorado Volunteers in the Philippine insurrection and was commissioned in the Regular Army in 1901. In January 1936 he was promoted to brigadier general and made commanding general, First Cavalry Division. After serving as commanding general, Pacific Sector, Panama Canal Department, from November 1938 to October 1940, he was promoted to lieutenant general and became commanding general, Second Army, until April 1943. He was temporarily commanding general, Army Ground Forces, from April to June 1943, and then he served on the Secretary of War's Personnel Board. From July 1944 to January 1945, he was commanding general, Army Ground Forces, replacing McNair, and then he was assigned to the ETO as deputy commanding general until July 1945. He retired in December 1945.

21. Collins badly needed a bridge over the Rhine near Bonn, so he "offered to buy beer for every man working on it if the total construction time did not exceed ten hours." The 237th Engineer Combat Battalion, assisted by the 238th Engineer Combat and the Twenty-third Armored Engineer battalions and 990th Treadway Bridge Company, were assigned to build a floating Treadway bridge over the Rhine. Work began at 0615 on 21 March, and the first vehicles drove over the 1,340-foot bridge to the east bank at 1625, a total time of 10 hours, 10 minutes. Collins accepted that as close enough and on the twenty-second hosted a beer party for the engineers in Bonn to celebrate what became known in engineer lore as the "Beer Bridge." See Alfred M. Beck et al., *The Corps of Engineers: The War against Germany* (Washington, DC: U.S. Army Center of Military History, 1985), 515.

22. Thomas North (28 April 1893–26 June 1990). Corps of Engineers and Field Artillery. North enlisted in the Eleventh Engineers (Railway) in May 1917 and served with it in France until December 1917. He was commissioned in the engineers in September 1918 and entered the Regular Army in the field artillery in July 1920. North was detailed to the American Battle Monuments Commission in October 1923 and opened its Paris office in April 1924, where he also served from 1931 to 1933. He was assigned to the Training Section, Office, Chief of Field Artillery, from July 1940 to March 1942, when he moved to the Operations Division, War Department General Staff. He was chief, Current Section, Logistics Group, from June 1942 to 31 January 1944, when he became chief, Current Group. From April 1946 to April 1953, North was secretary, American Battle Monuments Commission, and directed the construction of the World War II cemeteries and monuments overseas. Although he retired on 30 April 1953, he was immediately recalled and remained as secretary. He was promoted to major general in May 1957. See also Ancell, *Biographical Dictionary*, 241.

23. Dan Gilmer (14 September 1909–20 May 1982). U.S. Military Academy, 1932. Infantry. Gilmer served with the Fourth Infantry Division in 1939–1940. He was deputy chief of staff, Second Corps, in England from July to September 1942 and then secretary, General Staff, Allied Forces Headquarters, in the ETO and the Mediterranean until January 1944, when he became secretary, General Staff, for SHAEF. He returned to the Operations Division, War Department General Staff, in Washington as chief, European–African–Middle East Section, from April 1944 to June 1945. He was then chief, Pacific-Alaskan Section. Operations Division, War Department General Staff, until April 1946, when he became chief of staff, U.S. Delegation, UN Military Committee, until July 1948. He commanded the Seventh Cavalry Regiment, First Cavalry Division, in Korea in 1951–1952. He retired as a colonel in 1962.

24. Marion P. Echols (5 June 1899–19 March 1974). U.S. Military Academy, 1919. Field Artillery. Echols was an instructor at the Field Artillery School from June 1938 to November 1942. He was then made chief of staff, 102nd Division, until February 1944, when he became deputy chief of staff, Sixteenth Corps. In January 1945 he was made commander of the 417th Field Artillery Group. In 1945–1946 he was assigned to Headquarters, Army Ground Forces, in the Public Information Section, and then went to General Headquarters, Far East Command, as public information officer, until 1951. He retired in 1953 as a colonel.

25. Operation Varsity was planned to assist Montgomery's Twenty-first Army Group in Operation Plunder, its crossing of the Rhine River near the town of Wesel. On the morning of 24 March 1945, 1,696 transports and 1,348 gliders were used to land more than twenty-two thousand men of the First Allied Airborne Army east of the Rhine near Wesel. The British Sixth and U.S. Seventeenth Airborne divisions took part in the operations, which were successful but costly. The value and effectiveness of Varsity were seriously questioned

later because the German forces holding the east bank offered little opposition to the ground forces that crossed the river in the same area. See MacDonald, "The Rhine Crossings in the North," in *The Last Offensive*, 294–320.

8. Exploitation of the Remagen Bridgehead, 25 March–18 April 1945

1. Victor Morven Fortune (1883–1949). Royal Military College, Sandhurst. Commissioned in the Black Watch in December 1903, Fortune served throughout World War I with the Black Watch, winning a Distinguished Service Order and commanding the First Battalion from September 1916 to January 1918. He was promoted to brigadier and given command of the Forty-sixth Brigade, Fifteenth (Scottish) Division, in June 1918. He was returned to his permanent rank of captain (brevet major) after the war. He held various command posts in the 1930s, ending as commander of the Fifty-first Highland Division in January 1938. He took the Fifty-first to France as part of the British Expeditionary Force in September 1939 and in June 1940 was captured along with his division at St. Valery after holding off the German attack on Dunkirk and allowing thousands of British and French soldiers to be evacuated. He spent the remainder of the war as a prisoner of war. See "Victor Morven Fortune (1883–1949)" at University of Birmingham, Centre for First World War Studies, http://firstworldwar.bham.ac.uk.

2. Samuel I. Rosenman (13 February 1896–24 June 1973). Lawyer and judge. Columbia University, AB, 1915; LL.B., 1919. Rosenman was an informal political associate of President Franklin D. Roosevelt, serving as his counsel from 1929 to 1932 while FDR was governor of New York. FDR appointed him to the New York Supreme Court, on which he served from 1932 to 1943, when he resigned to work for the president. He was the personal counsel and chief speechwriter for President Roosevelt from 1943 to April 1945. He was special counsel to President Truman in 1945–1946. See *World Notables*, vol. 5 (1969–1973), 620.

3. Junior J. Spurrier (James I. Spurrier Jr.) (14 December 1922–25 February 1984). Spurrier received the Distinguished Service Cross (DSC) and Medal of Honor for heroism while serving in Company G, Second Battalion, 134th Infantry Regiment, Thirty-fifth Infantry Division, in France. He received the DSC for heroism on 16 September 1944 at Lay–St. Christophe and the Medal of Honor for his actions at Achain on 13 November 1944. See Hugh M. Cole, *The Lorraine Campaign* (Washington, DC: Historical Division, Department of the Army, 1950), 93n, 350.

4. John J. McCloy (21 March 1895–11 March 1989). Amherst College, 1916. McCloy served in the AEF as a captain in the field artillery. He received his law degree from Harvard Law School in 1921 and was a member of several large law firms in New York City. McCloy became an expert consultant to the secretary of war in October 1940 and was appointed assistant secretary of war in

April 1941. McCloy's primary concerns during the war were with the organization and maintenance of the army and the political aspects of the surrender and postwar occupation. He served as chairman of the Combined Civil Affairs Committee, Combined Chiefs of Staff, which dealt with postwar occupation and military-government problems. He was also the War Department's representative on the State, War, Navy Coordinate Committee, which coordinated policy at the highest levels in Washington. In November 1945 he returned to New York to practice law, but in 1947–1949 he became president of the World Bank. He then replaced Gen. Lucius D. Clay as U.S. High Commissioner for Germany from 1949 to 1952 and played a significant role in the rebirth of Germany. He was chairman of the board of Chase Manhattan Bank from 1955 to 1961, when President John F. Kennedy named him to head the administration's disarmament activities. He was associated with the law firm of Milbank, Tweed, Hadley, and McCloy for a number of years as well as serving as chairman of the Council on Foreign Relations (1954–1970). He was a member of the Warren Commission on President Kennedy's assassination and an adviser to every president after World War II. See *World Notables*, vol. 10, 1989–1993, 234.

5. Howard A. Craig (22 December 1897–1 October 1977). Air Corps. Craig served in the Aviation Section, Signal Corps, as an enlisted man and officer during World War I and remained in the Air Service after the war. He was assistant to the chief, air war plans, Office of the Chief of the Air Corps, from May 1940 until February 1942, when he became assistant chief, Air War Plans Division. From June to August 1942 he was assistant chief of staff, G-3, ETO. Following his promotion to brigadier general in August 1942, he became deputy chief of staff, Air, ETO and then Allied Forces Headquarters and commanding general, Twelfth Air Support Command, until February 1943. He was then chief of staff, Mediterranean Air Command, until August 1943, when he returned to Headquarters, Army Air Forces, as assistant chief of the Air Staff, Operations, A-3. He became a major general in February 1944 and moved to the Operations Division, War Department General Staff, as chief, Theater (Operations) Group, in October 1944. He remained with the Operations Division until June 1946, when he became commanding general, Alaskan Department, until January 1947 and a lieutenant general. He was commander in chief, Alaskan Command, from February to October 1947, when he became deputy chief of staff, materiel, in the newly established Headquarters, U.S. Air Force. From September 1949 to July 1952 he was inspector general of the air force and then served as commandant, National War College, until his retirement in June 1955.

6. Lloyd H. Gibbons (10 October 1895–7 April 1945). Infantry. Gibbons served as an enlisted man and officer in the Eighty-ninth Division in World War I and remained in the army after the war. At the time of his death, he was assistant division commander. He was posthumously promoted to brigadier general. See also Ancell, *Biographical Dictionary*, 116.

7. John B. Wogan (1 January 1890–30 September 1968). U.S. Military Acad-

emy, 1915. Cavalry and Field Artillery. Wogan served with the cavalry during the Mexican border campaign of 1916 and went to France with the Coast Artillery Corps in September 1917. He commanded the Sixty-eighth Armored Field Artillery Regiment at Fort Knox from June 1940 to August 1941, when he became chief of staff, Fifth Armored Division. From January to July 1942, he commanded Combat Command B, Second Armored Division, and was promoted to brigadier general in February 1942. He was given command of the Thirteenth Armored Division in July 1942 and was promoted to major general in September. Prior to the Thirteenth's shipment to the ETO in 1944, Wogan was attached to the Fourth Armored Division, Third Army, and served with it throughout the Battle of the Bulge. He rejoined his division when it arrived in the ETO in January 1945. He was severely wounded on 15 April during the fighting to destroy the Ruhr pocket and was evacuated. He retired on disability in October 1946 and managed the Veterans' Administration Hospital at Asheville (Oteen), North Carolina, for some years thereafter.

8. The Seventy-ninth Infantry and Seventeenth Airborne divisions occupied the main Krupp iron and steel works. Krupp was one of the largest industrial combines in the world and the leading armaments manufacturer in Germany since the nineteenth century.

9. The Rose pocket was an American name for the Ruhr pocket in which German Army Group B was encircled. It was so called in honor of Maj. Gen. Maurice Rose, commander of the Third Armored Division, who was killed in action on 30 March 1945.

10. The western Allies envisioned the possibility of a national or alpine redoubt that might be formed in the Alps of southern Bavaria and Austria by withdrawing German army and Waffen-SS units in a last-ditch effort to stave off final defeat. The collapse of German resistance prevented any concerted German plans to organize such a defensive zone. See MacDonald, "The Myth of the Redoubt," in *The Last Offensive*, 407–42.

11. Orlando Ward (4 November 1891–5 February 1972). U.S. Military Academy, 1914. Cavalry and Field Artillery. Ward served as a battery and battalion commander and regimental adjutant with the 113th Field Artillery until August 1918, when he became assistant G-3, Third Army. He was promoted to brigadier general in August 1941 and given command of the Tank Brigade, First Armored Division. In February–March 1942 he commanded the Eighth Armored Division and, upon promotion to major general, received command of the First Armored Division. He led the division to the United Kingdom and then North Africa in 1942–1943. As a result of the First Armored Division's poor showing at Kasserine Pass in February 1943, Ward was returned to the United States and given command of the Tank Destroyer Center from June 1943 to January 1944. After serving as commandant, Field Artillery School, until October 1944. He returned to the ETO in command of the Twentieth Armored Division in January 1945. After commanding the Sixth Infantry Division

in Korea from October 1946 to February 1949, he was chief of military history, Special Staff, U.S. Army, until his retirement in January 1953.

12. Harris M. Melasky (11 April 1893–24 October 1972). U.S. Military Academy, April 1917. Infantry. Melasky served in France in World War I. He headed the Testing Section, Infantry Board, at Fort Benning through June 1941 and was intimately involved in the earliest development of the U.S. Army airborne forces. He then commanded the 550th Infantry (Airborne) at Quarry Heights, Canal Zone, which tested many of the concepts developed at Fort Benning. He later served in the Canal Zone as assistant chief of staff, G-3, Headquarters, Caribbean Defense Command, until June 1942, when he became assistant division commander, Eighty-sixth Infantry Division. In July 1942 he received his first star and then became commanding general, Eighty-sixth Infantry Division, in January 1943. He became a major general in February 1943. The Eighty-sixth Division arrived in Europe in March 1945 and moved to the Pacific in August. Melasky commanded the division through December 1945 and retired in September 1946.

13. John S. D. Eisenhower (3 August 1922–). U.S. Military Academy, 1944. Infantry. Eisenhower completed the Infantry School in 1944 and was assigned to the 3323rd Signal Intelligence and Monitoring Company in Europe from February to April 1945. He then joined the First Division, remaining there until June 1945. He remained in the occupation forces in Germany and Austria until 1947. After teaching in the English department at West Point until 1951, he served as S-3, Fifteenth Infantry, and Headquarters, Third Division, in Korea in 1952–1953. From 1958 to 1961 he was White House liaison officer to his father, President Dwight D. Eisenhower. He remained assigned to the former president until 1963, when he resigned from the U.S. Army and entered the U.S. Army Reserve. During 1969 to 1971, he was U.S. ambassador to Belgium. He was promoted brigadier general in the reserve in 1974. He is the author of a number of historical works. See *Who's Who in America 2006*, vol. 1(A—L) (New Providence, NJ: Marquis Who's Who, 2005), 1323.

14. Colditz, a castle dating back to 1014 in Saxony, was officially Oflag IVC (Officer Prisoner Camp) but was a special high-security POW camp for those prisoners considered to be most dangerous and important. Allied POWs who had records of escapes were usually sent there. See Dear, *Oxford Guide to World War II*, 191.

15. Ralph McT. Pennell (18 August 1882–17 April 1973). U.S. Military Academy, 1906. Field Artillery. Pennell served in the Philippines and the United States during World War I. He commanded the Fifty-second Field Artillery Brigade from October 1940 to October 1941 and was promoted to brigadier general in January 1941. He then commanded the Twenty-seventh Infantry Division in the Pacific until October 1942, receiving his second star in March 1942. After duty with the War Department until March 1943, he was made commanding general, Field Artillery Training Center, Fort Sill, Oklahoma, in

April 1943. From September 1944 to October 1945 he was commandant, Field Artillery School. He retired as a major general in March 1946 and was president, Fort Sill National, Bank, for many years thereafter.

16. Benjamin O. Davis (1 July 1877–26 November 1970). Davis enrolled in Howard University in 1897 but left in 1898 to accept a commission as a second lieutenant in the Eighth U.S. Volunteer Infantry during the Spanish-American War. After the war, he enlisted in the Ninth Cavalry and served as a private and corporal until February 1901, when he received a commission as second lieutenant of cavalry. He was professor of military science and tactics at Wilberforce University from 1905 to 1907, 1915 to 1917, 1929 to 1930, and 1937 to 1938 and at Tuskeegee Institute from 1920 to 1924. In October 1940 Davis became the first black soldier to reach the rank of general in the U.S. Army. He commanded the Fourth Cavalry Brigade, Second Cavalry Division, from January 1941 until his retirement in June of that year. He was soon recalled to active duty and assigned to the Inspector General's Office in Washington. He served in the ETO as adviser to General Eisenhower on race relations and then returned to his duties as assistant inspector general in November 1945. He retired again in 1948. See Boatner, *Biographical Dictionary*, 120–21.

17. Apparently Konteradmiral (Rear Admiral) Werner Scheer, then commander of Recruiting District Headquarters, Essen I, was captured in the Ruhr pocket. See "Ruhr Pocket" at http://feldgrau.net.

18. A number of important German army commanders were captured in the Ruhr pocket: Gen. Gustav von Zangen, Fifteenth Army; Gen. Friedrich Köchling, Eighty-first Corps; Lt. Gen. Fritz Bayerlein, Fifty-third Corps; Gen. Smilo Freiherr von Lüttwitz, Forty-seventh Panzer Corps; Gen. Siegfried von Waldenburg, 116th Panzer Division; Gen. Walter Denkert, Third Panzer Grenadier Division; Gen. Wolfgang Lange, 183rd Volks Grenadier Division; and Gen. Josef Harpe, Fifth Panzer Army. In addition, Franz von Papen, the last chancellor before Hitler's accession to power, and later German ambassador to Turkey, was also captured. See MacDonald, *The Last Offensive*, 370.

19. Edward L. Bowles (9 December 1897–5 September 1990). After serving in the U.S. Army as a lieutenant of field artillery during World War I, Bowles received his BS in electrical engineering from Washington University, St. Louis, in 1920 and his MS from Massachusetts Institute of Technology in 1922. In 1920–1921 he was an assistant in the Department of Electrical Engineering at MIT and then became an instructor until 1925. He was assistant professor, electrical communications, until 1927 and then associate professor until 1937. He was professor, Communications Division, Department of Electrical Engineering, MIT from 1937 to 1963 and a central figure in the development of the MIT Radiation Laboratory. He was secretary, Microwave Section, National Defense Research Council, 1940–1942, and then consultant to the secretary of war, 1942–1947. He was consultant to the commanding general, Army Air Forces, on communications and radar, from 1943 to 1946. He later was scientific con-

sultant to the U.S. Air Force from 1947 to 1951; scientific warfare adviser to the Weapon Systems Evaluation Group, Office, Secretary of Defense, 1950–1952; and consultant to the secretary of the army, 1950–1952. See *World Notables,* vol. 10 (1989–1993), 40.

20. Eclipse was the Allied code name for operations and actions that would take place in case of a sudden termination of hostilities with Germany. The code name was originally Rankin and then Talisman but was changed to Eclipse in November 1944 because it was thought that the original name was compromised; these plans underwent constant revision as the war in Europe progressed through 1944 and into 1945. As time passed, the plans became the overall procedures to be adopted during the occupation and disarmament of Germany. See MacDonald, *The Last Offensive,* 334.

21. Field Marshal Walther Model, commander of Army Group B, which was encircled in the Ruhr pocket, refused to surrender because, as he had long told his associates, "a field marshal does not become a prisoner. Such a thing is not possible." On 21 April 1945, Model shot himself in a woods north of Düsseldorf and was buried by his aides in an unmarked grave. His body was later disinterred and is now buried in the German Military Cemetery near Germeter, Germany. See MacDonald, *The Last Offensive,* 372.

22. In the Ruhr pocket, the First and Ninth U.S. armies captured approximately 317,000 German prisoners of war, but there is no reliable estimate of the number of German soldiers and civilians killed in the fighting. See MacDonald, *The Last Offensive,* 372.

23. Frank S. Ross (9 March 1893–6 May 1970). Infantry. Ross served as an enlisted man in the Fourth Infantry, Texas National Guard, in 1916–1917 and was then commissioned and served in the infantry in World War I. From July 1940 to March 1942 he was assigned to the War Department General Staff's Supply Division, G-4. He then was assigned as chief of transportation, Headquarters, Services of Supply, and Headquarters, ETOUSA, until March 1946. He was promoted to brigadier general in June 1943 and major general in June 1944. After serving briefly in Headquarters, Army Service Forces, Ross was commanding general, Port of Embarkation, New York, until his retirement in September 1946. See also Ancell, *Biographical Dictionary,* 282.

9. Final Operations, 19 April–7 May 1945

1. Edward W. Timberlake (3 January 1895–11 February 1980). U.S. Military Academy, August 1917. Infantry and Coast Artillery Corps. Timberlake served in the infantry in World War I and with the American Forces in Germany in 1919–1922. He transferred to the Coast Artillery Corps in 1920. From May 1939 to October 1942, he was commander of the Washington, D.C., area command of the Seventy-first Anti-Aircraft Artillery (AAA) Regiment. He then commanded the Thirty-sixth AAA Brigade and the AAA Command, Military

District of Washington until June 1943, when he was promoted to brigadier general and made commanding general, Forty-ninth AAA Brigade, ETO. Timberlake commanded the brigade until March 1946 and also was commanding general, antiaircraft artillery, First Army, in 1945–1946. After the war he was professor of military science and tactics at Utah State University from 1946 until he retired in July 1950.

2. Fritz Sauckel (27 October 1894–16 October 1946). Sauckel joined the Nazi Party in 1923 and became the *Gauleiter*, or governor, of Thuringia from 1933 to 1942. In March of that year he was made plenipotentiary general for the allocation of labor, which placed him in charge of the importation of foreign slave labor into Germany. It is estimated that during his years in charge over five million people were brought into Germany to maintain the war effort. The vast majority of these people were forcibly removed to Germany, where many of them subsequently died from malnutrition and inhuman treatment. Sauckel was arrested after the war. He was tried before the International Military Tribunal at Nuremberg, found guilty of crimes against humanity, and executed on 16 October 1946. See Wistrich, *Who's Who in Nazi Germany*, 266–67.

3. The Nazi Party was organized into *Partiegaue*, or regions, each of which came under a *Gauleiter*, or regional party political leader, who reported to Hitler and the party leadership. This strictly Nazi Party organization formed part of a confusing and competing administrative structure in Nazi Germany that included the new *Reichsgaue* (Reich Districts), *Wehrkreise* (Military Districts or Corps Areas), and other structures that slowly came to replace the traditional *Länder* (states or lands) into which Germany was divided, and became in fact the government of the local regions. There were eventually forty-two Gauleiters (a forty-third Gau was for all foreign party matters involving German citizens) who ruled their areas with virtually dictatorial powers. As Germany expanded in the wake of its conquests, especially in the east, Gauleiters were established in the reclaimed areas, such as Austria, Czech Sudetenland, and the Polish Corridor. Gauleiters came to handle almost all political matters as well as economic affairs, propaganda, and labor. See Martin Kitchen, *Nazi Germany at War* (New York: Longman, 1995); Neumann, *Behemoth*; Dear, *Oxford Guide to World War II*, 365.

4. Gleb Vladimirovich Baklanov (1910–1976). Baklanov commanded a rifle regiment and brigade in 1941–1942 before becoming commander of the 299th Rifle Division at Stalingrad in 1942–1943. He then commanded the Thirteenth Guards Rifle Division in 1943–1944 and the Thirty-fourth Guards Rifle Corps, Fifth Guards Army, in 1944–1945. In 1960–1964, he was commander in chief of the Siberian Military District and then commander in chief, Northern Group of Forces, until he retired as a colonel-general in 1976. See "Colonel-General Gleb Vladimirovich Baklanov" at "The Generals of WWII" at http://www.generals.dk.

5. For information on the "Phantom Section," see note 53, chapter 5.

6. Air Marshal Sir Norman Bottomley (18 September 1891–13 August 1970). Bottomley served in the infantry in World War I before joining the Royal Flying Corps in 1915. From 1938 to 1940, he was senior Air Staff officer, Headquarters, Bomber Command, and he then commanded No. 5 Group, Bomber Command, during 1940–1941. In 1942 he became assistant chief of the Air Staff and in 1943 was made deputy chief of the Air Staff. In 1945 he replaced Arthur Harris as air officer in Command, Bomber Command. He was the RAF's inspector general in 1947–1948 and retired in 1948 as an air chief marshal. See "Air Chief Marshal Sir Norman Bottomley" at "RAF History: Bomber Command" at http://www.raf.mod.uk/bombercommand.

7. Emil Ludwig (25 January 1881–17 September 1948) was educated at Heidelberg University and was a famous writer living in Switzerland from 1907 until 1940, when he moved to the United States. Among his most notable books were *Napoleon* (1926), *Goethe* (1926), and *Bismarck* (1927). See *Who Was Who in America*, vol. 2 (1943–1950), 332–33.

8. Robert W. Grow (14 February 1895–11 March 1985). University of Minnesota, 1916. Cavalry. Grow served in the cavalry in World War I. He was assistant chief of staff, G-3, Second Armored Division, and commanded the Thirty-fourth Armored Regiment from July 1940 to April 1942, when he was promoted to brigadier general and took command of Combat Command B, Eighth Armored Division. In June 1942 he moved to Combat Command B, Tenth Armored Division, and in May 1943 became commanding general, Sixth Armored Division. He was promoted to major general in September 1943 and led the Sixth throughout the war in Europe. From July to November 1945 he commanded the Third Armored Division in Germany and then briefly commanded the Twenty-sixth Infantry Division. In July 1950 he was assigned as the U.S. Army attaché in Moscow. During a conference in Frankfurt in 1951, his personal diary containing secret information was photographed by East German agents working undercover in U.S. Army housing and publicized. Grow was later court-martialed and convicted for compromising classified information. He retired in January 1953. See also Ancell, *Biographical Dictionary*, 125.

9. Aleksei Semenovich Zhadov (1901–1977). Zhadov was the chief of staff, Third Army, in 1941–1942 and then commanded the Eighth Cavalry Corps before being wounded in 1942. He then commanded the Sixty-sixth Army at Stalingrad in 1942–1943 and remained as commander when it was redesignated the Fifth Guards Army in April 1943 in recognition of its service at Stalingrad. Zhadov commanded the Fifth Guards Army through 1946, when he became deputy commander in chief, ground forces. From 1950 to 1954, he headed the Frunze Military Academy in Moscow and then commanded the Soviet Central Group of Forces in Germany in 1954–1955. He was once again deputy commander in chief, ground forces, from 1955 to 1964 when he became deputy chief inspector, ministry of defense. He retired as General of the Army. See "Aleksei Semenovich Zhadov (1901–1977)" at "The Generals of WWII" at http://www.

generals.dk; Albert Z. Conner and Robert G. Poirer, *Red Army Order of Battle in the Great Patriotic War* (Novato, CA: Presidio Press, 1985), 25–26, 72.

10. Douglas MacArthur (28 January 1880–5 April 1964). U.S. Military Academy, 1903. Corps of Engineers and Infantry. After duty in the Philippines and United States, MacArthur served as aide to President Theodore Roosevelt (1906–1907) and was attached to the General Staff (1913–1915, 1916–1917). During World War I he helped organized the Forty-second Division as chief of staff and later served as commander of the Forty-second's Eighty-fourth Infantry Brigade (receiving two Distinguished Service Crosses) and of the division itself at the end of the war in France. From 1919 to 1922 he was superintendent of the U.S. Military Academy and then again served in the Philippines until 1925, when he was promoted to major general. From 1928 to 1930 he commanded the Department of the Philippines and was appointed chief of staff of the army in November 1930. Upon leaving this post he reverted to his permanent rank in October 1935. He once again went to the Philippines, this time as military adviser to the commonwealth government. He was promoted to the rank of field marshal of the Philippine army in 1936 and resigned from the U.S. Army in 1937. In June 1941 he was recalled to active duty as commanding general, U.S. Army Forces Far East, in the Philippines and was charged with preparing the defense of the islands against possible Japanese attack. When the Japanese did attack in December 1941, the American and Filipino forces had little chance. In March 1942 President Roosevelt ordered MacArthur to Australia to command the continued Allied resistance and also awarded him a Medal of Honor. In April 1942 MacArthur became supreme commander, Southwest Pacific Area, and was responsible for the war against Japan from New Guinea northward to the Philippines and Japan itself. In December 1944, he was promoted to General of the Army and became commanding general, U.S. Army Forces Pacific, in April 1945. With the end of the war in the Pacific, he became supreme commander, Allied Powers , in complete command of the occupation of Japan and its postwar restructuring. At the same time, he commanded U.S. Army Forces Far East and the Joint U.S. Far East Command. When the North Koreans invaded the Republic of Korea in June 1950, he led the American and later United Nations Command operations. In the spring of 1951, he publicly disagreed with President Truman's policy in Korea and was removed from command and retired. See also Boatner, *Biographical Dictionary*, 331–36.

Bibliography

Books and Journals

Ancell, R. Manning, with Christine M. Miller. *The Biographical Dictionary of World War II Generals and Flag Officers: The U.S. Armed Forces.* Westport, CT: Greenwood Press, 1996.

Association of Graduates, U.S. Military Academy. *Register of Graduates and Former Cadets of the United States Military Academy West Point, New York, 2000.* West Point, NY: Association of Graduates, 1999.

Astor, Gerald. *Terrible Terry Allen: Combat General of World War II; The Life of an American Soldier.* New York: Ballantine Books, 2003.

Baxter, James Phinney, III. *Scientists against Time.* Boston: Little, Brown, 1946.

Beck, Alfred M., Abe Bortz, Charles W. Lynch, Lida Mayo, and Ralph F. Weld. *The Corps of Engineers: The War against Germany.* Washington, DC: U.S. Army Center of Military History, 1985.

Bekke, Douglas. "Norwegian-Americans and the 99th Infantry Battalion (Separate)," Military Historical Society of Minnesota, Minnesota National Guard, www.minnesotanationalguard.org.

Benz, Wolfgang. *A Concise History of the Third Reich.* Berkeley and Los Angeles: University of California Press, 2006.

Beschloss, Michael. *The Conquerors: Roosevelt, Truman and the Destruction of Hitler's Germany, 1941–1945.* New York: Simon & Schuster, 2002.

Black, Robert W. *Rangers in World War II.* New York: Ballantine Books, 1992.

Blumenson, Martin. *Breakout and Pursuit.* Washington, DC: Office of the Chief of Military History, 1961.

Boatner, Mark M., III. *The Biographical Dictionary of World War II.* Novato, CA: Presidio Press, 1996.

Bradley, Omar N. *A Soldier's Story.* New York: Henry Holt, 1951.

Bradley, Omar N., and Clay Blair Jr. *A General's Life.* New York: Simon & Schuster, 1983.

Butcher, Harry C. *My Three Years with Eisenhower: The Personal Diary of Captain Harry C. Butcher, USNR, Naval Aide to General Eisenhower, 1942–1945.* New York: Simon & Schuster, 1946.

Cacutt, Len, ed. *The World's Greatest Aircraft.* New York: Exeter Books, 1988.

Carafano, James Jay. *After D-Day: Operation Cobra and the Normandy Breakout.* Boulder, CO: Lynne Rienner, 2000.

Caraley, Demetrios. *The Politics of Military Unification: A Study of Conflict and the Policy Process.* New York: Columbia University Press, 1966.

Cecil, Robert. *The Myth of the Master Race: Alfred Rosenberg and Nazi Ideology.* New York: Dodd Mead, 1972.

Chandler, Alfred D., Jr., and Stephen E. Ambrose, eds. *The Papers of Dwight David Eisenhower: The War Years,* vol. 4. Baltimore: Johns Hopkins University Press, 1970.

Clarke, Jeffrey J., and Robert Ross Smith. *Riviera to the Rhine.* Washington, DC: U.S. Army Center of Military History, 1993.

Codman, Charles R. *Drive.* Boston: Little, Brown, 1957.

Cole, Hugh M. *The Ardennes: Battle of the Bulge.* Washington, DC: U.S. Army Center of Military History, 1988.

———. *The Lorraine Campaign.* Washington, DC: Historical Division, Department of the Army, 1950.

Coll, Blanche D., Jean E. Keith, and Herbert H. Rosenthal. *The Corps of Engineers: Troops and Equipment.* Washington, DC: Office of the Chief of Military History, 1958.

Collins, J. Lawton. *Lightning Joe: An Autobiography.* Baton Rouge: Louisiana State University Press, 1979.

Conner, Albert Z., and Robert G. Poirer. *Red Army Order of Battle in the Great Patriotic War.* Novato, CA: Presidio Press, 1985.

Cooper, Matthew. *The German Army 1933–1945: Its Political and Military Failure.* Lanham, MD: Scarborough House, 1990.

Craven, Wesley Frank, and James Lea Cate. *The Army Air Forces in World War II.* Vol. 3, *Europe: Argument to V-E Day January 1944 to May 1945.* Washington, DC: Office of Air Force History, 1983.

De Guingand, Francis W., Sir. *Operation Victory.* New York: Charles Scribner's Sons, 1947.

Dickson, Paul. *War Slang: American Fighting Words and Phrases from the Civil War to the Gulf War.* New York: Pocket Books, 1994.

Dear, I. C. B., ed. *The Oxford Guide to World War II.* Oxford: Oxford University Press, 1995.

DuPre, Flint O. *U.S. Air Force Biographical Dictionary.* New York: Franklin Watts, 1965.

Eisenhower, Dwight D. *Crusade in Europe.* Garden City, NY: Doubleday, 1948.

Evans, Richard J. *The Third Reich in Power.* New York: Penguin Books, 2006.

Forty, George. *US Army Handbook 1939–1945.* New York: Barnes & Noble, 1995.

Franks, Norman L. *The Battle of the Airfields, 1st January 1945.* London: Grub Street, 2000.

Freeman, Roger A. *Mighty Eighth War Manual.* New York: Jane's, 1984.

Green, Constance McL., Harry C. Thomson, and Peter C. Roots. *The Ordnance Department: Planning Munitions for War.* Washington, DC: Office of the Chief of Military History, 1955.

Greenwood, John T. "Building the Road to Alaska." In *Builders and Fighters: U.S. Army Engineers in World War II,* edited by Barry W. Fowle, 117–35. Fort Belvoir, VA: Office of History, U.S. Army Corps of Engineers, 1992.

Gunston, Bill. *American Warplane.* New York: Salamander Books, 1986.

Harrison, Gordon A. *Cross-Channel Attack.* Washington, DC: Office of the Chief of Military History, 1951.

Helfers, M. C. "The Employment of V-Weapons by the Germans during World War II." Unpublished monograph. U.S. Army Center of Military History, Washington, DC.

Hoegh, Leo A., and Howard J. Doyle. *Timberwolf Tracks: The History of the 104th Infantry Division, 1942–1945.* Washington, DC: Infantry Journal Press, 1946.

Hogan, David W., Jr. *A Command Post at War: First Army Headquarters in Europe, 1943–1945.* Washington, DC: U.S. Army Center of Military History, 2000.

Jones, R. V. *The Wizard War: British Scientific Intelligence, 1939–1945.* New York: Coward, McCann, and Geoghegan, 1978.

Kitchen, Martin. *Nazi Germany at War.* New York: Longmans, 1995.

Kleitmann, K-G. *Die Waffen-SS: Eine Documentation* (The Waffen-SS: A Documentation). Osnabrück, Germany: Verlag "Der Freiwillige," 1965.

Lewin, Ronald. *Ultra Goes to War.* New York: Pocket Books, 1978.

Lüdeke, Alexander. *Weapons of World War II.* New York: Parragon, 2007.

MacDonald, Charles B. *A Time for Trumpets: The Untold Story of the Battle of the Bulge.* New York: William Morrow, 1985.

———. *The Last Offensive.* Washington, DC: Office of the Chief of Military History, 1973.

———. *The Siegfried Line Campaign.* Washington, DC: Office of the Chief of Military History, 1963.

McManus, John C. *Alamo in the Ardennes: The Untold Story of the American Soldiers Who Made the Defense of Bastogne Possible.* New York: John Wiley & Sons, 2007.

Millett, John D. *The Organization and Role of the Army Service Forces.* Washington, DC: Office of the Chief of Military History, 1954.

Mitcham, Samuel W., Jr. *German Order of Battle.* Vol. 2, *291st–999th Infantry Divisions, Named Infantry Divisions, and Special Divisions in World War II.* Mechanicsburg, PA: Stackpole Books, 2007.

———. *German Order of Battle.* Vol. 3, *Panzer, Panzer Grenadier, and Waffen SS Divisions in World War II.* Mechanicsburg, PA: Stackpole Books, 2007.

Mossman, Billy C. *Ebb and Flow, November 1950–July 1951.* Washington, DC: U.S. Army Center of Military History, 1990.

Murray, G. E. Patrick. "Courtney Hodges: Modest Star of WW II." *American History Illustrated* 7 (January 1973): 12–25.

Neumann, Franz. *Behemoth: The Structure and Practice of National Socialism 1933–1944.* New York: Harper Torchbooks, 1963.

Oldfield, Barney. *Never a Shot in Anger.* Santa Barbara, CA: Capra Press, 1989.

Parrish, Thomas, ed. *The Simon and Schuster Encyclopedia of World War II.* New York: Simon & Schuster, 1978.

Phillips, Robert F. *To Save Bastogne.* Burke, VA: Borodino Books, 1996.

Pogue, Forrest C. *The Supreme Command.* Washington, DC: U.S. Government Printing Office, 1954.

———. *George C. Marshall. Ordeal and Hope, 1939–1942.* New York: The Viking Press, 1965.

"Precise Puncher." *Time,* 16 October 1944.

Putnam, William Lowell. *A Yankee Image: The Life and Times of Roger Lowell Putnam.* West Kennebunk, ME: Phoenix Publishing for the Lowell Observatory, 1991.

Quick, John. *Dictionary of Weapons and Military Terms.* New York: McGraw-Hill, 1973.

Rottman, Gordon L. *FUBAR: Soldier Slang of World War II.* New York: Osprey Publishing, 2007.

Ruppenthal, Roland G. *Logistical Support of the Armies.* Vol. 1, *May 1941–September 1944.* Washington, DC: Office of the Chief of Military History, 1953.

———. *Logistical Support of the Armies.* Vol. 2, *September 1944–May 1945.* Washington, DC: Office of the Chief of Military History, 1959.

Sarnecky, Mary T. *A History of the U.S. Army Nurse Corps.* Philadelphia: University of Pennsylvania Press, 1999.

Schofield, B. B. *Operation Neptune.* Annapolis, MD: Naval Institute Press, 1974.

Schoenbaum, David. *Hitler's Social Revolution: Class and Status in Nazi Germany, 1933–1939.* Garden City, NY: Anchor Books, 1966.

Shirer, William L. *The Rise and Fall of the Third Reich: A History of Nazi Germany.* New York: Simon & Schuster, 1960.

Short, Neil. *Germany's West Wall: The Siegfried Line.* Oxford, UK: Osprey Publishing, 2004.

———. *Hitler's Siegfried Line.* Stroud, UK: Sutton Publishing, 2002.

Simon, Leslie E. *Secret Weapons of the Third Reich: German Research in World War II.* Old Greenwich, CT: WE, 1971.

Starr, Joseph R. *Fraternization with Germans in World War II.* Occupation Forces in Europe Series, 1945–46. Frankfurt-am-Main, Germany: Office of the Chief Historian, U.S. European Command, 1947.

Taylor, John W. R., ed. *Combat Aircraft of the World from 1909 to the Present.* New York: G. P. Putnam's Sons, 1969.

Terraine, John. *A Time for Courage: The Royal Air Force in the European War, 1939–1945.* New York: Macmillan, 1985.

U.S. Air Force. Ninth U.S. Air Force. *Condensed Analysis of the Ninth Air Force in the European Theater of Operations.* Washington, DC: Office of Air Force History, 1984.

U.S. Army. European Theater of Operations, Office of the Theater Historian. *Order of Battle of the United States Army World War II: European Theater of Operations; Divisions.* Paris, 1946. Copy in U.S. Army Center of Military History, Washington, DC.

U.S. Army. First U.S. Army. *Report of Operations, 20 October 1943–1 August 1944,* vol. 1. N.d, n.p.

———. *Report of Operations, 1 August 1944–22 February 1945,* vol. 1. Washington, DC: U.S. Government Printing Office, 1946.

———. *Report of Operations, 23 February 1945–8 May 1945.* Vol. 1, *Commanding General First U.S. Army and Headquarters Staff Sections.* Washington, DC: U.S. Government Printing Office, 1946.

———. *Combat Operations Data First Army: Europe, 1944–1945.* Governor's Island, NY: Headquarters, First U.S. Army, 1946.

U.S. Army. Historical Division, Department of the Army. *Combat Chronicle: An Outline History of U.S. Army Divisions.* Washington, DC: U.S. Army Center of Military History, 1948.

U.S. Army. VII Corps. *Mission Accomplished: The Story of the Campaigns of the VII Corps United States Army in the War against Germany, 1944–1945.* Leipzig, Germany: J. J. Weber for VII Corps, 1945.

U.S. Congress. Senate. Elbridge Colby. *The First Army in Europe, 1943–1945,* Senate Document 91–25, 91st Congress, 1st Session, 1969.

U.S. War Department. Field Manual 100–5 (FM 100–5), *Field Service Regulations, Operations,* 22 May 1941 and 15 June 1944. U.S. Army Center of Military History, Washington, DC.

———. Technical Manual 8–5. *Medical Department Units of a Theater of Operations.* May 1945. U.S. Army Center of Military History, Washington, DC.

———. Technical Manual TM-E 30–451. *Handbook on German Military Forces,* 15 March 1945 Washington, DC: U.S. Government Printing Office, 1945.

Webster's Biographical Dictionary. Springfield, MA: G. & C. Merriam, 1972.

Weingartner, James J. *Crossroads of Death: The Story of the Malmedy Massacre and Trial.* Berkeley and Los Angeles: University of California Press, 1979.

Who Was Who in America: A Companion Biographical Reference Work to Who's Who in America, Vol. 2: 1943–1950. Chicago: A. N. Marquis, 1963.

———. Vol. 3: 1951–1960. Chicago: A. N. Marquis, 1963.

Who Was Who in America with World Notables. Chicago: Marquis Who's Who, 1968–1985.

Who Was Who in America with World Notables. New Providence, NJ: Marquis Who's Who, 1989–1996. *Who's Who in America 2006.* Vol. 1: *A-L.* New Providence, NJ: Marquis Who's Who, 2005.

Wilson, John B. *Maneuver and Firepower: The Evolution of Divisions and Separate Brigades.* Washington, DC: U.S. Army Center of Military History, 1998.

————. *Armies, Corps, Divisions and Separate Brigades.* Washington, DC: U.S. Army Center of Military History, 1987.

Wolk, Herman S. *Planning and Organizing the Postwar Air Force, 1943–1947.* Washington, DC: Office of Air Force History, 1984.

Web Sites

For select biographies of U.S. Navy admirals, see "People—United States" at U.S. Naval Historical Center Online Library, at http://www.history.navy.mil.

For biographies of German general officers captured in Europe and held as prisoners of war in Wales during and after the war, see "Island Farm Prisoner of War Camp: 198/Special Camp: XI, Bridgend, South Wales," at http://www.islandfarm.fsnet.co.uk, and also "Island Farm Special Camp XI. POWs Held at Bridgend," at http://www.specialcamp11.fsnet.co.uk.

For U.S. Air Force general officers, see Air Force Link Biographies at http://www.af.mil/bios/.

For British, German, and Soviet Generals, see "The Generals of WWII" at http://www.generals.dk.

Britannica Online Encyclopedia at http://www.britannica.com.

Centre for First World War Studies, University of Birmingham, UK, at http://www.firstworldwar.bham.ac.uk.

U.S. National Archives and Records Administration. Access to Archival Databases (AAD). "World War II Prisoners of War Date File, 12/7/1941–11/19/1946," at http://aad.archives.gov.

For selected German naval officers, see "Deutsche Marinesoldaten" at http://www.deutsche-marinesoldaten.de.

For Royal Air Force, Bomber Command, information, see "Bomber Command" at http://www.raf.mod.uk/bombercommand/.

Index